C000262712

USGS Director of

Report of the Secretary of the Interior

Vol. 4, Part 3

USGS Director of

Report of the Secretary of the Interior
Vol. 4, Part 3

ISBN/EAN: 9783337812225

Printed in Europe, USA, Canada, Australia, Japan

Cover: Foto ©Suzi / pixelio.de

More available books at **www.hansebooks.com**

REPORT

OF THE

SECRETARY OF THE INTERIOR;

BEING PART OF

THE MESSAGE AND DOCUMENTS

COMMUNICATED TO THE

TWO HOUSES OF CONGRESS

AT THE

BEGINNING OF THE SECOND SESSION OF THE FIFTY-FOURTH CONGRESS.

IN FIVE VOLUMES.

VOLUME IV—IN THREE PARTS.
PART 3.

WASHINGTON:
GOVERNMENT PRINTING OFFICE.
1896.

SEVENTEENTH ANNUAL REPORT

OF THE

UNITED STATES GEOLOGICAL SURVEY.

PART III.—MINERAL RESOURCES OF THE UNITED STATES, 1895,
METALLIC PRODUCTS AND COAL.

CONTENTS.

CONTENTS.

XIV   CONTENTS.

SOAPSTONE, BY EDWARD W. PARKER.

CEMENT.

17 GEOL, PT 3——2

Page

Infusorial earth 947
    Occurrence 947
    Production 948
Garnet 948
    Occurrence 948
    Use 949
    Production 949
Quartz crystal 950
Tripoli 950

PHOSPHATE ROCK.

Production 951
Imports 954
A phosphate prospect in Pennsylvania, by M. C. Ihlseng 955

SULPHUR AND PYRITES, BY EDWARD W. PARKER.

Sulphur 958
    Occurrence 958
    Production 958
    Review of the industry 959
    Imports 960
    The Louisiana sulphur mine 965
    The Texas sulphur deposits 966
    The Sicilian sulphur industry 967
        Prices of Sicilian sulphur 969
        Exports of sulphur from Sicily 969
        Ports in the United States receiving Sicilian sulphur 971
Pyrites 973
    Production 973
    Imports 974
    Consumption 974
    Occurrences in the United States 975
        Southern Appalachian States 975
        Arkansas 977

GYPSUM, BY EDWARD W. PARKER.

Occurrence 978
Production 978
    Comparative statistics of production for six years 980
Imports 982

SALT, BY EDWARD W. PARKER.

Production 984
Review of the industry in 1895 991
Imports and exports 992

FLUORSPAR AND CRYOLITE.

Fluorspar 998
Cryolite 998
    Imports 999

MICA.

Production 1000
Imports 1001
Uses 1001

ILLUSTRATIONS.

LETTER OF TRANSMITTAL.

DEPARTMENT OF THE INTERIOR,
UNITED STATES GEOLOGICAL SURVEY,
DIVISION OF MINERAL RESOURCES,
Washington, D. C., July 20, 1896.

SIR: I have the honor to transmit herewith the manuscript of the twelfth report on the mineral resources of the United States, the volume bearing the title "Mineral Resources of the United States, 1895."

As indicated in the title, the volume carries the statistical record of the mineral developments in the United States to December 31, 1895. The descriptive matter has been brought up to a much later date, as it has all been prepared during the present year, 1896.

In accordance with your instructions, the report for the calendar year 1896 is already in preparation.

I take this opportunity to express my hearty appreciation not only of the increased facilities which you have secured for this work but for the attention which you have given to the many demands made by it on your time.

Very respectfully, your obedient servant,

DAVID T. DAY,
Geologist in Charge.

Hon. CHARLES D. WALCOTT,
Director United States Geological Survey.

1

INTRODUCTION.

In this report, the twelfth of the series Mineral Resources of the United States, the scope has been limited more to the statistics of production of the minerals of the United States and to statements of the conditions of their occurrence, and less space devoted to the technical features of development. In the preceding volume much information was given in regard to the mineral resources of foreign countries. This it has not seemed necessary to repeat in the present volume.

Sources of information.—The census method of obtaining information, by receiving from each producer in the United States a return covering the statistics of production, is followed more closely year by year as the producers acquire a better understanding of the purpose and usefulness of these publications. The statistics of production of gold and silver are those of the Director of the Mint, which are accepted as official in this report. The statistics of imports and exports are obtained through the courtesy of the Chief of the Bureau of Statistics of the Treasury Department. The names of the experts who give only a part of their time to the work of this report are printed at the heads of the chapters which they have contributed. It is impossible to acknowledge the great assistance which has been so freely rendered, not only by the producers of minerals themselves but by the voluntary contributions of many local experts.

A brief review of the principal statistical results shown by the report is given in the pages which immediately follow.

MINERAL RESOURCES OF THE UNITED STATES, 1895.

DAVID T. DAY, *Chief of Division.*

SUMMARY.

The total value of the mineral products of the United States for the year 1895 increased nearly one hundred million dollars beyond the value for 1894, or from $527,144,381 to $622,687,668. This increase is a long step toward recovery from the depression to which the mineral industry, like all others, has been subjected. The total value is slightly less than the greatest we have ever known, which was over $648,000,000, in 1892. In terms of quantities produced, instead of value received, 1895 is greatest. In other words, prices are lower.

If we consider for a moment the total values recorded in these reports since 1880 the increase from $369,319,000 to $622,687,668 is significant, and while it is impossible to select any year as a normal one from which to note increases and decreases and to record the permanent increase in the mining industry, still the average for these sixteen years gives a fair approximation to what our normal mineral product should have been half way between these dates, or in 1888. Comparing this computed normal product with the actual products, we see that the average yearly gain due to the general growth of the industry should be about $25,000,000, or the product for 1895 should have been $670,000,000. The great products of 1892 and 1895 show the ease with which the mines can respond to any unusual demand. They show that the capacity is significantly greater than the ability to market the product. In fact, it is difficult to confine the large capacity to actual requirements. With very slight encouragement the product takes a phenomenal stride. In 1892 and 1895 the product most difficult to hold in check was iron. This product easily controls the variations in the total value, either by the quantity produced or by the changes in price.

While the coal product is so great as to make a significant factor in the total value it is much steadier, and in spite of the extra demand for it in order to produce any extra supply of iron. The increased output of iron in 1895 was necessary because of the great retrenchment in 1894. The railroads ordered as little iron as possible in that year, but ordered freely in 1895 to take advantage of prices while they were still low but advancing. This advance was a marked industrial feature of the year, and continued until September.

5

The United States shared in the general increase in gold production, the increase being shown in nearly all the gold-producing States, but coming principally from Cripple Creek and other new camps in Colorado. The gain in the quantity of petroleum, but especially the phenomenal increase in its price, was one of the great features of the year.

METALS.

Iron and steel.—The declining tendency in production in 1894 noted in the previous report was changed in 1895 to one of the most remarkable increases in production of pig iron known in the history of the industry in the United States, it being from 6,657,388 long tons in 1894 to 9,446,308 tons in 1895, or nearly 42 per cent. This is the largest product ever attained in this country, the nearest approach to it being in 1890, when the output was 9,202,703 tons. The value also increased from $65,007,247 to $105,198,550, or from $9.76 to $11.14 per ton. The value per ton in 1890, the year of nearest approach to 1895, was $16.43.

Iron ores.—The production of iron ores in 1895 was 15,957,614 long tons, valued at $18,219,684, as compared with 11,879,679 long tons, with a value of $13,577,325, in 1894. Twenty-five States and Territories contributed to make up this total in 1895, an amount exceeded only by the outputs of the years 1890 and 1892. A comparison between the quantities reported indicates an increased production in 1895 of 34.33 per cent on the total for 1894, and with but six exceptions all of the iron-ore producing States participated in this advance. Owing to contracts that were made in advance, the average price per ton of iron ore was not so high in 1895 as in years previous to 1894, but the value per ton in 1896 bids fair to be much higher.

Steel.—The total value in the United States of all forms of steel in 1895 was $117,500,000. Of this total $31,640,000 was for steel rails and $85,860,000 for other forms of steel. The value of the steel other than rails is that for the raw and intermediate forms, not for the most finished forms.

Limestone for iron flux.—This product naturally followed the course of the iron industry and showed a large increase, or from 3,698,550 long tons in 1894, worth $1,849,275, to 5,247,949 tons in 1895, worth $2,623,974.

Gold and silver.—The steady increase in the gold product of the United States since 1892 was kept up during 1895, increasing from 1,910,816 ounces in 1894 to 2,254,760 ounces in 1895. The value of these products was $39,500,000 and $46,610,000, respectively. The production of silver also increased from 49,501,122 ounces in 1894 to 55,727,000 ounces in 1895 with coining values, respectively, of $64,000,000 and $72,051,000.

Copper.—Copper production followed the upward tendency of the other metals and increased from 354,188,374 pounds in 1894 to 380,613,404 pounds in 1895. The value increased from $32,171,220 in 1894 to $37,497,490 in 1895. All of the foregoing was from domestic ores.

In addition 10,678,434 pounds in 1894, worth $969,922, and 12,026,560 pounds in 1895, worth $1,184,857, were produced from imported pyrites.

Lead.—The production of lead increased from 159,331 short tons in 1894 to 170,000 in 1895. The value was $9,942,254 in 1894 and $11,220,000 in 1895.

Zinc.—The rapidly increasing product of this metal, which was checked in 1893 and 1894, was resumed in 1895, when 89,686 short tons were produced, worth $6,278,020, as compared with 75,328 short tons in 1894 worth $5,288,026.

Quicksilver.—The increase in production noted in 1894 was continued in 1895, the figures being 36,104 flasks in 1895, as compared with 30,416 flasks in 1894. The value of this product increased from $934,000 in 1894 to $1,337,131 in 1895.

Manganese.—The production of manganese ore increased from 6,308 long tons in 1894 to 9,547 in 1895. This increase came mostly from two States, Arkansas and Georgia, these alone producing more than the entire product in 1894. The Virginia product continued to decline. The manganiferous iron ore product declined quite markedly in 1895, or from 205,488 long tons, valued at $408,597, in 1894, to 125,729 long tons, valued at $233,988, in 1895. The manganiferous zinc ores increased in quantity and value in 1895.

Aluminum.—Aluminum continued its increased product in 1895, the quantity rising from 550,000 pounds in 1894 to 920,000 pounds in 1895. The value increased from $316,250 in 1894 to $464,600 in 1895.

Antimony.—The antimony product increased from 200 short tons in 1894 to 450 tons in 1895, and the value from $36,000 in 1894 to $68,000 in 1895. The product was from California, Nevada, and Montana. This includes the metal produced from imported ores, there having been but 86 tons of domestic ore raised during the year.

Nickel.—The product of nickel in the United States in 1895 increased slightly over that of 1894, or from 9,616 pounds to 10,302 pounds, while the value decreased from $3,269 in 1894 to $3,091 in 1895. The Nevada and Oregon mines are still nonproducers. There are vague reports of new deposits in Minnesota, and two companies have been organized to develop them.

Tin.—No tin was produced in the United States in 1895.

Platinum.—The platinum product, all of which comes from the Pacific Coast, continues small, though there was a slight increase in the product—from 100 ounces, worth $600 in 1894, to 150 ounces, worth $900 in 1895.

FUELS.

Coal.—The total product of coal of all kinds in 1895 was 172,426,366 long tons, or 193,117,530 short tons, compared to 152,447,791 long tons, or 170,741,526 short tons, in 1894, an increase of 22,376,004 long tons, or 25,061,124 short tons, or 13 per cent. The value of the product increased from $186,141,564 to $197,769,043, a gain of $11,627,479, or about 6 per cent, showing that the percentage of increase in value was less than half of that of the increase in product. The product in 1895 was made up of 51,785,122 long tons of Pennsylvania anthracite (against 46,358,144 long tons in 1894), valued at $82,019,272, and

120.641,244 long tons of bituminous coal (against 106,089,647 long tons in 1894), valued at $115,749,771. The bituminous product includes scattering lots of anthracite from Colorado and New Mexico.

The year was marked by a production considerably in excess of the market demands, and values were much reduced in consequence. The average price obtained for the anthracite coal marketed was $1.72 per long ton at the mines, against $1.85 in 1894 and $1.94 in 1893. In arriving at this average price the amount of coal consumed at the collieries is not considered. This factor consists of the culm or slack, which would otherwise be thrown on the dump or wasted. In determining the value of bituminous coal all the coal mined and sold or used is included. The average price for this product shows a decline from 91 cents per short ton in 1894 to 86 cents in 1895. This decline in value was general throughout the United States, there being but three or four comparatively unimportant States whose value was larger in proportion in 1895 than in 1894.

Petroleum.—The most notable features in connection with the production of crude petroleum in 1895 are: (1) The notable increase in production, especially in Ohio, Indiana, and California; (2) the decrease in stocks; (3) the rise in prices, and (4) the extension southward of the profitable producing districts in the Appalachian range.

Briefly summarized, the facts regarding these four features of 1895 are as follows:

1. The production of petroleum in the United States increased from 49,344,516 barrels in 1894 to 52,983,526 barrels in 1895, most of the important producing districts sharing in this increase. The production of Pennsylvania increased from 18,077,559 barrels in 1894 to 18,231,442 barrels in 1895, an increase of 153,883 barrels, or 0.85 of 1 per cent; of Ohio, from 16,792,154 barrels in 1894 to 19,545,233 barrels in 1895, an increase of 2,753,079 barrels, or 16.4 per cent. This increase in Ohio was fairly distributed throughout the two important producing districts. The production of Indiana increased from 3,688,666 barrels in 1894 to 4,386,132 barrels in 1895, an increase of 697,466 barrels, or nearly 19 per cent, while the production of California, owing to the new discoveries at Los Angeles, increased from 705,969 barrels in 1894 to 1,208,482 barrels in 1895, an increase of 71 per cent, the largest percentage increase of any of the States.

2. The stocks of crude petroleum in the Appalachian oil field at the close of 1895 were 5,344,784 barrels, as compared with 6,499,880 barrels at the close of 1894. The largest stocks at the close of any one month in 1895 were 5,859,348 barrels in January, as compared with 11,755,219 barrels, the largest stocks in 1894, which were also at the close of January. The smallest stocks at the close of any one month in 1895 were those of June, the stocks being 4,275,506 barrels, while the smallest stocks at the close of any one month in 1894 were those of December, as noted above. The average stocks at the close of each month in 1895 were 4,879,770 barrels.

3. The average value of certificate oil in the Pennsylvania field in 1895 was $1.35⅞, as compared with 83⅝ cents in 1894. This is the highest average price since 1877. The highest average price during any one month in 1895 was $1.79, in April; the lowest, 99 cents, in January. In the Lima field the average price advanced from 48 cents a barrel in 1894 to 71¾ cents in 1895. The total value of the 49,344,516 barrels produced in the United States in 1894 was $35,522,095, or nearly 72 cents a barrel, while the total value of the 52,983,526 barrels produced in 1895 was $57,691,279, or about $1.09.

Coke.—The total product of coke in the United States in 1895 was 13,333,741 short tons, as compared with 9,203,632 short tons in 1894. These two amounts represent the largest and smallest product of coke in recent years. The fluctuation was caused by the rise and decline of the pig-iron product, in the manufacture of which almost the entire coke output is consumed. The production of coke-smelted iron, or with a mixture of coke and anthracite, increased from 6,314,891 long tons in 1894 to 9,164,365 tons in 1895.

Natural gas.—This is one of the few important mineral products which showed a decline in value in 1895. The value decreased from $13,954,400 in 1894 to $13,006,650 in 1895. Among the notable features may be mentioned:

1. The decreasing pressure in all the natural gas fields, but greatest in Pennsylvania.

2. Resulting from the above: A great falling off in the product of gas per well, which has led to a great increase in the number of wells so as to maintain the supply.

3. The life of each well has been greatly shortened. In some cases in western Pennsylvania the average life of a well is only six months.

STRUCTURAL MATERIALS.

Stone.—The value of the total product of stone of all kinds decreased from $37,055,030 in 1894 to $34,688,816 in 1895. All the varieties except sandstone participated in this decrease.

Soapstone.—The production of soapstone in the form of slabs, etc., in 1895 amounted to 21,495 short tons, valued at $266,495, which was a decrease from 1894, when the product was 23,144 tons, valued at $401,325. The production of fibrous talc also showed a slight decrease, or from 39,906 short tons in 1894, worth $435,060, compared with 39,240 short tons, valued at $370,895, in 1895.

Clays.—The value of the brick clays aggregated $9,000,000, practically the same amount as in 1894. The product of all other clays, i. e., potters' clays, amounted to $800,000, showing no essential change from 1894.

The value of the clay products in the United States in 1895 was $65,319,806 as compared with $64,575,385 in 1894.

Fuller's earth.—This variety of clay was discovered in considerable quantity near Quincy, Fla., and began to compete with the imported material for filtering oils. Up to the close of 1895, 6,900 tons were produced, worth $41,400 at the point of shipment. Other deposits have been located near River Junction and near Ocala and Tampa, Fla. Extensions of the Quincy deposits have been found along the creeks to the north near Whigham, Ga.; and deposits, the value of which has not yet been established, have been noted in North Carolina, Virginia, and South Dakota.

Cement.—Natural rock cement showed the same slight increase which it did in 1894—from 7,563,488 barrels (of 300 pounds each), worth $3,635,731 in 1894 to 7,741,077 barrels, worth $3,895,424 in 1895. Meanwhile the Portland cement industry progressed markedly from a product of 798,757 barrels in 1894, worth $1,383,473, to 990,324 barrels in 1895, worth $1,586,830. The number of works decreased from 24 to 22.

ABRASIVES.

Millstones.—These increased from a value of $13,887 in 1894 to $22,542 in 1895.

Grindstones.—This industry shows a slight decline from a value of $223,214 in 1894 to $205,768 in 1895.

Corundum and emery.—The year 1895 shows an increase from 1,495 long tons in 1894, worth $95,936, to 2,102 tons, worth $106,256. The industry is still governed largely by the importation of low-priced emery from Asia Minor.

Oilstones.—There is little change in the trade, the old sources of supply increasing the product slightly from a value of $136,873 in 1894 to $155,881 in 1895.

CHEMICAL MATERIALS.

Phosphate rock.—In 1895, for the first time, the product reached a million long tons, i. e., 1,038,551, worth $3,606,094. The chief feature of interest is the fierce competition of the river-pebble deposits on Peace River in Florida. It is probable that the present low prices will gradually rise in this year. Phosphate rock from western Tennessee has become a permanent factor in the Western trade.

Gypsum.—This product increased from 239,312 short tons in 1894 to 265,503 tons in 1895 with about a constant price.

Salt.—The principal feature of interest was the discovery of a very thick deposit of rock salt on Orange Island, Louisiana, near the old mines of Avery's Island. The total product of salt in the United States increased from 12,967,417 in 1894 to 13,669,649 barrels in 1895, but the total value decreased from $4,739,285 to $4,423,084.

Bromine.—The industry shows an increase. Including the bromine in bromide of sodium, made directly, in 1895, the total product was 517,421 pounds, worth $134,343. In 1894, 379,444 pounds were made with a proportionate value.

Sulphur.—The point of principal interest is Sulphur Station, Louisiana, where the efficiency of the Frasch process has been increased by an air-lift pump by which two or three thousand tons were brought to the surface, partly in 1896, but not yet sold. In addition, the Utah deposits sold about 1,000 tons.

Pyrite.—This industry shows a decline from 105,940 long tons in 1894 to 99,549 tons in 1895.

Borax.—The product declined from 14,680,130 pounds in 1894 to 11,918,000 in 1895, with a similar decline in value.

Fluorspar.—The product decreased in two years from 12,400 short tons in 1893 to 4,000 tons in 1895.

Chromic iron ore.—The product declined from 3,680 long tons in 1894 to 1,740 tons in 1895. The greater supply is imported from Smyrna, but there are prospects of some future imports from Canada.

PIGMENTS.

Metallic paint.—The product shows a substantial increase, both in amount and value, over 1894. The product in 1895 was 28,859 short tons, valued at $319,142, against 25,375 short tons, valued at $284,883 in 1894, a gain of 3,484 short tons, or about 14 per cent in amount, and of $34,259, or something over 12 per cent in value.

Ocher, umber, etc.—The product of ocher increased in nearly the same proportion as that of metallic paint, from 9,768 short tons in 1894, valued at $96,935, to 12,045 tons, valued at $139,328 in 1895, a gain of 2,277 short tons, or about 23 per cent in amount, but having the advantage of a greater increase in value, proportionately—$42,393, more than 43 per cent. The production of umber increased from 265 short tons, valued at $3,830, to 320 short tons, valued at $4,350. The sienna output increased from 160 tons to 275 tons, with a value more than doubled—from $3,250 to $6,950. The amount of soapstone ground for pigment increased to 270 short tons, valued at $3,200, from 75 tons, worth $525 in 1894. Pigment from slate increased from 2,650 tons to 4,331 tons.

Venetian reds.—A product of 4,595 short tons, valued at $102,900, is reported for 1895, against 2,983 short tons, worth $73,300 in 1894. With the exception of 1892, this was the largest product ever reported.

Barytes.—The product declined again, or from 23,335 long tons, worth $86,983, in 1894, to 21,529 long tons, worth $68,321 in 1895.

Cobalt oxide.—The product is limited to amount extracted from the speiss obtained in lead smelting. It amounted to 14,458 pounds, worth $20,675.

Zinc white.—The production rallied slightly, or from 19,987 short tons in 1894, worth $1,399,090, to 20,710 short tons, worth $1,449,700, in 1895.

MISCELLANEOUS.

Precious stones.—The rough gems of domestic production were valued at $113,621 in 1895, against $132,250 in 1894.

Mica.—The industry continues in the unsatisfactory condition mentioned in the preceding report, though the value of the product was slightly in excess of that of 1894. The mines yielded 44,325 pounds of cut mica, valued at $49,218; and 148 tons of scrap mica, worth $5,450. Added to this was about 40,000 pounds of small-sized sheet mica, worth $1,163, making a total value for the product in 1895 of $55,831. The value of all kinds of mica produced in 1894 was $52,388.

Feldspar.—The product increased 35 per cent, or from 17,200 long tons in 1894, worth $98,900, to 23,400 long tons in 1895, worth $133,400.

Flint.—The flint used in pottery, etc., in 1895, amounted to 36,800 long tons, worth $117,760.

Asphaltum.—The value of the product was about the same in 1895 as in 1894, being $348,281, and $353,400, respectively. This, taken in connection with an increase in output from 60,570 to 68,163 short tons, indicates a sympathy with the general depression in values. The product was from California, Kentucky, Texas, and Utah.

Asbestos.—Owing to the development of asbestos mines in Georgia, the product increased considerably, notwithstanding a large decrease in California's output. The product in 1895 was 795 short tons, worth $13,525, against 325 tons, valued at $4,463, in 1894. The Wyoming properties have not yet assumed commercial importance.

Infusorial earth.—The product in 1894 was small, having a value of but $11,718, little more than half that of 1893. Better conditions prevailed in 1895, and the value of the product advanced to $20,514.

Magnesite.—This product still comes from California, and increased from 1,440 short tons in 1894, worth $10,240, to 2,200 short tons in 1895, worth $17,000.

Mineral waters.—The product was almost stationary, i. e., 21,569,608 gallons sold at $3,741,846 in 1894, and 21,463,543 gallons in 1895, which sold at the higher value of $4,254,237.

Metallic products of the United States in 1895.

Product.	Quantity.	Value.
Pig iron....................long tons..	9,446,308	$105,198,550
Silver, coining value.........troy ounces..	55,727,000	72,051,000
Gold, coining value ....do....	2,254,760	46,610,000
Copper....................pounds..	392,639,964	38,682,347
Lead......................short tons..	170,000	11,220,000
Zinc......................do....	89,686	6,278,020
Quicksilver....................flasks..	36,104	1,337,131
Aluminium....................pounds..	920,000	464,600
Antimony ....short tons..	450	68,000
Nickel ....pounds..	10,302	3,091
Platinum ....troy ounces..	150	900
Total		281,913,639

Nonmetallic products of the United States in 1895.

Product.	Quantity.	Value.
Bituminous coal ....short tons..	135, 118, 193	$115, 749, 771
Pennsylvania anthracite.........long tons..	51, 785, 122	82, 019, 272
Building stone		34, 688, 816
Petroleum.........................barrels..	52, 983, 526	57, 691, 279
Natural gas		13, 006, 650
Brick clay		9, 000, 000
Clay (all other than brick) ......long tons..	360, 000	800, 000
Cement.........................barrels..	8, 731, 401	5, 482, 254
Mineral waters ....gallons sold..	21, 463, 543	4, 254, 237
Phosphate rock.................long tons..	1, 038, 551	3, 606, 094
Salt ....barrels..	13, 669, 649	4, 423, 084
Limestone for iron flux ....long tons..	5, 247, 949	2, 623, 974
Zinc white...................short tons..	20, 710	1, 449, 700
Gypsum ....do....	265, 503	807, 447
Borax ....pounds..	11, 918, 000	595, 900
Mineral paints...............short tons..	50, 695	621, 552
Grindstones		205, 768
Fibrous talc................short tons..	39, 240	370, 895
Asphaltum.......................do....	68, 163	348, 281
Soapstone........................do....	21, 495	266, 495
Precious stones		113, 621
Pyrites.......................long tons..	99, 549	322, 845
Corundum and emery ....short tons..	2, 102	106, 256
Oilstones, etc		155, 881
Mica		55, 831
Barytes (crude) ....long tons..	21, 529	68, 321
Bromine ....pounds..	517, 421	134, 343
Fluorspar ....short tons..	4, 000	24, 000
Feldspar ....long tons..	23, 400	133, 400
Manganese ore ....do....	9, 547	71, 760
Flint ....do....	36, 800	117, 760
Monazite......................pounds..	1, 573, 000	137, 150
Graphite		52, 582
Bauxite.....................long tons..	17, 069	44, 000
Sulphur ....short tons..	1, 800	42, 000
Fuller's earth ....do....	6, 900	41, 400
Marls ....do....	60, 000	30, 000
Infusorial earth..................do....	4, 954	20, 514
Millstones................................		22, 542
Chromic iron ore ....long tons..	1, 740	16, 795
Cobalt oxide ....pounds..	14, 458	20, 675
Magnesite...................short tons..	2, 200	17, 000
Asbestos ....do....	795	13, 525
Rutile.........................pounds..	100	350
Total		339, 774, 029

Résumé of the mineral products of the United States in 1895.

Total value of metallic products.. $281, 913, 639
Total value of nonmetallic products.................................... 339, 774, 029
Estimated value of mineral products unspecified 1, 000, 000

Grand total.. 622, 687, 668

Mineral products of the United States

Products.	1880.	
	Quantity.	Value.
METALLIC.		
1 Pig iron, value at Philadelphia.......long tons..	3, 375, 912	$89, 315, 569
2 Silver, coining value.................troy ounces..	30, 320, 000	39, 200, 000
3 Gold, coining value...........................do....	1, 741, 500	36, 000, 000
4 Copper, value at New York City.........pounds..	60, 480, 000	11, 491, 200
5 Lead, value at New York City........short tons..	97, 825	9, 782, 500
6 Zinc, value at New York City.............do....	23, 239	2, 277, 432
7 Quicksilver, value at San Francisco......flasks..	59, 926	1, 797, 780
8 Nickel, value at Philadelphia............pounds..	329, 968	164, 984
9 Aluminum, value at Pittsburg.............do....		
10 Antimony, value at San Francisco....short tons..	50	10, 000
11 Platinum, value (crude) at San Francisco, ...troy ounces..	100	400
12 Total value of metallic products............		190, 039, 865
NONMETALLIC (spot values).		
13 Bituminous coal....................long tons..	38, 242, 641	53, 443, 718
14 Pennsylvania anthracite..................do....	25, 580, 189	42, 196, 678
15 Building stone....................................		18, 356, 055
16 Petroleum ....barrels..	26, 286, 123	24, 183, 233
17 Lime ....do....	28, 000, 000	19, 000, 000
18 Natural gas......................................		
19 Cement......................barrels..	2, 072, 943	1, 852, 707
20 Salt....................................do....	5, 961, 060	4, 829, 566
21 Phosphate rock.................long tons..	211, 377	1, 123, 823
22 Limestone for iron flux..................do....	4, 500, 000	3, 800, 000
23 Mineral waters.................gallons sold..	2, 000, 000	500, 000
24 Zinc white....................short tons..	10, 107	763, 738
25 Potters' clay...................long tons..	25, 783	200, 457
26 Mineral paints................short tons..	3, 604	135, 840
27 Borax ....pounds..	3, 692, 443	277, 233
28 Gypsum ....short tons..	90, 000	400, 000
29 Grindstones		500, 000
30 Fibrous talc ....short tons..	4, 210	54, 730
31 Pyrites.......................long tons..	2, 000	5, 000
32 Soapstone ....short tons..	8, 441	66, 665
33 Manganese ore ....long tons..	5, 761	86, 415
34 Asphaltum ....short tons..	444	4, 440
35 Precious stones......................		100, 000
36 Bromine ....pounds..	404, 690	114, 752
37 Corundum.....................short tons..	1, 044	29, 280
38 Barytes (crude) ....long tons..	20, 000	80, 000
39 Graphite ....pounds..		49, 800
40 Millstones............................		200, 000
41 Novaculite ....pounds..	420, 000	8, 000
42 Marls........................short tons..	1, 000, 000	500, 000
43 Flint.........................long tons..	20, 000	80, 000
44 Fluorspar....................short tons..	4, 000	16, 000
45 Chromic iron ore..............long tons..	2, 288	27, 808
46 Infusorial earth...............short tons..	1, 833	45, 660
47 Feldspar ....long tons..	12, 500	60, 000
48 Mica ....pounds..	81, 669	127, 825
49 Cobalt oxide ....do....	7, 251	24, 000
50 Slate ground as a pigment ....short tons..	1, 000	10, 000
51 Sulphur......................do....	600	21, 000
52 Asbestos ....do....	150	4, 312
53 Rutile........................pounds..	100	400
54 Lithographic stone ....short tons..		
55 Total value of nonmetallic mineral products.		173, 279, 135
56 Total value of metallic products		190, 039, 865
57 Estimated value of mineral products unspecified.		6, 000, 000
58 Grand total..........................		369, 319, 000

for the calendar years 1880 to 1895.

	1881.		1882.		1883.		
	Quantity.	Value.	Quantity.	Value.	Quantity.	Value.	
	4,144,254	$87,029,334	4,623,323	$106,336,429	4,595,510	$91,910,200	1
	33,077,000	43,000,000	36,197,695	46,800,000	35,733,622	46,200,000	2
	1,676,300	34,700,000	1,572,186	32,500,000	1,451,249	30,000,000	3
	71,680,000	12,175,600	91,646,232	16,038,091	117,151,795	18,064,807	4
	117,085	11,240,160	132,890	12,624,550	143,957	12,322,719	5
	26,800	2,680,000	33,765	3,646,620	36,872	3,311,106	6
	60,851	1,764,679	52,732	1,487,042	46,725	1,253,632	7
	265,668	292,235	281,616	309,777	58,800	52,920	8
					83	875	9
	50	10,000	60	12,000	60	12,000	10
	100	400	200	600	200	600	11
	....	192,892,408	....	219,755,109	....	203,128,859	12
	48,179,475	60,224,344	60,861,190	76,076,487	68,531,500	82,237,800	13
	28,500,016	64,125,036	31,358,264	70,556,094	34,336,469	77,257,055	14
	....	20,000,000	....	21,000,000	....	20,000,000	15
	27,661,238	25,448,339	30,510,830	24,065,988	23,449,633	25,790,252	16
	30,000,000	20,000,000	31,000,000	21,700,000	32,000,000	19,200,000	17
	....	....	....	215,000	....	475,000	18
	2,500,000	2,000,000	3,250,000	3,672,750	4,190,000	4,293,500	19
	6,200,000	4,200,000	6,412,373	4,320,140	6,192,231	4,211,042	20
	266,734	1,980,259	332,077	1,992,462	378,380	2,270,280	21
	6,000,600	4,100,000	3,850,000	2,310,000	3,814,273	1,907,136	22
	3,700,000	700,000	5,000,000	800,000	7,529,423	1,119,603	23
	10,000	700,000	10,000	700,000	12,000	810,000	24
	25,000	200,000	30,000	240,000	32,000	250,000	25
	6,000	100,000	7,000	105,000	7,000	84,000	26
	4,046,000	304,461	4,236,291	338,903	6,500,000	585,000	27
	85,000	350,000	100,000	450,000	90,000	420,000	28
	....	500,000	....	700,000	....	600,000	29
	5,000	60,000	6,000	75,000	6,000	75,000	30
	10,000	60,000	12,000	72,000	25,000	137,500	31
	7,000	75,000	6,000	90,000	8,000	150,000	32
	4,895	73,425	4,532	67,980	6,155	92,325	33
	2,000	8,000	3,000	10,500	3,000	10,500	34
	....	110,000	....	150,000	....	207,050	35
	300,000	75,000	250,000	75,000	301,100	72,264	36
	500	80,000	500	80,000	550	100,000	37
	20,000	80,000	20,000	80,000	27,000	108,000	38
	400,000	30,000	425,000	34,000	575,000	46,000	39
	....	150,000	....	200,000	....	150,000	40
	500,000	8,580	600,000	10,000	600,000	10,000	41
	1,000,000	500,000	1,080,000	540,000	972,000	486,000	42
	25,000	100,000	25,000	100,000	25,000	100,000	43
	4,000	16,000	4,000	20,000	4,000	20,000	44
	2,000	30,000	2,500	50,000	3,000	60,000	45
	1,000	10,000	1,000	8,000	1,000	5,000	46
	14,000	70,000	14,000	70,000	14,100	71,112	47
	100,000	250,000	100,000	250,000	114,000	285,000	48
	8,280	25,000	11,653	32,046	1,090	2,795	49
	1,000	10,000	2,000	24,000	2,000	24,000	50
	600	21,000	600	21,000	1,000	27,000	51
	200	7,000	1,200	36,000	1,000	30,000	52
	200	700	500	1,800	550	2,000	53
	50	1,000	....	....	....	....	54
	....	206,783,144	....	231,340,150	....	243,812,214	55
	....	192,892,408	....	219,755,109	....	203,128,859	56
	....	6,500,000	....	6,500,000	....	6,500,000	57
	....	406,175,552	....	457,595,259	....	453,441,073	58

Mineral products of the United States for

	Products.	1884.	
		Quantity.	Value.
	METALLIC.		
1	Pig iron, value at Philadelphia.......long tons..	4, 097, 868	$73, 761, 624
2	Silver, coining value.................troy ounces..	37, 744, 605	48, 800, 000
3	Gold, coining value.......................do....	1, 489, 949	30, 800, 000
4	Copper, value at New York City.........pounds..	145, 221, 931	17, 789, 687
5	Lead, value at New York City........short tons..	139, 897	10, 537, 012
6	Zinc, value at New York City.............do....	38, 544	3, 422, 707
7	Quicksilver, value at San Francisco.......flasks..	31, 913	936, 327
8	Nickel, value at Philadelphia............pounds..	64, 550	48, 412
9	Aluminum, value at Pittsburg.............do....	150	1, 350
10	Antimony, value at San Francisco....short tons..	60	12, 000
11	Platinum, value (crude) at San Francisco, ...troy ounces..	150	450
12	Total value of metallic products...........	------------	186, 109, 599
	NONMETALLIC (spot values).		
13	Bituminous coal...................long tons..	73, 730, 539	77, 417, 066
14	Pennsylvania anthracite..................do....	33, 175, 756	66, 351, 512
15	Building stone....................................		19, 000, 000
16	Petroleum.....................barrels..	24, 218, 438	20, 595, 966
17	Lime.......................................do....	37, 000, 000	18, 500, 000
18	Natural gas	------------	1, 460, 000
19	Brick clay......................................		
20	Clay (all other than brick)...........long tons..	35, 000	270, 000
21	Cement......................barrels..	4, 000, 000	3, 720, 000
22	Salt.......................................do....	6, 514, 937	4, 197, 734
23	Phosphate rock...................long tons..	431, 779	2, 374, 784
24	Limestone for iron flux..................do....	3, 401, 930	1, 700, 965
25	Mineral waters.................gallons sold..	10, 215, 328	1, 459, 143
26	Zinc white..................short tons..	13, 000	910, 000
27	Mineral paints ....do....	7, 000	84, 000
28	Borax.......................pounds..	7, 000, 000	490, 000
29	Gypsum....................short tons..	90, 000	390, 000
30	Grindstones....................................		570, 000
31	Fibrous talc ....short tons..	10, 000	110, 000
32	Pyrites......................long tons..	35, 000	175, 000
33	Soapstone ....short tons..	10, 000	200, 000
34	Manganese ore ....long tons..	10, 180	122, 160
35	Asphaltum ....short tons..	3, 000	10, 500
36	Precious stones................................		222, 975
37	Bromine.....................pounds..	281, 100	67, 464
38	Corundum...................short tons..	600	108, 000
39	Barytes (crude) ....long tons..	25, 000	100, 000
40	Graphite...................pounds..	------------	
41	Millstones.....................................		150, 000
42	Oilstones, etc.................pounds..	800, 000	12, 000
43	Marls.....................short tons..	875, 000	437, 500
44	Flint.......................long tons..	30, 000	120, 000
45	Fluorspar ....short tons..	4, 000	20, 000
46	Chromic iron ore...............long tons..	2, 000	35, 000
47	Infusorial earth...............short tons..	1, 000	5, 000
48	Feldspar ....long tons..	10, 900	55, 112
49	Mica.......................pounds..	147, 410	368, 525
50	Cobalt oxide ....do....	2, 000	5, 100
51	Slate ground as a pigment...........short tons..	2, 000	20, 000
52	Sulphur ....do....	500	12, 000
53	Asbestos ....do....	1, 000	30, 000
54	Rutile.......................pounds..	600	2, 000
55	Lithographic stone ....short tons..	------------	------------
56	Total value of nonmetallic mineral products....	------------	221, 879, 506
57	Total value of metallic products...........	------------	186, 109, 599
58	Estimated value of mineral products unspecified..	------------	5, 000, 000
59	Grand total.......................	------------	412, 989, 105

the calendar years 1880 to 1895—Continued.

	1885.		1886.		1887.	
	Quantity.	Value.	Quantity.	Value.	Quantity.	Value.	
4,044,425	$64,712,400	5,683,329	$95,195,760	6,417,148	$121,925,800	1
39,910,279	51,600,000	39,445,312	51,000,000	41,269,240	53,350,000	2
1,538,376	31,800,000	1,881,250	35,000,000	1,596,500	33,000,000	3
170,962,607	18,292,999	161,235,381	16,527,651	185,227,331	21,115,916	4
129,412	10,469,431	130,629	12,200,749	145,700	13,113,000	5
40,688	3,539,856	42,641	3,752,408	50,340	4,782,300	6
32,073	979,189	29,981	1,060,000	33,825	1,429,000	7
277,904	179,975	214,992	127,157	205,566	133,200	8
283	2,550	3,000	27,000	18,000	59,000	9
50	10,000	35	7,000	75	15,000	10
250	187	50	100	448	1,838	11
....	181,586,587	....	214,897,825	....	248,925,054	12
64,840,668	82,347,648	73,707,957	78,481,056	87,887,360	98,004,656	13
34,228,548	76,671,948	34,853,077	76,119,120	37,578,747	84,552,181	14
	19,000,000		19,000,000		25,000,000	15
21,847,205	19,198,243	28,064,841	19,996,313	28,278,866	18,877,094	16
40,000,000	20,000,000	....	....			17
....	4,857,200		10,012,000	....	15,817,500	18
			6,200,000		7,000,000	19
36,000	275,000	40,000	325,000	43,000	340,000	20
4,150,000	3,492,500	4,500,000	3,990,000	6,692,744	5,674,377	21
7,038,653	4,825,345	7,707,081	4,736,585	7,831,962	4,093,846	22
437,856	2,846,064	430,549	1,872,936	480,558	1,836,818	23
3,356,956	1,678,478	4,717,163	2,830,297	5,377,000	3,226,200	24
9,148,401	1,312,845	8,950,317	1,284,070	8,259,609	1,261,463	25
15,000	1,050,000	18,000	1,440,000	18,000	1,440,000	26
3,950	43,575	18,800	315,000	22,000	330,000	27
8,000,000	480,000	9,778,290	488,915	11,000,000	550,000	28
90,405	405,000	95,250	428,625	95,000	425,000	29
....	500,000	....	250,000		224,400	30
10,000	110,000	12,000	125,000	15,000	160,000	31
49,000	220,500	55,000	220,000	52,000	210,000	32
10,000	200,000	12,000	225,000	12,000	225,000	33
23,258	190,281	30,193	277,636	34,524	333,844	34
3,000	10,500	3,500	14,000	4,000	16,000	35
....	209,900	....	119,056	....	163,600	36
310,000	89,900	428,334	141,350	199,087	61,717	37
600	108,000	615	116,196	600	108,000	38
15,000	75,000	10,000	50,000	15,000	75,000	39
327,883	26,231	415,525	33,212	416,000	31,000	40
	100,000		140,000		100,000	41
1,000,000	15,000	1,160,000	15,000	1,200,000	16,000	42
875,000	437,500	800,000	400,000	600,000	300,000	43
30,000	120,000	30,000	120,000	32,000	185,000	44
5,000	22,500	5,000	22,000	5,000	20,000	45
2,700	40,000	2,000	30,000	3,000	40,000	46
1,000	5,000	1,200	6,000	3,000	15,000	47
13,600	68,000	14,900	74,500	10,200	56,100	48
92,000	161,000	40,000	70,000	70,000	142,250	49
68,723	65,373	35,000	36,878	18,340	18,774	50
1,975	24,687	....	....			51
715	17,875	2,500	75,000	3,000	100,000	52
300	9,000	200	6,000	150	4,500	53
600	2,000	600	2,000	1,000	3,000	54
						55
....	211,312,093	....	230,088,769	....	271,041,320	56
....	181,586,587	....	214,897,825	....	248,925,054	57
....	5,000,000	....	800,000	....	800,000	58
....	427,898,680	....	445,786,594	....	520,766,374	59

Mineral products of the United States

	Products.	1888.	
		Quantity.	Value.
	METALLIC.		
1	Pig iron, value at Philadelphia ....long tons..	6,489,738	$107,000,000
2	Silver, coining value ....troy ounces..	45,783,632	59,195,000
3	Gold, coining value.........................do....	1,604,927	33,175,000
4	Copper, value at New York City ....pounds..	231,270,622	33,833,954
5	Lead, value at New York City........short tons..	151,919	13,399,256
6	Zinc, value at New York City..............do....	55,903	5,500,855
7	Quicksilver, value at San Francisco ......flasks..	33,250	4,113,125
8	Aluminum, value at Pittsburg...........pounds..	19,000	65,000
9	Antimony, value at San Francisco....short tons..	100	20,000
10	Nickel, value at Philadelphia ....pounds..	204,328	127,632
11	Tin ....do....		
12	Platinum, value (crude) at San Francisco, ...troy ounces..	500	2,000
13	Total value of metallic products............		253,731,822
	NONMETALLIC (spot values).		
14	Bituminous coal.....................short tons..	102,039,838	101,860,529
15	Pennsylvania anthracite..............long tons..	41,624,611	89,020,483
16	Building stone		25,500,000
17	Petroleum..........................barrels..	27,612,025	17,947,620
18	Natural gas		22,629,875
19	Brick clay..		7,500,000
20	Clay (all other than brick)...........long tons..	36,750	300,000
21	Cement..............................barrels..	6,503,295	5,021,139
22	Mineral waters ....gallons sold..	9,578,648	1,679,302
23	Phosphate rock.....................long tons..	448,567	2,018,552
24	Salt................................barrels..	8,055,881	4,374,203
25	Limestone for iron flux ....long tons..	5,438,000	2,719,000
26	Zinc white ....short tons..	20,000	1,600,000
27	Gypsum ....do....	110,000	550,000
28	Borax ....pounds..	7,589,000	455,340
29	Mineral paints.....................short tons..	26,500	405,000
30	Grindstones.......................		281,800
31	Fibrous talc......................short tons..	20,000	210,000
32	Asphaltum.............................do....	53,800	331,500
33	Soapstone.............................do....	15,000	250,000
34	Precious stones		139,850
35	Pyrites..........................long tons..	54,331	167,658
36	Corundum........................short tons..	589	91,620
37	Oilstones, etc....................pounds..	1,500,000	18,000
38	Mica ....pounds..	48,000	70,000
39	Barytes (crude)....................long tons..	20,000	110,000
40	Bromine ....pounds..	307,386	95,290
41	Fluorspar ....short tons..	6,000	30,000
42	Feldspar ....long tons..	8,700	50,000
43	Manganese ore.........................do....	29,198	279,571
44	Flint ....do....	30,000	175,000
45	Graphite ....pounds..	400,000	33,000
46	Bauxite..........................long tons..		
47	Sulphur.........................short tons..		
48	Marls................................do....	300,000	150,000
49	Infusorial earth......................do....	1,500	7,500
50	Millstones		81,000
51	Chromic iron ore..................long tons..	1,500	20,000
52	Cobalt oxide ....pounds..	8,491	15,782
53	Magnesite ....short tons..		
54	Asbestos ....do....	100	3,000
55	Rutile ....pounds..	1,000	3,000
56	Ozocerite (refined) ....do....	43,500	3,000
57	Total value of nonmetallic mineral products.		286,197,614
58	Total value of metallic products..............		253,731,822
59	Estimated value of mineral products unspecified..		900,000
60	Grand total		540,829,436

for the calendar years 1880 to 1895—Continued.

1889.		1890.		1891.		
Quantity.	Value.	Quantity.	Value.	Quantity.	Value.	
7,603,642	$120,000,000	9,202,703	$151,200,410	8,279,870	$128,337,985	1
51,354,851	66,396,988	54,500,000	70,464,645	58,330,000	75,416,565	2
1,590,869	32,886,744	1,588,880	32,845,000	1,604,840	33,175,000	3
231,246,214	26,907,809	265,115,133	30,848,797	295,812,076	38,455,300	4
156,397	13,794,235	143,630	12,668,166	178,554	15,534,198	5
58,860	5,791,824	63,683	6,266,407	80,873	8,033,700	6
26,484	1,190,500	22,926	1,203,615	22,904	1,036,386	7
47,468	97,335	61,281	61,281	150,000	100,000	8
115	28,000	129	40,756	278	47,007	9
252,663	151,598	223,488	134,093	118,498	71,099	10
				125,289	25,058	11
500	2,000	600	2,500	100	500	12
	267,247,033		305,735,670		300,232,798	13
95,685,543	94,504,745	111,320,016	110,420,801	117,901,237	117,188,400	14
40,714,721	65,879,514	41,489,858	66,383,772	45,236,992	73,944,735	15
	42,809,706		47,000,000		47,294,746	16
35,163,513	26,963,340	45,822,672	35,365,105	54,291,980	30,526,553	17
	21,097,099		18,742,725		15,500,084	18
	8,000,000		8,500,000		9,000,000	19
294,344	635,578	350,000	756,000	400,000	900,000	20
7,000,000	5,000,000	8,000,000	6,000,000	8,222,792	6,680,951	21
12,780,471	1,748,458	13,907,418	2,600,750	18,392,732	2,996,259	22
550,245	2,937,776	510,499	3,213,795	587,988	3,651,150	23
8,005,565	4,195,412	8,776,991	4,752,286	9,987,945	4,716,121	24
6,318,000	3,159,000	5,521,622	2,760,811	5,000,000	2,300,000	25
16,970	1,357,600		1,600,000	23,700	1,600,000	26
267,769	764,118	182,995	574,523	208,126	628,051	27
8,000,000	500,000	9,500,000	617,500	13,380,000	869,700	28
34,307	483,766	47,732	681,992	49,652	678,478	29
	439,587		450,000		476,113	30
23,746	244,170	41,354	389,196	53,054	493,068	31
51,735	171,537	40,811	190,416	45,054	242,261	32
12,715	231,708	13,670	252,309	16,514	243,981	33
	188,807		118,833		235,300	34
93,705	202,119	99,854	273,745	106,536	338,880	35
2,245	105,565	1,970	89,395	2,265	90,230	36
5,982,000	32,980		69,909	1,375,000	150,000	37
49,500	50,000	60,000	75,000	75,000	100,000	38
19,161	106,313	21,911	86,505	31,069	118,363	39
418,891	125,667	387,847	104,719	343,000	54,880	40
9,500	45,835	8,250	55,328	10,044	78,330	41
6,970	39,370	8,000	45,200	10,000	50,000	42
24,197	240,559	25,684	219,050	23,416	239,129	43
11,113	49,137	13,000	57,400	15,000	60,000	44
	72,662		77,500		110,000	45
728	2,366	1,850	6,012	3,900	12,675	46
1,150	7,850			1,200	39,600	47
139,522	63,956	153,620	69,880	135,000	67,500	48
3,466	23,372	2,532	50,210		21,988	49
	35,155		23,720		16,587	50
2,000	30,000	3,599	53,985	1,372	20,580	51
13,955	31,092	6,788	16,291	7,200	18,000	52
				439	4,390	53
30	1,800	71	4,560	66	3,960	54
1,000	3,000	400	1,000	300	800	55
50,000	2,500	350,000	26,250	50,000	7,000	56
	282,583,219		312,776,503		321,768,846	57
	267,247,033		305,735,670		300,232,798	58
	1,000,000		1,000,000		1,000,000	59
	550,830,252		619,512,173		623,001,644	60

Mineral products of the United States

	Products.	1892.	
		Quantity.	Value.
	METALLIC.		
1	Pig iron, value at Philadelphia........long tons..	9, 157, 000	$131, 161, 039
2	Silver, coining value..............troy ounces..	63, 500, 000	82, 099, 150
3	Gold, coining value ....do....	1, 596, 375	33, 000, 000
4	Copper, value at New York City.........pounds...	352, 971, 744	37, 977, 142
5	Lead, value at New York City........short tons..	173, 654	13, 892, 320
6	Zinc, value at New York City..............do....	87, 260	8, 027, 920
7	Quicksilver, value at San Francisco ......flasks..	27, 993	1, 245, 689
8	Aluminum, value at Pittsburg...........pounds..	259, 885	172, 824
9	Antimony, value at San Francisco....short tons...	....	56, 466
10	Nickel, value at Philadelphia ....pounds..	92, 252	50, 739
11	Tin ....do....	162, 000	32, 400
12	Platinum, value (crude) at San Francisco, ...troy ounces..	80	550
13	Total value of metallic products..........	....	307, 716, 239
	NONMETALLIC (spot values).		
14	Bituminous coal.................short tons..	126, 856, 567	125, 124, 381
15	Pennsylvania anthracite.............long tons..	46, 850, 450	82, 442, 000
16	Building stone		48, 706, 625
17	Petroleum...................barrels..	50, 509, 136	26, 034, 196
18	Natural gas		14, 800, 714
19	Brick clay		9, 000, 000
20	Clay (all other than brick) ....long tons..	420, 000	1, 000, 000
21	Cement ....barrels..	8, 758, 621	7, 152, 750
22	Mineral waters ....gallons sold..	21, 876, 604	4, 905, 970
23	Phosphate rock ....long tons..	681, 571	3, 296, 227
24	Salt.........................barrels..	11, 698, 890	5, 654, 915
25	Limestone for iron flux............long tons..	5, 172, 114	3, 620, 480
26	Zinc white ....short tons..	27, 500	2, 200, 000
27	Gypsum ....do....	256, 259	695, 492
28	Borax........................pounds..	13, 500, 000	900, 000
29	Mineral paints ....short tons..	51, 704	767, 766
30	Grindstones.......................	....	272, 244
31	Fibrous talc..................short tons...	41, 925	472, 485
32	Asphaltum........................do....	87, 680	445, 375
33	Soapstone ....do....	23, 908	437, 449
34	Precious stones...................		312, 050
35	Pyrites ....long tons..	109, 788	305, 191
36	Corundum ....short tons..	1, 771	181, 300
37	Oilstones, etc..................pounds...	....	146, 730
38	Mica ....pounds..	75, 000	100, 000
39	Barytes (crude)................long tons..	32, 108	130, 025
40	Bromine......................pounds..	379, 480	64, 502
41	Fluorspar ....short tons..	12, 250	89, 000
42	Feldspar ....long tons..	15, 000	75, 000
43	Manganese ore....................do....	13, 613	129, 586
44	Flint ....do....	20, 000	80, 000
45	Monazite ....pounds..	....	....
46	Graphite ....do....		104, 000
47	Bauxite......................long tons..	9, 200	29, 900
48	Sulphur....................short tons..	2, 688	80, 640
49	Fuller's earth ....do....		
50	Marls ....do....	125, 000	65, 000
51	Infusorial earth.................do....	....	43, 655
52	Millstones.......................	....	23, 417
53	Chromic iron ore.............long tons..	1, 500	25, 000
54	Cobalt oxide ....pounds..	7, 869	15, 738
55	Magnesite ....short tons..	1, 004	10, 040
56	Asbestos ....do....	104	6, 416
57	Rutile.........................pounds..	100	300
58	Ozocerite (refined) ....do....	60, 000	8, 000
59	Total value of nonmetallic mineral products.	....	339, 954, 559
60	Total value of metallic products..........		307, 716, 239
61	Estimated value of mineral products unspecified..	....	1, 000, 000
62	Grand total	....	648, 670, 798

for the calendar years 1880 to 1895—Continued.

	1893.		1894.		1895.	
Quantity.	Value.	Quantity.	Value.	Quantity.	Value.	
7,124,502	$84,810,426	6,657,388	$65,007,247	9,446,308	*105,198,550	1
60,000,000	77,575,757	49,501,122	64,000,000	55,727,000	72,051,600	2
1,739,0~1	35,950,000	1,910,816	39,500,000	2,254,760	46,610,000	3
339,785,972	32,054,601	364,866,808	33,141,142	392,639,964	38,682,347	4
163,982	11,839,590	159,331	9,942,254	170,000	11,220,000	5
78,832	6,306,560	75,328	5,288,026	89,686	6,278,020	6
30,164	1,108,527	30,416	934,000	36,104	1,337,131	7
339,629	266,903	550,000	316,250	920,000	464,600	8
250	45,000	200	36,000	450	68,000	9
49,399	22,197	9,616	3,269	10,302	3,091	10
8,938	1,788	....	....	....	....	11
75	517	100	600	150	900	12
....	249,981,866	....	218,168,788	....	281,913,639	13
128,385,231	122,751,618	118,820,405	107,653,501	135,118,193	115,749,771	14
48,185,306	85,687,078	46,358,144	78,488,063	51,785,122	82,019,272	15
....	33,885,573	....	37,055,030	....	34,688,816	16
48,412,666	28,932,326	49,344,516	35,522,095	52,983,526	57,691,279	17
....	14,316,250	....	13,954,400	....	13,006,650	18
....	9,000,000	....	9,000,000	....	9,000,000	19
400,000	900,000	360,000	800,000	360,000	800,000	20
8,002,467	6,262,841	8,362,245	5,030,081	8,731,401	5,482,254	21
23,544,495	4,246,734	21,569,608	3,741,846	21,463,543	4,254,237	22
941,368	4,136,070	996,949	3,479,547	1,038,551	3,606,094	23
11,816,772	4,054,668	12,967,417	4,739,285	13,669,649	4,423,084	24
3,958,055	2,374,833	3,698,550	1,849,275	5,247,949	2,623,974	25
24,059	1,804,420	19,987	1,399,090	20,710	1,449,700	26
253,615	696,615	239,312	761,719	265,503	807,447	27
8,690,000	652,425	14,680,130	974,445	11,918,000	595,900	28
37,724	530,384	41,926	498,093	50,695	621,552	29
....	338,787	....	223,214	....	205,768	30
35,861	403,436	39,906	435,060	39,240	370,895	31
47,779	372,232	60,570	353,400	68,163	348,281	32
21,071	255,067	23,144	401,325	21,495	266,495	33
....	261,041	....	132,250	....	113,621	34
75,777	256,552	105,940	363,134	99,549	322,845	35
1,713	142,325	1,495	95,936	2,102	106,256	36
....	135,173	....	136,873	....	155,881	37
66,971	88,929	....	52,388	....	55,831	38
28,970	88,506	23,335	86,983	21,529	68,321	39
348,399	104,520	379,444	102,450	517,421	134,313	40
12,400	84,000	7,500	47,500	4,000	24,000	41
18,391	68,037	17,200	98,900	23,400	133,400	42
7,718	66,614	6,308	53,635	9,547	71,769	43
29,671	63,792	38,000	145,920	36,800	117,760	44
130,000	7,600	546,855	36,193	1,573,000	137,150	45
843,103	63,232	918,000	64,010	....	52,582	46
9,079	29,507	11,021	35,818	17,069	44,000	47
1,200	42,000	500	20,000	1,800	42,000	48
....	....	....	....	6,900	41,100	49
75,000	40,000	75,000	40,000	60,000	30,000	50
....	22,582	....	11,718	4,954	20,511	51
....	16,645	....	13,887	....	22,512	52
1,450	21,750	3,680	53,231	1,740	16,795	53
8,422	10,346	6,763	10,145	14,458	20,675	54
704	7,040	1,440	10,240	2,200	17,000	55
50	2,500	325	4,463	795	13,525	56
		150	450	100	350	57
				None.	None.	58
....	323,249,448	....	307,975,593	....	339,774,029	59
....	249,981,866	....	218,168,788	....	281,913,639	60
....	1,000,000	....	1,000,000	....	1,000,000	61
....	574,231,314	....	527,144,381	....	622,687,668	62

IRON ORES.

By John Birkinbine.

Twenty-five States and Territories contributed to make up the total production of 15,957,614 long tons of iron ore for the United States in 1895, an amount exceeded only by the reported outputs of the years 1890 and 1892.

A comparison between the quantities reported indicates an increased production in the year 1895 of 34.33 per cent on the total for 1894, and with but six exceptions all of the iron-ore-producing States participated in this advance.

SUMMARY OF PRODUCTION OF IRON ORES IN THE UNITED STATES, 1889 TO 1895.

The following summarizes the statistics of iron-ore production during the seven years for which detailed reports have been collected by the United States Geological Survey, and shows for each year the number of States and Territories which reported iron-ore production, the total outputs, the percentage which these amounts bore to the maximum of 1892, and the total quantity of pig iron produced:

Production of iron ores in the United States from 1889 to 1895.

Year.	Number of producing States.	Total iron-ore production.	Percentage of maximum output.	Production of pig iron.
		Long tons.		*Long tons.*
1889	28	14,518,041	89.09	7,603,642
1890	25	16,036,043	98.40	9,202,703
1891	25	14,591,178	89.53	8,279,870
1892	24	16,296,666	100.00	9,157,000
1893	25	11,587,629	71.10	7,124,502
1894	24	11,879,679	72.92	6,657,388
1895	25	15,957,614	97.90	9,446,308
Average		14,409,550		8,210,202
Total for seven years		100,866,850		57,471,413

23

PRODUCTION OF BESSEMER AND OTHER PIG IRONS IN THE UNITED STATES, 1889 TO 1895.

The annual production of pig iron, as reported by the American Iron and Steel Association, is given to indicate the general relation between the quantities of iron ores mined and the amounts of pig iron made in each year, for most of the iron ores are smelted in blast furnaces to produce pig metal. This relation is but general, as it is affected by the stocks of domestic iron on hand, the amounts of foreign iron ores brought into the country, and the quantities of mill cinder and other materials used as ore in blast furnaces. The relation, however, as exhibited, is sufficient to indicate a growing demand for ores carrying high percentages of iron, which fact may be further emphasized by considering the quality of ores employed. For this purpose a comparative statement is given below of the quantities of pig iron produced in the various years which was sufficiently low in phosphorus to be classed as of Bessemer grade, and the total outputs. As some iron ores not within the Bessemer limit of phosphorus were used in admixture with low phosphorus ores in the production of Bessemer pig iron, and as many of the ores used for producing foundry and mill irons carry lower percentages of metal than those smelted in the production of Bessemer pig iron, the proportion of Bessemer ore will not be as great as that shown for the pig metal, but the percentages are sufficiently close to indicate the growing increase in the employment of such material.

Production of Bessemer and other pig irons in the United States from 1889 to 1895.

Year.	Total production.	Product of Bessemer grade.	Proportion of Bessemer to total pig iron.
	Long tons.	Long tons.	Per cent.
1889	7,603,642	3,151,414	41.4
1890	9,202,703	4,092,343	44.5
1891	8,279,870	3,472,190	41.9
1892	9,157,000	4,444,041	48.5
1893	7,124,502	3,568,598	50.1
1894	6,657,388	3,808,567	57.2
1895	9,446,308	5,623,695	59.5

It would be difficult to determine closely the amount of iron ore mined which was within the Bessemer limits prescribed by the steel manufacturers, for this limit has been narrowed to meet the conditions of trade. While metal which does not exceed one part of phosphorus in 1,000 of iron by weight is by common consent within the Bessemer limit, late specifications for steel rails do not accept 0.1 phosphorus, but demand 0.085 phosphorus, and as a rule the adaptability of an ore is influenced by the phosphorus in the fuel and flux employed, as well as by the composition of other ores available at a given blast furnace.

The combination of mine operators lately formed to regulate the production of Bessemer ores includes some which produce ore exceeding 1 part of phosphorus to 1,000 of iron, although the basis of sales is upon ore carrying 62 per cent of iron and 0.045 per cent of phosphorus, and advance prices are allowed only on such ores as give a smaller proportion than 1 of phosphorus to 1,300 of iron. However, in determining the relative values of ores produced by mines represented in this combination, all the various elements entering into the composition of the ore are considered.

THE IRON-ORE INDUSTRY IN VARIOUS STATES.

The distribution of the iron-ore product by States continued the same relations as in 1894 between those which contributed over 500,000 long tons, with the exception of Pennsylvania, which this year takes precedence of Virginia, but both Wisconsin and Tennessee have been added to the States producing over half a million tons of iron ore.

Michigan still leads with an output for 1895 of 5,812,444 long tons, an increase over the figures for 1894 of 31.5 per cent; but the quantity mined last year was below that reported in the statistics collected by the United States Geological Survey for the other years from 1889 to 1895, except in 1893 and 1894. This decreased output may in part be credited to a protracted strike in the Marquette range, which affected not only the mining of ore, but prevented shipments from stock piles.

Minnesota in 1895 approximated the output of Michigan in 1894, and showed a total of 3,866,453 long tons, an increase over the previous year of 30.25 per cent.

The product for Alabama, 2,199,390 long tons, while indicating an advance of 47.30 per cent over 1894, is below the returns collected in 1892, but exceed those reported for any other year.

Pennsylvania, which this year returned to fourth position, contributed 900,340 long tons, an increase over the previous year of 69.21 per cent, exceeding her output of 1893 and 1894, but not of other years.

The quota contributed by Virginia was 712,241 long tons, an increase of 18.60 per cent, and the maximum output for the State with the exception of the year 1892.

Wisconsin, while not reaching the figures attained in the years 1889, 1890, and 1892, mined 301,850 long tons, or 86.86 per cent, more in 1895 than in 1894, bringing the total up to 649,351 long tons.

Tennessee's output of 519,796 long tons, an advance of 77.51 per cent over the 1894 product, was the largest record for the State with the exception of the year 1891.

PRODUCTION OF IRON ORE BY STATES, 1889 TO 1895.

The following table shows the quantities of iron ore returned as being produced in the various States for the seven years for which statistics have been collected by the United States Geological Survey, and also the totals for the entire country and the amounts of foreign iron ores imported.

Production of iron ore, by States, from 1889 to 1895.

State.	1889.	1890.	1891.	1892.	1893.	1894.	1895.
	Long tons.	Long tons.	Long tons.	Long tons.	Long tons.	Long tons.	Long tons.
Michigan	5,856,169	7,141,656	6,127,001	7,543,541	4,668,324	4,419,071	5,812,444
Alabama	1,570,319	1,897,815	1,986,830	2,312,071	1,742,410	1,493,046	2,199,390
Pennsylvania	1,560,234	1,361,622	1,272,928	1,084,017	697,985	532,087	900,310
New York	1,217,537	1,253,393	1,017,216	891,099	534,122	212,759	907,256
Wisconsin	837,399	948,965	589,481	790,179	439,429	347,501	619,351
Minnesota	864,508	891,910	945,105	1,255,465	1,499,927	2,968,463	3,866,453
Virginia	498,154	543,583	658,916	711,027	a616,965	a600,562	712,241
New Jersey	415,510	405,808	525,612	465,455	336,150	277,183	282,433
Tennessee	473,294	465,695	543,923	406,578	372,996	292,831	519,796
Georgia	218,020	244,088	250,755	185,054	b186,015	b174,691	b272,011
Missouri	265,718	181,690	106,949	118,494	77,863	81,926	12,512
Ohio	254,294	163,088	104,487	93,768	68,141	58,493	44,834
Colorado	109,136	114,275	110,942	141,769	171,670	250,199	210,937
Montana, Oregon, New Mexico, and Utah	c86,405	81,632	d93,730	44,875	d38,716	h44,438	i47,026
Kentucky	77,487	77,685	65,089	50,523	36,711	42,548	42,093
Maryland	e29,380	35,657	37,379	40,171	13,830	7,915	981
Massachusetts	46,242	32,934	47,502	44,941	40,732		
Connecticut	29,690	26,058	30,923	31,324		30,259	39,112
West Virginia	13,101	25,116	6,200	6,000			
North Carolina	10,125	22,873	19,210	23,379	(g)	(g)	(a)
Texas	13,000	22,000	51,000	22,908	25,620	15,361	8,571
Maine	12,319	2,500					
Total	14,518,011	16,036,043	14,501,178	16,296,666	11,887,629	11,879,679	15,957,614
Foreign ore imported	853,573	1,246,830	912,861	806,585	526,951	167,307	521,153

a Including West Virginia.
b Including North Carolina.
c Including Idaho.
d Including Delaware.
e Including Idaho and Washington.
f See Virginia.
g See Georgia.
h Omitting Oregon and including Nevada.
i Omitting Oregon and including Nevada, Wyoming, and Idaho.

QUANTITIES OF DIFFERENT CLASSES OF IRON ORE PRODUCED IN THE UNITED STATES IN 1895.

The report for 1894 showed graphically and by tables the proportions of the four general classes of iron ores mined in each of the years named, the classes being those described in previous reports, which need not be repeated, but the following table will indicate the quantities of each class produced in 1895 in the various States:

Quantities of different classes of iron ore produced in the United States in the year 1895, by States.

State.	Red hematite.	Brown hematite.	Magnetite.	Carbonate.	Total.
	Long tons.	*Long tons.*	*Long tons.*	*Long tons.*	*Long tons.*
Michigan	5,741,582	10,986	59,876	....	5,812,444
Minnesota	3,866,453	....	....	....	3,866,453
Alabama	1,830,987	368,403	....	....	2,199,390
Pennsylvania	29,606	239,153	628,999	2,582	900,340
Virginia	36,815	674,926	500	....	712,241
Wisconsin	636,301	13,000	50	....	649,351
Tennessee	257,502	255,583	....	6,711	519,796
New York	6,769	26,462	260,139	13,886	307,256
New Jersey	....	....	282,433	....	282,433
Georgia and North Carolina	53,642	215,181	3,191	....	272,014
Colorado	14,520	199,250	27,167	....	240,937
Missouri	12,512	....	....	....	12,512
Montana, New Mexico, Nevada, Idaho, Wyoming, and Utah	24,343	16,816	5,867	....	47,026
Ohio	....	....	....	44,834	44,834
Kentucky	2,963	35,085	....	4,045	42,093
Connecticut and Massachusetts	....	39,142	....	....	39,142
Texas	....	8,371	....	....	8,371
Maryland	....	....	....	981	981
Totals	12,513,995	2,102,358	1,268,222	73,039	15,957,614
Percentage	78.42	13.17	7.95	0.46	....

The total amount of zinc residuum produced in 1895 was 36,372 long tons.

The total amount of magnetically concentrated ore produced during the year 1895 was 19,926 long tons.

Comparing the proportions of the various classes of ores produced in 1895, it is found that the percentage of red hematite, which had risen from 62.38 in 1889 to 78.68 in 1894, was 78.42 in 1895. The percentage of brown hematite, which decreased from 17.38 to 12.40 in the same interval, recovered sufficiently to show 13.17 per cent in 1895. The magnetite, which in 1889 represented 17.26 per cent and in 1894 8.18 per cent, decreased to 7.95 per cent in 1895. The amount of carbonate ore mined is now relatively insignificant, and has continually decreased from 2.98 per cent in 1889 to 0.46 per cent in 1895.

The substitution of red hematite for the other classes of iron ores is explained in part by the numerous deposits which produce large quantities, much of which is of Bessemer grade. While pure magnetite may contain more iron than pure red hematite, and while there is some of the former of most excellent quality, most of the deposits of magnetic iron ore wrought in this country are comparatively lean, or, if rich in iron, carry phosphorus, sulphur, or titanium in excess of what is now considered desirable.

THE LAKE SUPERIOR REGION.

The Lake Superior iron-ore region at present comprises five districts, or "ranges," as they are locally designated, which were developed in the order named:

The Marquette range, in Michigan, opened in 1849; shipments commenced in 1856.

The Menominee range, in Michigan and Wisconsin, opened in 1877.

The Gogebic range, in Michigan and Wisconsin, opened in 1884.

The Vermilion range, in Minnesota, opened in 1884.

The Mesabi range, in Minnesota, opened in 1892.

The iron-ore product of the Lake Superior mines in the year 1892 was double the maximum annual output of the noted Bilbao district of Spain and one-half greater than the largest amount credited to the Cleveland district in England in any one year; and the average quality of the ores obtained from the Lake Superior mines is not equaled by any other large producing district. In 1895 the quantity of iron ore taken from the Lake Superior region was 10,268,978 tons, or 704,590 long tons in excess of the previous maximum of 1892.

The importance of the Lake Superior region as a source of iron-ore supply for the United States is set forth in the following table, in which are given for seven years—

(1) The total apparent supply of iron ore as represented by the production of domestic and the importations of foreign iron ores without regard to stocks.

(2) The production of the Lake Superior region as represented by the output of all the iron-ore mines of Michigan and Minnesota, and those of Wisconsin which are in the Menominee and Gogebic ranges.

(3) The proportion which this product of the Lake Superior region bore to the total apparent supply.

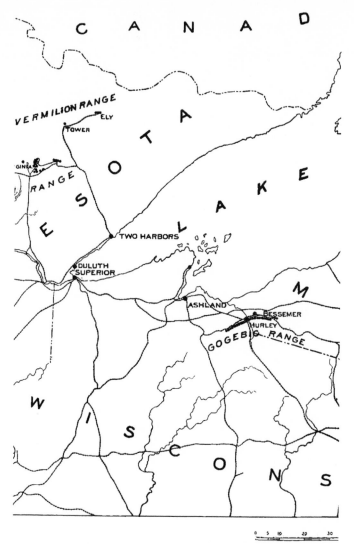

MAP OF THE LAKE SUPERIOR REGION, SHO

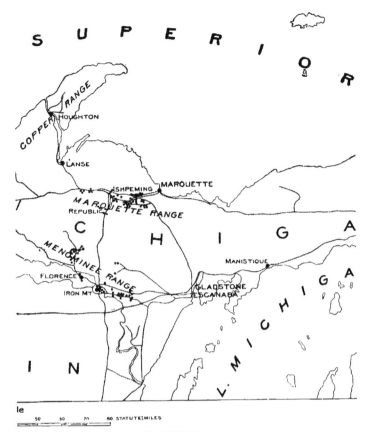

While this table is not claimed to show actual consumption, it does so approximately, the stocks on hand at the beginning or close of each year, the ore used for flux, silver smelting, etc., and the cinder and scale used as ore all influencing the actual consumption.

Proportion of iron ore supplied by Lake Superior district from 1889 to 1895.

Year.	Total apparent supply of iron ore.	Total product of Lake Superior region.	Proportion furnished by Lake Superior region.
	Long tons.	*Long tons.*	*Per cent.*
1889	15,371,614	7,519,614	48.92
1890	17,282,873	8,944,031	51.75
1891	15,504,042	7,621,465	49.16
1892	17,103,251	9,564,388	55.92
1893	12,114,580	6,594,618	54.44
1894	12,046,986	7,692,548	63.85
1895	16,481,767	10,268,978	62.31

When the great ice fields moved over what is now the State of Minnesota, they planed down ridges and deposited glacial drift in interlacing valleys, leaving about 2,000 feet above tide the watershed dividing the streams which ultimately find their way by diverse channels into the Atlantic Ocean. Three small streams heading within a few miles of the iron-ore mines at Hibbing, Minn., discharge through the Mississippi River into the Gulf of Mexico, through the Rainy and Winnipeg lakes into Hudson Bay, and through the St. Louis River to and through the great system of lakes and out into the ocean via the St. Lawrence River and Bay.

Close to this divide are the iron-ore deposits of the Mesabi and Vermilion ranges, which, by their quantity and quality, have in a decade advanced Minnesota from a nonproducer to second rank as a contributor to the country's supply, furnishing a larger amount of iron-ore per annum than any other State except Michigan, and more than any foreign country except Great Britain, Germany, and Spain.

To reach the ore bodies of Minnesota, over 400 miles of standard-gauge railroad have been built and equipped with modern locomotives and cars through what was a trackless wilderness ten years ago, and in fact much of the active producing country was visited only as hunting ground within three or four years.

The total average water and rail haul from the mines on the Marquette range to lower lake ports is less, and from those on the Vermilion and Mesabi ranges greater, than the average haul from the two other ranges, and the present relative transportation facilities may therefore be rated in the following order, subject to the cargoes offering return freight or for competitive East-bound transportation: (1) Marquette range; (2) Menominee range; (3) Gogebic range; (4) Vermilion range; (5) Mesabi range.

To overcome permanently the natural disadvantage of the longer total hauls, the Minnesota ores mined must be of superior grade or be produced at a cost (royalty included) below what other similar ores nearer to consumers can be marketed for. The proportion of Minnesota ores, which are of Bessemer grade according to general acceptance, is as great as, if not greater than, the proportion obtained from eastern Michigan, and the problem of future competition for Bessemer or non-Bessemer ores will resolve itself practically into a determination of the expense of mining (royalties included) per unit of iron in the ore won.

The objection to the physical condition of some Mesabi ores may be considered merely as of temporary character, and the statement that blast-furnace managers can not use finely comminuted ores is a reflection upon the ability of men who have accomplished greater results than that of adapting their plants and their practice to the use of a deposit of such magnitude and character as has been developed on the Mesabi range. Men who have mastered the problems of producing pig iron within the narrow limits of chemical constituents acceptable to consumers, and who have reduced fuel consumption to a point approaching theoretical possibility, will find means to use liberally ore of good quality which can be supplied in quantity, whatever its physical condition. The engineering skill which has designed blast furnaces to produce liberal amounts of metal, and are maintained in blast for long campaigns, can also perfect modifications in the machinery equipment, in the method of charging, in the shape of furnace, in the gas-removal appliances, or in other structural features, which will reduce to a minimum any permanent annoyances from comminuted ores. It is remarkable, considering the objections raised, that the Mesabi ores obtained such a strong foothold when their introduction was largely at a time when furnace proprietors were expending little or nothing in improvements and managers were not encouraged in experiments, but it is questionable whether this introduction was not, as a rule, at prices which left no profit for producers.

The Mesabi ores are in the market as a permanent factor, but not necessarily as supplanters of other ores of acceptable quality which are economically mined. The low cost of winning ores from some of the underground mines in other ranges which have obtained considerable depth evidences conscientious attention to details, and demonstrates the necessity of strict economy in competitive mines which obtain ore from large bodies close to the surface. While the steam shovel and milling mines of the Mesabi range are very attractive and appear to offer extraordinary advantages in mining, experience has already shown that the cost of removing and of securing ground for depositing large quantities of stripping, in which bowlders form no inconsiderable proportion, is not insignificant. A rigorous climate gives underground

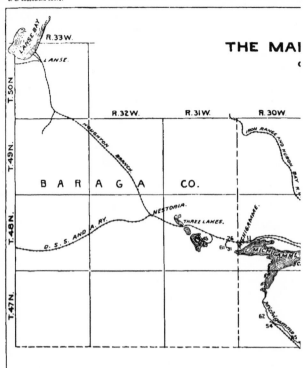

THE MAI

ACTIVE MINES.

No.	Name of mine.	Kind of ore.	Remarks.	No.	N:
1	Cambria	Soft red hematite	Leased from Teal Lake I. Co.	25	Blue...
2	Champion	Magnetic and specular.		26	Bessie
3	Cheshire	Soft red hematite	Escanaba River Land and Iron Co.	27	Cliffs
4	Cleveland	Soft red hematite and specular.	Cleveland Cliffs Iron Co.	28	Foster
5	Davis	Soft red hematite	Leased.	29	Hartf
6	Dexter	Soft red hematite and manganiferous ore.	Do.	30	Humb
7	Jackson	Specular and soft red hematite.		31	Imper
8	Lake Superior	do	"Hard Ore," "Hematite," "Sec. 16," "Sec. 21," "Lowthian," "New Burt," etc.	32	Lowth
				33	Lucy
				34	Mitch
				35	River
				36	Volun
9	Lillie	Soft red hematite	Leased from Teal Lake I. Co.		
10	Consolidated Mg. Co.	Siliceous	Leased; Gribben, Richards, etc.		
11	Michigamme	Magnetic and specular.	Little done since 1892.		
12	Negaunee	Soft red hematite	Leased.		
13	Pittsburgh and Lake Angeline.	do			
14	Platt	do	Do.	40	Ameri
15	Queen	do	Queen, Buffalo, S. Buffalo, Prince of Wales.	41	Albio
				42	Allen
16	Republic	Magnetic and specular.		43	Barto
17	Salisbury	Soft red hematite	Cleveland Cliffs Iron Co.	44	Bay S
18	Star West	Siliceous	Leased; formerly Wheat.	45	Brandl
19	Winthrop	Soft red hematite		46	Carr
				47	Chica
				48	Clevel
				49	Colum
				50	Courn
				51	East I
				52	Detroi
				53	East C

E. JOPLING

Note: The numbers on the Map refer to
the list of mines below.

Scale

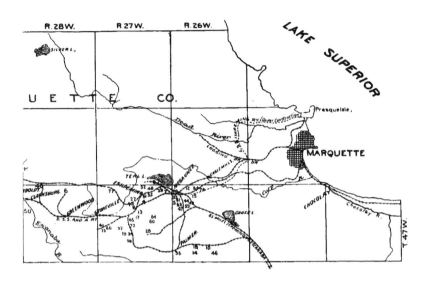

ABANDONED MINES—Continued.

No.	Name of mine	Kind of ore	Remarks
54	Erie	Magnetic and specular	
55	East New York	Soft red hematite	
56	Gibson	Limonite	
57	Goodrich	Hard hematite	
58	Howell & Heppech	Soft red hematite	
59	Hinrod	do	
60	Iron Mountain	Siliceous	
61	Manganese	Manganiferous ore	
62	Magnetic	Magnetic and specular	
63	Milwaukee	Soft red hematite	
64	Marquette	Siliceous	
65	National	Specular and soft red hematite	L. S. I. Co.
66	New Burt	do	Do.
67	New York	Specular	
68	North Champion	Limonite	Hortense.
69	Norwood	do	
70	Pendill	Soft red hematite	E. Jackson.
71	Phenix	Limonite	Dalliba.
72	Parsons	Specular and soft red hematite	L. S. I. Co.
73	Pascoe	Limonite	
74	Pioneer	Soft red hematite	
75	Saginaw	Specular and soft red hematite	
76	Spurr	Magnetic and specular	
77	St. Lawrence	Limonite	
78	Samson	Magnetic and specular	Lincoln, Edwards, Argyle
79	Taylor	Soft red hematite	
80	Titan	Limonite	
81	Webster	do	
82	Washington	Magnetic and specular	
83	West Republic	do	

...DED MINES.

...f ore	Remarks
...atite	Leased.
	Leased from Michigan L. and I. Co
	Cleveland Cliffs Iron Co.
...natite and	Do.
...atite	Leased from Teal Lake I. Co.
...d specular	Washington Iron Co.
	Mich. L. and I. Co.
...natite	Lake Superior I. Co.
	Pitts. and L. A. I. Co.
...d specular	Mich. L. and I. Co.

...NED MINES.

	Remarks
	Boston and Sterling.
...te	
	Cleveland Cliffs Iron Co.
...atite	Indiana.
...atite	Cleveland Cliffs Iron Co.
...d specular	Kloman.
...atite	Lackawanna.
...I specular	Keystone.

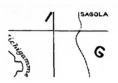

SAGOLA

ichigamme

G

MENOMINEE IRON RA

MICHIGAN & WISCONSIN

COMPILED BY

JAMES E. JOPLING

1895

Note: *The numbers on the Map refer to the list of*

Scale

6   0   6 MILES.

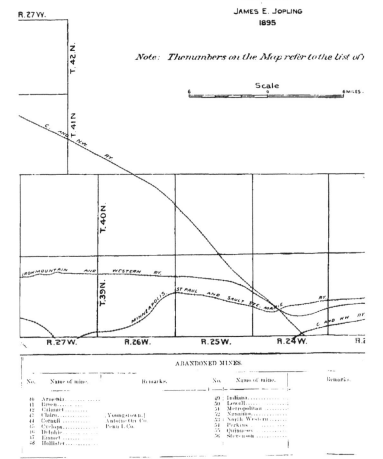

R.27 W.

T.42 N.

T.41 N.

C. AND N.W. RY.

T.40 N.

IRON MOUNTAIN AND WESTERN RY.

T.39 N.

MINNEAPOLIS ST PAUL AND SAULT STE MARIE RY.

C. AND N.W. RY.

R.27 W.   R.26 W.   R.25 W.   R.24 W.   R.2

ABANDONED MINES.

No.	Name of mine.	Remarks.	No.	Name of mine.	Remarks.
40	Armenia		49	Indiana	
41	Breen		50	Lowell	
42	Calumet		51	Metropolitan	
43	Claire	, Youngstown.	52	Nanaimo	
44	Cornell	Antoine Ore Co.	53	North Western	
45	Cyclops	Penn I. Co.	54	Perkins	
46	Debbie		55	Quinnesec	
47	Emmet		56	Stevenson	
48	Hollister				

mining advantages over methods which are interfered with by inclement weather, and, taking into consideration the royalties paid, there is little reason to expect great differences in the cost of supplying ores from the best mines in the various ranges of the Lake Superior district. The variations in phosphorus contents of some ores and the cost of repeated samplings and analyses to properly sort the product is another factor at the present limitation and market rates of Bessemer and non-Bessemer ores, the necessity of taking out both grades forcing the sale of the less desirable in competition with ores of practically similar character produced nearer to points of consumption.

It will not be surprising if in the future a portion of the Minnesota ores find a market at or near to the head of the Lakes, for, notwithstanding the apparently unsatisfactory outcome of ventures in iron and steel production at Duluth and West Superior, enough was accomplished to demonstrate that when ample capital is at command to erect the necessary converting and manufacturing plant, to buy material best suited to requirements, and to introduce the product into a market already supplied by established industries, projects of this class will become profitable.

With the wealth of iron ores convenient, and the low rates at which fuel can be brought to Lake Superior, the production of metal for the growing territory to the west seems to offer many opportunities. A failure to treat ore not at present apparently valuable so that it may in the future be obtained for use would evidence a want of faith in the future of the Northwest, and it is well for those who have at command ores below the accepted standard to remember that the average yield of all the iron ores used in the United States does not exceed 54 per cent, while the phosphorus in non-Bessemer Mesabi ores is below that of the average non-Bessemer ores of the country.

The longer rail and water transportation now required to bring the ores of Minnesota to blast furnaces which can use them gives the ores from other ranges an advantage equivalent to from 60 to 80 per cent of the net mining cost, and the limitations placed upon ores acceptable as of Bessemer grade restrict the output of the Mesabi range. But its large reserves of ore, which are above the average in iron and below the average in phosphorus of domestic ores now used, will seek a utilization, and it is not improbable that these deposits will further stimulate the present rapid development of the basic open-hearth method of steel production.

The development of the Vermilion and Mesabi ranges in Minnesota practically repeats, with local modifications, what took place on the Marquette, the Menominee, and the Gogebic ranges of Michigan and Wisconsin. The early exploitation of the Marquette iron-ore mines shares with the initial work in the copper mines the credit of opening up northern Michigan within half a century, and the iron ores of the Menominee range were responsible for the development of the interior section of the Upper Peninsula less than two decades ago. Similarly, the timber clearings, railroad and town building, etc., on the Gogebic range of Michigan and Wisconsin to secure the soft ores, which lay unused until slightly over ten years past, were contemporaneous with the bold venture which brought into market the excellent ores from the Vermilion range in Minnesota.

The Gogebic iron range trends nearly east and west and is about 10 miles south of Lake Superior, the mines being located at from 1,400 to 1,600 feet above the lake level. The ores find their principal outlet by railroad hauls of from 40 to 50 miles to Ashland, Wis. The mines of the Marquette range are from 12 to 40 miles west of Marquette, and at elevations above Lake Superior of from 800 to 1,000 feet, while those of the Menominee range, farther south, are at elevations of from 1,200 to 1,400 feet above Lake Superior, or 1,800 to 2,000 feet above tide. The Marquette range ore is carried to the ports of Marquette and Escanaba, that from the Menominee range going to Escanaba and Gladstone on Lake Michigan. The mines comprised in the Vermilion range are from 70 to 95 miles from the shipping port to Two Harbors, Minn., and from 825 to 990 feet above Lake Superior. The Mesabi range mines have elevations of 825 to 950 feet above Lake Superior, and their product is forwarded to Two Harbors and Duluth, Minn., and Superior, Wis., by rail hauls of from 80 to 110 miles, the average approximating 90 miles.

THE MESABI RANGE.

The quantities of ore "in sight," the apparent ease of mining, and the grade of material won on the Mesabi range may be pronounced marvelous; but the other ranges each in turn were surprises, and have done their part in making the Lake Superior region the greatest iron-ore producing district of the world, for no other section has in forty years supplied 100,000,000 tons of this mineral.

No other iron range so far discovered possesses greater apparent reserves than the Mesabi; conservative estimates formulated from the records of properties now exploited and worked, together with others determined by systematic explorations and analyses, show that the Mesabi range can supply ore (which will equal in average iron and phosphorus contents) double the quantity which the entire Lake Superior region has produced in fifty years. In this estimate there are not included a number of properties which have been imperfectly explored.

The occurrence of the Mesabi ores in nearly horizontal deposits differs materially from the lenses predominating in the other ranges, which as a rule have steeper angles; consequently, an exploration in the Mesabi range covers a greater area, and the ordinary foot and hanging walls are not readily discernible. In but few instances is there any covering over the ore other than glacial drift. These conditions, added to the limitation placed upon ores of Bessemer grade, have necessitated very

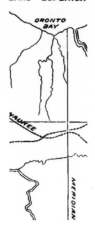

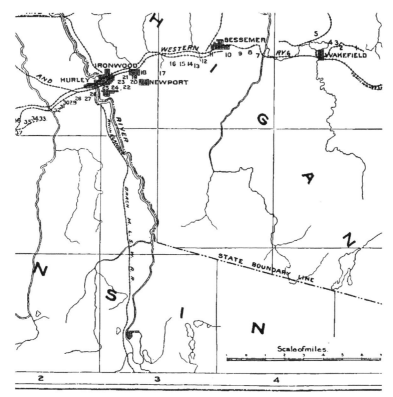

G THE LOCATION OF IRON-ORE MINES.

thorough methods of exploring by pits and by drills, which are generally accompanied by analyses of the ore for every 10 feet of depth, and it is upon determinations obtained in this way that the above estimate was prepared.

The Geological Survey of Minnesota is to be congratulated upon having pointed to the region now known as the Mesabi range as a probable iron-producing district prior to active explorations and exploitations, and the limits in which workable bodies of commercial ore have been found correspond closely with the conclusions arrived at by the geologists as to the probable existence of this mineral.

On the Mesabi range progress has been phenomenal, and the youngest of the five iron-ore ranges has in its fourth year of development supplied 27.65 per cent of the total iron ore obtained from the Lake Superior region.

The record of the production of the mines of this range as reported to the division of mineral resources of the United States Geological Survey shows the rapidity of its development, and the shipments as reported to the Iron Trade Review emphasize the progress made.

Production and shipments of iron ore on the Mesabi range, Minnesota.

Year.	Production.	Shipment.
	Long tons.	*Long tons.*
1892	29, 245	4, 245
1893	684, 194	613, 620
1894	1, 913, 234	1, 793, 052
1895	2, 839, 350	2, 781, 587

These quantities will be better appreciated by comparisons with the maximum production of certain States not in the Lake Superior region, as far as this is determinable from official reports.

Output of some prominent States in 1893, 1894, and 1895.

State.	Production.		
	1893.	1894.	1895.
	Long tons.	*Long tons.*	*Long tons.*
Alabama	1, 742, 410	1, 493, 086	2, 190, 390
Pennsylvania	697, 985	532, 087	900, 340
Virginia and West Virginia	616, 965	600, 562	712, 241
New York	531, 122	242, 759	307, 256

No other range has supplied so much ore in a year except the Marquette range in 1890 and 1892, and the Gogebic range in the same years, and no State but Michigan has ever produced so much ore in

17 GEOL, PT 3——3

one year as the Mesabi range contributed in 1895 to the quota of Minnesota.

It is probable that the protracted strike in the Marquette range was in part responsible for the record of the Mesabi range in 1895, but making the fullest allowance for this, the progress of the Mesabi range is approached only by the earlier history of the Gogebic range in the Lake Superior region, which was as follows. No figures of production were collected, but those given are shipments taken from the Iron Trade Review.

Early shipments of iron ore on the Gogebic range.

Year.	Shipment.
	Long tons.
1877	1,022
1878	119,860
1879	753,362
1880	1,322,878

The Vermilion and Gogebic ranges produce ores mainly of Bessemer grade—the former generally hard and quite high in iron, the latter, as a rule, soft and somewhat lower in iron; the condition of some of the prominent mines indicating that the latter range has produced its maximum, and will be comparatively a less important factor than in the past.

The Marquette and Mesabi ranges have closely approximated each other in supplying 40 per cent of Bessemer and 60 per cent of non-Bessemer ores, although the latter may in the future outrank the former in the proportion of Bessemer ores.

The Menominee range produces mainly non-Bessemer ores, which are carried by railroad an average of 50 miles before obtaining water shipment, and has its outlet on Lake Michigan, avoiding delays due to canal passage, with shorter vessel carriage and at present deeper draft for much of its output. It is also closer than any other range to blast furnaces in Illinois and Wisconsin which can receive the ore by all-rail routes, and the season when ice obstructs navigation is shorter than on Lake Superior.

While most of the ores found in the Menominee range are non-Bessemer, it is an important source of supply for steel works, for one of its large mines produces liberally ore very low in phosphorus, and the ore obtained from its largest producer, while outside of the Bessemer limit as to phosphorus, is largely used in Bessemer mixtures.

The advantage of this shorter vessel haul is also shared by a considerable portion of the ores from the Marquette district, and some from the Gogebic range have reached water transportation on Lake Michigan by a railroad haul of 150 miles. But with the completion of the two large locks at Sault Ste. Marie and the deepening of channels

THE
MINNESOTA IRON DISTRICTS

Scale of miles

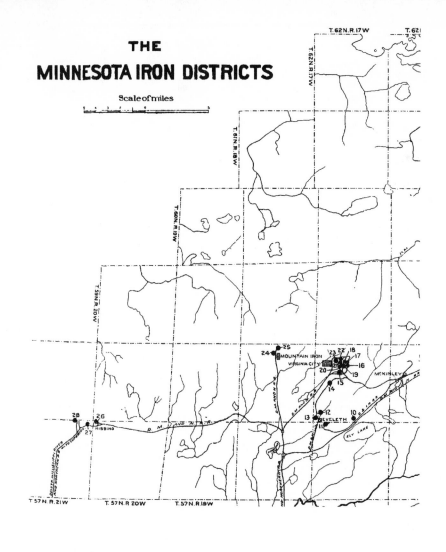

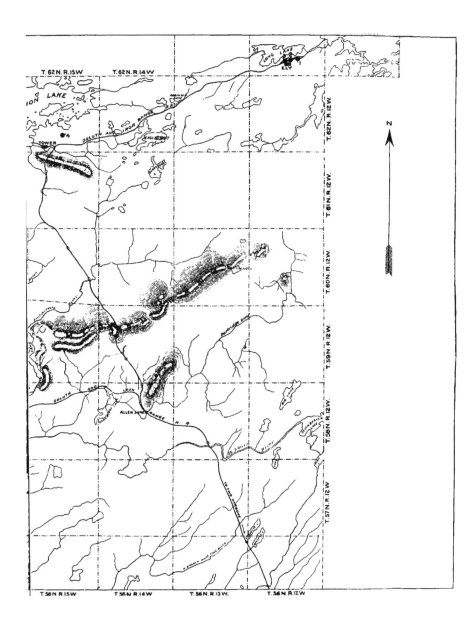

connecting Lakes Erie, Huron, and Superior, the encouragement to send ores from the Marquette range via Lake Michigan will be less pronounced, except for such as are supplied to furnaces on or adjacent to that lake.

DIMENSIONS OF SHIPPING DOCKS FOR LAKE SUPERIOR ORES.

There are now on Lakes Superior and Michigan 23 docks constructed to secure economical shipping facilities (including those in course of construction), having a total of 4,624 pockets, with an aggregate capacity of 633,804 long tons, which have cost $6,849,529. These docks are of the dimensions given and are located as shown in the following statement:

Dimensions of shipping docks for Lake Superior iron ores.

Location.	Height of dock.		Length of dock.	Number of pockets.	Total capacity.	Number of railroad tracks.	Cost.
	Ft.	*In.*	*Feet.*		*Long tons.*		
Two Harbors:							
No. 1..........	47	0	1,056	162	20,250	2	
No. 2..........	46	0	1,056	141	17,620	2	
No. 3..........	51	6	590	90	14,400	4	$1,650,000
No. 4..........	51	6	1,056	168	26,880	4	
No. 5..........	54	0	1,056	168	30,000	4	
Duluth:							
No. 1..........	53	8¼	2,304	384	57,600	4	597,811
No. 2..........	57	8¼	1,152	192	34,560	....	262,210
Superior	54	0	1,563	250	37,500	....	413,619
Ashland:							
No. 1..........	54	0	1,404	234	36,036	4	586,576
No. 2..........	45	0	1,404	234	25,740	3	
No. 3..........	54	6	1,908	314	40,000	4	356,000
Marquette:							
No. 1..........	45	0	1,715	270	28,000	3	
No. 3..........	44	0	1,260	213	14,000	4	
No. 4..........	47	6	1,280	200	30,000	4	1,733,304
(Building)	54	0	1,250	200	35,000	6	
St. Ignace..........	42	0	650	100	10,000	3	
L'Anse¹	38	0	550	100	8,000	2	
Escanaba:							
No. 1..........	46	0	1,104	184	24,104	2	
No. 2..........	39	0	1,152	192	20,928	2	
No. 3..........	39	0	1,356	226	30,284	2	1,122,000
No. 4..........	46	0	1,500	250	32,750	2	
No. 5..........	51	10	1,392	232	43,152	2	
Gladstone..........	47	0	768	120	17,000	5	128,069

¹ Abandoned.

IMPORTANT IRON-ORE-PRODUCING MINES.

As would naturally be expected, with the increased total production of the country in the year ending December 31, 1895, the number of large producing operations was also augmented, the statistics showing that in the year 1895 seventy-two mines, or groups of mines, produced each 50,000 long tons or over, the total being 13,406,322 long tons, or 84.01 per cent of the total for the United States, the highest percentage yet reached, the next highest being in 1894, when 77.26 per cent of the amount mined in the United States came from the larger operations, forty-four in number. Of these seventy-two operations whose output exceeded 50,000 tons in 1895, one produced over 700,000 tons, three over 600,000 tons, three over 500,000 tons, two over 400,000 tons, five over 300,000 tons, eight over 200,000 tons, twenty over 100,000 tons, and thirty between 50,000 and 100,000 tons. The average amount per operation was 186,199 long tons.

Of these more prominent mines, fifty-four supplied ore of the red hematite variety, with a total production of 11,493,146 long tons; twelve contributed a total of 837,880 long tons of brown hematite ore; four operations mined 830,804 long tons of magnetite ore, and the remaining two produced 244,492 tons of mixed red hematite and magnetite, the former variety predominating. Twenty-seven of these mines were located in Michigan, sixteen in Minnesota, ten in Alabama, four each in Wisconsin and Tennessee, three in Virginia, two each in Georgia, New York, and Pennsylvania, and one each in Colorado and New Jersey.

The following table gives the name, general location, and production of such of the larger mining operations as expressed no objection to this publication:

Production of more prominent iron-ore mines during the year 1895.

Name of mine.	Production.
Metropolitan Iron and Land Co., Michigan:	
East Norrie 124,280	
Norrie 486,253	*Long tons.*
North Norrie 142,086	752,619
Cornwall, Pennsylvania..........................	614,598
Ishkooda and Spalding, Alabama.........................	602,477
Chapin, Michigan	601,352
Alice, Fossil, Redding, Muscado, and Wares (group), Alabama.......................	548,025
Chandler, Minnesota.............................	546,448
Mesabe Mountain and Lone Jack, Minnesota...............	500,376
Tilden 1 and 2 and Rand, Michigan	462,855
Minnesota Iron Co., Minnesota....................	412,636
Auburn, Minnesota	382,524
Lake Superior, Michigan............................	327,171

Production of more prominent iron-ore mines during the year 1895—Continued.

Name of mine.	Production.
	Long tons.
Pittsburg and Lake Angeline, Michigan	320,761
Franklin, Minnesota	317,591
Mountain Iron, Minnesota	304,453
Pewabic, Michigan	260,295
Canton, Minnesota	260,000
Biwabik, Minnesota	244,620
Cleveland Iron Mining Co., Michigan:	
Hard ore ... 23,626	
Lake ore ... 172,272	
Hematite ... 48,518	
	244,416
Aurora, North Aurora, and Vaughn, Michigan	222,142
Commonwealth and Badger, Wisconsin	221,600
Pabst, Michigan	215,644
Penn Iron Mining Co., Michigan	193,757
Fayal, Minnesota	187,795
Newport and Bonnie, Michigan	181,724
Sloss, Alabama	164,517
Montreal, Wisconsin	154,964
Cliff's Shaft, Michigan	152,058
Queen Mining Co., Michigan	150,732
Aragon, Michigan	149,929
Ashland, Michigan	143,992
Irondale, Michigan	138,756
Winthrop Iron Co., Michigan:	
Winthrop ... 62,917	
Open Pit ... 70,898	
	133,815
Republic and West Republic, Michigan	131,187
Brown Mining Co., Tennessee	130,006
Iron Belt, Wisconsin	125,481
Champion, Michigan	111,305
Orient, Colorado	103,920
Negaunee, Michigan	100,676
Richards, New Jersey	100,466
Norman, Minnesota	93,392
Scotia, Pennsylvania	93,215
Atlantic, Wisconsin	85,754
Lillie, Michigan	84,425
Dunn, Michigan	83,545
Longdale, Virginia	80,943
Eureka and Welcker, Tennessee	76,000
Lake Superior, Minnesota	74,317

Production of more prominent iron-ore mines during the year 1895—Continued.

Name of mine.	Production.
	Long tons.
Pioneer, Minnesota	68, 019
Adams, Minnesota	67, 881
Columbia, Michigan	66, 431
Palms, Michigan	65, 654
Rathbun, Minnesota	64, 900
Champion, Alabama	63, 500
Greeley, Alabama	62, 699
Loretto, Michigan	56, 828
Anvil, Michigan	56, 306
Jackson, Michigan	54, 606
Upland, Virginia	50, 180
14 other mines, not mentioned by name, aggregating	1, 140, 014
Total for 72 operations	13, 406, 322
Average per mine	186, 199

Up to 1885 a list of twenty mines would have included all which had in any one year reached or approximated an output of 100,000 tons, while in 1895 forty-four mines exceeded this amount.

A résumé of the figures reported to the United States Geological Survey for the years for which they have been collected indicate a generally growing increase in the number of large mines and in their average annual product. This is set forth in the following statement:

Number, average product, and percentage of total production of mines producing over 50,000 tons in 1889, 1892–1895.

Year.	Number of mines producing over 50,000 tons.	Average product per mine.	Proportion of total production supplied by large mines.
		Long tons.	*Per cent.*
1889	65	159, 869	71. 58
1892	71	176, 928	77. 08
1893	54	153, 743	71. 65
1894	44	208, 589	77. 26
1895	72	186, 199	84. 01

STOCKS OF ORE.

The stock of ore on hand at the mines December 31, 1895, throughout the whole of the United States amounted to 2,976,494 long tons, or 18.65 per cent of the amount produced in 1895. This was a decline of 259,704 long tons, or 8.02 per cent, from the 1894 total stock of 3,236,198 long tons.

The following table shows the stocks of ore on hand at mines December 31, 1895, by States. Michigan heads the list with a total of 1,460,238 tons, while the smallest stock reported is in Colorado, where but 250 tons were on hand December 31, 1895:

Stocks of iron ore on hand December 31, 1895 and 1894, by States.

State.	1895.	1894.
	Long tons.	Long tons.
Michigan	1,460,238	1,546,612
Minnesota	517,975	504,861
Alabama	17,496	7,700
Pennsylvania	62,180	85,778
Virginia	51,941	27,295
Wisconsin	326,661	394,484
Tennessee	61,118	26,700
New York	144,384	214,509
New Jersey	68,897	63,317
Georgia and North Carolina	7,092	11,261
Colorado	250	10,875
Missouri	175,868	212,859
Montana, Nevada, New Mexico, Idaho, Utah, and Wyoming	3,185	a 12,280
Ohio	38,115	83,635
Kentucky	22,282	15,785
Connecticut and Massachusetts	3,156	3,847
Texas	8,010	14,400
Maryland	7,646	None. (?)
Total	2,976,494	3,236,198

a Does not include Idaho and Nevada.

As would naturally be expected, the largest stocks on hand were from the Lake Superior region. Most of this ore is sent forward by water, and as during the five colder months of the year navigation is suspended, large stocks are accumulated at the mines to await the opening of the shipping season, usually about May 1. The figures given, however, do not include the stocks of ore which are carried at the receiving ports on the lower lake, the statistics of this report being confined, as in former years, to mining operations.

In this connection, however, the statement of the stocks of Lake Superior ore at the lower lake ports at the opening and closing of navigation, published by the Iron Trade Review, are given to indicate the quantity of ore held to meet the furnace demand when transportation by water is impracticable.

Stocks at lower lake ports at opening and closing of navigation from 1893 to 1896.

Year.	Stock at opening, May 1.	Stock at closing, December 1.
	Long tons.	Long tons.
1893	2, 095, 797	4, 070, 710
1894	2, 588, 370	4, 834, 247
1895	2, 642, 980	4, 415, 712
1896	1, 949, 698	....

There is usually a considerable amount of the ore carried as stock, some of which is hurried forward toward the close of navigation, having been sold to consumers.

VALUE OF IRON ORES.

The total valuation of the 15,957,614 long tons of iron ore produced in the United States in 1895, as reported by the various mines, was $18,219,684, giving an average value at the mine of $1.14. This was the same average price as was recorded in 1894, and is the lowest average value per ton which has yet been reached. With but few exceptions it can not be considered as yielding a reasonable profit on the ore won, and the prices announced for 1896 show that the probable value of the iron ore produced this year will be higher than in the last two years.

Speaking generally, the prices in the Lake Superior region and in the West are slightly higher in 1895 than in 1894, but this was offset by a decreased valuation in the Southern and Middle States. The highest average value recorded is $2.92 per ton in Colorado, where a considerable portion of the iron ore produced was used in the smelters and commanded a value on account of its silver or manganese contents. The large red hematite operations in the Birmingham district, where quantities of ore are cheaply won, aided in making the average value of the iron ore of Alabama but 66 cents per ton, this State reporting the lowest average value.

The following table has been prepared showing the total amount of iron ore produced by States, its total valuation, and the average value per ton. In analyzing this table it should be remembered that where ores of Bessemer grade or of unusually high percentages of iron predominate the average value per ton is liable to be increased, and where the operations are small or the exploitation difficult the contrary may be expected. The figures given in the table are the values of iron ore as shipped from the mine and do not include transportation charges.

Valuation of the iron ore produced during the year ending December 31, 1895, by States.

State.	Production of iron ore.	Valuation.	
		Total.	Per ton.
	Long tons.		
Michigan..............................	5,812,444	$8,403,958	$1.45
Minnesota............................	3,866,453	2,803,452	.73
Alabama	2,199,390	1,460,600	.66
Pennsylvania........................	900,340	997,719	1.11
Virginia..............................	712,241	987,077	1.39
Wisconsin............................	649,351	633,165	.98
Tennessee	519,796	447,852	.86
New York .....:.....................	307,256	598,313	1.95
New Jersey..........................	282,433	612,671	2.17
Georgia and North Carolina...........	272,014	250,116	.92
Colorado	240,937	702,520	2.92
Missouri.............................	12,512	16,968	1.36
Montana, Nevada, Idaho, Utah, New Mexico, and Wyoming...............	47,026	82,993	1.76
Ohio	44,834	63,487	1.42
Kentucky	42,093	54,516	1.30
Connecticut and Massachusetts	39,142	96,037	2.45
Texas	8,371	6,278	.75
Maryland	981	1,962	2.00
Total........................	15,957,644	18,219,684	1.14

IMPORTATION OF FOREIGN IRON ORES.

The Bureau of Statistics of the Treasury Department has, as formerly, furnished data in regard to the amounts and values of iron ores imported into the United States for the year ending December 31, 1895, by countries and also by customs districts, as follows:

Quantity and value of iron ores imported into the United States in the calendar year 1895.

From—	Amount.	Total value.
	Long tons.	
Cuba................................	367,255	$446,799
Spain	77,594	174,055
French Africa and Oceanica...........	27,731	59,133
Italy...............................	24,259	69,195
Greece	18,425	18,415
British Columbia.....................	1,136	3,153
England	195	4,817
Other countries	7,558	10,640
Total	524,153	786,207

Distribution by customs districts of foreign iron ores imported in 1895.

Port.	Quantity.	Total value.
	Long tons.	
Philadelphia, Pa	311,957	$460,641
Baltimore, Md	209,793	321,190
New York, N. Y	221	602
Boston, Mass	36	115
Total Atlantic ports	522,007	782,548
Vermont	35	132
Chicago, Ill		6
Total lake ports	35	138
Puget Sound, Wash	1,136	3,153
Total Pacific ports	1,136	3,153
Paso del Norte, Tex	969	329
Total Gulf ports	969	329
Miscellaneous	6	39
Total imports	524,153	786,207

The five maps appearing in this paper are presented to illustrate the condition of the iron-ore mining in the Lake Superior region at the time of this report. The general map of the Lake Superior region shows the location of the different ranges.

The map of the Marquette range shows the location of the mines on the Marquette range and their railroad connections, a list of the names indicating by corresponding numbers the location of each mine.

The third map is a similar presentation of the Menominee range, and indicates the active, the temporarily suspended, and the abandoned mining enterprises. For this map the Geological Survey is under obligations to Mr. James E. Jopling, mining engineer of Marquette, Mich.

The map of the Gogebic range shows the location of the mines which are producing or which have produced ore in quantity from the Gogebic range, and their railroad connections, but no attempt has been made to locate the numerous properties which can not be regarded as more than explorations.

The map of the Minnesota district, illustrating the location of producing mines in Minnesota, was compiled from data supplied by Mr. Robert Angst, C. E., chief engineer of the Duluth and Iron Range Railroad, and Mr. W. J. Olcott, M. E., general manager of the Lake

Superior Consolidated Iron Mines. This map does not indicate a number of properties on the Mesabi range which have been sufficiently explored to determine, by the approximate extent and character of ore, their availability for mining operations. As no exploitation followed, mention of these properties is omitted, for it is not within the scope of this report to determine which have and which have not sufficient commercial ore to entitle them to a place among prospective producers. It is, however, just to say that some explored areas give promise of adding largely to the supply of iron ore obtainable from Minnesota, and that these extend the productive area beyond the limits indicated by the locations of the numbered mines. The figures are used to indicate only such mines as have produced ore and have reported their output to the United States Geological Survey.

PRESENT CONDITION OF THE IRON AND STEEL INDUSTRIES OF THE UNITED STATES.

—

By JAMES M. SWANK,

General Manager of the American Iron and Steel Association.

.. —

In previous contributions to Mineral Resources I have dwelt chiefly upon the growth of the iron and steel industries of the United States and of foreign countries. In the present paper the condition of these industries in the United States on January 1, 1896, as it is of record in the office of the American Iron and Steel Association, will alone be considered. The statistics which will be presented will note first the number, character, and location of the iron and steel works of the country at the time mentioned, and will show afterwards the production of the various kinds of iron and steel in 1895 and the immediately preceding years. The phraseology of recent publications of the association will be followed in some instances because of its exactness, but the details which are essential in these publications but are unnecessary in a general review or summary will be omitted. For instance, scarcely any mention will be made of furnaces, rolling mills, and steel works that were in course of erection in January, 1896.

NUMBER, CAPACITY, AND LOCATION OF THE IRON AND STEEL WORKS IN THE UNITED STATES.

In the accompanying tables are given the number, capacity, and location of the iron and steel works in the United States on January 1, 1896, these works embracing blast furnaces, rolling mills, steel works, tin-plate works, and forges and bloomaries which make blooms for sale from iron ore, pig iron, and scrap iron. These branches of our iron and steel industries include the production from raw materials of all iron and steel in their crude forms as well as in some of their more finished

45

forms—pig iron, steel ingots, iron and steel rails, structural iron and steel, plate and sheet iron and steel, tin plates, wire rods, cut nails and wire nails, and all miscellaneous forms of rolled iron and steel. Foundries which produce iron castings, and machine shops and similar reproductive branches, with the exception of cut and wire nail works, already mentioned, are not included in the tables. Forges which make axles, anchors, anvils, shafting, and other forgings are not included.

Number and capacity of iron and steel works of the United States in January, 1890.

Number of completed blast furnaces—256 bituminous, 117 anthracite and coke, and 96 charcoal; total	469
Annual capacity of completed blast furnaces, long tons	17,373,637
Annual capacity of the bituminous furnaces, long tons	13,118,600
Annual capacity of the anthracite furnaces, long tons	3,156,487
Annual capacity of the charcoal furnaces, long tons	1,098,550
Number of completed rolling mills and steel works	505
Number of single puddling furnaces (a double furnace counting as two single ones)	4,408
Number of heating furnaces	3,356
Annual capacity of completed rolling mills, double turn, long tons	14,763,920
Number of rolling mills having cut-nail factories	53
Number of cut-nail machines	4,598
Number of wire-nail works	53
Number of completed standard Bessemer steel works	43
Number of standard Bessemer converters	99
Annual capacity of works (built and building) in ingots and direct castings, long tons	9,472,350
Number of completed Clapp-Griffiths steel works	3
Number of Clapp-Griffiths converters	5
Number of completed Robert-Bessemer steel works	3
Number of Robert-Bessemer converters	5
Number of Walrand-Legenisel steel works	1
Number of completed open-hearth steel works	88
Number of open-hearth steel furnaces	225
Annual capacity of works (built and building) in ingots and direct castings, long tons	2,430,450
Number of completed crucible steel works	45
Number of steel-melting pots which can be used at each heat	3,094
Annual capacity of works in ingots and direct castings, long tons	98,700
Number of completed tin-plate works	69
Number of forges making wrought iron from ore	9
Annual capacity of forges in blooms and billets, double turn, long tons	17,075
Number of pig and scrap iron bloomaries	14
Annual capacity of bloomaries in blooms, double turn, long tons	37,650

Number and capacity of blast furnaces in January, 1896.

State.	Furnaces completed Jan. 1. 1896.				Annual capacity of completed furnaces Jan. 1, 1896, in long tons.			
	Anthracite.	Bituminous.	Charcoal.	Total.	Anthracite.	Bituminous.	Charcoal.	Total long tons.
Massachusetts................			3	3	....	....	15,000	15,000
Connecticut................			6	6	....	....	28,500	28,500
New York......	15	3	5	23	446,600	245,000	33,000	724,600
New Jersey	12			12	252,162	....	....	252,162
Pennsylvania ..	90	76	13	179	2,457,725	4,575,500	48,350	7,081,575
Maryland		5	4	9	....	367,000	26,900	393,900
Virginia............		24	4	28	....	808,500	22,750	831,250
West Virginia......		4	....	4	....	231,000	....	231,000
Kentucky		6	3	9	....	207,000	49,500	256,500
Tennessee		12	9	21	....	507,000	116,000	653,000
North Carolina.....		2	....	2	....	40,200	....	40,200
Georgia		2	3	5	....	63,000	38,000	101,000
Alabama		39	12	51	....	1,804,000	168,500	1,972,500
Texas		4		4	....	....	52,000	52,000
Ohio..............		53	10	63	....	2,377,200	40,050	2,417,250
Indiana		2	....	2	....	27,000	....	27,000
Illinois...........		17	....	17	....	1,350,700	....	1,350,700
Michigan........			15	15	....	....	321,000	321,000
Wisconsin........		4	2	6	....	200,500	67,000	267,500
Minnesota........		1	....	1	....	50,000	....	50,000
Missouri		3	1	4	....	105,000	17,000	122,000
Colorado..........		3	....	3	....	160,000	....	160,000
Oregon...........			1	1	....	....	15,000	15,000
Washington....			1	1	....	....	10,000	10,000
Total.....	117	256	96	469	3,156,487	13,118,600	1,098,550	17,373,637

In preparing the above table we have transferred to the abandoned list 54 furnaces which were classed in 1894 among the furnaces that were then active or likely to become active at some future time. Work has also been suspended upon 1 furnace which was being rebuilt two years ago and was then counted as a completed furnace, and this furnace has therefore been placed among the partly erected furnaces, making a total of 55 furnaces which have been taken from the active list of 1894. Since the beginning of that year there have been built and revived 5 furnaces, making the net reduction in the list of completed furnaces from 1894 to 1896 exactly 50.

Number of rolling mills, steel works, tin-plate works, and forges and bloomaries in January, 1896.

State.	Rolling mills and steel works.	Iron and steel rolling mills.	Cut-nail machines.	Steel works.						Tin-plate works.	Forges and bloomaries.
				Bessemer.	Clapp-Griffiths.	Robert-Bessemer.	Walrand-Legenisel.	Open-hearth.	Crucible.		
Maine	1	1									
New Hampshire	1	1						1			
Massachusetts	11	10	268		1			4		1	
Rhode Island	1	1									
Connecticut	7	7							3		
New York	23	20		1				3	4	4	7
New Jersey	20	18	193					4	6		1
Pennsylvania	223	207	1,401	19	2	1		46	21	32	11
Delaware	9	8						1			
Maryland	7	7		1					1	4	1
Virginia	9	9	137	1						1	
West Virginia	7	7	852	2						2	
Kentucky	9	9	126	1				2		1	
Tennessee	5	4	41	1				1	1		1
North Carolina											1
Georgia	1	1									
Alabama	9	8	77					2			1
Texas	2	2									
Ohio	67	62	795	7				10	2	13	
Indiana	33	29	316	3			1	3	1	6	
Illinois	27	25	279	5		1		7	1	3	
Michigan	5	4				1		1	1	1	
Wisconsin	5	3		1					2		
Minnesota	3	3						1			
Missouri	7	6	50					1		1	
Iowa	2	1							1		
Kansas	1								1		
Colorado	2	2		1							
Wyoming	1	1									
Washington	1	1									
Oregon	1	1									
California	5	5	63						1		
Total	505	463	4,598	43	3	3	1	88	45	69	23

COMMENTS UPON THE TABLES.

Blast furnaces.—In 1876, twenty years ago, we enumerated and described 713 blast furnaces which were then active or which it was supposed would some day become active, their total annual capacity being 4,856,455 long tons. In the accompanying tables we enumerate 469 furnaces, or just 244 less than in 1876. Yet with this great reduction in the number of active furnaces or of furnaces that may some day become active the annual capacity has increased to 17,373,637 tons in 1896. With 244 fewer furnaces than in 1876 we now have more than three and a half times the furnace capacity of that year. In 1876 the average annual capacity of all the furnaces was 6,811 long tons; in 1896 the average annual capacity is 37,044 tons.

These figures indicate a very great change in furnace construction and management in the last twenty years. Merciless competition, better methods of manufacture, better ores and better fuel, favored manufacturing localities, the constant tendency to lower prices, and the crushing effects of financial panics have combined to place the manufacture of pig iron in this country in 1896 in few and strong hands.

Of the 469 furnaces now enumerated 96 use charcoal as fuel and 373 use anthracite and bituminous coal and coke. The total annual capacity of the 96 charcoal furnaces is 1,098,550 long tons, and the total annual capacity of the 373 mineral fuel furnaces is 16,275,087 tons. The furnaces classified as anthracite use, with few exceptions, a mixture of anthracite and coke, while those classified as bituminous use coke almost exclusively, a very few using a mixture of raw coal and coke. The average annual capacity of the charcoal furnaces in 1896 is 11,443 tons, and the average annual capacity of all the furnaces using mineral fuel in 1896 is 43,633 tons.

Rolling mills and steel works.—In the tables given we enumerate and describe 505 completed rolling mills and steel works, of which 463 contain trains of rolls and 42 have no rolls.

Puddling furnaces.—The number of puddling furnaces connected with rolling mills in January, 1896, each double furnace being considered as the equivalent of two single furnaces, was 4,408, against 4,715 early in 1894, a decrease of 307 furnaces. The highest number of puddling furnaces reported was in 1884, when 5,265 were enumerated. In 1892 there were still 5,120 in existence. Since that year the number has steadily declined. The most notable abandonment of puddling furnaces that has taken place in recent years has occurred at the American works of Jones & Laughlins, Limited, at Pittsburg. In 1894 this firm reported 92 single puddling furnaces as still forming part of its plant; in the tables only 15 single puddling furnaces are included, and on February 8 the last of these 15 furnaces was dismantled. Hereafter this firm will manufacture only steel.

Bessemer steel works.—Since January, 1894, there have been built 5 new standard Bessemer steel plants—one at Lorain, Ohio, by the Johnson Company, to make girder and T rails and street railroad specialties; one at Youngstown, Ohio, by the Ohio Steel Company, to make sheet and tin-plate bars, slabs, and small billets; one at Columbus, Ohio, by the King, Gilbert and Warner Company, to make steel slabs, billets, and sheet bars; one at Alexandria, Ind., by the Union Steel Company, to make ingots, billets, bars, sheets, small rails, shapes, etc.; and one 1,000-pound converter at East Chicago, Ind., by the Potter and Hollis Foundry Company, of Chicago, to make steel castings by the Walrand-Legenisel process. The company removed its plant in 1896 to Chicago, where it is now in operation. A 2-long-ton Robert-Bessemer converter was also built at East Chicago, Ind., in 1894 by the Drexel Railway Supply Company, of Chicago, for the production of steel castings, but it was abandoned in 1895.

Since January, 1894, 5 standard Bessemer steel plants, containing 7 converters, have been abandoned—1 in Pennsylvania, 2 in Ohio, 1 in Tennessee, and 1 in Illinois—and in the same period 1 Clapp-Griffiths and 2 Robert-Bessemer steel plants have been abandoned. In addition to the above the partly completed 4-long-ton standard Bessemer converter at Sharon, Pa., work upon which was commenced in 1891 by the Sharon Steel Casting Company, has also been abandoned.

Including the Walrand-Legenisel plant we now have 44 standard Bessemer steel works, with 99 converters. We also have 3 Clapp-Griffiths and 3 Robert-Bessemer steel plants, with 10 converters, but even these are not all in operation. The annual converting capacity of all the standard Bessemer steel plants in January, 1896, built and building, was 9,472,350 long tons of ingots and direct castings, against 7,740,900 tons in January, 1894. This is a very great increase in capacity, but it will be seen that the tendency is to reduce rather than to increase the number of Bessemer steel plants. But few direct castings are made at Bessemer steel works.

Open-hearth steel works.—Eleven new open-hearth steel plants have been built since January, 1894, while 4 have been burned or abandoned, showing a net increase of 7 plants. We now have 88 completed open-hearth steel plants. The annual capacity in ingots and direct castings of the open-hearth steel plants in January, 1896, built and building, was 2,430,450 long tons, against 1,740,000 tons in January, 1894, a surprisingly large increase. During the past two years rapid progress has been made in the production of basic steel in open-hearth furnaces.

In 1894 there were 28 open-hearth plants which were prepared to make direct castings, and in 1896 there are 35 plants which are similarly equipped. The production of open-hearth steel castings has grown rapidly in late years.

Basic steel.—The manufacture of basic steel in this country is now wholly confined to works which have open-hearth steel plants. At a large number of these works basic steel is now regularly manufactured, and at some works it is almost, if not altogether, exclusively manufactured. About one-half the open-hearth steel works of the country which produce ingots now make basic steel. While the manufacture of basic Bessemer steel has no existence in this country to-day, it is worthy of mention that the Troy Steel Company proposes to make basic Bessemer steel with three 15-long-ton converters at its new works now being erected on Breaker Island, New York.

Crucible steel works.—In the tables, we enumerate 3 crucible steel plants less than in 1894, 8 plants having been abandoned in the meantime and 5 having been built. We now have 45 completed crucible steel plants, against 48 completed and 1 building in 1894. The aggregate annual capacity of the existing crucible steel works is 98,700 long tons.

Cut-nail machines.—In January, 1892, there were 65 rolling mills which were devoted in whole or in part to the manufacture of cut nails and cut spikes, containing 5,546 nail machines. In January, 1894, there were 55 mills and 5,094 nail machines. In January, 1896, there were 53 mills and 4,598 nail machines. These figures show a decrease of 948 nail machines in four years.

Wire rods.—We enumerate in the tables 23 works which are equipped for rolling iron or steel wire rods.

Wire-nail works.—In 1894 we enumerated 54 completed and 1 partly erected wire-nail works. In the accompanying tables we enumerate 53 completed wire-nail works. The capacity of the wire-nail works is now much greater than in 1894, the nominal decline in the whole number possessing no significance.

Iron and steel rails.—The manufacture of iron rails in the United States is practically an abandoned industry, although as late as 1872 we made 808,866 long tons of iron rails. In 1895 we made only 5,810 tons of iron rails. In the same year we made 697 tons of open-hearth steel rails. Practically, therefore, all rails now made in the United States are made of Bessemer steel.

Structural iron and steel.—The works which make structural iron and steel are classified with the rolling mills and steel works. Of these there are about 40, but a few are now idle and others make only small sizes of structural material. Most of the large works make only steel shapes. During the past two years our capacity for the production of structural material has greatly increased.

Plate and sheet mills.—Included with the rolling mills and steel works are the plate and sheet mills. Of these we enumerate 156 completed plants. In 1890, before our tin-plate industry had obtained a foothold, there were 129 plate and sheet mills and 3 in course of erection. Most of the new mills that have since been built have been designed to meet the demand for black plates, or sheets, for tinning and terne plating, and many of the mills which were in existence in 1890 have been enlarged or changed to meet the same demand. In 1896 there are 41 completed rolling mills which make black plates for tinning. Our armor-plate works are included with the plate works.

Tin-plate works.—In April, 1891, we announced that at 3 works in the country bright tin plates were then manufactured, and that terne plates were manufactured at another works, while 2 additional tin-plate plants were in course of erection. We also stated that "other firms and companies are reported to be considering the advisability of engaging in the manufacture of tin plates and terne plates." In 1892 we enumerated and described 20 works which were either making or were prepared to make tin plates or terne plates, and 10 additional works were in course of erection. In 1894 we described 56 completed works, 2 building, and 1 additional works which was partly erected. In the accompanying tables we enumerate 69 completed works.

Forges and bloomaries.—Under this classification we enumerate only the works which make wrought iron direct from the ore and works which make blooms from pig iron or scrap iron for sale. Works which make blooms in connection with rolling mills and for use exclusively in these rolling mills are not separately classified, as they are auxiliary and not independent enterprises. In the tables we enumerate 23 forges and bloomaries, most of which are pig-and-scrap forges. In the whole South, where formerly there were literally hundreds of Catalan forges, making small quantities of wrought iron directly from the ore, there is now only one active forge of this character left—Helton Forge, at Crumpler, Ashe County, N. C. In 1876 there were 27 forges in New York which made iron directly from the ore; there are now only 7, and all of these are not actively employed.

Natural gas.—In 1896 there are 89 rolling mills and steel works which use natural gas in whole or in part, exactly 10 more than two years ago—45 in Allegheny County, Pa., 16 in other counties of western Pennsylvania, 1 in West Virginia, 5 in Ohio, and 22 in Indiana. One steel works which has just been built in Indiana will also use natural gas. It is in Indiana chiefly that the use of natural gas in iron and steel works has been extended during the last few years. In January, 1892, only 6 works in that State used this fuel. It must be added, however, that the total consumption of natural gas in the iron and steel works of the country is growing less and less from year to year. Even the Indiana natural-gas fields are showing signs of exhaustion.

WIDE DISTRIBUTION OF OUR IRON AND STEEL INDUSTRIES.

The blast furnaces of the United States are located in 24 States. Twenty States made pig iron in 1895. Indiana, Minnesota, Washington, and Oregon did not make pig iron in that year. None of the Territories make pig iron.

Bessemer steel works are located in 14 States. Bessemer steel, including the production of the Clapp-Griffiths and Robert-Bessemer converters, was made in 8 States in 1895, namely, Pennsylvania, West Virginia, Kentucky, Ohio, Indiana, Illinois, Michigan, and Colorado. The three leading Bessemer steel producing States are Pennsylvania, Illinois, and Ohio, in the order mentioned. These States also lead in the production of Bessemer steel rails.

The open-hearth steel works are located in 16 States. The open-hearth steel made in 1895 was produced in 11 States—New Hampshire, Massachusetts, New York, New Jersey, Pennsylvania, Kentucky, Ohio, Indiana, Illinois, Missouri, and California.

The crucible steel works are located in 13 States, 12 of which made crucible steel in 1895, namely, Connecticut, New York, New Jersey, Pennsylvania, Maryland, Tennessee, Ohio, Indiana, Illinois, Michigan, Wisconsin, and Kansas.

Rolling mills are to be found in 30 States. Twenty-seven States rolled either iron or steel or both iron and steel in 1895. Nearly all these States make bar iron.

Only 8 States made iron and steel rails in 1895, namely, Pennsylvania, Tennessee, Alabama, Ohio, Illinois, Colorado, Wyoming, and California. All these States made Bessemer steel rails except Tennessee and Wyoming.

Works for the manufacture of structural iron and steel, about 40 in all, are located in 16 States, namely, Maine, Massachusetts, New York, New Jersey, Pennsylvania, Maryland, Kentucky, Tennessee, Alabama, Ohio, Indiana, Illinois, Wisconsin, Minnesota, Colorado, and California. Only 10 States, however, made structural shapes in 1895.

There are 156 works which roll iron and steel plates and sheets, of which 4 are in New York, 2 are in New Jersey, 76 are in Pennsylvania, 6 are in Delaware, 6 are in Maryland, 4 are in West Virginia, 5 are in Kentucky, 2 are in Alabama, 30 are in Ohio, 9 are in Indiana, 6 are in Illinois, and 1 each is in New Hampshire, Connecticut, Michigan, Wisconsin, Missouri, and California. Works making only nail plate, tack plate, skelp, or shovel plate are not included in the above enumeration.

The 53 cut-nail works, which are connected with rolling mills, are located in 13 States—3 in Massachusetts, 2 in New Jersey, 22 in Pennsylvania, 1 in Virginia, 5 in West Virginia, 1 each in Kentucky, Tennessee, and Missouri; 2 in Alabama, 7 in Ohio, 3 in Indiana, 3 in Illinois, and 2 in California.

There are 23 works which roll wire rods, of which 9 are in Pennsylvania, 4 are in New Jersey, 4 are in Ohio, 2 are in Illinois, and 1 each is in Massachusetts, Connecticut, New York, and Indiana.

The 53 wire-nail works are located in 15 States, as follows: Massachusetts, 6; Rhode Island, 1; Connecticut, 1; New York, 6; New Jersey, 1; Pennsylvania, 8; West Virginia, 1; Ohio, 6; Indiana, 3; Illinois, 10; Wisconsin, 3; Missouri, 1; Kansas, 1; Washington, 2; and California, 3.

The 69 tin-plate works in January, 1896, were located in 12 States, as follows: Massachusetts, 1; New York, 4; Pennsylvania, 32; Maryland, 4; Virginia, 1; West Virginia, 2; Kentucky, 1; Ohio, 13; Indiana, 6; Illinois, 3; Michigan, 1; and Missouri, 1.

The 23 forges and bloomaries which make blooms and bar iron for the general market, from iron ore and pig and scrap iron, are located in 7 States. This is a decaying branch of our iron and steel industries.

MAXIMUM YEARLY PRODUCTION.

When the year 1895 opened all forms of iron and steel in this country had touched the lowest prices ever recorded, so complete had been the prostration of our iron and steel industries after the panic of 1893. The production and prices of the leading forms of iron and steel had steadily fallen in 1893 and 1894, and it seemed at the beginning of 1895 as if there could be no favorable reaction in that year, at least none worthy of special note. But early in the spring of 1895 a marked change for the better occurred; demand increased and prices began to tend upward, and before May and June had passed this favorable movement resulted in great activity in every branch, with steadily advancing prices. In July, August, and September this activity developed into a genuine boom. The demand in some branches was greater than the supply, and prices still further advanced. In September the boom weakened and in October it ended. During the remainder of the year the demand was much less urgent and most prices slowly receded, but production remained active, owing to the impetus which had been given to it from May to October. During the first six months of 1896 production has been well maintained, although upon a smaller scale than in the active months of 1895, but prices, in most cases, have again fallen to unprofitably low figures.

In most branches of our iron and steel industries the largest production ever recorded was achieved in 1895. Steel rails form the only notable exception to the rule of largest production in that year. A summary of the leading results established by the statistical details to be presented hereafter shows that in 1895 the United States made 9,446,308 long tons of pig iron, 4,909,128 tons of Bessemer steel ingots, 1,137,182 tons of open-hearth steel, and 6,114,834 tons of steel of all kinds, and rolled in all 6,189,574 tons of finished iron and steel, including rails. There were also shipped in the same year 10,438,268 tons of Lake Superior iron ore and 8,244,438 short tons of Connellsville coke.

The shipments of Lake Superior iron ore increased 2,689,336 tons in 1895 over the shipments of 1894, or 34.7 per cent; the shipments of Connellsville coke increased 2,789,987 tons, or over 51 per cent; the production of pig iron increased 2,788,920 tons, or 41.9 per cent; spiegeleisen and ferro-manganese, 51,544 tons, or 42.9 per cent; Bessemer steel ingots, 1,337,815 tons, or 37.5 per cent; open-hearth steel, 352,246 tons, or 44.9 per cent; all kinds of steel, 1,702,802 tons, or 38.6 per cent; structural shapes, 157,615 tons, or 43.7 per cent; plates and sheets, 308,559 tons, or 45.2 per cent; Bessemer steel rails, 283,615 tons, or 27.9 per cent; wire rods, 117,728 tons, or 17.5 per cent; all rolled iron and steel, including rails, 1,547,363 tons, or 33.3 per cent.

We present below a table showing the production of all leading forms of iron and steel in 1895, compared with the production in 1894; also the shipments of Lake Superior iron ore and Connellsville coke in these two years.

Production of iron ore and the leading forms of iron and steel in 1895 compared with 1894.

[Long tons, except nails and coke.]

Articles.	1894.	1895.
Shipments of iron ore from Lake Superior	7,748,932	10,438,268
Shipments of Connellsville coke (short tons)	5,454,451	8,244,438
Production of pig iron, including spiegel and ferro.	6,657,388	9,446,308
Production of spiegeleisen and ferro-manganese...	120,180	171,724
Production of Bessemer steel ingots	3,571,313	4,909,128
Production of open-hearth steel ingots and castings.	784,936	1,137,182
Production of all kinds of steel	4,412,032	6,114,834
Production of structural shapes, not including plates	360,305	517,920
Production of plates and sheets	682,900	991,459
Production of all rolled iron and steel, except rails.	3,620,439	4,883,438
Production of Bessemer steel rails	1,016,013	1,299,628
Total production of rails	1,021,772	1,306,135
Production of street rails, included above	157,457	163,109
Production of iron and steel cut nails, in kegs	2,425,060	2,129,894
Production of iron and steel wire nails, in kegs	5,681,801	5,841,403
Production of iron and steel wire rods	673,402	791,130
Production of all rolled iron and steel, including rails	4,642,211	6,189,574

The shipments of iron ore from Lake Superior and of coke from the Connellsville region are given in this connection because these products are raw materials in the production of pig iron and because the statistics of the movement of these raw materials show how quickly the demand for them is influenced by the condition of our iron and steel industries. This reference to the interdependence of leading American industries could be extended to embrace many interesting and instructive details.

We will now present in detail the statistics of the production of leading articles of iron and steel in 1895 and immediately preceding years, which we preface with a brief reference to the shipments of iron ore from leading iron-ore-producing districts.

SHIPMENTS OF IRON ORE FROM LEADING DISTRICTS.

For a number of years the American Iron and Steel Association has regularly ascertained the annual shipments of iron ore from the leading iron-ore districts of the country. These shipments, in the last three years, including the consumption by local furnaces, were as follows. They must not be confounded with the total production of the districts in the years mentioned nor with the total production of the country.

Shipments of iron ore from leading districts.

District.	1893.	1894.	1895.
	Long tons.	*Long tons.*	*Long tons.*
Lake Superior mines of Michigan and Wisconsin	4,621,987	5,008.246	6,582,134
Vermilion Lake and Mesabi mines of Minnesota....................	1,438,505	2,740,686	3,856,134
Missouri mines	60,862	14,147	49,454
Cornwall mines, Pennsylvania	439,705	371,710	614,598
New Jersey mines	328,028	277,483	285,417
Chateaugay mines, on Lake Champlain...........................	29,584	10,000	20,937
Crown Point mines, New York	19,001	5,190	6,339
Port Henry mines, New York	153,902	59,656	166,965
Other Lake Champlain mines, New York	1,570	....	10,595
Hudson River Ore and Iron Co......	38,442	12,334	13,089
Tilly Foster mines, New York	27,623	66,953	41,216
Forest of Dean mines, New York....	18,185	12,510	6,881
Salisbury region, Connecticut.......	17,024	14,000	11,402
Alleghany County, Virginia.........	175,140	142,808	209,619
Cranberry mines, North Carolina....	9,098	300	2,019
Tennessee Coal, Iron, and Railroad Co.'s Inman mines in Tennessee...	73,428	26,477	19,900
Tennessee Coal, Iron, and Railroad Co.'s mines in Alabama...........	722,976	813,587	1,186,999
Calhoun, Etowah, and Shelby counties, Ala..........................	200,370	81,933	218,819
Total	8,375,430	9,658,020	13,302,517

PRODUCTION OF PIG IRON.

The total production of pig iron in 1895 was 9,446,308 long tons, against 6,657,388 tons in 1894, 7,124,502 tons in 1893, 9,157,000 tons in 1892, 8,279,870 tons in 1891, and 9,202,703 tons in 1890. The production of 1895 was the largest in our history, exceeding by 2,788,920 tons, or nearly 42 per cent, that of 1894, and by 243,605 tons that of 1890, when our largest previous production was attained. The production of pig iron in the first half of 1895 was 4,087,558 tons, and in the last half of 1895 it was 5,358,750 tons. The following table gives the production of pig iron by States in 1894 and 1895, in the order of their prominence in 1895:

Production of pig iron in 1894 and 1895, by States

State.	1894.	1895.	State.	1894.	1895.
	Long tons.	*Long tons.*		*Long tons.*	*Long tons.*
Pennsylvania...	3,370,152	4,701,163	New Jersey.....	63,273	55,502
Ohio	900,029	1,463,789	Georgia	40,268	31,034
Illinois.........	604,795	1,006,091	Missouri	6,522	27,518
Alabama	592,392	854,667	Maryland	5,600	10,916
Virginia........	298,086	346,589	Connecticut....	7,416	5,615
Tennessee	212,773	248,129	Massachusetts..	156	4,710
New York	175,185	181,702	Texas	4,671	4,682
Wisconsin.....	91,595	148,400	North Carolina.		323
West Virginia..	80,781	141,968	Oregon.........	1,000	....
Michigan.......	95,171	91,222			
Kentucky	33,854	63,780	Total.......	6,657,388	9,446,308
Colorado	73,669	58,508			

The production of pig iron of Bessemer quality in 1895 was 5,623,695 tons, against 3,808,567 tons in 1894. Much more than half of the pig iron we annually produce is of Bessemer quality, the remainder being foundry and forge pig iron, basic pig iron, spiegeleisen, and ferro-manganese. The production of spiegeleisen and ferro-manganese in 1895 was 171,724 long tons, against 120,180 tons in 1894. The production of 1895 was in New Jersey, Pennsylvania, Illinois, and Colorado.

The whole number of furnaces which were in blast at the close of 1895 was 242, against 185 at the close of 1894 and 137 at the close of 1893.

PRODUCTION OF BESSEMER STEEL.

The production of Bessemer steel ingots in the United States in 1895 was 4,909,128 long tons, against 3,571,313 tons in 1894, 3,215,686 tons in 1893, and 4,168,435 tons in 1892. There was an increase of 1,337,815 tons, or over 37 per cent, in 1895 as compared with 1894. The production in 1895 was much the largest in our history. The following table shows the production by States of Bessemer steel ingots in the last five years. The production by the Clapp-Griffiths and the Robert-Bessemer works is included. Direct castings are counted as ingots.

Production of Bessemer steel for five years.

State.	1891.	1892.	1893.	1894.	1895.
	Long tons.	*Long tons.*	*Long tons.*	*Long tons.*	*Long tons.*
Pennsylvania........	2,048,330	2,397,981	2,126,220	2,334,518	2,978,924
Illinois.............	605,921	879,952	314,829	581,540	866,531
Ohio	333,666	409,855	348,141	363,974	719,954
Other States........	259,500	480,644	426,496	291,251	343,719
Total.........	3,247,417	4,168,435	3,215,686	3,571,313	4,909,128

Sixteen standard Bessemer steel plants did not make steel in 1895. Two of the three Clapp-Griffiths steel plants were idle in 1895. Of the four Robert-Bessemer plants in existence in 1895 one did not make steel in that year.

PRODUCTION OF OPEN-HEARTH STEEL.

Our statistics of the production of open-hearth steel in the United States include steel made in the open hearth by the basic process. Direct castings are included with ingots. The production of open-hearth steel in 1895 was 1,137,182 long tons, against 784,936 tons in 1894, an increase of 352,246 tons, or over 44 per cent. The increased production in 1895 was largely a result of the growing popularity of basic open-hearth steel. The following table shows the production of open-hearth steel ingots and direct castings, by States, during the past six years:

Production of open-hearth steel for six years.

State.	1890.	1891.	1892.	1893.	1894.	1895.
	Long tons.	*Long tons.*	*Long tons.*	*Long tons.*	*Long tons.*	*Long tons.*
New England.......	12,586	14,316	18,620	24,759	26,204	36,733
New York .... New Jersey.........	} 15,049	18,499	19,511	17,591	21,363	32,203
Pennsylvania	417,512	472,607	551,010	616,516	659,969	904,352
Ohio...............	58,823	51,524	60,834	50,385	54,182	75,637
Illinois .... Other States........	} 9,262	22,807	19,914	28,639	23,218	{ 49,500 38,757
Total	513,232	579,753	669,889	737,890	784,936	1,137,182

PRODUCTION OF CRUCIBLE STEEL.

The production of crucible steel in the United States in 1895 amounted to 67,666 long tons, against 51,702 tons in 1894, 63,613 tons in 1893, 84,709 tons in 1892, 72,586 tons in 1891, and 71,175 tons in 1890. Of the total production in 1895 New England contributed 957 tons; New York, 5,999 tons; New Jersey, 8,711 tons; Pennsylvania, 49,889 tons: the Western States, 1,600 tons; and the Southern States, 510 tons.

PRODUCTION OF MISCELLANEOUS STEEL.

The production of steel in the United States in 1895 by various minor processes amounted to 858 long tons, against 4,081 tons in 1894, 2,806 tons in 1893, 4,548 tons in 1892, 4,484 tons in 1891, and 3,793 tons in 1890.

TOTAL PRODUCTION OF STEEL.

The production of all kinds of steel in the United States in 1895 was as follows: Bessemer steel, 4,909,128 long tons; open-hearth steel, 1,137,182 tons; crucible steel, 67,666 tons; all other steel, 858 tons; total, 6,114,834 tons, against 4,412,032 tons in 1894, 4,019,995 tons in 1893, and 4,927,581 tons in 1892.

PRODUCTION OF IRON AND STEEL RAILS.

The production of all kind of rails, including light and heavy rails, and street, electric, and mine rails, in the United States in 1895 was 1,306,135 long tons, against 1,021,772 tons in 1894, an increase of 284,363 tons, or almost 28 per cent. The production of 1895 was composed of 1,266,081 tons of Bessemer steel rails rolled by the producers of domestic ingots; 33,547 tons of Bessemer steel rails rolled from purchased blooms and old steel rails; 697 tons of open-hearth steel rails; and 5,810 tons of iron rails. The open-hearth steel rails were all made in Pennsylvania and California. The iron rails were made in Pennsylvania, Tennessee, Alabama, Illinois, Colorado, Wyoming, and California.

Of the total production of Bessemer steel rails in 1895 Pennsylvania made 864,499 tons, as compared with 714,935 tons in 1894; Illinois, 327,618 tons, against 226,306 tons in 1894; and the remainder of the country 107,511 tons, against 74,772 tons in 1894.

The rails reported to us which are definitely known to have been rolled for street and electric railways in 1895 amounted to 163,109 long tons, against 157,457 tons in 1894, an increase of 5,652 tons. All of these rails were made of steel.

PRODUCTION OF IRON AND STEEL STRUCTURAL SHAPES.

Our statistics of iron and steel structural shapes embrace the production of beams, beam girders, zee bars, tees, channels, angles, and other structural forms, but do not include plate girders made from plates. Nearly all the structural shapes and plates used for structural purposes in 1895 and recent years were made of steel, both Bessemer

and open-hearth steel being used. The total production in 1894 and
1895 was as follows, in long tons:

Production of iron and steel structural shapes in 1894 and 1895, by States.

State.	1894.	1895.	State.	1894.	1895.
	Long tons.	Long tons.		Long tons.	Long tons.
New England .			Ohio	15,018	18,417
New York	1,897	1,542	Wisconsin.....		
New Jersey ...	15,701	20,884	Minnesota.....	614	....
Pennsylvania..	313,312	464,410	Colorado		
Kentucky			California......	7,170	5,251
Tennessee.....	6,593	7,413			
Alabama			Total	360,305	517,920

The increased production of iron and steel structural shapes in 1895
over 1894 was 157,615 tons, or over 43 per cent.

PRODUCTION OF PLATES AND SHEETS.

The production of plate and sheet iron and steel in the United States
in 1895, excluding nail plate, amounted to 991,459 long tons, against
682,900 tons in 1894, 674,345 tons in 1893, and 751,460 tons in 1892.
Skelp iron and steel are not included.

The following table gives the production of iron and steel plates and
sheets, not including nail plate, in 1894 and 1895, in long tons. We
have separated plates and sheets by gauges, observing the following
classification: Plates, up to No. 8, inclusive; firebed, No. 9 to No. 19,
inclusive; sheets, No. 20 to No. 25, inclusive, and No. 26 and thinner
gauges. The production was as follows:

Production of iron and steel plates and sheets by gauges in 1894 and 1895.

Gauges.	1894.	1895.
	Long tons.	Long tons.
Plates, up to No. 8 gauge, inclusive................	375,117	508,343
Firebed, No. 9 to No. 19 gauge, inclusive..........	80,099	112,537
Sheets, No. 20 to No. 25 gauge, inclusive..........	73,968	91,449
Sheets thinner than No. 25 gauge.................	153,716	279,130
Total plates and sheets....................	682,900	991,459

The production of "black plates for tinning" alone in 1895 is reported
to us to have amounted to 129,615 long tons, against 52,359 tons in
1894, an increase of 77,256 tons, or over 147 per cent.

PRODUCTION OF TIN PLATES.

In the following table we give the production of tin plates and terne plates in the United States in the four years beginning with July 1, 1891, and ending with June 30, 1895. The authority for this table is Col. Ira Ayer, special agent of the Treasury Department.

Production of tin plates and terne plates in the United States.

Periods.	Tin plates.	Terne plates.	Total.
	Pounds.	*Pounds.*	*Pounds.*
July 1, 1891, to September 30, 1891....	152,489	674,433	826,922
October 1, 1891, to December 31, 1891..	215,911	1,193,910	1,409,821
January 1, 1892, to March 31, 1892.....	1,099,656	2,109,569	3,209,225
April 1, 1892, to June 30, 1892.........	3,071,534	5,129,217	8,200,751
Total for first year..............	4,539,590	9,107,129	13,646,719
July 1, 1892, to September 30, 1892....	3,611,367	7,341,358	10,952,725
October 1, 1892, to December 31, 1892..	6,138,739	13,617,752	19,756,491
January 1, 1893, to March 31, 1893.....	15,244,574	14,321,825	29,566,399
April 1, 1893, to June 30, 1893.........	20,748,427	18,795,160	39,543,587
Total for second year...........	45,743,107	54,076,095	99,819,202
July 1, 1893, to September 30, 1893....	13,861,163	13,284,317	27,145,480
October 1, 1893, to December 31, 1893..	14,682,045	12,669,196	27,351,241
January 1, 1894, to March 31, 1894.....	26,313,561	11,946,850	38,260,411
April 1, 1894, to June 30, 1894.........	26,752,996	19,713,339	46,466,335
Total for third year............	81,609,765	57,613,702	139,223,467
July 1, 1894, to September 30, 1894....	30,185,684	18,159,949	48,345,633
October 1, 1894, to December 31, 1894..	18,971,166	14,299,864	33,271,030
January 1, 1895, to March 31, 1895.....	28,299,454	16,311,687	44,611,141
April 1, 1895, to June 30, 1895.........	42,871,615	24,701,624	67,573,269
Total for fourth year...........	120,327,949	73,473,124	193,801,073
Grand total for four years.......	252,220,411	194,270,050	446,490,461

In the four years covered by the above table the total production of tin plates and terne plates amounted to 199,326 long tons.

PRODUCTION OF WIRE RODS.

The production of iron and steel wire rods in the United States in 1895 was 791,130 long tons, against 673,402 tons in 1894, an increase of 117,728 tons. Nearly all wire rods are now made of steel. The following table shows the production of wire rods, by States, during the past six years in long tons.

Production of wire rods in the past six years.

State.	1890.	1891.	1892.	1893.	1894.	1895.
	Long tons.	Long tons.	Long tons.	Long tons.	Long tons.	Long tons.
New England and New York	96,338	114,507	111,432	79,618	88,913	91,513
New Jersey	18,755	20,589	20,943	23,013	20,880	22,290
Pennsylvania	134,249	166,255	197,708	227,257	246,101	278,406
Ohio	131,282	147,272	176,007	140,047	173,272	210,058
Indiana and Illinois ..	76,505	87,984	121,739	67,337	144,236	188,863
Total	457,099	536,607	627,829	537,272	673,402	791,130
Iron	17,677	13,623	15,422	1,125	5,772	2,840
Steel	439,422	522,984	612,407	536,147	667,630	788,290

PRODUCTION OF WIRE NAILS.

The production of wire nails in 1895 was 5,841,403 kegs, against 5,681,801 kegs in 1894, an increase of 159,602 kegs. In the following table we give the production of wire nails, by States, in the last seven years, in kegs of 100 pounds. The production of 1895 represented 260,777 tons.

Production of wire nails in the past seven years.

Year.	New England.	New York and New Jersey.	Pennsylvania.	Ohio.	Indiana and Illinois.	Other States.	Total.
	Kegs.	Kegs.	Kegs.	Kegs.	Kegs.	Kegs.	Kegs.
1889...	110,000	170,000	816,000	944,000	46,000	349,000	2,435,000
1890..	167,135	168,460	1,061,639	1,115,320	47,507	575,850	3,135,911
1891..	193,668	128,159	1,460,252	1,659,396	381,950	290,960	4,114,385
1892..	107,477	91,470	1,676,684	1,800,742	796,406	246,745	4,719,524
1893..	129,108	147,930	2,177,495	1,556,160	802,106	283,146	5,095,945
1894..	121,283	78,043	2,396,482	1,830,000	950,507	305,486	5,681,801
1895..	168,365	144,657	2,129,951	1,534,690	1,479,465	384,275	5,841,403

The "other States" referred to in 1895 were West Virginia, Wisconsin, Missouri, Kansas, Washington, and California.

PRODUCTION OF CUT NAILS.

Our statistics of the production of iron and steel cut nails and cut spikes in the United States do not embrace railroad and other spikes made from bar iron or machine-made horseshoe nails. Cut spikes are included with cut nails.

The total production of cut nails in 1895 was 2,129,894 kegs of 100 pounds each, against 2,425,060 kegs in 1894, a decrease of 295,166 kegs, or over 12 per cent. There has been a steady decline in the production of cut nails since 1886, in which year the maximum production of 8,160,973 kegs was reached. In 1895 our production of wire nails exceeded our production of cut nails by over 3,700,000 kegs. Ten States made cut nails in 1895.

TOTAL PRODUCTION OF ROLLED IRON AND STEEL.

The production of all iron and steel rolled into finished forms in the United States in 1895 was 6,189,574 long tons, against 4,642,211 tons in 1894, an increase of 1,547,363 tons, or over 33 per cent. The following table gives the aggregate production, by States, of iron and steel rolled into all kinds of finished forms in 1894 and 1895, in long tons.

Total production of rolled iron and steel in 1894 and 1895.

State.	1894.	1895.	State.	1894.	1895.
	Long tons.	Long tons.		Long tons.	Long tons.
Maine..........	2,786	4,631	Ohio	577,080	893,665
New Hampshire	3,100	5,050	Indiana	156,763	227,035
Massachusetts..	79,392	107,711	Illinois.........	432,598	626,342
Rhode Island...	10,420	10,445	Michigan	11,445	27,696
Connecticut	18,912	28,493	Wisconsin......	64,932	85,006
New York	128,389	119,811	Minnesota......	4,530	3,796
New Jersey	77,596	91,482	Missouri	20,391	35,005
Pennsylvania ..	2,719,796	3,491,935	Iowa...........	5,200	....
Delaware	27,652	43,024	Colorado	71,637	52,836
Maryland	5,283	8,003	Wyoming	5,372	4,185
Virginia	24,378	27,504	Washington....		
West Virginia..	103,319	167,531	Oregon.........	20,345	32,318
Kentucky	34,449	42,632	California......		
Tennessee......	5,120	8,247			
Alabama	28,326	45,191	Total	4,642,211	6,189,574

PRODUCTION OF IRON BLOOMS AND BILLETS.

The iron blooms and billets produced in forges directly from the ore in 1895 amounted to 40 long tons, against 40 tons in 1894, 864 tons in 1893, 2,182 tons in 1892, 5,290 tons in 1891, 7,094 tons in 1890, and 11,078 tons in 1889. The only ore blooms produced in 1894 and 1895 were made at the Helton Forge of W. J. Pasley, at Crumpler, Ashe County, N. C., and these were converted on the spot into bar iron.

The iron blooms produced in forges from pig and scrap iron in 1895, and which were for sale and not intended for the consumption of the makers, amounted to 7,185 long tons, against 3,221 tons in 1894 and 6,605 tons in 1893. All the pig and scrap blooms so made in 1895 were produced in Pennsylvania and Maryland. At the Exeter Steam Forge, in Berks County, Pa., bar iron is still hammered from charcoal blooms and wrought scrap iron.

IMPORTS OF IRON AND STEEL.

The following table, which has been compiled by the Bureau of Statistics of the Treasury Department, gives in detail the quantities and values of our imports of iron and steel and manufactures thereof in the calendar years 1894 and 1895:

Imports of iron and steel in 1894 and 1895.

Articles.	1894.		1895.	
	Long tons.	Value.	Long tons.	Value.
Pig iron, spiegel, and ferrosilicon	15,582	$407,638	53,232	$1,337,978
Scrap iron and scrap steel	2,380	43,710	6,066	103,523
Bar iron........................	9,228	377,397	20,049	772,822
Iron and steel rails	300	4,292	1,447	27,076
Cotton ties.....................	5	120	3,485	102,309
Hoop, band, and scroll iron or steel	805	51,111	15	2,925
Steel ingots, billets, blooms, slabs, etc	9,494	809,184	26,255	1,610,889
Sheet, plate, and taggers iron or steel	28,795	1,197,671	14,531	727,638
Tin plates......................	215,068	12,053,167	219,545	11,482,380
Wire rods, of iron or steel.......	22,607	923,675	26,834	1,090,707
Wire and wire rope, of iron or steel	4,288	514,484	5,773	716,901
Anvils	406	57,614	502	70,901
Chains	291	35,910	474	87,097
Cutlery	....	1,220,707	....	2,092,038
Files, file blanks, rasps, and floats............................	....	49,413	....	61,083
Firearms	....	294,230	....	623,760
Machinery	....	1,189,965	....	2,199,518
Needles	....	286,655	....	314,416
All other, including baling hoops.	....	1,326,633	....	2,348,175
Total	309,249	20,843,576	378,208	25,772,136

EXPORTS OF IRON AND STEEL.

We are indebted to the Bureau of Statistics of the Treasury Department for the following details of the quantities and values of our exports of iron and steel in the calendar years 1894 and 1895:

Exports of iron and steel in 1894 and 1895.

Commodities.	1894.		1895.	
	Quantity.	Value.	Quantity.	Value.
Pig iron............long tons..	24,482	$309,222	26,164	$371,297
Bar iron ....do....	3,147	130,207	3,329	117,798
Band, hoop, scroll iron...do....	100	5,380	198	8,169
Car wheels..........number..	14,662	113,172	14,106	113,195
Castings, not elsewhere specified.		484,675	....	751,664
Cutlery	....	160,879	....	170,166
Firearms..........................	....	640,099	....	845,110
Steel ingots, bars, rods...tons..	1,463	50,911	3,147	117,250
Builders' hardware..............	....	2,452,732	....	2,766,532
Machinery		10,715,520	....	12,115,118
Cut nails and spikes......tons..	8,180	331,133	7,875	339,825
Horseshoe and wire nails..do...	1,738	196,175	2,367	239,610
Iron plates and sheets.....do...	2,227	111,586	423	32,170
Steel plates and sheets.....do...	829	53,641	812	60,889
Printing presses, and parts of...	....	160,303	....	217,678
Iron rails.................tons..	1,327	32,306	6,792	139,470
Steel rails.................do...	12,229	323,880	8,807	222,661
Saws and tools..................	....	2,019,199	....	2,012,000
Scales and balances..............	....	292,055	....	387,710
Sewing machines, and parts of..	....	2,064,787	....	2,988,006
Fire engines ....number..	11	22,138	2	2,145
Locomotives ....do....	189	1,567,464	217	2,110,244
Stationary engines.......do....	291	257,350	308	192,985
Boilers and parts of engines....	....	582,683	....	436,091
Stoves, and parts of	....	240,936	....	289,462
Wire.................tons..	26,512	1,304,794	29,475	1,375,195
Other iron and steel manufactures..................		5,320,502	....	6,610,398
Total	....	29,943,729	....	35,062,838
Agricultural implements, additional		4,765,793	....	5,319,885

IMPORTS OF IRON ORE.

In the following table we give our total imports of iron ore in the calendar years from 1879 to 1895. Previous to 1879 the imports never amounted in any one year to 100,000 tons. In recent years most of our imports of iron ore have come from Cuba. We have compiled this table from data obtained from the Bureau of Statistics, above referred to.

Imports of iron ore since 1879.

Year.	Long tons.	Year.	Long tons.	Year.	Long tons.
1879........	281,141	1885........	390,786	1891........	912,856
1880........	493,408	1886........	1,039,433	1892........	806,585
1881........	782,887	1887........	1,194,301	1893........	526,951
1882........	589,655	1888........	587,470	1894........	168,541
1883........	490,875	1889........	853,573	1895........	524,153
1884........	487,820	1890........	1,246,830		

PRICES OF IRON AND STEEL.

In the following table we give the average prices of leading articles of iron and steel during the last ten years. The prices given are yearly averages of average monthly quotations, and are per long ton. They have been compiled from the records of the American Iron and Steel Association. Prices for earlier years, going back in some instances to the closing years of the last century, may be found on page 514 of our History of the Manufacture of Iron in All Ages, and in our earlier Annual Reports and in the Report for 1889.

Average prices of various leading articles of iron and steel since 1886.

Year.	No. 1 anthracite foundry pig iron at Philadelphia.	Gray forge pig iron at Philadelphia.	Gray forge pig iron, lake ore, at Pittsburg.	Bessemer pig iron at Pittsburg.	Steel billets, at mills, at Pittsburg.	Steel rails, at mills, in Pennsylvania.	Best refined bar iron, from store, at Philadelphia.	Best refined bar iron, at Pittsburg.
1886........	$18.71	$16.40	$16.58	$18.96	$31.75	$34.50	$43.12	$38.08
1887........	20.92	17.79	19.02	21.37	32.55	37.08	49.37	43.59
1888........	18.88	16.21	15.99	17.38	28.78	29.83	44.99	39.67
1889........	17.75	15.48	15.37	18.00	29.45	29.25	43.40	38.30
1890........	18.40	15.82	15.78	18.85	30.32	31.75	45.92	41.25
1891........	17.52	14.52	14.06	15.95	25.32	29.92	42.56	38.38
1892........	15.75	13.54	12.81	14.37	23.63	30.00	41.81	36.79
1893........	14.52	12.73	11.77	12.87	20.44	28.12	38.08	33.53
1894........	12.66	10.73	9.75	11.38	16.58	24.00	29.96	26.86
1895........	13.10	11.49	10.94	12.72	18.48	24.33	32.29	28.09

DEPRESSED CONDITION OF THE AMERICAN IRON TRADE IN THE FIRST HALF OF 1896.

It has already been stated that the reaction from the brief boom of 1895 in the American iron trade set in in the autumn months of that year and that it continued during the first six months of 1896. We now submit the statistics of the production of pig iron in these six months, and of the stocks of unsold pig iron at their close. This information, coupled with a table of prices of iron and steel in the same period, which will also be given, will accurately show the extent of the reaction referred to, measured in tons and in dollars and cents, but it will fail to indicate the depth of the depression which now prevails in the American iron trade, and which is as great as it has been at any time since the panic of 1893. Since July 1, 1896, both production and prices have still further declined.

The total production of pig iron in the United States in the first half of 1896 was 4,976,236 long tons, against 4,087,558 tons in the first half of 1895 and 5,358,750 tons in the second half of 1895. As compared with the first half of 1895 there was an increase in the first half of 1896 of 888,678 tons, but as compared with the second half of 1895 there was a decrease of 382,514 tons.

The production of pig iron of Bessemer quality in the first half of 1896 was 2,793,672 long tons, against 2,402,023 tons in the first half of 1895 and 3,221,672 tons in the second half. The decreased production of 428,000 tons in the first half of 1896 as compared with the second half of 1895 is doubtless due in large part to the increasing demand for open-hearth steel and particularly for basic open-hearth steel.

The shrinkage in the total production of pig iron in Pennsylvania in the first half of 1896 as compared with the second half of 1895 was 367,029 tons, which is almost equal to the total shrinkage of 382,514 tons in the whole country. The decreased production of Bessemer pig iron in Pennsylvania in the first half of 1896 as compared with the second half of 1895 was 348,092 tons, which figures fall very little below the total shrinkage in Pennsylvania above mentioned.

The production of spiegeleisen and ferro-manganese in the first half of 1896 was 83,010 long tons, against 73,011 tons in the first half of 1895 and 98,713 tons in the second half.

The whole number of furnaces in blast on June 30, 1896, was 196, against 242 in blast on December 31, 1895. The number of furnaces out of blast on June 30, 1896, was 273.

The statistics of unsold stocks of pig iron on June 30, 1896, show a marked increase over the unsold stocks on December 31, 1895. On June 30 the stocks which were unsold in the hands of manufacturers or their agents, and which were not intended for their own consumption, amounted to 644,887 long tons, against 444,332 tons on December

31, an increase of 200,555 tons, or over 45 per cent. These figures do not include pig iron sold and not removed from the furnace bank, nor pig iron manufactured by rolling mill proprietors for their own use, nor stocks in warrant yards which had passed out of the hands of the manufacturers.

The following table shows the production of pig iron in each of the pig-iron producing States in the first half of 1895, the second half of 1895, and the first half of 1896, with the number of furnaces in blast in each of the States at the end of each of the last two half-yearly periods mentioned:

Production of pig iron in 1895 and the first half of 1896.

State.	Blast furnaces.				Production (includes spiegeleisen).		
	In blast Dec. 31, 1895.	June 30, 1896.			First half of 1895.	Second half of 1895.	First half of 1896.
		In.	Out.	Total.			
					Long tons.	Long tons.	Long tons.
Massachusetts	1	1	2	3	2,194	2,516	893
Connecticut	1	2	4	6	2,438	3,177	3,656
New York	6	5	18	23	88,369	93,333	99,870
New Jersey	4	3	9	12	28,112	27,390	34,435
Pennsylvania	103	79	99	178	2,087,381	2,613,782	2,246,753
Maryland	1	1	8	9		10,916	51,807
Virginia	17	11	17	28	142,580	204,009	231,685
North Carolina	1		2	2		323	2,151
Georgia	2	1	4	5	11,535	19,499	7,593
Alabama	22	20	30	50	390,553	464,114	464,205
Texas	1	1	3	4	2,502	2,180	1,131
West Virginia	3	2	2	4	62,567	79,401	68,421
Kentucky	4	3	6	9	19,285	44,495	41,450
Tennessee	8	9	12	21	114,169	133,960	131,354
Ohio	40	31	33	64	632,571	831,218	743,444
Indiana			2	2			
Illinois	15	13	4	17	376,401	629,690	638,186
Michigan	6	8	8	16	45,868	45,354	65,193
Wisconsin	5	4	2	6	53,750	94,650	102,586
Minnesota			1	1			
Missouri	1	1	3	4	2,267	25,251	4,758
Colorado	1	1	2	3	25,016	33,492	30,665
Oregon			1	1			
Washington			1	1			
Total	242	196	273	469	4,087,558	5,358,750	4,976,236

PRICES OF IRON AND STEEL IN FIRST HALF OF 1896.

In the following table we give the average monthly prices of leading articles of iron and steel in the first six months of 1896, per long ton of 2,240 pounds, except for bar iron, steel tees, and steel beams, which are quoted by the pound, and tin plates, which are quoted by the box of 108 pounds. The prices of some of the articles mentioned in the table have been maintained during this period and others have been advanced by artificial methods, while the prices of most of the other articles in the sale of which competition has been unchecked have steadily fallen. It is also necessary to add that the prices of pig iron have been largely influenced in these six months by the advance in the prices of coke and iron ore which occurred in the fall of 1895, and has since been maintained. But for this advance the prices of pig iron would already have fallen this year below the lowest prices ever recorded. It will be remembered that prices at the close of 1895 had fallen very far below the prices which had ruled only a few months before.

Prices of iron and steel in the first six months of 1896.

Month.	Old iron T rails at Philadelphia.	No. 1 anthracite foundry pig iron at Philadelphia.	Gray forge pig iron at Philadelphia.	Gray forge pig iron lake ore, at Pittsburg.	Bessemer pig iron at Pittsburg.	Steel rails, at mills in Pennsylvania.
	Per long ton.	*Per long ton.*	*Per long ton.*	*Per long ton.*	*Per long ton.*	*Per long ton.*
January........	$14.25	$13.56	$11.55	$10.90	$11.81	$28.00
February......	14.75	13.50	11.50	11.00	12.95	28.00
March..........	15.00	13.45	11.30	10.92	12.25	28.00
April..........	14.87	13.25	11.19	10.85	13.32	28.00
May	14.43	12.83	11.00	10.79	12.83	28.00
June	14.00	12.75	11.00	10.62	12.47	28.00

Month.	Steel billets, at mills, at Pittsburg.	Best refined bar iron, from store, Philadelphia.	Best refined bar iron, at Pittsburg.	Steel tees, on dock, at New York.	Steel beams, on dock, at New York.	Foreign coke tin plates at New York.	Domestic coke tin plates at New York.
	Per long ton.	*Cents per pound.*	*Cents per pound.*	*Cents per pound.*	*Cents per pound.*	*Per box.*	*Per box.*
January........	$16.60	1.45	1.25	1.62½	1.57½	$3.86	$3.80
February......	17.19	1.40	1.25	1.60	1.50	3.88	3.78
March..........	17.19	1.35	1.21	1.60	1.55	3.85	3.75
April..........	19.80	1.40	1.20	1.60	1.60	3.80	3.70
May	19.55	1.40	1.20	1.60	1.67½	3.72	3.55
June	19.12	1.40	1.20	1.60	1.70	3.70	3.55

IMPORTS AND PRICES OF TIN PLATES IN THE UNITED STATES.

In framing the McKinley tariff, which became a law on October 1, 1890, Congress provided for increased duties on tin plates and on articles made from them, to take effect on the 1st of July, 1891. The new duty on tin plates, terne plates, and taggers tin provided as follows:

On and after July 1, 1891, all iron or steel sheets, or plates, or taggers iron coated with tin or lead or with a mixture of which these metals or either of them is a component part, by the dipping or any other process, and commercially known as tin plates, terne plates, and taggers tin, shall pay 2.2 cents per pound.

This duty took the place of a duty of 1 cent per pound which had been provided in the tariff of 1883. Immediately after the McKinley tariff became a law several enterprising iron and steel manufacturers and others commenced the manufacture of tin plates and terne plates for the general market, and ever since the number of establishments engaged in turning out these products has steadily increased.

IMPORTS OF TIN PLATES.

The following table, compiled from the publications of the Bureau of Statistics of the Treasury Department, shows the quantities of tin plates imported into the United States in each calendar year from 1872 to 1895, with their foreign values, Great Britain furnishing virtually all the tin plates that were imported during the whole period:

Imports of tin plates from 1872 to 1895.

Year.	Long tons.	Value.	Year.	Long tons.	Value.
1872	85,629	$13,893,450	1884	216,181	$16,858,650
1873	97,177	14,240,868	1885	228,596	15,991,152
1874	79,778	13,057,658	1886	257,822	17,504,976
1875	91,054	12,098,885	1887	283,836	18,699,145
1876	89,946	9,416,816	1888	298,238	19,762,961
1877	112,479	10,679,028	1889	331,311	21,726,707
1878	107,864	9,069,967	1890	329,435	23,670,158
1879	154,250	13,227,659	1891	327,882	25,900,305
1880	158,049	16,478,110	1892	268,472	17,102,487
1881	183,005	14,886,907	1893	253,155	15,559,423
1882	213,987	17,975,161	1894	215,068	12,053,167
1883	221,233	18,156,773	1895	219,545	11,482,380

The total quantity of tin plates imported into the United States in the twenty-four years from 1872 to 1895 was 4,823,992 long tons, the foreign value being $379,492,793.

PRICES OF TIN PLATES.

In the following table we have compiled, from quotations in the Iron Age, the wholesale prices per box. of "full weight," 108 pounds, of imported coke Bessemer tin plates, I. C., 14 by 20, at New York, freight and duty paid, from January, 1890, to March, 1896:

Prices of tin plates, by months, from 1890 to 1896.

Month.	Price.	Month.	Price.	Month.	Price.
January, 1890	$4.72	February, 1892	$5.30	March, 1894 ...	$5.20
February	4.61	March	5.30	April..........	5.19
March	4.46	April..........	5.30	May	5.15
April........	4.42	May	5.30	June	5.14
May	4.42	June	5.29	July	5.12
June	4.43	July	5.25	August........	5.12
July	4.49	August........	5.21	September	5.10
August.......	4.66	September	5.20	October.......	4.09
September ...	5.17	October	5.27	November.....	4.10
October	5.49	November.....	5.45	December	4.00
November	5.44	December	5.49	January, 1895 .	3.96
December	5.24	January, 1893 .	5.35	February	3.87
January, 1891	5.35	February	5.35	March	3.80
February	5.47	March	5.44	April..........	3.80
March	5.36	April..........	5.50	May	3.80
April........	5.26	May	5.50	June	3.80
May	5.17	June	5.41	July	3.82
June	5.35	July	5.31	August........	3.90
July	5.28	August........	5.30	September	3.95
August.......	5.39	September	5.26	October	4.00
September ...	5.43	October	5.37	November.....	3.95
October	5.37	November.....	5.35	December	3.82
November	5.31	December	5.32	January, 1896 .	3.86
December	5.30	January, 1894 .	5.27	February	3.88
January, 1892	5.30	February	5.22	March	3.85

During the first four months of 1896 the price of American I. C. "full-weight" tin plates at New York averaged about 10 cents per box below that quoted for similar grades of foreign tin plates.

The duty on tin plates was reduced by the Wilson tariff of August, 1894, to 1.2 cents per pound. That our tin-plate manufacturers were able to meet the low prices of foreign tin plates after the Wilson tariff became a law was due partly to the skill and experience they had acquired, but mainly to the fortunate coincidence that the prices of steel billets and steel tin-plate bars, the raw materials of manufacture, had fallen in 1894 and 1895 to the lowest figures ever known.

GOLD AND SILVER.

PRODUCTION.

The product of both gold and silver increased in 1895. According to the returns of the Director of the Mint, the increase in gold production was very significant, i. e., from 1,910,813 ounces in 1894, valued at $39.500,000, to 2,254,760 ounces in 1895, worth $46,610,000.

The silver product increased also from 49,500,000 ounces in 1894 to 55,727,000 ounces in 1895. This rather unexpected increase in the silver product was to some extent the result of increased copper production in Montana, where the Anaconda ore also carries silver. This State alone shows an increase of 4,749,019 ounces of silver.

The product by States is shown in the following tables:

Approximate distribution, by producing States and Territories, of the product of gold and silver in the United States for the calendar year 1895, as estimated by the Director of the Mint.

State or Territory.	Gold.		Silver.		Total value.
	Fine ounces.	Value.	Fine ounces.	Coining value.	
Alaska	78, 140	$1, 615, 300	67, 200	$86, 880	$1, 702, 180
Arizona	95, 072	1, 965, 300	986, 900	1, 275, 990	3, 241, 290
California	722, 171	14, 928, 600	653, 700	845, 180	15, 773, 780
Colorado	643, 634	13. 305, 100	23. 398, 500	30, 252, 600	43, 557, 700
Georgia	6, 192	128, 000	400	520	128, 520
Idaho	86, 088	1, 779, 600	3, 110, 600	4, 021, 780	5, 801, 380
Michigan	2, 075	42, 900	37, 300	48, 220	91, 120
Montana	198, 405	4, 101, 400	17, 569, 100	22, 715, 600	26, 817, 000
Nevada	75, 088	1, 552, 200	956, 200	1, 236, 290	2, 788, 490
New Mexico....	23, 810	492, 200	694, 800	898, 320	1, 390, 520
North Carolina.	2, 622	54, 200	400	520	54, 720
Oregon..........	42, 972	888, 300	51, 000	65, 930	954, 230
South Carolina.	6, 212	128, 400	400	520	128, 920
South Dakota..	187, 187	3, 869, 500	159. 300	205, 960	4, 075, 460
Texas			450, 000	581, 810	581. 810
Utah...........	66, 419	1, 373, 000	7, 468, 100	9, 655, 720	11, 028, 720
Washington....	16, 980	351, 000	122, 700	158, 640	509, 610
Alabama					
Connecticut					
Minnesota......					
Nebraska	1, 693	35, 000	400	520	35, 520
Tennessee					
Virginia........					
Wyoming					
Total	2, 254, 760	46, 610, 000	55, 727, 000	72. 051, 000	118, 661, 000

Product of gold and silver for the calendar year 1894, by States and Territories.

State or Territory.	Gold.		Silver.		Total value.
	Fine ounces.	Value.	Fine ounces.	Coining value.	
Alabama	194	$4,007	66	$85	$4,092
Alaska	62,047	1,282,623	4,422	5,717	1,288,340
Arizona	96,313	1,990,966	1,539,453	1,990,404	3,981,370
California......	670,636	13,863,282	229,967	297,331	14,160,613
Colorado	513,571	10,616,463	23,747,915	30,704,375	41,320,838
Georgia	4,772	98,652	343	443	99,095
Idaho	111,687	2,308,775	3,774,349	4,879,966	7,188,741
Maryland	47	976	2	2	978
Michigan.......	2,150	44,444	35,122	45,410	89,854
Montana	187,135	3,868,429	13,638,967	17,634,220	21,502,649
Nevada	59,051	1,220,700	771,504	997,500	2,218,200
New Mexico....	40,128	829,519	214,060	276,764	1,106,283
North Carolina.	2,330	48,167	3,682	4,760	52,927
Oregon.........	102,234	2,113,356	8,006	10,351	2,123,707
South Carolina.	4,758	98,366	307	397	98,763
South Dakota ..	187,122	3,868,155	82,256	106,351	3,974,506
Tennessee......	16	329	....	....	329
Texas..........	209	4,320	429,314	555,073	559,393
Utah...........	54,570	1,128,062	6,534,182	8,448,235	9,576,297
Virginia	369	7,621	17	22	7,643
Washington....	11,260	232,761	9,683	12,520	245,281
Total.....	2,110,599	43,629,973	51,023,617	65,969,926	109,599,899

The following tables show the increase or decrease in the silver product in each State for recent years:

Production of silver in the United States in 1891 and 1892 and the increase or decrease in each year, by States and Territories.

State or Territory.	1891.	1892.	Increase.	Decrease.
	Fine ounces.	Fine ounces.	Fine ounces.	Fine ounces.
Alaska	8,000	8,400	400	....
Arizona	1,480,000	1,161,900	....	318,100
California	750,000	392,200	....	357,800
Colorado	21,160,000	26,632,300	5,472,300	....
Georgia	400	400	....	....
Idaho	4,035,000	3,461,200	....	573,800
Michigan..............	73,000	65,600	....	7,400
Montana	16,350,000	19,038,800	2,688,800	....
Nevada	3,520,000	2,454,500	....	1,065,500
New Mexico	1,325,000	1,176,700	....	148,300

Production of silver in the United States in 1891 and 1892 and the increase or decrease in each year, by States and Territories—Continued.

State or Territory.	1891.	1892.	Increase.	Decrease.
	Fine ounces.	*Fine ounces.*	*Fine ounces.*	*Fine ounces.*
North Carolina	5,000	9,800	4,800	....
Oregon	320,000	54,200	....	175,800
South Carolina	500	400	....	100
South Dakota	100,000	58,100	....	41,900
Texas	375,000	328,100	....	46,900
Utah	8,750,000	8,490,800	....	259,200
Washington	165,000	165,700	700	....
Alabama				
Maryland				
Tennessee				
Vermont	3,100	900	....	2,200
Virginia				
Wyoming				
Total	58,330,000	63,500,000	8,167,000	2,997,000
Net increase	....	....	5,170,000	....

Production of silver in the United States in 1892 and 1893, and the increase or decrease in each year, by States and Territories.

State or Territory.	1892.	1893.	Increase.	Decrease.
	Fine ounces.	*Fine ounces.*	*Fine ounces.*	*Fine ounces.*
Alaska	8,400	9,600	1,200	....
Arizona	1,161,900	2,935,700	1,773,800	....
California	392,200	470,100	77,900	....
Colorado	26,632,300	25,838,600	....	793,700
Georgia	400	500	100	....
Idaho	3,461,200	3,910,700	449,500	....
Michigan	65,600	43,500	....	22,100
Montana	19,038,800	16,906,400	....	2,132,400
Nevada	2,454,500	1,561,300	....	893,200
New Mexico	1,176,700	458,400	....	718,300
North Carolina	9,800	13,400	3,600	....
Oregon	54,200	11,800	....	42,400
South Carolina	400	500	100	....
South Dakota	58,100	140,400	82,300	....
Texas	328,100	349,400	21,300	....
Utah	8,490,800	7,196,300	....	1,294,500
Washington	165,700	152,700	....	13,000
Alabama				
Maryland				
Tennessee				
Vermont	900	700	....	200
Virginia				
Wyoming				
Total	63,500,000	60,000,000	2,409,800	5,909,800
Net decrease	....	....	....	3,500,000

Production of silver in the United States in 1893 and 1894, and the increase or decrease in each year, by States and Territories.

State or Territory.	1893.	1894.	Increase.	Decrease.
	Fine ounces.	*Fine ounces.*	*Fine ounces.*	*Fine ounces.*
Alaska	9,600	22,261	12,661	
Arizona	2,935,700	1,147,204		1,788,496
California	470,100	717,368	247,268	
Colorado	25,838,600	23,281,399		2,557,201
Georgia	500	325		175
Idaho	3,910,700	3,288,548		622,152
Michigan	43,500	35,122		8,378
Montana	16,906,400	12,820,081		4,086,319
Nevada	1,561,300	1,035,151		526,149
New Mexico	458,400	632,183	173,783	
North Carolina	13,400	352		13,048
Oregon	11,800	26,171	14,371	
South Carolina	500	305		195
South Dakota	140,400	58,973		81,427
Texas	349,400	429,314	79,914	
Utah	7,196,300	5,891,901		1,304,399
Washington	152,700	113,160		39,540
Alabama				
Maryland				
Tennessee				
Virginia	700	182		518
Vermont				
Wyoming				
Total	60,000,000	49,500,000	527,997	11,027,997
Net decrease				10,500,000

Production of silver in the United States in 1894 and 1895, and the increase or decrease in each year, by States and Territories.

State or Territory.	1894.	1895.	Increase.	Decrease.
	Fine ounces.	*Fine ounces.*	*Fine ounces.*	*Fine ounces.*
Alaska	22,261	67,200	44,939	
Arizona	1,147,204	986,900		160,304
California	717,368	653,700		63,668
Colorado	23,281,399	23,398,500	117,101	
Georgia	325	400	75	
Idaho	3,288,548	3,110,600		177,948
Michigan	35,122	37,300	2,178	
Montana	12,820,081	17,569,100	4,749,019	
Nevada	1,035,151	956,200		78,951

Production of silver in the United States in 1894 and 1895, and the increase or decrease in each year, by States and Territories—Continued.

State or Territory.	1894.	1895.	Increase.	Decrease.
	Fine ounces.	Fine ounces.	Fine ounces.	Fine ounces.
New Mexico............	632, 183	694, 800	62, 617	....
North Carolina	352	400	48	....
Oregon	26, 171	51, 000	24, 829	....
South Carolina.........	305	400	95	....
South Dakota	58, 973	159, 300	100, 327	....
Texas	429, 314	450, 000	20, 686	....
Utah..................	5, 891, 901	7, 468, 100	1, 576, 199	....
Washington............	113, 160	122, 700	9, 540	....
Alabama				
Connecticut.............				
Minnesota...............				
Nebraska	182	400	218	....
Tennessee				
Virginia				
Wyoming				
Total.............	49, 500, 000	55, 727, 000	6, 707, 871	480, 871
Net increase.............			6, 227, 000	....

Rank of the States and Territories in the production of gold and silver in 1894.

Rank.	Gold.	Rank.	Silver.	Rank.	Total.
1	California.	1	Colorado.	1	Colorado.
2	Colorado.	2	Montana.	2	Montana.
3	Montana.	3	Utah.	3	California.
4	South Dakota.	4	Idaho.	4	Utah.
5	Idaho.	5	Arizona.	5	Idaho.
6	Oregon.	6	Nevada.	6	Arizona.
7	Arizona.	7	Texas.	7	South Dakota.
8	Alaska.	8	California.	8	Nevada.
9	Nevada.	9	New Mexico.	9	Oregon.
10	Utah.	10	South Dakota.	10	Alaska.
11	New Mexico.	11	Michigan.	11	New Mexico.
12	Washington.	12	Washington.	12	Texas.
13	Georgia.	13	Oregon.	13	Washington.
14	South Carolina.	14	Alaska.	14	South Carolina.
15	North Carolina.	15	North Carolina.	15	Georgia.
16	Michigan.	16	Georgia.	16	Michigan.
		17	South Carolina.	17	North Carolina.

Ranks of the States and Territories in the production of gold and silver in 1895.

Rank.	Gold.	Rank.	Silver.	Rank.	Total.
1	California.	1	Colorado.	1	Colorado.
2	Colorado.	2	Montana.	2	Montana.
3	Montana	3	Utah.	3	California.
4	South Dakota.	4	Idaho.	4	Utah.
5	Arizona.	5	Arizona.	5	Idaho.
6	Idaho.	6	Nevada.	6	South Dakota.
7	Alaska.	7	New Mexico.	7	Arizona.
8	Nevada.	8	California.	8	Nevada.
9	Utah.	9	Texas.	9	Alaska.
10	Oregon.	10	South Dakota.	10	New Mexico.
11	New Mexico.	11	Washington.	11	Oregon.
12	Washington.	12	Alaska.	12	Texas.
13	South Carolina.	13	Oregon.	13	Washington.
14	Georgia.	14	Michigan.	14	South Carolina.
15	North Carolina.		Georgia.	15	Georgia.
16	Michigan.	15	North Carolina.	16	Michigan.
			South Carolina.	17	North Carolina.

The contributions of the several States to the marked increase in the gold product is also shown in the following table:

Production of gold in the United States in 1894 and 1895.

State or Territory.	1894.	1895.	Increase.	Decrease.
	Fine ounces.	*Fine ounces.*	*Fine ounces.*	*Fine ounces.*
Alaska	53,868	78,140	24,272	....
Arizona	86,324	95,072	8,748	....
California	656,468	722,171	65,703	....
Colorado	459,152	643,634	184,482	....
Georgia	4,728	6,192	1,464	....
Idaho	100,682	86,088	....	14,594
Michigan	2,150	2,075	....	75
Montana	176,637	198,405	21,768	....
Nevada	55,042	75,088	20,046	....
New Mexico	27,465	23,810	....	3,655
North Carolina	2,254	2,622	368	....
Oregon	68,792	42,972	....	25,820
South Carolina	4,733	6,212	1,479	....
South Dakota	159,594	187,187	27,593	....
Utah	41,991	66,419	24,428	....
Washington	9,438	16,980	7,542	....
Alabama Connecticut Minnesota Nebraska Tennessee Virginia Wyoming	1,495	1,693	198	....
Total	1,910,813	2,254,760	388,091	44,144
Net increase	....	....	343,947	....

Product of gold and silver in the United States from 1792.

[The estimate for 1792–1873 is by Dr. R. W. Raymond, United States Mining Commissioner, and since by the Director of the Mint.]

Year.	Total.	Gold.	Silver.
April 2, 1792–July 31, 1834	$14,000,000	$14,000,000	(a)
July 31, 1834–Dec. 31, 1844	7,750,000	7,500,000	$250,000
1845	1,058,327	1,008,327	50,000
1846	1,189,357	1,139,357	50,000
1847	939,085	889,085	50,000
1848	10,050,000	10,000,000	50,000
1849	40,050,000	40,000,060	50,000
1850	50,050,000	50,000,000	50,000
1851	55,050,000	55,000,000	50,000
1852	60,050,000	60,000,000	50,000
1853	65,050,000	65,000,000	50,000
1854	60,050,000	60,000,000	50,000
1855	55,050,000	55,000,000	50,000
1856	55,050,000	55,000,000	50,000
1857	55,050,000	55,000,000	50,000
1858	50,500,000	50,000,000	500,000
1859	50,100,000	50,000,000	100,000
1860	46,150,000	46,000,000	150,000
1861	45,000,000	43,000,000	2,000,000
1862	43,700,000	39,200,000	4,500,000
1863	48,500,000	40,000,000	8,500,000
1864	57,100,000	46,100,000	11,000,000
1865	64,475,000	53,225,000	11,250,000
1866	63,500,000	53,500,000	10,000,000
1867	65,225,000	51,725,000	13,500,000
1868	60,000,000	48,000,000	12,000,000
1869	61,500,000	49,500,000	12,000,000
1870	66,000,000	50,000,000	16,000,000
1871	66,500,000	43,500,000	23,000,000
1872	64,750,000	36,000,000	28,750,000
1873	71,750,000	36,000,000	35,750,000
1874	70,800,000	33,500,000	37,300,000
1875	65,100,000	33,400,000	31,700,000
1876	78,700,000	39,900,000	38,800,000
1877	86,700,000	46,900,000	39,800,000
1878	96,400,000	51,200,000	45,200,000
1879	79,700,000	38,900,000	40,800,000
1880	75,200,000	36,000,000	39,200,000
1881	77,700,000	34,700,000	43,000,000
1882	79,300,000	32,500,000	46,800,000
1883	76,200,000	30,000,000	46,200,000

a Insignificant.

Product of gold and silver in the United States from 1792—Continued.

[The estimates for 1792-1873 is by Dr. R. W. Raymond, United States Mining Commissioner, and since by the Director of the Mint.]

Year.	Total.	Gold.	Silver.
1884	$79,600,000	$30,800,000	$48,800,000
1885	83,400,000	31,800,000	51,600,000
1886	86,000,000	35,000,000	51,000,000
1887	86,350,000	33,000,000	53,350,000
1888	92,370,000	35,175,000	59,195,000
1889 { mint	97,446,000	32,800,000	64,646,000
1889 { census	99,282,866	32,886,180	66,396,686
1890	103,330,714	32,845,000	70,485,714
1891	108,591,565	33,175,000	75,416,565
1892	115,101,000	33,000,000	82,101,000
1893	113,531,000	35,955,000	77,576,000
1894	103,500,000	39,500,000	64,000,000
1895	118,661,000	46,610,000	72,051,000

COPPER.

By CHARLES KIRCHHOFF.

GENERAL TRADE CONDITIONS.

The copper industry of the world has had a fairly prosperous year during 1895, the characteristic feature having been the rapid expansion in the consumption, notably in Europe. In the United States the copper trade participated in the quick, but short-lived, improvement in the demand, which extended to all branches of the iron and metal trades during the summer and early fall.

Production expanded in the United States, until now this country contributes more than one-half to the world's output, and has treble the output of its nearest rival as a producer of copper. No new developments opening sources of supply in hitherto unworked sections have taken place. Some new enterprises have been started, but they do not promise to enter in the near future into the ranks of the first ten or twelve large mines. What expansion has taken place has occurred with the well-established older concerns.

One fact has been growing more and more conspicuous in recent years, and that is the preponderating influence of a few large groups of producers in the copper trade of the United States. Foremost stands the Anaconda, with a product of 100,000,000 to 120,000,000 pounds per year. The Calumet and Hecla can produce from 85,000,000 to 90,000,000 pounds, and the interests controlling the Boston and Montana, Tamarack, Osceola, and Old Dominion represent 75,000,000 to 80,000,000 pounds more. There are a number of smaller groups, but none of them attain 25,000,000 pounds per annum. In Europe the Rothschilds control the Rio Tinto and the Boleo, with a capacity of 100,000,000 pounds for both, and in conjunction with the Exploration Company have a very large holding in the Anaconda property. In other words, the four large interests named have possession of mines which, in the aggregate, produce very nearly one-half of the whole copper product in the world, and possess even far greater influence when it is considered that nearly everyone of the mines in question can sell copper at much lower figures than the normal market price.

17 GEOL, PT 3——6

PRODUCTION.

The following table shows the production of copper in the United States from its first rise to the dignity of an industry. For the earlier years the best available sources have been drawn upon for the estimates given. Since 1882 the figures are those collected by this office:

Production of copper in the United States from 1845 to 1895.

[Long tons.]

Year.	Total production.	Lake Superior.	Calumet and Hecla.	Percentage of Lake Superior of total product.
1845	100	12		12
1846	150	26		17.3
1847	300	213	....	71
1848	500	461	....	92.2
1849	700	672	....	96
1850	650	572	....	88
1851	900	779	....	86.6
1852	1,100	792	....	72
1853	2,000	1,297	....	64.9
1854	2,250	1,819	....	80.8
1855	3,000	2,593	....	86.4
1856	4,000	3,666	....	91.7
1857	4,800	4,255	....	88.6
1858	5,500	4,088	....	74.3
1859	6,300	3,985	....	63.3
1860	7,200	5,388	....	74.8
1861	7,500	6,713	....	89.5
1862	9,000	6,065	....	67.4
1863	8,500	5,797	....	68.2
1864	8,000	5,576	....	69.7
1865	8,500	6,410	....	75.4
1866	8,900	6,138	....	69
1867	10,000	7,824	603	78.2
1868	11,600	9,346	2,276	80.6
1869	12,500	11,886	5,497	95.1
1870	12,600	10,992	6,277	87.2
1871	13,000	11,942	7,242	91.9
1872	12,500	10,961	7,215	87.7
1873	15,500	13,433	8,414	86.7
1874	17,500	15,327	8,984	87.6
1875	18,000	16,089	9,586	89.4
1876	19,000	17,085	9,683	89.9

Production of copper in the United States from 1845 to 1895—Continued.

[Long tons]

Year.	Total production.	Lake Superior.	Calumet and Hecla	Percentage of Lake Superior of total product.
1877	21,000	17,422	10,075	83
1878	21,500	17,719	11,272	82.4
1879	23,000	19,129	11,728	83.2
1880	27,000	22,204	14,140	82.2
1881	32,000	24,363	14,000	76.1
1882	40,167	25,439	14,309	62.9
1883	51,574	26,653	14,788	51.6
1884	64,708	30,961	18,069	47.8
1885	74,052	32,269	21,093	43.5
1886	70,430	36,124	22,553	51.3
1887	81,017	33,941	20,543	41.9
1888	101,054	38,604	22,453	38.2
1889	101,239	39,364	21,727	38.7
1890	115,966	45,273	26,727	38.9
1891	126,839	50,992	....	40.2
1892	151,018	54,999	....	35.7
1893	147,033	50,270	....	34.2
1894	158,120	51,031	....	32.3
1895	169,917	57,737	34,455	34

In detail, the production of copper, territorially distributed, has been as follows since 1883:

Total copper production in the United States, 1883 to 1887.

Sources.	1883.	1884.	1885.
	Pounds.	Pounds.	Pounds.
Lake Superior	59,702,404	69,353,202	72,147,889
Arizona	23,874,963	26,734,345	22,706,366
Montana	24,664,346	13,093,054	67,797,864
New Mexico	823,511	59,450	79,839
California	1,600,862	876,166	469,028
Utah	341,885	265,526	126,199
Colorado	1,152,652	2,013,125	1,146,460
Wyoming	962,468	....	....
Nevada	288,077	100,000	8,871
Idaho	....	46,667	40,381
Missouri	260,306	230,000	....

Total copper production in the United States, 1883 to 1887—Continued.

Sources.	1883.	1884.	1885.
	Pounds.	*Pounds.*	*Pounds.*
Maine and New Hampshire........	212, 124	249, 018	
Vermont.........................	400, 000	655, 405	211, 602
Southern States	395, 175	317, 711	40, 199
Middle States....................	64, 400	2, 114	190, 641
Lead desilverizers, etc............	782, 880	950, 870	910, 144
Total domestic copper	115, 526, 053	144, 946, 653	165, 875, 483
From imported pyrites and ores....	1, 625, 742	2, 858, 754	5, 086, 811
Total (including copper from imported pyrites).........	117, 151, 795	147, 805, 407	170, 962, 324

Sources.	1886.	1887.
	Pounds.	*Pounds.*
Lake Superior	80, 918, 460	76, 028, 697
Arizona	15, 657, 035	17, 720, 462
Montana	57, 611, 621	78, 699, 677
New Mexico	558, 385	283, 664
California	430, 210	1, 600, 000
Utah	500, 000	2, 500, 000
Colorado	409, 306	2, 012, 027
Wyoming	....	....
Nevada...........................	50, 000	....
Idaho		....
Missouri..........................		....
Maine and New Hampshire.........		
Vermont..........................	315, 719	200, 000
Southern States...................	29, 811	....
Middle States.....................	....	....
Lead desilverizers, etc	1, 282, 496	2, 432, 804
Total domestic copper..............	157, 763, 043	181, 477, 331
From imported pyrites and ores..................	4, 500, 000	3, 750, 000
Total (including copper from imported pyrites)......................	162, 263, 043	185, 227, 331

Since 1888 the production has been as follows, in detail:

Total copper production in the United States, 1888 to 1893.

Sources.	1888.	1889.	1890.
	Pounds.	*Pounds.*	*Pounds.*
Lake Superior	86,472,034	88,175,675	101,410,277
Arizona	31,797,300	31,586,185	34,796,689
Montana	97,897,968	98,222,444	112,980,896
New Mexico	1,631,271	3,686,137	850,034
California	1,570,021	151,505	23,347
Utah	2,131,047	65,467	1,006,636
Colorado, including copper smelters(a)	1,621,100	1,170,053	3,585,691
Wyoming	232,819	100,000	....
Nevada	50,000	26,420	....
Idaho	50,000	156,490	87,243
Washington	....	....	....
Maine and New Hampshire }
Vermont }	271,631	72,000	378,840
Southern States	18,201	18,144	
Middle States	....	....	
Lead desilverizers, etc. (b)	2,618,074	3,345,442	4,643,439
Total domestic copper	226,361,466	226,775,962	259,763,092
From imported pyrites and ores	4,909,156	5,190,252	6,017,041
Total (including copper from imported pyrites)	231,270,622	231,966,214	265,780,133

Sources.	1891.	1892.	1893.
	Pounds.	*Pounds.*	*Pounds.*
Lake Superior	114,222,709	123,198,460	112,605,078
Arizona	39,873,279	38,436,099	43,902,824
Montana	112,063,320	163,206,128	155,209,133
New Mexico	1,233,197	1,188,796	280,742
California	3,397,405	2,980,914	239,682
Utah	1,562,098	2,209,428	1,135,330
Colorado, including copper smelters (a)	6,336,878	7,593,674	7,695,826
Wyoming	....	....	....
Nevada	....	....	20,000
Idaho	146,825	226,000	36,367

a Copper smelters in Colorado, purchasing argentiferous copper ores and mattes in the open market, sources not known. The quantity of Montana matte which goes to one of these works has been deducted.

b For 1891 the quantity stated covers only that part of the incidental copper product the source of which could not be ascertained.

Total copper production in the United States, 1888 to 1895—Continued.

Sources.	1891.	1892.	1893.
	Pounds.	*Pounds.*	*Pounds.*
Washington...........................	....	....	39, 785
Maine and New Hampshire.........			
Vermont...........................			
Southern States...................	296, 463	467, 448	732, 793
Middle States.....................			
Lead desilverizers, etc. (b)........	4, 989, 590	5, 491, 702	7, 456, 838
Total domestic copper......	284, 121, 764	344, 998, 679	329, 354, 398
From imported pyrites and ores and regulus..................	11, 690, 312	7, 973, 065	10, 431, 574
Total (including copper from imported pyrites)........	295, 812, 076	352, 971, 744	339, 785, 972

Sources.	1894.	1895.
	Pounds.	*Pounds.*
Lake Superior	114, 308, 870	129, 330, 749
Arizona	44, 514, 894	47, 953, 553
Montana	183, 072, 756	190, 172, 150
New Mexico	31, 884	143, 719
California	120, 000	218, 332
Utah	1, 147, 570	2, 184, 708
Colorado, including copper smelters (a)	6, 481, 413	6, 079, 243
Wyoming	....	....
Nevada...................................	....	....
Idaho	....	1, 425, 914
Washington	....	
Maine and New Hampshire..................		
Vermont		
Southern States............................	2, 374, 514	3, 105, 036
Middle States..............................		
Lead desilverizers, etc. (b)	2, 136, 473	....
Total domestic copper....................	354, 188, 374	380, 613, 404
From imported pyrites and ores and regulus....	10, 678, 434	12, 026, 560
Total (including copper from imported pyrites)	364, 866, 808	392, 639, 964

a Copper smelters in Colorado, purchasing argentiferous copper ores and mattes in the open market, sources not known. The quantity of Montana matte which goes to one of these works has been deducted.

b For 1894 the quantity stated covers only that part of the incidental copper product the source of which could not be ascertained.

The available supply for the domestic markets may be computed as follows:

Supply of copper for the United States in 1891, 1892, 1893, 1894, and 1895.

	1891.	1892.	1893.
	Pounds.	*Pounds.*	*Pounds.*
Production of domestic copper....	284, 121. 764	344. 998. 679	329, 354. 398
Imports:			
Fine copper in ore, entered for consumption...................	8, 931, 554	7, 669, 978	7, 256, 015
Fine copper in regulus, entered for consumption	2, 403, 919	303, 087	3, 175, 559
Bars and ingots...............	2, 556	22, 097	551, 318
Old copper...................	134, 407	71, 485	59, 375
Total.....................	295, 594, 200	353, 065, 326	340, 399, 695
Exports:			
Ingots and bars...............	69, 279, 024	30, 515, 736	138, 984. 128
Estimated fine copper contents of matte	50, 000, 000	66, 000, 000	50, 000, 000
Total.....................	119, 279. 024	96, 515, 736	188, 984, 128
Available supply.............	176, 315. 176	256, 549. 596	151, 415, 567

	1894.	1895.
	Pounds.	*Pounds.*
Production of domestic copper...................	354, 188, 374	380, 613, 404
Imports:		
Fine copper in ore, entered for consumption.	4, 804, 614	8, 921, 320
Fine copper in regulus, entered for consumption................	5, 873, 820	3, 104, 640
Bars and ingots	606, 415	7, 979. 322
Old copper	160, 592	1, 336, 901
Total	365, 633, 815	401, 956, 187
Exports:		
Ingots and bars	162, 393, 000	121, 328. 390
Estimated fine copper contents of matte.....	5, 750. 000	15, 200, 000
Total	168, 143, 000	136, 528. 390
Available supply	197, 490, 815	265, 427. 797

This statement leaves out of account the stocks concerning which no reliable data are obtainable.

Since July, 1892, Mr. John Stanton, of New York, has collected monthly, from sworn returns, figures showing the production of the leading mines of Lake Superior, Montana, and Arizona. The estimate of outside sources is drawn, particularly recently, from official returns of the principal smaller mines.

American product of copper.

[Long tons.]

Year and month.	Reporting mines.	Outside sources.	Total.
1892.			
July	9,294	924	10,218
August	10,807	870	11,677
September	9,710	994	10,704
October	9,668	1,289	10,957
November	9,888	1,036	10,924
December	9,872	1,174	11,046
Total	59,239	6,287	65,526
1893.			
January	9,187	989	10,176
February	8,213	1,042	9,245
March	9,065	1,321	10,386
April	11,775	1,042	12,817
May	12,706	1,042	13,748
June	11,524	1,042	12,566
July	11,049	1,042	12,091
August	11,745	1,042	12,787
September	11,750	1,042	12,792
October	11,503	1,042	12,545
November	10,705	1,042	11,477
December	10,538	1,042	11,580
Total	129,760	12,730	142,480
1894.			
January	10,832	1,340	12,172
February	10,245	1,340	11,585
March	13,759	1,340	15,099
April	12,475	1,340	13,815
May	12,668	1,340	14,608
June	13,972	1,340	15,312
July	12,639	1,340	13,979
August	11,815	1,500	13,315
September	11,257	1,500	12,757
October	12,692	1,500	14,192

American product of copper—Continued.

[Long tons.]

Year and month.	Reporting mines.	Outside sources.	Total.
1894.			
November	11,044	1,600	12,644
December	9,145	1,600	10,745
Total	142,543	17,080	159,623
1895.			
January	10,094	1,600	11,694
February	11,120	1,600	12,720
March	12,553	1,600	14,153
April	11,944	1,600	13,544
May	13,260	1,600	14,860
June	11,641	1,100	12,741
July	12,524	1,100	13,624
August	14,290	1,100	15,390
September	14,251	1,100	15,351
October	15,045	1,100	16,145
November	15,330	1,100	16,430
December	13,445	1,100	14,545
Total	155,497	15,700	171,197
1896.			
January	14,872	1,200	16,072
February	16,316	1,200	17,516
March	16,722	1,200	17,922
April	15,912	1,200	17,112
May	15,533	1,200	16,733
June	14,825	1,200	16,025
July	15,395	1,200	16,595
First 6 months 1896	94,180	7,200	101,380
First 6 months 1895	70,612	9,100	79,712

The product of the foreign reporting mines was as follows:

Foreign reporting mines.

Year and month.	Long tons.	Year and month.	Long tons.
1892.		**1894—continued.**	
July	6,358	August	7,367
August	6,888	September	7,110
September	5,478	October	7,231
October	6,476	November	6,961
November	6,789	December	7,606
December	7,666		
		Total	88,531
Total last 6 months.	39,655	**1895.**	
		January	6,737
1893.		February	6,739
January	5,736	March	7,424
February	6,762	April	7,219
March	6,896	May	7,400
April	6,913	June	6,965
May	6,806	July	6,988
June	7,935	August	7,129
July	6,095	September	6,947
August	7,057	October	7,753
September	6,303	November	7,728
October	7,081	December	7,149
November	6,953		
December	7,248	Total	86,178
Total	81,785	**1896.**	
		January	6,834
1894.		February	7,096
January	8,145	March	6,910
February	7,217	April	6,865
March	6,922	May	7,495
April	7,385	June	7,055
May	8,013	July	7,847
June	7,611		
July	6,960	Total first 7 months	50,102

These include the principal mines of the Peninsula, the Cape, Australia, Germany, and Mexico.

According to the compilations by Mr. John Stanton, the exports of fine copper from the United States were as follows:

United States exports.

Year and month.	Long tons.	Year and month.	Long tons.
1892.		**1894—continued.**	
July	3,450	October	5,057
August	1,545	November	4,785
September	1,458	December	6,793
October	3,144		
November	3,897	Total first 6 months	39,769
December	4,486	Total last 6 months	37,758
		Total year 1894	77,527
Total last 6 months	17,980	**1895.**	
1893.		January	7,144
January	3,171	February	3,450
February	1,815	March	3,914
March	2,334	April	5,677
April	3,450	May	5,430
May	4,482	June	8,600
June	5,109	July	6,035
July	7,181	August	4,493
August	9,127	September	4,106
September	16,131	October	3,773
October	11,478	November	4,874
November	7,821	December	7,226
December	8,293		
		Total first 6 months	34,215
Total first 6 months	20,361	Total last 6 months	30,507
Total last 6 months	60,031		
		Total year 1895	64,722
Total year 1893	80,392	**1896.**	
1894.		January	8,168
January	7,717	February	8,296
February	5,590	March	10,892
March	7,137	April	10,684
April	6,209	May	10,481
May	6,140	June	9,797
June	6,976	July	10,885
July	7,622		
August	6,408	Total first 7 months	69,203
September	7,093		

THE LAKE SUPERIOR MINES.

The following is, in detail, the output of the Lake Superior mines, as reported by the companies, from 1884 to 1890:

Production of Lake Superior copper mines, 1884 to 1890.

Mines.	1884.	1885.	1886.	1887.
	Pounds.	*Pounds.*	*Pounds.*	*Pounds.*
Calumet and Hecla.....	40,473,585	47,247,990	50,518,222	46,016,123
Quincy.................	5,650,436	5,848,530	5,888,511	5,603,691
Osceola	4,247,630	1,945,208	3,560,786	3,574,972
Franklin..............	3,748,652	4,007,105	4,264,297	3,915,838
Allouez	1,928,174	2,170,476	1,725,463	885,010
Atlantic	3,163,585	3,582,633	3,503,670	3,611,865
Pewabic	227,831	....	....	....
Central	1,446,747	2,157,408	2,512,886	2,199,133
Grand Portage	255,860	....	....	....
Conglomerate	1,198,691	....	....	....
Mass..................	481,396	363,500	217,179	....
Copper Falls..........	891,168	1,150,538	1,378,679	719,150
Phœnix	631,004	344,355	1,101,804	11,600
Hancock	562,636	203,037	150,000	....
Huron	1,927,660	2,271,163	1,992,695	1,881,760
Ridge.................	74,030	63,390	158,272	81,902
St. Clair	139,407	....	....	....
Cliff	28,225	....	22,312	....
Wolverine	751,763	328,610	3,125	2,300
Nonesuch	23,867	28,484	....	....
Isle Royale...........	16,074	....	....	....
National	87,368	162,252	184,706	25,187
Minnesota.............	1,144	12,608	....	....
Belt	130,851	27,433	7,300	....
Sheldon and Columbia..	9,828	....	....	....
Adventure	4,333	4,000	1,000	....
Peninsula.............	1,225,981	....	....	....
Tamarack.............	....	181,669	3,646,517	7,396,529
Ogima	1,106	12,000	....	....
Kearsarge.............	....	....	....	21,237
Evergreen Bluff........	954	1,500	1,000	....
Ash Bed	1,517	....	....	....
Sundry companies— tributers	21,696	31,000	50,000	50,000
Total	69,353,202	72,147,889	80,918,460	76,028,697

Production of Lake Superior copper mines, 1884 to 1890—Continued.

Mines.	1888.	1889.	1890.
	Pounds.	*Pounds.*	*Pounds.*
Calumet and Hecla...............	50, 295, 720	48, 668, 296	59, 868, 106
Quincy.........................	6, 367, 809	6, 405, 686	8, 064, 253
Osceola	4, 134, 320	4, 534, 127	5, 294, 792
Franklin.......................	3, 655, 751	4, 346, 062	5, 638, 112
Allouez	314, 198	1, 762, 816	1, 407, 828
Atlantic.......................	6, 974, 877	3, 698, 837	3, 619, 972
Pewabic			
Central	1, 817, 023	1, 270, 592	1, 413, 391
Grand Portage..................			
Conglomerate			
Mass		58, 349	62, 187
Copper Falls	1, 199, 950	1, 440, 000	1, 330, 000
Phœnix			
Hancock			
Huron	2, 370, 857	2, 219, 473	1, 736, 777
Ridge..........................	50, 924	28, 000	21, 569
St. Clair......................			
Cliff			
Wolverine......................			
Nonesuch			
Isle Royale....................			
National		454, 134	123, 879
Minnesota......................			
Belt...........................			
Sheldon and Columbia...........			
Adventure		692	15, 485
Peninsula		736, 507	1, 108, 660
Tamarack.......................	11, 411, 325	10, 605, 451	10, 106, 741
Ogima			
Kearsarge	829, 185	1, 918, 849	1, 598, 525
Evergreen Bluff		21, 580	
Ash Bed........................			
Sundry companies—tributers	50, 000	6, 224	
Total	86, 472, 031	88, 175, 675	101, 410, 277

The permission to publish the report of the Calumet and Hecla Company since 1891 has not been given. According to the return by the company in Michigan, the product was 79,769,293 pounds in 1894 and 79,137,399 pounds in 1895.

The following table records only the output of the other leading producers in that district:

Production of Lake Superior copper mines in 1891, 1892, 1893, 1894, and 1895.

Mines.	1891.	1892.	1893.	1894.	1895.
	Pounds.	Pounds.	Pounds.	Pounds.	Pounds.
Tamarack	16, 161, 312	16, 426, 633	15, 085, 113	15, 375, 281	14, 810, 000
Quincy.........	10, 542, 519	11, 103, 926	14, 398, 477	15, 484, 014	16, 304, 721
Osceola	6, 543, 358	7, 008, 656	6, 715, 870	6, 918, 592	6, 270, 373
Franklin	4, 319, 840	3, 769, 605	3, 501, 244	3, 556, 487	3, 086, 933
Atlantic........	3, 653, 671	3, 703, 875	4, 221, 933	4, 437, 609	4, 832, 497
Kearsarge	1, 727, 390	1, 467, 758	1, 627, 030	1, 908, 710	1, 916, 163
Tamarack, jr....	....	796, 769	1, 610, 259	2, 349, 329	2, 605, 000
Peninsula	1, 599, 670	973, 217	....	....	....
Copper Falls ...	1, 427, 000	1, 350, 000	750, 000	....	....
Huron	1, 257, 059	461, 499	562, 776	....	....
Allouez	1, 241, 423	546, 530	....	....	....
Central	1, 237, 500	1, 625, 982	1, 180, 040	584, 590	379, 020
Centennial	531, 983	106, 801	....	....	....
Wolverine......	312, 112	500, 074	1, 025, 062	1, 665, 255	1, 815, 391

LAKE SUPERIOR.

During the fiscal year ended April 30, 1896, the Calumet and Hecla Company produced mineral equivalent to 83,963,775 pounds of refined copper. The product in refined copper was 85,552,756 pounds, as compared with 62,466,414 pounds during the fiscal year 1894-95. The company does not publish any statement of income or expenditure, but reports only assets and liabilities. The Red Jacket shaft has reached a vertical depth of 4,900 feet, the deepest point to which it is proposed to sink. The rock temperature at this depth is 87.6° F., a temperature which, the report says, will not interfere with active mining operations.

The report of the Tamarack Company covers the period of eighteen months from June 30, 1894, to December 31, 1895. It does not contain any figures with reference to product, but deals only with income and finances. The gross receipts for copper were $2,143,201.78, the running costs being $1,324,641.52 at the mine and $341,785.71 for smelting, transportation, and expenses of marketing. This shows a mining profit of $476,774.55. Dividends aggregating $600,000 were paid. The outlay for construction account and sinking shafts was $449,698.54. On the other hand, there was received from the sale of new stock $684,911.88, and there was still due from the sale of new stock, less commission to underwriters, $265,988.12. In August, 1895, work was begun on shaft No. 5, which is to reach the lode at a depth of 4,700 feet. On February 19 Mr. W. E. Parnell, the superintendent, reported the depth of the shafts of the company as 3,232.9 feet for No. 1, 3,535 feet for No. 2, 4,450 feet each for No. 3 and No. 4, and 226 feet for No. 5.

In 1895 the Quincy produced 16,304,721 pounds of refined copper, which realized $1,657,701.05, to which has been added $3,745.53 for the sale of silver and $8,415.21 for interest on loans, etc. The running expenses at the mine were $763,018.82, and the smelting, transportation, and other expenses were $206,353.55, making the net income of the year $700,489.42. The dividends paid during the fiscal year were $600,000, so that the balance of assets was $1,007,500.68 on January 1, 1896, that sum including $909,410.72 cash and copper. During the year there were received 563,360 tons of rock, of which there were hoisted 506,058 tons, and treated in the stamp mill 495,402 tons. The product of the stamp mill was 14,670,530 pounds of mineral, and from the rock houses 5,062,440 pounds.

The following table shows the operations of the Quincy mine for a series of years. It illustrates well the steady increase in production, the fluctuations in the yield, the heavy decline in the price of copper, the crowding down of cost through improvements, in spite of increasing depth, and the remarkable uniformity of wages paid. It should be stated that the average price realized is calculated from the gross income and the product, the reports failing to show the quantity of copper on hand at the beginning of each fiscal year, and the values at which it was put in:

Operations of the Quincy mine.

Year.	Product.	Yield fine copper per fathom broken.	Price obtained.	Cost per pound.	Number of miners on contract.	Average monthly contract wages.
	Pounds.	*Pounds.*	*Cents.*	*Cents.*		
1864	2,498,574	562	44.8	26.7	242	$65.50
1865	2,720,980	501	....	....	212	57.53
1866	2,114,220	451	31.3	29	227	53.16
1867	1,921,620	526	22.7	18.9	167	50.83
1868	1,417,941	447	25.2	23.1	157	50.41
1869	2,417,365	446	21.9	16.7	210	51.10
1870	2,496,774	528	21.5	15.3	181	46.09
1871 (a)	2,409,501	441	22.8	15.2	104	47.08
1872	2,269,104	391	32.5	22.9	233	60.62
1873	2,621,087	491	26.5	18.6	223	62.42
1874	3,050,154	577	21.9	15.1	234	43.38
1875	2,798,281	485	22.7	15.8	217	46.74
1876	3,073,171	507	20.0	15.7	227	47.13
1877	2,837,014	467	18.6	15.1	217	43.79

a Introduction of steam drills.

Operations of the Quincy mine—Continued.

Year.	Product.	Yield fine copper per fathom broken.	Price obtained.	Cost per pound.	Number of miners on contract.	Average monthly contract wages.
	Pounds.	*Pounds.*	*Cents.*	*Cents.*		
1878	2,991,050	395	14.9	14	234	$41.50
1879	2,639,958	403	16.3	13.7	212	38.76
1880	3,609,250	563	18.5	11.8	192	49.10
1881	5,702,606	767	18.7	10	212	48.54
1882	5,682,663	800	17.1	9.5	152	48.83
1883	6,012,239	850	13.7	8.9	165	46.02
1884	5,680,087	722	12.2	8.6	157	43.35
1885	5,848,497	710	11.4	7.5	132	44.00
1886	5,888,517	638	11.1	6.8	140	45.80
1887	5,603,691	781	11.7	8.6	142	48.40
1888	6,367,809	690	15.9	10.1	158	49.60
1889	6,405,686	690	12	9.4	145	49.15
1890	8,064,253	769	15.7	8.2	146	52.60
1891	10,542,519	685	12.8	9.1	182	53.40
1892	11,103,926	572	11.27	8.8	238	53.75
1893	14,398,477	574	10.4	7.1	259	49.60
1894	15,484,014	584	9.5	5.7	285	50.70
1895	16,304,721	517	10.1	5.9	336	50.00

The Osceola suffered from a calamity in 1895, 30 men having been lost through a fire in No. 3 shaft. Costs were also affected through the sinking of No. 6 shaft. In spite of the loss of product the total outlay per pound of copper was only very slightly increased. The annual report no longer furnishes the details submitted in former years. The product of mineral was 7,399,846 pounds, yielding 6,270,373 pounds of refined copper, or at the rate of 437 pounds of refined copper per cubic fathom of ground broken. The percentage of fine copper in the stamp rock was 1.34. The total mining cost per ton of rock hoisted was $1.77, while the total cost per pound of copper was 8.75 cents against 8.70 cents in 1894, 9.48 cents in 1893, and 9.12 cents in 1892. The total income was $669,907.33 and the total costs $548,445.12, leaving a mining profit of $121,462.21. Dividends aggregating $125,000 were paid, reducing the balance on assets to $273,062.65.

Toward the end of November, 1895, fire destroyed the engine house, boiler house, and a large part of the machinery of the Franklin mine, so that the product was smaller than usual. The mine produced 3,086,933 pounds of refined copper from 3,721,458 pounds of mineral obtained by crushing 126,990 tons of rock, 141,061 tons having been hoisted. The receipts were $333,363.51, including $2,867.88 for interest.

The running expenses at the mine were $248,583.73, and the other expenses for freight, smelting, etc., were $44,111.75, thus showing a mining profit of $40,668.03, from which is deducted $9,926.67 for construction, leaving a net income of $30,741.36. Exploration work on the territory of the Franklin, jr., has been pushed, but nothing of value has been discovered in the extensions of the Calumet, Osceola, or Pewabic veins. The expense of equipping and working the Franklin, jr., during the year amounted to $49,533.62.

In the low cost of handling material the management of the Atlantic Mining Company continues its records:

Cost of copper at the Atlantic mine per ton of rock treated.

Items of cost.	1888.	1889.	1890.	1891.
	Cents.	Cents.	Cents.	Cents.
Mining, selecting, breaking, and all surface expenses, including taxes	83.73	87.87	104.14	95.29
Transportation to mill	3.47	3.88	3.46	3.86
Stamping and separating	26.89	27.78	27.78	25.82
Freight, smelting, marketing, and New York expenses	21.42	20.22	20.37	18.47
Total working expenses	135.51	139.75	155.75	143.44
Total expenditures, including construction	142.82	153.27	166.70	154.51
Net profit	54.36	6.23	27.71	0.16
Yield of copper, per cent	0.667	0.663	0.650	0.615

Items of cost.	1892.	1893.	1894.	1895.
	Cents.	Cents.	Cents.	Cents.
Mining, selecting, breaking, and all surface expenses, including taxes	83.98	79.49	75.18	75.25
Transportation to mill	3.33	3.28	3.03	4.08
Stamping and separating	25.09	24.95	23.30	22.20
Freight, smelting, marketing, and New York expenses	17.67	18.22	17.71	18.81
Total working expenses	130.07	125.94	119.22	120.34
Total expenditures, including construction	133.51	160.24	165.07	156.05
Yield of copper, per cent	0.615	0.669	0.703	0.730

During 1895 the moving of the machinery from the old mill on Port-age Lake to the new stamping mill on Lake Superior was completed and the necessary railroad built. The mill has an equipment of 6 18-inch Ball stamps, 24 separators, 168 wire jigs, and 28 slime tables. Provision has been made for an extension. The mill is able to handle all the rock which the hoisting facilities can supply. During the year there were stamped 334,058 tons of rock, which produced 6,239,000 pounds of mineral, yielding 4,832,497 pounds of refined copper. The yield showed some improvement, being 241 pounds of refined copper per cubic fathom of ground broken, as compared with 219 pounds in 1894. The receipts were $508,252.47 for copper and $760.27 for interest, a total of $509,012.74. The working expenses at the mine were $336,131.06, and the freight, smelting, and other outlays $62,282.21, leaving a gross profit of $110,599.47, to which is added $2,687 as the amount credited real estate for stumpage. The construction account at the mine amounted to $19,585.34; at the new mill $91,587.24, and on the new railroad $6,933.04. This shows an excess of expenditures over receipts of $4,819.15, and reduces the surplus to $150,874.97.

The report for the Wolverine Copper Mining Company covers the fiscal year ended June 30, 1896. The product of the mine was 2,325,875 pounds of mineral, which yielded 2,011,638 pounds of refined copper. The mine hoisted 106,190 tons of rock, of which 85,155 tons were stamped, thus showing a yield of 1.344 per cent as compared with 0.9668 per cent during the previous year. The cost per pound of copper at the mine was 7.10 cents, while the cost of smelting, transportation, etc., was 1.26 cents, making a total of 8.36 cents. In the preceding year the figures were 7.23, 1.22, and 8.45 cents, respectively. The total income was $219,187.19, while the outlay was $168,256.81, leaving a mining profit of $50,930.38.

The Kearsarge Company produced 1,946,163 pounds of refined copper from 2,292,805 pounds of mineral, the ground broken having yielded 409 pounds of fine copper per cubic fathom, while the percentage of fine copper from the stamp rock was 1.51. The mining cost per ton of rock hoisted was $1.72, and the total cost of copper sold was 9.22 cents. The total receipts were $209,783.65 and the total costs $179,434.66, leaving a net income of $30,348.99. With the net income of 1894 of $18,197.24 this permitted the declaration of a dividend of $40,000.

The Central produced a small amount of copper as an incident to its explorations, which did not lead to any finds in 1895.

MONTANA.

The growth in importance of Montana as a copper producer is shown in the following table:

Montana's proportion of the copper product.

Year.	United States.	Montana.		Lake Superior.
	Pounds.	Pounds.	Per cent.	Per cent
1882...................	90, 646, 232	9, 058, 281	10. 0	62. 9
1883...................	115, 526, 053	24, 664, 346	21. 4	51. 6
1884...................	144, 946, 653	43, 093, 054	29. 7	47. 8
1885...................	165, 875, 483	67, 797, 864	40. 9	43. 5
1886...................	157, 763, 043	57, 611, 621	36. 7	51. 6
1887...................	181, 477, 331	78, 699, 677	43. 4	41. 9
1888...................	226, 361, 466	97, 897, 968	43. 3	38. 2
1889...................	226, 775, 962	98, 222, 444	43. 3	38. 9
1890...................	259, 763, 092	112. 980, 896	43. 5	39. 0
1891...................	284, 121, 764	112, 063, 320	39. 4	40. 2
1892...................	344, 998, 679	163, 206, 128	47. 3	35. 7
1893...................	329, 351, 398	155, 209, 133	47. 1	34. 2
1894...................	354, 188, 374	183, 072, 756	51. 6	32. 3
1895...................	380, 613, 404	190, 172, 150	50. 0	34. 0

During the year some interesting figures relative to the operations of the Anaconda Mining Company have been published. They deal with the financial results obtained during the period from February 1, 1891, to December 31, 1893, with the year 1894, and with the first six months of 1895. During the first period the mines were closed for eight months.

Financial results of the operations of the Anaconda Mining Company from February 1, 1891, to December 31, 1893.

	Amount.
Receipts—	
From sale of copper...............................	$18, 471, 269. 94
From sale of silver and gold........................	1, 991, 386. 16
From sale of Baltimore bullion	740, 404. 10
From sale of Anaconda bullion	724, 417. 49
Total..	21, 927, 477. 69
Amount of stuff produced, not realized (estimated)......	3, 174, 425. 00
Total gross proceeds from entire output............	25, 101, 902. 69
Cost of operating expenses and supplies used at mines.....	14, 350. 124. 55
Amount of gross profit on production............	10, 751, 778. 14

Financial results of the operations of the Anaconda Mining Company, etc.—Continued.

	Amount.
Toll charges for treating and selling copper, commissions and expenses on sales, allowance on silver and gold in refining copper, and expenses paid by the New York office	$5, 502, 473. 02
Profit	5, 249, 305. 12
Sundry receipts from royalties, dividends, rents, etc	206, 615. 04
Total	5, 455, 920. 16
Sundry expenditures for taxes, prospecting, assessment work on claims, etc	164, 311. 20
Net profit	5, 291, 608. 96

Financial results of the operations of the Anaconda Mining Company, 1894, and first six months of 1895.

	Year 1894.	First 6 months, 1895.
Receipts:		
From the sale of copper	$8, 727, 377. 46	$3, 828, 733. 11
From the sale of silver and gold	1, 042, 263. 42	117, 711. 78
From the sale of Baltimore bullion	1, 210, 057. 30	561, 977. 80
From the sale of Anaconda bullion	372, 743. 29	298, 782. 54
From sale of ore at mines	3, 359. 17	
Total	11, 355, 800. 64	4. 807, 205. 23
Amount of product not realized (estimated)	3, 174, 425. 00	3, 477, 527. 34
Amount realized on output	8, 181, 375. 64	1, 329, 677. 89
Amount of stuff produced, but not realized at end of period (estimated)	3, 477, 527. 34	4, 945, 891. 25
Total gross proceeds from output	11, 658, 902. 98	6, 275, 569. 14
Cost of operating expenses and supplies used at mines	6, 499, 914. 44	3, 641, 471. 09
Amount of gross profit on production	5, 158, 988. 54	2, 634, 098. 05
Toll charges for treating and selling copper, commissions and expenses on sales, allowance on silver and gold in refining copper, and expenses paid by the New York office	2, 125, 927. 16	664, 800. 36
Profit	3, 033, 061. 38	1, 969, 297. 69

Financial results of the operations of the Anaconda Mining Company, etc.—Continued.

	Year 1894.	First 6 months, 1895.
Sundry receipts from royalties, dividends, rents, etc....................	$170,077.03	$69,214.72
Total	3,203,138.41	2,038,512.41
Sundry expenditures for taxes, prospecting, assessment work on claims, etc..................................	216,654.22	107,204.81
Net profit	2,986,484.19	1,931,307.60

The balance sheet on June 30, 1895, was as follows:

Balance sheet of the Anaconda Mining Company June 30, 1895.

	Amount.
Liabilities:	
Capital stock...................................	$25,000,000.00
Sundry creditors................................	3,626,054.66
Total...................................	28,626,054.66
Assets:	
Properties, improvements, and investments..........	27,281,184.07
Inventory of supplies, etc. (estimated)..............	436,167.32
Product not realized on June 30, 1895 (estimated)....	4,945,891.25
Furniture and fixtures at New York office...........	4,050.77
Cash in hands of J. B. Haggin, treasurer.............	3,042,921.40
Cash in hands of Marcus Daly, superintendent......	320,656.09
Sundry debtors.................................	1,056,221.22
Total...................................	37,087,092.12
Excess of assets over liabilities...................	8,461,037.46
Profit for period from February 1, 1891, to December 31, 1893, adjusted	5,242,643.22
Profit for year ending December 31, 1894.................	2,973,604.19
Profit for half year ending June 30, 1895.................	1,931,307.60
Total..................................	10,147,555.01
Anaconda Old Company, balance of account.............	313,482.45
Total..................................	10,461,037.46
Less stock dividend..................................	2,000,000.00
Balance	8,461,037.46

The principal event in the recent history of the Anaconda has been the sale of two blocks (each of 270,000 shares) of stock to English capitalists—the Exploration Syndicate, largely interested in South African mining ventures, and the Rothschilds. The only important recent addition to the plant is the extension of the electrolytic refinery, which, when completed, will permit the company to handle monthly 3,000 net tons of copper out of a total product of about 5,000 net tons monthly.

The Boston and Montana Company had gross receipts from sales of copper, silver, and gold of $4,999,231.39 in 1895, as compared with $3,630,526.96 in 1894. The running expenses at Butte and Great Falls were $2,086,161.88 in 1895, against $2,019,205.29 in 1894, and the expenses of handling copper were $555,365.90 and $623,876.25, respectively; so that the total running expenses were almost equal in the two years—$2,643,081.54 in 1894 and $2,641,527.78 in 1895. The gross profit in 1895 was $2,357,703.61, as contrasted with $987,455.42 in 1894. Interest on the bonded debt figured up $86,392.15; $150,000 went to sinking fund, and $37,769.37 was paid for mining property. The dividends amounted to $1,050,000 in 1895, as compared with $300,000 in 1894. Out of a total issue of $2,100,000 in 7 per cent bonds there were still outstanding on December 31, 1895, $1,247,000, there being available on that date for redemption a balance of $135,207.76.

The ore shipments at Great Falls were 225,859 tons, but they went partly to increasing the supply of ore and concentrates at the smelting works at Great Falls by one-third. These were estimated in the 1894 report to contain 7,000,000 pounds of copper. This would indicate that the cost, placed entirely upon the copper, was less than 6 cents per pound of copper sold, the precious metals being profit. Mr. Thomas Couch, the superintendent, reports that the reserves increased during the year, being estimated at 956,233 tons. At the Great Falls smelting plant an addition has been built to the power house to contain five new No. 7 Connersville blowers, which, with the old equipment, will suffice for five large blast furnaces. A new power house is planned to contain a pair of horizontal turbines to drive two Westinghouse generators for the electrolytic plant, which has been brought up to a capacity of over 2,000,000 pounds monthly, or about one-half the usual product. At the smelting works a series of modern roasting furnaces is contemplated, to replace the Brueckner cylinders.

ARIZONA.

The only new producer is the United Globe mines, with which the same interests are identified which control the Copper Queen and the Detroit properties. A furnace has been started (in 1896) which has been producing about 300,000 pounds per month, and a larger plant is to be put in. At the Detroit a set of converters is being erected, which will probably lead to a somewhat greater product. At Globe the Old Dominion has been expanding its operations, and is reaching a higher output.

CALIFORNIA.

What is regarded as the most notable deposit upon which development has been begun in recent years is the Iron Mountain mine in California. Although the copper is only an incident, the main value lying in the precious metal contents, yet it is believed that the mine may become a copper producer of some moment. The smelting plant at Keswick, California, consists as yet of only one furnace, having a capacity of 100 tons of ore per day. The matte ultimately produced is to be Bessemerized and the copper treated by electrolysis.

IMPORTS.

The imports of fine copper contained in ores, and of regulus and black copper, and of ingot copper, old copper, plates not rolled, rolled plates, sheathing metal, and manufactures not otherwise specified, and of brass, are given in the following tables:

Fine copper contained in ores, and regulus and black copper imported and entered for consumption in the United States, 1867 to 1895, inclusive.

Year ending—	Fine copper contained in ores.		Regulus and black copper. (a)		Total value.
	Quantity.	Value.	Quantity.	Value.	
	Pounds.		*Pounds.*		
June 30, 1867.....	....	$936,271	....	....	$936,271
1868.....	3,496,994	197,203			197,203
1869.....	24,960,604	448,487			448,487
1870.....	1,936,875	134,736	....	....	134,736
1871.....	411,315	42,453	499	$60	42,513
1872.....	584,878	69,017	1,247	1,083	70,100
1873.....	702,086	80,132	1,444,239	279,631	359,763
1874.....	606,266	70,633	28,880	5,397	76,030
1875.....	1,337,104	161,903	12,518	2,076	163,979
1876.....	538,972	68,922	8,584	1,613	70,535
1877.....	76,637	9,756	1,874	260	10,016
1878.....	87,039	11,785	....	....	11,785
1879.....	51,959	6,199	....	....	6,199
1880.....	1,165,283	173,712	2,201,394	337,163	510,875
1881.....	1,077,217	124,477	402,640	51,633	176,110
1882.....	1,473,109	147,416	224,052	30,013	177,429
1883.....	1,115,386	113,349	....		113,349
1884.....	2,204,070	219,957	2,036	204	220,161
1885.....	3,665,739	343,793	285,322	20,807	364,600
Dec. 31, 1886.....	4,503,400	341,558	1,960	98	341,656
1887.....	3,886,192	194,785	27,650	1,366	196,151

a Not enumerated until 1871.

Fine copper contained in ores, and regulus and black copper imported and entered for consumption in the United States, 1867 to 1895, inclusive—Continued.

Year ending —	Fine copper contained in ores.		Regulus and black copper. (a)		Total value.
	Quantity.	Value.	Quantity.	Value.	
	Pounds.		*Pounds.*		
Dec. 31, 1888.....	4,859,812	$381,477	4,971	$324	$381,801
1889.....	3,772,838	274,649	60,525	4,244	278,893
1890.....	3,448,237	241,732	221,838	15,688	257,420
1891.....	8,931,554	774,057	2,403,919	214,877	988,934
1892.....	7,669,978	453,474	303,087	17,390	470,864
1893.....	7,256,015	435,448	3,175,559	202,197	637,645
1894.....	4,804,614	260,402	5,873,820	144,832	405,234
1895.....	8,921,920	213,689	3,104,640	125,853	339,542

a Not enumerated until 1871.

Copper imported and entered for consumption in the United States, 1867 to 1895, inclusive.

Year ending—	Bars, ingots, and pigs.		Old, fit only for remanufacture.		Old, taken from bottoms of American ships abroad. (a)	
	Quantity.	Value.	Quantity.	Value.	Quantity.	Value.
	Pounds.		*Pounds.*		*Pounds.*	
June 30, 1867...	1,635,953	$287,831	569,732	$81,930	....	....
1868...	61,394	6,935	318,705	42,652	....	....
1869...	13,212	2,143	290,780	34,820	.....	....
1870...	5,157	418	255,386	31,931	....	
1871...	3,316	491	369,634	45,672	....	....
1872...	2,638,589	578,965	1,144,142	178,536	....	
1873...	9,697,608	1,984,122	1,413,040	255,711	32,307	$4,913
1874...	713,935	134,326	733,326	137,087	9,500	930
1875...	58,475	10,741	396,320	55,564	11,636	1,124
1876...	5,281	788	239,987	35,545	10,304	1,981
1877...	230	30	219,443	28,608	41,482	5,136
1878...	1	1	198,749	25,585	....	6,004
1879...	2,515	352	112,642	11,997	11,000	1,107
1880...	1,242,103	206,121	695,255	91,234	....	
1881...	219,802	36,168	541,074	63,383	14,680	1,504
1882...	6,200	836	508,901	59,629	16,075	1,629
1883...	....	....	330,495	36,166	9,415	666
1884...	b542	107	149,701	12,099	....	554
1885...	914	172	81,312	6,658	....	1,160
Dec. 31, 1886...	276	37	37,149	2,407	....	584
1887...	212	22	39,957	2,374	....	129

a Not enumerated until 1873.   b Includes "plates not rolled" since 1884.

Copper imported and entered for consumption in the United States, etc.—Continued.

Year ending—	Bars, ingots, and pigs.		Old, fit only for remanufacture.		Old, taken from bottoms of American ships abroad. (a)	
	Quantity.	Value.	Quantity.	Value.	Quantity.	Value.
	Pounds.		*Pounds.*		*Pounds.*	
Dec. 31, 1888...	1,787	$299	37,620	$2,535	....	....
1889...	3,160	522	19,912	1,176	....	....
1890...	5,189	859	284,789	26,473	....	....
1891...	2,556	389	134,407	9,685	....	....
1892...	22,097	2,588	71,485	6,114	....	....
1893...	554,348	58,480	59,375	6,945	....	$6,326
1894...	606,415	42,688	160,592	15,726	....	1,143
1895...	7,979,322	726,347	1,336,901	109,340	....	....

Year ending—	Plates not rolled.		Plates rolled, sheets, pipes, etc.	
	Quantity.	Value.	Quantity.	Value.
	Pounds.		*Pounds.*	
June 30, 1867...........	....	....	....	$1,101
1868...........	....	....	....	1
1869...........	....	....	....	39
1870...........	....	....	....	2,039
1871...........	430	$129	....	7,487
1872...........	148,192	33,770	....	18,895
1873...........	550,431	97,888	....	4,514
1874...........	....	....	....	27
1875...........	8	4	....	617
1876...........	5,467	600	....	326
1877...........	....	....	....	203
1878...........	....	....	....	1,201
1879...........	27,074	4,496	....	786
1880...........	120	11	....	1,131
1881...........	20	3	....	82
1882...........	....	....	5,855	1,551
1883...........	....	....	2,812	379
1884...........	....	....	6,529	2,330
1885...........	....	....	470	120
Dec. 31, 1886...........	....	....	3,770	339
1887...........	....	....	37,925	5,493
1888...........	....	....	5,208	737
1889...........	....	....	13,848	2,082
1890...........	....	....	1,209	917
1891...........	....	....	122,219	23,291

a Not enumerated until 1873.

Copper imported and entered for consumption in the United States, etc.—Continued.

Year ending —	Plates not rolled.		Plates rolled, sheets, pipes, etc.	
	Quantity.	Value.	Quantity.	Value.
	Pounds.		*Pounds.*	
Dec. 31, 1892			1,788	$600
1893			7,056	1,065
1894			12,681	1,821
1895			27,156	2,586

Year ending—	Sheathing metal, in part copper. (a)		Manufactures not otherwise specified.	Total value.
	Quantity.	Value.	Value.	
	Pounds.			
June 30, 1867	220,889	$37,717	$15,986	$424,565
1868	101,488	18,852	21,492	89,932
1869	43,660	6,592	43,212	86,806
1870			485,220	519,608
1871			668,894	722,673
1872			1,007,744	1,817,910
1873			869,281	3,216,429
1874	282,406	50,174	123,708	448,252
1875	136,055	23,650	35,572	127,272
1876	18,014	2,903	29,806	71,949
1877	110	22	41,762	75,761
1878	647	55	35,473	68,319
1879	300	20	39,277	58,035
1880	6,044	693	130,329	432,522
1881	39,520	4,669	284,509	390,318
1882			77,727	141,372
1883	6,791	1,047	40,343	78,601
1884	19,637	926	55,274	71,290
1885	86,619	9,894	61,023	79,027
Dec. 31, 1886	21,573	1,917	31,871	37,155
1887	18,189	1,867	37,289	47,174
1888	23,622	2,696	14,567	20,834
1889	23,520	2,572	13,430	19,782
1890	37,458	4,467	24,752	57,468
1891	228,486	29,112	12,926	75,403
1892	417,134	51,380	49,764	110,446
1893	1,670	167	16,166	89,149
1894	8,422	1,470	3,851	66,699
1895	5,698	389	13,166	851,828

a Does not include copper sheathing in 1867, 1868, and 1869.

The source of the imports of fine copper in ore into the United States during 1893 and 1894 is shown in the following table. For 1895 the tonnage of material is given.

Imports of fine copper in ore in 1893, 1894, and 1895.

Countries from which imported.	1893. Quantity.	1893. Value.	1894. Quantity.	1894. Value.
	Pounds.		*Pounds.*	
Spain	166, 870	$11. 680	....	....
Dominion of Canada:				
Nova Scotia, New Brunswick, etc............	1, 344	48	....	....
Quebec, Ontario	4, 795, 704	307. 000	4, 599, 505	$312, 790
British Columbia.......	7, 790	778	78, 380	7, 838
Newfoundland and Labrador................	1, 788, 261	91, 099	2, 028, 261	113, 931
Mexico	639, 606	41, 201	303, 782	18, 356
Venezuela...............	257, 112	12, 570	236, 750	11, 099
All other countries........	66, 700	3, 612	*a* 4, 479	408
Total	7, 723, 387	467, 988	7, 251. 157	494, 422

Countries from which imported.	1895 (Ore and regulus). Quantity.	1895 (Ore and regulus). Value.
	Tons.	
Spain	....	....
Dominion of Canada:		
Nova Scotia, New Brunswick, etc............	....	....
Quebec, Ontario........................	1, 168	$72, 099
British Columbia......................	1, 135	117, 888
Newfoundland and Labrador..............	5, 467	15, 510
Mexico...............................	1, 853	198. 171
Venezuela.............................	....	....
All other countries....................	11	771
Total	9, 631	404, 439

a All from Peru.

For the year 1893 the above table includes 467,372 pounds which were either reexported or entered in bonded warehouses and not withdrawn during 1893, so that the actual amount of imported fine copper contained in ores consumed in the United States in 1893 was 7,256,015 pounds, as given in the table on page 104.

The imports of copper in ore and in the form of pigs, bars, and old, monthly, are presented in the following table:

Imports of copper in ore and as pigs and bars, monthly, in 1893, 1894, and 1895.

Month.	Ore and regulus.	Fine, in ore.	
	1895.	1894.	1893.
	Tons.	Pounds.	Pounds.
January	867	690,633	611,548
February	122	330,673	462,659
March	259	628,267	530,864
April	819	395,236	733,067
May	487	441,541	191,861
June	371	225,538	654,119
July	5,143	549,200	620,746
August	119	583,662	646,294
September	166	{ a 38 / 15,342 }	1,157,942
October	339	{ 10,677 / a 75 }	736.691
November	157	a 877	876,420
December	783	a 1,877	501,176
Total			7,723,387
Dutiable		3,870,769	
Free	9,634	a 2,867	

Month.	Pigs, bars, ingots, and old.		
	1895.	1894.	1893.
	Pounds.	Pounds.	Pounds.
January	773,531	673,200	965.539
February	298,491	129,765	198,009
March	520,491	95,225	262,206
April	614,688	42,326	1,581.453
May	245,257	132,902	301.336
June	199,737	302,269	32,628
July	253,817	170,575	114,610
August	1,334,874	743,062	193,470
September	2,190,881	174,354	1,112,794
October	1,465,750	521,606	85,241
November	653,281	275,530	234,710
December	831,002	185,910	454,694
Total			5,536,690
Dutiable		2,289,324	
Free	9,381,800	1,157,400	

a Tons.

The increase in the imports of ingots during the months of August, September, and October is due to the temporary scarcity in this country, which induced a return of the American copper.

EXPORTS.

The exports of copper in the form of ore (including matte), ingots, and manufactured copper for a series of years have been as follows:

Copper and copper ore of domestic production exported from the United States, 1864 to 1895.

[Cwts. are long hundredweights of 112 pounds.]

Year ending—	Ore and matte.		Pigs, bars, sheets, and old.	
	Quantity.	Value.	Quantity.	Value.
	Cwts.		*Pounds.*	
June 30, 1864	109,581	$181,298	102,831	$43,229
1865	225,197	553,124	1,572,382	709,106
1866	215,080	792,450	123,444	33,553
1867	87,731	317,791	a4,637,867	303,048
1868	92,612	442,921	1,350,896	327,287
1869	121,418	237,424	1,134,360	233,932
1870	a19.198	537,505	2,214,658	385,815
1871	a54,445	727,213	581,650	133,020
1872	35,564	101,752	267,868	64,844
1873	45,252	170,365	38,958	10,423
1874	13,326	110,450	503,160	123,457
1875	a51,305	729,578	5,123,470	1,042,536
1876	15,304	84,471	14,304,160	3,098,395
1877	21,432	109,451	13,461,553	2,718,213
1878	32,947	169,020	11,297,876	2,102,455
1879	23,070	102,152	17,200,739	2,751,153
1880	21,623	55,763	4,206,258	667,242
1881	9.958	51,499	4,865,407	786,860
1882	25,936	89,515	3,340,531	565,295
1883	112,923	943,771	8,221,363	1,293,947
1884	386,110	2,930,895	17,044,760	2,527,829
1885	432,300	4,739,601	44,731,858	5,339,887
Dec. 31, 1886	417,520	2,344,164	19,553,421	1,968,772
1887	501,280	2,774,464	12,471,393	1,247,928
1888	794,960	6,779,294	31,706,527	4.906,805
1889	818,500	8,226,206	16,813,410	1,896,752
1890	431,411	4,413,067	10,971,899	1,365,379
1891	672,120	6,565,620	69,279,024	8,844,304
1892	b943,040	6,479,758	30,515,736	3,438,048
1893	835,040	4,257,128	138,984,128	14,213,378
1894	87,040	440,129	162,393,000	15,324,925
1895	276,480	1,631,251	121,328,390	12,222,769

a Evidently errors in quantities.   b Corrected figures.

Copper and copper ore of domestic production exported, etc.—Continued.

[Cwts. are long hundredweights of 112 pounds.]

Year ending—	Value of manufactured product.	Total value.
June 30, 1861	$208,043	$432,570
1865	282,640	1,544,870
1866	110,208	936,211
1867	171,062	791,901
1868	152,201	922,409
1869	121,342	592,698
1870	118,926	1,042,246
1871	55,198	915,431
1872	121,139	287,735
1873	78,288	259,076
1874	233,301	467,208
1875	43,152	1,815,266
1876	343,544	3,526,410
1877	195,730	3,023,394
1878	217,446	2,488,921
1879	79,900	2,933,205
1880	126,213	849,218
1881	38,036	876,395
1882	93,646	748,456
1883	110,286	2,348,004
1884	137,135	5,595,859
1885	107.536	10,187,024
Dec. 31, 1886	76,386	4,386,322
1887	92,064	4,114,456
1888	211,141	11,897,240
1889	86,764	10,209,722
1890	139,949	5,918,395
1891	293,619	15,703,543
1892	245,064	10,162,870
1893	464,991	18,935,497
1894	378,040	16,143,094
1895	1,084,289	14,938,309

The destination of the copper exports during the years 1893, 1894, and 1895 is shown in the following table from the reports of the Bureau of Statistics:

Destination of exports of copper bars and ingots.

Country.	1893.	1894.	1895.
	Pounds.	Pounds.	Pounds.
Germany	17, 677, 887	20, 359, 111	14, 962, 257
United Kingdom	42, 649, 832	67, 621, 830	24, 064, 694
France	27, 960, 616	20, 419, 969	25, 266, 032
Other countries in Europe	49, 914, 487	53, 447, 119	56, 236, 915
Other countries..............	781, 276	544, 968	798, 492
Total...................	138, 984, 128	162, 393, 000	121, 328, 390

The Bureau of Statistics has prepared in further detail the following statement, showing the destination of exports monthly during the year 1895:

Exports of copper bars and ingots in 1895.

Month.	United Kingdom.	Austria.	Belgium.	France.	Germany.
	Pounds.	Pounds.	Pounds.	Pounds.	Pounds.
January ...	4, 695, 566	830, 250	988, 752	2, 137, 868	334, 923
February ..	1, 985, 221	225, 000	425, 844	1, 293, 418	402, 362
March	2, 940, 013	....	895, 868	1, 625, 346	535, 067
April	2, 272, 199	....	100, 925	3, 476, 405	1, 739, 861
May	2, 034, 490	....	946, 318	2, 863, 535	2, 432, 253
June	2, 505, 008	505, 169	1, 268, 170	3, 653, 067	1, 242, 186
July	918, 535	135, 126	1, 476, 456	2, 334, 871	1, 318, 423
August.....	627, 086	382, 151	781, 666	2, 355, 077	824, 257
September .	604, 672	405, 000	49, 738	899, 652	1, 650, 665
October	328, 555	....	49, 996	1, 342, 111	1, 287, 269
November ..	1, 766, 566	403, 448	314, 436	1, 264, 283	1, 615, 900
December ..	3, 386, 783	342, 401	1, 086, 826	2, 020, 399	1, 579, 091
Total ..	24, 064, 694	3, 228, 545	8, 384, 995	25, 266, 032	14, 962, 257

Exports of copper bars and ingots in 1895—Continued.

Month.	Italy.	Netherlands.	Russia (Baltic).	Sweden and Norway.	Other Europe (Denmark).
	Pounds.	*Pounds.*	*Pounds.*	*Pounds.*	*Pounds.*
January ...	29,909	2,778,740	....	....	....
February ..	43,750	2,960,329	....	....	....
March	....	3,542,547	....	....	....
April	134,125	2,724,925	....	22,470	....
May	22,500	4,561,815	....	....	....
June.......	112,500	4,375,915	688,419	96,856	....
July	89,663	4,829,015	192,787	37,568	....
August.....	....	2,794,171	898,963	30,692	....
September .	....	2,640,190	850,332	35,550	....
October	222,538	3,098,109	337,500	34,532	....
November ..	78,500	3,000,347	....	....	....
December ..	168,000	3,145,277	....	....	44,841
Total ..	901,485	40,451,380	2,968,001	257,668	44,841

Month.	British North America.	Mexico.	West Indies and Bermuda.	Other countries.	Total.
	Pounds.	*Pounds.*	*Pounds.*	*Pounds.*	*Pounds.*
January....	28,700	25,000	....	....	11,849,708
February ..	....	24,741	....	....	7,360,665
March......	56,194	33,988	....	....	9,629,023
April.......	2,500	5,510	....	....	10,478,920
May........	....	14,494	1,721	13,300	12,890,426
June	27,500	6,856	....	8,500	14,490,146
July	65,320	13,990	....	....	11,411,754
August.....	38,960	8,902	....	....	8,741,925
September .	28,090	422	....	....	7,164,311
October	91,242	5,190	....	224,401	7,021,443
November ..	60,400	5,298	....	....	8,509,178
December ..	....	7,273	....	....	11,780,891
Total ..	398,906	151,664	1,721	246,201	121,328,390

This report is particularly interesting as showing the exports to the Netherlands, practically all of this metal going into Germany for consumption there.

THE COPPER MARKETS.

The following table summarizes the highest and lowest prices obtained for Lake copper monthly in the New York markets from 1860 to 1895, both inclusive:

Highest and lowest prices of Lake Superior ingot copper, by months, from 1860 to 1895.

[Cents per pound.]

Year.	January.		February.		March.		April.		May.		June.	
	Highest.	Lowest.	Highest.	Lowest.	Highest.	Lowest.	Highest.	Lowest.	Highest.	Lowest.	Highest.	Lowest.
1860......	24	23½	24	23¾	23¾	23	23½	23	23¼	22½	22¾	21¾
1861......	20	19	19½	19	19¾	19¼	19¾	19	19¾	19¼	19	18
1862......	28	27	28	25	25	23	23	21½	21½	20¾	23	20¼
1863......	35	31	37	35	37	31	31	30	30½	30	30½	30
1864......	41¼	39	42	41¼	42½	41½	44	42½	44	43	49	44
1865......	50½	46	46	44	44½	34	35	34	34	30	30½	28½
1866......	42	38	38	35½	35½	29½	30	28½	31	29	33	31
1867......	29¼	27	27¾	27½	27½	24	24½	23½	24¼	24	24½	24
1868......	23½	21½	24	22½	24	23¼	24¼	23¼	24¼	24	24	23⅛
1869......	26¼	23¾	27	26	26¾	24	24	23¼	24¼	23¾	23¾	22
1870......	22	21⅛	21¼	20⅞	20¾	19	19¾	19¼	19½	19	20⅝	19
1871......	22⅞	22	22⅜	21⅞	22	21½	21¾	21¼	21¾	21⅜	21½	21¼
1872......	28½	27⅛	28⅝	28¼	30½	28⅜	44	30½	42	36	34¾	33
1873......	35	32½	35	34	35	34½	34½	33½	33½	32	31½	29½
1874......	25	24½	25	24⅛	24¾	24	25	24¾	25	24½	24¾	24¼
1875......	23½	21½	22¾	21¾	21¾	21½	21¾	21½	23¼	22⅝	23	23
1876......	23¼	23	22⅞	22½	22¼	22	22⅝	22	22⅛	21	21	19¼
1877......	19½	19	20½	19½	19¼	19	19½	19¼	19¼	19	19⅝	19
1878......	17⅝	17¼	17½	17⅛	17⅛	16⅞	17	16⅞	16¾	16¼	16⅝	16¼
1879......	16	15½	15½	15½	15¾	15¾	16	15¾	16¼	16	16¼	16½
1880......	25	21⅜	24½	24	24	22¾	22½	24	21	18	18½	17⅞
1881......	19⅝	19⅜	19⅜	19⅛	19⅜	19	19	18¾	18⅞	18¼	18¼	16⅝
1882......	20⅜	20¼	20	19	19¼	18⅞	18⅞	17⅞	18¼	18	18¼	18
1883......	18⅛	:8	17⅞	17¾	17⅝	17⅛	16	15¾	16	15⅞	15⅞	15
1884......	15	14⅞	15	14⅞	15	14⅞	15	14½	14¼	14⅛	14¼	14
1885......	11½	10⅜	11⅛	10⅗	11⅛	10⅗	11¼	10 1/10	11½	9⅗	11½	11
1886......	11⅝	11⅜	11⅝	11⅜	11½	11⅜	11½	11⅝	11⅛	10	10⅛	10
1887......	12	11⅛	11⅛	10⅗	10½	10⅜	10⅗	10	10	9 13/20	10¼	10
1888......	17 4/10	15 17/20	16 9/10	16	16 7/20	15 13/20	16 3/10	16	16¾	16 3/10	16 13/20	16 [illegible]
1889......	17½	16½	16¾	16½	15¾	15	16	15½	12⅛	12	12¼	12
1890......	14½	14¼	14¼	14¼	14¼	14	14½	14¼	15¼	14⅝	16¾	15¼
1891......	15	14⅝	14⅞	14¼	14¼	13⅝	13¾	13½	13¾	12¾	13	12⅞
1892......	11	10¾	10¾	10½	12	10¾	12	11¾	12¼	12	11⅞	11½
1893......	12½	12¼	12¼	12	12	11¾	11½	11¼	18⅛	11	11	10¾
1894......	10¼	10	10	9⅝	9⅝	9⅝	9½	9⅝	9⅝	9¼	9⅛	9
1895......	10	9⅞	9⅞	9½	9½	9¼	9¾	9⅝	10⅝	9¾	10¾	10⅜

Highest and lowest prices of Lake Superior ingot copper, by months, etc.—Continued.

[Cents per pound.]

Year.	July.		August.		September.		October.		November.		December.	
	Highest.	Lowest.	Highest.	Lowest.	Highest.	Lowest.	Highest.	Lowest.	Highest.	Lowest.	Highest.	Lowest.
1860......	21¾	21½	21½	21½	22	21¼	22	21½	21½	20¼	20¼	19¾
1861......	18	17½	19	17¾	20¼	19	20¼	20	22½	20¼	27	22½
1862......	24½	22½	24½	24	27	24¼	32⅞	27	32⅞	30½	31½	30½
1863......	32	29	31	29	32¼	31	34¼	32¼	38½	34½	38¾	38½
1864......	55	49	52½	50	52½	47½	48	47	49	47	50	48½
1865......	30¼	28	32	30½	32¾	31½	33	32½	45½	33	45½	39¼
1866......	33½	31	31	30	31½	30¾	31	30¾	30¾	26½	29	26½
1867......	26	24	26¼	25¾	27¼	26¼	26¾	22¾	23	22¾	23	21½
1868......	21½	23⅛	24¼	24	24	23¾	24	23	24	22½	24½	23¾
1869......	22¼	21⅞	23⅛	21⅞	23	22	22¾	22	22½	22	22	21½
1870......	20½	20⅝	21⅜	20⅛	21½	20¾	21¾	21½	23⅝	21¾	22⅝	22¼
1871......	22¼	21⅝	23	22⅜	23⅞	22⅞	23⅞	23¼	24¼	23¼	27	24½
1872......	34	33	35	32½	35¼	33	34¾	31¼	32¼	30¾	32½	30½
1873......	29	26⅝	27½	27	27	25½	25½	24	24	21	25	23
1874......	24¼	20	21	19	21¼	21	22¼	21¼	23¾	22¼	23¼	23¼
1875......	23	22⅝	23⅜	23	23⅞	23⅛	23¼	23	23¼	23	23⅜	23⅜
1876......	20	19½	19½	18¾	21	18¾	21¼	20½	20½	20	20	19⅝
1877......	19¼	19	19	17⅞	18½	17⅞	18	17¾	17¾	17⅝	17¾	17½
1878......	16¼	16	16	16	16¼	16	16	15½	15⅞	15½	16	15⅞
1879......	16⅛	16	16⅜	16	17	16¼	21½	18	21¾	21	21½	21
1880......	18⅞	18½	19⅛	19	18⅞	18¾	18⅞	18¾	18⅞	18¾	19⅛	18⅞
1881......	16½	16	16⅝	16⅜	18⅛	16¾	18⅜	18	19	18⅛	20⅜	19¼
1882......	18¼	18⅛	18¼	18⅛	18¼	18	18¼	18	18⅛	18	18	17⅞
1883......	15⅛	15	15	15	15¼	15⅛	15¼	15⅛	15	14⅞	15	14⅞
1884......	14⅛	13⅞	14	13⅞	13⅛	13	13⅛	12⅞	13	12½	12⅛	11
1885......	11¼	10⅞	11¼	11	11½	10 19/20	11⅛	10⅘	11⅛	10⅘	11½	11 1/10
1886......	10⅛	10	10¼	10	11⅛	10¼	11¾	11⅛	12	11¾	12⅛	11⅞
1887......	10¾	10⅛	10¾	10⅗	11	10⅝	12 3/20	10 3/10	14 13/20	11 11/20	17¾	14 13/20
1888......	16 9/10	16 13/20	17	16⅗	17 7/10	16 9/10	17⅗	17 7/20	17⅗	17¼	17 9/20	17 1/10
1889......	12	12	12	12	12	11	11	11	13¼	11¼	14½	14
1890......	17¼	16½	17¼	17	17	17	16⅞	16¾	16¾	16¾	16	15
1891......	12⅞	12½	12⅜	12	12½	12⅛	12⅜	11⅜	11½	11	11⅛	10¼
1892......	11¾	11¼	11¾	11 6/10	11 6/10	11 1/10	11¾	11 1/10	12	11¾	12⅜	12¼
1893......	10½	10¼	10⅛	9⅗	9⅞	9¾	9¾	9¾	10¼	9¾	10½	10⅜
1894......	9⅛	9	9⅛	9	9⅞	9⅛	9¾	9½	9½	9⅝	10	9½
1895......	11¾	10½	12¼	11¾	12¼	12	12	11¾	11⅝	11	11	10

The market in 1895 was one of quick changes. From a period of keen depression earlier in the year to a time of sharply quickened hopes was a matter of a few weeks. Then came months of relatively high prices, with a lively demand, followed by a relapse to the level of prices at which the year started. The sales to consumers late in 1894, at 10 cents for Lake copper, had supplied the trade for some time, and under pressure from producers the market weakened, and in February became very irregular because of the threatening financial situation. Great eagerness was shown to market metal in Europe.

In March somewhat better domestic buying was brought out by the low prices, which touched 9.25 cents. There were further considerable export sales and a stronger feeling developed, the metal entering April with Lake copper at 9.35 cents. Then came the announcement of a sale of over 25,000,000 pounds of copper by the Calumet and Hecla Company to home consumers at $9\frac{1}{2}$ cents for delivery over five months. It became evident that consumption was expanding rapidly in this as in other metals. In the meantime negotiations were being carried on between American and European producers looking to a reduction of exports on the part of the former to 60,000 tons per annum, from July 1, and to a lowering of the production by the latter by 5 to $7\frac{1}{2}$ per cent. The refusal of the two leading producers in this country to accede to the plan led to a sharp reaction in Europe, but did not greatly influence our markets, because a good demand from consumers developed for autumn delivery. Early in June there was a brief period of a weakening tendency, due to manipulation, but later in the month good sales for fall delivery stiffened the market to $10\frac{3}{4}$ cents. In July there were again heavy sales for delivery to the end of the year at 11 cents, the market rising to $11\frac{3}{4}$ cents before the close of the month. Such was the pressure that purchases of Lake and Arizona copper were made in Liverpool for return to this country, the quantity involved being about 6,000,000 pounds. Yet the market rose, and consumers again took hold at 12 cents, the Calumet and Hecla Company again selling about 20,000,000 pounds at 12 cents for delivery over four months. The market was moderately active during September at the range of 12 to $12\frac{1}{4}$ cents, and early October brought some good sales for the balance of the year at 12 cents; but as the month progressed the market became easier, since consumption fell off in a disappointing manner. Efforts were made to effect sales in Europe, but it was possible only at a sacrifice in prices, which reflected on our markets. This condition of affairs was emphasized in November, and in December the adverse financial situation caused a relapse bordering on demoralization. Toward the close of the month consumers contracted for three months' supplies, in moderate quantity, at 10 cents per pound.

The following table shows the fluctuations in prices in the English market:

Average values of copper in England.

Year.	Chilo bars or G. O. B.			Ore, 25 per cent.		Precipitate.	
	Long ton.			Per unit.		Per unit.	
	£	s.	d.	s.	d.	s.	d.
1880	62	10	0	12	9	12	11
1881	61	10	0	12	6	13	8$\frac{3}{16}$
1882	66	17	0	13	6$\frac{1}{4}$	13	10$\frac{1}{16}$
1883	63	5	10	12	4$\frac{1}{2}$	12	10$\frac{7}{16}$
1884	54	9	1	10	5$\frac{1}{4}$	11	1
1885	44	0	10	8	4	9	0$\frac{1}{4}$
1886	40	9	3	7	9	8	3$\frac{1}{2}$
1887	43	16	11	8	6	8	11$\frac{1}{4}$
1888	79	19	4$\frac{1}{2}$	14	3$\frac{1}{4}$	16	3
1889	49	10	5	9	6$\frac{1}{2}$	....
1890	54	5	5	10	7	....
1891	51	9	8$\frac{1}{4}$	9	7	....
1892	45	12	8$\frac{1}{4}$	8	7	....
1893	43	15	6$\frac{1}{4}$	8	5	....
1894	40	7	4	7	6$\frac{1}{2}$	....
1895	42	19	7	8	4$\frac{1}{4}$	....

In detail, the fluctuations, monthly, of good merchant copper in the English market were as follows in 1892, 1893, 1894, and 1895:

Fluctuations in good merchant copper in England in 1892, 1893, 1894, and 1895.

[Per long ton.]

Month.	1892.			1893.			1894.			1895.		
	£	s.	d.	£	s.	d.	£	s.	d.	£	s.	d.
January	45	13	7$\frac{1}{4}$	46	1	8	42	1	6$\frac{1}{4}$	40	13	9$\frac{1}{4}$
February	44	1	5$\frac{1}{4}$	45	13	2$\frac{1}{4}$	41	6	8$\frac{1}{4}$	39	14	3$\frac{1}{4}$
March	46	1	1	45	11	7$\frac{1}{4}$	40	19	5$\frac{1}{4}$	39	1	9$\frac{1}{4}$
April	45	16	10	44	18	7$\frac{1}{2}$	40	10	10$\frac{1}{4}$	40	3	6$\frac{1}{4}$
May	46	10	4	43	15	1$\frac{3}{4}$	39	10	5$\frac{1}{4}$	43	0	0
June	45	19	9	44	4	3$\frac{1}{4}$	38	10	4$\frac{1}{4}$	42	15	6$\frac{1}{4}$
July	44	19	5$\frac{1}{4}$	42	17	6$\frac{1}{4}$	38	12	8$\frac{1}{4}$	44	0	2$\frac{1}{4}$
August	44	12	2$\frac{1}{2}$	41	10	2	39	12	4$\frac{1}{4}$	46	13	2$\frac{1}{4}$
September	44	5	2	42	13	2$\frac{1}{4}$	41	1	0	46	15	7$\frac{1}{4}$
October	45	14	4	42	1	2$\frac{1}{4}$	41	2	10$\frac{1}{4}$	46	4	10
November	46	13	10$\frac{1}{4}$	42	11	10$\frac{1}{2}$	40	3	2$\frac{1}{4}$	43	16	3$\frac{1}{4}$
December	47	4	10$\frac{1}{2}$	43	8	2$\frac{1}{4}$	40	16	5$\frac{1}{4}$	42	15	11

THE WORLD'S PRODUCTION.

Henry R. Merton & Co., of London, have compiled the following statement of the world's production, the figures being modified by this office where official statistics are available:

The copper production of the world, 1888 to 1895, inclusive.

[Long tons.]

Country.	1895.	1894.	1893.	1892.
EUROPE.				
Great Britain	a 400	a 400	425	495
Spain and Portugal:				
Rio Tinto	32, 985	31, 061	31, 954	31, 539
Tharsis	12, 000	11, 000	11, 000	11, 258
Mason and Barry...........	a 4, 100	a 4, 200	a 4, 400	a 4, 400
Sevilla......................	1, 050	1, 170	1, 270	1, 070
Portugueza	....	205	625	1, 192
Poderosa and others	a 4, 300	a 4, 600	a 5, 600	a 6, 800
Germany:				
Mansfeld	14, 860	14, 990	14, 150	15, 360
Other German	1, 695	2, 210	2, 000	1, 935
Austria	1, 100	1, 810	1, 215	1, 100
Hungary	200	271	343	285
Sweden	515	350	535	735
Norway	2, 685	1, 885	1, 860	1, 410
Italy............................	a 2, 500	2, 600	2, 500	2, 500
Russia	a 5, 000	5, 000	5, 000	4, 900
Total Europe............	83, 390	81, 752	82, 877	84, 979
NORTH AMERICA.				
United States	169, 917	158, 120	147, 033	154, 072
Canada	3, 924	3, 500	3, 620	3, 600
Newfoundland..................	1, 800	1, 900	2, 040	2, 390
Mexico:				
Boleo	10, 450	10, 370	7, 980	6, 415
Other Mexican	1, 170	1, 400	900	900
Total North America......	187, 261	175, 290	161, 573	167, 377
SOUTH AMERICA.				
Chile	22, 075	21, 340	21, 350	22, 565
Bolivia:				
Corocoro	2, 250	2, 300	2, 500	2, 860
Peru	450	440	460	290

a Estimated.

The copper production of the world, 1888 to 1895, inclusive—Continued.

[Long tons.]

Country.	1895.	1894.	1893.	1892.
SOUTH AMERICA—continued.				
Venezuela:				
New Quebrada	....	2,500	2,850	3,100
Argentina	150	230	160	200
Total South America	24,925	26,810	27,320	29,015
AFRICA.				
Algiers	35	....		
Cape of Good Hope:				
Cape Company	5,350	5,000	5,200	5,670
Namaqua	1,730	1,500	890.	450
Total Africa	7,115	6,500	6,090	6,120
ASIA.				
Japan	18,430	20,050	18,000	19,000
Total Asia	18,430	20,050	18,000	19,000
AUSTRALIA.				
Australia	10,000	9,000	7,500	6,500

Country.	1891.	1890.	1889.	1888.
EUROPE.				
Great Britain	720	935	905	a1,500
Spain and Portugal:				
Rio Tinto	31,827	30,000	29,500	a32,000
Tharsis	a11,100	a10,300	a11,000	a11,500
Mason and Barry	a4,150	a5,600	a5,250	a7,000
Sevilla	875	810	1,350	1,700
Portugueza	890	565	670	1,250
Poderosa and others	a5,500	a4,225	a6,500	a7,000
Germany:				
Mansfeld	14,250	15,800	15,500	13,380
Other German	1,900	1,825	a1,850	a1,850
Austria	965	1,210	1,225	1,010
Hungary	285	a300	a300	858
Sweden	655	830	830	1,036
Norway	1,247	1,390	1,357	1,570
Italy	2,200	2,200	3,500	3,500
Russia	4,800	4,800	4,070	4,700
Total Europe	81,364	80,790	83,813	89,854

a Estimated.

The copper production of the world, 1888 to 1895, inclusive—continued.

[Long tons.]

Country.	1891.	1890.	1889.	1888.
NORTH AMERICA.				
United States....................	126,839	115,966	101,239	101,054
Canada	3,500	3,050	2,500	a 2,250
Newfoundland...................	2,040	1,735	2,615	2,050
Mexico:				
Boleo	4,175	3,450	3,280	2,566
Other Mexican	1,025	875	500	200
Total North America......	137,579	125,076	110,134	108,120
SOUTH AMERICA.				
Chile..........................	19,875	26,120	24,250	31,210
Bolivia:				
Corocoro	2,150	1,900	a 1,200	1,450
Peru	280	150	275	250
Venezuela:				
New Quebrada	6,500	5,640	6,068	4,000
Argentina.....................	210	150	190	150
Total South America......	29,015	33,960	31,983	37,090
AFRICA.				
Algiers.........................	120	120	160	50
Cape of Good Hope:				
Cape Company	5,100	5,000	a 7,700	7,500
Namaqua.....................	900	1,450		
Total Africa	6,120	6,570	7,860	7,550
ASIA.				
Japan..........................	18,500	17,972	16,125	13,054
Total Asia.................	18,500	17,972	16,125	13,054
AUSTRALIA.				
Australia.......................	7,500	7,500	8,300	7,550

a Estimated.

The copper production of the world, 1888 to 1895, inclusive—Continued.

RECAPITULATION.

[Long tons.]

Country.	1895.	1894.	1893.	1892.
Europe	83,390	81,752	82,877	84,979
North America	187,261	175,290	161,573	167,377
South America	24,925	26,810	27,320	29,015
Africa	7,115	6,500	6,090	6,120
Asia	18,430	20,050	18,000	19,000
Australia	10,000	9,000	7,500	6,500
Total	331,121	319,402	303,360	312,991

Country.	1891.	1890.	1889.	1888.
Europe	81,364	80,790	83,813	89,854
North America	137,579	125,076	110,134	108,120
South America	29,015	33,960	31,983	37,090
Africa	6,120	6,570	7,860	7,550
Asia	18,500	17,972	16,125	13,054
Australia	7,500	7,500	8,300	7,550
Total	280,078	271,868	258,215	263,218

THE ENGLISH COPPER TRADE.

Since England is one of the leading copper markets of the world, the following tables, showing the import and export movement, are of great interest:

British imports and exports of copper.

Year.	Imports of—		Total imports.	Exports.	Apparent English consumption.
	Bars, cakes, and ingots.	Copper in ores and furnace products.			
	Long tons.	*Long tons.*	*Long tons.*	*Long tons.*	*Long tons.*
1860	13,142	13,715	26,857	26,117	....
1865	23,137	23,922	47,059	41,398	....
1870	30,724	27,025	57,749	53,006	....
1871	33,228	23,671	56,899	56,633	....
1872	49,000	21,702	70,702	53,195	....
1873	35,840	26,756	62,596	55,716	....
1874	39,906	27,894	67,800	59,742	....
1875	41,931	29,483	71,414	51,870	....

British imports and exports of copper—Continued.

| Year. | Imports of— | | Total imports. | Exports. | Apparent English consumption. |
	Bars, cakes, and ingots.	Copper in ores and furnace products.			
	Long tons.	*Long tons.*	*Long tons.*	*Long tons.*	*Long tons.*
1876	39,145	36,191	75,336	52,468	....
1877	39,743	53,582	93,325	54,088	....
1878	39,360	48,212	87,572	55,001	....
1879	46,670	50,421	97,091	62,412	30,774
1880	36,509	56,225	92,734	59,482	32,879
1881	32,170	54,057	86,227	61,689	31,607
1882	35,509	58,366	93,875	55,683	42,877
1883	35,653	63,493	99,146	59,350	40,469
1884	39,767	69,623	109,390	64,691	51,263
1885	41,933	81,616	123,549	62,080	54,323
1886	42,969	65,046	108,015	60,511	41,158
1887	29,198	73,891	103,089	69,453	53,096
1888	44,063	90,867	135,470	*a* 72,066	42,562
1889	*b* 38,576	101,407	139,983	75,627	65,759
1890	*c* 49,461	91,788	141,249	89,747	66,170
1891	44,213	94,403	138,616	76,056	59,223
1892	*d* 35,015	99,356	134,371	82,542	*e* 48,367
1893	41,829	88,003	129,832	70,986	66,817
1894	56,158	68,851	125,009	54,689	61,330
1895	42,135	77,806	119,941	65,990	62,692

a Including 22,557 tons of Chile bars transferred to France.
b Including 1,166 tons of Chile bars transferred from France to England.
c Including 3,501 tons of Chile bars transferred from France to England.
d Including 3,585 tons of Chile bars transferred from France to England.
e Add 4,001 tons for comparison with former years, the difference arising from the new method of making up stock.

The following figures from the board of trade returns, supplemented by James Lewis & Son, of Liverpool, for the past nine years show in detail the form in which the copper is brought into Great Britain and in what form it is exported:

Imports of copper into Great Britain from 1887 to 1895, inclusive.

[Long tons.]

Character.	1887.	1888.	1889.	1890.	1891.
Pure in pyrites	14,940	15,448	16,097	16,422	15,406
Pure in precipitate ..	21,819	26,366	25,110	25,563	29,326
Pure in ore	15,148	19,452	22,219	18,000	14,172
Pure in matte	21,984	29,601	37,981	31,803	35,499
Bars, cakes, etc......	29,198	44,603	38,576	49,461	44,213
Total	103,089	135,470	139,983	141,249	138,616

Character.	1892.	1893.	1894.	1895.
Pure in pyrites	15,110	15,320	15,401	14,561
Pure in precipitate	28,444	24,988	24,878	26,508
Pure in ore.....................	13,585	11,701	12,804	15,240
Pure in matte	42,217	35,994	15,767	21,497
Bars, cakes, etc.................	35,015	41,829	56,158	42,135
Total	134,371	129,832	125,008	119,941

The following table gives the details relating to the British imports of precipitate and matte:

Imports of precipitate and matte into Great Britain from 1887 to 1895, inclusive.

[Long tons.]

Country.	1887.		Fine copper.		
	Precipitate and matte.	Fine copper.	1888.	1889.	1890.
Portugal	10,758	} 24,754	30,119	28,157	28,018
Spain	37,892				
Chile	1,595	718	734	1,919	2,122
United States	24,229	15,039	20,752	26,581	18,897
Other countries	5,366	2,292	4,362	6,431	8,329
Total	79,840	42,803	55,967	63,091	57,366

Imports of precipitate and matte into Great Britain from 1887 to 1895, inclusive—Cont'd.

[Long tons.]

Country.	Fine copper.				
	1891.	1892.	1893.	1894.	1895.
Portugal .... } Spain	32,425	32,509	29,359	28,645	30,196
Chile	595	2,040	2,714	626	212
United States	19,109	24,668	20,700	2,133	8,337
Other countries	12,696	11,444	8,209	9,242	9,660
Total	64,825	70,661	60,982	40,646	38,405

Messrs. James Lewis & Son, of Liverpool, estimate as follows the imports of copper product into Liverpool, London, and Swansea during the years from 1887 to 1895, which represent the total imports, with the exception of precipitate, into Newcastle and Cardiff, reliable returns of which can not be obtained, but which was estimated to vary from 8,000 to 10,000 tons fine per annum in former years, and in the last few years has been placed as high as 25,000 tons:

Imports of copper product into Liverpool, Swansea, and London.

[Long tons.]

Country.	1887.	1888.	1889.	1890.	1891.
Chile	20,008	24,479	22,070	22,909	14,378
United States	16,534	25,730	30,729	20,171	26,120
Spain and Portugal..	5,178	5,915	5,189	5,202	4,734
Spain and Portugal (precipitate).......	13,042	15,568	17,192	18,430	17,439
Spain and Portugal (pyrites)	14,940	15,448	16,097	16,422	15,406
Australia	6,047	6,746	6,285	6,561	6,265
Cape of Good Hope ..	8,271	8,829	11,507	9,927	7,452
Venezuela	2,261	3,574	4,299	5,215	5,017
Japan	200	4,469	2,523	10,674	7,852
Italy	1,055	1,058	1,043	953	619
Norway		545	234	80	30
Canada..............	94	156	181	264	189
Newfoundland.......	359	465	631	1,552	1,617
Mexico	61	158	3,938	3,325	3,616
Peru	13	202	271	254	279
La Plata River.......	167	135	184	143	211
Other countries......	1,074	4,051	1,389	225	236
Total tons fine..	89,304	117,531	123,762	122,337	111,490

Imports of copper product into Liverpool, Swansea, and London—Continued.

[Long tons.]

Country.	1892.	1893.	1894.	1895.
Chile	17,619	15,875	16,971	18,197
United States	26,475	35,617	30,495	17,098
Spain and Portugal	5,372	5,674	4,674	3,288
Spain and Portugal (precipitate)	14,831	10,296	10,642	12,612
Spain and Portugal (pyrites)	15,110	15,320	15,401	14,561
Australia	5,547	6,393	6,481	8,223
Cape of Good Hope	8,092	5,472	6,112	6,524
Venezuela	5,028	1,434	2,327	360
Japan	4,989	2,370	3,299	4,258
Italy	725	1,091	763	283
Norway	38	....	30	486
Canada	120	50	105	....
Newfoundland	3,229	2,265	1,279	3,244
Mexico	869	1,185	1,408	4,623
Peru	287	462	443	449
La Plata River	196	160	229	148
Other countries	1,245	1,944	855	930
Total tons fine	109,772	105,638	101,514	95,284

The apparent decline in the shipments to this country is due to the fact that the copper is now sent direct to the Continent instead of being forwarded to England and subsequently transshipped.

The quantities of copper in different forms which were imported from the United States to Great Britain and France are given in the following table:

Imports of copper from the United States in England and France.

[Long tons.]

	1886.	1887.	1888.	1889.	1890.
England:					
Ore	420	26	298	349	5
Matte	10,853	15,039	20,752	26,581	18,897
Bars and ingots	2,210	1,469	4,680	3,799	1,269
Total	13,483	16,534	25,730	30,729	20,171
France	4,167	3,910	6,496	1,058	1,733
United States into England and France	17,650	20,444	32,226	31,787	21,904
Chile into England and France	35,448	29,019	32,947	22,020	24,641

Imports of copper from the United States in England and France—Continued.

[Long tons.]

	1891.	1892.	1893.	1894.	1895.
England:					
• Ore	4	18	23	5	....
Matte	19, 109	24, 668	20, 700	2, 133	8, 337
Bars and ingots.....	7, 007	1, 427	14, 924	28, 357	12, 250
Total.............	26, 120	26, 113	35, 647	30, 495	20, 587
France.................	8, 329	4, 340	12, 483	9, 248	11, 806
United States into England and France......	34, 449	30, 453	48, 130	39, 743	32, 393
Chile into England and France...............	18, 820	19, 840	19, 717	20, 783	22, 161

The exports of copper from Great Britain, estimating the fine contents of alloys, were as follows:

Exports of copper from Great Britain from 1887 to 1895, inclusive.

[Long tons.]

Character.	1887.	1888.	1889.	1890.	1891.
English, wrought and unwrought, and sheets	40, 700	32, 058	48, 189	58, 571	51, 765
Yellow metal, at 60 per cent..................	10, 153	4, 513	9, 195	10, 514	8, 547
Brass, at 70 per cent....	3, 146	2, 650	3, 773	3, 721	3, 992
Total	53, 999	39, 221	61, 157	72, 806	64, 304
Fine foreign............	15, 454	a32, 845	14, 470	16, 941	11, 752
Total	69, 453	72, 066	75, 627	89, 747	76, 056

Character.	1892.	1893.	1894.	1895.
English, wrought and unwrought, and sheets......................	58, 518	45, 349	34, 874	45, 299
Yellow metal, at 60 per cent	8, 853	8, 745	9, 514	8, 978
Brass, at 70 per cent..............	3, 783	4, 049	3, 808	3, 747
Total	71, 154	58, 143	48, 196	58, 024
Fine foreign..................	11, 388	12, 843	6, 493	7, 966
Total	82, 542	70, 986	54, 689	65, 990

a Including 22,557 tons Chile bars transferred to France.

IMPORTS INTO FRANCE.

The direct imports of copper from different countries into France were as follows for a series of years:

Direct imports into France from 1887 to 1895, inclusive.

[Long tons.]

Year.	Chile.	United States.	Mexico.	Other countries.	Total.
1887....................	9,011	3,910	....	1,048	13,969
1888....................	8,468	6,496	2,700	6,905	24,569
1889....................	2,470	1.058	738	1,715	5,981
1890....................	2,803	1,733	....	975	5,511
1891....................	4,442	8,329	....	2,118	14,889
1892....................	2,221	4,340	2,515	2,208	11,284
1893....................	3,842	12,483	7,620	2,908	26,853
1894....................	3,312	9,248	6,299	1,588	20,947
1895....................	3,964	11,806	4,520	2,505	22,795

THE GERMAN COPPER TRADE.

Efforts have been made in Germany in the last few years to trace the source of the copper imported into that country. Since the United States is the largest contributor, this undertaking possesses special interest for us. The matter is beset with a good deal of difficulty. It is not possible to trace how much American copper was forwarded via Great Britain whose ultimate destination was Germany. On the other hand, it is an open question, too, whether copper sent directly and indirectly to Germany does not to a considerable extent find final lodgment in Russia.

The official statistics show that the copper imported into Germany was derived from the following sources:

Source of German copper imports.

Country.	1894.	1895.
	Metric tons.	Metric tons.
United States	23,795	31,311
England	7,430	7,363
Holland	109	139

Aron Hirsch & Sohn, of Halberstadt, Germany, have reviewed these figures, and are inclined to the belief that the official statistics credit the United States with too large a total. They point out that while the import figures for Germany return England with 7,363 tons and Holland with 139 tons—a total of 7,502 tons—the English Board of Trade returns put down the exports to Germany at 6,629 tons and to Holland at 6,942 tons, a total of 13,571 tons. It is difficult to escape the conclusion, however, that a very large part of the 6,069 tons of difference was really American copper in transit through England to Germany. In fact, were it possible to trace the copper extracted in English smelting works from American furnace material some of the metal credited to England and bearing English brands would be found to be of American origin. Our own statistics of exports to Germany and Holland show a total of 24,738 long tons, but possibly a part of the 3,743 long tons shipped to Belgium may have gone to that country also.

The importance of Germany as a growing consumer of copper is well shown in the following statistics, compiled by Aron Hirsch & Sohn, of Halberstadt. Since the production includes metal obtained from foreign ores and pyrites, an allowance is made for it:

Copper consumption of Germany.

[Metric tons.]

	1891.	1892.	1893.	1894.	1895.
Imports	46,153	44,514	51,806	52,504	59,712
Exports	9,973	9,817	11,304	10,406	10,893
Excess of imports	36,180	34,697	40,502	42,098	48,819
Production	24,688	25,406	24,011	25,857	a 26,000
Total	60,868	60,103	64,513	67,955	74,819
Imports of copper ore and iron pyrites	4,000	4,000	4,000	5,000	4,500
Home consumption	56,868	56,103	60,513	62,955	70,319

a Estimated.

THE LEADING FOREIGN PRODUCERS.

The Rio Tinto Company had a very prosperous year in 1895. The table on the following page shows the production of the company for a series of years.

Pyrites and copper statistics at Rio Tinto, Spain.

Year.	Pyrites extracted.				Pyrites consumed (average copper contents).		Copper produced at mines.
	For shipment.	For local treatment.	Total.	Average copper contents.	Tons.	Per cent.	
	Tons.	*Tons.*	*Tons.*	*Per cent.*	*Tons.*	*Per cent.*	*Tons.*
1876......	189,962	159,196	349,158	1.5	158,597	1.5	946
1877......	251,360	520,391	771,751	2.375	211,487	2	2,495
1878......	218,818	652,289	871,107	2.78	211,403	2.18	4,184
1879......	243,241	663,359	906,600	2.78	236,849	2.45	7,179
1880......	277,590	637,567	915,157	2.865	274,210	2.481	8,559
1881......	249,098	743,949	993,047	2.75	256,827	2.347	9,466
1882......	259,924	688,307	948,231	2.805	272,826	2.401	9,740
1883......	313,291	786,682	1,099,973	2.956	288,104	2.387	12,295
1884......	312,028	1,057,890	1,369,918	3.234	314,751	2.241	12,668
1885......	406,772	944,694	1,351,466	3.102	354,501	2.27	14,593
1886......	336,548	1,041,833	1,378,381	3.046	347,024	2.306	15,863
1887......	362,796	819,642	1,182,438	3.047	385,842	2.283	17,813
1888......	434,316	969,317	1,403,633	2.949	393,149	2.208	18,522
1889......	389,943	824,380	1,214,323	2.854	395,081	2.595	18,708
1890......	396,349	865,405	1,261,754	2.883	397,875	2.595	19,183
1891......	464,027	972,060	1,436,087	2.649	432,532	{ 2.651 / 1.309 }	21,227
1892......	406,912	995,151	1,402,063	2.819	435,758	{ 2.569 / 1.465 }	20,017
1893......	477,656	854,346	1,332,002	2.996	469,339	{ 2.659 / 1.544 }	20,887
1894......	498,540	888,555	1,387,095	3.027	485,441	{ 2.594 / .988 }	20,606
1895......	525,195	847,181	1,372,376	2.821	518,560	{ 2.595 / .986 }	20,762

The copper produced by treatment at the mines was 20,762 tons, and the fine copper contents of the pyrites shipped was 12,223 tons, making the total product of the Rio Tinto Company 32,985 tons. The quantities actually brought to market were 20,230 tons of refined copper and 11,065 tons of copper in pyrites. Some idea of the magnitude of the deposit of the Rio Tinto is conveyed by the estimate of the engineers relative to the reserves. These are placed at 135,000,000 tons; enough at the present rate of production to last ninety-seven years. Of this quantity it is estimated that 35,000,000 tons consist of ore poor in copper, leaving 100,000,000 tons of a quality not under the average of what has been worked in the past.

The profit on the product of the Rio Tinto Company was £626,287 in 1895; to which are added £6,297 for other profits and rents £25,087 by balance, £15 for transfer fees, and £70,996 for adjustment of exchange account. The interest on debentures figured up £158,900; taxes, etc., £22,041; expense of administration, £65,223, interest and commissions £713, allowance to directors £596 and redemption of mortgage debt £70,031, leaving a balance on revenue account of £411,178. The net profit was £534,068, from which there has been written off £17,859, extension and development account, £50,500 for redemption of bonds, an increase of £25,000 of the general depreciation account, £10,000 reduction of over-burden account, and £19,531 for plant gone out of use, leaving a balance of £411,178. Out of this dividends of 22 shillings per share, or £357,500, have been paid, and £25,000 has been carried to reserve account, making the total of that fund £100,000. During 1895 the outstanding 5 per cent mortgage bonds were converted into 4 per cent bonds, the issue being £3,600,000, while the capital stock is £3,250,000. The saving due to the lowering of interest will be £74,000 annually.

The Tharsis Company made a net profit of £219,491 in 1895, and declared a dividend of 17½ per cent. In 1894 the net profit was £120,346, and a dividend of 10 per cent, or £125,000, was declared. In 1893 the profit was £170,852. From the Tharsis and Calanas mines there were produced 612,483 long tons in 1895, as compared with 588,427 tons in 1894, 610,822 tons in 1893, and 504,706 tons in 1892. There were shipped for export 218,037 tons in 1895, against 208,362 tons in 1894, 250,250 tons in 1893, and 235,162 tons in 1892. There were delivered to consumers in 1895 222,269 tons of pyrites, and in 1894, 203,010 tons. The quantity of ore for local treatment was 612,483 tons in 1895, against 588,427 in 1894. The product of copper precipitate, owing to good rainfalls, was 9,600 tons in 1895 as compared with 7,386 tons in 1894, 7,330 tons in 1893, and 7,686 tons in 1892.

The operations of the third large company of the peninsula, the Mason & Barry, fell off somewhat in 1895. In that year the amount of ore broken was 185,463 long tons, as compared with 196,922 tons in 1894, and 209,814 tons in 1893. The shipments, exclusive of the material sent to the cementation works, were 186,368 tons in 1895, 242,386 tons in 1894, and 172,376 tons in 1893. There were invoiced for sulphur value in 1895, 189,448 tons, and in 1894, 233,729 tons. The production of copper precipitate was 3,059 tons fine copper in 1895, 3,321 tons in 1894, and 3,566 tons copper in 1893. The net profit for 1895 was £16,155 13s., to which were added dividends on the Sabine mine of £8,177 7s. 5d., and revenue from miscellaneous sources of £3,587 6s. 8d., making a total profit of £27,920 7s. 1d., as compared with £29,494 in 1894.

The Namaqua Copper Company of South Africa produced in 1895 6,672 long tons of dressed ore, against 5,433 long tons in 1894, the average price realized being 8s. 4¾d. and 7s. 7¾d. per unit, respectively, while the cost was £8 6s. 8d. and £8, respectively, per ton of dressed ore. The profit rose from £6,875 in 1894 to £21,313 in 1895, a dividend of 7½ per cent being paid in the latter year.

17 GEOL, PT 3——9

LEAD.

By Charles Kirchhoff.

INTRODUCTION.

The year 1895 has been characterized by a notable expansion in the demand for lead, which has, however, been covered principally by importations, which were double those of the year 1894. American production expanded only about 9,000 short tons, while duty was paid on 74,865 short tons of lead in pig and ores, as compared with 36,044 short tons in 1894, a striking proof of the great importance which foreign competition has attained.

PRODUCTION.

The following table presents the figures of the total gross production of lead in the United States from 1825. Up to the year 1882 the figures have been compiled from the best data available. Since 1882 the statistics are those collected by this office, with the exception of the year 1889, when they were gathered by the Census Office:

Production of refined lead in the United States from 1825 to 1895, both inclusive.

Year.	Total production. (a)	Desilverized lead. (a)	Soft lead. (b)	From foreign ores and base bullion.	Net American product.
	Short tons.	Short tons.	Short tons.	Short tons.	Short tons.
1825.........	1,500				
1830.........	8,000				
1831.........	7,500				
1832.........	10,000				
1833.........	11,000				
1834.........	12,000				
1835.........	13,000				
1836.........	15,000				
1837.........	13,500				
1838.........	15,000				

a Including foreign base bullion refined in bond.
b Including a small quantity of lead produced in the Southern States.

Production of refined lead in the United States from 1825 to 1895, both inclusive—Cont'd.

Year.	Total production. (a)	Desilverized lead. (a)	Soft lead. (b)	From foreign ores and base bullion.	Net American product.
	Short tons.	*Short tons.*	*Short tons.*	*Short tons.*	*Short tons.*
1839	17,500				
1840	17,000				
1841	20,500				
1842	21,000				
1843	25,000				
1844	26,000				
1845	30,000				
1846	28,000				
1847	28,000				
1848	25,000				
1849	23,500				
1850	22,000				
1851	18,500				
1852	15,700				
1853	16,800				
1854	16,500				
1855	15,800				
1856	16,000				
1857	15,800				
1858	15,300				
1859	16,400				
1860	15,600				
1861	14,100				
1862	14,200				
1863	14,800				
1864	15,300				
1865	14,700				
1866	16,100				
1867	15,200				
1868	16,400				
1869	17,500				
1870	17,830				
1871	20,000				
1872	25,880				
1873	42,540	20,159	22,381		

a Including foreign base bullion refined in bond.
b Including a small quantity of lead produced in the Southern States.

Production of refined lead in the United States from 1825 to 1895, both inclusive—Cont'd.

Year.	Total production. (a)	Desilverized lead. (a)	Soft lead. (b)	From foreign ores and base bullion.	Net American product.
	Short tons.	*Short tons.*	*Short tons.*	*Short tons.*	*Short tons.*
1874.........	52,080	....	....	....	....
1875.........	59,640	34,909	24,731	....	....
1876.........	64,070	37,649	26,421	....	....
1877.........	81,900	50,748	31,152	....	....
1878.........	91,060	64,290	26,770	....	....
1879.........	92,780	64,650	28,130	....	....
1880.........	97,825	70,135	27,690	....	....
1881.........	117,085	86,315	30,770	....	....
1882.........	132,890	103,875	29,015	....	....
1883.........	143,957	122,157	21,800	....	....
1884.........	139,897	119,965	19,932	....	....
1885.........	129,412	107,437	21,975	....	....
1886.........	135,629	114,829	20,800	c 5,000	c 130,629
1887.........	160,700	135,552	25,148	c 15,000	c 145,700
1888.........	180,555	151,465	29,090	28,636	151,919
1889.........	182,967	153,709	29,258	26,570	156,397
1890.........	161,754	130,403	31,351	18,124	143,630
1891.........	d 202,406	171,009	31,397	23,852	178,554
1892.........	e 213,262	181,584	31,678	39,957	173,305
1893.........	f 229,333	196,820	32,513	65,351	163,982
1894.........	219,090	181,404	37,686	59,739	g 162,686
1895.........	241,882	201,992	39,890	76,173	g 170,000

a Including foreign base bullion refined in bond.
b Including a small quantity of lead produced in the Southern States.
c Estimated.
d Including 4,043 tons antimonial lead.
e Including 5,039 tons of antimonial lead.
f Including 5,013 tons of antimonial lead.
g Arrived at from direct returns from smelters.

The following is a comparison of half-yearly periods, including the first six months of the current year:

Comparison of half-yearly periods.

	1896.	1895.		1894.	
	First half.	Second half.	First half.	Second half.	First half.
	Short tons.	*Short tons.*	*Short tons.*	*Short tons.*	*Short tons.*
Desilverized lead	109,592	114,035	87,957	94,632	86,772
Soft lead	21,103	21,877	18,013	22,076	15,610
Total production refined lead	130,695	135,912	105,970	116,708	102,382
Refined in bond	26,119	37,238	17,458	17,243	21,392
From base bullion produced in the United States........	104,576	98,664	88,512	99,465	80,990

Included in the product of desilverized lead for the first six months of 1896 was 3,869 short tons of hard lead.

The method of arriving at the total production of lead derived from ores mined in the United States, which was initiated in 1894, has been carried on for 1895. Returns were received from all the smelters and refiners showing the lead contents of the ores treated by them, distributed by States and Territories. The results obtained are embodied in the following table:

Source of lead in American ores smelted by silver lead smelters and refiners.

State or Territory.	1894.	1895.
	Short tons.	*Short tons.*
Colorado	50,613	46,984
Idaho	33,308	31,638
Utah	23,190	31,305
Montana	9,637	9,802
Nevada	2,254	2,583
New Mexico.................................	2,973	3,040
Arizona	1,480	2,053
California	478	949
Washington, Oregon, Alaska, South Dakota........	150	381
Missouri, Kansas, Wisconsin......................	8,614	13,706
Total lead contents ores smelted	132,697	142,441
Contents Mexican ores..................	*a* 21,000	16,437
Contents Canadian ores..................		5,010

a Estimated.

Assuming that the waste and loss in smelting and refining amounted to 6 per cent, then there were derived from the ores mined in the United States, worked by smelters and desilverizers, 124,700 short tons in 1894 and 134,900 short tons in 1895. Adding the production of soft lead from Kansas, Missouri, Iowa, Illinois, and Virginia ores, which was 37,686 short tons in 1894 and 39,890 short tons in 1895, the following amounts are reached as closely representing the product of lead from American ores: 162,386 short tons in 1894 and 174,790 short tons in 1895.

According to direct returns the total production of desilverized lead was 201,992 short tons. Of this, according to direct returns, 54,696 short tons were from refining Mexican and Canadian base bullion and 21,477 short tons from foreign ores. Making an allowance for waste of 6 per cent on ores, there was therefore included in the above 201,992 short tons of desilverized lead and 74,885 tons of foreign metal, leaving 127,107 short tons of lead from domestic metal which passed through the works of desilverizers. This compares with 134,900 tons found by estimating on the basis of direct returns of the lead contents of the ores handled by smelters. This apparent discrepancy is probably accounted for by changes in the stocks of base bullion carried by refiners, by changes in the quantity of material in transit from smelters to desilverizers, and by the difference between the actual metallurgical loss and that estimated.

Drawing an average between these figures and adding the product of soft lead, we reach the estimate of 170,000 short tons, which has been accepted as being the closest attainable of the lead product of the United States for 1895 from domestic ores. This estimate of course does not influence, by its necessarily approximate character, the exactness of the returns as to the total quantity of commercial lead available for the domestic market and exportable.

The principal increase in the production of lead has taken place in the Mississippi Valley. It may be placed at 46,000 tons in 1894 and 53,000 tons in 1895, so that now it has attained the position of contributing nearly one-third to the total of lead produced from native ores. A large share in the recent increase is due to the larger amount of lead ore raised in the Galena district, Kansas.

IMPORTS AND EXPORTS.

The following tables show the imports and exports of lead and its manufactures for a series of years:

Lead imported and entered for consumption in the United States, 1867 to 1895.

Year ending—	Ore and dross.		Pigs and bars.	
	Quantity.	Value.	Quantity.	Value.
June 30—	*Pounds.*		*Pounds.*	
1867............	611	$25	65, 322, 923	$2, 812, 668
1868............	6, 945	239	63, 254, 677	2, 668, 915
1869............	....	....	87, 865, 471	3, 653, 481
1870............	5, 973	176	85, 895, 724	3, 530, 837
1871............	316	10	91, 496, 715	3, 721, 096
1872............	32, 231	1, 425	73, 086, 657	2, 929, 623
1873............	....	....	72, 423, 641	3, 233, 011
1874............	....	....	46, 205, 154	2, 231, 817
1875............	13, 206	320	32, 770, 712	1, 559, 017
1876............	....	....	14, 329, 366	682, 132
1877............	1, 000	20	14, 583, 845	671, 482
1878............	....	....	6, 717, 052	294, 233
1879............	....	....	1, 216, 500	42, 983
1880............	....	....	6, 723, 706	246, 015
1881............	5, 981	97	4, 322, 068	159, 129
1882............	21, 698	500	6, 079, 304	202, 603
1883............	600	17	4, 037, 867	130, 108
1884............	419	13	3, 072, 738	85, 395
1885............	4, 218	57	5, 862, 474	143, 103
1886............	715, 588	9, 699	17, 582, 298	491, 310
Dec. 31—				
1887............	153, 731	21, 487	7, 716, 783	219, 770
1888............	88, 870	2, 468	2, 582, 236	69, 891
1889............	328, 315	7, 468	2, 773, 622	76, 243
1890............	11, 213, 883	528, 757	19, 336, 233	593, 671
1891............	40, 692, 478	1, 120, 273	3, 392, 562	104, 184
1892............	54, 249, 291	1, 278, 114	1, 549, 771	110, 953
1893............	58, 487, 319	1, 004, 295	3, 959, 781	163, 484
1894............	33, 020, 250	437, 999	39, 168, 529	895, 496
1895............	45, 050, 674	687, 222	104, 551, 082	2, 052, 209

Lead imported and entered for consumption in the United States, 1867 to 1895—Continued.

Year ending—	Sheets, pipe, and shot.		Shot.		Not otherwise specified.	Total value.
	Quantity.	Value.	Quantity.	Value.		
June 30—	*Pounds.*		*Pounds.*			
1867............	185, 825	$9, 560	....		$6, 222	$2, 828, 475
1868............	142, 137	7, 229	....		6, 604	2, 682, 987
1869............	307, 424	15, 531	....		18, 885	3, 687, 897
1870............	141, 681	6, 879	....		10, 444	3, 548, 336
1871............	86, 712	4, 209	....		8, 730	3, 734, 045
1872............	15, 518	859	....		20, 191	2, 952, 098
1873............	105	12	420	$50	21, 503	3, 254, 576
1874............	....	....	30, 219	1, 349	36, 484	2, 269, 650
1875............	....	....	58	4	25, 774	1, 585, 115
1876............	....	....	20, 007	1, 204	27, 106	710, 442
1877............	....	....	16, 502	1, 242	1, 041	673, 785
1878............	....	....	15, 829	963	113	295, 309
1879............	....	....	3, 748	209	930	44, 122
1880............	....	....	1, 120	54	371	246, 440
1881............	....	....	900	65	1, 443	160, 734
1882............	....	....	1, 469	99	2, 449	205, 651
1883............	....	....	1, 510	79	8, 030	138, 234
1884............	15, 040	630	....		1, 992	88, 030
1885............	971, 951	22, 217	....		1, 372	166, 749
1886............	27. 357	1, 218	....		964	503, 191
Dec. 31—						
1887............	27, 941	1, 280	....		302	242, 845
1888............	23, 103	1, 202	....		977	74, 538
1889............	35, 859	1, 417	....		1, 297	86, 425
1890............	68, 314	3, 338	....		1, 133	1, 130, 665
1891............	334, 179	12, 406	....		604	1, 237, 466
1892............	90, 135	6, 207	....		2, 063	1, 397, 336
1893............	59, 798	2, 955	....		1, 691	1, 136, 701
1894............	44, 680	2, 050	....		536	1, 336, 082
1895............	128, 008	5, 030	....		1, 277	2, 745, 738

Old and scrap lead imported and entered for consumption in the United States, 1867 to 1889, inclusive.

Year ending—	Quantity.	Value.	Year ending—	Quantity.	Value.
June 30—	*Pounds.*		June 30—	*Pounds.*	
1867	1,256,233	$53,202	1880	213,063	$5,262
1868	2,465,575	101,586	1881	123,018	2,729
1869	2,983,272	123,068	1882	220,702	5,949
1870	3,756,785	150,379	1883	1,094,133	31,724
1871	2,289,688	94,467	1884	160,356	4,830
1872	4,257,778	171,324	1885	4,866	106
1873	3,545,098	151,756	Dec. 31—		
1874	395,516	13,897	1886	24,726	882
1875	382,150	13,964	1887	136,625	4,323
1876	265,860	9,534	1888	33,100	904
1877	249,645	8,383	1889	50,816	1,494
1878	106,342	3,756	1890	(a)	(a)
1879	42,283	1,153			

a Included in pigs and bars after 1889.

Lead and manufactures of lead, of domestic production, exported from the United States.

Year ending—	Manufactures of—			Pigs, bars, and old.		Total value.
	Lead.		Pewter and lead.			
	Quantity.	Value.	Value.	Quantity.	Value.	
	Pounds.			*Pounds.*		
Sept. 30, 1790	13,440	$810	....	....	....	$810
1803(a)..	900	....	....	....	....	....
1804	19,804	....	....	....	....	....
1805	8,000	....	....	....	....	....
1808	40,583	....	....	....	....	....
1809	126,537	....	....	....	....	....
1810	172,323	....	....	....	....	....
1811	65,497	....	....	....	....	....
1812	74,875	....	....	....	....	....
1813	276,940	....	....	....	....	....
1814	43,600	....	....	....	....	....
1815	40,245	....	....	....	....	....
1816	35,844	....	....	....	....	....
1817	111,034	9,993	....	....	....	9,993
1818	281,168	22,493	....	....	....	22,493
1819	94,362	7,549	....	....	....	7,549
1820	25,699	1,799	....	....	....	1,799

a Barrels.

Lead and manufactures of lead, of domestic production, etc.—Continued.

Year ending—	Manufactures of—			Pigs, bars, and old.		Total value
	Lead.		Pewter and lead.			
	Quantity.	Value.	Value.	Quantity.	Value.	
	Pounds.			*Pounds.*		
Sept. 30, 1821.....	56,192	$3,512	....	....	....	$3,512
1822.....	66,316	4,244	....	....	....	4,244
1823.....	51,549	3,098	....	....	....	3,098
1824.....	18,604	1,356	....	....	....	1,356
1825.....	189,930	12,697	....	....	....	12,697
1826.....	47,337	3,347	$1,820	....	....	5,167
1827.....	50,160	3,761	6,183	....	....	9,944
1828.....	76,882	4,184	5,545	....	....	9,729
1829.....	179,952	8,417	5,185	....	....	13,602
1830.....	128,417	4,831	4,172	....	....	9,003
1831.....	152,578	7,068	6,422	....	....	13,490
1832.....	72,439	4,483	983	....	....	5,466
1833.....	119,407	5,685	2,010	....	....	7,695
1834.....	13,480	805	2,224	....	....	3,029
1835.....	50,418	2,741	433	....	....	3,174
1836.....	34,600	2,218	4,777	....	....	6,995
1837.....	297,488	17,015	3,132	....	....	20,147
1838.....	375,231	21,747	6,461	....	....	28,208
1839.....	81,377	6,003	12,637	....	....	18,640
1840.....	882,620	39,687	15,296	....	....	54,983
1841.....	2,177,164	96,748	20,546	....	....	117,294
1842.....	14,552,357	523,428	16,789	....	....	540,217
June 30, 1843 (a) .	15,366,918	492,765	7,121	....	....	499,886
1844.....	18,420,407	595,238	10,018	....	....	605,256
1845.....	10,188,024	342,646	14,404	....	....	357,050
1846.....	16,823,766	614,518	10,278	....	....	624,796
1847.....	3,326,028	124,981	13,694	....	....	138,675
1848.....	1,994,704	84,278	7,739	....	....	2,017
1849.....	680,249	30,198	13,196	....	....	43,394
1850.....	261,123	12,797	22,682	....	....	35,479
1851.....	....	....	16,426	229,448	$11,774	28,200
1852.....	....	....	18,469	747,930	32,725	51,194
1853.....	....	....	14,064	100,778	5,540	19,604
1854.....	....	....	16,478	404,247	26,874	43,352
1855.....	....	....	5,233	165,533	14,298	19,531
1856.....	....	....	5,628	310,029	27,512	33,110
1857.....	....	....	4,818	870,544	58,624	63,442

a Nine months.

Lead and manufactures of lead, of domestic production, etc.—Continued.

Year ending—	Manufactures of—		Pewter and lead.	Pigs, bars, and old.		Total value.
	Lead.					
	Quantity.	Value.	Value.	Quantity.	Value.	
	Pounds.			*Pounds.*		
June 30, 1858	....	....	$27,327	900,607	$48,119	$75,446
1859	....	....	28,782	313,988	28,575	57,357
1860	....	....	56,081	903,468	50,446	106,527
1861	....	....	30,534	109,023	6,241	36,775
1862	....	....	28,832	79,231	7,334	36,166
1863	....	....	30,609	237,239	22,634	53,243
1864	....	....	30,411	223,752	18,718	49,129
1865	....	....	29,271	852,895	132,666	161,937
1866	....	....	44,483	25,278	2,323	46,806
1867	....	....	27,559	99,158	5,300	32,859
1868	....	....	37,111	438,040	34,218	71,329
1869	....	....	17,249	....	....	17,249
1870	....	$28,315	....	....	....	28,315
1871	....	79,880	....	....	....	79,880
1872	....	48,132	....	....	....	48,132
1873	....	13,392	....	....	....	13,392
1874	....	302,044	....	....	....	302,044
1875	....	429,309	....	....	....	429,302
1876	....	102,726	....	....	....	102,726
1877	....	49,835	....	....	....	49,835
1878	....	314,904	....	....	....	314,904
1879	....	280,771	....	....	....	280,771
1880	....	49,899	....	....	....	49,899
1881	....	39,710	....	....	....	39,710
1882	....	178,779	....	....	....	178,779
1883	....	43,108	....	....	....	43,108
1884	....	135,156	....	....	....	135,156
1885	....	123,466	....	....	....	123,466
Dec. 31, 1886	....	136,666	....	....	....	136,666
1887	....	140,065	....	....	....	140,065
1888	....	191,216	....	....	....	194,216
1889	....	161,614	....	....	....	161,614
1890	....	181,030	....	....	....	181,030
1891	....	173,887	....	....	....	173,887
1892	....	154,375	....	....	....	154,375
1893	....	508,090	....	....	....	508,090
1894	....	456,753	....	....	*a* 41,240	497,993
1895	....	164,083	....	1,696,879	50,773	214,856

a Not enumerated between 1868 and July 1, 1894.

From records kept by Mr. A. E. Caswell, the imports of lead during the calendar years from 1860 to 1888, both inclusive, were as follows, the official figures in the table presented covering only fiscal years to 1886:

Imports of lead in calendar years from 1860 to 1888.

Year.	In pigs.	In ores.	Total.
	Short tons.	*Short tons.*	*Short tons.*
1860	21,425	....	21,425
1861	15,720	....	15,720
1862	32,900	....	32,900
1863	12,600	....	12,600
1864	27,900	....	27,900
1865	13,600	....	13,600
1866	27,200	....	27,200
1867	23,330	....	23,330
1868	23,225	....	23,225
1869	35,111	....	35,111
1870	28,600	....	28,600
1871	28,000	....	28,000
1872	26,355	....	26,355
1873	22,114	....	22,114
1874	17,674	....	17,674
1875	7,305	....	7,305
1876	4,685	....	4,685
1877	745	....	745
1878	285	....	285
1879	2,461	....	2,461
1880	3,228	....	3,228
1881	3,492	....	3,492
1882	2,518	....	2,518
1883	1,085	....	1,085
1884	2,508	....	2,508
1885	2,682	....	2,682
1886	9,760	8,800	18,560
1887	4,312	15,060	19,372
1888	1,642	27,018	28,660

The Bureau of Statistics has published the following data relative to the imports of lead entered for consumption during half-yearly periods, from 1891 to 1895, together with the duty collected:

Imports of lead, half-yearly, with duty collected from 1891 to 1895.

Period.	Lead in ore and dross.	Duty paid.	Lead in bars and pigs.	Duty paid.
	Short tons.		*Short tons.*	
First half 1891	8,778	*263,333	766	*30,661
Second half 1891	11,568	317,054	930	37,190
First half 1892	13,702	411,073	440	17,619
Second half 1892	13,422	402,667	834	33,376
First half 1893	16,484	494,519	1,153	86,830
Second half 1893	12,755	382,791	827	33,061
First half 1894	6,159	184,784	1,040	41,617
Second half 1894	10,351	158,660	18,544	372,486
First half 1895	12,247	191,138	22,847	456,939
Second half 1895	9,779	146,682	29,429	588,571

In addition to this, small quantities of manufactured lead were imported.

During the period of "exempt" lead, the actual quantities of foreign lead which went into United States consumption were larger than those indicated above.

According to the returns of the Treasury Department, the imports of lead in 1894 and 1895 were as follows:

Sources of imports of lead.

Country.	1894.	1895.
	Pounds.	*Pounds.*
United Kingdom..........................	6,357,937	8,161,411
Germany	1,792,305	1,113,148
Other Europe............................	14,452,179	36,618,228
Total refined pig lead..............	22,602,421	45,892,787
British North America	4,969,993	15,860,906
Mexico	112,148,130	138,312,146
Total ore and base bullion	117,118,123	154,173,052
Other countries........................	241,367	931,116
Total imports.......................	139,961,911	200,996,955

As against the 77,552 short tons of imports exclusive of refined pig lead shown in the Treasury statement, 76,174 short tons are recorded in the direct returns of refiners and desilverizers.

Duty was paid in 1895 on 149,729,764 pounds of lead, this including 45,050,674 pounds in ore and dross, 104,551,082 pounds in pigs and bars, and 128,008 pounds of sheet, pipe, and shot.

Through the courtesy of Mr. R. E. Preston, Director of the Mint, the following statement is presented, showing the base bullion, base silver ore, and copper bullion imported from Mexico and British Columbia, with the metal contents thereof:

Importations of base bullion, base silver ore, and copper bullion in 1895.

Description.	From Mexico.	From British Columbia.
	Pounds.	*Pounds.*
Base bullion...............................	49,872,054	4,949,024
Base silver ore............................	211,961,651	63,277,236
Copper bullion	766,370	....

The metal contents of this material are stated in the following table:

Metal contents of base bullion imported in 1895.

Description.	From Mexico.	From British Columbia.	Total.
Gold ....ounces..	1,245,472	43,026	1,288,498
Silver ....do....	28,839,872	1,538,762	30,378,634
Lead ....pounds..	78,206,955	14,442,723	92,649,678
Copper...................do....	4,126,802	1,947,704	6,074,506

These figures do not agree, so far as the importations of base bullion are concerned, with the returns from the desilverizers, who reported that they obtained from Mexican and Canadian bullion 54,696 short tons of refined lead. The report given above covers only 27,411 short tons of base bullion, equal to about 26,000 tons of lead.

All the Mexican base bullion which is imported into New York goes to Newark, N. J., and also since May, 1895, to Perth Amboy, for refining. The Bureau of Statistics has compiled the following table to show this movement:

Lead entered, withdrawn from, and remaining in warehouse at Newark, N. J., and Perth Amboy, N. J.

Month.	Remaining in warehouse on first day of each month.	Entered warehouse.	Withdrawn for export.
1894.	*Pounds.*	*Pounds.*	*Pounds.*
January	6, 605, 020	4, 592, 990	6, 096, 700
February	5, 029, 350	3, 481, 975	5, 687, 755
March	2, 504, 035	8, 891, 190	5, 760, 625
April	4, 646, 540	6, 090, 055	5, 588, 950
May	4, 278, 335	8, 190, 940	4, 473, 181
June	7, 207, 515	6, 857, 531	5, 311, 544
July	8, 005, 311	8, 121, 595	5, 366, 594
August	9, 923, 826	8, 439, 605	2, 989, 150
September	13, 482, 060	5, 115, 980	3, 777, 121
October	7, 951, 860	7, 180, 115	4, 325, 165
November	6, 244, 370	6, 072, 995	3, 542, 033
December	6, 898, 775	9, 741, 690	3, 360, 288
Total, 1894		a 82, 776, 661	56, 279, 106
1895.			
January	10, 569, 875	6, 841, 810	1, 940, 684
February	9, 966, 590	4, 881, 100	224, 012
March	11, 092, 510	8, 231, 965	2, 188, 784
April	11, 037, 170	10, 322, 050	3, 248, 315
May	13, 693, 310	6, 507, 655	4, 647, 528
June	12, 973, 900	7, 616, 649	1, 942, 923
July	15, 513, 730	13, 347, 712	1, 873, 135
August	20, 271, 197	8, 696, 142	585, 117
September	21, 606, 439	5, 631, 965	4, 652, 361
October	17, 850, 727	3, 898, 745	3, 638, 353
November	11, 592, 370	10, 350, 429	6, 352, 884
December	10, 847, 672	11, 845, 622	2, 967, 630
Total, 1895		98, 171, 844	34, 261, 726
1896.			
January	15, 771, 667	7, 951, 581	3, 298, 096
February	12, 158, 590	b 5, 837, 395	3, 405, 272
March	10, 321, 569		

a 2,249 pounds added to previous entry by liquidation.
b 3,081 pounds added to previous entry by liquidation.

Lead entered, withdrawn from, and remaining in warehouse, etc.--Continued.

Month.	Withdrawn for transportation (a).	Withdrawn for consumption.	Deductions from previous entries by liquidation.
1894.	*Pounds.*	*Pounds.*	*Pounds.*
January		71,960	
February		319,535	
March		152,905	835,155
April		102,070	767,240
May		149,712	638,867
June		1,660	746,531
July		100,022	736,464
August		1,486,110	407,060
September		6,183,994	685,465
October		3,514,397	1,048,943
November		1,351,623	524,934
December		2,112,016	598,286
Total, 1894		15,546,004	6,988,945
1895.			
January		5,149,195	355,216
February		3,355,714	175,454
March		5,756,063	342,458
April		4,020,770	396,825
May		2,124,132	455,405
June		2,996,429	137,467
July		6,402,395	314,715
August	1,407,170	5,200,954	167,659
September	1,550,422	2,809,778	375,116
October	4,116,018	1,974,945	427,786
November	4,084,197	35,010	623,036
December	2,481,826	755,846	716,325
Total, 1895	13,639,633	40,581,231	4,487,462
1896.			
January	5,331,876	497,447	2,437,239
February	3,209,970	875,987	
March			

a Exported from the port of New York.

17 GEOL, PT 3——10

CONSUMPTION.

Based on these data the following estimate of consumption of lead in 1894 and 1895 is presented, the stocks of domestic lead being based upon partial direct returns from producers:

Estimate of United States consumption in 1894 and 1895.

	1894.	1895.
Supply:		
Product, desilverized lead (including lead refined in bond)	*Short tons.* 181,404	*Short tons.* 201,992
Soft lead	37,686	39,890
Imports foreign refined lead	8,200	22,917
Stock, domestic, January 1, 1894	7,496	8,586
Stock, foreign in bond, January 1, 1894	3,302	7,181
Total	238,088	280,596
Deduct:		
Foreign refined in bond and exported	29,000	17,282
Lead in manufactures exported under drawback	950	2,000
Stock, domestic, January 1, 1895	8,586	9,557
Stock, foreign in bond, January 1, 1895	7,181	9,865
Total	45,717	38,704
Consumption	192,371	241,892

Another method is to add to the domestic production from United States sources, found to be 170,000 short tons, the quantity of lead on which duty was paid, 74,865 short tons; and allowing for the increase in stock, this leads to a consumption of about 245,000 short tons in 1895, from which some deduction must be made for waste in smelting foreign ores, which would carry it to 244,000 short tons. These figures indicate a very remarkable expansion in the demand in 1895, which is, however, somewhat counteracted by the fact that during the latter part of the year large consuming interests purchased heavily, but did not actually turn the metal into manufactured goods, so that some manufacturers entered the year 1896 with unusually large stocks. Even when making full allowance for this fact, it is true that 1895 witnessed a very notable increase in the consumption as compared with 1894. In this respect the experience in lead has merely been a repetition of that in iron and the other leading metals.

DOMESTIC PRODUCERS.

SOUTHEASTERN MISSOURI.

The lead-mining district of southeastern Missouri is growing in importance, but its further development is imperiled by the low prices of lead, which in the summer of 1896 had fallen below all previous records. Mining is only possible after a heavy investment of capital, relatively speaking. The geological features of the district and the distribution of the ore have been admirably described by Prof. Arthur Winslow in the recent Bulletin No. 132 of the United States Geological Survey, entitled The Disseminated Lead Ores of Southeastern Missouri.

The necessity for extensive exploration, of preparation for mining by power drills, and of building concentrating plants to handle large quantities of ore precludes any sudden increase in the production. The district, on the other hand, has a capacity for resisting for a relatively long time periods of depression and low prices, although recent experience has shown that a drop below 3 cents for lead in New York tries the majority of producers severely, and will soon drive them to enforced idleness.

The largest producer is the St. Joe Lead Company at Bonne Terre, which also controls the Doe Run Company in the Flat River district. In the same district, which has developed most rapidly in recent years, are the Desloge, the Central, Taylor, Donnelly, Derby, and Leadington. Of these only the Desloge and Central market their product as pig lead. The others sell what concentrates they produce in the open market, the lead desilverizers being the principal buyers.

By far the largest producer is the St. Joe Lead Company, which controls the Bonne Terre and the Doe Run mines, the latter being in the Flat River district. The production has been increased until now the company is turning out lead at the rate of nearly 20,000 tons per annum. The mine La Motte, at the extreme south of the belt, has fluctuated very little in its output for a number of years. The two most important recent additions to the district are the Desloge and the Central, concerning whose equipment the following data are submitted:

The Desloge Consolidated Mining Company first began the development of its tract of 2,500 acres in 1892, and is now completing the work which is ultimately to bring its mining, dressing, and smelting plant into harmonious cooperation to produce 6,000 tons of pig lead per annum. Until now the bulk of the ore, which yields from 4 to 8 per cent on the average, has been taken from No. 2 shaft, situated three-fourths of a mile from the dressing works and smelting plant. No. 3 shaft, 300 feet deep and 600 feet from the works, is being equipped for a larger production of ore, higher in grade. A large Cornish pump, with 12-inch plunger and 6-foot stroke, is being put in and is expected to handle 700 gallons of water per minute when operating its companion pump from the same gear. A novel and handy equipment of these shafts is a large bumping table, upon which the rock is dumped as it is hoisted from the mines. During its progress to the rock breaker the rock is culled.

The dressing plant is housed in a heavily timbered structure 110 feet wide, 175 feet long, and 55 feet high. The crushed ore is conveyed from the mines in self-dumping 20-ton cars, which delivers into a large ore bin along the entire length of the building. From it the ore passes over a set of six revolving screens, which take out all stuff under 15 millimeters, which goes directly to the corresponding dressing plant. The greater part of the material coarser than 15 millimeters is delivered to six pairs of Cornish rolls, 36 inches in diameter by 14-inch face, running at thirty-five revolutions per minute. The product of these rolls passes over grizzlies, the finer product being delivered direct to three sets of fine crushing rolls, 36 inches in diameter and 15-inch face, running fifty revolutions a minute. The coarse grizzly product is delivered to an elevator, which carries it to the coarse revolving screens.

The mill proper is divided into six distinct and independent sections, so that any one of them can be stopped or started without interfering with the others, and thus admitting of prompt repairs.

The ore is sized by revolving screens into 15, 10, 7, and 4 millimeter material. The 15-millimeter ore is delivered automatically to 12 slide-motion jigs, which produce a clean product ready for the furnaces and middlings, which are reduced and prepared for further treatment. The 10, 7, and 4 millimeter sizes are handled on eccentric jigs. The middlings from all the jigs are crushed in a 5-foot Huntingdon and Bryan mill and are sized and classified by hydraulic classifiers. The coarser particles are treated on 16 three sieve eccentric jigs, and the fine slimes are conveyed to Clausthal spitzkasten, from whence the material goes direct to 14 Evans slime tables, which finish it. All the pulp from the basement to the jig and table floors is raised 18 feet by No. 4 centrifugal pumps, the total number being 7.

The plant is furnished with steam by two Heine water-tube boilers, rated at 300 horsepower each, room being provided for a third. The engine plant consists of a 300-horsepower compound condensing Reynolds-Corliss engine with 18 and 32 inch cylinders, and 42-inch stroke. This also drives a Norwalk compound condensing air compressor with 18 and 28 inch steam cylinders and 30-inch stroke, to drive the drills at the adjacent plant.

The daily quantity of ore now treated by this dressing plant is 300 tons, and its average product is 1,000,000 pounds of concentrates per month. A doubling of the output is contemplated in the near future.

The Desloge Company does not treat the table concentrates produced in the concentrating plant. The coarse stuff, which is equal to about two-thirds of the whole yield and which averages 65 to 70 per cent of lead, is worked in the smelting plant of the company. This consists of two Flintshire and two Tarnowitz furnaces having in the aggregate a capacity to produce 250 tons of pig lead per month by running two shifts to a furnace. A larger product might be attained by working three shifts. The reaction process is used, a small quantity of fluor-spar being employed. The slag made, averaging about 100 tons per month, is not treated at the works, but is sold.

The Central Lead Company has developed a large tract on Flat River by sinking a shaft 380 feet deep, equipped with an admirably arranged plant, including a compound Worthington pump, Norwalk air compressors, a counterbalanced Lidgerwood hoisting engine, three 8 by 16 inch rock breakers, machine and pattern shops, and a sawmill.

From the rock breakers at the shaft the rock is discharged into what may be called bin cars, which have a capacity of 10 tons and are handled by horses on a standard-gauge track to the concentrating mill, a distance of 1,500 feet. This system has proved exceedingly convenient and is very cheap.

The mill proper is built on the slope of the bluff overlooking Flat River, the terraces being cut into the solid rock, thus affording an excellent foundation and reducing the handling to a minimum. It is a two-section mill. The rock first goes to coarse rolls, 16-inch face and 30 inch diameter, running at a speed of 28 revolutions, with a capacity of 200 tons per twenty-four hours each. The crushed material is sized in trommel to 12, 6, and 3 millimeters. Everything over 12 millimeters goes to four coarse jigs, which sometimes yield concentrates and sometimes middlings. All middlings produced by these four coarse jigs go to one set of coarse rolls, whose product is returned to the 12-millimeter trommel.

Turning back to the material sized by the trommels of the rock rolls, the stuff between 6 and 12 millimeters may first be dealt with. It is delivered to 4 jigs on one side and 6 jigs on the other side. The material passed through the 6 to 3 millimeter meshes of the main trommel is treated on 4 jigs on each side. The middlings from these jigs, handling the 12 to 6 millimeter and the 6 to 3 millimeter sizes, are crushed in one pair of fine rolls, 30 inches in diameter, running at a speed of 45 revolutions.

The product of the first trommel which was below the 3-millimeter size flows to 2 two-compartment classifiers. The larger material from the first compartment of the classifiers is delivered to 4 three-compart-ment jigs, while the material from the second compartment of the classifiers goes to 4 three-compartment jigs. The overflow from the classifiers is handled in a spitzkasten with two compartments, the material from each of which is concentrated on a two-deck rotating table.

All of the concentrates come down one launder for each of the two elements of the mill, and are transferred by a car to an elevator alongside one end of the mill, which delivers the concentrates to a set of fine crushing rolls. The concentrates are loaded into a car, weighed, and conveyed to the smelting works. The equipment of the mill, which has a capacity of 300 to 400 tons per day, double turn, is therefore 2 sets of coarse crushing rolls, 2 sets of fine rolls, 38 jigs, and 2 tables. All the jigs, it may be noticed incidentally, are provided individually with tight and loose pulleys. Power is furnished by 2 flue boilers, 18 feet by 60 inches, with 4-inch flues, and a Reynolds-Corliss 16 by 36 inch engine. The water service is provided for by a plunger pump, with 18-inch cylinder and 7-foot stroke.

During the year 1895 the Central Lead Company built a smelting plant, which went into operation in March, 1896. It consists of a roasting plant connected by tramway with the concentrator, containing three roasting furnaces. These have each eleven doors on each side and are 67 feet long. The charge made every six hours is 4,000 pounds of concentrates, which is finally sintered with the aid of about 4 to 5 per cent of river sand, the average time required to work a charge being thirty hours. Four men are employed per shift, two on each side, whose wages are $1.60 and $1.50 per day, respectively. The fuel consumption is 3 tons of Illinois coal per day. The roasted product goes to a 50-inch water-jacketed shaft furnace, the fuel consumption being about 14 per cent of coke. A small elevator is used to return, to the charging floor, dross and such incidental products of the furnace which can be charged directly to it. The principal flux is iron furnace cinder, drawn from St. Louis. What matte is produced is roasted in open heaps.

The pigs made at the water-jacket furnace are melted in a liquation furnace and run into a kettle, and are subjected to a steaming for about thirty minutes, this refining the lead. By means of a siphon the metal is drawn into molds on a rotary casting table 16 feet in diameter. The metal is loaded on cars at the refinery.

The plant of the Central Lead Company is so arranged that it can produce about 3,500 tons of lead per annum, a limitation set by the water supply available in Flat River, supplemented by the water pumped from the mine proper. The latter amounts to about 300 gallons per minute.

The annual report of Mr. Francis A. La Grave, State mine inspector of Missouri, says that the production of lead ore in St. Francois County for the fiscal year ending June 30, 1895, was 34,510 short tons, and for Madison County, 3,546 short tons. It should be understood, however, that these figures refer to concentrates. In the first six months of 1896, when practically no concentrates were sold to outside interests, the production of pig lead from these two counties was 12,821 tons. The figures for the production of pig lead during the calendar year 1895 are not given, because during that year notable quantities of concentrates were sold to desilverizers.

There are a number of smaller producers in Washington County who convert the ore raised on their properties into pig lead, but in the aggregate the metal so produced is small in quantity.

Southwestern Missouri and southeastern Kansas have continued to be the scene of active mining, and a gradual extension of the territory southwestward is observed. In the majority of the mines lead and zinc ore are produced from the same shafts. The zinc ore, however, usually predominates in quantity and value. The system of leasing small tracts of mineral lands prevails, so that there are a large number of small groups of producers. The life of individual mines is naturally short, but in the aggregate the district contributes very largely to the lead product of the country. The dressed ore is sold to the local smelters, the Picher Lead Company, Granby, or Case and Serage, or goes to more distant silver-lead smelters or desilverizers. According to the report of the mine inspector of Missouri, the product of lead ore in the fiscal years ending June 30, 1892, 1893, 1894, and 1895 was 18,472 short tons, 13,892 short tons, 20,019 short tons, and 20,391 short tons, respectively. If this whole ore went into pig lead this would represent about 12,000 tons annually. A considerable quantity, however, is used for the manufacture of sublimed lead.

For the calendar year 1895 the Joplin Herald estimates the product of the district at 28,337 tons, basing the estimate on the weekly report of sales. This, however, probably includes the product of the Galena district, stated by local authorities to have been 12,538 tons, leaving 15,799 tons for southwest Missouri.

KANSAS.

A very notable expansion has taken place during recent years in the production of the Galena district, Cherokee County, Kans. The producing territory has been considerably enlarged in a southwest direction. New finds have been made south of Shoal Creek and also in the Indian Territory. The following statement shows the production of the district:

Output of lead and zinc ores, Galena district, Cherokee County, Kans., from 1886 to 1895.(a)

Year.	Zinc ore.	Amount sold for zinc.	Lead ore.	Amount sold for lead.	Total value of output.
	Short tons.		*Pounds.*		
1886......	31,768	$587,708.00	5,924,284	$174,766.38	$762,474.38
1887......	32,795	623,105.00	6,152,380	161,499.98	784,604.98
1888......	33,391	701,211.00	5,248,000	81,344.00	782,555.00
1889......	32,950	790,800.00	7,985,000	183,655.00	974,455.00
1890......	21,675	498,525.00	8,347,927	176,176.28	674,701.28
1891......	20,641	454,102.00	7,204,420	182,271.83	636,373.83
1892......	23,811	476,237.78	14,376,340	301,903.14	778,140.92
1893......	25,028	471,789.00	10,279,180	195,314.42	667,103.42
1894......	28,670	490,257.00	11,631,980	195,794.66	686,051.66
1895......	41,232	812,792.00	25,075,290	482,518.75	1,295,340.75
Total...	291,961	5,906,526.78	102,227,801	2,135,271.44	8,011,801.22

a December estimated.

The work done by concentrating mills, as far as reported for 1895, was as follows:

The number of pounds of rough ore milled was 131,298,720, which produced 39,730,590 pounds of zinc ore and 1,880,680 pounds of lead ore. Had all mills reported this would be considerably increased.

The smelting of the lead ore is done by works in southwest Missouri and by desilverizers, but the 1895 product represents a tonnage probably close to 9,000 short tons of lead.

UPPER MISSISSIPPI VALLEY REGION.

The Upper Mississippi lead-zinc region, which includes adjacent territory in Wisconsin, Iowa, and Illinois, produces only small quantities of lead. Mr. A. G. Leonard, in his report, entitled "The lead and zinc deposits of Iowa," for the Iowa Geological Survey, estimates the production of that State at 750,000 pounds of ore in 1895.

ROCKY MOUNTAIN REGION.

So far as the Rocky Mountain region is concerned, no developments have taken place which might foreshadow the rise of another great lead-producing section. The statistics show that the quantity of lead produced has not undergone any material changes. Mining has been aided in a number of districts by reductions in rates of freights to smelters.

In Colorado, Leadville has more than held its own. According to the Herald-Democrat the mines produced in 1895 330,933 tons of ore, of which 70,429 tons were carbonate, 86,243 tons iron, 116,975 tons sulphide, and 57,286 tons silicate. The leading producers of carbonate were the Maid of Erin, with 27,614 tons; the Starr lease, 7,497 tons; Bon Air, 4,929 tons; Bison, 4,100 tons, and Welden, 3,931 tons. The Wolf Tone raised 35,508 tons of sulphides, the A. Y. and Minnie 25,765 tons, Boreel 10,172 tons, Union Leasing Company 13,233 tons, and the Small Hopes 9,917 tons. From the smelters' returns it appears that they treated 394,710 tons of Leadville ores, containing 31,236 tons of lead.

By far the greater part of the Idaho product, of over 30,000 tons in 1895, is derived from the Cœur d'Alene district, which early in the year was affected by labor troubles and litigation, but was more active later on. The capacity of the mines and concentrating plants is very much greater than the actual output in recent years.

PRICES.

The following table gives the highest and lowest prices monthly for a series of years, compiled from market quotations:

Highest and lowest prices of lead at New York City, monthly, from 1870 to 1895, inclusive.

[Cents per pound.]

Year.	January.		February.		March.		April.	
	Highest.	Lowest.	Highest.	Lowest.	Highest.	Lowest.	Highest.	Lowest.
1870	a 6.30	6.20	6.25	6.17	6.20	6.10	6.25	6.15
1871	a 6.30	6.15	6.25	6.20	6.20	6.15	6.20	6.10
1872	a 6	5.90	6	5.87	6	5.87	6.12	5.90
1873	a 6.37	6.25	6.50	6.40	6.50	6.25	6.50	6.25
1874	a 6	5.90	6.25	6	6.25	6.12	6.25	5.90
1875	a 6.20	6	5.90	5.85	5.75	5.62	5.87	5.80
1876	a 6	5.87	6.37	6	6.50	6.40	6.40	6.12
1877	b 6.15	6.12	6.40	6.20	6.75	6.50	6.50	6.25
1878	4.35	4	3.87	3.65	3.87	3.62	3.75	3.50
1879	4.50	4	4.50	4.50	4.50	3.25	3.25	2.87
1880	6.10	5.50	6	5.87	5.95	5.30	5.75	5.40
1881	5	4.30	5.10	4.80	4.85	4.62	4.85	4.37
1882	5.15	4.95	5.20	5	5.12	4.85	5	4.90
1883	4.70	4.60	4.60	4.50	4.65	4.50	4.62	4.40
1884	4.50	3.75	4.10	3.75	4.15	4.10	4.05	3.62½
1885	3.70	3.55	3.70	3.60	3.70	3.62½	3.70	3.62½
1886	4.70	4.50	4.90	4.60	4.95	4.85	4.90	4.65
1887	4.45	4.15	4.50	4.25	4.45	4.25	4.32½	4.20
1888	4.90	4.50	5.15	4.60	5.25	5	5.05	4.55
1889	3.90	3.75	3.75	3.60	3.75	3.65	3.67½	3.60
1890	3.85	3.80	3.85	3.75	3.95	3.85	4.07½	3.85
1891	4.50	4.05	4.50	4.25	4.37½	4.25	4.32½	4.10
1892	4.30	4.10	4.25	4.05	4.22½	4.10	4.30	4.20
1893	3.90	3.85	3.95	3.90	4.05	3.85	4.05	4.15
1894	3.25	3.15	3.35	3.20	3.45	3.25	3.45	3.37½
1895	3.12½	3.05	3.12½	3.07½	3.10	3.07½	3.12½	3.05

a Gold.   b Currency.

Highest and lowest prices of lead at New York City, monthly, etc.—Continued.

[Cents per pound.]

Year.	May.		June.		July.		August.	
	Highest.	Lowest.	Highest.	Lowest.	Highest.	Lowest.	Highest.	Lowest.
1870	6.25	6.20	6.25	6.20	6.30	6.20	6.37	6.32
1871	6.18	6.10	6 15	6.12	6.15	6.10	6.12	6
1872	6.62	6.25	6.62	6.40	6.62	6.40	6.50	6.40
1873	6.62	6.35	6.55	6.12	6.12	6	6.25	6
1874	6	5.75	6	5.62	5.80	5.62	5.80	5.65
1875	5.95	5.90	5.90	5.75	6	5.95	5.95	5.87
1876	6.50	6.10	6.50	6.25	6.35	6.20	6.37	6.25
1877	6	5.55	5.70	5.60	5.60	5.37	5.12	4.90
1878	3.50	3.25	3 50	3.12	3.62	3.25	3.50	3.20
1879	3.12	2.87	3.80	3.12	4.10	3.90	4.05	4.60
1880	5.25	4.40	4.75	4.50	4.75	4.25	5	4.30
1881	4.70	4.25	4.50	4.25	4.90	4.50	4.95	4.75
1882	4.85	4.60	4.90	4.55	5.15	4.90	5.10	4.95
1883	4.55	4.40	4.45	4.40	4.40	4.30	4.30	4.20
1884	3.75	3.52½	3.65	3.57½	3.70	3.55	3.70	3.52½
1885	3.75	3.60	3.85	3.62½	4.15	3.87½	4.25	4.12
1886	4.75	4.65	4.90	4.65	4.90	4.75	4.80	4.75
1887	4.70	4.30	4.70	4.50	4.67½	4.40	4.62½	4.55
1888	4.62½	4	4.10	3.65	4.07½	3.85	4.97½	4.15
1889	3.87½	3.60	4.05	3.90	4.05	3.80	3.95	3.75
1890	4.35	4	4.50	4.25	4.50	4.40	4.72½	4.35
1891	4.37½	4.20	4.50	4.35	4.45	4.30	4.53	4.40
1892	4.25	4.20	4.20	4.05	4.25	4	4.15	4
1893	4	3.75	3.90	3.45	3.60	3.30	3.75	3.25
1894	3.40	3.30	3.37½	3.25	3.65	3.37½	3.70	3.30
1895	3.25	3.07½	3.30	3.25	3.50	3.30	3.55	3.50

Year.	September.		October.		November.		December.	
	Highest.	Lowest.	Highest.	Lowest.	Highest.	Lowest.	Highest.	Lowest.
1870	6.37	6.30	6.37	6.25	6.35	6.20	6.35	6.25
1871	6.10	6	6	5.87	6	5.90	6	5.75
1872	6.50	6.30	6.62	6.40	6.60	6.50	6.60	6.42
1873	6.62	6.37	6.75	6.25	6.50	6	6.12	6
1874	6.10	5.65	6.35	6.10	6.50	6.25	6.40	6.12
1875	5.87	5.70	5.65	5.60	5.87	5.65	5.95	5.87
1876	6.25	6	6	5.80	5.80	5.70	5.70	5.65
1877	4.85	4.75	4.85	4.25	4.75	4.50	4.60	4.50
1878	3.45	3.25	3.60	3.37	3.95	3.60	4	3.90

Highest and lowest prices of lead at New York City, monthly, etc.—Continued.

[Cents per pound.]

Year.	September.		October.		November.		December.	
	Highest.	Lowest.	Highest.	Lowest.	Highest.	Lowest.	Highest.	Lowest.
1879.............	4	3.75	5.50	4	5.62	5	5.60	5.50
1880.............	4.90	4.80	4.87	4.65	4.85	4.75	4.75	4.25
1881.............	5.37	4.95	5.25	4.87	5.25	4.90	5.25	5
1882.............	5.15	4.95	5.15	4.85	4.90	4.50	4.75	4.50
1883.............	4.32	4.30	4.32	4.12	4.05	3.65	3.75	3.60
1884.............	3.75	3.55	3.75	3.60	3.55	3.37½	3.75	3.50
1885.............	4.25	4	4.25	4	4.60	4	4.67½	4.50
1886.............	4.70	4.45	4.30	4	4.40	4.10	4.35	4.25
1887.............	4.55	4.25	4.40	4.20	4.75	4.25	5.15	4.90
1888.............	5.12½	4.90	5.12½	3.62½	3.82½	3.60	3.82½	3.60
1889.............	4	3.85	3.90	3.75	3.90	3.75	3.90	3.75
1890.............	5	4.67½	5.25	5.	5.25	4.60	4.60	4.05
1891.............	4.55	4.40	4.55	4.10	4.35	4.10	4.25	4.25
1892.............	4.15	4	3.95	3.85	3.85	3.70	3.85	3.70
1893.............	3.95	3.75	3.75	3.25	3.37½	3.30	3.30	3.20
1894.............	3.30	3.10	3.15	3.05	3.12½	3.10	3.12½	3.02½
1895.............	3.45	3.32½	3.35	3.30	3.27½	3.15	3.30	3 20

THE LEAD MARKET.

The year opened with a dull market, but, under a somewhat livelier demand, stimulated by the shut down at the Idaho mines, the market rose from 3.02½ cents early in January to 3.12½ cents toward the close. February brought increasing weakness, but a somewhat more confident tone developed in March. Partly owing to lower rates of freight from the Missouri River, the market reacted to 3.05 cents in the middle of April. Later large consumers entered the market without materially affecting prices. It was not until the middle of May that further heavy purchases caused a rise to 3.25 cents, from which there was a reaction toward the end of the month, caused by free offerings on the part of some refining interests. In June the market fluctuated within narrow limits, and in July the principal event was the flurry caused by the report of fire in the Broken Hill mines, Australia. August brought a heavier demand and the highest prices of the year, the market toward the end being influenced by lower prices in Europe. There were good sales early in September, but later on the market relapsed into dullness, until in October greater activity checked the downward tendency temporarily. That tendency, however, gathered strength in November, which was characterized by symptoms of a collapse in the iron trade and other metal industries. In December the market showed some strength at first, but toward the close of the year sagged off to 3.20 cents.

WORLD'S PRODUCTION.

The following table gives the world's production of lead during the years 1886 to 1894, inclusive, compiled by the Metallgesellschaft of Frankfurt a. Main.

The world's production of lead during the years 1886 to 1894, inclusive.

[Metric tons.]

Country.	1886.	1887.	1888.	1889.	1890.
Germany	91,000	95,000	97,000	100,000	101,000
Spain................	a 102,000	a 119,000	129,200	136,900	140,300
Great Britain	a 51,000	a 50,000	a 50,000	a 47,800	49,800
Austria	8,000	7,800	8,000	8,000	8,300
Hungary	2,100	1,800	2,000	2,300	1,200
Italy	19,000	a 19,000	17,000	18,000	17,700
Belgium	10,000	10,000	11,000	9,400	9,600
France..............	4,000	a 5,000	6,500	5,400	4,600
Greece..............	a 10,000	12,500	14,500	13,500	14,200
Other European countries..............	a 2,000	a 2,000	a 2,000	a 2,000	a 2,000
United States........	119,387	132,150	137,790	141,852	130,272
Mexico	16,000	18,100	30,100	27,500	22,300
Australia (b).........	a 5,000	a 10,000	a 19,000	a 35,000	40,500
Other countries	a 1,000	a 1,000	a 1,000	a 1,000	a 1,000
Total..........	440,487	483,350	525,090	548,752	542,772

Country.	1891.	1892.	1893.	1894.
Germany......................	95,000	98,000	95,000	101,000
Spain	145,700	152,300	157,100	157,700
Great Britain...................	49,000	44,900	38,200	42,800
Austria	7,600	7,300	7,200	7,500
Hungary......................	2,100	2,300	2,500	a 2,500
Italy........................	18,500	22,000	19,900	19,600
Belgium	12,700	10,100	12,000	13,500
France......................	6,700	8,800	8,100	a 8,100
Greece	13,300	14,400	12,800	12,700
Other European countries.......	a 2,000	a 2,500	a 3,000	a 4,000
United States	161,948	157,187	147,627	147,600
Mexico......................	30,200	47,500	61,000	57,000
Australia (b)...................	56,000	54,000	58,000	50,000
Other countries.................	a 1,000	a 1,000	a 1,000	a 1,000
Total	601,748	622,287	626,427	625,000

a Estimated.   b Exclusive of that part of product not exported to Europe and America.

For the United States the figures collected by this office have been accepted.

SPAIN.

There are puzzling discrepancies in the statistics of the production of lead in Spain. The official figures for 1894 show a production of 64,189 metric tons of lead and 88,433 metric tons of argentiferous lead or base bullion, a total of 152,622 metric tons. Making an allowance of 4 per cent for waste in desilverizing and for silver contents, this would represent a total of 146,000 tons. Yet the exports of that year were 160,316 tons, to which must be added the lead contents of 12,164 tons of ore exported, which, at 65 per cent yield, would carry the total to about 168,000 tons. This ignores entirely the domestic consumption. It does not seem likely that this discrepancy of 22,000 tons can be explained by a withdrawal for export of stocks of the metal in Spain.

Ramon Oriol, in the Revista Minera, of Madrid, makes the following estimate of the production of Spain for 1895 by provinces, the figures for 1894 and 1895 being those of the Junta Superior Facultativa de Mineria:

Production of lead in Spain.

Province.	1895. R. Oriol's estimate.	1894. Official figures.
	Metric tons.	Metric tons.
Murcia	92,000	85,465
Jaén (Linares)	42,500	31,529
Córdova	20,500	17,795
Almeria	15,000	13,295
Guipúzcoa	5,000	4,536
Total	175,000	152,620
Export pig lead	151,129	160,316
Export lead ore	9,203	12,164

It will be observed that while Mr. Oriol estimates a liberal increase in the production, the official export statistics display a falling off in both the exports of lead and of ore. The official returns, so far as details are concerned, are not available for 1895. The report shows a product for the whole country of 124,195 metric tons of lead ore and 181,433 tons of argentiferous lead ore. The smelting works produced 76,808 metric tons of pig lead and 83,978 tons of argentiferous base bullion. This shows a total lead product of 160,786 tons.

FRANCE.

Official statistics published in the *Annales des Mines* show the following:

Lead statistics of France.

Year.	Production from domestic and imported ores.	Exports.	Imports.	Apparent home consumption.
	Metric tons.	Metric tons.	Metric tons.	Metric tons.
1882	8,076	5,301	65,369	68,144
1883	7,770	5,629	69,038	71,179
1884	6,293	4,939	57,536	58,890
1885	4,806	5,890	57,696	56,012
1886	3,874	14,367	61,681	51,188
1887	5,939	10,857	63,338	58,420
1888	6,406	8,850	54,001	51,557
1889	5,305	10,569	61,249	55,985
1890	4,544	9,895	67,754	62,403
1891	6,680	10,957	74,748	70,471
1892	8,776	10,057	73,045	71,764
1893	8,119	9,243	77,679	76,555
1894	8,696	8,133	84,674	85,237

GREAT BRITAIN.

The lead-mining industry of Great Britain has declined almost uninterruptedly for many years. The official statistics show that the mines produced the following quantities of dressed ores since 1880:

Production of dressed lead ore in Great Britain during the years 1880 to 1894, inclusive.

Year.	Long tons.	Year.	Long tons.	Year.	Long tons.
1880	72,245	1885	51,302	1890	45,651
1881	64,702	1886	53,420	1891	43,859
1882	65,001	1887	51,563	1892	40,024
1883	56,487	1888	51,259	1893	40,808
1884	54,485	1889	48,465	1894	40,599

In 1894 England participated in the total with 22,538 tons of dressed ore, from which 15,813 tons of lead are estimated to have been "obtainable by smelting." Wales contributed 8,317 tons of dressed ore, with 6,589 tons obtainable by smelting; Scotland, with 4,028 and 3,087 tons, respectively; Ireland, with 92 and 64 tons, and the Isle of

Man with 5,624 tons of ore, estimated equivalent to 4,134 tons of metal. The product of silver from these ores was 274,100 ounces.

According to the board of trade returns the exports of English lead in recent years have been as follows:

Exports of English lead during the years 1892, 1893, and 1894.

	1892.	1893.	1894.
	Long tons.	*Long tons.*	*Long tons.*
Ore	5	29	....
Pig lead.......................................	39, 178	29, 535	27, 801
Rolled, sheet, pipe, etc......................	18. 984	19, 336	19, 259

The principal countries to which this metal was shipped were the following:

Destination of English lead exports in 1893 and 1894.

Destination.	Pig lead.		Manufactured lead.	
	1893.	1894.	1893.	1894.
	Long tons.	*Long tons.*	*Long tons.*	*Long tons.*
Russia	9, 852	10, 434	3, 661	3, 730
Germany	2, 479	....	309	....
Holland	1, 053	....	15	....
France	4, 645	4, 287	....	14
British East Indies	574	544	6, 831	6, 683
China	4, 804	3, 856	78	23
Hongkong	1, 706	625	383	114
Japan..............................	264	351	1, 939	2, 296
United States	....	1, 901	....	30

The exports of foreign lead were as follows:

English exports of foreign lead in 1892, 1893, and 1894.

	1892.	1893.	1894.
	Long tons.	*Long tons.*	*Long tons.*
Ore	2, 586	2, 348	3, 916
Pig lead and sheet.............................	15, 613	18, 836	13, 836

The greater part of the ore, 2,440 tons, was shipped to Italy. The following countries received the principal quantities of the pig lead and sheet lead exported:

Country.	1893.	1894.	Country.	1893.	1894.
	Long tons.	*Long tons.*		*Long tons.*	*Long tons.*
Russia	3,070	2,809	France	3,697	....
Germany	1,626	....	Japan	220	....
Holland	850	1,023	United States .	....	1,175
Belgium	8,210	7,875			

GERMANY.

According to official statistics, the production of lead in Germany has been as follows:

Production of lead in Germany during the years 1884 to 1895, inclusive.

Year.	Metric tons.	Year.	Metric tons.
1884	94,809	1890	101,781
1885	93,134	1891	95,615
1886	92,520	1892	97,742
1887	94,921	1893	94,659
1888	96,995	1894	100,751
1889	100,601	1895	114,491

Germany has steadily increased her imports of lead during a series of years, while her exports have declined. The following table presents the figures since 1888:

German imports and exports of lead during the years 1888 to 1895, inclusive.

Year.	Imports.	Exports.	Year.	Imports.	Exports.
	Metric tons.	*Metric tons.*		*Metric tons.*	*Metric tons.*
1888	7,358	34,889	1892	17,500	25,657
1889	9,527	32,793	1893	23,856	23,944
1890	12,766	32,115	1894	24,280	24,354
1891	17,624	24,973	1895	28,449	27,855

The imports of litharge were 840 tons, while the exports were 2,725 tons. In white lead the imports were only 479 tons, while the exports footed up to 14,260 tons.

The Mechernich Company did better in 1895, the loss being only 311,738 marks, as compared with a loss of 1,105,307 marks in 1894.

AUSTRIA.

Austria produced in 1894, 7,563 metric tons of lead, of which the Government works turned out 2,046 tons. Carinthia contributed 4,746 tons, Bohemia 1,974 tons, and Carniola 843 tons. The old mines and works of the Bleiberg Bergwerks Union made profit in 1895 of 84,759 florins, paying a dividend of 4½ per cent, which absorbed 84,000 florins. The mines at Bleiberg produced 2,502 tons, and Windisch Bleiberg 134 tons.

Austria imported in 1895, 8,974 metric tons of lead, and exported 60 tons.

Mines in Hungary yielded 2,514 tons of lead in 1893, and 2,113 tons in 1894.

AUSTRALIA.

The product of the Broken Hill Proprietary has fallen off quite heavily in 1895, as is shown in the table given below. Efforts are being made to deal with additional quantities of ore, and a concentrating plant capable of handling 6,000 tons of ore per week is being erected. The management has estimated that there is in sight down to the 400-foot level at the northern boundary and to the 500-foot level at the southern boundary, 2,019,000 tons of ore, containing on an average 24.3 per cent of lead, 21.9 per cent of zinc, and 18.5 ounces of silver. The reserve of oxidized ores is estimated at 1,250,000 tons, with 12 per cent of lead and 15 ounces of silver. The company now refines all its own bullion, and is putting in a parting plant. Up to the close of 1895 the company has paid in cash dividends £6,416,000, and £1,744,000 par value of stock in subsidiary companies. During the six months ending May 31, 1896, the company made a profit of £244,914, the ore treated having averaged 7 per cent of lead and 19 ounces of silver. During that period the value of the ore treated was £3 8s. 6d. and the average cost of treatment was £2 6s.

Production of Broken Hill Proprietary Company.

Half year ending—	Ore treated.	Product of silver.	Product of lead.
	Long tons.	Ounces.	Long tons.
May 31, 1890	103,912	3,855,381	15,399
November 30, 1890	103,912	3,872,546	14,938
May 31, 1891	138,645	4,918,124	24,222
November 30, 1891	147,473	5,028,944	17,165
May 31, 1892	180,852	5,754,940	26,813
November 30, 1892	73,973	2,310,208	9,653
May 31, 1893	230,463	5,972,194	21,734
November 30, 1893	260,047	6,533,232	25,609
May 31, 1894	269,245	7,287,337	25,638
November 30, 1894	325,919	6,767,056	23,955
May 31, 1895	300,558	....	19,359
November 30, 1895	222,324	4,158,551	13,712
May 31, 1896	230,451	4,107,578	11,958

Production of Broken Hill Proprietary Company—Continued.

Half year ending—	Value of ore per ton.			Cost per ton.			Profit per ton.		
	£.	s.	d.	£.	s.	d.	£.	s.	d.
May 31, 1890	8	8	9	3	15	9	4	12	4
November 30, 1890	9	7	7	4	5	2	5	1	10
May 31, 1891	8	3	9	3	18	7	4	5	2
November 30, 1891	7	18	1	3	12	2	4	5	11
May 31, 1892	6	11	11	3	14	1	2	17	10
November 30, 1892	5	12	9	3	14	10	1	17	11
May 31, 1893	4	16	0	2	8	10	1	17	2
November 30, 1893	4	8	9	2	13	10	1	14	11
May 31, 1894	4	2	0	2	12	6	1	9	6
November 30, 1894	3	4	8	2	3	7	1	1	1
May 31, 1895	3	3	10	2	0	11	1	2	11
November 30, 1895	3	13	3	2	6	11	1	6	4

Since its completion the refinery of the company has handled the following quantities of material:

Product of refinery of the Broken Hill Proprietary Company.

Half year ending—	Lead.	Silver.	Gold.	Cost.		
	Long tons.	Ounces.	Ounces.	£	s.	d.
May 31, 1891	3,989	642,604	365	2	0	9
November 30, 1891	2,196	821,928	440	2	14	7½
May 31, 1892	7,969	1,684,210	1,352	1	14	5¼
November 30, 1892	3,725	729,825	473	1	19	3
May 31, 1893	10,994	2,857,722	1,848	1	8	2¼
November 30, 1893	11,309	3,154,233	1,431	1	12	1¼
May 31, 1894	10,117	3,083,014	1,341	1	9	3¼
November 30, 1894	11,070	3,667,555	2,737	1	8	8½
May 31, 1895	11,687	3,773,539	2,914	1	9	0¼
November 30, 1895	12,986	3,864,362	2,287	1	4	6¼

Some of the smaller mines in the district are expanding. Thus the Broken Hill Block 10 is putting up a new concentrating plant to handle 2,000 tons of ore per week.

ZINC.

By Charles Kirchhoff.

PRODUCTION.

Like all the metals, spelter recovered somewhat in 1895 from the depression following the panic of 1893, and the production expanded so that the industry resumed its onward course. The production of 1892 was exceeded and a new record established.

For a series of years the production of spelter has been as follows:

Production of spelter in the United States.

Year.	Short tons.	Year.	Short tons.
1873	7,313	1888	55,903
1875	15,833	1889	58,860
1880 a	23,239	1890	63,683
1882	33,765	1891	80,873
1883	36,872	1892	87,260
1884	38,544	1893	78,832
1885	40,688	1894	75,328
1886	42,641	1895	89,686
1887	50,340		

a Census year ending May 31.

For a series of years the production has been as follows:

Production of spelter in the United States, by States.

Year.	Eastern and Southern States.	Illinois.	Kansas.	Missouri.	Total.
	Short tons.	Short tons.	Short tons.	Short tons.	Short tons.
1882	5,698	18,201	7,366	2,500	33,765
1883	5,340	16,792	9,010	5,730	36,872
1884	7,861	17,594	7,859	5,230	38,544
1885	8,082	19,427	8,502	4,677	40,688
1886	6,762	21,077	8,932	5,870	42,641
1887	7,446	22,279	11,955	8,660	50,340
1888	9,561	22,445	10,432	13,465	55,903

Production of spelter in the United States, by States—Continued.

Year.	Eastern and Southern States.	Illinois.	Kansas.	Missouri.	Total.
	Short tons.	*Short tons.*	*Short tons.*	*Short tons.*	*Short tons.*
1889...................	10, 265	23, 860	13, 658	11, 077	58, 860
1890.................	9, 114	26, 243	15, 199	13, 127	63, 683
1891................	a8, 945 b4, 217	28, 711	22, 747	16, 253	80, 873
1892..............	9, 582 4. 913	c31, 383	24, 715	16, 667	87, 260
1893..............	8, 802 3, 882	c29, 596	22, 815	13, 737	78, 832
1894..............	7, 400 1, 376	c28, 972	25, 588	11, 992	75, 328
1895	9, 484 3, 697	c35, 732	25, 775	14, 998	89, 686

a Eastern.   b Southern.   c Including Indiana.

The production during the first six months of 1896 has been as follows:

Production of zinc during the first half of 1896.

States.	Short tons.
Eastern..	4, 517
Southern...	1, 200
Illinois and Indiana...	16, 305
Kansas...	11, 351
Missouri...	5, 548
Total..	38, 921

This shows a considerable falling off in the rate of production.

STOCKS.

A partial statement of stocks shows the following changes:

States.	January 1—			
	1893.	1894.	1895.	1896.
	Short tons.	*Short tons.*	*Short tons.*	*Short tons.*
Eastern	3, 316	1, 587	1, 779	2, 333
Southern......................		1, 437	914	1, 108
Illinois and Indiana	12	826	1, 348	1, 169
Kansas.........................	483	590	665	675
Missouri	349	129	205	517
Total.....................	4, 160	4, 569	4, 911	5, 802

The principal event in the industry was the consolidation of a considerable number of plants under the name of the Cherokee-Lanyon Spelter Company, which purchased outright some of the works and leased others, like those of S. H. Lanyon & Bro. and the Girard Zinc Company, for a period of years. The companies under the control of the consolidation are the Cherokee Zinc Company, with two works, at Weir and at Pittsburg, Kans.; Robert Lanyon & Co., with two works, at Nevada, Mo., and at Pittsburg, Kans.; the old and the new Girard plants; that of the Pittsburg and St. Louis Zinc Company; the Rich Hill Zinc Works; S. H. Lanyon & Bro., and the Columbia Zinc Company. The magnitude of the new company, in which a leading New York firm of metal merchants is largely interested, is readily appreciated when the fact is taken into account that the consolidated works produced, in 1893, 27,029 short tons; in 1894, 31,392 short tons, and in 1895, 30,560 short tons of spelter. In the latter year, therefore, the consolidated companies made one-third of the metal produced in the United States. Actually this does not, however, measure its influence upon the market, because a very large proportion of the total amount of spelter made by the two greatest Illinois smelters is rolled into sheet zinc and does not therefore affect the spelter market, and because, secondly, the greater part of the spelter produced in the South and East is of special quality and is little used in the channels into which Western spelter chiefly goes. Under the circumstances the dominating influence of interests controlling so large a share of the product will be readily understood.

The principal producing district of zinc ore in the United States is southwest Missouri and southeast Kansas, the belt stretching into the Indian Territory. So far as southwest Missouri is concerned the reports of the State mine inspector, Francis A. La Grave, furnish data bearing on the production. Unfortunately, they cover fiscal years ending June 30.

Production of zinc ore in southwest Missouri.

Fiscal year.	Amount.	Average price.	Total value.
	Short tons.		
1890–1891	123,752	$21.60	$2,673,063.36
1891–1892	131,488	21.76	2,862,475.08
1892–1893	108,591	20.57	2,245,028.80
1893–1894	89,150	15.00	1,337,910.36
1894–1895	101,294	16.86	1,707,665.40

From weekly reports of sales the Joplin Herald compiles a statement showing that the total product in 1895 was 139,043 short tons of zinc ore. This, however, includes the ore put on the market by the Galena district in southeast Kansas. According to local reports this district has produced during the last six calendar years the following quantities of zinc ore:

Zinc product of the Galena district, Kansas.

Year.	Short tons.	Amount realized.
1890	21,675	$198,525.00
1891	20,641	454,102.00
1892	23,811	476,237.78
1893	25,028	471,789.00
1894	28,670	490,257.00
1895	41,232	812,792.00

In the East the only development of interest is the erection of a plant at Sterling, N. J., for concentrating the ores of the famous Franklin mines with the Wetherill magnetic separators. This will make available for spelter production a large amount of ore available hitherto only for producing zinc white, and is likely to lead to some expansion in the output of high-grade spelter.

IMPORTS AND EXPORTS.

Zinc imported and entered for consumption in the United States, 1867 to 1895, inclusive.

Year ending—	Blocks or pigs.		Sheets.	
	Quantity.	Value.	Quantity.	Value.
	Pounds.		*Pounds.*	
June 30, 1867	5,752,611	$256,366	5,142,417	$311,767
1868	9,327,968	417,273	3,557,448	203,883
1869	13,211,575	590,332	8,306,723	478,646
1870	9,221,121	415,497	9,542,687	509,860
1871	11,159,040	508,355	7,646,821	409,243
1872	11,802,247	522,524	10,704,944	593,885
1873	6,839,897	331,399	11,122,143	715,706
1874	3,593,570	203,479	6,016,835	424,504
1875	2,034,252	101,766	7,320,713	444,539
1876	947,322	56,082	4,611,360	298,308
1877	1,266,894	63,250	1,311,333	81,815
1878	1,270,184	57,753	1,255,620	69,381
1879	1,419,791	53,294	1,111,225	53,050
1880	8,092,620	371,920	4,069,310	210,230
1881	2,859,216	125,457	2,727,324	129,158
1882	18,408,391	736,964	4,413,042	207,032
1883	17,067,211	655,503	3,309,239	141,823
1884	5,869,738	208,852	952,253	36,120
1885	3,515,840	113,268	1,839,860	64,781

*Zinc imported and entered for consumption in the United States, etc.—*Continued.

Year ending—	Blocks or pigs.		Sheets.	
	Quantity.	Value.	Quantity.	Value.
	Pounds.		*Pounds.*	
Dec. 31, 1886.........	4, 300, 830	$136, 138	1, 092, 400	$40, 320
1887.........	8, 387, 647	276, 122	926, 150	32, 526
1888.........	3, 825, 947	146, 156	295, 287	12, 558
1889.........	2, 052, 559	77, 845	1, 014, 873	43, 356
1890.........	1, 997, 524	101, 335	781, 366	43, 495
1891.........	808, 094	41, 199	21, 948	1, 460
1892.........	297, 969	16, 520	27, 272	2, 216
1893.........	425, 183	22, 790	28, 913	1, 985
1894.........	387, 788	13, 788	39, 947	2, 061
1895.........	744, 301	26, 782	42, 513	2, 773

Year ending—	Old.		Value of manufactures.	Total value.
	Quantity.	Value.		
	Pounds.			
June 30, 1867	....	....	$1, 835	$569, 968
1868	....	....	1, 623	622, 779
1869	....	....	2, 083	1, 071, 061
1870	....	....	21, 696	947, 053
1871	....	....	26, 366	943, 964
1872	....	....	58, 668	1, 175, 077
1873	....	....	56, 813	1, 103, 918
1874	....	....	48, 304	676, 287
1875	....	....	26, 330	572, 635
1876	....	....	18, 427	372, 817
1877	....	....	2, 496	147, 561
1878	....	....	4, 892	132, 026
1879	....	....	3, 374	109, 718
1880	....	....	3, 571	585, 721
1881	....	....	7, 603	262, 218
1882	....	....	4, 940	948, 936
1883	....	....	5, 606	802, 932
1884	....	....	4, 795	249, 767
1885	....	....	2, 054	180, 103
Dec. 31, 1886	....	....	9, 162	185, 620
1887	....	....	11, 329	319, 977
1888	....	....	12, 080	170, 794
1889	....	....	19, 580	140, 781
1890	....	....	9, 740	154, 570
1891	....	....	....	42, 659
1892	115, 293	$6, 556	20, 677	45, 969
1893	265	21	16, 479	41, 275
1894	27, 754	530	11, 816	28, 195
1895	61, 398	899	9, 953	40, 407

Imports of zinc oxide from 1885 to 1895, inclusive.

Year ending—	Dry.	In oil.	Year ending—	Dry.	In oil.
	Pounds.	*Pounds.*		*Pounds.*	*Pounds.*
June 30, 1885..	2,233,128	98,566	Dec. 31, 1891..	2,839,351	128,140
Dec. 31, 1886..	3,526,289	79,788	1892..	2,442,014	111,190
1887..	4,961,080	123,216	1893..	3,900,749	254,807
1888..	1,401,312	51,985	1894..	3,371,292	59,291
1889..	2,686,861	66,240	1895..	4,546,019	129,343
1890..	2,631,458	102,298			

Exports of zinc and zinc ore of domestic production, 1864 to 1895, inclusive.

Year ending—	Ore or oxide.		Plates, sheets, pigs, or bars.		Value of manufactures.	Total value.
	Quantity.	Value.	Quantity.	Value.		
	Cwt.		*Pounds.*			
June 30, 1864..	14,810	$116,431	95,738	$12,269	....	$128,700
1865..	99,371	114,149	184,183	22,740	....	136,889
1866..	4,485	25,091	140,798	13,290	....	38,381
1867..	3,676	32,041	312,227	30,587	....	62,628
1868..	8,344	74,706	1,022,699	68,214	....	142,920
1869..	....	65,411	....	....	....	65,411
1870..	15,286	81,487	110,157	10,672	....	92,159
1871..	9,621	48,292	76,380	7,823	....	56,115
1872..	3,686	20,880	62,919	5,726	....	26,606
1873..	234	2,304	73,953	4,656	....	6,960
1874..	2,550	20,037	43,566	3,612	....	23,649
1875..	3,083	20,659	38,090	4,245	$1,000	25,904
1876..	10,178	66,259	134,542	11,651	4,333	82,243
1877..	6,428	34,468	1,419,922	115,122	1,118	150,708
1878..	16,050	83,831	2,545,320	216,580	567	300,978
1879..	10,660	40,399	2,132,919	170,654	....	211,053
1880..	13,024	42,036	1,368,302	119,264	....	161,300
1881..	11,390	16,405	1,491,786	132,805	168	149,378
1882..	10,904	13,736	1,489,552	124,638	....	138,374
1883..	3,045	11,509	852,333	70,981	734	83,224
1884..	4,780	16,685	126,043	9,576	4,666	30,927
1885..	6,840	22,824	101,685	7,270	4,991	35,085
Dec. 31, 1886..	26,620	49,455	917,229	75,192	13,526	138,173
1887..	4,700	17,286	136,670	9,017	16,789	43,092
1888..	4,560	18,034	62,234	4,270	19,098	41,402
1889..	26,760	73,802	879,785	44,049	35,732	153,583
1890..	77,360	195,113	3,295,584	126,291	23,587	344,991
1891..	115,820	149,435	4,294,656	278,182	38,921	466,538
1892..	18,380	41,186	12,494,335	669,549	166,794	877,529
1893..	980	1,271	7,446,934	413,673	224,787	639,731
1894..	5	5	3,607,050	144,074	99,406	243,485
1895..	480	1,008	3,060,805	153,175	50,051	204,234

PRICES.

The market for spelter dragged along with a weakening tendency during the first ten months of 1895, declining from 3.35 cents at New York early in January to 3.10 cents in February. Then the market hardened and held its own steadily during March and April. May brought a quickening demand, both at home and abroad, and there was a rapid advance, which established a price of 3¾ cents early in June, followed by a slight reaction. July developed more firmness, and then followed the excitement incident to the consolidation of the works in Kansas and Missouri, already alluded to. The price was advanced to 4.35 cents at New York in September, but when the tide of heavy consumption in the whole metal trades receded, in October and November, the price declined steadily, until 3.40 to 3.50 cents was reached in December.

The following table summarizes the prices of spelter since 1875:

Prices of common Western spelter in New York City, 1875 to 1895, inclusive.

[Cents per pound; figures in parentheses are combination prices.]

Year.	January.		February.		March.		April.	
	Highest.	Lowest.	Highest.	Lowest.	Highest.	Lowest.	Highest.	Lowest.
1875	6.75	6.37	6.67	6.25	6.50	6.20	(7)	6.50
1876	(7.60)	7.40	(7.75)	7.50	(7.75)	7.62	(8)	7.60
1877	6.50	6.25	6.62	6.50	6.50	6.37	6.37	6.25
1878	5.75	5.50	5.62	5.25	5.62	5.25	5.25	5
1879	4.50	4.25	4.62	4.40	4.62	4.37	4.75	4.25
1880	6.50	5.87	6.75	6.37	6.75	6.50	6.50	6.12
1881	5.25	4.87	5.25	5.12	5	4.87	5.12	4.75
1882	6	5.75	5.75	5.62	5.62	5.37	5.50	5.25
1883	4.62	4.50	4.62	4.50	4.75	4.62	4.75	4.60
1884	4.37	4.20	4.40	4.25	4.60	4.40	4.65	4.50
1885	4.50	4.12	4.30	4.25	4.30	4.12	4.30	4.12
1886	4.50	4.30	4.55	4.30	4.60	4.50	4.60	4.50
1887	4.60	4.50	4.60	4.40	4.60	4.40	4.65	4.45
1888	5.37	5.20	5.35	5.25	5.25	4.87	4.87	4.60
1889	5	5	5	4.90	4.87	4.70	4.65	4.65
1890	5.45	5.35	5.35	4.20	5.20	5	5	4.90
1891	6	5.25	5.25	5	5.10	5	5.10	4.90
1892	4.70	4.60	4.60	4.55	4.60	4.50	4.80	4.60
1893	4.35	4.30	4.30	4.25	4.25	4.20	4.50	4.30
1894	3.60	3.50	4	3.60	3.85	3.80	3.75	3.50
1895	3.35	3.20	3.20	3.10	3.20	3.15	3.30	3.25

*Prices of common Western spelter in New York City, 1875 to 1895, inclusive—*Continued.

[Cents per pound; figures in parentheses are combination prices.]

Year.	May. Highest.	Lowest.	June. Highest.	Lowest.	July. Highest.	Lowest.	August. Highest.	Lowest.
1875	(7.25)	7.15	(7.25)	7.15	(7.35)	7.25	(7.25)	7.10
1876	(8)	7.75	(8)	7.25	7.25	7.12	7.25	7
1877	6.25	6	6.12	5.87	5.87	5.62	5.90	5.80
1878	5	4.62	4.62	4.25	4.75	4.50	4.87	4.50
1879	4.50	4.25	4.37	4.12	4.75	4.37	5.62	4.80
1880	6	5.62	5.50	5.12	5	4.87	5.25	4.87
1881	5	4.87	5	4.75	5	4.75	5.12	5
1882	5.62	5.25	5.37	5.25	5.37	5.12	5.50	5.12
1883	4.75	4.50	4.62	4.37	4.50	4.30	4.40	4.30
1884	4.60	4.45	4.60	4.45	4.55	4.45	4.62	4.52
1885	4.25	4.10	4.10	4	4.40	4.10	4.60	4.40
1886	4.60	4.40	4.40	4.35	4.40	4.30	4.40	4.30
1887	4.65	4.45	4.65	4.50	4.50	4.50	4.60	4.55
1888	4.65	4.60	4.60	4.50	4.55	4.50	4.87	4.50
1889	4.85	4.62	5	5	5.10	5	5.20	5.15
1890	5.45	5	5.60	5.35	5.60	5.40	5.55	5.40
1891	4.90	4.85	5.10	4.90	5.10	5.05	5.10	5
1892	4.90	4.80	4.90	4.80	4.85	4.70	4.70	4.65
1893	4.40	4.20	4.25	4.15	4.15	3.90	3.90	3.55
1894	3.55	3.45	3.50	3.40	3.50	3.45	3.45	3.40
1895	3.65	3.30	3.75	3.30	3.85	3.70	4.20	4

Year.	September. Highest.	Lowest.	October. Highest.	Lowest.	November. Highest.	Lowest.	December. Highest.	Lowest.
1875	(7.25)	7.10	(7.40)	7.15	(7.40)	7.15	(7.40)	7.15
1876	7.12	6.80	6.75	6.62	6.62	6.37	6.50	6.37
1877	5.87	5.75	5.90	5.70	5.87	5.62	5.75	5.50
1878	4.87	4.75	4.82	4.50	4.75	4.50	4.37	4.25
1879	6	5.62	6.37	6	6.25	5.87	6.25	6
1880	5.12	4.75	5	4.87	4.90	4.65	4.75	4.65
1881	5.25	5	5.37	5.25	5.87	5.50	6	5.87
1882	5.37	5.12	5.37	5.12	5.12	4.87	4.87	4.50
1883	4.50	4.40	4.45	4.35	4.40	4.37	4.37	4.35
1884	4.62	4.50	4.55	4.40	4.40	4.30	4.25	4
1885	4.62	4.50	4.62	4.50	4.60	4.45	4.60	4.45
1886	4.40	4.25	4.30	4.25	4.30	4.25	4.50	4.35
1887	4.65	4.60	4.65	4.50	4.80	4.52	5.87	5
1888	5.12	4.75	5.12	4.87	5.12	4.87	5.12	4.87

Prices of common *Western spelter* in *New York City, 1875 to 1895, inclusive*—Continued.

[Cents per pound; figures in parentheses are combination prices.]

Year.	September.		October.		November.		December.	
	Highest.	Lowest.	Highest.	Lowest.	Highest.	Lowest.	Highest.	Lowest.
1889............	5.15	5.10	5.15	5.10	5.25	5.05	5.35	5.30
1890............	5.65	5.50	6	5.65	6.10	5.90	6	5.90
1891............	5	4.85	5.15	4.95	4.90	4.75	4.75	4.65
1892............	4.65	4.50	4.50	4.35	4.40	4.35	4.40	4.35
1893............	3.75	3.65	3.70	3.55	3.85	3.60	3.80	3.70
1894............	3.50	3.40	3.50	3.37	3.40	3.35	3.35	3.25
1895............	4.35	4.15	4.20	3.90	3.80	3.45	3.50	3.40

FOREIGN SPELTER PRODUCTION.

EUROPE.

Messrs. Henry R. Merton & Co., of London, make the following report on the spelter production of Europe:

Estimate of the production of zinc in Europe.

[Long tons.]

Country.	1895.	1894.	1893.	1892.	1891.	1890.	1889.
Rhine district and Belgium...............	172,135	152,420	149,750	143,305	139,695	137,630	134,648
Silesia	93,620	91,145	90,310	87,760	87,080	87,475	85,653
Great Britain.........	29,495	32,065	28,375	30,310	29,410	29,145	30,806
France and Spain.....	22,895	21,245	20,585	18,662	18,360	18,240	16,785
Austria	8,355	8,580	7,560	5,020	6,440	7,135	6,330
Poland...............	4,960	5,015	4,530	4,270	3,760	3,620	3,026
Total	331,460	310,470	301,110	289,327	284,745	283,215	277,248

Country.	1888.	1887.	1886.	1885.	1884.	1883.	1882.
Rhine district and Belgium...............	133,245	130,995	129,020	129,754	129,240	123,891	119,193
Silesia	83,375	81,375	81,630	79,623	76,116	70,405	68,811
Great Britain.........	26,783	19,839	21,230	24,299	29,259	29,161	26,081
France and Spain.....	16,140	16,028	15,305	14,817	15,311	14,671	18,075
Austria	4,977	5,338	5,000	5,610	6,170	6,267	6,709
Poland..............	3,785	3,580	4,145	5,019	4,161	3,733	4,400
Total	268,305	257,155	256,330	259,152	260,290	248,128	243,269

The output of the works in the different districts was as follows:

Production of zinc by principal foreign producers.

[Long tons.]

District.	1895.	1894.	1893.	1892.
Rhine district and Belgium:				
Vieille Montagne	63,545	54,0.0	54,305	53,770
Stolberg Co	16,385	15,170	15,135	14,950
Austro-Belge	9,855	9,595	9,855	9,720
G. Dumont & Frères..........	10,080	9,415	8,680	8,675
Rhein-Nassau Co	9,085	8,165	8,205	8,040
L. de Laminne.................	6,440	6,930	6,920	6,845
Escombrera Bleyberg.........	5,690	5,750	5,775	6,070
Grillo	6,195	5,615	5,625	5,550
Märk, Westf., Bergw., Ver.....	6,155	5,620	5,620	5,540
Nouvelle Montagne	6,815	5,290	5,290	5,240
Berzelius.....................	5,535	5,350	5,345	5,290
Eschger Ghesquiere & Co.....	4,205	4,375	4,370	4,100
Société Prayou	7,330	4,110	4,250	4,085
Société de Boom..............	7,155	7,065	7,110	5,430
Zinkmaatshappy in Limburg .	....	a 700	a 2,000	....
Société Campine.............	4,200	a 2,810	a 700	....
Schulte & Co..................	3,465	2,430	565	....
Total	172,135	152,420	149,750	143,305
Silesia:				
Schlesische Actien-Gesell-schaft.....................	25,950	25,230	25,255	24,915
G. von Giesche's Erben........	19,860	19,385	18,920	18,295
Herzog von Ujest.............	21,140	17,265	17,210	17,085
Graf H. Henckel von Don-nersmarck..................	11,680	12,005	11,695	11,115
Graefin Schaffgotsch..........	3,570	6,940	6,885	6,070
Graf G. Henckel von Don-nersmarck..................	4,400	4,185	4,215	4,070
H. Roth	3,320	1,805	1,775	1,845
Wünsch	2,155	1,980	2,075	2,120
Vereinigte Königs & Laura-hütte	1,400	1,270	1,170	1,230
Baron v. Horschitz'sche Erben.	....	935	960	875
Fiscus.......................	145	145	150	140
Total.......................	93,620	91,145	90,310	87,760

a Estimated.

Production of zinc by principal foreign producers—Continued.

[Long tons.]

District.	1895.	1894.	1893.	1892.
Great Britain:				
Vivian & Sons	6,970	8,005	7,060	7,791
English Crown Spelter Co., Limited	5,700	5,515	5,380	5,527
Dillwyn & Co	4,935	4,870	3,450	3,759
Swansea Vale Spelter Co	2,375	2,380	2,105	2,063
Villiers Spelter Co	2,155	2,300	2,050	1,920
Pascoe, Grenfell & Sons	1,680	1,455	1,260	1,080
Nenthead & Tynedale Co	1,775	1,870	1,855	1,600
John Lysaght, Limited	1,805	2,915	2,760	3,000
Staffordshire Knot	....	....	....	....
Minera Mines	....	....	....	1,350
H. Kenyon & Co	500	505	500	500
Leeswood Co	a 1,600	1,750	1,495	1,720
Dynevor Co. and sundries	....	500	460	....
Total	29,495	32,065	28,375	30,310
France and Spain:				
Asturienne	17,915	18,695	18,695	18,462
St. Amand	2,520	2,550	1,890	200
Malfidano	2,460	....	....	....
Total	22,895	21,245	20,585	18,662
Austria:				
Sagór	1,080	1,225	1,360	1,475
Cilli	1,990	2,580	2,510	1,710
Siersza-Niedzieliska	4,300	4,420	3,690	3,550
Merklin	985	355	....	....
Total	8,355	8,580	7,560	6,735
Poland	4,960	5,015	4,530	4,270

District.	1891.	1890.	1889.	1888.
Rhine district and Belgium				
Vieille Montague	53,820	52,865	52,016	51,670
Stolberg Co	15,040	14,855	14,634	14,036
Austro-Belge	9,425	9,250	9,245	9,140
G. Dumont & Frères	8,370	8,350	8,863	8,759
Rhein-Nassau Co	8,075	7,960	7,470	7,586
L. de Laminue	6,810	6,760	6,693	6,597

a Estimated.

Production of zinc by principal foreign producers—Continued.

[Long tons.]

District.	1891.	1890.	1889.	1888.
Rhine district and Belgium—C't'd.				
Escombrera Bleyberg.........	5,770	5,630	5,560	4,930
Grillo......................	5,390	5,490	5,353	5,299
Märk, Westf., Bergw., Ver	5,600	5,485	5,805	5,537
Nouvelle Montagne...........	5,550	5,350	5,090	5,032
Berzelius...................	5,155	5,175	4,910	4,818
Eschger Ghesquiere & Co.....	3,810	4,065	4,303	4,137
Société Prayon	4,130	4,100	3,956	3,906
Société de Boom.............	2,720	2,295	a 750	1,798
Zinkmaatshappy in Limburg..	....	....	....	....
Société Campine.............	....	....	....	....
Schulte & Co................	....	....	....	....
Total	139,695	137,630	134,648	133,245
Silesia:				
Schlesische Actien-Gesell- schaft....................	25,245	24,840	23,675	22,917
G. von Giesche's Erben.......	18,700	18,550	18,206	17,594
Herzog von Ujest............	16,795	16,355	16,202	15,456
Graf H. Henckel von Don- nersmarck..................	11,230	11,670	11,392	11,193
Graefin Schaffgotsch..........	5,310	6,265	6,405	6,402
Graf G. Henckel von Don- nersmarck..................	3,905	4,090	3,943	4,114
H. Roth....................	1,730	1,750	1,660	1,555
Wünsch	1,920	1,880	1,907	1,906
Vereinigte Königs & Laura- hütte	1,180	1,020	1,130	1,166
Baron v. Horschitz'sche Erben.	850	830	963	935
Fiscus	215	225	170	137
Total	87,080	87,475	85,653	83,375
Great Britain:				
Vivian & Sons..............	7,235	6,605	6,842	6,510
English Crown Spelter Co., Limited	5,180	4,945	4,981	4,980
Dillwyn & Co	3,580	3,930	4,540	3,904
Swansea Vale Spelter Co......	1,840	1,615	2,161	2,150
Villiers Spelter Co...........	2,125	1,890	2,180	1,993
Pascoe Grenfell & Sons	1,060	1,160	1,272	1,330
Nenthead & Tynedale Co.....	1,440	1,530	1,507	1,516
John Lysaght, Limited.......	4,185	4,450	5,113	3,750

a Estimated.

Production of zinc by principal foreign producers—Continued.

[Long tons.]

District.	1891.	1890.	1889.	1888.
Great Britain—Continued.				
Staffordshire Knot............	....	350	1,100	150
Minera Mines.................	2,265	2,170	610	....
H. Kenyon & Co..............	500	500	500	500
Leeswood Co.................	....	....	....	....
Dynevor Co. and sundries.....	....	....	....	....
Total	29,410	29,145	30,806	26,783
France and Spain:				
Asturienne	18,360	18,240	16,785	16,140
St. Amand..................	....	....	....	....
Malfidano	....	....	....	....
Total.....................	18,360	18,240	16,785	16,140
Austria:				
Sagor	1,280	1,430	1,210	1,087
Cilli......................	1,810	1,880	1,670	1,240
Siersza-Niedzieliska	3,350	3,825	3,450	2,650
Merklin	....	....	....	....
Total.....................	6,440	7,135	6,330	4,977
Poland......................	3,760	3,620	3,026	a 3,785

a Estimated.

Production of zinc mines of Silesia.

Year.	Calamine.	Blende.	Total.
	Metric tons.	Metric tons.	Metric tons.
1888	319,316	212,264	531,580
1889	325,705	246,955	572,660
1890	368,495	261,921	630,416
1891	391,891	271,277	663,168
1892	358,230	291,617	649,817
1893	348,654	287,375	636,029
1894	....	....	571,335
1895	273,151	267,673	540,824

The number of persons employed in the mines and dressing works in Silesia was 10,039, of whom 7,703 were men and 2,336 women, the latter employed above ground. The average annual wages for men were 654.81 marks, or $160; and for women 184.04 marks, or $45. The total wages were 5,480,463 marks. The average value of the calamine was 5.35 marks and of the blende 17.08 marks per metric ton.

The production of zinc in Silesia was 92,546 metric tons in 1894 and 95,430 tons in 1895.

Official statistics published in the Annales des Mines furnish the following statement relative to the production, exports, and imports of zinc ore for France:

Production, exports, and imports of zinc ore in France, 1880 to 1894, inclusive.

Year.	Production.	Exports.	Imports.
	Metric tons.	*Metric tons.*	*Metric tons.*
1880	12,139	2,394	38,299
1881	12,943	2,683	32,288
1882	8,372	5,419	33,332
1883	5,491	6,721	36,882
1884	3,120	4,587	30,993
1885	5,078	4,807	38,730
1886	11,103	7,961	32,560
1887	13,321	10,586	31,623
1888	20,702	14,492	32,556
1889	34,290	20,468	35,582
1890	47,540	24,050	39,473
1891	55,785	31,662	36,737
1892	67,069	32,023	41,931
1893	74,398	47,426	34,221
1894	76,949	58,281	34,955

The statistics of spelter, including production, exports, imports, and apparent home consumption, were as follows:

French statistics of spelter.

Year	Production.	Exports.	Imports.	Home consumption.
	Metric tons.	*Metric tons.*	*Metric tons.*	*Metric tons.*
1880	16,232	4,754	31,245	42,723
1881	18,509	5,595	43,359	56,273
1882	18,525	4,551	34,167	48,141
1883	15,915	3,578	39,398	51,735
1884	16,884	3,023	39,740	53,601
1885	15,108	3,237	33,214	45,085
1886	16,132	2,566	33,547	47,113
1887	16,712	4,905	35,527	47,334
1888	16,960	5,146	27,643	39,457
1889	17,982	5,606	27,786	40,162
1890	19,372	5,156	29,356	43,572
1891	20,596	5,177	31,604	47,023
1892	20,609	7,034	30,862	44,437
1893	22,419	8,819	35,200	48,800
1894	23,387	7,282	35,368	51,473

On the whole the foreign producers have been quite prosperous. The Stolberg Company, which is also a large producer of lead, made a gross profit in 1895 of 1,978,111 marks, paying 7 per cent on its preferred and 2 per cent on its common stock. The Rheinisch Nassau B. & H. A. G. wound up the year with a profit of 99,208 marks in 1895, as against 80,054 marks in 1894, and paid a dividend of 1 per cent. The Berzelius Company made net 206,662 marks in 1895, as compared with 159,934 marks in 1894. The Schlesische Zink-Hütten-Gesellschaft made a gross profit of 3,626,526 marks and a net profit of 3,312,294 marks in 1895.

The annual report of the Vieille Montagne Company shows a notable increase in the production. In 1895 the output was 64,497 metric tons of crude zinc, as compared with 54,839 metric tons in 1894. The average price dropped from 374.42 francs per metric ton in 1894 to 353.26 francs in 1895. In 1893 it was 422.30 francs. The company produced 57,000 tons of sheet zinc in 1895, as compared with 54,515 tons in 1894. The output of zinc white was 8,988 tons and 7,669 tons, respectively. The decline in prices during recent years is due to the collapse of the syndicate. The president of the company, M. Saint-Paul de Sinçay, states that overtures have been made during 1895 looking toward a reestablishment of the international syndicate, but have not led to any result. The Vieille Montagne Company during 1895 acquired from the Nenthead and Tyndale Company the right to work the zinc mines at Alston, Cumberland, England. The gross profit in 1895 was 4,556,482.73 francs, as compared with 4,859,718.37 francs in 1894. There was written off for general expenses, interest, exchange, discounts, etc., 593,622.10 francs, leaving a net profit for 1895 of 3,962,860.63 francs, as compared with 4,194,453.50 francs in 1894. There was written off 846.973.13 francs on mining and furnace property; for reserve according to law, 533,177.50 francs; 10 per cent to the administration, 266,588.75 francs, and 2½ per cent to the management, 66,647.18 francs, leaving available for dividends paid 2,250,000 francs, and practically the same balance.

The Prayon Company made a gross profit of 120,219.32 francs during 1895, out of which there were paid 95,000 francs in dividends. An issue of 2,000 shares at 300 francs par was made to cover the cost of enlarging the works, the net premium of 87,000 francs which was received going to reserve account.

The Asturienne Company, which mines zinc ore in Spain and produced 18,181 metric tons of spelter in Spain and France in 1895, had a profit in that year of 2,713,830 francs. The company has quick assets of 20,203,439 francs, its plant standing on the books at the nominal sum of 10 francs.

QUICKSILVER.

PRODUCT.

After being stationary at 30,000 flasks for two years, the product advanced to 36,067 flasks (of 76½ pounds each), the largest output for twelve years. Better prices offered the chief incentive to production, and there seemed to be little difficulty in marketing the supply.

No effort was made to develop the deposit in Texas, which was referred to in the last report, and, as usual, the product came from California. The Altoona mine, in Trinity County, excited interest by its increased output, due to a richer strike as the mine was deepened.

The usual statistical tables follow.

Total product of quicksilver in the United States.

[Flasks of 76½ pounds, net.]

Year.	New Almaden.	New Idria.	Redington.	Sulphur Bank.	Great Western.	Napa Consolidated.
1850........	7,723					
1851........	27,779					
1852........	15,901					
1853........	22,284					
1854........	30,004					
1855........	29,142					
1856........	27,138					
1857........	28,204					
1858........	25,761					
1859........	1,294					
1860........	7,061					
1861........	34,429					
1862........	39,671		444			
1863........	32,803		852			
1864........	42,489		1,914			
1865........	47,194	(a)	3,545			
1866........	35,150	6,525	2,254			
1867........	24,461	11,493	7,862			
1868........	25,628	12,180	8,686			
1869........	16,898	10,315	5,018			

a Production from 1858 to 1866 was 17,455 flasks; no yearly details obtainable. they are in the product of ''various mines.''

Total product of quicksilver in the United States—Continued.

[Flasks of 76½ pounds, net.]

Year.	New Almaden.	New Idria.	Redington.	Sulphur Bank.	Great Western.	Napa Consolidated.
1870........	14,423	9,888	4,546	....	....	....
1871........	18,568	8,180	2,128	....	....	....
1872........	18,574	8,171	3,046	....	....	....
1873........	11,042	7,735	3,294	....	310	....
1874........	9,084	6,911	6,678	573	1,122	....
1875........	13,648	8,432	7,513	5,372	3,384	....
1876........	20,549	7,272	9,183	8,367	4,322	573
1877........	23,996	6,316	9,399	10,993	5,856	2,229
1878........	15,852	5,138	6,686	9,465	4,963	3,049
1879........	20,514	4,425	4,516	9,249	6,333	3,605
1880........	23,465	3,209	2,139	10,706	6,442	4,416
1881........	26,060	2,775	2,194	11,152	6,241	5,552
1882........	28,070	1,953	2,171	5,014	5,179	6,842
1883........	29,000	1,606	1,894	2,612	3,869	5,890
1884........	20,000	1,025	881	890	3,292	4,307
1885........	21,400	1,144	385	1,296	3,469	3,506
1886........	18,000	1,406	409	1,449	1,949	5,247
1887........	20,000	1,890	673	1,490	1,446	5,574
1888........	18,000	1,320	126	2,164	625	5,024
1889........	13,100	980	812	2,283	556	4,590
1890........	12,000	977	505	1,608	1,334	3,429
1891........	8,200	792	442	1,375	1,844	4,454
1892........	5,563	848	728	1,393	5,867	5,680
1893........	6,614	869	1,012	1,200	3,187	6,120
1894........	7,235	1,005	1,200	348	5,341	4,930
1895........	7,050	1,100	163	2,703	5,023	5,400
Total ..	951,021	135,880	103,298	91,702	81,984	90,417

Year.	Great Eastern.	Mirabel.	Ætna.	Altoona.	Abbott.	Various mines.	Total yearly production of California mines.
1850......						....	7,723
1851......						....	27,779
1852......						4,099	20,000
1853......						....	22,284
1854......						....	30,004
1855......						3,858	33,000
1856......						2,862	30,000
1857......						....	28,204
1858......						5,239	31,000

Total product of quicksilver in the United States—Continued.

[Flasks of 76½ pounds, net.]

Year.	Great Eastern.	Mirabel.	Ætna.	Altoona.	Abbott.	Various mines.	Total yearly production of California mines.
1859........						11,706	13,000
1860........						2,939	10,000
1861........						571	35,000
1862........						1,885	42,000
1863........						6,876	40,531
1864........						3,086	47,489
1865........						2,261	53,000
1866........						2,621	46,550
1867........						3,184	47,000
1868........						1,234	47,728
1869........						1,580	33,811
1870........						1,220	30,077
1871........						2,810	31,686
1872........						1,830	31,621
1873........						5,231	27,642
1874........						3,388	27,756
1875........	412					11,489	50,250
1876........	387					22,063	72,716
1877........	565					20,101	79,395
1878........	1,366					17,361	63,880
1879........	1,455					23,587	73,684
1880........	1,279					8,270	59,926
1881........	1,065					5,812	60,851
1882........	2,124					1,379	52,732
1883........	1,669					185	46,725
1884........	332					1,186	31,913
1885........	446					427	32,073
1886........	735					786	29,981
1887........	689	1,543				520	a 33,825
1888........	1,151	3,848				992	33,250
1889........	1,345	1,874				924	26,464
1890........	1,046	1,290				737	22,926
1891........	1,660	1,686				2,451	22,901
1892........	1,630	3,208	1,592	....	672	812	27,993
1893........	1,445	5,211	3,795	....	133	578	30,161
1894........	1,368	4,214	3,575	....	1,200	....	30,416
1895........	1,813	3,900	3,300	3,926	1,223	466	36,067
Total ..	23,922	26,774	12,262	3,926	3,228	188,606	1,713,020

a Includes 65 flasks from Oregon.

PRICES.

Highest and lowest prices of quicksilver in 1895.

[Per flask.]

Month.	Price in San Francisco.		Price in London.					
	Highest.	Lowest.	Highest.			Lowest.		
			s.	*s.*	*d.*	*s.*	*s.*	*d.*
January	$37.00	$36.00	6	12	6	6	12	6
February	37.00	35.90	6	12	6	6	10	0
March	37.00	36.00	6	10	0	6	10	0
April	38.50	36.50	7	0	0	6	10	0
May	41.00	38.50	7	10	0	7	0	0
June	41.00	41.00	7	10	0	7	10	0
July	41.00	39.50	7	10 · 0		7	5	0
August	41.00	39.50	7	5	0	7	5	0
September	41.00	37.00	7	5	0	7	5	0
October	41.00	38.00	7	7	6	7	0	0
November	40.00	39.00	7	7	6	7	7	6
December	40.00	39.00	7	7	6	7	7	6
Extreme range	41.00	35.90	7	10	0	6	10	0

Highest and lowest prices of quicksilver during the past forty-six years.

[Per flask.]

Year.	Price in San Francisco.		Price in London.					
	Highest.	Lowest.	Highest.			Lowest.		
			£.	*s.*	*d.*	£.	*s.*	*d.*
1850	$114.75	$84.15	15	0	0	13	2	6
1851	76.50	57.35	13	15	0	12	5	0
1852	61.20	55.45	11	10	0	9	7	6
1853	55.45	55.45	8	15	0	8	2	6
1854	55.45	55.45	7	15	0	7	5	0
1855	55.45	51.65	6	17	6	6	10	0
1856	51.65	51.65	6	10	0	6	10	0
1857	53.55	45.90	6	10	0	6	10	0
1858	49.75	45.90	7	10	0	7	5	0
1859	76.50	49.75	7	5	0	7	0	0
1860	57.35	49.75	7	0	0	7	0	0
1861	49.75	34.45	7	0	0	7	0	0
1862	38.25	34.45	7	0	0	7	0	0
1863	45.90	38.25	7	0	0	7	0	0

Highest and lowest prices of quicksilver during the past forty-six years—Continued.

[Per flask.]

Year.	Price in San Francisco.		Price in London.					
	Highest	Lowest.	Highest.			Lowest.		
			£	s.	d.	£	s.	d.
1864	45.90	45.90	9	0	0	7	10	0
1865	45.90	45.90	8	0	0	7	17	6
1866	57.35	45.90	8	0	0	6	17	0
1867	45.90	45.90	7	0	0	6	16	0
1868	45.90	45.90	6	17	0	6	16	0
1869	45.90	45.90	6	17	0	6	16	0
1870	68.85	45.90	10	0	0	6	16	0
1871	68.85	57.35	12	0	0	9	0	0
1872	66.95	65.00	13	0	0	10	0	0
1873	91.80	68.85	20	0	0	12	10	0
1874	118.55	91.80	26	0	0	19	0	0
1875	118.55	49.75	24	0	0	9	17	6
1876	53.55	34.45	12	0	0	7	17	6
1877	44.00	30.60	9	10	0	7	2	6
1878	35.95	29.85	7	5	0	6	7	6
1879	34.45	25.25	8	15	0	5	17	6
1880	34.45	27.55	7	15	0	6	7	6
1881	31.75	27.90	7	0	0	6	2	6
1882	29.10	27.35	6	5	0	5	15	0
1883	28.50	26.00	5	17	6	5	5	0
1884	35.00	26.00	6	15	0	5	2	6
1885	33.00	28.50	6	15	0	5	10	0
1886	39.00	32.00	7	10	0	5	16	3
1887	50.00	36.50	11	5	0	6	7	6
1888	47.00	36.00	10	0	0	6	12	6
1889	50.00	40.00	9	15	0	7	10	0
1890	58.00	47.00	10	10	0	9	1	0
1891	51.00	39.50	8	12	6	7	5	0
1892	47.50	41.50	7	10	0	6	2	6
1893	43.50	30.00	6	17	6	6	2	0
1894	37.00	28.50	6	15	0	5	7	6
1895	41.00	35.90	7	10	0	6	10	0
Extreme range	118.55	25.25	26	0	0	5	2	6

SHIPMENTS.

Quicksilver shipments in 1894 and 1895.

By sea to—	1894.	1895.
	Flasks.	Flasks.
New York	10,300	14,000
Mexico	4,060	3,919
China	2,000	
Australia		50
Central America	800	310
Canada	200	
New Zealand		
British Columbia	4	10
Japan	5	
Total by sea	17,369	18,289
Total by rail	a 7,881	a 8,703
Total shipments	25,250	26,992

a To Mexico.

IMPORTS.

In the following table is given a statement of the imports of quicksilver from 1867 to 1895:

Quicksilver imported and entered for consumption in the United States, 1867 to 1895, inclusive.

Year ending—	Quantity.	Value.	Year ending—	Quantity.	Value.
	Pounds.			Pounds.	
June 30, 1867		$15.248	June 30, 1882	597,898	$233,057
1868	152	68	1883	1,552,738	593,367
1869		11	1884	136,615	44,035
1870	239,223	107,646	1885	257,659	90,416
1871	301,965	137,332	Dec. 31, 1886	629,888	249,411
1872	370,353	189,943	1887	419,934	171,431
1873	99,898	74,146	1888	132,850	56,997
1874	51,202	52,093	1889	341,514	162,064
1875	6,870	20,957	1890	802,871	445,807
1876	78,902	50,164	1891	123,966	61,355
1877	38,250	19,558	1892	96,318	40,133
1878	291,207	135,178	1893	41,772	17,400
1879	519,125	217,707	1894	7	6
1880	116,700	48,463	1895	15,001	7,008
1881	138,517	57,733			

MANGANESE.

By Joseph D. Weeks.

[The ton used in this report is the long ton of 2,240 pounds, if not otherwise designated.]

THE ORES OF MANGANESE.

The ores of manganese mined in the United States are, with rare exceptions, oxides. Indeed, as a rule, the commercial ores of this metal are either one or the other of the three well-known oxides, or mixtures of two or more of them. Carbonate of manganese is mined in Merionethshire, Wales, and at Chevron, Belgium, and possibly at one other locality, and carbonate deposits are reported in the United States. Manganese silicates have also been mined, the deposit at Blue-hill, Me., being described as such. The carbonates and silicates, however, are of but little value commercially, the manganese ores that are almost exclusively mined the world over being psilomelane, pyrolusite, braunite, and wad, and these are all oxides, most of them containing more or less water of hydration.

These oxides are rarely found pure, but are usually intimately associated with other metallic oxides, as those of iron and zinc, and with the carbonate ores of silver, so much so that it is difficult at times to decide whether the mineral shall be classed as a manganese ore or as an iron, silver, or zinc ore. This mixture of the ores of other metals with manganese has given rise to the classification of manganese-bearing ores herein noted, i. e., (1) manganese ores; (2) manganiferous iron ores; (3) manganiferous silver ores; (4) manganiferous zinc ores.

The characteristics of these four classes were given in the last report.[1]

MINING LOCALITIES IN THE UNITED STATES.

By far the larger proportion of the manganese ore produced in the United States is mined in three localities, the Valley of Virginia, Cartersville, Ga., and Batesville, Ark. Manganese is found, however, in many places in the United States. Its occurrence is almost coextensive with brown hematite iron ores. It is found all along the western slope of the eastern ridge of the Appalachian Mountains from Maine to Georgia. Considerable manganese ore is found associated with the hematite ores of the Lake Superior region, and in Arkansas, southwest from

[1] Sixteenth Ann. Rept. U. S. Geol. Survey, Part III, p. 390. Washington, 1895.

Batesville. The indications are that there are large deposits in the Rocky Mountain region, and on the California coast very large deposits of manganese ore have been observed. In many cases, however, the ore is so far from railroads and from the points of consumption as to make it impossible to mine it profitably, while in other cases it is too high in phosphorus to make it largely available for steel manufacture.

Outside of the three districts named above, with few exceptions, the deposits are small and the indications not such as to justify the expenditure of large amounts of money in mining and washing plants, which are usually necessary for the economical production of manganese. It is not to be understood that there are no localities outside of those named in which manganese can be profitably mined. The production of manganese ore, however, is one of the most uncertain undertakings in mining. The amount of manganese produced in the country is much smaller than is generally believed; its mining, as a rule, is not profitable, and the risks are very great by reason of the pockety character of the deposits.

The largest proportion of the manganiferous iron ore produced in the United States is from the Lake Superior region, where it is found associated with the iron ores of that section. These, as a rule, carry very low percentages of manganese, and in most cases have but little added value because of their manganese content. In Virginia ore of this character is also mined, though oftentimes in quantities so small as not to justify its separation from the other manganese produced in that State, and therefore the whole product is reported as manganese ore. In Colorado manganiferous iron ore is found associated with or in close proximity to the manganiferous silver ore, which is the chief manganese product of that State. This ore is used chiefly at Pueblo and occasionally at Chicago in the manufacture of spiegeleisen. All of the Colorado ore is from the Leadville district.

Manganiferous silver ores are of quite frequent occurrence in the silver regions of the West, though, as it is usually classed as a silver ore, no attempt is made to ascertain the amount produced except in the Leadville district of Colorado and in Montana. Only small amounts are produced in Montana at present, though the indications justify the belief that manganiferous silver ore will be produced in this State in increasing quantities.

All of the manganiferous zinc ores are from Sussex County, N. J.

PRODUCTION OF MANGANESE ORES.

The production of manganese ores proper in the United States in 1895 shows an increase of some 50 per cent over the production of 1894, the total production in 1895 being 9,547 tons, as compared with 6,308 tons in 1894 and 7,718 tons in 1893. Every State which produced in both 1895 and 1894 shows an increased production in 1895 over that in 1894 except one. The production of Arkansas increased from 1,934 tons in 1894 to 2,991 tons in 1895; California, from 278 tons in 1894 to 525 tons in 1895; Georgia, from 1,277 tons in 1894 to 3,856 tons in 1895. On the other hand, Virginia shows a decline from 1,797 tons in 1894 to 1,715 tons in 1895. Tennessee and West Virginia, which were producers in 1894, produced no manganese in 1895; while Pennsylvania, which did not appear as a producer in 1894, produced 460 tons in 1895.

The total value of the 9,547 tons of manganese ore mined in 1895 was $71,769, or $7.52 a ton, as compared with a total value of $53,635 in 1894, or an average of $8.50 a ton. The average price in 1893 was $8.63 a ton. Thus, while the production and total value in 1895 showed an increase over 1894 and 1893, the average value of the ore per ton in 1895 was less than in either 1894 or 1893.

The amount and value of manganese ores produced in the United States in 1894 and 1895 are shown in the following table:

Amount and value of manganese ores produced in the United States in 1894 and 1895.

State.	1894.			1895.		
	Product.	Total value.	Value per ton.	Product.	Total value.	Value per ton.
	Long tons.			*Long tons.*		
Arkansas.......	1,934	$19,564	$10.13	2,991	$20,997	$7.02
California.....	278	1,800	6.47	525	5,400	10.29
Georgia.......	1,277	8,620	6.74	3,856	27,416	7.11
Tennessee	922	5,993	6.50	0	0	0
Pennsylvania...	0	0	0	460	2,300	5.00
Virginia........	1,797	16,658	9.27	1,715	15,656	9.13
West Virginia.	100	1,000	10.00	0	0	0
Total....	6,308	53,635	a8.50	9,547	71,769	a7.52

a Average.

The following table shows the production of manganese ores in the United States from 1880 to 1895, the output of the three chief producing States being reported separately, while the product of the other States is consolidated:

Production of manganese ores from 1880 to 1895.

Year.	Virginia.	Arkansas.	Georgia.	Other States.	Total.	Total value.
	Long tons.	*Long tons.*	*Long tons.*	*Long tons.*	*Long tons.*	
1880...	3,661	....	1,800	300	5,761	$86,415
1881...	3,295	100	1,200	300	4,895	73,425
1882...	2,982	175	1,000	375	4,532	67,980
1883...	5,355	400	....	400	6,155	92,325

Production of manganese ores from 1880 to 1895—Continued.

Year.	Virginia.	Arkansas.	Georgia.	Other States.	Total.	Total value.
	Long tons.	*Long tons.*	*Long tons.*	*Long tons.*	*Long tons.*	
1884...	8,980	800	....	400	10,180	$122,160
1885...	18,745	1,483	2,580	450	23,258	190,281
1886...	20,567	3,316	6,041	269	30,193	277,636
1887...	19,835	5,651	9,024	14	34,524	333,844
1888...	17,646	4,312	5,568	1,672	29,198	279,571
1889...	14,616	2,528	5,208	1,845	24,197	240,559
1890...	12,699	5,339	749	6,897	25,684	219,050
1891...	16,248	1,650	3,575	1,943	23,416	239,129
1892...	6,079	6,708	826	....	13,613	129,586
1893...	4,092	2,020	724	882	7,718	66,614
1894...	1,797	1,934	1,277	1,300	6,308	53,635
1895...	1,715	2,991	3,856	985	9,547	71,769
Total.	158,312	39,407	43,428	18,032	259,179	2,543,979

No words can show better than this table the uncertainty of the production of manganese ores. In 1887, nine years ago, the total production of manganese in the United States was 34,524 tons. In 1895 it had fallen to 9,547 tons. The total value of the production in 1887 was $333,844, as compared with $71,769 in 1895. The production of Virginia alone in 1887 was more than 10,000 tons in excess of the total production of the United States in 1895.

PRODUCTION OF MANGANIFEROUS IRON ORES.

No attempt has been made to collect the statistics of manganese-bearing iron ores except in cases where they have been used in the manufacture of spiegeleisen, or where the iron ore has an added value because of the percentage of manganese contained in it. Under this limitation we have reports from but two localities producing manganiferous iron ores, namely, the Leadville district of Colorado, and the Lake Superior region. Some of the ores produced in other States and reported among the manganese ores proper should be strictly classed as manganiferous iron ores—a portion of them falling below 44¼ per cent of metallic manganese, which has been assumed as the dividing line between manganese and manganiferous iron ores; but as the average manganese in the shipments of ore from these localities has exceeded the 44¼ per cent limit, they are classed as manganese ores.

The following table shows the production of manganiferous iron ores in the United States in 1895:

Production of manganiferous iron ores in the United States in 1895.

Locality.	Product.	Per cent of manganese.	Value per ton.	Total value.
	Long tons.			
Colorado	13,464	28.05	$3.02	$40,661
Lake Superior........	112,265	3.5 to 8	1.72	193,337
Total...........	125,729	3.5 to 28.05	1.86	233,998

From this table it will be seen that the total production of manganiferous iron ores in the United States in 1895 was 125,729 tons, as compared with 205,488 tons in 1894. The total value of the ore produced in 1895 was $233,998, an average of $1.86 a ton, as compared with $408,597, or $1.99 a ton, in 1894.

The following table shows the total production of manganiferous iron ores in the United States, and their value for each year from 1889 to 1895:

Total production of manganiferous iron ores in the United States from 1889 to 1895.

Year.	Total product.	Total value.	Value per ton.
	Long tons.		
1889.................................	83.434	$271,680	$3.26
1890.................................	61,863	231,655	3.74
1891.................................	132,511	314,099	2.37
1892.................................	153,373	354,664	2.31
1893.................................	117,782	283,228	2.40
1894.................................	205,488	408,597	1.99
1895.................................	125,729	233,998	1.86

PRODUCTION OF MANGANIFEROUS SILVER ORES.

Under this classification no silver ores are included unless the presence of manganese is considered as giving the ore either a technical or a commercial value.

The manganiferous silver ores produced in the United States were chiefly from the Leadville district of Colorado, with some small amounts from Montana.

The total production of ores in 1895 was 54,163 tons, valued at $229,651, or $4.24 a ton. The production in 1894 was 31,687 tons, valued at $148,292, or $4.91 a ton. While no value was given for the ore produced in Montana, we have assumed that its average value was the same as that produced in Colorado.

The total production of manganiferous silver ores in the United States, with the content of manganese and the value per ton, for each year from 1889 to 1895, for which returns have been received, is given in the following table:

Production of manganiferous silver ores in the United States from 1889 to 1895.

Year.	Containing 20 per cent and over.	Containing less than 20 per cent.	Total.	Total value.	Average value per ton.
	Long tons.	Long tons.	Long tons.		
1889	9,987	55,000	61,987	$227,455	$3.50
1890	7,826	44,014	51,840	181,440	3.50
1891	19,560	59,951	79,511	397,555	5.00
1892	17,047	45,262	62,309	323,794	5.20
1893	12,642	a 43,320	a 55,962	258,695	4.75
1894	12,460	a 19,227	a 31,687	148,292	4.91
1895	11,789	42,374	54,163	229,651	4.24

a Including 1,500 tons from Montana for which no value is given.

PRODUCTION OF MANGANIFEROUS ZINC ORES.

The manganiferous zinc ores, including only the residuum or clinker left from working the zinc ores at Franklin, N. J., are used in the manufacture of spiegeleisen at the furnaces of the New Jersey Zinc and Iron Company and the Passaic Zinc Company, in New Jersey, and the Lehigh Zinc and Iron Company at Bethlehem, Pa. The total consumption at these blast furnaces of this class of ores in 1895 was 43,249 tons, valued at $24,451, or 56½ cents per ton. In 1894 the consumption was but 26,981 tons, valued at $20,464. The amount given as the value of this ore is only an approximation to its actual value. Much of the residuum is used at the spiegel furnaces of the zinc producers themselves and is charged to the furnace at simply the cost of handling and freight to the furnace, the clinker itself being regarded as of no value; in other cases an arbitrary value is placed on the ore; in still others the cost of the ore delivered at the furnace is that given as its price. The ore used contained on an average from 8 to 11 per cent of manganese. At one furnace the average of the ore used for the year was 8 per cent of manganese and 22 per cent of iron. At the other furnaces it averaged about 11 per cent of manganese.

In the following table will be found a statement of the product of the manganiferous zinc ores in the United States and their value for each year from 1889 to 1895.

Product of manganiferous zinc ores in the United States from 1889 to 1895.

Year.	Quantity.	Value.
	Long tons.	
1889	43,648	$54,560
1890	48,560	60,700
1891	38,228	57,432
1892	31,859	25,937
1893	37,512	30,535
1894	26,981	20,464
1895	43,249	24,451

PRODUCTION OF ALL CLASSES OF MANGANESE ORES.

On the basis of the classification and statistics herein given, the total production of manganese and manganiferous ores in the United States in 1895 was as follows:

Production of manganese and manganiferous ores in the United States in 1895.

Kinds of ore.	Quantity.	Total value.	Value per ton.
	Long tons.		
Manganese	9,547	$71,769	$7.52
Manganiferous iron ore	125,729	233,998	1.86
Manganiferous silver ore	54,163	229,651	4.24
Manganiferous zinc ore	43,249	24,451	.565
Total	232,688	559,869	a 2.41

a Average.

From the above table it appears that the total production of all grades of manganese and manganiferous ores in the United States in 1895 was 232,688 tons, valued at $559,869, or $2.41 a ton. The total production is 1894 was 270,464 tons, valued at $630,988, or $2.33 a ton.

PRICES OF MANGANESE AND MANGANIFEROUS ORES.

In connection with the statements of production in the several States the price is given free on board at the mines at which the various classes of manganese-bearing ores have been sold. The prices paid, however, by the Carnegie Steel Company, Limited, are of considerable importance. A memorandum of prices paid by this company is as follows:

Prices are based on ores containing not more than 8 per cent of silica and not more than 0.10 per cent of phosphorus, and are subject to deductions as follows: For each 1 per cent of silica in excess of 8 per cent, 15 cents per ton; for each 0.02 per cent of phosphorus in excess of 0.1 per cent, 1 cent per unit of manganese.

Prices paid for manganese ores delivered at Bessemer, near Pittsburg, Pa.

Manganese.	Price per unit.	
	Iron.	Manganese.
	Cents.	Cents.
Ore containing above 49 per cent..........	6	28
46 to 49 per cent.....................	6	27
43 to 46 per cent.....................	6	26
40 to 43 per cent.....................	6	25

Settlements are based on analyses of samples dried at 212° F., the percentage of moisture in samples when taken being deducted from the weight.

These prices are subject to change without notice, unless otherwise specially agreed upon.

The above prices ruled in 1894, as well as in 1895.

The unit of manganese or iron is 1 per cent of either of these metals in the metallic state contained in the ore dried at 212° F. For instance, if an ore contain 49 per cent manganese and 5 per cent of iron, there would be 49 units of manganese and 5 units of iron. The price of such an ore, according to the above table, would be 6 cents a unit for the iron and 28 cents a unit of manganese, provided the silica and phosphorus were within the limits named. This would make the iron in the ore worth 30 cents and the manganese $13.72; the total value of the ore being therefore $14.02 delivered at Bessemer, which is practically a Pittsburg delivery.

The prices given in the above table practically govern the price of all the manganese ore produced in the United States. The price at the mine would be the price obtained for the ore at Bessemer less the transportation charges. Prices for ore delivered at either Chicago or Johnstown would be practically based on these same rates, with allowances for difference in location, freight charges, etc.

IMPORTS OF MANGANESE.

The following table shows the amount of manganese, including both that classed as manganese ore and that classed as oxide of manganese, imported and entered for consumption into the United States in the years 1889 to 1895, these imports being for calendar years.

Manganese imported and entered for consumption into the United States, 1889–1895.

Year.	Ore.		Oxide of.	
	Quantity.	Value.	Quantity.	Value.
	Long tons.		*Long tons.*	
1889.................	4,135	$72,391	151	$6,000
1890.................	33,998	509,704	156	7,196
1891.................	28,624	371,594	201	9,024
1892.................	58,364	830,006	208	10,805
1893.................	67,717	860,832	396	19,406
1894.................	a 44,655	432,561	....	....
1895.................	a 86,111	747,910	....	....

a Classified as ore and oxide.

THE PRODUCTION BY STATES AND COUNTRIES.

ALABAMA.

Though frequent examinations indicate that manganese of a very high grade exists in some quantity in Alabama, the only ore shipped from this State of which we have any record was in 1886, from Stock's Mills, in Cherokee County. The total amount was only 75 tons. In 1875 a manganiferous iron ore was used in the manufacture of some 1,000 tons of spiegeleisen, the first made in the United States from true manganese ores, in the Woodstock furnace at Anniston. So far as has been learned, these are the only two amounts of ores from the mines of this State that have been used commercially as manganese ores, though manganese is frequently found associated with the iron ores of the State.

CALIFORNIA.

The two manganese deposits of California described in previous volumes of Mineral Resources are the only ones supplying manganese in commercial quantities. They produced a larger amount of ore in 1895 than usual, the total production being 525 tons, valued at $5,400. The ore carries from 62 to 72 per cent of binoxide of manganese, and is worth on an average about $10 a ton.

Until quite recently but little exact information has been available regarding the production of manganese in California. It is used only in a small way in the manufacture of chlorine for gold-smelting purposes. It is estimated that the total amount produced up to the close of 1890 was between 5,000 and 6,500 tons. This estimate is made on the basis that 5,000 tons were mined for shipment to England from 1867 to 1874. After 1874 but small amounts were produced each year, none being produced in 1892. In 1893 the production was 400 tons, and in 1894 but 278 tons. As nearly as can be ascertained, the following

17 GEOL, PT 3——13

table represents the production of manganese in California from the beginning of mining until the close of 1895:

Total production of manganese in California to December 31, 1895.

Year.	Tons.	Year.	Tons.
1871 to 1888	6,000	1893	400
1889	53	1894	278
1890	386	1895	525
1891	705	Total	8,347
1892			

COLORADO.

Colorado produces two classes of manganese-bearing ores—manganiferous iron ores, used to some extent in the production of spiegeleisen, and manganiferous silver ores, used as a flux in the smelting of silver-lead ores. Both classes of ores are from the upper workings of the Leadville silver deposits, and carry manganese in varying quantities, from 5 to 25 per cent, and occasionally as much as from 30 to 35 per cent of manganese, with 0 to 20 ounces of silver and occasionally a little gold, 0 to 4 per cent of lead, 4 to 18 per cent of silica, and from 11 to 50 per cent of iron. In most of the silver mines in the Leadville district more or less iron and manganese are found.

The occurrence and character of these ores, as well as their uses and the terms on which they are bought and sold, have been thoroughly discussed in previous volumes of Mineral Resources, especially the volume for 1894. There are one or two additional facts, however, to which attention should be called.

The deposits of manganese-bearing ores in Colorado are like most manganese deposits the world over—they are extremely variable, both in quantity and character. For a while a mine will produce a considerable quantity of ore rich in manganese, though varying somewhat in the proportion, and then for weeks and even months not the least evidence of manganese will be found. One Colorado mine which produced several thousand tons in 1894, and considerable amounts in January and February, 1895, then gave out and yielded no more, though operations were continuous until June. The mine produced manganese ore during this month and July, when the deposit again gave out. No more was found during the remainder of the year.

The amount of manganese in the ore varies greatly, not only in different mines but even at different times in the same mine. For example, the manganese percentages in seven consecutive shipments from a certain Colorado mine were as follows: 16.85, 31, 19.1, 19.1, 22.6, 17.5, and 18.2.

The production of manganese of both grades in Colorado in 1895 showed considerable increase over the production of 1894. The total output of silver-bearing ores in 1895 was 53,506 tons, as compared with 30,187 tons in 1894. Of this total of 53,506 tons, 11,789 tons contained 20 per cent and over of manganese, while 41,717 tons carried less than 20 per cent. The prices of this ore, however, were less in 1895 than in 1894. In some cases ore carrying from 10 to 20 per cent of silver sold at from $3 to $4.50 a ton, and ore with 13 to 21 per cent of manganese sold at $2.07 to $2.27 a ton. The range in price was from $2.07 to $7, an actual average of $4.24, as compared with $4.93 in 1894.

The total production of manganiferous iron ores in Colorado in 1895 was 13,464 tons, containing an average of 28.05 per cent of manganese, valued at the mines at $3.02 a ton. The total production in 1894 of this class of ores was but 7,022 tons. The total production of these ores in 1895 was sold to the Colorado Fuel and Iron Company. Some years ago the Illinois Steel Company, of Chicago, purchased some of their manganese ores in Colorado, but the cost of freight from Leadville to Chicago was so great that the ores could not compete with those brought from abroad, especially the Russian ores, and shipments stopped. This office is advised, however, that this company has made a contract for a quantity of Colorado ores to be delivered in 1896, and that shipments have already begun (March, 1896). The closing of this contract, it is understood, was made possible through lower freight rates.

The statistics of the production of manganese-bearing ore in Colorado from 1889 to 1895 are as follows:

Production of manganiferous ores in Colorado from 1889 to 1895.

[Long tons.]

	1889.	1890.	1891.	1892.
Manganiferous iron ores used for spiegeleisen..............	2,075	....	961	3,100
Manganiferous silver ores with 20 per cent and over of manganese	9,987	7,826	19,560	17,017
Manganiferous silver ores with less than 20 per cent of manganese	55,000	44,014	59,951	45,262
Total	67,062	51,840	80,475	65,409

	1893.	1894.	1895.
Manganiferous iron ores used for spiegeleisen	5,766	7,022	13,464
Manganiferous silver ores with 20 per cent and over of manganese ...	12,642	12,460	11,789
Manganiferous silver ores with less than 20 per cent of manganese	41,820	17,727	41,717
Total.....................	60,228	37,209	66,970

GEORGIA.

Georgia is again the largest manganese-producing State in the Union. Its production in 1895 reached 3,856 tons, the largest since 1889. Of this total production, 164 tons should be classed, strictly speaking, as manganiferous iron ore, its percentage being a trifle below 41¼ per cent of metallic manganese, which we have assumed as the dividing line between manganese ore and manganiferous iron ore. This production is so small, however, and the average content of manganese so high for a manganiferous iron ore, that these 164 tons are included with the manganese ores. The entire production was from the Cartersville district, the oldest of the manganese ore regions of the United States, mining having begun here as early as 1866 and having been prosecuted continuously ever since, with the exception of the years 1883 and 1884.

The ore produced in 1895 contained an average of 47½ per cent of manganese, and was valued at $27,416, or $7.11 a ton. Some of the ore netted as low as $4.50 a ton on carts at the mine, while other portions, very highly crystalline in character, and used for chemical purposes, sold for $11 a ton.

The following table shows the production of manganese ore in Georgia since 1866:

Production of manganese ore in Georgia from 1866 to 1895, inclusive.

Year.	Quantity.	Year.	Quantity.
	Long tons.		Long tons.
1866	550	1881	1,200
1867		1882	1,600
1868		1883	
1869		1884	
1870	5,000	1885	2,580
1871		1886	5,981
1872		1887	9,024
1873		1888	5,568
1874	2,400	1889	8,208
1875	2,400	1890	719
1876	2,400	1891	3,575
1877	2,400	1892	826
1878	2,400	1893	724
1879	2,400	1894	1,277
1880	1,800	1895	3,856

INDIAN TERRITORY.

No manganese ore was mined in Indian Territory in 1895. A description of the large deposit found some 15 miles west of Lehigh, as well as analyses of the ore, will be found in the report of 1894. Some 209 tons were mined in 1892 and 1893, since which time operations have been entirely suspended. There seems to be little doubt of the existence of a large body of manganese ore of a good quality at the locality named. Transportation facilities are lacking, and until these are provided there is little hope of mining operations being resumed. The owner of the property reports that negotiations are in progress which will probably result in furnishing the needed transportation.

LAKE SUPERIOR REGION.

Strictly speaking, there are no manganese mines in the Lake Superior district, but a number of iron-ore mines produce an ore sufficiently high in manganese to justify its grading, usually into three classes, sometimes into two only, one grade being the iron ore proper and the other grades those manganiferous iron ores containing 4 per cent or more of manganese. At times thin streaks of high-grade ore are found in the iron-ore beds, but they are rarely of sufficient extent to justify the separation of this high-grade ore from the ordinary iron ore. The manganese ores are found, in connection with the hematite of the district, in pockets of greater or less extent. When the amount of manganese is small it is ignored; when it reaches 4 per cent or more it is frequently mined and sold separately. By reason of the pockety character of the ores, however, it often happens that a mine will report a production of manganiferous ores one year and none the next.

The total production of manganiferous iron ore in the Lake Superior region in 1895 was 112,265 tons, as compared with 198,466 tons in 1894. The proportion of manganese ranged from 3.536 per cent to 8 per cent, 60,480 tons having over 7¼ per cent and 51,785 tons about 3½ per cent. The value per ton ranged from $1.30 to $1.90 on board cars at mine. The total value was $193,337, or $1.72 a ton, as compared with $1.92 a ton in 1894.

The total production of manganiferous iron ore in the Lake Superior region since 1886, so far as the same has been ascertained, together with the percentage of manganese in the ores, is shown in the following table:

Production of manganiferous iron ore in the Lake Superior region from 1886 to 1895.

Year.	Product.	Average per cent of manganese.	Year.	Product.	Average per cent of manganese.
	Tons.			*Tons.*	
1886........	100,000	2	1888........	189,574	4
	157,000	4		11,562	11
Total....	257,000		Total....	201,136	
1887........	200,000	4	1889........	50,018	6.74
	10,000	10		31,341	9+
Total....	210,000		Total....	81,359	

Production of manganiferous iron ore in the Lake Superior region from 1886 to 1895—Continued.

Year.	Product.	Average per cent of manganese.	Year.	Product.	Average per cent of manganese.
	Tons.			*Tons.*	
1890........	61,863			5,051	10.40
			1893...... {	7,833	14
	13,711	4.68–17.96		300	22
1891...... {	11,015	10	Total....	110,618	
	9,213	9.68			
	98,572	5.38		50,763	3.07
				57,872	3.55
Total....	132,511			6,264	6.50
			1894...... {	61,817	7.26
	6,710	4.893		14,610	7.75
	102,695	5		7,140	18
1892...... {	7,500	8	Total....	198,466	
	8,272	9.998			
	22,254	12.028		13,752	8
				10,228	7.608
Total....	147,431		1895...... {	10,000	7.5
	27,353	4.67		26,500	7.26
1893...... {	55,009	7.61		51,785	3.536
	15,102	7.77	Total....	112,265	

MISSOURI.

Though deposits of both manganese and manganiferous iron ores are known to exist in Missouri, but little, if any, of either grade has been produced in this State since 1881. In that year some 2,000 tons of ore were taken from one mine, the manganese being associated with iron ore. It is not at all improbable that manganese may yet be produced in Missouri, though at present no commercial deposits of this ore are known which can be sent to market cheaply.

MONTANA.

But little can be added to what was said in the report for 1894 as to the extent and character of the manganiferous silver ores of this State. Owing to the depression in the price of silver, there was a falling off in 1895 in the output of these ores.

The production for the three years for which we have reports is as follows:

Production of manganiferous silver ores in Montana, 1893 to 1895.

Year.	Quantity.	Manganese contained.
	Tons.	*Per cent.*
1893...............................	1,500	7
1894...............................	1,049	7.70
1895...............................	657	7 to 12

No value is given for the product, for reasons that have been explained in previous volumes, namely, that the ore is a silver ore, its value being determined chiefly by its content of silver, the manganese in the ore having value only as a flux.

NEW JERSEY.

The manganese-bearing ores produced in New Jersey are the zinc ores of Sussex County. The residuum which is obtained from working these ores for the zinc, and which is used in the manufacture of spiegeleisen, has been termed manganiferous zinc ore. The character and occurrence of these ores, as well as the nature and analyses of their residuum, have been thoroughly discussed in previous volumes of Mineral Resources.

The total production of manganiferous zinc ores in 1895, by which is meant the amount of residuum used in blast furnaces in making spiegeleisen, was 43,249 tons, valued at $24,451, or 56½ cents a ton. This ore carried from 8 to 11 per cent of manganese.

The total production of these ores for a series of years has been as follows:

Product of manganiferous zinc ores from 1889 to 1895.

Year.	Quantity.	Value.
	Long tons.	
1889	43,618	$54,560
1890	48,560	60,700
1891	38,228	57,432
1892	31,859	25,937
1893	37,512	30,535
1894	26,981	20,464
1895	43,249	24,451

NORTH CAROLINA.

A small amount of ore was mined in North Carolina in 1895, but none was shipped, the mining being for development purposes only. It is claimed that the ore showed 40 to 54 per cent metallic manganese.

The amount of manganese mined in this State of which we have reports is shown in the following table:

Production of manganese in North Carolina from 1886 to 1895.

Year.	Long tons.	Year.	Long tons.
1886	15	1891	
1887	11	1892	
1888	50	1893	20
1889	47	1894	
1890	11	1895	

PENNSYLVANIA.

The only manganese produced in this State in 1895 was from the deposit at the base of South Mountain in Cumberland County, described in the report for 1894. This deposit is black oxide, and though somewhat high in phosphorus it is so low in silica and high in manganese that it is being used to some considerable extent in the manufacture of basic open-hearth steel. A washing plant has been erected, and the ore was put in better shape for the market in 1895 than in 1894. About 460 tons of ore were mined in 1895, of which 260 tons were shipped and the balance left on the stock pile awaiting washing. The ore carries from 40 to 45 per cent metallic manganese and is valued at $5 a ton.

The following table shows the production and value of manganese in this State for the years 1894 and 1895:

Amount and value of manganese ores produced in Pennsylvania in 1894 and 1895.

Year.	Production.	Value.
	Tons.	
1894	35	
1895	460	$2,300

SOUTH CAROLINA.

Quite extensive operations were undertaken in 1895 by the Southern Manganese Company on the manganese property of this company near Blacksburg. This property was carefully examined by Mr. H. B. C. Nitze, the well-known geologist of Baltimore. Mr. Nitze examined the lead of the ore for some 7 miles, extending from a point on the Charleston, Cincinnati and Chicago Railroad about 3½ miles below Blacksburg in a general northeasterly direction toward Kings Mountain. Two leads of ore were traced for a distance of 5 miles, where they join and continue as one. At points one lead measured 7 or 8 feet in width; the other about 25 feet. The following statement is condensed from Mr. Nitze's report: The outcrops appear as a very dark, bluish stratification of shales and slates, impregnated with manganese dioxide, disseminated through which—especially in the small cracks—may be found small pebbles or particles of crystalline pyrolusite and psilomelane. The outcrop is naturally impure, which is common to all mineral veins.

On Gold's place a shaft 28 feet in depth had been sunk on the vein. In descending, the black shales seem to grow gradually richer in manganese, small streaks of ore appearing between the same, until at a depth of about 25 feet solid ore is reached, in a matrix of shale and some quartzite, the foot wall of hard yellow shale appearing on one side. The character of the ore was hard, crystalline, and very pure.

The quality of the ore is shown by the following analyses:

Analyses of South Carolina manganese.

	1	2	3	4	5
	Per cent.	Per cent.	Per cent.	Per cent.	Per cent.
Silica	2.920	7.370	4.660	1.000	2.450
Metallic iron	1.435	1.980	2.000	.670	.780
Metallic manganese...	57.353	53.160	51.150	60.380	57.830
Phosphorus	.050	.050	.055	.029	.032
Baryta					
Lime.................			3.500		

These analyses were made on samples taken from the bottom of the shaft, and represent an average. No. 1 was made by Dr. Henry Froehling, of Richmond, Va. No. 2 was made at the laboratory of Carnegie Bros. & Co., Pittsburg, Pa. No. 3 was made by H. B. C. Nitze, Baltimore, Md. Nos. 4 and 5 were made by Dr. Froehling from the exploiting work of the company during 1895.

During the year 1895 work on this property was carried on under the general direction of the company.

This company writes that the work done by them in 1895 was for purposes of exploration and prospecting. The examination already shows that the outcroppings extend a distance of some 7 miles, and upon working down to the veins they found marketable ore in beds. As all the ore mined by this company in 1895 was simply for development, no report is made of production.

The total production since 1885, so far as the returns show, has been as follows:

Total production of manganese ore in South Carolina.

Year.	Tons.	Year.	Tons.
1885 and 1886...........	300	1888....................	50
1887.....................	45	1889....................	124

TENNESSEE.

Notwithstanding the promising developments of manganese ore in Tennessee in 1893 and 1894, which led to a considerable production in these years, no manganese, so far as learned, was produced from these mines in 1895, though operations have been resumed in 1896 at one mine which was worked in 1894.

Mr. William McGovern, who has recently made an investigation into several manganese deposits in southwestern Virginia and eastern Tennessee, has furnished a report on the results of his examination, from which the following is extracted regarding some deposits in Johnson County, Tenn. :

Manganese ore occurs in considerable quantities in Shady Valley, in the eastern part of Johnson County, Tenn., and near the Virginia line. At what is known as the Heberlin mine an opening was made some years ago and about 800 tons of a superior quality of manganese taken out, which still remains piled near the mouth of the mine. When work was stopped the ore apparently continued in about the same quantity under the low ridge in which it was found. The amount was won in a space 15 feet wide by 40 in length. About 100 yards from the main opening another was made, disclosing the ore in about the same quantity. Across a small stream, on another, but somewhat higher, range of hills, manganese has been found at several places, although not so plentifully as at the main opening from which the pile of stock ore was taken. The ore here is principally psilomelane, while in the other openings in the valley it is pyrolusite.

Next to the Heberlin the most important showing of manganese in Shady Valley is at the Wright property, farther up and near the head of the valley. During the past summer, 1895, an opening was made on the ore and about 150 tons were taken out. The ore here is in massive form, about 6 feet under ground and about the same number of feet in thickness, and at a distance has somewhat the appearance of a seam of coal. When work on it was stopped the ore showed no signs of exhaustion, and it probably exists at this place in considerable quantity.

At about a mile from the Wright opening, in the bed of a small stream, a manganese ore was found in the shape of a ledge with upturned edge 4 feet wide by 6 feet deep. About 10 tons of ore have been mined at this place.

In the lower end of the valley, on lands of the estate of P. W. Sheafer, some prospecting has been done and the ore exposed in several places. From the several openings on this property some 15 or 20 tons of manganese have been raised.

As the distance from Shady Valley to the railroad is 20 miles, over bad roads, the work so far done has been for the purpose of development and to prove the existence of manganese ore in quantity. Aside from the places before mentioned, manganese has been noted at more than thirty other localities in the valley, and it is believed that this section may prove the most important manganese district along the entire line of the valley of Virginia and Tennessee.

Analyses of these ores are given below:

Analyses of manganese ores from Johnson County, Tenn.

	Silica.	Metallic iron.	Metallic manganese.	Phosphorus.
	Per cent.	Per cent.	Per cent.	Per cent.
Heberlin bank, pile of stock ore	1.62	4.6	51.05	.075
Heberlin bank, pile of washed ore ..	1.1	3.0	55.00	.099
Alex. Coles, at small stream.........	1.4	2.3	53.09	.177
Wright bank	7.6	7.1	41.44	.066
Sheafer bank	4.12	5.2	50.25	.16
King bank	1.7	16.1	40.87	.052

Outside of Johnson, manganese is known to be found in Carter, Unicoi, Sevier, and Monroe counties, on about the line which marks the lowest limit of the Silurian rocks. In this connection a close study has developed certain facts which may be of interest from both an economic and a scientific standpoint.

1. The nearer manganese ore occurs to the line of the stratified or Lower Silurian rocks the more likely is it to be a psilomelane, changing gradually to the form of pyrolusite as it enters the lower rocks.

2. Where found in deposits of Lower Silurian or Cambrian age it is more or less associated with iron ore, becoming more nearly manganese as its position in older rocks is encountered.

3. When an ore holds manganese and iron in the proportions of about 40 and 15 per cent metallic, and is low in silica, the percentage of phosphorus will be low, but increasing as these proportions are left in either direction. Whether this is only a feature of the east Tennessee deposits, or holds elsewhere, is not known.

The total production of manganese ore in this State since the beginning of operations is given in the following table:

Total production of manganese in Tennessee.

Year.	Production.	Year.	Production.
	Tons.		Tons.
Prior to 1886	800	1890...................	0
1886.....................	50	1892...................	0
1887.....................	0	1893...................	482
1888.....................	16	1894...................	922
1889.....................	30	1895...................	175

VERMONT.

Manganese mining in this State has been of an exceedingly fitful character. The production in 1888 was 1,000 tons; in 1889, 1,576 tons; in 1890, nothing; and in 1891, 49 tons; since which time none has been produced, though it is learned from the owner of the most important mine that he purposes resuming operations in the spring.

The table is repeated showing the production of manganese in this State from 1888 to 1891, the only years for which there are figures.

Production of manganese in Vermont from 1888 to 1891.

Year.	Long tons.
1888	1,000
1889	1,576
1890	0
1891	49

VIRGINIA.

Virginia is in some respects the most important manganese-producing State in the Union. There are more known deposits of this mineral in Virginia, they are spread over a greater extent of territory, more localities have been worked, and more manganese has been raised than in any other State, and yet in 1895 it was the third State in rank as a producer of manganese, its total production in that year being but 1,715 tons, as compared with 3,856 tons produced in Georgia and 2,991 tons produced in Arkansas.

The history, conditions of occurrence, and chief deposits, as well as the character of the manganese mined in Virginia, are thoroughly described in the report Mineral Resources for 1894, and need not be discussed here.

The entire production for 1895, as well as for 1894, was from the midland and valley districts of the State. The largest amount of ore produced in 1895 was from the mines of Messrs. Kendall and Flick, near Elkton, in Rockingham County. These mines produced 1,367 tons, containing from 47 to 48 per cent of manganese, as compared with 1,190 tons produced in 1894.

The total production of manganese ores in 1895 was 1,715 tons, as compared with 1,797 tons in 1894. The total value of the ore produced in 1895 was $15,656, or $9.13 a ton, as compared with $9.27 a ton in 1894. The range of the value of the ore produced in 1895 was from $4 to $9.37 a ton on board cars at mines.

Neither the Crimora mine nor the adjoining mine, the Old Dominion, produced any ore in 1895.

The total production of manganese ore in Virginia from 1880 to 1895, inclusive, is shown in the following table:

Production of manganese ore and manganiferous iron ore in Virginia from 1880 to 1895.

Year.	Manga-nese ore.	Manganif-erous iron ore.	Year.	Manga-nese ore.	Manganif-erous iron ore.
	Tons.	Tons.		Tons.	Tons.
1880.........	3,661	....	1888.........	17,646	....
1881.........	3,295	....	1889.........	14,616	....
1882.........	2,982	....	1890.........	12,689	....
1883.........	5,355	....	1891.........	16,248	....
1884.........	8,980	....	1892.........	6,079	2,842
1885.........	18,745	....	1893.........	4,092	1,188
1886.........	20,567	....	1894.........	1,797	132
1887.........	19,835	....	1895.........	1,715	0

It will be noted that the production of manganese in Virginia in 1895 was the smallest in its history.

WEST VIRGINIA.

The mines at Glenmore, in Greenbrier County, W. Va., some 7 miles north of White Sulphur Springs, which gave such promise in 1894, 100 tons of ore having been produced in that year, seem to have greatly belied this promise, at least so far as concerns production, no ore having been mined here in 1895. This seems to have been due, at least so far as the report made to us indicates, to no want of confidence in the existence of manganese at this point, but to other reasons.

The total production of manganese in this State, so far as has been ascertained, was the 100 tons above referred to, produced in 1894.

CANADA.

Most of the manganese mined in Canada is from the deposits which have been described in Nova Scotia and New Brunswick, though small amounts are from time to time mined in Quebec.

According to the Mineral Production of Canada, published by the Geological Survey of Canada, the total production of manganese ore in the Dominion, and its value, from 1886 to 1895, were as follows:

Production and value of Canadian manganese ore from 1886 to 1895.

Year.	Product.	Value.	Year.	Product.	Value.
	Tons.			Tons.	
1886.........	1,789	$11,499	1891.........	255	$6,691
1887.........	1,245	43,658	1892.........	115	10,250
1888.........	1,801	47,914	1893.........	228	14,458
1889.........	1,455	32,737	1894.........	74	4,180
1890.........	1,328	32,550	1895.........	125	8,464

The exports of manganese ore from Canada are usually regarded as equivalent to the production. The figures furnished by the Customs Department differ somewhat from those given by the Geological Survey. The Customs Department figures are as follows:

Exports of manganese from the Dominion of Canada during the fiscal year ending June 30, 1895.

Province.	Quantity.	Value.
	Tons.	
Nova Scotia	83	$5,293
New Brunswick	45	2,400
Total	128	7,693

The difference in the figures is evidently due to the year covered by the reports, that of the Geological Survey being for the calendar year 1895, while the Customs Department report is for the fiscal year ending June 30, 1895.

Regarding the ore mined in New Brunswick and Nova Scotia, it may be said that it is of a very high grade, and is very highly prized by glass makers for its freedom from impurities. The ore from Markhamville, New Brunswick, carries $96\frac{1}{2}$ to $98\frac{3}{4}$ per cent of peroxide of manganese, with a little over one-half of 1 per cent of silica and three-fourths of 1 per cent of iron. When granulated or powdered and packed in barrels, this ore is worth 5 cents a pound. The Teny Cape manganese ores of Nova Scotia are of similar character. The ore is a fibrous pyrolusite, and after a slight hand dressing has in some years brought as much as $125 a ton at the mine.

The only statements of production of ore in New Brunswick are exports. From these the following statement of production of manganese in this Province since 1868 is compiled:

Production of manganese ores in New Brunswick, 1868 to 1895, and value of same.

Year.	Product.	Value.	Year.	Product.	Value.
	Long tons.			*Long tons.*	
1868	861	$19,019	1882	771	$14,227
1869	332	6,174	1883	1,013	16,708
1870	140	3,580	1884	469	9,035
1871	951	8,180	1885	1,607	29,595
1872	1,075	24,495	1886	1,377	27,484
1873	1,031	20,192	1887	837	20,572
1874	776	16,961	1888	1,094	16,073
1875	194	5,314	1889	1,377	26,326
1876	391	7,316	1890	1,729	34,248
1877	785	12,210	1891	233	6,131
1878	520	5,971	1892		
1879	1,732	20,016	1893	10	112
1880	2,100	31,707	1894	0	0
1881	1,504	22,532	1895	45	2,400

The production of manganese in Nova Scotia since 1861, so far as figures have been ascertained, is given in the following table:

Production of manganese in Nova Scotia from 1861 to 1895.

Year.	Product.	Value.	Year.	Product.	Value.
	Tons.			Tons.	
1861 to 1871 ..	1,500	$10,500	1884..........	302	$23,830
1872..........	40	1,400	1885..........	354	....
1873..........	131	....	1886..........	465	13,849
1874..........	6	12	1887..........	665	21,683
1875..........	7	....	1888..........	106	6,460
1876..........	21	723	1889..........	200	....
1877..........	97	5,335	1890..........	112	....
1878..........	127	6,505	1891..........	41	....
1879..........	145	7,170	1892..........	111	8,691
1880..........	283	14,831	1893..........	123½	12,499
1881..........	231	18,022	1894..........	65	4,875
1882..........	209	11,520	1895..........	83	5,293
1883..........	150	12,462			

CUBA.

Owing to the disturbances in Cuba, no report of the production of manganese in this island has been received for the last two years. Indeed, it seems probable that little was mined; at least, little seems to have been exported. The total imports of manganese ore from Cuba into the United States for the fiscal year ending June 30, 1895, are reported by the Bureau of Statistics as but 1,609 pounds. It may be assumed, therefore, that in 1895, at least, but little manganese was produced.

A complete description of the manganese deposits near Santiago, from which most, if not all, of the ore mined is produced, will be found in Mineral Resources for 1892, page 212.

The exportation of manganese ore from these mines since 1888, so far as we have received reports of the same, is given in the following table:

Exportation of manganese ores from Santiago district, Cuba, from 1888 to 1893.

Year.	Tons.
1888	1,942
1889	704
1890	21,810
1891	21,987
1892	18,751
1893 (first six months)........................	10,640
Total	75,834

CHILE.

There are two manganese mining operations in Chile, known as the "Coquimbo," in a province of the same name, the port of shipment also being Coquimbo, and "Carrizal," or "Huasco," in the Province of Atacama. The mining districts in Atacama take their names from the ports of shipment, which are from 35 to 40 miles distant from the mines.

The Coquimbo ore carries from 45 to 55 per cent of manganese, averaging 52 per cent. It contains considerable peroxide, and is softer than that from the Carrizal district. The ore of the latter district averages 50 per cent of metallic manganese, is hard and brittle, with a glassy fracture, and requires blasting.

No report of the production of manganese in Chile since 1893 has been received.

The production of Coquimbo since 1885, and of Carrizal since 1886, and the total production of Chile since 1885, in tons of 2,240 pounds, are as follows:

Production of Chilean manganese, 1885 to 1893.

Year.	Coquimbo.	Carrizal.	Total Chile.
	Long tons.	Long tons.	Long tons.
1885	4,041	....	4,041
1886	23,701	227	23,928
1887	38,234	9,287	47,521
1888	12,132	6,581	18,713
1889	9,145	19,538	28,683
1890	23,409	24,577	47,986
1891	16,462	18,000	34,462
1892	22,535	25,359	47,894
1893	16,556	19,540	36,096

The imports of manganese ore into the United States from Chile for the fiscal year ending June 30, 1895, were 19,177,200 pounds, or 8,561 tons of 2,240 pounds each, valued at $51,947, or $6.07 per ton.

The imports of manganese ore from Chile into the United Kingdom of Great Britain and Ireland were 30,174 tons in 1893, valued at $456,209, or $15.12 per ton, and 29,903 tons in 1894, valued at $434,608, or $14.54 per ton.

COLOMBIA.

The Caribbean Manganese Company, composed chiefly of American capitalists, which owns large manganese deposits in the Republic of Colombia, began shipments in 1895. The first cargo reached Baltimore in June of that year.

The deposits of the ore belonging to this company are located about 10 miles inland from the port of Nombre-de-Dios. So far as prospected the deposits seem to consist chiefly of masses or bowlders, varying in size from a few pounds to over 1,000 tons. The shipments thus far made have been principally surface ore, and have varied in metallic contents according to the care that has been exercised in sorting. The last cargo received in this country, early in 1896, of about 1,500 tons, contained 57.50 per cent of manganese, 4.16 per cent of silica, and 0.04 per cent of phosphorus, with moisture varying from $1\frac{1}{2}$ to 2 per cent. The greater part of the ore shows a hard, steely-blue fracture. Until further and more systematic explorations are made no definite statement can be given regarding the extent of the deposits, though the quantity of ore seems to be very considerable.

The total imports of manganese into the United States from Colombia for the calendar year 1895 were 8,849,000 pounds, or 3,950 long tons. The ore imported for the fiscal year ending June 30, 1895, was 5,601,000 pounds, or 2,500 tons, valued at $11,685, or $4.674 per ton.

AUSTRIA-HUNGARY.

Manganese is found in three of the great divisions of Austria-Hungary, namely: Austria, Hungary, and Bosnia.

In the following table is given the production of manganese in Austria proper from 1876 to 1893:

Production of manganese in Austria from 1876 to 1893.

Year.	Product.	Year.	Product.
	Long tons.		Long tons.
1876	3, 337	1885	3, 030
1877	3, 888	1886	4, 550
1878	2, 059	1887	4, 582
1879	1, 690	1888	3, 225
1880	4, 367	1889	1, 912
1881	4, 483	1890	3, 940
1882	4, 143	1891	2, 598
1883	4, 617	1892	2, 261
1884	3, 908	1893	2, 657

In the following table is shown the production of manganese in Hungary from 1889 to 1893:

Production of manganese in Hungary from 1889 to 1893.

Year.	Long tons.
1889	96
1890	1, 422
1891	126
1892	612
1893	86

The production of manganese ore in Bosnia from 1890 to 1894 was as follows:

Production of manganese in Bosnia from 1890 to 1894.

Year.	Long tons.
1890	5,413
1891	8,707
1892	7,818
1893	7,286
1894	6,484

BELGIUM.

The manganese-bearing ores of Belgium are found chiefly in the Province of Liege. They are largely manganiferous iron ores. The following table gives the quantity and value of manganese ore produced in this country since 1880, so far as ascertained:

Production of manganese ore in Belgium from 1880 to 1894.

Year.	Product.	Value.	Year.	Product.	Value.
	Long tons.			Long tons.	
1880	689	$772	1888	27,348	$62,725
1881	758	772	1889	20,575	47,864
1882	340	338	1890	14,030	33,968
1883	807	791	1891	18,206	49,138
1884	738	724	1892	16,510	40,202
1885			1893	16,535	38,793
1886	738	1,737	1894	21,700	53,596
1887	12,519	30,079			

FRANCE.

The total production of manganese in France in 1894 was 32,239 long tons. This was produced from 11 mines. Most of the ore is a carbonate from the Las Cabeses mine, in the department of Ariége, in the extreme southeastern portion of France, on the borders of Spain. In 1894 this mine produced 7,000 metric tons of raw carbonate and 11,000 tons of calcined, a total of 18,000 metric tons, out of a total production for the country in 1894 of 32,751 metric tons. From the department of Saône-et-Loire, 11,000 metric tons of binoxide were produced from the workings of Romaneche and Grand-Filon. The remainder of the production was binoxide from the departments of Allier, Aude, Indre, and Lozère.

The total production of manganese in France in 1894 was 32,239 long tons, valued at $192,264, or $5.96 per ton, as compared with a total production in 1893 of 37,406 long tons, valued at $290,073, or $7.75 per ton. Of the 1894 production, 17,719 long tons were carbonate and 14,520 long tons manganese ores proper.

The production and value of manganese ores in France from 1873 to 1894 are given in the following table:

Production and value of manganese ores in France from 1873 to 1894.

Year.	Production.	Total value.	Value per ton.
	Long tons.		
1873	12,182	$160,781	$13.20
1874	11,212	110,675	9.87
1875	8,874	93,237	10.51
1876	4,790	44,033	9.19
1877	7,061	59,126	8.37
1878	9,234	61,165	6.62
1879	5,874	65,356	11.13
1880	9,499	106,543	11.22
1881	13,491	98,466	7.30
1882	7,419	48,028	6.47
1883	6,469	39,557	6.12
1884	4,463	32,540	7.29
1885	3,370	20,647	6.13
1886	7,555	53,099	7.03
1887	11,932	50,501	4.23
1888	10,873	60,757	5.59
1889	9,842	59,000	5.99
1890	15,731	89,517	5.69
1891	15,101	90,316	5.98
1892	31,894	205,074	6.43
1893	37,406	290,073	7.75
1894	32,239	192,264	5.96

GERMANY.

The chief occurrence of manganese ores in Germany is on the right bank of the river Rhine, in the districts of Wiesbaden and Coblentz. Some small amounts are also found in Thuringia.

The total production of manganese ores in the German Empire in 1894 was 43,012 tons, valued at $111,756.

The production of manganese in Germany from 1890 to 1894 is given in the following table:

Production of manganese in Germany from 1890 to 1894.

Year.	Long tons.
1890	41,180
1891	39,698
1892	32,341
1893	40,057
1894	43,012

While the above table gives the production of manganese in the entire German Empire, the production of this mineral in Prussia, from which most of the manganese produced in Germany is derived, as well as the value of the same, is given in the following table:

Production and value of manganese ores in Prussia from 1891 to 1894.

Year.	Product.	Value.	Year.	Product.	Value.
	Long tons.			Long tons.	
1881.........	10,911	$79,104	1888.........	26,877	$147,250
1882.........	4,597	33,745	1889.........	43,311	216,384
1883.........	4,502	28,423	1890.........	39,497	174,428
1884.........	7,629	43,118	1891.........	36,278	174,624
1885.........	14,464	81,302	1892.........	30,892	101,844
1886.........	24,649	177,066	1893.........	38,384	93,506
1887.........	35,957	228,439	1894.........	41,854	94,992

GREAT BRITAIN.

Though Great Britain is the largest consumer of manganese ores in the world, chiefly in steel production and chemical manufacture, her production of the mineral is quite small. The total production for 1894 was 1,809 tons, valued at $3,582, or $1.98 a ton. Of this amount 67 tons were produced in England, 36 tons being from Derbyshire and 31 tons from Devonshire, where the ore occurs in the Lower Silurian in the form of psilomelane with some pyrolusite. The production of Wales was 1,742 tons, 59 tons being from Carnarvonshire and 1,683 tons from Merionethshire. This Welsh ore is chiefly, but not entirely, carbonate.

The following table shows the annual production and value of manganese ore raised in the United Kingdom from 1873 to 1894, no figures being available as yet for 1895:

Production and value of manganese ore in the United Kingdom from 1873 to 1894.

Year.	Quantity.	Value.	Year.	Quantity.	Value.
	Tons.			Tons.	
1873.........	8,671	$279,587	1884.........	909	$6,921
1874.........	5,778	141,328	1885.........	1,688	11,669
1875.........	3,205	76,985	1886.........	12,763	52,722
1876.........	2,797	47,350	1887.........	13,777	53,772
1877.........	3,039	38,517	1888.........	4,312	9,361
1878.........	1,586	15,106	1889.........	8,852	31,354
1879.........	816	7,333	1890.........	12,444	32,588
1880.........	2,839	27,109	1891.........	9,476	30,071
1881.........	2,884	31,174	1892.........	6,078	21,461
1882.........	1,548	18,910	1893.........	1,336	3,688
1883.........	1,287	14,404	1894.........	1,809	3,582

As showing the amount of manganese ore imported into the United Kingdom, as well as the wide range of countries from which it draws its supply, the following table is given of the amount of ore imported in 1893 and 1894:

Manganese ore imported into the United Kingdom in 1893 and 1894.

Country imported from.	1893.		1894.	
	Quantity.	Value.	Quantity.	Value.
	Tons.		Tons.	
Australasia................	917	$9,390	2,571	$26,117
British North America....	....	....	1	29
Russia	59,478	853,326	58,809	710,541
Sweden	2,293	29,781	308	3,543
Belgium...................				
France...................	8,836	113,217	3,005	36,934
Italy.....................			1	24
Portugal	1,970	28,604	6,848	83,945
Spain	2,278	32,326	7,684	89,613
Turkey...................			3,085	37,897
United States	183	2,773	....	....
Chile......	30,174	456,209	29,903	434,608
Other countries...........	15,644	197,337	15,766	214,605
Total	121,773	1,722,963	127,981	1,637,856

The imports of manganese ore into the United Kingdom, and the value of the same per ton, from 1880 to 1894, are shown in the following table:

Imports of manganese ore into the United Kingdom, and value of same per ton, from 1880 to 1894.

Year.	Quantity.	Value.	Year.	Quantity.	Value.
	Tons.	Per ton.		Tons.	Per ton.
1880..........	16,058	$20.18	1888..........	72,088	$13.50
1881..........	18,743	18.39	1889..........	96,031	14.18
1882..........	29,766	16.65	1890..........	140,174	15.00
1883..........	22,362	17.81	1891..........	101,449	15.54
1884..........	26,048	14.04	1892..........	109,823	15.05
1885..........	47,581	16.50	1893..........	121,773	14.13
1886..........	73,424	15.83	1894..........	127,981	12.78
1887..........	90,383	14.62			

GREECE.

Two grades of manganese ores are produced in Greece, a manganese ore proper and a manganiferous iron ore, the production of the latter being by far the larger.

The production of manganese ores proper from 1888 to 1894 is shown in the following table:

Production of manganese ores in Greece from 1888 to 1894.

Year.	Long tons.
1888	1,452
1889	10,492
1890	13,333
1891	13,240
1892	11,531
1893	5,167
1894	9,172

The production of iron that contained a percentage of manganese high enough for its classification as manganiferous iron ore, from the years 1890 to 1894, is given in the following table:

Production of manganiferous iron ores in Greece from 1890 to 1894.

Year.	Long tons.
1890	124,619
1891	107,015
1892	155,263
1893	119,435
1894	156,567

ITALY.

The chief manganese-producing mines in Italy are the Apennines, though some small mines in Sardinia are producing. In 1894 there were four mines in this country producing manganese ore proper, and one producing manganiferous iron ore. The total production of manganese was 748 tons, valued at $6.06 a ton, or a total value of $4,536. Carrara, in the Apennines, produced 590 tons; Iglesias, in Sardinia, 148 tons, and Torino 10 tons.

The total production of manganiferous iron ore was 5,718 tons, valued at $1.57 per ton, or a total value of $8,971. This was all produced in Firenze, in the Apennines.

In the following table is given the production of manganese and manganiferous iron ore in Italy from 1887 to 1894, so far as the figures have been obtained:

Production of manganese and manganiferous iron ore in Italy.

Year.	Manganese.		Manganiferous iron ore.	
	Product.	Value.	Product.	Value.
	Long tons.		Long tons.	
1887	4,364	$21,872	....	....
1888	3,573	15,054	....	....
1889	2,168	9,998	....	....
1890	2,113	9,949	....	....
1891	2,391	12,467	....	....
1892	1,220	8,106	4,549	$8,320
1893	797	6,320	8,666	14,439
1894	748	4,536	5,718	8,971

PORTUGAL.

But little information has been collected regarding the deposits of manganese ore in Portugal. It is evident, however, from the large exports to Great Britain that they must be of some importance. It was reported that in 1893 ninety mines of this mineral were working in Portugal, the character of the ore being very high. In 1891, 9,906 tons were produced. The following table gives the number of tons of manganese exported to Great Britain since 1888, as far as obtainable. These statements of exports are the only ones we have giving anything of the production of Portugal, and in the absence of more correct figures they may be assumed to represent the production:

Exports of manganese ore from Portugal to Great Britain.

Year.	Tons.
1888	5,638
1889	....
1890	....
1891	3,105
1892	4,188
1893	1,970
1894	6,848

RUSSIA.

For its supply of manganese the world is dependent chiefly upon the mines of Russia, and especially upon those in the Caucasus region. Compared with the production of this country, that of other nations is exceedingly small. The production of the last five years has averaged considerably over 150,000 tons a year, an amount in excess of the production of the rest of the world.

Manganese is mined in three provinces of Russia—the Caucasus, South Russia, and the Urals. The districts were thoroughly described in Mineral Resources for 1893, page 138. Of these districts the Caucasus is much the most important.

In the following table are given the shipments of the Caucasian manganese ore from the ports of Poti and Batoum for 1893 and 1894, these shipments being somewhat less than the production, quantities of ore awaiting transportation from the mines. It has been usual, however, to regard the exports as the production:

Shipment of manganese ore from the ports of Poti and Batoum in 1893 and 1894.

To—	1893.		1894.	
	From Poti.	From Batoum.	From Poti.	From Batoum.
	Tons.	Tons.	Tons.	Tons.
Great Britain.........	49,230	....	65,110	....
Germany.............	36,305	4,100	44,840	6,615
United States	36,070	....	9,890	....
Belgium.............	400	2,725	28,300	....
France	3,500	600	....	2,520
Total..........	125,505	7,425	148,140	9,135

The total production of manganese ore in Russia since 1881, so far as it has been ascertained, is shown in the following table. In making up this table 62.1 poods are taken as the equivalent of a long ton of 2,240 pounds, the pood being regarded as 36.0678 pounds:

Production of manganese in Russia from 1881 to 1894.

Year.	Caucasus.	Ural.	Ekaterino-slav.	Total.
	Long tons.	Long tons.	Long tons.	Long tons.
1881...................	11,048	....	....	11,048
1882...................	12,498	1,933	....	14,431
1883...................	15,971	1,081	....	17,052
1884...................	20,688	1,446	....	22,134
1885...................	59,636	896	....	60,532
1886...................	69,486	819	4,095	74,400
1887...................	53,680	819	3,708	58,207
1888...................	29,857	1,355	1,468	32,680
1889...................	69,504	2,934	5,594	78,032
1890...................	171,467	2,351	8,650	182,468
1891...................	100,314	1,926	10,811	113,081
1892...................	168,950	819	29,412	199,181
1893...................	167,526	1,417	76,321	245,264
1894...................	180,243	2,567	57,371	240,181

From the above table it will be seen that the total production in the Caucasus in 1893 was 167,526 tons; in 1894, 180,243 tons.

SPAIN.

The manganese deposits of Spain were described in the report for 1894. As to production, it may be said that the statistics are of little value. Not only do the official reports contain evident errors, but manganese and manganiferous iron and iron ores are confounded in a way that is extremely puzzling to the statistician.

The official report of the production of manganese in Spain from 1890 to 1894 is as follows:

Production of manganese ores in Spain from 1890 to 1894.

Year.	Long tons.
1890	9,716
1891	6,883
1892	16,643
1893	1,437
1894	423

The great falling off in production in 1893 and 1894 will be noted, and yet the statements of exports for these two years show that in 1893 9,480 tons, and in 1894, 7,319 tons of manganese ore were exported from Spain. In 1893, 2,278 tons of manganese ore were sent from Spain to Great Britain, and in 1894, 7,684 tons. It is believed that in preparing the manganese ore for export, especially that ore that is shipped from Carthagena, two grades of ore are mixed. These manganiferous iron ores are bought on a guarantee basis of 18 per cent of manganese, 30 per cent of iron, and 10 per cent of silica, and the cargoes come very close to the guarantee analysis. For instance, a cargo of such ores in use at a spiegel furnace in the United States analyzed: Manganese, 18.65 per cent; iron, 28.15 per cent; silica, 9.155 per cent. It appears that, as stated above, these cargoes are composed of a mixture of two grades of ore, one running higher and one lower in manganese than the guaranteed analysis.

Much of the iron ore exported from the Province of Murcia can be put down as manganiferous. On the basis that two-thirds of this iron ore is manganiferous, the production of manganiferous iron ores from this Province would be 287,000 tons for the fiscal year ending June 30, 1891, and 245,000 tons for the fiscal year ending June 30, 1892.

SWEDEN.

Through the kindness of Mr. K. A. Wallroth, of the Geological Survey of Sweden, we were enabled to give in the report for 1893 a very complete statement regarding the manganese ores of that country.

Mr. Wallroth states that Swedish manganese ores are of three different types: First, pyrolusite with manganite; second, hausmannite with braunite; and third, manganous carbonate and silicates of manganese, accompanying iron ores.

Ores of the first type occur at Bölet and other places in Vestergötland; at Spexeryd, Höhult, Jacobsberg, and Ludwigsberg, in Smaland; at Skidberg and Nälberg, in the parish of Leksand, Dalarne; and at Spethult, Dalsland. The soft Bölet ore contains from 53 to 61 per cent of manganese; hard ore, somewhat less; an ore graded as No. 4 carries about 25 per cent; a picked ore, 38 to 40 per cent; and washed ore about 35 per cent. An analysis made in 1889 of good soft ore showed 53.17 per cent of manganese, while the average content of manganese in good hard ore, analyzed in 1890, was 48.88 per cent.

The production of manganese ore in the Bölet field from 1886 to 1894 is as follows:

Product of manganese ores in the Bölet field, Sweden.

Year.	Long tons.
1886	102
1887	1,111
1888	2,020
1889	1,942
1890	1,629
1891	1,599
1892	1,833
1893	1,418
1894	1,610

In the Smaland district the occurrence of the ore is very similar to the divisions under which it is found in Bölet. It is divided into three grades for the market, from which samples of the first quality carry about 48.20 per cent of manganese.

The production of this district since 1885 is as follows:

Product of manganese ores in the Smaland district, Sweden.

Year.	Long tons.
1885	2,828
1886	3,792
1887	4,809
1888	5,485
1889	4,409
1890	5,996
1891	4,164
1892	3,795
1893	3,574
1894	508

The deposits of Dalarne and Dalsland are of no commercial importance.

Ores of the second class occur at Paisberg, Långban, and Nordmarken, including Jacobsberg, in Vermland, and in the Sjö mine, in Nerike. The ore consists of hausmannite and braunite mixed, but also contains jacobsite. Several silicates of manganese also occur. In all these places the ore is found stratified with limestone or dolomite, usually in the vicinity of strata of iron ore. At Långban the ore is concentrated by washing: in the other places the ore is graded in two numbers.

The ore from Paisberg (Harstigs mine) contains 39.10 per cent of manganese, the ore from Långban 41.36 per cent; concentrated ore contains 52.77 per cent. The ore from Nordmarken contains: Ore No. 1, 41.71 per cent of manganese; ore No. 2, 24.50 per cent. The ore from Sjö mine contains, on an average, 40.30 per cent of manganese.

The production of manganese ores from this field from 1885 to 1894 was as follows:

Production of manganese ores in Vermland and Nerike (in tons of 2,240 pounds).

Locality.	1885.	1886.	1887.	1888.	1889.
Paisberg, Vermland	1,144	1,736	374	132	19
Långban, Vermland	2,023	1,600	1,670	1,617	2,045
Nordmarken, including Jacobsberg, Vermland			363	228	14
Sjö mine, Nerike		4	184	25	81

Locality.	1890.	1891.	1892.	1893.	1894.
Paisberg, Vermland					
Långban, Vermland	2,839	2,976	2,179	1,958	1,151
Nordmarken, including Jacobsberg, Vermland	66	197			
Sjö mine, Nerike					

The manganiferous iron ores form the third class. They are in greater part magnetic ores, chiefly hematite.

The content of manganese in these ores seldom exceeds 6 per cent, though there are some places where the percentage is higher, as at Röebergs field in Norberg, with as much as 26 per cent of manganese; Gladkärn, with 20 per cent; Svartberg, with 15 per cent; Skinnarvang and Knipgrufvan, with about 12 per cent; Penning and Hilläng field, with 10 per cent; and Långvik, with 8 per cent.

In many fields which produce ores of this type there are collections of manganiferous silicates, as, for instance, knebelite at Dannemora, but no use is made of them.

The products of these manganiferous iron ores in the principal fields in Sweden from 1888 to 1894, with percentage of manganese, are given in the following table:

Production of manganiferous iron ores in Sweden from 1888 to 1894.

[Long tons.]

Locality.	Metallic manganese.	Production.		
		1888.	1889.	1890.
	Per cent.			
Dannemora	1.38	55,548	60,816	62,579
Burängsberg	2.59	10,200	11,190	8,035
Viker	3.31	3,982	3,163	3,374
Klackberg and Kolningsberg	4.40	60,032	51,356	52,339
Långvik	6.72	6,976	6,238	6,632
Hilläng	9.95	1,944	3,808	2,163
Svartberg	14.09	....	1,535	2,598
Total		138,682	138,106	137,720

Locality.	Production.			
	1891.	1892.	1893.	1894.
Dannemora	58,704	60,729	57,697	50,815
Burängsberg	8,907	6,964	8.552	7,976
Viker	1,486	2,524	1.739	1,949
Klackberg and Kolningsberg	50,675	44,448	67,721	60.083
Långvik	9,960	8,486	8,349	6,634
Hilläng	2,037	1,781	1,640	1.945
Svartberg	2,812	2,543	2,030	1,665
Total	134,581	127,475	117.728	131,067

The percentages of manganese in the above table are the average of analyses made by R. Åkermann and Adolph Tamm.

EAST INDIES.

Speaking of the pyrolusite deposits at Gosalpur, Jabalpur district, Mr. F. R. Mallett states that the existence of manganese ore at Gosalpur appears to have been known for a long time past, and the mineral has been in use to a slight extent among native glass makers in the neighborhood.

It was first brought to the notice of the Government by Mr. W. G. Olpherts in 1875. Although the nature of the deposit is more or less obscure, there seems no reason to doubt that a large supply of this ore may be depended on at Gosalpur.

The ore is a dark steel-gray, finely crystalline pyrolusite, mixed with a varying proportion of psilomelane. It contains 54.66 per cent of manganese and 3.17 of iron, with 0.28 of phosphoric acid, and no sulphuric acid. It contains 15.26 per cent of available oxygen, equivalent to 83 per cent of peroxide. As an oxidizing agent, therefore, it is of high value, the average run of manganese ores met with in commerce containing only 60 to 75 per cent, but the presence of some psilomelane reduces it some $3\frac{1}{2}$ per cent. A considerable quantity of psilomelane occurs with the manganiferous micaceous iron at Gosalpur. If the latter were worked in connection with iron making, the psilomelane would be raised at the same time and would be available as an ore of manganese. On assay it yielded 83.20 per cent of available peroxide, or about the same amount as the pyrolusite.

From both sources combined it may reasonably be hoped that a considerable supply of the ore will be procurable when there is a demand for it. The following are analyses of the ore as mined:

Analyses of Indian manganese ores.

Pyrolusite from Gosalpur.	Per cent.
Silica	3.27
Peroxide of manganese	82.40
Protoxide of manganese	2.84
Peroxide of iron	2.01
Alumina	3.19
Lime	Trace.
Baryta	2.94
Magnesia	Trace.
Phosphoric acid (= phosphorus 0.16)	.36
Sulphuric acid	Trace.
Carbonic acid	
Oxide of zinc	Trace.
Combined water	2.81
Moisture	.44
Total	100.26
Metallic manganese	54.29

Psilomelane from Gosalpur.	No. 1	No. 2.
	Per cent	Per cent.
Iron oxide	3.13	9.13
Alumina	.14	.60
Manganese oxide	75.34	73.00
Lime	1.66	2.40
Copper oxide	.40	....
Cobalt	.51	....
Nickel	.16	....
Phosphoric acid	.39	.27
Silica	8.20	5.20
Water	7.75	7.32
Total	97.68	97.92

TURKEY.

While considerable manganese is known to exist in Turkey, no exact statistics concerning its production are obtainable, nor are there descriptions of the character of the ore or its occurrence.

In the calendar year 1894, 3,085 tons of manganese ores, valued at $37,897, were imported from Turkey into Great Britain, while in the fiscal year ending June 30, 1895, 2,500 tons, valued at $17,501, or $7 a ton, were imported from this country into the United States.

JAPAN.

The chief sources of supply of manganese ore in the United States, naming them in the order of imports, for the fiscal year ending June 30, 1895, were Russia, Chile, and Japan. Descriptions of the occurrence of the mineral in Japan have been given in previous volumes. The ore is of a high grade, produced chiefly from surface or shallow workings by the natives, who take it down the mountains and rivers in small quantities to the dealers, who grade and export it.

The production of manganese in Japan from 1881 to 1893 is as follows:

Production of manganese in Japan from 1881 to 1893.

Year.	Product.	Year.	Product.
	Long tons.		*Long tons.*
1881................	2	1888................	813
1882................	156	1889................	945
1883................	151	1890................	2,604
1884................	125	1891................	3,178
1885................	123	1892................	4,948
1886................	404	1893................	13,945
1887................	312		

The imports of manganese from Japan into the United States for the fiscal year ending June 30, 1895, were 7,158½ long tons, valued at $51,419, or $7.18 a ton.

NEW SOUTH WALES.

But little attention has been given to the mining of manganese in New South Wales, though there is no doubt that this mineral occurs in considerable quantities in the country. The difficulty is that the ores can not at present be profitably worked, owing to the cost of carriage to the seaboard. There seems to have been no production of manganese ores in New South Wales prior to 1890. The production since the latter date is given in the official report tabulated on the following page.

Production and value of manganese in New South Wales from 1890 to 1894.

Year.	Product.	Value.
	Tons.	
1890....	100	$1,573
1891....	138	1.646
1892....	16	227
1893....	0	0
1894....	14	213

NEW ZEALAND.

But little can be learned definitely as to the character of the manganese ores of New Zealand. This ore first appeared among the exports from this island in 1878. The production since this date is given in the following table, the exports being regarded as equivalent to production:

Production of manganese ores in New Zealand from 1878 to 1894.

Year.	Product.	Value.	Year.	Product.	Value.
	Tons.			Tons.	
1878........	2,516	$50,413	1887........	305	$4,332
1879........	2,140	40,356	1888........	1,085	11,635
1880........	2,611	50,447	1889........	1,080	5,227
1881........	1,271	15,890	1890........	1,170	12,741
1882........	2.181	33,701	1891........	1,153	12,801
1883........	384	5,590	1892........	521	5,022
1884........	318	3,911	1893........	319	4,561
1885........	602	8,305	1894........	531	5,595
1886........	328½	6,369			

QUEENSLAND.

Manganese ores have been found from time to time in Queensland, but production has been exceedingly uncertain. Only four tons were mined in 1889, and none in 1892 and 1893. The following table shows the production of manganese ores in Queensland since 1881:

Production and value of manganese in Queensland from 1881 to 1894.

Year.	Product	Value.	Year.	Product.	Value.
	Tons.			Tons.	
1881........	87	$1,263	1890........	5	$97
1882........	100	1,694	1891........	10	126
1883........	20	290	1892........		
1884........	55	799	1893........		
1889........	4	87	1894........	140	1,936

SOUTH AUSTRALIA.

In past years considerable manganese has been produced in South Australia. We have no statement regarding the character of the ores or their occurrence. The production since 1882, so far as we have any records, is as follows:

Production and value of manganese in South Australia from 1882 to 1893.

Year.	Product.	Value.	Year.	Product.	Value.
	Tons.			*Tons.*	
1882.........	136	$3,214	1888.........	1,021	$16,971
1883.........	333	10,062	1889.........	1,596	24,718
1884.........	59	1,142	1890.........	2,764	33,991
1885............		4,061	1891.........	847	8,349
1886.........	1,550	53,163	1892.........	704	7,416
1887.........	1,452	27,801	1893.........	2,428	30,778

WORLD'S PRODUCTION.

In the following table will be found a statement showing the world's production of manganese, so far as the same has been ascertained, for the latest year for which we have returns at the time this report goes to press.

World's production of manganese.

Country.	Year.	Manganese.		Manganiferous.	
		Product.	Value.	Product.	Value.
North America:		*Long tons.*		*Long tons.*	
United States	1895	9,547	$71,769	223,141	$488,100
Canada	1895	125	8,464	....	....
Cuba............	1895	0	0	....	....
South America:					
Chile............	1893	36,096	219,103	....	....
Colombia	1895	3,950	18,462	....	....
Europe:					
Austria-Hungary .	1893	2,743	....		
Bosnia	1894	6,484	....	....	....
Belgium..........	1894	....	....	21,700	53,596
France	1894	14,520	....	17,719	....
Germany	1894	43,012	....		
Great Britain.....	1894	67	....	1,742	....
Greece	1894	9,172	....	156,567	....

World's production of manganese—Continued.

Country.	Year.	Manganese.		Manganiferous.	
		Product.	Value.	Product.	Value.
Europe—Continued.		*Long tons.*		*Long tons.*	
Italy	1894	748	$4,536	5,178	$8,971
Portugal	1894	6,848	....	....	....
Russia	1894	240,181	....	....	....
Spain	1894	7,684	....	275,000	....
Sweden	1894	3,269	....	131,067	....
Asia:					
Turkey...........	1894	9,000	....	....	....
Oceanica:					
Japan	1893	13,945	....	....	....
New South Wales.	1894	14	....	....	....
New Zealand	1894	534	....	....	....
Queensland.......	1894	140	....	....	....
Total...........	....	408,079	....	832,114	....

In many instances it has been difficult to distinguish between manganese ores proper and manganiferous ores. The table, however, shows the best results we have been able to obtain.

17 GEOL, PT 3——15

TIN.

INTRODUCTION.

No effort was made during 1895 to develop the deposits of tin ore known in the United States, i. e., at South Riverside, Cal., in the Black Hills of South Dakota, the Cash Mine in Rockbridge County, Va., and at Kings Mountain, North Carolina.

Meanwhile the following report on the conditions of occurrence and the methods of mining and smelting tin ore on the islands of Banca and Billiton was received too late for publication in the comprehensive report on the tin deposits of the world, by Mr. Charles M. Rolker, E. M., which appeared in the last report of this series:

THE OCCURRENCE OF TIN ORE IN THE ISLANDS OF BANCA AND BILLITON.

By O. H. Van der Wyck.

GENERAL GEOLOGY.

The present sketch refers specially to the island of Banca, which is much larger and better known than Billiton. The geological formation, the mining, and the smelting being very similar in both the islands, a description of the more important one will be sufficient.

It should be borne in mind that the survey of Banca by the Royal Mining Engineers was chiefly technical, in search of tin-ore deposits, scientific investigations and pure geological researches having been governed by commercial and technical considerations.

The greater part of the island consists of stratified rocks of very great age, forming a hilly country characterized by central mountain masses [massifs] varying greatly in size. Minor groups and lower peaks, often wanting any visible connection with other distant ones, form at several localities a strongly indented country. The nucleus of the more important massifs is granite. This is evident at the northwest extremity of the island (district of Muntok), in a larger massif at the north and northeast part of it (districts of Djeboes and Blinjoe), and in a still more extensive series in the southeastern part of the island, along the margin of the districts of Toboaly and Koba, and in some other localities. In the northeastern part of the island the axis of this granite nucleus trends northwest and southeast; in the southeastern part almost west and east.

Post-Tertiary formations are represented by many lowlands, which skirt the river banks, locally stretching up the river valleys to a great extent; by sandy plains at the seashore; by swamps of enormous extent at the mouths of many rivers, and by the valleys.

All strata incline at considerable angles, this steepness increasing in the vicinity of the granite. Though the strata are much folded and cracked, they show an average trend nearly northwest and southeast. The steep inclination, almost reaching the vertical, the great weathering, and the luxuriant tropical vegetation are serious obstacles to geological investigation.

The sedimentary strata are sandstones, argillaceous or quartzose, often real quartzites or argillites of different description, superposed in numerous repeating alternations, with some interposed conglomerate beds. Limestone is entirely wanting. In the northern part of the island mica-schist rests immediately upon the granite, forming a flat, softly-undulating country. Any trace of organic life being wanting, as well as other determinative characteristics, it is impossible to state the geological age of the sedimentary strata or to recognize the geologic place of a single one of the great series of alternating beds, even within a restricted locality. This repeating alternation results from the great inclination of the strata. All banks show an altered character when in contact with the granite and in its vicinity. At the contact both the sedimentary strata and the granite are much fissured and intersected by dikes and veins, and the granite is more quartzose.

The granite varies from coarse to fine grained. Fine-grained granite forms dikes in the coarse grained, and coarse-grained granite forms dikes in fine-grained granite. Generally speaking, all Banca granite is light colored, dark varieties being of subordinate occurrence. The quartz is generally gray or milky white, more or less transparent. The feldspar is light-colored orthoclase, often with pearly luster. Oligoclase is seldom intermixed. The mica is generally dark-colored biotite, green or brown, often black, and commonly forms small aggregates. White mica is found in weathered granites only. Besides these, several other minerals are found in the granite.

Amphibole (hornblende) is not rare. When the mica is partly or totally substituted by amphibole the granite turns to syenite and assumes a dark color. Often the granite shows a porphyritic structure, or forms granite-porphyry; occasionally the last turns into felsitic rock. In exceptional cases graphitic granite has been found.

Some medium or fine-grained granites show distinct stratification. On the west coast of the Svengei Liah district such a granite of favorable mixture, quartz not prevailing, exists for 800 meters. Regular joints trending northeast and southwest from one-half to 1 meter apart, allow the rock to be easily broken out and used for building purposes.

Other minerals found in the granite are: Tourmaline, very frequent; garnet, occasional; chlorite often intermixed, and pyrite, usually iron pyrite, very frequent. Tin ore is occasionally found forming fine stringers, and manganese ore (commonly polianite) also occurs. Wolfram was detected once in a single locality.

In the district of Svengei Liah agalmatolite veins have been found crossing the granite. They contain quartz and show copper ore, some galena, iron pyrite, and some fluorspar. Quartz dikes and veins frequently appear in the granite.

Mica-schist occurs chiefly in the northern part of the island, along the granite massifs. Inclinations of 80 degrees have been noted. The rock is very susceptible to weathering. In contact with the granite it has turned to gneiss; at a distance from the granite it assumes the character of quartzite. These quartzites are always most distinctly fissile and often shaly. Occasionally they are dark colored and fit for touchstones.

The sandstones are partly argillaceous, partly quartzose, frequently fairly ferruginous and manganiferous. Often they are friable and easily affected by weathering; even when quartzose they are often very hard and resistant. Quartz sandstones containing a great deal of quartz, both as fragmentary crystals and as a compact or crypto-grained mass, are altered to quartzite when in contact with the granite. This quartzite stands out in several lofty peaks, including the highest peak of the island—one of the Maras summits (701 meters), which overtower the neighboring granite. By its abrupt slopes and angular forms sandstone, and particularly quartzite, contrasts most obviously with the smoother and rounder shape of the granite mountains. According to its components, the quartzite is always very hard and light colored. The common argillaceous sandstone frequently contains mica leaves, generally of a light-colored variety, black mica being an exception. The fine-grained argillaceous sandstones contain much mica, which causes the rock to be foliated and gives it a striking resemblance to mica-schist.

Polianite, magnetic, and other iron ores frequently form secretions on the cleavage faces of all sandstones, and manganese ore often forms a thin film on them. Psilomelane was found in a pocket within the sandstone in the Koba district, forming great blocks, the sandstone being very much disintegrated.

In the neighboring island of Lucipara the sandstone is coarse grained, quite hard, and contains many minute fragments of hornblende and augite (pyroxene). Quartz veins intersect the rock in all directions.

Clay rocks form large, undulating, and hilly regions and prominences overreaching the granite locally. The characteristic roof slate is very rare; siliceous and sandy slates are more frequent, colored brown or red, showing a hardness which varies according to the proportion of quartz and iron oxide they contain. By weathering, these slates pass easily into a sandy clay. Often sandy slates turn into sandstones or quartz slate, the quartz being prevalent.

In the southern part of the island (district of Toboaly) the clay rock is altered in contact with the granite for 17 kilometers to a compact rock resembling "hornfels," where foliation has entirely disappeared.

In the Svengei Liah district claystone banks assume a burnt appearance, growing more siliceous in the vicinity of the granite. Slates are frequently very ferruginous, and especially so in the vicinity of the granite.

Brown iron ore and iron ocher have been noted locally as forming small layers between common clay slate and mica-schists. Pyrolusite, psilomelane, and scaly specular iron ore (itabiryte) are often deposited on the cleavage faces, even of metamorphosed clay slates in the neighborhood of granite. Magnetic iron ore has been found over a limited extent on the east slope of Mount Plardan, in the southeastern part of the island. In this locality the magnetic iron ore occurs near to the granite. Away from the granite the iron ore is brown.

Manganese often forms in the joints of claystones and clay slates and forms stringers in the bulk of the rock.

Claystones are most differently colored—white (kaolin), gray-brown, red, dark blue, green, and black. The blue varieties often contain iron pyrite.

At several localities conglomerates are found. The pebbles originate from the other rocks—especially from claystones, slates, and sandstones—and are associated with quartz and occasionally some feldspar fragments. Being chiefly light-colored, they are most conspicuous in the generally dark-colored matrix. Rarely the cement is clayish. Most frequently it is ferruginous and siliceous, often mixed with a great deal of manganese oxide, replacing iron oxide.

The tin ore has been referred to as forming stringers in the granite; it is found also in quartz veins intersecting it, but its occurrence in the granite has been proved. At several localities tin ore has been panned out of the weathered products of the granite deposited in cavities. At several others it has been panned out of crushed, not weathered, granite. Tin ore can not be detected by microscopical study in granites from Billiton. That it does not occur in the Billiton granite may be possible; nevertheless, its occurrence in Banca granite is beyond question. Tin ore veins and pockets have been found in the island of Banca, but less frequently than in Billiton.

At Sambong Giri Hill sandstones altered into quartzite, trending nearly northwest and southeast, overlie slates metamorphosed at the contact with the granite upon which they rest. The granite is much weathered, claystone and sandstone being in contact, and both of these are much crumbled and intermingled. Near the contact the sandstone alternates with a hard, brown claystone which has a metamorphic appearance and contains pyrolusite. The sandstone is intersected here by stringers of tourmaline and tourmaline-bearing clay, inclosing rutile and showing a thickness locally increasing to a few centimeters. These stringers are often thrown by the joints of the stratum; often they come abruptly to an end in the bulk of the rock.

Near this locality a small vein formed almost exclusively of tin ore has been noted, showing a thickness of a few centimeters. This vein follows the joints of the sandstone, dipping 30 degrees. Here and there the tin ore is impacted in a clayish substance of remarkable luster, feeling greasy ("steinmark"). At a distance of 20 meters the sandstone grows harder, turning finally into quartzite. It contains scattered tin ore and molds of tin ore crystals. Within its vicinity the sandstone shows distinct jointing, trending here almost north and nearly perpendicularly to the direction of the mountain. Another vein was found in the quartzite, following its joints and dipping 70 degrees. Down to the depth of a few meters it increases in thickness and forms a valuable pocket of limited extent. The neighboring sandstones are intersected by minute veins of hardened clay. The ore deposit runs out at a small depth, probably by forming minute stringers following the joints. A small vein was found containing a little tin ore with mica and some polianite. After increasing to a small depth, the vein ends soon in a worthless stringer. Veins of notable size and persistence have not been found.

At Salinta Hill (district of Pangkal Pinang) claystone and sandstone banks are both in contact with weathered granite, and trend nearly north-northwest; likewise all banks in this district. The claystone has a burnt appearance and is very hard; the sandstone turns into quartzite. On the cleavage faces are found small deposits of tourmaline crystals and tin ore, mixed in different proportions. Remnants found in the upper grounds show tin ore crystals. Small veins of quartz occur, too, containing wolfram. Occasionally some notable piece was found and a few well-formed crystals. The vein has but an insignificant extent.

In the Doesbec Valley (district of Djeboes) the soil consists of an alternation of clay and sand clay rocks. The proper character of each is almost obliterated by weathering. The main vein strikes W. 10° N., and dips almost vertically, and is formed of ferruginous quartz rock. It is nearly 50 centimeters thick and contains scattered granules of tin ore. Deviating to the north is a minute quartz vein which was stated to contain some scattered tin ore. Another vein, about 30 centimeters thick, dipping 30 degrees, was so much weathered that the components could hardly be determined. Some quartz forming stringers were found, and a great deal of tourmaline crystals, and fine angular tin-ore granules could be found by panning. The amount was insignificant. A few minute veins, showing the same character, were found to contain small granules of tin ore, not visible to the naked eye. In the worked-out grounds several fragments and tin-ore crystals were found, rendering it probable that the previously existing outcrop was richer than the portion now visible.

In the neighborhood of the mine No. 16 (Soenon), district of Djeboes, a tin-ore vein was found in the worked-out grounds, dipping at a very low angle, trending W. 20° S. At two spots a small welling or minute fault was observed, with a maximum thickness of 50 centimeters.

In the island of Billiton the ore veins have the same character. They pinch out everywhere or grow barren with increasing depth. Iron-ore veins are tin ore bearing in the upper parts only, and pass into pyrite with increasing depth, inclosing tin ore either in insignificant quantity, or not at all. Such a vein of iron ore was found in the district of Tandjang Pandan, in sedimentary rocks, and proved to contain tin ore near to the outcrop exclusively.

At the Goenoeng Tadjaoe a lode was found trending east and west, pinching out very soon. It follows the joints of quartzite and clay slate, impregnating the clay stone rock. The fault rock consists of very ferruginous clay, clay slate, pyrite, quartz, and tin ore. The thickness was 1.60 meters, including the neighboring clay-slate layer. Beyond the depth of 17 meters the tin ore was much diminished.

At the Mengkosboeng mine (district of Manggar) a vein, filled up with iron hydrate, and crossing clay-slate and sandstone layers trending east and west dipping 75 degrees to the south, shows a thickness of 2 meters near the outcrop. The thickness diminishes within a small depth, and was only rich in tin ore near the outcrop.

In the mine No. 13A (district of Manggar) a small iron-ore vein occurs in sandstone, reaching a thickness of 0.2 meters near the outcrop, but diminishing with increasing depth. The vein trends east and stands vertically. At the depth of 15 meters the vein rock consisted almost entirely of pyrite with a trace of tin ore. At the outcrops the thickness of the ferruginous rock was greater.

In mine No. 61, in the Manggar district, a vein was found inclosing quartz stringers which bore tin ore. The outcrop only has been worked, the tin ore diminishing with increasing depth. The trend is southeast, the dip 80 degrees to the south.

In a few other localities the tin-ore-bearing veins have shown the same character. Mineral-bearing veins and quartz dikes are found in all the rocks. Veins of brown iron ore, manganese ore, and tourmaline are very frequent. They are of small size and occur chiefly near the contact of granite and stratified rocks. Brown iron ore alone often forms minute veins, or impregnates the rocks. Hematite is very rare. It has exceptionally been found showing a "glashof" structure. Specular iron is also very rare. A valuable but small deposit of magnetite occurring in sandstone is known in the district of Koba from a very isolated locality. Titanic iron must occur in that district, for titanic-iron-bearing sand is found yielding 10 per cent of tin ore.

Manganese ore has already been mentioned. It occurs as polianite, as a substitute for iron oxide, or forms thin films on the joints of the rocks. Pyrolusite and psilomelane have been noticed occurring in sandstone. Occasionally these ores are also found in the valleys. Large quantities were found in sandstone on the west slope of Goe-noeng Plawan (district of Sei Selan). Fortunately, wolfram has only been found in a single locality.

Gold has been found on the east shore of the district of Sei Liah, in the sands derived from the neighboring reefs, these being outcrops of sandstone banks, much weathered and intersected by small quartz veins standing at great angles of declivity. The sandstone resembles that of Mount Sambong Giri. The gold-bearing quartz fragments are milky white.

Greenstone fragments have been found in the district of Koba, in the north of Goenoeng Pading. The proper seat is unknown. Green-stone diabase covers conformably a very fine-grained sandstone along the north coast of the Island of Siantoe, which shows, like the others in the Gaspar Strait, the same geological features as in Banca and Billiton. The sandstone in Siantoe trends nearly as do the strata of Billiton.

A remarkable feature of both the islands of Banca and Billiton are the tracts called "padangs." These are flat or very slightly undu-lating plains, nearly horizontal, and covered exclusively by jungle, tall trees being entirely wanting, except in the wet ground. Such padangs, occurring in the upper grounds, are often more or less rich "koolit" beds, but they are not workable, it being impossible to sup-ply them with water. The surface is commonly very sandy, showing coarse-grained quartz sand, covering a dark-colored sheet called "fo san kak," formed out of quartz sands bound by a cement of organic nature, under which the tin ore occurs.

The valleys, both present and buried, are the main seat of valuable tin ore deposits in the island of Banca. In the island of Billiton they may be inferior or equal to the "koolit" beds, a name given the tin ore-bearing grounds on the valley banks or distant from them in the upper grounds, the workable tracts of valley grounds being called "kollong."

The question where valuable ore deposits were to be expected has of course stimulated investigation in order to deduce prospecting rules. Experience has proved that the presence of granite is most frequently of great influence on the occurrence of tin ore, but only as a general rule. Though many of the granite massifs show a great number of tin-bearing valleys, working and outworked mines, yet, on the contrary, several show none within their boundary. In the district of Svengei

Liah the main deposits are generally found in the most ferruginous and sandy banks along the granite massifs. Often rich deposits occur at considerable distance from the granite, in sandstone. The favorable influence of the granite is not evident everywhere. The Mangkol massif of granite is one of the most valuable in affecting the occurrence of tin ore in valleys and upper grounds on its southern slope; at the northern slope, on the contrary, no valuable ore deposit has been found.

At the northern slope of Goenoeng Ladi, a granite hill in the district of Pangkal Pinang, rich ore deposits are found; at the northwestern slope also, but they are wanting at the south side of the hill.

As a general rule the majority of valuable tin ore deposits are found in the grounds near to the contact of the granite with stratified rocks, and are workable to a distance from the granite not exceeding 4 kilometers. Besides the kollong and the koolit deposits already mentioned, there is a third category called "koolit-kollong." These are stream-like deposits occurring in the upper grounds, or more or less distanced from the river banks, and showing a considerable depth down to the ore sheet. Probably they are buried ancient stream beds.

Originating from a single locality, the workable valley tracts seldom exceed 3 kilometers in length. Generally the ore deposit is workable only up to a certain distance from the valley heads. Exceptionally they are workable almost to the head, in which case the upper valley and the heads are surrounded or accompanied by workable koolit grounds.

A section of the ore-bearing valleys shows most commonly the following alternation of sheets: As a rule the tin ore is deposited immediately upon the weathered rock in situ, called "khong," and is covered by a sheet of coarse-grained sand or fine gravel superposed by a layer of fine-grained sand. The overlying sheets of clay, more or less sandy, at several localities inclosing a sheet of fine white kaolin, are covered by bituminous clay, often a very muddy sheet, which is covered by vegetable earth. Occasionally two tin ore sheets are found separated by layers of clay and sand. The total thickness of all layers, from the vegetable earth down to the khong, is commonly 8 to 10 meters; kollongs with a depth to 12 meters are exceptions.

The yield of the total mass varies from about 10 to 60 kilograms of tin ore per cubic meter, and on the average 20 to 40 kilograms, being about 1 to 2 per cent. The thickness of the ore layer is but 3 to 6 decimeters.

In the koolit grounds the deposits are very shallow, the ore being often covered by a thin clay layer and vegetable earth only. Often the ore is scattered even through the vegetable earth, and occasionally the whole groundmass yields diffused tin ore down to the khong. The common size of the ore grains is nearly 3 millimeters, the coarse-grained ore seldom exceeding 5 millimeters in size. Koolit and kollong ore are chiefly distinguished by the size and partly by the luster, the koolit ore surpassing generally the kollong ore in both these respects. The ore is generally larger in the upper parts of the valley, growing smaller with increasing distance from the valley heads. It is generally dark brown, often nearly black. Lighter colored, rather gray, tin ore is not very rare; exceptionally, white, yellow, and zircon-red particles are found. These are very much valued by the Chinese miners. In this regard it ought to be observed that the very dark-colored ore is most commonly rather fine grained and has therefore a tendency to be blown away by the blast in the furnaces.

A striking resemblance has often been observed between ores found in the same group of adjoining mines, forming a natural group by topographical situation, originating from the same mountain series. An initiated person will be enabled by this likeness to point out the group of mines furnishing a given specimen of ore. By this means it is sometimes possible to follow the different streams which have contributed to the formation of a tin-ore deposit in the valley, the ore of the different confluents running often for a considerable distance alongside of each other.

All tin ore is cassiterite (tin oxide) and occurs in crystalline grains or aggregates, sometimes in well-formed small crystals, often adhering to quartz, but very seldom to tourmaline. Though fragments and granules of all components of the rocks may be found in the ore layer, most frequently quartzose rock fragments occur only as quartzite, quartz, and sandstone, the feldspar being weathered into clay and flooded away. Tourmaline is frequently mixed in the ore layer; also pebbles of agalmatolite or similar silicates. Iron pyrite generally accompanies the tin ore, but in very small quantities, the greater part being weathered or deposited in the lower parts of the valley, where mining would not be lucrative. Magnetic iron ore fragments are found occasionally. Titanic iron happened to be found in a single locality; also, wolfram, which has been noted in but one valley in the district of Panghal Pinang. Polianite is found occasionally, too, both in kollong and in koolit grounds.

Gold is found in but one valley, in the district of Merawang, the panned ore yielding 0.036 per cent gold. Within the same ore deposit remarkable abnormalities are often observed in respect to thickness, extent, and persistence. Locally more or less extensive pockets are met with, occasionally showing a great depth, sometimes of a very limited area, as is proved by borings all around. Often the ore layer disappears and reappears at a considerable distance. Often the ore layer narrows or enlarges locally.

MINING.

The lack of reliable tin indications has been referred to, and it has been remarked how difficult it is to note the contact of granite with the stratified rocks, how irregularly the tin ore is deposited in the valleys, and how often it occurs distant from them. It is therefore incumbent on the Royal Mining Engineers to find out the deposits and to indicate accurately the workable tracts therein. They are also required to trace for any mining company every year a parcel to be worked out within that year, in accordance with all circumstances affecting the mining work and its results. Such governing circumstances are: The number of the miners, the water supply, the difficulties to be met with in working and draining, the hardness and thickness of the overlying beds, the depth down to the ore sheet, and several other conditions.

A parcel being pointed out, the first thing to be done is to lay hand upon an abundant or sufficient supply of water, which is indispensable for mining, pumping, washing, smelting, and domestic purposes. A strong dam is built in the upper valley, beyond the workable tract, if possible. This dam accumulates the water, drains the parcel, and forms an extensive reservoir. Occasionally neighboring valleys are dammed in the same way, their waters being made tributary to the main reservoir. On both the valley banks a large canal is dug. One of these, the working canal, "loi-soei-hoeno," leads the water to the mine, the other, "pisoeikong," discharges the dam, ends in the valley beneath the workable tract, and joins the third canal. This, the "gan keaew," dug from the lower part of the parcel down to the deepest water course in the valley, is the draining and flooding canal. While these canals are being dug the whole parcel is cleared by the natives (Malays). The method of working causes the lowest parcels of the workable tracts to be worked first.

The mining work in particular begins by leading a vigorous water stream along one of the margins of the parcel. The adjacent soil, loosened by means of large crowbars, is thrown therein and immediately flooded down to the gan keaew, when a parcel is the first one attacked of a tract, or to the last worked-out "kollong." The progress of this work, called "katnaipi," varies with the velocity, the quantity, and the purity of the water. A considerable streak being washed away, the stream is compelled to run along the newly formed margin, which is now attacked and washed down in the same way. This work proceeds over the whole extent of the parcel, down to a varying depth, fixed by the level of the gan keaew, commonly being about 1 meter, exceptionally 1.50 meters.

When katnaiping is not possible any longer the water stream is led into wooden channels, called "khaan," placed upon wooden blocks or supports, increasing in height with augmenting depth of the "kollong" mine. The miners throw the ground into the khaans with their "pazols"—peculiar spades. As depression of the mine bottom proceeds, earth, gravel, and clay are heaped upon "poenkies"—horseshoe-shaped baskets, twisted of rattan and furnished with two handles. One miner loads the poenkie, another flings its contents overhead into the khaan by elevating it and pulling it vigorously at the handle. By still greater increase of depth two or three series of miners work above each other. This work is called "totjauw," and increases the depth by about 2 meters at the maximum.

When this method is no longer practicable the ground is carried out of the kollong by the miners, no economy being realized by mechanical digging and transportation. This work, called "tam-nai-si," is the most laborious of all. Two loaded poenkies are suspended at the ends of a bamboo. The miners, placing the bamboo over their shoulders, carry it out of the mine, scaling a strong beam, and come back, descending another beam, after having thrown away the ground in a suitable place, commonly the last worked-out kollong.

The mining work preceding it is necessary in order that the mine may be drained by pumping. Commonly all mines employ wooden Chinese chain pumps, of a length up to 25 meters, run by small water wheels, with a diameter of 1 meter up to 1.80 meters.

All the ground is worked out down to the ore layer, which is carried out in the same way and deposited separately, that it may easily be washed afterwards. This work is called "tjoekaksa." To that end a short and broad canal is dug and lined with bark or planks. A strong water stream is turned in and the ore, poured in the canal at the lower end of it, is worked ahead by an experienced miner, who breaks up the lumps, and mixing and turning the sand over and over again, pushes it toward the upper end of the canal, that the water course may flood away all the tailings. The whole stock of ore remains in this canal. It is once more carefully washed over before it is smelted. This final washing is effected by means of a plank placed vertically in the upper part and drawn by two or four miners through the ore from the lower end of the canal up to the upper end while the water course is running in the inverse direction.

As the upper layers of the parcel are sometimes ore-bearing, this ore would be lost by katnaipiing and totjauwing. A small quantity of fine-grained ore is also flooded away by washing. With a view to these possibilities, women, girls, and children of the miners try to gather this ore by panning the detritus, flooded into the prolonged loysoeikeeuw and frequently realize a small profit by selling the ore to the "kongsi" (mining company).

The mass of ground worked per man within one year is variable, the local conditions for the mining work being very unlike in different and even in neighboring localities.

The nature of the ground, especially the more sandy or more clayey character of the layers, their hardness and coherence, their thickness, the occurrence of mud sheets, the depth down to the ore layer on one hand, the abundance or the scarcity of working water, the distance to the forest, providing wood and rattan, the local circumstances, more or less favorable to katnaipiing and totjauwing, the presence or the absence of a worked-out kollong, the variability of yield of the ore layer and of features of the superposed layers, even in adjacent kollongs, and the variable distribution of the ore, cause prospecting and rating beforehand to be a most complex, difficult, and hazardous task for the engineers.

It ought to be noticed here that the mining work includes all work and all business the mining company has to deal with, including not only the technical work but also the administration business and the household exigencies, embracing the whole existence of the mine and its working up to the delivery of the tin. Consequently the whole household management, the wood charring, the washing and reduction, and the transport of the metal are included in the "mining work," and this reduces, of course, the effect per man regarding the mining work in particular; being thus greater than it will appear in the following note:

Considering circumstances, neither too difficult nor too advantageous, it may be adopted that working 300 days a year—as the Chinese do—the worked ground per year per man is to be rated as follows:

Down to a depth of—	Cubic meters.
3 meters............	600–900
3–4 meters.........	450–600
4–5 meters.........	375–450
5–6 meters.........	350–375
6–7 meters.........	325–350
7–8 meters.........	300–325
8–9 meters.........	275–300
9–10 meters.......	130–275

THE ORE TREATMENT.

The simple washing process, already traced, is sufficient to obtain a most concentrated ore, almost totally free from all foreign accompaniments. The ore being cassiterite of remarkable purity, the treatment consists in a mere reducing process yielding the pure tin metal directly.

The furnaces in the small mines are built entirely of siliceous clay mixed with sand and some salt. Their shape is much like that of a Chinese smith's oven, and table-like. The shaft, forming a niche, is cut out within the mass near to the back, where a wall is formed in order to protect the blast and to enable the "melter" to heap charcoal standing out at the shaft. In the midst of the forefront another conical niche is cut out in the table, the top of which communicates with the other niches by means of an inclined hole 2 inches in diameter. The basis of this conical niche is the orifice of a recipient, dug in the ground in order to gather the metal, issuing steadily in a fine stream.

The blast is formed out of a wood trunk, carefully hollowed, or of two parts, correctly assembled. The wooden portion is adjusted by means of cockfeathers, no other material being a sufficient substitute with a view to efficacy, adherence, durability, and insignificant friction. It is managed by three miners, running to and fro.

The work is performed at night only, on account of the great heat. Commonly the night work begins about 5 o'clock in the afternoon and is stopped at 4 or 5 o'clock in the morning. The furnace having been warmed the first "night" several hours before the work is to begin, charcoal and ore are loaded in alternating sheets, the furnace being kept constantly filled. At the end of the night charcoal is exclusively loaded. The work proceeding, a small mass of slag is removed from the molten metal, accumulating in the recipient; for fear of oxidation, the tin is covered by charcoal. The "melter" takes care that the hole discharging the molten metal—the "eye"—does not get choked up, by cleaning it diligently with a long, flexible branch.

The blasting pipe enters the furnace on a higher level than the eye, and is covered by refractory clay or furnished with a tuyere formed of refractory clay. The blast is in the direction of the "eye."

Out of the recipient the upper part of the tin is spooned into cast-iron moulds. A few impurities resting and forming a film upon the tin are scraped away. Before the tin is caught it is tested with a view to its rupture and its "crying."

The slags are molded in the same night in order to extract the inclosed tin and to reduce the ore grains possibly diffused in it.

The tin near the bottom of the recipient is kept aside and molten afterwards once or twice in order to liberate it from the tin iron, which, when present, will accumulate in the lowest part of the recipient.

In the larger furnaces of this kind—the "Chinese furnaces"—the output of one night is about 25 piculs of tin. The charge is 40 piculs tin ore and about 30 piculs of charcoal (1 picul is the weight of 61.761 kilograms, or about one-sixteenth of a ton).

The larger mines generally employ quadrangular furnaces, and of a height of about 6 feet. The circular shaft is clothed with refractory bricks imported from Europe.

According to the capacity of the furnace, one, two, or three blast pipes are employed. The blast is an iron rotary fan, run by a water-wheel. The work is the same as at the Chinese furnaces, but the output is greater, and amounts to about 73 per cent.

The tin issuing from the furnaces and accumulated in the receptacle comes to a second basin, out of which the upper parts are spooned into the molds.

The slags are gathered, stamped, and washed in the washing canals, melted together with the ore.

THE REFINING PROCESS.

The last four or five blocks (one "block" weighs on the average 35 kilograms of tin) got in one night by the reducing process, as well as those from the treatment of the slags, come, together with the blocks rejected during the night or at the following examination, to the refining process, a mere melting, the pure metal being decanted into iron pans.

The arrangement is as follows:

In a furnace, the interior of which has the shape of a horizontal retort, a large wood fire is blown by a hand ventilator. The long flame, projecting at the opposite side, embraces the tin blocks, which are piled up in an adjacent oblong basin of small depth. This is the "melting basin" in which the tin blocks are progressively melted, the metal flowing into an adjacent oblong receptacle. The flame of a second firing furnace, similar to the first-mentioned one, is forced to cover the molten metal in this receptacle. An iron pan adjusted above the lower end of the flame causes it to extend regularly over the whole surface. This pan is utilized for melting a few blocks.

The foundation of the receptacle and basin is a sheet of sand, in the dug-out ground. The purpose of this is to secure the escaping tin, as the receptacle or basin occasionally cracks. This precaution is necessary, since the molten tin has been stated to penetrate the warmed ground down to a depth of 4 meters. The sand stops and retains the molten metal. The basin and the receptacle have both a capacity of about 200 blocks of tin. Out of the receptacle the metal is forced to flow into the "controlling pan," having a capacity of about 15 blocks. From here the tin is decanted into a large iron pan, which is heated exclusively at its bottom, out of which the metal is spooned into the molds. All things being right, not the least trace of tin iron is to be found at the bottom of the "controlling pan." As soon as a sample taken from its bottom proves to be less pure tin the process is stopped. The molten metal is carefully gathered and brought back into the basin in order to be melted over once more. The receptacle is carefully cleaned and the tin iron deposited at the bottom of it totally eliminated. This tin iron forms a viscous mass and is successively carried out from the receptacle during the process by iron spoons, pierced by a multitude of holes, allowing the molten metal to filter through, the tin-iron mass adhering to the spoon in consequence of its viscosity. The tin iron is gathered and melted once more in order to extract the remaining particles of tin. This final melting is performed in small furnaces especially constructed for this purpose out of the same clay mass as the Chinese and the other furnaces. These walls inclose such a furnace, which communicates at the back side with a chimney.

The wood fire warms a trap-like surface, inclined to about 30°, formed out of iron plates with turned up edges.

The tin iron, being melted once more, forms a crystalline mass, which is put upon the second plate from the lower end of the inclined surface just alluded to. The first plate is not charged, it being reserved for the granules of sand and particles of earth which were adhering to the tin.

The tin blocks placed upon the second plate soften and are successively spooned and transferred upon the third plate, new blocks being put upon the second one. These blocks growing soft, the mass is transferred from the third plate to the fourth, and so on. The tin melting, flows downward to an iron pan placed at the foot of the furnace. The tin-iron mass, depositing at last on the highest iron plate, is a sandy mass. It is put aside, being worthless for the moment.

The loss of the metal occasioned by the whole refining process amounts scarcely to 2 per cent. In ratio to the total production of tin metal the loss by refining amounts to 0.25 per cent, and most probably it will be reduced to 0.20 per cent. The expenses of producing the metal are increased by the refining process by about 0.11 f. per picul.

In the island of Billiton the refining process consists in melting the rejected tin blocks by means of a wood fire, above which the blocks are suspended. The molten metal, trickling through the wood fire, falls upon the inclined iron plates, which lead the metal to an iron pan.

The sliding tariff, on the basis of which the Chinese work the parcels in the island of Billiton, varies according to the prospecting drilling from 20 fan in minimum to 41 fan in maximum per picul of tin delivered in the magazines.

The Billiton Mining Company provides also the kongsis with tools and other necessary articles, at a price inferior to that at which the kongsis would be able to buy them elsewhere.

In the island of Banca the tin grounds are worked by the kongsis, which engage the miners at the rate of 10 fan a month with plentiful supply of food.

The kongsis are provided by the Government with rice, tools, and other articles, and cash money on account, which is settled at the end of the mining year. The Chinese year begins now in February or March. With a view to the tin prices, the tin is paid to the kongsis, with 40 fan as a maximum.

The following table gives a note regarding the mining work in the island of Banca during the last years:

Recent tin production in Banca.

Mining year.	Number of miners.	Production.	Average expenses paid to the kongsis per picul.	Total of expenses per picul.	Production per miner.
		Piculs.	Fan.	Fan.	Piculs.
1889–90	8,818	89,691.11	20.01	27.62	10.17
1890–91	8,814	107,189.85	19.22	26.32	12.16
1891–92	9,245	93,622.83	22.105	29.22	10.12
1892–93	9,734	121,736.06	21.56	28.18	12.49
1893–94	10,345	139,513.42	22.46	29.135	11.55
1894–95	11,795	129,951.16	20.57	26.87	11.02

The "total expenses" include also the transportation of metal from Banca to Batavia, and from there to the market at Amsterdam.

Note regarding the production of tin in the islands of Banca and Billiton during the last six years:

Production of tin in Banca and Billiton for six years.

Mining year.	Production.	
	Island of Banca.	Island of Billiton.
	Piculs.	*Piculs.*
1890-91	107,189.85	96,487.88
1891-92	93,622.83	106,245.75
1892-93	121,736.06	8,270.17
1893-94	119,513.42	78,594.51
1894-95	129,951.16	82,424.62

All the tin produced in the island of Banca is transported to Europe.

The production of the island of Singkep has been as noted in the following table:

Tin product of Singkep.

Mining year.	Production.
	Piculs.
1890-91	448.72
1891-92	1,392.87
1892-93	2,746.25
1893-94	4,240.27
1894-95	a 8,500.00

a Approximately.

ALUMINUM.

INTRODUCTION.

With the extension of the producing capacity of the aluminum plant at Niagara Falls the product in the United States increased to nearly a million pounds—920,000 pounds. The price averaged $50\frac{1}{2}$ cents per pound, showing that there have been practically little difficulty in marketing the supply.

Besides the metallurgic uses as an addition to cast iron and steel, the metal is becoming a recognized material for a host of fancy articles of cheaper grade than silver, a use which must certainly expand markedly as the value of Moissan's advice is recognized, i. e., to avoid all traces of sodium and other impurities, which, though slight in quantity, effect rapid loss of brightness. It is also interesting to note the new use of plates—the largest which have been rolled—among the interior fittings of some of the United States cruisers.

PRODUCTION AND IMPORTS.

The increase in production during recent years, as well as the imports and exports, are shown in the tables which follow.

Production of aluminum in the United States from 1883 to 1895.

Year.	Pounds.	Year.	Pounds.
1883	83	1891	150, 000
1884	150	1892	259, 885
1885	283	1893	333, 629
1886	3, 000	1894	550, 000
1887	18, 000	1895	920, 000
1888	19, 000	Total	2, 362, 779
1889	47, 468		
1890	61, 281		

243

Imports of crude and manufactured aluminum from 1891 to 1895.

Calendar year.	Crude.		Leaf.		Manufactures.	Total value.
	Pounds.	Value.	Packs of 100.	Value.		
1891...........	3,922	*6,266	10,033	*1,135	*1,161	*8,562
1892...........	43	51	14,510	1,202	1,036	2,289
1893...........	7,816	4,683	18,700	1,903	1,679	8,265
1894...........	5,306	2,514	10,780	1,210	386	4,110
1895...........	25,294	7,814	6,610	646	1,811	10,301

Aluminum imported and entered for consumption in the United States from 1870 to 1891.

Year ending—	Quantity.	Value.	Year ending—	Quantity.	Value.
	Pounds.			Pounds.	
June 30, 1870...	....	$98	June 30, 1882....	566.50	*6,459
1871...	....	341	1883....	426.25	5,079
1873...	2	2	1884....	595	8,416
1874...	683	2,125	1885....	439	4,736
1875...	434	1,355	Dec. 31, 1886....	452.10	5,369
1876...	139	1,412	1887....	1,260	12,119
1877...	131	1,551	1888....	1,348.53	14,086
1878...	251	2,978	1889....	998	4,810
1879...	284.44	3,423	1890....	2,051	7,062
1880...	340.75	4,042	1891....	3,922	6,266
1881...	517.10	6,071			

Bauxite.—This raw material for aluminum, in so far as produced in the United States, came from Georgia and Alabama in the following quantities, from the well-established mines referred to in previous volumes:

Production of bauxite in the United States from 1889 to 1895, by States.

Calendar year.	Georgia.	Alabama.	Total.
	Long tons.	Long tons.	Long tons.
1889..............................	728	....	728
1890..............................	1,850	....	1,850
1891..............................	3,300	600	3,900
1892..............................	2,000	7,200	9,200
1893..............................	2,315	6,764	9,079
1894..............................	2,005	9,016	11,021
1895..............................	....	....	17,069

The characteristics of foreign bauxites for use in making aluminum are referred to in the following pages on the manufacture of aluminum abroad.

ALUMINUM MANUFACTURE IN EUROPE.

By ALFRED E. HUNT.

The first works on a commercial scale in Europe, and, indeed, in the world, for the manufacture of aluminum, were located in France. From the early commercial work of Deville at Javel, under the auspices of Emperor Napoleon III, and of Charles and Alexander Tissier at Rouen, in 1854–55 (who sold their metal at from $2 to $4 per ounce), the Société Anonyme de l'Aluminium, for working and selling aluminum, came into existence with works for making the metal first at Glacière, then at Nanterre, and later at the chemical works of H. Merle & Co. at Salindres, where for many years under their proprietorship, and later of Pechiney & Co., the manufacture of aluminum was successfully conducted.

In their first successful work, cryolite (the double fluoride of sodium and aluminum) was used as the ore from which to reduce the metal, and later, and more efficiently, chloride of aluminum ($Al_2 Cl_6$) was used as the salt of the metal from which to reduce it by the means of sodium.

This concern produced some of the best aluminum that has ever been put upon the market, and earned for the metal praises for properties which later experience with inferior and more impure metal has often not substantiated, to the serious retarding of the introduction of the metal in the arts.

Too much praise can not be bestowed upon these early manufacturers of the metal, who for more than thirty years from the year 1857 were not only pioneers, but practically were alone in the field.

These works enjoyed a practical monopoly of the aluminum business of the world for more than twenty-five years, although there were unsuccessful business enterprises started in England, the first in 1859, by C. H. Gerhart, at Battersea, a suburb of London, which only ran for a short time, and later, in 1860, by Bell Brothers, at Newcastle-on-Tyne, who made aluminum in a desultory sort of a way up to the year 1874.

In 1882, the selling price of aluminum, which had been reduced to about $12 to $14 per pound, was further lowered by the process of an Englishman named Webster, who started a company called the Webster Aluminium Company. Mr. Webster's improvements consisted in a cheaper production of aluminum chloride, used as the salt from which the metal was best reduced by the sodium process.

The business of this concern was further strengthened by the purchase of the patented process of Mr. H. Y. Castner for making the reducing agent, sodium, by an improvement by which a more intimate contact is effected of the carbon used as a reducing agent of the sodium from molten caustic soda.

This company developed, in June, 1887, into the Aluminium Company, Limited, with a share capital of £400,000, and put up expensive works at Oldbury, near Birmingham, England, for working aluminum chloride, metallic sodium, and from them metallic aluminum. Among the shareholders of this company were some of the best chemists and metallurgists, as well as some of the most prominent politicians of Great Britain.

Early in the year 1888 another rival company to the Aluminium Company, Limited, was started at Wallsend, a suburb of Newcastle-on-Tyne, to work the process of Carl Netto. This process consisted in using molten cryolite as the salt from which to reduce the aluminum, the metallic sodium being made in a furnace by the trickling of molten caustic soda over incandescent coke.

Soon after getting into operation these two companies unfortunately got into legal complications regarding their relative patent rights, and the curious spectacle was presented of these two large and strong financial companies fighting over the patent rights to a process that was destined to prove, before the settlement of the suit, uneconomical as compared with the Hall electrolytic process that was even at that time being successfully developed in Pittsburg, Pa.

Both of these concerns in the year 1890 stopped the manufacture of aluminum by the modifications of the old Deville process of reduction by means of metallic sodium.

Early in the year 1891 the firm of Pechiney & Co. also ceased operations in the manufacture of aluminum, for by this time the selling price of aluminum had been reduced to $1.50 per pound—a rate far below the cost of manufacture of aluminum by the sodium process.

In August, 1891, the selling price was again reduced to 50 cents per pound.

The European price for pure aluminum fell, to meet the American competition, to the following prices:

European prices of aluminum.

Date.	Wholesale price per pound.	Retail price per pound.
September 1, 1890, to March, 1891	$1.67	$1.83
March to July 20, 1891	1.32	1.45
July 20 to October 1, 1891	.78	.88
October, 1891	.70	.88
November, 1891, to July, 1893	.55	.66

This rate of 50 cents per pound was far lower than it could be hoped that any sodium-reducing process for the manufacture of aluminum could attain, and they all forthwith quit the business, although the meritorious Castner process of manufacturing sodium was developed by the Aluminium Company, Limited, within the next three years to the rate of about 25 cents per pound, that company having achieved financial success in the manufacture and sale of metallic sodium made by the Castner electrolytic process at Oldbury, England.

Ludwig Grabau, of Hanover, Germany, in 1889, devised processes for making cheaply fluoride of aluminum from kaolin by means of decomposition with sulphuric and hydrofluoric acids; also pure and cheap metallic sodium by the electrolysis of fused common salt, and made some very pure aluminum in 1890. His work was also one of those ruthlessly cut short by the drop in price to 50 cents per pound.

There were several poorly devised processes, in which the use of an electric current had been called into service, that were as well "given their quietus" by the drop in price to 50 cents per pound for aluminum in 1891; among these being the concerns named below.

1. Aluminium and Magnesium Fabrik, at Hemelingen, near Bremen. This concern at first, from 1884 to 1887, used the process of Grätzel, who suggested the electrolysis of the chloride or fluoride of aluminum, using compound anodes of part carbon and part alumina. The process was a failure because of the polarization around and excessive wear of the anodes and because of the noncontinuity of the process, as well as because of the expense of the aluminum halogen salts used as the source of the decomposition by the electrolytic action. This concern later (1888–1890) used a modification of the Deville sodium process, under the direction of their works manager, Herr Saarburger.

2. The process of Dr. Edward Kleiner, of Zurich, Switzerland, patented in England early in the year 1886, of the electrolysis of cryolite, which was electrolyzed after being first melted by the aid of the electric current, as had been first suggested by the work of Sir Humphry Davy and later was published in many forms during the interim between his day and the time when cheap and efficient electrical generators made such a process as Hall's a practicable undertaking.

The Kleiner process was started at Hope Mills, Tyddesley, Lancashire, England, and failed, like its predecessor, the Grätzel process, for similar reasons. Its last hopes as a successful process, indeed, waned with the reduction of price to $1.50 per pound, in 1889. The electrical plant of the Kleiner concern was purchased by the Pittsburgh Reduction Company, to be used in working their foreign patents.

3. The process of Adolph Minet, which consisted in the electrolysis of a molten bath of fluoride of aluminum, together with the chloride of sodium, fed by the addition of fresh aluminum fluoride and alumina. From 1888 to 1890 this process was experimented on at Creil, in France, and in 1890 was started on a larger scale at St. Michel, using a water-

power of the Vaillorette, a stream running into the Arc River in High Savoy. This process was worked by the Bernard Brothers, of Paris, who lost money upon the unsuccessful working of the process. Their plant, like that of Kleiner, has since been sold to a concern working under the Hall patents.

4. The Hérault process for manufacture of aluminum alloys, first put into practical operation on July 30, 1888, at the works of the Société Métallurgique Suisse at the Falls of the Rhine, Neuhausen, Switzerland. In this process alumina is reduced in the presence of carbon and a cloaking metal, like copper or iron, to alloy with the reduced aluminum, by means of the intense heat produced in a powerful electric arc.

The Hérault alloy process was abandoned upon the advent of the 50-cent rate for aluminum, in works that have been in operation under the proprietorship of a stock company (the Aluminium-Industrie-Actien-Gesellschaft) at Neuhausen, Switzerland, and at Froges (Isère), in France, as well as at Boonton, in the State of New Jersey.

The Aluminium-Industrie-Actien-Gesellschaft, formed with a share capital of 10,000,000 marks by the uniting of the Société Électro-Métallurgique Suisse and the Allgemeine Electricität-Gesellschaft of Berlin in November, 1888, purchased the Hérault Continental patents and continued the work of manufacturing aluminum at Neuhausen. This new concern soon found that the aluminum alloys made by their Hérault alloy process, which was not essentially an electrolytic process were superseded in the world's market by the pure aluminum made by the electrolytic process. They consequently gave up their more expensive alloy furnaces early in the year 1890, after having experimented with the pure aluminum process for some months, and devoted their attention to producing pure aluminum. From the year 1891 they have manufactured almost exclusively pure aluminum.

Their present plant—which, by the way, is just at present considerably curtailed in its output of aluminum, on account of their going into the manufacture of carbide of calcium with a portion of their available water power—is limited to the taking from the River Rhine at the Rhine Falls, Neuhausen, of 20 cubic meters of water, equivalent to 700 cubic feet per second, which they conduct through steel penstocks to a fall of 20 meters, giving them at a maximum about 5,500 effective mechanical horsepower, which they utilize in a manner to obtain about 3,000 horsepower in electrical current. The plant now consists of one 300-horsepower turbine, two 600-horsepower turbines, and five 610-horsepower turbines of the Jouval type; one of the turbines being kept as a spare. The turbines have vertical shafts, and each actuates above it a generator of 7,500 amperes at a tension of 55 volts, or 553 electrical horsepower. With this plant running at full time, an output of between 3,000 and 4,000 pounds per day has been produced since the middle of the year 1893. This concern has also secured further water-power rights by means of a canal and expensive tunnel which is proposed to be driven later, when business will warrant, lower down at the Höllenhaken Rapids, Rheinfelden, on the Rhine, near Basle, where it is proposed to erect a plant having 20,000-horsepower capacity. They have also secured another water-power right at or near Salzburg, Austria.

Following the parent company, the Aluminium Industrie Actien Gesellschaft, the Société Électro-Métallurgique Française, which had established works at Froges (Isère) to manufacture aluminum alloys by the Hérault process in early 1889, soon gave up their alloy business, and in 1891 commenced to sell pure aluminum made by the electrolytic process of dissolving alumina in a molten bath of the fluoride of aluminum together with the fluoride of some metal or metals more electropositive than aluminum, passing a direct electric current through the bath, and producing aluminum by the electrolysis of the alumina thus dissolved. Their plant at Froges was abandoned in 1893, and a much larger one at La Praz, on the River Arc, in Savoy, was established in 1894, designed only to make pure aluminum. This plant consists of two turbines, each running a generator of about 1,500 electrical horsepower, and their capacity is about 3,000 pounds of aluminum per day.

In the "survival of the fittest," with the lowered selling price of the metal, it will be seen from the above hasty sketch of the history of the development of aluminum that a report upon the present state of the art of aluminum manufacture in the years 1893, 1894, and 1895 would have shown in manufacturing operation in Europe only the works of the Aluminium-Industrie-Actien-Gesellschaft at Neuhausen, Switzerland, the works of the Société Électro-Métallurgique Française, whose works during this period were removed from Froges (Isère) to La Praz, near Modane, on the River Arc, in Savoy, and the works at St. Michel, which during this period were transferred from the hands of Bernard Brothers, who had been working the Minet process, to the Société Industrielle de l'Aluminium, a concern who had bought the French patents of Hall from the Pittsburgh Reduction Company. These concerns, with the Pittsburgh Reduction Company in America, with works at New Kensington, Westmoreland County, Pa., near Pittsburg, and at Niagara Falls, N. Y., were the only ones in the world that were in commercial operation during this period.

So far in the development of the metallurgy of aluminum, France, England, Germany, Switzerland, and the United States have been the only countries of the world dividing the honors. In the future the countries having good water powers will undoubtedly compete for the world's trade; and already, as before referred to, the Aluminium-Industrie-Actien-Gesellschaft have secured, in addition to another power on the Rhine near Basle, Switzerland, a water power in Austria for a future development of works. In Russia, there are several large landed interests with water powers, the advantages of which they are considering for the manufacture of aluminum. In Norway and Sweden, there are also good water powers which the new development in electro-metallurgy are bringing into favorable consideration. A plant in Norway, at Sarpsfos, has been definitely decided upon; this plant having a capacity of 10,000 horsepower steadily during the entire year, the fall of the water which it is proposed to utilize being about 80 feet. There is a very large volume of water that can be utilized. This plant will probably not be in operation before the year 1898.

The disadvantages of most of the European water powers that would seem to be in other ways available are their periods of low water in the winter and early spring season, when the snows of the mountain glaciers which feed their head waters, where water powers are situated, are frozen up. Owing to the comparative slowness of operation of the present successful electrolytic process of manufacture of aluminum, continuity of operation seems to be an almost necessary prerequisite to economical manufacture, and a plant that would be forced to lie idle or work at a greatly reduced output for three months out of the twelve will undoubtedly be so seriously handicapped as to be unable to compete for the business of the future.

As to methods of manufacture, all the aluminum now being made in the world is practically made by the general process of the electrolytic decomposition of alumina dissolved in a molten flux consisting of the fluoride of aluminum together with the fluorides of a metal or metals more electro-positive than aluminum; the idea being to use a flux which dissolves the ore with the most facility, remains molten the longest, is least subject to decomposition, allows the best circulation around the anodes, and is the easiest to manage continuously without caking up.

Hérault suggested, and in his patents only mentions cryolite, a specific mineral composed of aluminum fluoride, 40.25 per cent; sodium fluoride, 59.75 per cent. Hall preferred, and in his patents, besides his broad claim, suggests several mixtures containing much larger proportions of aluminum fluoride, with the additions of the fluorides of other electro-positive metals, notably, the fluoride of calcium, as giving better results than with the use of cryolite alone as a flux.

The Pittsburgh Reduction Company, in their experience, have found some of these mixtures to give not only a greater yield per unit of electrical current, but a considerably less cost in operating, due to the freedom from caking from the results of the decomposition of the bath; and, more important still, have found that these special mixtures of the electrolyte have produced metal much freer from the impurities of sodium, carbon, and occluded gases than it would be possible to obtain with cryolite alone used as the flux.

In this, the examination of the metal made in Europe for these impurities, as compared with that made by the Pittsburgh Reduction Company, by the French chemist Moissan, has been confirmatory.

Bauxite has become recognized as the best native ore of aluminum, and as the purification of its contained alumina from silica, oxide of iron, and titanic acid has shown that the silica is the bête noir of the operation, the location of bauxites rich in alumina and at the same time low in contained silica is an important factor to the manufacturer of aluminum.

So far the red bauxite of the department of Var, in South France, has been the great, and, in fact, the only large commercial source of such ore in Europe. The Styrian Alps have furnished some bauxite low in silica, and late reports have been that there had been some large deposits of such ore recently opened up, but it is a fact that up to the year 1896 no large commercial shipments have been made of it and that the operators in Southern France have furnished from the district of the Var practically all of the bauxite ore used in the manufacture of aluminum in Europe, with the exception of some few shipments of bauxite from America.

The bauxites low in silica in the Var in France and in similar large deposits in America are all at the surface, with no superincumbent strata except a few feet of surface earth and clay to be stripped, and the mining is all of an open quarrying operation upon faces of the ore from 20 to 50 feet in thickness.

The British Aluminium Company, Limited, are now building a works at Foyers Falls, in Scotland, to manufacture aluminum. The water is taken from the river bed about three-quarters of a mile above the falls, and is carried through a circular brick-lined tunnel 9 feet in diameter to the slope of a hill, at the base of which, toward Loch Ness, the power house of the proposed works is situated. The water is to be conveyed from the tunnel to a basin, from which five lines of cast-iron pipe ($28\frac{1}{2}$ inches internal diameter) convey it down the slope of the hill to the power house, 45 feet wide, 90 feet long, and 26 feet high, on posts, where each pipe is to feed a turbine water wheel at the very considerable head of about 325 feet.

This plant is estimated to have a maximum of about 4,000 horse-power when the high-water level in the tunnel can be maintained. The British Aluminium Company, Limited, have purchased the water rights to a very large tract of land in the hills above their present source of supply, and intend increasing the natural drainage basin of their watershed and increasing the capacity of the locks which form their storage reservoirs.

The British Aluminium Company, Limited, up to this writing (February, 1896) have not manufactured any aluminum, but have acted as British selling agents for the Aluminium Industrie Action Gesellschaft, whose patents for the manufacture of aluminum in Great Britain, as well as those of the Cowles Company, they have bought.

This concern and another at Sarpsfos, in Norway, are the only new ones now in actual progress of erection for the manufacture of aluminum that are known to the public at this time.

NICKEL AND COBALT.

PRODUCTION.

The nickel ores of Oregon, Nevada, and elsewhere have not yet been systematically mined, and the only nickel (and cobalt) mined in the United States in 1895 was that produced at Mine La Motte, Missouri, which yielded 180,737 pounds of matte, containing 14,458 pounds of cobalt and 10,302 pounds of nickel. In addition to this the smelting of foreign matte makes the total product of nickel larger than heretofore. The price of nickel ranged from 28 cents to 38 cents per pound, according to quantity and fineness, and that of cobalt oxide from $1.40 to $1.45 per pound.

USES.

The effect of nickel upon steel and iron has become a favorite subject of experiment, discussion, and some speculation in the last three or four years, since its use was found to be advantageous in armor plates. A paper on the manufacture, properties, and applications of nickel steel by O. Vogel, in Stahl und Eisen, 1895, page 718 et seq., gives a comprehensive review of the subject, the substance of which is here reproduced. The author quotes from a chemical work by Christofle Girtanner, published in 1792, to show that it was then known that iron would unite with nickel. Later, in 1820, Faraday made nickel-iron alloys by melting the two metals together, and he was followed by a number of experimenters. Nickel steel seems to have been first made by a manufacturer named Wolf, in Schweinfurt, Germany, in 1832, and was described by Liebig as resembling damascened steel. It was introduced into trade, although not very extensively, under the name of "meteor" steel, but it was not until 1888–89 that nickel steel was successfully introduced into large use, when the attention of Governments was drawn to it.

The preferred methods of making nickel steel consist in adding the desired proportion of nickel to the molten metal in a Martins furnace, for example, and the nickel is introduced either as oxide, together with a reducing agent, or in the metallic state as ferro-nickel.

The author gives several tables showing the composition of various nickel steels and the results of the tests made upon them. The tests were made by the Canadian Copper Company and the Cleveland Rolling Mill Company in this country, and in several places in Europe.

The results show that in steels having very nearly an identical composition, except that one contains nickel while the other does not, the steel containing nickel is superior in strength and elasticity under the same conditions. One table may be given in illustration of this point.

The nickel steel had the following composition: C, 0.08; Mn, 0.36; P, 0.045; S, 0.038; Ni, 2.69.

Experiments of the Cleveland Rolling Mill.

Number of test.	Diminution of cross section.	Elongation.	Limit of elasticity per square mm.	Breaking strain per square mm.
	Per cent.		*Kilograms.*	*Kilograms.*
1....................	53.0	23.25	....	45.05
2....................	53.3	26.0	33.11	46.66
3....................	56.3	25.0	31.42	46.40
4....................	45.1	24.5	33.32	47.17
5....................	54.4	26.0	33.25	45.55
6....................	49.7	23.75	34.37	46.54

COMPARISON TEST.

1....................	45.6	26.0	25.10	39.01
2....................	45.8	26.0	24.95	38.38
3....................	52.9	27.5	23.06	37.89
4....................	61.8	32.0	23.94	36.91
5....................	63.0	27.0	24.95	37.75
6....................	62.0	26.0	25.94	39.72

The steel used for comparision in the above test had the following composition: C, 0.10; Mn, 0.27; P, 0.048; S, 0.039.

In France, Messrs. Cholat and Harmet made a series of studies on nickel-iron and nickel-iron-chromium alloys, of which Herr Vogel gives the following summary:

1. Nickel-iron alloys, with 2.5 per cent to 25 per cent nickel. The addition of nickel to pure iron causes a rapid increase in strength and elasticity. At about 10 per cent of nickel this increase ceases, and at about 15 per cent of nickel the elasticity and strength begin to decrease. Elongation and contraction decrease, but with 25 per cent nickel the elongation begins to increase again.

2. Nickel-iron alloys, with 2.5 per cent nickel and 0.1 per cent to 1 per cent carbon. The hardened tests showed that the elasticity and strength were increased, while the contraction was slightly lessened. Therefore, hardening improves nickel carbon steel.

3. Nickel iron alloys, with 15 per cent nickel and 0.1 per cent to 1 per cent carbon. The greatest strength was found to be with about 15 per cent nickel and 0.3 per cent carbon. The breaking strain reached

150 kilograms. Hardened in oil, the strength was 195 kilograms, while the expansion and contraction decreased.

4. Alloys with 25 per cent nickel and 0.1 per cent to 1 per cent carbon. The elongation and contraction increased with increase in carbon, and the metal did not become brittle.

5. Nickel chromium-iron alloys, with 2.5 per cent nickel and 0.25 per cent to 2.5 per cent chromium. They showed great strength and elasticity, which two properties increased with increasing chromium. Chromium seems to increase the strength and elasticity given by the nickel.

6. Alloys with 15 per cent nickel and 0.25 per cent to 2.5 per cent chromium. The strength increased with the increase of chromium, but brittleness also increased. Hardening decreased the strength and elasticity, but increased the contraction and elongation. Chromium may therefore replace nickel and carbon to some extent. The alloy is not unlike a carbon nickel iron alloy.

7. With 25 per cent nickel and 0.25 per cent to 2.5 per cent chromium, the effect of the chromium was remarkable when the test was hardened and heated. It acted like carbon in No. 4.

8. With 2.5 per cent nickel and 1 per cent to 5 per cent silicon, the silicon was found to act as on nickel-free iron, viz, it increased the strength and elasticity, but caused great brittleness.

The conclusions drawn from these experiments are that—

1. Carbon improves the properties of hardened nickel steel strikingly, without making it brittle, as usual.

2. The limit of the beneficial effect of nickel on the metal seems to be reached at about 15 per cent; with a greater proportion the effect is less advantageous.

3. By the addition of chromium to a metal with 15 per cent nickel the advantageous effects due to the latter are enhanced and the metal reaches a tenacity of 180 kilograms, a degree hitherto unknown, but the nickel does not lessen the brittleness due to the chromium as it does with carbon; therefore a lower chromium percentage is indicated. These important results were utilized in the manufacture of armor plates, and in France nickel chrome steel has been patented for this purpose. The new material, made at St. Chamond since 1891, may be described as a nickel chrome steel in which chromium is the hardener in place of carbon. As both nickel and chromium have a hardening effect, it is obvious that, in the presence of these constituents, the Harvey process should not be carried so deep as in steels free from them.

Other comparative tests of nickel and nonnickel steel are cited in Herr Vogel's paper, which go to show the superiority of the nickel steel for certain purposes. Its greater elasticity and tensile strength have suggested many new uses for this steel, which are mentioned in a paper by Mr. A. G. Charleton, published in the Journal of the Society of Arts May 24, 1895. Among these are shafting and boilers especially for marine engines, where much weight could be dispensed with. parts of locomotives, and many others.

On the other hand, Mr. H. H. Campbell has published the results of tests made by the Pennsylvania Steel Company.[1] His paper contains several tables, and he draws the conclusion from the tabulated results of the tests that "it seems doubtful if the nickel steel offers such marked improvement in quality that it can be employed profitably in ordinary engineering work."

METALLURGY.

It remains to report further progress in the extraction of nickel from its ores. Several processes have been patented since the last report was prepared. Of these some are worthy of mention because they help to make the record of this industry continuous, and the Mond process should be preserved in this report because of its inherent scientific interest. The patent of Garnier of January 2, 1894, No. 511,886, describes a process of reducing nickel oxide in a basic-lined apparatus somewhat resembling a converter. The specification states that the molten nickel is apt to clog if it is pure. To avoid this the oxide is reduced in contact with basic slags in the basic-lined apparatus and carbon and silicon are added to it in the process of reduction in the form of highly carbonized and siliconized nickel. The melted metal is then blown, as in a converter, to remove carbon and silicon, and the metal, after blowing, is run upon the siliceous hearth of a Siemens furnace to remove the basic material mechanically mixed with it. He adds ferromanganese or ferro-aluminum to effect final deoxidation.

C. G. Richardson's patent, April 10, 1894, No. 518,117, is for a process of refining nickel and cobalt mattes, which is as follows: The finely pulverized matte is roasted to convert the sulphides into oxides. The oxides are then placed in a suitable furnace—e. g., a Brückner furnace—and dry hydrochloric acid gas is passed over them while in a heated state, which converts them into chlorides. By managing the temperature, the chloride of iron formed by the action of the gas may be distilled off, leaving nickel chloride behind. If copper is present the nickel chloride can then be separated from the copper chloride by distillation at the proper temperature. The nickel chloride is roasted to oxide, which can be reduced to metal. The hydrochloric acid gas is returned by suitable means to the chloridizing chamber and re-used.

A. L. Grant and C. G. Richardson patented a process for refining nickel and copper mattes on April 23, 1895, No. 538,212, according to which the matte, containing copper, nickel, and iron, is finely crushed and then roasted to complete oxidation in a reverberatory or other suitable furnace. The resulting oxides are placed in a suitable receptacle, provided with means for stirring the contents, and subjected to

---

[1] Trans. Am. Soc. Civil Eng., October, 1895, p. 285.

heat and the action of a reducing gas until complete reduction has taken place. This leaves the metals in a finely divided condition, which is best suited to the action of an acid. The metals are then subjected to the action of dilute sulphuric acid, which dissolves the iron and nickel to sulphates, but leaves the copper. As some copper is, however, dissolved, it is removed by adding to the solution a fresh portion of the finely divided metals. The solution is filtered off, oxidized by chlorine or a current of air, to peroxidize the iron and cobalt, when the latter oxides are precipitated (by lime or in any usual way), leaving nickel sulphate to be used in the manufacture of nickel salts, or for obtaining nickel in any of the ordinary ways. The patentees prefer to crystallize out the nickel sulphate and then roast it to oxide, which is then reduced.

Manhes's bessemerizing process (D. R. P. 80,467), which is an improvement on an earlier one, consists, first, in the oxidation of the iron contained in a matte and solution of the oxide so produced in special basic or alkaline fluxes added in the converter to form a slag; and, secondly, in the removal of the sulphur under the same conditions, also by means of alkaline or basic slag reagents combined with chlorides of the same bases. The reagents for slagging off the iron oxide may be alkaline salts, but lime borate, or boracite, is preferred, and for removing sulphur lime and chloride of lime (chlorkalk) are used. In carrying out the process the matte containing nickel and iron is run into the converter and blown; the sulphur is partly removed as SO_2 and the iron is speedily oxidized. The iron oxide so produced would remain in a pasty condition and interfere with the process unless it was removed. The slag forming reagents are therefore added to dissolve the iron oxide as it is formed. After the iron has been almost completely removed, which is shown by the color of the flame, the blast is stopped and the slag run off. Then the second set of reagents—the lime and chloride of lime for removing sulphur—is added and the blast turned on again. The remaining sulphur forms an alkaline salt, and pure nickel remains in the converter, which can be poured. In case an alloy or mixture of iron and nickel, such as would result from smelting ores containing no sulphur, were used in the converter the process would be the same as above described, except that no treatment for sulphur would be necessary. The same process would apply to cobalt as to nickel.

A process which is very interesting from its history, and because it affords another instance of the direct transfer of a chemical process from the laboratory to industry, is that of L. Mond, F. R. S., which he described in a paper read before the New York section of the Society of Chemical Industry and published in the journal of the society (14, p. 945). The discovery of this process was due to an accident. Mr. Mond was engaged in experiments with a view to recovering the chlorine from the chloride of ammonium formed in the Solvay process. It was necessary to construct a plant for volatilizing the chloride, and it was found that the metal valves of the apparatus were attacked by the vapors of the chlorides. Valves made of nickel proved among the most resisting in the laboratory experiments, but even these were soon acted upon when used on the large scale. The faces of these valves were covered with a black crust which was found to contain carbon, which must have been derived from carbon monoxide gas (or carbonyl, CO), a small proportion of which was known to be present in the carbonic acid gas used to sweep the ammonia out of the apparatus. This discovery led to a study of the action of carbonic oxide gas upon nickel, when it was found that that metal is capable of taking a part of the carbon from the monoxide (CO) within certain temperatures, leaving carbonic acid (CO_2). In the course of these experiments the compound of nickel and carbonyl was discovered, which was described a few years ago. It was then found, as the experimenters (Mr. Mond and Dr. Langer), gained facility in the manipulations, that they could produce nickel carbonyl in quantity, having discovered the exact conditions. Then came the idea of making a practical application of this method in separating nickel from other metals on a manufacturing scale. Mr. Mond erected a plant at Birmingham, and after several years' experimenting reduced the process to a practical method, by which he was able to produce with the Birmingham plant a ton and a half of nickel a week from Canadian nickel-copper matte. The process is as follows: The matte, which contains about 40 per cent of nickel and an equal quantity of copper, is carefully roasted to drive off the sulphur, and is then subjected to the action of a reducing gas in a suitable apparatus, the temperature of which is under perfect control and is not allowed to exceed 400° C. From this apparatus (called the reducer) the metallic material is taken through air-tight conveyors and elevators to another apparatus (called the volatilizer), where it is subjected, at a temperature not exceeding 80° C., to the action of CO gas. The apparatus, consists of an iron cylinder provided with shelves and a stirring device which gradually moves the material from the top to the bottom while the gas passes in the opposite direction. The CO is prepared by passing pure CO_2 through incandescent coke, the pure CO_2 being made by passing the flue gas of a boiler or fire through a solution of carbonate of potash and subsequently boiling the solution. The CO gas, charged with nickel, is passed through a series of tubes or chambers heated to about 180° C. in which the nickel is deposited in various forms, according to the speed of the gas current, the richness of the gas, and the existing temperature. The CO gas thus freed from nickel is taken back by means of a blower and used over again in the volatilizer, so that the quantity consumed is limited to the very small amount of unavoidable loss through leakage of the plant. The material under treatment is repeatedly taken from the volatilizer to the reducing chamber, and vice versa, by means of air-tight conveyors until the amount of nickel volatilized begins to fall off. It is then roasted to remove the sulphur which it still retains, and is treated with sulphuric acid to remove part of the copper. The residue is treated over again as above described until the nickel is removed as far as practicable, when this residue is melted into matte again. If the nickel is deposited slowly at a carefully regulated temperature it can, Mr. Mond states, easily be obtained from the gas as a coherent metallic film, so that it is possible to coat any substance which can stand heating to 150° C. with a perfect covering of metallic nickel. It is also possible to make articles of metallic nickel for direct use; the finest delineations of a mold can be reproduced in this manner. Hollow nickel goods could be made in this way which at present can not be made at all, or only by the use of hydraulic machinery. The cost of the process, if carried out on a sufficiently large scale, Mr. Mond declares, would be inconsiderable, as the consumption of material would be very small, the main expense consisting in providing careful superintendence of the operation. (The Mond process was patented in this country December 10, 1895, No. 551,220.)

ORIGIN OF NICKEL ORES.

In Mineral Resources for 1893, a summary was given of the opinions which petrographers were coming to entertain of the origin of nickel and cobalt ores. It was shown that these metals were brought to the earth's surface in the first instance by basic rocks, of which, in some cases, they were original constituents in the form of sulphides, as in the case of pyrrhotites in the gabbro-diorite of Sudbury, in Canada, and in Sweden, according to Professor Vogt. Since that review was prepared a long and very complete discussion of the nickel and cobalt deposits of the Rhine, by Laspeyres, has appeared.[1] His conclusion, based on a most laborious and careful study of the minerals and their geological occurrence, including the literature relating to the subject, is that the nickel and cobalt were brought to the surface by the diabase of the region (a basic rock) which is of Devonian age, and that from this original source all the numerous veins of the region were supplied.

[1] Verhandl. Naturh. Ver. preuss. Rheinl. und Westfalens, vol. 50, 1893.

IMPORTS.

In the following tables are given the statistics of the imports of nickel and cobalt oxide into the United States from 1868 to 1895:

Nickel imported and entered for consumption in the United States, 1868 to 1895, inclusive.

Year ending—	Nickel.		Oxide and alloy of nickel with copper.		Total value.
	Quantity.	Value.	Quantity.	Value.	
	Pounds.		*Pounds.*		
June 30, 1868		$118,058			$118,058
1869		134,327			134,327
1870		99,111			99,111
1871	17,701	48,133	4,438	$3,911	52,044
1872	26,140	27,144			27,144
1873	2,842	4,717			4,717
1874	3,172	5,883			5,883
1875	1,255	3,157	12	,36	3,193
1876			156	10	10
1877	5,978	9,522	716	824	10,346
1878	7,486	8,837	8,518	7,847	16,684
1879	10,496	7,829	8,314	5,570	13,399
1880	38,276	25,758	61,869	40,311	66,069
1881	17,933	14,503	135,744	107,627	122,130
1882	22,906	17,924	177,822	125,736	143,660
1883	19,015	13,098	161,159	119,386	132,484
1884			a 194,711	129,733	129,733
1885			105,603	64,166	64,166
Dec. 31, 1886			277,112	141,546	b 141,546
1887			439,037	205,232	c 205,232
1888			316,895	138,290	d 138,290
1889			367,288	156,331	e 156,331
1890	f 566,571	260,665	247,299	115,614	376,279
1891	355,455	172,476	g 10,245,200	148,687	321,163
1892			h 4,487,890	428,062	428,062
1893			h 12,427,986	386,740	386,740
1894			h 9,286,733	310,581	310,581
1895			h 20,355,749	629,910	629,910

a Including metallic nickel.
b Including $465 worth of manufactured nickel.
c Including $879 worth of manufactured nickel.
d Including $2,281 worth of manufactured nickel.
e Including $131 worth of manufactured nickel.
f Classified as nickel, nickel oxide, alloy of any kind in which nickel is the element or material of chief value.
g Classified as nickel and nickel matte.
h Includes all nickel imports except manufactures.

Cobalt oxide imported and entered for consumption in the United States, 1868 to 1895, inclusive.

Year ending—	Oxide.		Year ending—	Oxide.	
	Quantity.	Value.		Quantity.	Value.
	Pounds.			*Pounds.*	
June 30, 1868		$7,208	June 30, 1882	17,758	$12,764
1869		2,330	1883	13,067	22,323
1870		5,019	1884	25,963	43,611
1871		2,766	1885	16,162	28,138
1872		4,920	Dec. 31, 1886	19,366	29,543
1873	1,480	4,714	1887	26,882	39,396
1874	1,404	5,500	1888	27,446	46,211
1875	678	2,604	1889	41,455	82,332
1876	4,440	11,180	1890	33,338	63,202
1877	19,752	11,056	1891	23,643	43,188
1878	2,860	8,693	1892	32,833	60,067
1879	7,531	15,208	1893	28,884	42,694
1880	9,819	18,457	1894	24,020	29,857
1881	21,844	13,837	1895	36,155	39,839

CHROMIC IRON, WITH REFERENCE TO ITS OCCURRENCE IN CANADA.

By WILLIAM GLENN.

HISTORICAL.

In another place,[1] the writer has related the manner in which the problem of the constitution of the mineral "Siberian red lead" entertained the chemists of Europe for nearly forty years, until, on the 4th of November, 1797, Vauquelin, then a subprofessor of chemistry in the Polytechnique at Paris, announced its solution. He had learned that the mineral now called crocoite (Dana) was a native crystallized salt of lead, the acid of which was easily reduced to an oxide, which he believed to have a metallic base called by him chrôme. Later on he gave the process by which he reduced the oxide and isolated the metal, whose characteristics he describes. Following usage in such cases, the element subsequently came to be known as chromium.

The discoverer learned that the salts of chromic acid, and more especially the oxides of chromium, afforded coloring matters which might have valuable application in the arts. But the supply of crude ore was almost nothing.

In the year following, P. Meder announced the discovery of the only commercial ore of chromium even as yet known to us. Under the title "Description of some new Russian minerals,"[2] he described what we now know as chromic iron. He states that it was found by Soymonof, then director of mines for the northern part of the Urals, upon the bank of a small river there; and that it was analyzed by Professor Lowitz, who found in it chromic acid, iron, and some silica and alumina. Meder calls the mineral "chromium-säure eisen," and not eisenchrom or chromeisenstein, as stated by most writers. He then gives a quite full description of the mineral, from which it is clear that he had before him the mineral known to us as chromite. Later on, he states that at about the time Soymonof found the mineral it was discovered by Metschnikow in the more southerly part of the Urals, perhaps 500 Russian versts distant from the point of Soymonof's discovery.

In 1799, there was sent to the Council of Mines at Paris, from the department of Var, a mineral not known to the council. It was analyzed by Tassaert, who printed his results under this title: "Analyse du chromate de fer de la bastide de la Carrade; par le cit. Tassaert."[3]

---

[1] Proc. Am. Inst. Min. Eng., Vol. XXV, p. 481. [2] Crell's Cemische Annalen, 1798, Vol. I, p. 493.
[3] Annales de chimie, Vol. XXXI, p. 220.

261

The author begins with a physical description of the mineral, in which he states that it resembles brown blende. And although he makes no mention of Lowitz's work, the latter mention leads one to suspect that he was aware of it, for Lowitz tells how to differentiate it from that very mineral (uraninite).

Tassaert first attempted to dissolve his mineral in acid, and met only failure. He then resolved to attack it with fusing alkali. I have taken the following translation from Nicholson.[1]

Two other grams were therefore taken and ignited with five times their weight of potash. After a quarter of an hour's application of fire the crucible was suffered to cool, and the matter was mixed with water. The fluid exhibited a beautiful lemon-yellow color, which led to the suspicion of chromic acid; and, in fact, when trial was made with the nitrates of lead, silver, and mercury, there remained no doubt of the presence; particularly when the slight residue left by the potash was treated with nitric acid it swelled up like a vegetable extract, which is one of the most prominent characteristics of chromic acid.

Then Tassaert fused 5 grams of the finely powdered mineral with eight times as much "potasse" for half an hour in a platinum crucible. The fusion was dissolved in water and then filtered; the undissolved residue was treated with hydrochloric acid and the solution again filtered. The mineral remaining was again fused with potash, and the operation repeated until all was in two solutions; Tassaert imagined that now he had all the chromic acid as alkali chromate, and all the iron separated as iron chloride. Following the methods of Vauquelin, he precipitated both elements and arrived at this conclusion: Chromic acid, 63.6 per cent; iron, 36 per cent; lost, 0.4 per cent, and so reported.

To understand how Tassaert succeeded in decomposing chromic iron in the way he mentions, we have but to recall that the French writers of his time used the expression "potasse" for the body we know as potassium hydroxide. Under the conditions stated, that reagent will decompose chromite; after which the liberated chromic oxide may be further oxidized to chromic acid simply by oxygen contained in the air which may reach the fusing mass. This fact enables us to understand why it was that Tassaert supposed he had found chromic acid in the mineral, when in fact it contains not a trace of it. In the year 1881, Morse and Day, then working in the Johns Hopkins University, printed a paper on the assay of chromic iron by the method of fusion with potassium hydroxide.[2] Evidently, they were not aware that they had evolved the means of decomposition used in the first analyses made of that mineral, except that their method is accurate and useful while that of Tassaert led him into grievous error and deductions.

CHARACTERISTICS OF CHROMITE.

Chromite (chromic iron) is a heavy, opaque mineral of submetallic luster, and in color varying from iron black to brownish black on fresh surfaces. Its impalpable powder invariably is brownish, the more so

---

[1] Nicholson's Jour., Vol. III, p. 314.   [2] Am. Chem. Jour., Vol. III, p. 163.

the more of chromic oxide contained in the specimen. Fracture, uneven. Specimens poor in chromic oxide often are magnetic. Hardness, about 5.5 in crystals. But all specimens will scratch window glass. Specific gravity, between 4.3 to 4.5, slightly more or less. Its structure usually is fine granular, or it may be massive. Some ores are exceedingly tough to blows from a hammer, while others may be rubbed to granules like coarse sand between one's fingers.

The form of crystals is octahedral, isometric. They are exceedingly rare. Parts of them have been observed in the ores of the Wood Pit, Pennsylvania, region. Perfect ones occur in that form of ore called sand chrome, but they are so small that one would not detect them unless a lens were used. The largest crystal ever found by the writer was about 6 millimeters long in its greatest axis. It is a perfect octahedron, and now is in the collection of Prof. William Simon at Baltimore.

Ideal chromite would consist of a molecule of ferrous oxide combined with a molecule of chromic oxide. It would have the symbol FeO,Cr_2O_3, affording ferrous oxide 32.11 per cent and 67.89 per cent of chromic oxide. But, so far as my knowledge extends, one or both of the metals are always more or less replaced by alumina, magnesia, lime, and silica, together with other bodies which occur in very small quantities. It is safe to assert that a part of the chromic oxide is replaced invariably to such a degree that ores having more than 50 per cent of it are by no means plentiful. The exhibit of Russia at the Centennial Exposition at Philadelphia contained specimens marked 59 per cent chromic oxide. I have seen a hand specimen which gave 56 per cent and a shipment of 54 per cent by my own assays; but I have not seen chromic iron richer than that, to my own knowledge.

USUAL COMPOSITION OF SHIPMENTS.

Of late, there has grown up among metallurgists some demand for chrome ores having special qualities as to constituents. To those who have not results obtained in their own laboratories, the writer begs to offer the following analyses as being typical of what may be expected in consignments of ore:

Typical analyses of chromic iron ore in bulk.

	No. 1.	No. 2.	No. 3.
	Per cent.	Per cent.	Per cent.
Silica	7.00	5.22	6.44
Chromic oxide..............	39.15	51.03	53.07
Ferrous oxide	27.12	13.06	15.27
Magnesium oxide...........	16.11	16.32	16.08
Calcium oxide..............	3.41	2.61	1.20
Aluminum oxide...........	7.00	12.16	8.01
Total	99.79	100.40	100.07

It will be observed that ores have from 5 per cent to 7 per cent of silica, rarely less and not often more. It is unusual to find consignments of ore as low as 7 per cent alumina; it is not unusual to find them containing twice that quantity. Apparently these are the elements which mostly interest metallurgists. As to chromic oxide, that represented by the first analysis would be regarded as very poor, the second sample as rich, and the third as very rich. The greater part of chrome ore now being offered in the market varies between 40 per cent and 46 per cent chromic oxide.

Since it is my hope to be of some service to those metallurgists who are but entering the field of chromium, it may be well to mention that when chrome ores reach the eastern seaboard of the United States, they consist of lumps varying in size from that of a man's head to that of sand grains and dust. Asiatic ores are friable and contain many small lumps and crushed material. Canadian ores are hard and tough; they stand transport and handling, and provide abundantly of large-sized stones. On the other hand, the ores of one of the Turkish mines are wonderfully friable; they afford almost no lumps and chiefly are in a condition resembling fine gravel and sand. A pile of it is not "iron black" at all, or "brownish black," but a yellowish shade of brown. In this respect it is unique. But upon fresh surfaces it is brownish black, and it scratches window glass, even though lumps of it may be crushed between one's fingers.

In the writer's paper, cited at the beginning of this account, he ventured to make this statement:

THE OCCURRENCE OF CHROMITE.

We now are familiar with the chromic iron deposits of the eastern part of America, from the Gulf of Mexico to the St. Lawrence; with the mines of California, from San Luis Obispo to the Washington boundary, and with those of Norway and of the Urals; with the deposits of the Danubian provinces, and of Asiatic Turkey and of Syria, and with those of the Gundagia-Tumut district of New South Wales. With this knowledge before us, we can say distinctly that wherever found at all, chromic iron is found in serpentine rocks. This is a most peculiar condition. It is an impressive fact that chromic iron is found in serpentine only, or in some rock nearly akin to it, and, like it, metamorphic.

The reader will observe that the statement refers to chromic iron deposits—that is, to mines of chrome ore. It was long ago pointed out that the oxides of chromium existed in many of the basic magnesian rocks to be found near the eastern seaboard of North America. Sir William Logan, writing in 1863, says:

In addition to the chrome and nickel which these serpentines have in common with similar rocks of the same age in Eastern Canada, it is worthy of remark that copper ores, with specular iron, have been found in the serpentines of Newfoundland and resembling the ores of the Quebec group in the eastern townships. A beautiful variety of steatite, holding traces of nickel and colored emerald green by oxide of nickel, occurs in these serpentines.[1]

---

[1] Geol. of Canada, note to p. 875.

Parenthetically, the writer begs to recall the somewhat careless habit of ascribing always to the oxides of chromium the green colors found so abundantly in these rocks, when, in fact, such colors often are due to nickel, which will afford even emerald green, as pointed out by Logan in the note just cited. And similarly, it is not unusual to see chromic iron mentioned as chromate of iron, thus reiterating the error made by Tassaert originally.

The late T. Sterry Hunt had an unusually wide knowledge of the rocks we now are considering; and he insisted that, in Canada, they often were marked by the presence of the oxides of chrome and nickel. In one of his early lectures, not printed until 1878, he has this to say:[1]

The great preponderance of magnesia in the forms of dolomite, magnesite, steatite, and serpentine is also characteristic of portions of this series. The latter, which forms great beds (ophiolites), is marked by the almost constant presence of small portions of the oxides of chrome and nickel. These metals are also common in other magnesian rocks of the series.

One of Dr. Hunt's colaborers on the Canadian Survey (whose name, unfortunately, I failed to note) made studies of the magnesian rocks found so abundantly in the eastern townships of Quebec. He writes:[2]

The magnesite of Bolton, where it forms an immense bed, resembles a crystalline limestone, and consists of about 60 per cent of carbonate of magnesia, 9 per cent of carbonate of iron, and 31 per cent of quartz in grains, besides small portions of nickel and chrome.

My own observations made on the magnesian rocks which may be found at intervals from central Alabama to the St. Lawrence in Quebec lead me to suppose that nearly always, if not invariably, the chromium found in them exists as sesquioxide, and not as chromite, unless in the serpentines. The single exception relates to a crystal of chromite found by me in the detritus from a rock mass which I regarded as peridotite (or chrysolite), which might be considered as anhydrous serpentine.

Those who know most of the matter are in agreement that coal seams are to be regarded as beds; that they are strata, occurring in an orderly way in a series of sedimentary rocks. That they are, indeed, one member of such a series. Since this is true, if we know the position and the figure of a coal seam at a given point, we can safely predict its position in the rocks at a point somewhat distant from the point given. That is to say, a coal seam has an orderly and persistent extension of figure. We can with much safety predict where it is to be found, when once we are familiar with its physical history.

Whatever opinions we may entertain regarding the genesis of the great pyrite deposits at Capelton, in the Province of Quebec, and of the neighboring and similar ones at Ely and at Elizabeth, in Vermont, we must agree that they lie conformably in the rocks; and that in some other respects they are like coal seams. They have a definite

[1] Chem. and Geol. Essays, p. 32.   [2] Geol. Survey Canada 1853, p. 422.

figure and a persistent position in the rock beds, so far as the latter are to be distinguished. We safely can predict the general extension of all such deposits, much as already has been said of coal seams; except, to emphasize our present opinion that their mode of deposit must have been different from that of coal beds, we say that such deposits are veins. The same designation is given to ore bodies, which are found within well-defined side walls which cut through or across the general stratification of the country rocks. And this we do without any mental reservation whatever. There is no reason for supposing that fissure veins have any near relation to coal seams.

Another form of ore deposits is that of the lead mines of Missouri, and of nearly all other useful metal deposits which occur similarly in limestone rocks. These ore bodies have no definite figure, or direction of extension. They occupy what are but shapeless holes in the rocks, mere pockets which are filled with ores of lead or zinc or copper or other metal. Knowing the position of a part of such a pocket, that of the remainder of the body cannot be foretold. And no matter what may be the extent of one of these, they are regarded as ore pockets, since they are neither veins nor fissures nor beds, and are in nowise of orderly occurrence, or of orderly figure, or extension in the rocks. With few exceptions, indeed, the same is true of chrome mines. They have no orderly mode of occurrence or of extension of figure. They are neither veins nor beds nor fissures, but are ore pockets, each one of which must be considered as a completed unit, having no relation whatever to any other pocket in the region in which it may exist. So far as concerns chrome mines, it would be futile to argue the position of an unknown pocket from the basis of any known one. It would be equally as rational to throw one's hat high into the air and to search at the point to which the wind might transport it, a method no little affected by the lead miner of Missouri.

The only rational way in which to search for a pocket of chrome ore is to hunt for the ore which erosion may have left in and upon the soil of the natural surface. The ore is obdurate to subaerial decay, far more so than are the rocks which inclose it; for which reason, more or less of it always is to be found in and upon the soil which usually overlies a mine. When the deposit is an ample one, and where the natural surface above it is not much inclined, it is usual to find some tons of the ore lying upon the surface. But upon a steep hillside, the ore set free by decay of the rocks may have been transported to a distance, and always downhill, of course. Since one may be sure that drift ore never flows uphill, the conditions of search are much narrowed.

The corundum mines of Dr. Lucas, near Franklin, in North Carolina, lie upon the rather sharply inclined north side of the valley of a tributary of the Tennessee. Near the river side, grains of corundum were found in the soil; by washing this in a shovel submerged in water, and in that way eliminating the lighter material, the heavier corundum particles were made more evident, because of their concentration into a less volume. In this way, by washing out shovelfuls of the soil, the flow of drift ore was followed uphill for quite a distance, perhaps a fourth of a mile; until at last there was found soil which contained no corundum. The upper end of the stream of drift ore had been found; and under that was the corundum mine, which has proved the richest yet known to exist.

This instance is cited as being typical of the method to be pursued when a deposit of any relatively heavy mineral is to be searched for; and because it is about the only rational one to adopt in the case of a chrome pocket, not made evident by stones of ore lying upon the clays which conceal the deposit in place.

Except among those having no knowledge of the subject, there is no such practice as shafting or tunneling for chrome ore which might lie concealed in the rocks. The methods in use have just been indicated; when they fail, we necessarily must wait for a further wearing down of the rocks which form the natural surface. In the present state of our knowledge, it would not seem philosophical to expect an alternative, since we know nothing of the method by which mines of chrome ore are formed; except that we may feel assured that the agencies by which chromite was concentrated into ore bodies are no longer active within the earth's extreme outer crust.

To the eastward of the Appalachian field, within the "crystalline rocks much older than the Paleozoic and part of that continent which yielded the materials of Paleozoic sediments" (Bailey Willis), are to be found more or less of exposures of serpentine and similar basic magnesian rocks. They occur in north Alabama, and at several points in Georgia, one exposure of which lies as far east as Washington, in that State. Small exposures of them may be seen in North Carolina, and in the Piedmont country of Virginia at Lynchburg and again in Loudoun County and elsewhere. But among the rocks we now are considering there is not known to me any very considerable exposure of magnesian rocks until the Baltimore region is reached.

Within the Paleozoic rocks, in the midst of the high mountains of North Carolina, are to be seen many small fields of serpentine or rocks nearly akin to it. Many of these exposures were described by J. Volney Lewis in a paper entitled "Corundum of the Appalachian Belt," read at the Atlanta meeting (October, 1895) of the American Institute of Mining Engineers.

From the Baltimore region northward there occur detached fields of serpentine until the Pennsylvania boundary is reached at the Texas region mentioned by Dana. Thenceforth they extend eastward along Mason and Dixon's line nearly to its beginning at the northeast corner of Maryland. These rocks were studied, in the last-named State, by the late Prof. George H. Williams.[1] That part of the bed lying in

---

[1] Bull. U. S. Geol. Survey No. 28, 1886.

Pennsylvania was studied by Prof. Frederick D. Chester.[1] These rocks are interesting as being the most important chromic iron field known to exist on this continent.

In similar position within the ancient crystallines, fields of basic magnesian rocks are to be found in Pennsylvania and in New York. A somewhat important one lies just upon the flank of the Housatonic Mountain, near Chester, in Massachusetts. From that point northward and at wide intervals the magnesian rocks occur to the eastward of the Green Mountains, in Vermont, from whence they may be traced across the frontier and into the Province of Quebec.

CHROMITE IN CANADA.

Exposures of magnesian rocks are somewhat abundant in the eastern townships of Quebec. They lie to the westward of the St. Francis River and its chain of lakes, reaching northeastward for more than a hundred miles and beyond the township of Thetford; after which point is passed, the writer has no further personal knowledge of them. And although the Geological Survey has as yet printed but little concerning their outcrops in the great stretch of country lying between Thetford and the Shickshock range in Gaspé, there is little doubt that more or less of them will yet be found to exist in that region. These rocks are the more interesting because they are the congeners of serpentine, the home of chromic iron, a mineral which has been useful always, and which of late has found favor in the eyes of the metallurgist of steel.

A great body of these rocks outcrops in what is known to the Survey as the eastern townships of Quebec. Its southward end is in the township of South Ham, from which it extends in an unbroken body for 15 miles through Garthby and into Wolfestown. The rocks are diorite, with fields of serpentine lying along its westward edge, the entire mass varying from 1 mile to 3 miles in width. To its northeasterly end is joined a field of serpentine reaching through Coleraine and Thetford and beyond, being more than 20 miles in length and of varying width, the detached fields being not less than 6 miles between Little Lake St. Francis and Black Lake, where occurs their greatest lateral extension. This is the largest field of serpentine to be seen along the eastern seaboard of North America, so far as my knowledge extends, and at present it is the most important one in Canada, since it contains all the commercially valuable chrome ore known to exist in the Dominion, in addition to the mines of asbestos everywhere famous. It may be well to add that this material is chrysotile and not asbestos truly.

From the Black Lake and Thetford region to the Gaspé Peninsula, a distance of 350 miles, the Canadian Survey seems, as yet, to have

[1] Second Geol. Survey Pennsylvania, Ann. Rept. for 1887.

printed but little concerning the rocks we are considering. It has, however, much of interest relating to the Shickshock range in Gaspé, and of the serpentine rocks to be seen there. Apparently, members of the Geological Survey of Canada visited the range in 1858 for the first time, when they discovered on Mount Albert the peculiar mineral chromite and the even more peculiar "well-stratified serpentine."[1] The following account is taken from the report for 1882, page 32 E:

> Among the prominent features of the Shickshock range are the two barren hills of serpentine, the one on the eastern extremity, overlooking the forks of the Ste. Anne River, and known as Mount Albert; the other 12 miles west on the Solomon Branch, and called by Sir W. E. Logan the South Mountain.

Referring to the latter, the account continues:

> The width of the mass of serpentine and associated rocks is about three-eighths of a mile. It rests upon the south flank of the hornblende schists, and terminates abruptly on the east bank of the branch. The serpentine of this mountain apparently lacks the stratification seen in that of Mount Albert, and no traces of asbestos or chromic iron were discovered.

Further account of the locality is given in the same report, beginning at page 7 F:

> The next day we ascended Mount Albert. The summit is about 3,000 feet above the bed of the river and 1½ miles distant. The top of Mount Albert is flat, and is rent by a deep gorge on the east side, which, near its head, splits into several smaller ones. The sides of the gorges are quite destitute of vegetation, and the bare serpentine rocks are weathered to a light buff color. On the top of the mountain blocks of serpentine are scattered around, and are partially covered by a thick growth of mosses and lichens. Sheltered places are occupied by a stunted growth of black spruce (*Abies nigra*), which rarely attains a height of 10 feet. The whole surface has a dead appearance, and reminds one of the pictures of the moon.
>
> [Page 19 F:] *Serpentine and olivine.*—These rocks are largely developed at the eastern extremity of the Shickshock range, and form the prominent peak of Mount Albert. They extend in a southwesterly course, making a total distance of 12 miles. The greatest breadth is 4 miles, on Mount Albert, but the average is not more than 2½ miles. The rocks are chiefly olivine, more or less changed into a dark green serpentine. All the rock seen on Mount Albert was altered into the above serpentine. Chromic iron is found associated with the green serpentine, and seems to be confined to certain beds of the rock, as it is found scattered along the strike in loose blocks, some of which are 10 inches in diameter.
>
> The ore was found to occur in small, widely separated pockets, scattered through the serpentine, and where seen is not in sufficient quantity for profitable mining.

As appropriate to the preceding sentence, the writer begs to observe that it is more than probable that good deposits of chromic iron will yet be found on Mount Albert. Experience teaches that serpentine fields so extensive, rarely are free from considerable pockets of that mineral. At this time it so happens that no important body of ore exists at the natural surface of the rocks.

In addition to that of Mount Albert, members of the Survey have reported upon the chrome ore of one other region. In 1888, Dr. Ells

---

[1] Geol. Survey Canada 1858, pp. 154, 164.

examined into the occurrences of it in the eastern townships, concerning which he writes:[1]

Chromic iron.—This valuable mineral is found at many points throughout the serpentine belt of the eastern townships from the boundary of Vermont to the Shickshock Mountains in Gaspé.

In the eastern townships while chromic iron is found at a number of places, the attempts to mine it have not been attended with much success. In the township of South Ham, on lot 40, range 2, a lenticular mass, having a thickness of 14 inches, was worked about thirty years since, and some 10 tons of 41 per cent ore extracted by Mr. Leckie, when the supply apparently gave out and the locality was abandoned. In Wolfestown, on lot 23, ranges 2 and 3, several pockets occurred in the serpentine, and were mined by Mr. William Grey, manager for Bell's asbestos mine at that place in 1886, about 25 tons in all being obtained, but the ore still remains unsold, presumably owing to the fact that it did not contain the requisite percentage of chromic oxide. In Leeds, on lot 10, range 10, a deposit of excellent ore was mined several years ago by Dr. Reed, of Inverness, and about 50 tons taken out, for which a ready sale was found, and in the township of Thetford, on lot 17, range 4, there is apparently a very extensive deposit which has been slightly opened up. A sample of this assayed in the laboratory of this Survey gave chromic oxide 35.46. This location is also owned by Dr. Reed.

The reader will notice that Dr. Ells did not write of his own knowledge concerning the 50 tons of ore said to have been mined in Leeds. There are reasons for supposing that the account was exaggerated.

As has been stated, chromic iron was known to exist in the eastern townships long before the year 1894; and it had even been mined in small quantities; but no industry had grown out of the discovery, which had shown no commercial vitality. The real discovery was made by a French Canadian, Provençal by name, by trade a carpenter, of the little commune of Black Lake.

In the early springtime of 1894, Provençal found some heavy black stones, seemingly iron ore, upon the desolate hills 2 miles to the southward of the village. Following the instincts of his race, he put them into the hands of Father Ouellet, the village priest, that they might be applied intelligently. Through the Father's acquaintance among the members of the Laval University at Quebec, it soon was learned that the stones were chromic iron and that they contained about 50 per cent of chromic oxide. When the snows had melted, the Provençal mine was opened. It proved a pocket, affording about 600 tons of merchantable chromic ore, which found its way to Baltimore promptly and there was used for manufacture of alkali bichromates.

This was a true discovery, and it had the usual effect of diffusing a spirit of industrious search into many people, and so fortunate were they that when the summer had ended there were known to exist in the township of Coleraine, not Provençal's mine alone, but twenty-one other deposits in addition; and in the adjoining township of Garthby there had been found at least one chromic-iron outcrop; but few of them, however, had any commercial value at all.

[1] Geol. Survey Canada, Vol. IV, new series, p. 111 K.

The best studies of the Black Lake mines are those made by Mr. J. Obalski, provincial mining engineer of Quebec, who in January of the present year gave some account of them in a paper read before the General Mining Association of the Province of Quebec,[1] at its meeting in Montreal. Mr. Obalski states:

Although chromic iron has been known to exist in the serpentines of the eastern townships, I do not suppose more than 50 tons were shipped until last year, the different deposits scattered through the country not being considered of commercial importance.

In the month of April, 1894, quite a large deposit (Nadeau[2] mine) having been discovered, more researches were made and many other important deposits were found, mainly in the township of Coleraine. As by returns kindly furnished by the Quebec Central Railway, the shipments in 1894 amounted to 915 long tons sent to Baltimore and Philadelphia.

For the year ending December 31, 1895, the shipments were as follows:

Shipments of chromic iron ore from Coleraine township, Canada, in 1895.

To —	Long tons.	To—	Long tons.
Philadelphia	807	Glasgow	41
Baltimore	725	Nova Scotia	54
Pittsburg	810		
Liverpool	400	Total	2,837

Besides there are about 1,200 tons of ore delivered at the Quebec Central Railway tracks or lying at the mines ready for shipment.

I would state that the larger part of the ore shipped was of the first quality, the chemical works of Baltimore and Philadelphia requiring that grade, while the ore used for metallurgy may be of an inferior grade. The most of the ore sent to England was of the third quality.

For fifteen minutes before reaching Black Lake it is noticed that the train is moving through a low, mountainous country which presents a barren and inhospitable aspect. And if he be at all familiar with such a landscape as is before him, he will be convinced that he is passing through a comparatively enormous field of serpentine. Such distressing poverty of foliage, the sharp crest lines of bleak and bare hills, such want of animate nature, all are expressive of that poverty of soil (and of no soil) typical of those rocks. But as the climate is cold and moist, the whole region is carpeted with cryptogamous plants, the lowly organisms which ask so little of mother earth. An abundance of lakes and their geographic position lead one to suppose that they were born of the glaciers which once moved over the land. And in some other respects the country recalls parts of the Adirondacks. One here is passing through the chromic iron field; and just beyond, at Black Lake station, the great asbestos (chrysotile) quarries come into

[1]Canadian Mining Review, January, 1896.

[2]Provençal took into partnership Nadeau, and shortly his discovery came to be known as Nadeau's.— W. G.

view. The more noted of them, however, lie yet 3 miles northward, at the station Thetford Mines.

Nearly always, chromic iron is found as a heavy, blackish, and nearly homogeneous rock; that is to say, it has no gangue which might be separated readily, and but little which could be separated at all. Slabs, wedges, and pockets of magnesian rocks are found scattered through the mass of the ore body, but they are readily eliminated in the mining operations; so that usually 90 per cent of the ore is ready for the market when it is taken from the mine. The remainder is such as has been taken from the confines of the ore body and from juxtaposition of its included rocks, so that it is attached to worthless matter, and must be separated from it by hammers.

One of the Black Lake mines is a prominent exception to the general order of occurrence just stated. It is a large body of chrome ore, together with more or less of gangue in intimate mixture, and so constituted that the ore and gangue may be separated by modern methods and at reasonable cost.

Chromite also occurs in small grains scattered at wide intervals through whole fields of serpentine; indeed, at intervals so wide that the occurrence of ore is not apt to be noticed at all. Erosion sets free the mineral, which is obdurate to decay, and running waters transport its minute grains to the beds of brooks and of rivers, where they are concentrated because of their relatively high specific gravity. When freed from foreign matter this form of chromic iron is called sand ore or stream ore, which is as valuable as rock ore.

It should be borne in mind that magnetite also occurs in serpentine fields in similar grains, similarly disposed, and that it forms deposits in brooks in the same way as does chromic iron. The father of the chrome industry in America (Isaac Tyson, jr., of Baltimore) once bought many tons of magnetite sand when he supposed he was buying sand chrome.

Recalling that nature does not delight in clear-cut and prominent boundary lines, we may inquire if what we call sand chrome is never found concentrated into mines. There are three such occurrences in the Wood Pit region of Pennsylvania, and all of them were industriously worked. But even the best one of them could scarcely be considered as a mine; because so little of ore was found in it. Unless the Black Lake mine, last mentioned, may be looked upon as a mine of sand chrome which had been concentrated in the rocks, there is no such occurrence known to me. My own opinion (for whatever that may be worth) is that it ought not to be so regarded.

USES OF CHROME IRON ORE.

More than ten years ago there was manufactured what was sold as chrome steel, even though a published analysis of it declared that it contained no chromium at all. It is a fact that the maker of it used chromic iron ore in his process, and there can be no doubt that he believed he was making an alloy containing chromium. That such alloys lately have been produced is clearly set forth in a late paper by F. L. Garrison on the "Alloys of iron and chromium."[1]

In this country alone considerable quantities of chrome ore are now being used in two or three metallurgical establishments, presumably for production of the alloys mentioned by Mr. Garrison. Previous to such use chromic iron was consumed alone by makers of chromic acid salts, who continue to be the chief buyers of it.

For forty years subsequent to the French Revolution the knowledge of chromium was centered in Paris, from which Vauquelin had announced the discovery of the element in the year 1797. Yet the great chromic-acid factories were not to be at Paris, or even in France. The first of these to live and flourish grew out of a chemical works in Scotland, through the guidance of John White, who had been a student under the teachers at Paris, and who had returned to his father's works at Glasgow. Subsequently these came to be known as the establishment of J. & J. White; which soon was devoted to the production of chromic acid salts, as they still are. The second successful establishment was the Baltimore Chrome Works, established by Isaac Tyson, jr., in the year 1844. From the beginning to the present these works have produced chromic acid salts alone.

Vauquelin believed that he had originated a coloring matter which would prove useful in the arts. As a matter of fact, his "chrôme" has been the basis of what probably is the most useful of all such matters. The manufacturer of textiles finds it indispensable for many shades of buff, red, brown, and black. Makers of painters' colors require it for the purer tints of red and yellow. It is used for colors and tints on pottery, and upon other kinds of objects. And while the tanner of skins has learned that alkali bichromates have a high value for him, and he uses them largely, yet the great field for chromic acid is the field of color.

-

[1] Sixteenth Ann. Rept. U. S. Geol. Survey, Part III, 1895, pp. 610-614.

ANTIMONY.[1]

By Edward W. Parker.

OCCURRENCE.

Antimonial ores are found in a number of the Western States, chiefly in Arkansas, California, Idaho, Montana, Nevada, and Utah. Dana mentions it as occurring also, but sparingly, in Maine and Maryland. The usual form in which antimony occurs is stibnite (sulphide of antimony), but it is also found in compounds with other minerals, among which are berthierite (with iron and sulphur), wolfsbergite (with copper and sulphur), boulangerite, and bleinierite (with lead and sulphur); also with silver and sulphur and as antimonial silver and antimonial nickel. It is sometimes, but rarely, found native. Oxide of antimony, known as valentinite, is occasionally found. It occurs to some extent in this form in Utah, but all of the commercial product obtained in the United States is in the common form of stibnite.

PRODUCTION IN 1895.

The production of metallic antimony in the United States in 1895 amounted to 450 short tons, valued at $68,000. It was obtained almost entirely from imported ores, the output of ore from the mines of the United States amounting to only 86 short tons; of this ore California produced 43 tons, Montana 30 tons, and Nevada 13 tons. The value of the domestic ore was $2,845. As the statistics of antimony production have heretofore been given for the metal, and as it is impossible to segregate the metallic antimony obtained from domestic and foreign ores, the product for 1895 is made uniform with the other years.

PRODUCTION IN PREVIOUS YEARS.

Mineral Resources for 1882 contained the first record of antimony production in the United States. The product in that year was 60 short tons of metallic antimony, valued at $200 per ton. The production in 1880 and 1881 was estimated at 50 tons each year, the metal being reduced by Starr and Mathison (afterwards the Mathison Smelting Company), of San Francisco, from ores mined in California and Nevada. From 1880 to 1887 the product averaged about 55 short tons per year, the smallest figure being 35 tons, in 1886, and the highest, 75 tons, in 1887. The price remained about stationary. In 1888, the product

[1] For fuller details regarding the domestic and foreign localities where antimony occurs the reader is referred to the article by Prof. W. P. Blake in Mineral Resources for 1883-84.

increased to 100 tons and continued to advance until 1892, but in 1893 and 1894 decreased. The decrease was due in great part to the uncertain supply of domestic ores. This uncertainty became so pronounced in 1894 that the Mathison Smelting Company (formerly Starr and Mathison) sold its works in San Francisco, constructed new ones on Staten Island, New York, and moved its office to New York City. This company is now using foreign ores or crude metal almost exclusively, while its successor in San Francisco, the Chaps Smelting Company, depends upon ores from Mexico and "crude" metal from Japan for the bulk of its supply.

In the following table is shown the annual production of antimony in the United States since 1880:

Production of antimony in the United States since 1880.

Year.	Quantity.	Value.	Year.	Quantity.	Value.
	Short tons.			Short tons.	
1880	50	$10,000	1889	115	$28,000
1881	50	10,000	1890	129	40,756
1882	60	12,000	1891	278	47,007
1883	60	12,000	1892:		
1884	60	12,000	Metallic	150	
1885	50	10,000	Ore	380	} 56,466
1886	35	7,000	1893	250	45,000
1887	75	15,000	1894	200	36,000
1888	100	20,000	1895	a 450	68,000

a Principally from imported ores.

USES.

Antimony is chiefly valuable as an alloy with other metals. It is used to large extent with lead in the manufacture of type metal, to which it gives hardness, and, what is more valuable, it possesses the peculiarity, when used as an alloy, of expanding at the moment of solidifying, thus giving to the type a clean, sharp impression. From 10 to 16 parts of antimony in 100 are used in making britannia metal. Pewter contains about 7 per cent. It is also used in the manufacture of babbitt metal, an antifriction alloy used in the journals of railroad locomotives and cars and other rapidly moving machinery. It has lately been used as an alloy with aluminum, to which it gives hardness and elasticity. Its effects on some metals is very injurious, particularly copper, an almost inappreciable amount (one part in a thousand) destroying its good qualities. The well known medicinal preparation, tartar emetic, is a tartrate of antimony and potassium. The trisulphide is also used to some extent in medicial practice. The sulphide was used to considerable extent by the ancients as a pigment, and women of the East are said to use it at the present day for darkening their eyebrows.

IMPORTS.

As will be seen from the following table, the antimony of domestic production supplies a very small proportion of the consumption. The value of the domestic product has exceeded $50,000 in one year only, while the imports have fallen below $300,000 only once in the past six years and have exceeded $400,000 twice in that time.

Antimony and antimony ore imported and entered for consumption in the United States, 1867 to 1895.

Year ending—	Crude and regulus.		Ore.		Ground. Value.	Total value.
	Quantity.	Value.	Quantity.	Value.		
	Pounds.		*Pounds.*			
June 30, 1867..	....	$63,919	....	......	......	$63,919
1868..	1,033,336	83,822	....	......	......	83,822
1869 .	1,315,921	129,918	....	......	......	129,918
1870..	1,227,429	164,179	....	......	......	164,179
1871..	1,015,609	148,264	....	$2,364	......	150,628
1872..	1,953,306	237,536	....	3,031	......	240,567
1873..	1,166,321	184,498	....	2,941	......	187,439
1874..	1,253,814	148,409	....	203	......	148,612
1875..	1,238,223	131,360	6,460	609	......	131,969
1876..	946,809	119,441	8,321	700	......	120,141
1877..	1,115,124	135,317	20,001	2,314	......	137,631
1878..	1,256,624	130,950	20,351	1,259	......	132,209
1879..	1,380,212	143,099	34,542	2,341	......	145,440
1880..	2,019,389	265,773	25,150	2,349	......	268,122
1881..	1,808,945	253,054	841,730	18,199	......	271,253
1882..	2,525,838	294,234	1,114,699	18,019	......	312,253
1883..	3,064,050	286,892	697,244	11,254	......	298,146
1884..	1,779,337	150,435	231,360	6,489	......	156,924
1885..	2,579,840	207,215	215,913	7,497	......	214,712
Dec. 31, 1886..	2,997,985	202,563	218,366	9,761	......	212,324
1887..	2,553,284	169,747	302,761	8,785	......	178,532
1888..	2,814,044	248,015	68,010	2,178	......	250,193
1889..	2,676,130	304,711	116,309	5,568	......	310,279
1890..	3,315,659	411,960	611,140	29,878	......	441,838
1891..	2,618,941	327,307	1,433,531	36,232	......	363,539
1892..	3,950,864	392,761	192,314	7,338	......	400,099
1893..	2,780,432	243,341	116,495	5,253	......	248,594
1894..	2,653,487	193,988	375,468	18,068	$737	212,793
1895..	3,499,901	223,968	668,610	14,718	......	238,686

PRICES.

There has been a steady and almost precipitons decline in the prices of antimony since 1890, so that in 1895 the average for the year was about one-third of what it was in the early part of the former year. At the beginning of 1890 the prices were 22½ cents per pound for higher grades. In 1895 they reached as low as 7¾ cents, and the highest price quoted in New York was 8⅝ cents. Toward the close of 1890 the price declined to 17 cents, but reacted to 18¾ to 19 cents for "Cookson's" in the early part of 1891. "Hallett's" was quoted at 16¼ to 16½ cents at that time. Prices gradually declined during the spring and summer of that year, until in September Cookson's was quoted at 11⅝ cents and Hallett's at 10 cents. This decline had been caused by reports that large supplies of ores would soon be put upon the market. As these did not materialize, the market improved during the last three months, December prices being 16¼ cents for Cookson's and 12¾ cents for Hallett's.

The prices for antimony during 1892 were low. The year opened with quotations slightly less than in December, 1891, and gradually declined, with the exception of a little improvement in May and June, until October, the prices for September being the lowest during the year. In October and the first of November an improved tone prevailed, but prices again weakened about the first of December, and the year closed with Cookson's and L. X. each 4 cents lower than at the beginning of the year, and Hallett's showing a decline of 2 cents. The following table exhibits the range of prices during the year:

Ruling prices for antimony during 1892.

[Cents per pound.]

Month.	Cookson's.	L. X.	Hallett's.
January	15½ to 16	12 to 15	12¼ to 12½
February	15 to 15½	12 to 14	11¼
March	14¾ to 15	11¾ to 13	10¾ to 11⅛
April	14¼ to 15½	12¼ to 12½	10⅞ to 11
May	15	12¾	11½
June	14½	12¾	11¼
July	13¼	12¼	10⅞
August	12	11½	10¾
September	11½ to 11¾	11 to 11¼	10 to 10¼
October	12	11¼	10⅝ to 10¾
November	11¾	11	10½
December	11¼	11	10¼ to 10⅝

During January and February, 1893, prices were still depressed, Cookson's being quoted as low as 10¾ cents, with L. X. at 10½ cents, and Hallett's from 9⅞ to 10¼ cents. In the early part of March a firmer tone prevailed for the cheaper grades, but fell off later in the month, with trade dull and lifeless. Prices continued to decline slowly, with an apathetic trade throughout the summer, until November, when the lowest prices in the year were quoted for the higher grades: Cookson's, 10 cents; L. X., 9¾ cents, and Hallett's, 9¼ to 9⅜. A better tone prevailed in December for Cookson's, which advanced about ⅛ or ¼ cent, but the cheaper grades continued to decline, the year closing with L. X. at 9½ to 9⅝ cents and Hallett's at 9⅛ to 9¼ cents. The following table shows the average prices which obtained throughout the year:

Ruling prices for antimony during 1893.

[Cents per pound.]

Month.	Cookson's.	L. X.	Hallett's.
January	11	10½	10¼
February	10¾	10½	9⅞ to 10
March	10¾	10 to 12	10
April	10¾	10⅜	10
May	10½	10¼	10
June	10½	10¼	9⅞
July	10⅜	10⅛	9⅞
August	10¼	10	9¾
September	10¼	10	9¾
October	10¼	10	9¾
November	10	9¾	9⅝
December	10⅛ to 10¼	9½ to 9⅝	9⅛ to 9¼

Prices continued to decline in 1894. The year opened with Cookson's quoted about the same as in December, 1893, and other grades slightly lower. Some fluctuations were noted during the spring and summer, but the general tendency was toward lower prices. The lowest figures reached were in November, when Cookson's was quoted at 8½ cents and Hallett's at 8¼. The following table shows the prices for each grade during the year:

Prices of antimony at New York in 1894, by months.

[Cents per pound.]

Month.	Cookson's.	Hallett's.	L. X.
January	10¼	9½	9⅛
February	10	9⅜	8⅞
March	10⅛	9½	8⅞
April	10⅛	9⅜	8⅞
May	10⅛	9¼	8¾
June	9¾	9⅛	8⅝
July	10	8¾	8⅝
August	10	8⅞	8¼
September	9½	8⅝	7⅞
October	9⅝	8¼	7½
November	8½	8¼	7⅝
December	8⅝	8⅛	7⅝

According to the metal market reports of the Iron Age, the opening prices in 1895 were, for Cookson's, from 8½ cents to 8⅝ cents, with only a fair jobbing trade. The downward tendency of prices continued during the year very slowly, not more than an eighth of a cent a pound at a time, the total decline being about three-fourths of a cent or one-sixteenth of a cent per month. December prices were, for Cookson's, 7¾ cents to 7⅞ cents, and for Hallett's, 6⅞ cents to 7 cents. Importations from Japan, either as regulus or crude, became a factor in the markets of 1895, and in April quotations on "Japanese" appeared in the market reports to the exclusion of what has previously been known as L. X. Prices for Japanese antimony were usually quoted about an eighth of a cent below Hallett's and about 1 cent lower than Cookson's.

The ruling prices for antimony during 1895, taken from the market reports to the Iron Age, were as follows:

Prices of antimony at New York in 1895, by months.

[Cents per pound.]

Month.	Cookson's.	Hallett's.	Japanese.
January	8½ to 8⅝	7⅛ to 7¼	
February	8¼ to 8½	7⅛ to 7¼	
March	8¼	7⅛ to 7¼	....
April	7⅞ to 8⅛	7 to 7⅛	6⅞ to 7
May	7⅞ to 8	7	6⅞
June	7⅞ to 8	7 to 7⅛	6⅞
July	8 to 8⅛	7⅛ to 7¼	7
August	8	7⅛	7
September	8	7⅛	6⅞ to 7
October	7¾ to 8	7 to 7⅛	6⅞
November	7¾ to 7⅞	7	6¾ to 6⅞
December	7¾ to 7⅛	6⅞ to 7	6¾ to 6⅞

PLATINUM.

DEVELOPMENTS IN THE UNITED STATES.

The usual small product was obtained in the United States in connection with the placers of California and Oregon. But little effort was made toward exploiting the black beach sands of Oregon, where indications favorable for platinum have been noted. To be sure, more intelligent prospecting and many assays have been made representing considerable areas of these sands, but this had not yet led to significantly favorable results.

DEVELOPMENTS IN NEW SOUTH WALES.

More important developments for the platinum industry have, meantime, been made in New South Wales, and they are entitled to still more attention from the investigations of their efficient Geological Survey. The report of Mr. J. B. Jaquet,[1] particularly, calls attention to the conditions of occurrence of platinum in the drift of an old river bed extending north and south for a little over a mile and from 60 to 150 feet wide, in the region of the newly surveyed townships of Fifield and Platina. These townships are situated about 26 miles northeast of Condobolin and are distant from one another 1½ miles. This is the commercial source of platinum in New South Wales.

The drift containing platinum was developed for the gold which it also yields. Both occur as waterworn grains in crevices in the surface of the bedrock and for perhaps 3 inches in the bottom of the drift.

In working the deposits, the wash dirt is first all puddled in machines worked by horses. During this process the soft layer of bedrock which is broken down with the drift is pulverized, and any which may be attached to it is set free. The clean gravel is afterwards washed in ordinary sluice boxes, and the gold and platinum obtained and separated in the ordinary way. The crude platinum is worth about $5.75 per ounce and is about 75 per cent pure, the chief impurities, as shown by Prof. J. C. H. Mingaye, being iron and osmiridium.

The conditions of occurrence of this platinum drift, as developed by Mr. Jaquet, are especially interesting since he traces the platinum to a series of horizontally bedded conglomerates or cemented drifts and

---

[1] Records of the Geological Survey of New South Wales, Vol. V, part 1, 1896.

shales in the vicinity of Fifield and Platina at an elevation of at least a hundred feet above the alluvial platiniferous drift. These conglomerates are composed of rounded or subangular quartz pebbles, tightly cemented by an infiltration of ferric oxide. The shales are highly ferruginous and much indurated. Upon the top of Jacks Lookout, a low hill, distant about 2 miles southeast from Fifield, these conglomerates contain waterworn grains of gold and platinum. Bowlders of the same cement have been found in the Fifield-Platina drift.

In this connection, the most interesting deposits in the colony, although not worked, are those in Little Darling Creek and Mulga Springs, near Broken Hill. Here the metal is found in iron ore, ferruginous clays, and decomposed gneiss. Samples assayed in the Department of Mines laboratory by Mr. J. C. H. Mingaye yielded from traces up to 1 ounce 9 pennyweights of platinum per ton.[1] Some of the samples contained small quantities of gold and silver, and the iron ore was generally more or less impregnated with carbonate of copper. No platinum could be seen in the ore. Experiments made to determine the condition in which it is present have resulted in failure, while attempts at concentration have only been partially successful.[2] These deposits have additional interest not only as tracing the deposits a step farther back from the alluvial drift, but because of the extended field that they give to prospectors elsewhere and from the fact of reports, still unconfirmed, of similar deposits in this country.

In connection with the recent announcement of vanadium and platinum in the ash of certain Australian coals, the following analyses of such coals are furnished by Messrs. Thirkell & Co. London:

Analysis of coal containing platinum and vanadium.

	Per cent.
Carbon	65.2
Hydrogen	4.6
Oxygen	21.8
Nitrogen	1.9
Sulphur	3.8
Water (lost at 100° C.)	0.7
Ash	1.7
Total	99.7

[1] Ann. Report Dept. Mines for 1889, p. 219.
[2] Ann. Report Dept. Mines and Agric. for 1891, p. 276.

Approximate composition of ash.

	Per cent.
Metallic vanadium	25. 1
Platinum metals	3. 6
Oxygen (combined with above metals)	44. 0
Sandy and other earthy matters	27. 3
Total	100. 0

As the coal contains 1.7 per cent of ash this means that it contains 0.44 per cent of vanadium and 0.063 per cent of platinum metals. In other words, 1 ton of the coal will yield 144 ounces 1 pennyweight 3 grains of metallic vanadium, and 20 ounces 13 pennyweights 11 grains of platinum metals. Thus 144 ounces of vanadium would be equal to about 488 ounces of chloride of vanadium.

Percentage of composition of ash of sample of coal drawn from bulk.

	Per cent.
Metallic vanadium	2. 90
Platinum metals	0. 23
Oxygen (combined with metals)	5. 10
Sand, carbonate of lime, etc	91. 77
Total	100. 00

The above is equal to 146 ounces 17 pennyweights 8 grains vanadium in 1 ton of coal, and 11 ounces 13 pennyweights 8 grains of platinum in 1 ton of coal.

COAL.

By Edward W. Parker.

INTRODUCTION.

The statistics of coal production in the United States during 1895 have been compiled from direct returns to the Geological Survey or its duly appointed agents, with the usual exception of Illinois. The bureau of labor statistics of Illinois, through its secretary, Mr. George A. Schilling, has for the past four years furnished the figures to the Survey, frequently in advance of its own publication. Prior to 1892 the statistics of coal production in Illinois were furnished by the then secretary of the bureau, Col. John S. Lord. The chief mine inspectors of Alabama and Kentucky, Messrs. James D. Hillhouse and C. J. Norwood, as a part of the duties imposed by their positions in the State governments, collect the statistics of coal production of their respective States, and in connection therewith have kindly acted as agents for the Survey, with highly satisfactory results.

The report on Pennsylvania anthracite has been prepared jointly by Messrs. John H. Jones and William W. Ruley, who have for several years furnished this feature of the chapter on coal production.

Contributions from secretaries of boards of trade and others regarding the movement of coal at the important trade centers and shipping ports are gratefully acknowledged here, and also by name in connection with the articles which will be found under the general head of Coal Trade Review. Where any reference has been made to the files of technical periodicals, due credit is given in the proper place.

Some confusion is apt to occur by the fact that both the long ton of 2,240 pounds and the short ton (2,000 pounds) are used in this chapter. This is unfortunate, but can not be avoided. Pennsylvania anthracite is always measured by the long ton. In cases where Pennsylvania bituminous coal is sold in the Eastern markets the long ton is used. The same is true of West Virginia and of the Tazewell and Wise County coals of Virginia. The laws of Maryland permit the use of the long ton only. In all other cases bituminous coal is sold by the short ton. For the sake of convenience the bituminous product has in this report been reduced to short tons, and when the anthracite and bituminous products are tabulated together the short ton is used. In the section devoted entirely to Pennsylvania anthracite the long ton only is used, and in the table of shipments from the Cumberland region this is also the case.

THE COAL FIELDS OF THE UNITED STATES.

For convenience the coal areas of the United States are divided into two great classes, the anthracite and bituminous.

In a commercial sense, particularly in the East, when the anthracite fields are mentioned the fields of Pennsylvania are considered, though Colorado and New Mexico are now supplying anthracite coal of good quality to the Rocky Mountain region, and small amounts are mined annually in Virginia. This small quantity from Virginia and a semi-anthracitic product from Arkansas are considered with the bituminous output. In previous years some coal which was classed as anthracite has been mined and sold in New England. The productive area was confined to the eastern part of Rhode Island and the counties of Bristol and Plymouth in Massachusetts. The classing of this product as anthracite coal was erroneous. The original beds have been metamorphosed into graphite or graphitic coal, and the product requires such a high degree of heat for combustion that it can be used only with other combustible material or under a heavy draft. It is, therefore, not an economical practice to use this product for fuel in competition with the anthracite coal from Pennsylvania or the bituminous coals from the New River and Pocahontas fields, which are now sent in large quantities to New England points, and its mining for fuel purposes has been abandoned.

The Bituminous division includes the following coal fields: (1) The Triassic field, embracing the coal beds of the Triassic or New Red Sandstone formation in the Richmond basin in Virginia and in the coal basins along the Deep and Dan rivers in North Carolina; (2) the Appalachian field, which extends from the State of New York on the north to the State of Alabama on the south, having a length northeast and southwest of over 900 miles and a width ranging from 30 to 180 miles; (3) the Northern field, which is confined exclusively to the central part of Michigan; (4) the Central field, embracing the coal areas in Indiana, Illinois, and western Kentucky; (5) the Western field, including the coal areas west of the Mississippi River, south of the forty-third parallel of north latitude and east of the Rocky Mountains; (6) the Rocky Mountain field, containing the coal areas in the States and Territories lying along the Rocky Mountains; (7) the Pacific Coast field, embracing the coal districts of Washington, Oregon, and California.

The various fields are described at some length in Mineral Resources for 1886, and also in the report for 1894. The latter also contains some historical information regarding the development of these fields. Mineral Resources for 1892 contains some interesting contributions from State geologists on the coal fields of several States.

The following table contains the approximate areas of the coal fields in the various States, grouped according to the divisions mentioned, with the total output from each from 1887 to 1895.

Classification of the coal fields of the United States.

	Area.	Product in—		
		1887.	1888.	1889.
Anthracite.	*Sq. miles.*	*Short tons.*	*Short tons.*	*Short tons.*
New England (Rhode Island and Massachusetts)	500	6,000	4,000	2,000
Pennsylvania	480	39,506,255	43,922,897	45,544,970
Colorado and New Mexico.	15	36,000	44,791	53,517
	995	39,548,255	43,971,688	45,600,487
Bituminous.(a)				
Triassic:				
Virginia	180	30,000	33,000	49,411
North Carolina	2,700	....	....	222
Appalachian:				
Pennsylvania	9,000	30,866,602	30,796,727	36,174,089
Ohio	10,000	10,301,708	10,910,946	9,976,787
Maryland	550	3,278,023	3,479,470	2,939,715
Virginia	2,000	795,263	1,040,000	816,375
West Virginia	16,000	4,836,820	5,498,800	6,231,880
Kentucky	11,180	950,903	1,193,000	1,108,770
Tennessee	5,100	1,900,000	1,967,297	1,925,689
Georgia	200	313,715	180,000	225,934
Alabama	8,660	1,950,000	2,900,000	3,572,983
	62,690	55,193,034	60,966,240	62,972,222
Northern:				
Michigan	6,700	71,461	81,407	67,431
Central:				
Indiana	6,450	3,217,711	3,140,979	2,845,057
Kentucky	4,500	982,282	1,377,000	1,290,985
Illinois	36,800	10,278,890	14,655,188	12,104,272
	47,750	14,478,883	19,173,167	16,240,314
Western:				
Iowa	18,000	4,473,828	4,952,440	4,045,358
Missouri	26,700	3,209,916	3,909,967	2,557,823
Nebraska	3,200	1,500	1,500	2,222,443
Kansas	17,000	1,596,879	1,850,000	
Arkansas	9,100	150,000	276,871	279,584
Indian Territory	20,000	685,911	761,986	752,832
Texas	4,500	75,000	90,000	128,216
	98,500	10,193,034	11,842,764	10,036,256

a Including lignite, brown coal, and scattering lots of anthracite.

Classification of the coal fields of the United States—Continued.

	Area.	Product in—		
		1887.	1888.	1889.
Bituminous(a)—Continued.				
Rocky Mountain, etc.:	*Sq. miles.*	*Short tons.*	*Short tons.*	*Short tons.*
Dakota		21,470	34,000	28,907
Montana		10,202	41,467	363,301
Idaho		500	400	
Wyoming		1,170,318	1,481,540	1,388,947
Utah		180,021	258,961	236,651
Colorado	2,913	1,755,735	2,140,686	2,544,144
New Mexico		508,034	626,665	486,463
		3,646,280	4,583,719	5,048,413
Pacific Coast:				
Washington		772,612	1,215,750	1,030,578
Oregon		31,696	75,000	64,359
California		50,000	95,000	119,820
		854,308	1,385,750	1,214,757
Total product sold		124,015,255	142,037,735	
Colliery consumption		5,960,302	6,621,667	
Total product, including colliery consumption		129,975,557	148,659,402	141,229,513

	Product in—		
	1890.	1891.	1892.
Anthracite.			
New England (Rhode Island and Massachusetts)	*Short tons.*	*Short tons.* 500	*Short tons.*
Pennsylvania	46,468,641	50,665,431	52,472,504
Colorado and New Mexico	(b)	(b)	64,963
	46,468,641	50,665,931	52,537,467
Bituminous. (a)			
Triassic:			
Virginia	19,346	17,290	37,219
North Carolina	10,262	20,355	6,679

a Including lignite, brown coal, and scattering lots of anthracite.
b Included in bituminous product.

Classification of the coal fields of the United States—Continued.

	Product in—		
	1890.	1891.	1892.
Bituminous (a)—Continued.			
Appalachian:	*Short tons.*	*Short tons.*	*Short tons.*
Pennsylvania	42, 302, 173	42, 788, 490	46, 694, 576
Ohio	11, 494, 506	12, 868, 683	13, 562, 927
Maryland	3, 357, 813	3, 820, 239	3, 419. 962
Virginia	764, 665	719, 109	637. 986
West Virginia........	7, 394, 494	9, 220, 665	9, 738, 755
Kentucky	1, 206, 120	1, 222, 918	1, 231. 110
Tennessee	2, 169, 585	2, 413, 678	2, 092, 064
Georgia	228, 337	171, 000	215, 498
Alabama	4, 090, 409	4, 759, 781	5, 529, 312
	73, 008, 102	77, 984, 563	83, 122, 190
Northern:			
Michigan	74, 977	80, 307	77, 990
Central:			
Indiana	3, 305, 737	2, 973, 474	3, 345, 174
Kentucky	1, 495, 376	1, 693, 151	1. 794, 203
Illinois	15, 292, 420	15, 660, 698	17, 862, 276
	20, 093, 533	20, 327, 323	23, 001, 653
Western:			
Iowa.................	4, 021, 739	3, 825, 495	3, 918, 491
Missouri	2, 735, 221	2, 674, 606	2. 733, 949
Nebraska............		1, 500	1, 500
Kansas..............	2, 259, 922	2, 716, 705	3. 007, 276
Arkansas............	399, 888	542, 379	535. 558
Indian Territory......	869, 229	1, 091, 032	1, 192, 721
Texas	184, 440	172, 100	245, 690
	10, 470, 439	11, 023, 817	11, 635, 185
Rocky Mountain, etc.:			
Dakota..............	30, 000	30, 000	40, 725
Montana	517, 477	541, 861	564, 648
Idaho			
Wyoming	1, 870, 366	2, 327, 841	2, 503, 839
Utah................	318, 159	371, 045	361, 013
Colorado	3, 094, 003	3, 512, 632	3, 447, 967
New Mexico..........	375, 777	462, 328	659, 230
Nevada			
	6, 205, 782	7, 245, 707	7, 577, 422

a Including lignite, brown coal, and scattering lots of anthracite.

Classification of the coal fields of the United States—Continued.

	Product in—		
	1890.	1891.	1892.
Bituminous(a)—Continued.			
Pacific Coast:	*Short tons.*	*Short tons.*	*Short tons.*
Washington	1, 263, 689	1, 056, 249	1, 213, 427
Oregon	61, 514	51, 826	34, 661
California	110, 711	93, 301	85, 178
	1, 435, 914	1, 201, 376	1, 333, 266
Total product, including colliery consumption	157, 788, 656	168, 566, 669	179, 329, 071

	Product in—		
	1893.	1894.	1895.
Anthracite.			
New England (Rhode Island and Massachusetts)	*Short tons.*	*Short tons.*	*Short tons.*
Pennsylvania	53, 967, 543	51, 921, 121	57, 999, 337
Colorado and New Mexico.	93, 578	71, 550	67, 179
	54, 061, 121	51, 992, 671	58, 066, 516
Bituminous. (a)			
Triassic:			
Virginia	19, 878	52, 079	57, 782
North Carolina	17, 000	16, 900	24, 900
Appalachian:			
Pennsylvania.........	44, 070, 724	39, 912, 463	50, 217, 228
Ohio	13, 253, 646	11, 909, 856	13, 355, 806
Maryland	3, 716, 041	3, 501, 428	3, 915, 585
Virginia	800, 461	1, 177, 004	1, 310, 542
West Virginia........	10, 708, 578	11, 627, 757	11, 387, 961
Kentucky	1, 245, 785	1, 218, 072	1, 490, 057
Tennessee	1, 902, 258	2, 180, 879	2, 535, 644
Georgia	372, 740	354, 111	260, 998
Alabama	5, 136, 935	4, 397, 178	5, 693, 775
	81, 207, 168	76, 278, 748	90, 167, 596

a Including lignite, brown coal, and scattering lots of anthracite.

Classification of the coal fields of the United States—Continued.

	Product in—		
	1893.	1894.	1895.
Bituminous (a)—Continued.			
Northern :	*Short tons.*	*Short tons.*	*Short tons.*
Michigan.............	45, 979	70, 022	112, 322
Central :			
Indiana...............	3, 791, 851	3, 423, 921	3, 995, 892
Kentucky	1, 761, 394	1, 893, 120	1, 867, 713
Illinois...............	19, 949, 564	17, 113, 576	17, 735, 864
	25, 502, 809	22, 430, 617	23, 599, 469
Western :			
Iowa.................	3, 972, 229	3, 967, 253	4, 156, 074
Missouri	2, 897, 442	2, 245, 039	2, 372, 393
Nebraska.............	....	....	....
Kansas...............	2, 652, 546	3, 388, 251	2, 926, 870
Arkansas.............	574, 763	512, 626	598, 322
Indian Territory......	1, 252, 110	969, 606	1, 211, 185
Texas	302, 206	420, 848	484, 959
	11, 651, 296	11, 503, 623	11, 749, 803
Rocky Mountain, etc. :			
Dakota...............	49, 630	42, 015	39, 197
Montana	892, 309	927, 395	1, 504, 193
Idaho	....	....	....
Wyoming	2, 439, 311	2, 417, 463	2, 246, 911
Utah.................	413, 205	431, 550	471, 836
Colorado	4, 018, 793	2, 776, 817	3, 027, 327
New Mexico..........	655, 112	580, 238	709, 130
Nevada	....	150	....
	8, 468, 360	7, 175, 628	7, 998, 594
Pacific Coast :			
Washington..........	1, 264, 877	1, 106, 470	1, 191, 410
Oregon...............	41, 683	47, 521	73, 685
California	72, 603	67, 247	75, 453
	1, 379, 163	1, 221, 238	1, 340, 548
Total product, including colliery consumption	182, 352, 774	170, 741, 526	193, 117, 530

a Including lignite, brown coal, and scattering lots of anthracite.

PRODUCTION.

The output from the coal mines of the United States in 1895 exceeded that of any previous year in the history of the country, aggregating 172,426,366 long tons, equivalent to 193,117,530 short tons. This was an increase of 22,376,004 short tons over the product of 1894, or an advance of about 13 per cent. The year of largest production previous to 1895 was 1893, when 182,352,774 short tons were mined. The output of 1895 exceeded this by about 10,000,000 tons, or a little more than 5 per cent. In considering the coal product these reports include not only the coal marketed, either by shipment to distant points or sold locally, but also that consumed by the mine employees and by the mine operators themselves in locomotives, under stationary boilers, etc., in working the mine, and technically known as colliery consumption. There are occasional exceptions, where operators use only slack or waste, which would otherwise be thrown on the dump and no record kept, the miner not even being paid for it. These exceptions are few and the amount so comparatively small as not to materially affect the total. Coal consumed in the manufacture of coke is also included in this report.

Excluding the colliery consumption, the product in 1895 was 169,389,630 long tons, or 189,716,386 short tons. This may be and usually is considered the marketable product.

Coincident with the increased production of coal in 1895, it is interesting to note the activity which prevailed in all branches of the iron and steel industry which have a direct bearing upon the demand for and production of coal. The production of pig iron, according to the annual report of the American Iron and Steel Association, increased from 6,657,388 long tons in 1894 to 9,446,308 long tons in 1895. Assuming the consumption of coal to be 1½ tons for each ton of pig iron produced, an increased production of coal to the amount of over 4,500,000 short tons is at once accounted for. But there was also an increased production of Bessemer and open-hearth steel, steel rails, structural iron and steel, plates and sheets, wire rods and nails, and in fact of all iron and steel products, with the exception of cut nails, which have been declining rapidly and steadily for several years. This increased activity had direct effect upon the coal production, but it can not satisfactorily account for the comparative decline in the value of the coal product, which, while the output increased about 22,000,000 tons, only advanced about $11,000,000, and was about $10,000,000 less than in 1892, when the product was 13,000,000 tons less than it was in 1895. How, in the face of such seemingly prosperous conditions, is the falling off in value to be accounted for?

The fact is that prices for bituminous coal have been on the decline since 1888, though in 1890, 1891, and 1892 they were about the same. In 1893 and 1894 they were lower than in any previous year of which we have any record. Similar conditions affected the other "raw materials" used in the manufacture of iron and steel. Mr. James M. Swank, in his Review of the American Iron Trade, states that in the depression of 1893, 1894, and the first half of 1895 "the best furnace coke this country can produce was sold on cars at 85 cents per ton of 2,000 pounds, and the best Lake Superior Bessemer ores were sold at less than $3 per gross ton delivered at Cleveland." This naturally allowed the finished products to be sold at greatly reduced prices, and it is fair to suppose that the increased demand for iron and steel products in 1895 was rather due to low prices than indicative of a healthier condition of trade. The fact that the year closed with slackened demand and reduced prices rather tends to this belief. The trade which had been developed by prices favorable to buyers fell off when values were advanced, and the year passes into history as one with the largest production in iron, steel, and coal, but one of very little, if any, profit to the producers.

ANTHRACITE.

The product of Pennsylvania anthracite in 1895 was 51,785,122 long tons, or 57,999,336 short tons, valued at $82,019,272. This was the largest output ever obtained, being 5,426,978 long tons, or about 11 per cent, in excess of that of 1894, and 3,599,816 long tons more than in 1893, the year of largest previous production. The value in 1895, however, while greater than that of 1894, was comparatively less, and there were four years prior to 1895 when, with a smaller output, the value was in excess of the year just closed. These years were 1887 ($84,552,181), 1888 ($89,020,483), 1892 ($82,442,000), and 1893 ($85,687,078). The average price per ton, obtained by dividing the total value by the total product, was $1.69 per long ton in 1894 and $1.58 in 1895, a decline of 11 cents. In quoting the average price per ton of anthracite, however, the item of colliery consumption is excluded as not having any value, only the marketable product being considered. The average price for the marketable grades was $1.85 in 1894 and $1.72 in 1895, a decline of 13 cents. In 1893 this average price was $1.94. Two reasons may be assigned for this decline, both of which probably had some effect—one the general depression in values, whose influence was felt in all branches of trade; the other the increased use of the smaller sizes of anthracite, which are sold at lower prices, and cause a comparative decrease in the total value of the coal marketed. As these sizes were previously a waste product and have now become a source of revenue, there is, in the product affected, an increased profit from the coal mined, though a decreased value for the coal marketed.

The number of men employed in the anthracite mines in 1895 was 142,917, who averaged 196 working days, against 131,603 men for 190 days in 1894.

In addition to the anthracite production of Pennsylvania in 1895 there were 67,179 short tons mined in Colorado and New Mexico, making the total output of anthracite coal in the United States 58,066,516 short tons. Except in the preceding tables, the anthracite product of Colorado and New Mexico, for sake of convenience, is included in the bituminous product, and, unless expressly stated to the contrary, reference in this chapter to anthracite production means that of Pennsylvania only.

BITUMINOUS.

The production of bituminous coal in 1895 (including lignite, brown coal, and scattering lots of anthracite, as previously mentioned) was 135,118,193 short tons, valued at $115,779,771, compared with 118,820,405 short tons, valued at $107,653,501, in 1894, indicating an increase in product of 16,297,788 short tons, or 14 per cent, and in value of $8,126,270, or 8 per cent. The conditions affecting the industry in 1895, and to which may be attributed the increase in product and comparative decrease in value, have already been discussed.

Among the more important coal-producing States nearly the same relative positions were maintained in 1895 as were held in 1894. Pennsylvania of course comes first, with about 37 per cent of the total bituminous product—but including her anthracite product, Pennsylvania produced 57 per cent of the total coal output. Illinois, second, contributed 13 per cent of the bituminous product and 9 per cent of the total. Ohio, third, produced 10 per cent of the bituminous output and 7 per cent of the total. West Virginia, fourth, yielded 7.5 per cent and 6.9 per cent, respectively. Alabama, fifth, produced 4.2 per cent of the bituminous output; and Iowa, yielding 3.1 per cent, ranked sixth. Indiana replaces Maryland for seventh place, each having a little less than 3 per cent. Kentucky and Colorado each advance one point, into ninth and tenth places, respectively, while Kansas falls from ninth to eleventh.

The total number of men employed in the bituminous coal mines in 1895 was 239,962, averaging 194 working days, against 244,603 employees for 171 days in 1894.

The following tables exhibit the production of all kinds of coal in the United States during 1894 and 1895:

Coal product of the United States in 1894, by States.

State or Territory.	Loaded at mines for shipment.	Sold to local trade and used by employees.	Used at mines for steam and heat.	Made into coke.
	Short tons.	*Short tons.*	*Short tons.*	*Short tons.*
Alabama	3, 269, 548	43, 911	130, 404	953, 315
Arkansas............	488, 077	7, 870	16. 679	....
California	52, 736	8. 143	6. 368	....
Colorado	2, 181, 048	56, 688	112, 414	481, 259
Georgia	178, 610	....	8, 978	166, 523
Illinois..............	13, 948, 910	2, 590, 414	570. 452	3, 800
Indiana	3, 085, 664	218. 398	67, 545	22, 314
Indian Territory......	923, 581	4, 632	30, 878	10, 515
Iowa................	3, 390, 751	511, 683	64, 819	....
Kansas..............	3, 066, 398	275, 565	45, 523	765
Kentucky	2, 734. 847	281. 235	47, 341	47, 766
Maryland	3, 435. 600	51, 750	14, 078	....
Michigan	60. 817	7, 055	2, 150	....
Missouri	1, 955, 255	242, 501	47, 283	....
Montana	861, 171	12, 900	17, 324	36, 000
Nevada	....	150	....	....
New Mexico	561, 523	8, 266	14, 365	13, 042
North Carolina	13, 500	1, 000	2, 400	....
North Dakota	37, 311	4, 480	224	....
Ohio	10, 636, 402	1, 101, 940	126, 397	45, 117
Oregon..............	45, 068	2, 171	282	....
Pennsylvania	29, 722, 803	1, 589, 595	342. 294	8, 257, 771
Tennessee	1, 571, 406	59, 985	28, 993	520, 495
Texas	417. 281	2. 412	1. 155	....
Utah................	364, 675	11. 173	6, 892	48, 810
Virginia	1. 015, 713	21, 162	4, 690	187, 518
Washington..........	1, 030, 232	10, 822	56, 853	8, 563
West Virginia........	9, 116, 314	428, 202	64, 126	2, 019, 115
Wyoming	2, 309, 934	21, 482	72, 362	13, 685
Total...........	96, 475, 175	7, 605, 585	1, 903, 272	12, 836. 373
Pennsylvania anthracite	46. 358, 144	1, 158, 953	4, 404, 024	....
Grand total.....	142, 833, 319	8. 764. 538	6, 307, 296	12, 836. 373

Coal product of the United States in 1894, by States—Continued.

State or Territory.	Total product.	Total value.	Average price per ton.	Average number of days active.	Average number of employees.
	Short tons.				
Alabama	4,397,178	$4,085,535	$0.93	238	10,859
Arkansas	512,626	631,988	1.22	134	1,493
California	67,247	155,620	2.31	232	125
Colorado	2,831,409	3,516,340	1.24	155	6,507
Georgia	354,111	299,290	.85	304	729
Illinois	17,113,576	15,282,111	.89	183	38,477
Indiana	3,423,921	3,295,034	.96	149	8,603
Indian Territory	969,606	1,541,293	1.59	157	3,101
Iowa	3,967,253	4,997,939	1.26	170	9,995
Kansas	3,388,251	4,178,998	1.23	164	7,339
Kentucky	3,111,192	2,749,932	.88	145	8,083
Maryland	3,501,428	2,687,270	.77	215	3,974
Michigan	70,022	103,049	1.47	224	223
Missouri	2,245,039	2,634,564	1.17	138	7,523
Montana	927,395	1,887,390	2.04	192	1,782
Nevada	150	475	3.15	60	2
New Mexico	597,196	935,857	1.57	182	985
North Carolina	16,900	29,675	1.76	145	95
North Dakota	42,015	47,049	1.12	156	77
Ohio	11,909,856	9,841,723	.83	136	27,105
Oregon	47,521	183,914	3.87	243	88
Pennsylvania	39,912,463	29,479,820	.74	165	75,010
Tennessee	2,180,879	2,119,481	.97	210	5,542
Texas	420,848	976,458	2.32	283	1,062
Utah	431,550	603,479	1.40	199	671
Virginia*	1,229,083	933,576	.76	234	1,635
Washington	1,106,470	2,578,441	2.33	207	2,662
West Virginia	11,627,757	8,706,808	.75	186	17,824
Wyoming	2,417,463	3,170,392	1.31	190	3,032
Total	118,820,405	107,653,501	.91	171	244,603
Pennsylvania anthracite	51,921,121	78,488,063	1.85	190	131,603
Grand total	170,741,526	186,141,564	1.09	178	376,206

Coal product of the United States in 1895, by States.

State or Territory.	Number of mines.	Loaded at mines for shipment.	Sold to local trade and used by employees.	Used at mines for steam and heat.	Made into coke.
		Short tons.	Short tons.	Short tons.	Short tons.
Alabama	60	3, 610, 433	272, 551	137, 021	1, 673, 770
Arkansas.............	13	576, 112	14, 935	7, 275	....
California............	5	60, 440	12, 171	2, 842	....
Colorado	87	2, 445, 578	49, 088	99, 055	489, 261
Georgia	2	135, 692	150	6, 256	118, 900
Illinois	a319	14, 456, 524	2, 684, 607	591, 133	3, 600
Indiana	113	3, 488, 876	392, 423	104, 695	9, 898
Indian Territory	16	1, 173, 399	3, 070	21, 935	12, 781
Iowa.................	177	3, 630, 867	460, 820	64, 387	....
Kansas..............	106	2, 587, 602	279, 739	59, 142	387
Kentucky	120	3, 012, 610	254, 028	50, 294	40, 838
Maryland	23	3, 840, 991	59, 950	14, 644	....
Michigan	9	80, 403	27, 019	4, 900	....
Missouri	122	2, 104, 452	231, 090	36, 851	....
Montana	22	1, 404, 862	19, 168	20, 463	59, 700
New Mexico..........	22	695, 634	13, 045	11, 292	683
North Carolina	3	23, 400	600	900	....
North and South Dakota	9	35, 380	3, 817	....	....
Ohio	407	11, 933, 686	1, 227, 224	152, 277	42, 619
Oregon	5	68, 108	5, 294	283	....
Pennsylvania	588	35, 164, 453	1, 732, 803	468, 381	12, 851, 591
Tennessee	44	1, 808, 056	51, 923	25, 477	650, 188
Texas...............	14	475, 157	7, 705	2, 097	....
Utah................	14	376, 459	25, 097	7, 253	63, 027
Virginia	22	1, 024, 200	15, 173	22, 338	306, 613
Washington..........	22	1, 108, 868	16, 320	43, 249	22, 973
West Virginia........	186	8, 858, 256	445, 023	50, 595	2, 034, 087
Wyoming	25	2, 106, 937	35, 628	81, 065	23, 281
Total	2, 555	106, 287, 435	8, 340, 461	2, 086, 100	18, 404, 197
Pennsylvania anthracite	349	52, 092, 854	1, 315, 044	4, 591, 439	....
Grand total	2, 904	158, 380, 289	9, 655, 505	6, 677, 539	18, 404, 197

a Shipping mines. The product includes also the output from 517 local mines.

Coal product of the United States in 1895, by States—Continued.

State or Territory.	Total product.	Total value.	Average price per ton.	Average number of days active.	Average number of employees.
	Short tons.				
Alabama	5,693,775	$5,126,822	$0.90	244	10,346
Arkansas	598,322	751,156	1.25	176	1,218
California	75,453	175,778	2.33	262	190
Colorado	3,082,982	3,675,185	1.20	182	6,125
Georgia	260,998	215,863	.83	312	848
Illinois	17,735,864	14,239,157	.80	182	38,630
Indiana	3,995,892	3,642,623	.91	189	8,530
Indian Territory	1,211,185	1,737,254	1.43	164	3,212
Iowa	4,156,074	4,982,102	1.20	189	10,066
Kansas	2,926,870	3,481,981	1.20	159	7,482
Kentucky	3,357,770	2,890,247	.86	146	7,865
Maryland	3,915,585	3,160,592	.81	248	3,912
Michigan	112,322	180,016	1.60	186	320
Missouri	2,372,393	2,651,612	1.12	163	6,299
Montana	1,504,193	2,850,906	1.89	223	2,184
New Mexico	720,654	1,072,520	1.49	190	1,383
North Carolina	24,900	41,350	1.66	226	61
North and South Dakota	39,197	42,046	1.07	139	65
Ohio	13,355,806	10,618,477	.79	176	24,644
Oregon	73,685	247,901	3.36	69	414
Pennsylvania	50,217,228	35,980,357	.72	206	71,130
Tennessee	2,535,644	2,349,032	.93	224	5,120
Texas	484,955	913,138	1.88	171	1,642
Utah	471,836	617,349	1.31	203	670
Virginia	1,368,324	869,873	.63	225	2,158
Washington	1,191,410	2,577,958	2.16	224	2,840
West Virginia	11,387,961	7,710,575	.68	195	19,159
Wyoming	2,246,911	2,977,901	1.33	184	3,449
Total	135,118,193	115,779,771	.86	194	239,962
Pennsylvania anthracite	57,999,337	82,019,272	1.41	196	142,917
Grand total	193,117,530	197,799,043	1.02	195	382,879

PRODUCTION IN PREVIOUS YEARS.

The following table shows the annual production of anthracite and bituminous coal since 1880. The quantities are expressed both in long tons of 2,240 pounds and in short tons of 2,000 pounds.

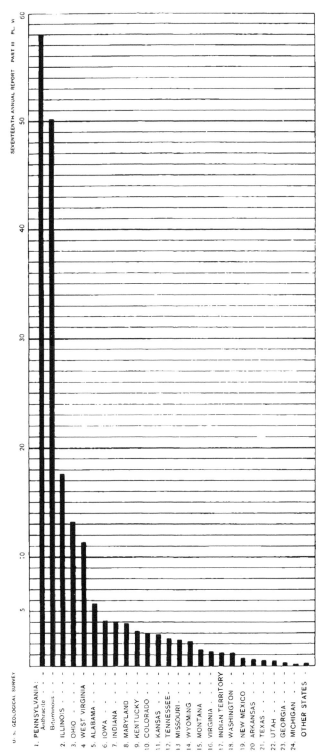

1. PENNSYLVANIA :
   Anthracite - - -
   Bituminous - - -
2. ILLINOIS - - -
3. OHIO - - - -
4. WEST VIRGINIA -
5. ALABAMA - - -
6. IOWA - - - -
7. INDIANA - - -
8. MARYLAND - - -
9. KENTUCKY - - -
10. COLORADO - - -
11. KANSAS - - -
12. TENNESSEE - -
13. MISSOURI - - -
14. WYOMING - - -
15. MONTANA - - -
16. VIRGINIA - - -
17. INDIAN TERRITORY
18. WASHINGTON - -
19. NEW MEXICO - -
20. ARKANSAS - - -
21. TEXAS - - - -
22. UTAH - - - -
23. GEORGIA - - -
24. MICHIGAN - - -
    OTHER STATES -

RANK OF COAL-PRODUCING STATES IN 1895, WITH COMPARATIVE PRODUCTION.

(In millions of tons.)

Annual production of coal in the United States since 1880.

Year.	Bituminous coal.		
	Long tons of 2,240 pounds.	Short tons of 2,000 pounds.	Value.
1880............................	38,242,641	42,831,758	$53,443,718
1881............................	48,365,341	53,961,012	60,224,344
1882............................	60,861,190	68,164,533	76,076,487
1883............................	68,531,500	76,755,280	82,237,800
1884............................	73,730,539	82,578,204	77,417,066
1885............................	64,840,668	72,621,548	82,347,648
1886............................	65,810,676	73,707,957	78,481,056
1887............................	78,470,857	87,887,360	98,004,656
1888............................	91,106,998	102,039,838	101,860,529
1889............................	85,432,628	95,685,543	94,504,745
1890............................	99,392,871	111,320,016	110,420,801
1891............................	105,268,962	117,901,237	117,188,400
1892............................	113,261,792	126,856,567	125,124,381
1893............................	114,629,671	128,385,231	122,751,618
1894............................	106,089,647	118,820,405	107,653,501
1895............................	120,641,244	135,118,193	115,779,771

Year.	Pennsylvania anthracite.		
	Long tons of 2,240 pounds.	Short tons of 2,000 pounds.	Value.
1880............................	25,580,189	28,649,811	$42,196,678
1881............................	28,500,016	31,920,018	64,125,036
1882............................	31,358,264	35,121,256	70,556,094
1883............................	34,336,469	38,456,845	77,257,055
1884............................	33,175,756	37,156,847	66,351,512
1885............................	34,228,548	38,335,974	76,671,948
1886............................	34,853,077	39,035,446	76,119,120
1887............................	37,578,747	42,088,197	84,552,181
1888............................	41,624,611	46,619,564	89,020,483
1889............................	40,665,152	45,544,970	65,721,578
1890............................	41,489,858	46,468,641	66,383,772
1891............................	45,236,992	50,665,431	73,944,735
1892............................	46,850,450	52,472,504	82,442,000
1893............................	48,185,306	53,967,543	85,687,078
1894............................	46,358,144	51,921,121	78,488,063
1895............................	51,785,122	57,999,337	82,019,272

Annual production of coal in the United States since 1880—Continued.

Year.	Total.		
	Long tons.	Short tons.	Value.
1880	63, 822, 830	71, 481, 569	$95, 640, 396
1881	76, 865, 357	85, 881, 030	124, 349, 380
1882	92, 219, 454	103, 285, 789	146, 632, 581
1883	102, 867, 969	115, 212, 125	159, 494, 855
1884	106, 906, 295	119, 735, 051	143, 768, 578
1885	99, 069, 216	110, 957, 522	159, 019, 596
1886	100, 663, 753	112, 743, 403	154, 600, 176
1887	116, 049, 604	129, 975, 557	182, 556, 837
1888	132, 731, 609	148, 659, 402	190, 881, 012
1889	126, 097, 780	141, 229, 514	160, 226, 323
1890	140, 882, 729	157, 788, 657	176, 804, 573
1891	150, 505, 954	168, 566, 668	191, 133, 135
1892	160, 115, 242	179, 329, 071	207, 566, 381
1893	162, 814, 977	182, 352, 774	208, 438, 696
1894	152, 447, 791	170, 741, 526	186, 141, 564
1895	172, 426, 366	193, 117, 530	197, 799, 043

The total amount and value of coal produced in the United States, by States, since 1886, is shown in the following table. The amounts in this table are expressed in short tons of 2,000 pounds.

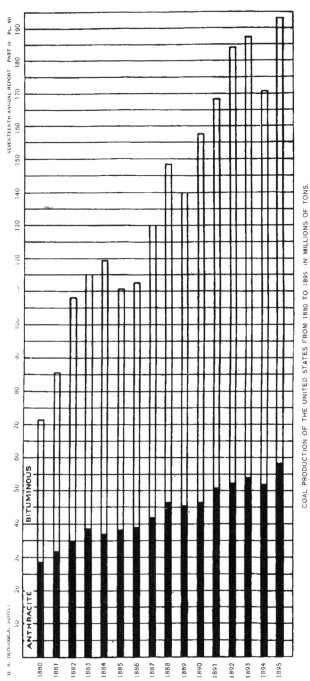

COAL PRODUCTION OF THE UNITED STATES FROM 1880 TO 1895, IN MILLIONS OF TONS.

(Quantity expressed in short tons of 2,000 pounds.)

Amount and value of coal produced in the United States, by States and Territories, from 1886 to 1895.

State or Territory.	1886.		1887.	
	Product.	Value.	Product.	Value.
	Short tons.		*Short tons.*	
Alabama	1,800,000	$5,574,000	1,950,000	$2,535,000
Arkansas	125,000	200,000	150,000	252,500
California	100,000	300,000	50,000	150,000
Colorado	1,368,338	3,215,594	1,791,735	3,941,817
Georgia	223,000	334,500	313,715	470,573
Idaho	1,500	6,000	500	2,000
Illinois	9,246,435	10,263,543	10,278,890	11,152,596
Indiana	3,000,000	3,450,000	3,217,711	4,324,604
Indian Territory	534,580	855,328	685,911	1,286,692
Iowa	4,312,921	5,391,151	4,473,828	5,991,735
Kansas	1,400,000	1,680,000	1,596,879	2,235,631
Kentucky	1,550,000	1,782,500	1,933,185	2,223,163
Maryland	2,517,577	2,391,698	3,278,023	3,114,122
Michigan	60,434	90,651	71,461	107,191
Missouri	1,800,000	2,340,000	3,209,916	4,298,994
Montana	49,846	174,460	10,202	35,707
Nebraska			1,500	3,000
New Mexico	271,285	813,855	508,034	1,524,102
North Carolina				
North Dakota	25,955	41,277	21,470	32,205
Ohio	8,435,211	8,013,450	10,301,708	9,096,848
Oregon	45,000	112,500	31,696	70,000
Pennsylvania:				
Anthracite	36,696,475	71,558,126	39,506,255	79,365,244
Bituminous	26,160,735	21,016,235	30,866,602	27,806,941
Rhode Island			6,000	16,250
Tennessee	1,714,290	1,971,434	1,900,000	2,470,000
Texas	100,000	185,000	75,000	150,000
Utah	200,000	420,000	180,021	360,042
Virginia	684,951	684,951	825,263	773,360
Washington	423,525	952,931	772,612	1,699,746
West Virginia	4,005,796	3,805,506	4,836,820	4,594,979
Wyoming	829,355	2,488,065	1,170,318	3,510,954
Total product sold.	107,682,209	117,112,755	124,015,255	173,595,996
Colliery consumption.	5,061,194		5,960,302	8,960,841
Total	112,743,403	147,112,755	129,975,557	182,556,837

Amount and value of coal produced in the United States, etc.—Continued.

State or Territory.	1888.		1889.	
	Product.	Value.	Product.	Value.
	Short tons.		*Short tons.*	
Alabama	2,900,000	$3,335,000	3,572,983	$3,961,491
Arkansas	276,871	415,306	279,584	395,836
California	95,000	380,000	184,179	434,382
Colorado	2,185,477	4,808,049	2,544,144	3,843,992
Georgia	180,000	270,000	226,156	339,382
Idaho	400	1,800		
Illinois	14,655,188	16,413,811	12,104,272	11,755,203
Indiana	3,140,979	4,397,370	2,845,057	2,887,852
Indian Territory	761,986	1,432,072	752,832	1,323,807
Iowa	4,952,440	6,438,172	4,095,358	5,426,509
Kansas	1,850,000	2,775,000	2,220,943	3,297,288
Kentucky	2,570,000	3,084,000	2,399,755	2,374,339
Maryland	3,479,470	3,293,070	2,939,715	2,517,474
Michigan	81,407	135,221	67,431	115,011
Missouri	3,909,967	8,650,800	2,557,823	3,479,057
Montana	41,467	145,135	363,301	880,773
Nebraska	1,500	3,375	1,500	4,500
New Mexico	626,665	1,879,995	486,463	870,468
North Carolina			(a)	
North Dakota	34,000	119,000	28,907	41,431
Ohio	10,910,946	10,147,180	9,976,787	9,355,400
Oregon	75,000	225,000	(b)	
Pennsylvania:				
Anthracite	43,922,897	85,649,649	c45,598,487	65,873,514
Bituminous	33,796,727	32,106,891	36,174,089	27,953,315
Rhode Island	4,000	11,000	2,000	6,000
Tennessee	1,967,297	2,164,026	1,925,689	2,338,309
Texas	90,000	184,500	128,216	340,620
Utah	258,961	543,818	236,651	377,456
Virginia	1,073,000	1,073,000	865,786	804,475
Washington	1,215,750	3,647,250	1,030,578	2,393,238
West Virginia	5,498,800	6,048,680	6,231,880	5,086,584
Wyoming	1,481,540	4,444,620	1,388,947	1,748,617
Total product sold	142,037,735	204,222,790	141,229,513	160,226,323
Colliery consumption	6,621,667	7,295,834		
Total	148,659,402	211,518,624		

a Product included in Georgia.
b Product included in California.
c Includes product of anthracite in Colorado and New Mexico.

Amount and value of coal produced in the United States, etc.—Continued.

State or Territory.	1890.		1891.	
	Product.	Value.	Product.	Value.
	Short tons.		*Short tons.*	
Alabama	4,090,409	$4,202,469	4,759,781	$5,087,596
Arkansas	399,888	514,595	542,379	647,560
California	110,711	283,019	93,301	204,902
Colorado	3,094,003	4,314.196	3,512,632	4,800,000
Georgia	228,337	238,315	171,000	256,500
Idaho				
Illinois	15,292,420	14,171,230	15,660,698	14,237,071
Indiana	3,305,737	3,259,233	2,973,474	3.070,918
Indian Territory	869,229	1,579,188	1,091,032	1,897,037
Iowa	4,021,739	4,995,739	3,825.495	4,867,999
Kansas	2,259,922	2,947,517	2,716,705	3,557,303
Kentucky	2,701,496	2,472,119	2,916,069	2,715,600
Maryland	3,357,813	2.899,572	3,820,239	3,082,515
Michigan	74,977	149,195	80,307	133,387
Missouri	2,735,221	3,382,858	2,674,606	3,283,242
Montana	517,477	1,252,492	541,861	1,228,630
Nebraska	1,500	4,500	1,500	4,500
New Mexico	375,777	504,390	462,328	779,018
North Carolina	10,262	17,864	20,355	39,365
North Dakota	30,000	42,000	30,000	42,000
Ohio	11,494,506	10,783,171	12,868,683	12,106,115
Oregon	61,514	177,875	51,826	155,478
Pennsylvania:				
Anthracite	46,468,641	66,383,772	50,665,431	73,944,735
Bituminous	42,302,173	35,376,916	42,788,490	37,271,053
Rhode Island			500	10,000
Tennessee	2,169,585	2,395,746	2,413,678	2,668,188
Texas	184,440	465,900	172,100	412,360
Utah	318,159	552,390	371,045	666,045
Virginia	781,011	589,925	736,399	611,654
Washington	1,263,689	3,426,590	1,056,249	2,437,270
West Virginia	7,394,654	6,208,128	9,220,665	7,359,816
Wyoming	1,870,366	3,183,669	2,327,841	3,555,275
Total product sold.	157,788,656	176,804,573	168,566,669	191,133,135

Amount and value of coal produced in the United States, etc.—Continued.

State or Territory.	1892.		1893.	
	Product.	Value.	Product.	Value.
	Short tons.		*Short tons.*	
Alabama	5,529,312	$5,788,898	5,136,935	$5,096,792
Arkansas	535,558	666,230	574,763	773,347
California	85,178	209,711	72,603	167,555
Colorado	3,510,830	5,685,112	4,102,389	5,104,602
Georgia	215,498	212,761	372,740	365,972
Idaho				
Illinois	17,862,276	16,243,645	19,949,564	17,827,595
Indiana	3,345,174	3,620,582	3,791,851	4,055,372
Indian Territory	1,192,721	2,043,479	1,252,110	2,235,209
Iowa	3,918,491	5,175,060	3,972,229	5,110,460
Kansas	3,007,276	3,955,595	2,652,546	3,375,740
Kentucky	3,025,313	2,771,238	3,007,179	2,613,569
Maryland	3,419,962	3,063,580	3,716,041	3,267,317
Michigan	77,990	121,314	45,979	82,462
Missouri	2,733,949	3,369,659	2,897,442	3,562,757
Montana	564,648	1,330,847	892,309	1,772,116
Nebraska	1,500	4,500		
Nevada				
New Mexico	661,330	1,074,601	665,094	979,044
North Carolina	6,679	9,599	17,000	25,500
North Dakota	40,725	39,250	49,630	56,250
Ohio	13,562,927	12,722,745	13,253,646	12,351,139
Oregon	34,661	148,546	41,683	164,500
Pennsylvania:				
Anthracite	52,472,504	82,442,000	53,967,543	85,687,078
Bituminous	46,694,576	39,017,164	44,070,724	35,260,674
Rhode Island				
Tennessee	2,092,064	2,355,441	1,902,258	2,048,449
Texas	245,690	569,333	302,206	688,407
Utah	361,013	562,625	413,205	611,092
Virginia	675,205	578,429	820,339	692,748
Washington	1,213,427	2,763,547	1,264,877	2,920,876
West Virginia	9,738,755	7,852,114	10,708,578	8,251,170
Wyoming	2,503,839	3,168,776	2,439,311	3,290,904
Total product sold.	179,329,071	207,566,381	182,352,774	208,438,696

Amount and value of coal produced in the United States, etc.—Continued.

State or Territory.	1894.		1895.	
	Product.	Value.	Product.	Value.
	Short tons.		*Short tons.*	
Alabama	4, 397, 178	$4, 085, 535	5, 693, 775	$5, 126, 822
Arkansas	512, 626	631, 988	598, 322	751, 156
California	67, 247	155, 620	75, 453	175, 778
Colorado	2, 831, 409	3, 516, 340	3, 082, 982	3, 675, 185
Georgia	354, 111	299, 290	260, 998	215, 863
Idaho				
Illinois	17, 113, 576	15, 282, 111	17, 735, 864	14, 239, 157
Indiana	3, 423, 921	3, 295, 034	3, 995, 892	3, 642, 623
Indian Territory	969, 606	1, 541, 293	1, 21·, 185	1, 737, 254
Iowa	3, 967, 253	4, 997, 939	4, 155, 074	4, 982, 102
Kansas	3, 388, 251	4, 178, 998	2, 926, 870	3, 481, 981
Kentucky	3, 111, 192	2, 749, 932	3, 357, 770	2, 890, 247
Maryland	3, 501, 428	2, 687, 270	3, 915, 585	3, 160, 592
Michigan	70, 022	103, 049	112, 322	180, 016
Missouri	2, 245, 039	2, 634, 564	2, 372, 393	2, 651, 612
Montana	927, 395	1, 887, 390	1, 504, 193	2, 850, 906
Nebraska				
Nevada	150	475		
New Mexico	597, 196	935, 857	720, 654	1, 072, 520
North Carolina	16, 900	29, 675	24, 900	41, 350
North Dakota	42, 015	47, 049	a 39, 197	a 42, 046
Ohio	11, 909, 856	9, 841, 723	13, 355, 806	10, 618, 477
Oregon	47, 521	183, 914	73, 685	247, 901
Pennsylvania :				
Anthracite	51, 921, 121	78, 488, 063	57, 999, 337	82, 019, 272
Bituminous	39, 912, 463	29, 479, 820	50, 217, 228	35, 980, 357
Rhode Island				
Tennessee	2, 180, 879	2, 119, 481	2, 535, 644	2, 349, 032
Texas	420, 848	976, 458	484, 959	913, 138
Utah	431, 550	603, 479	471, 836	617, 349
Virginia	1, 229, 083	933, 576	1, 368, 324	869, 873
Washington	1, 106, 470	2, 578, 441	1, 191, 410	2, 577, 958
West Virginia	11, 627, 757	8, 706, 808	11, 387, 961	7, 710, 575
Wyoming	2, 417, 463	3, 170, 392	2, 246, 911	2, 977, 901
Total product sold	170, 741, 526	186, 141, 564	193, 117, 530	197, 799, 043

a Includes South Dakota.

Comparing the amount and value of the product in 1895 with that of 1894, the following statement of increases and decreases is obtained:

Increases and decreases in coal production during 1895 compared with 1894, by States.

State or Territory.	Increases.		Decreases.	
	Short tons.	Value.	Short tons.	Value.
Alabama	1,296,597	$1,041,287		
Arkansas	85,696	119,168		
California	8,206	20,158		
Colorado	251,573	158,845		
Georgia			93,113	$83,427
Illinois	822,288			1,042,954
Indiana	571,971	347,589		
Indian Territory	241,579	195,961		
Iowa	188,821			15,837
Kansas			461,381	697,017
Kentucky	246,578	140,315		
Maryland	414,157	473,322		
Michigan	42,300	76,967		
Missouri	127,354	17,048		
Montana	576,798	962,516		
Nevada			150	475
New Mexico	123,458	136,663		
North Carolina	8,000	11,675		
North Dakota			2,818	5,003
Ohio	1,445,950	776,754		
Oregon	26,164	63,987		
Pennsylvania bituminous.	10,304,765	6,500,537		
Tennessee	354,765	229,551		
Texas	64,111			63,320
Utah	40,286	13.870		
Virginia	139,241			63,703
Washington	84,940			483
West Virginia			239,796	996,233
Wyoming			170,552	192,491
Total	16,297,788	8,126,270		
Pennsylvania anthracite..	6,078,216	3,531,209		
Grand total	22,376,004	11,657,479		

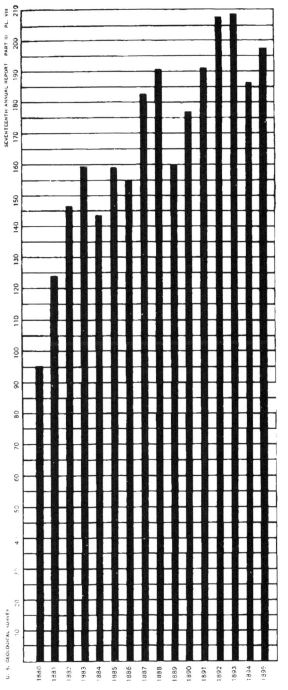

VALUE OF COAL PRODUCED IN THE UNITED STATES FROM 1880 TO 1895.

(In millions of dollars.)

LABOR STATISTICS.

The following table shows under one head the total number of employees in the coal mines of the United States for a period of six years, and the average time made by each:

Labor statistics of coal mining since 1890.

State or Territory.	1890. Number of days active.	1890. Average number employed.	1891. Number of days active.	1891. Average number employed.	1892. Number of days active.	1892. Average number employed.
Alabama	217	10,642	268	9,302	271	10,075
Arkansas	214	938	214	1,317	199	1,128
California	301	364	222	256	204	187
Colorado	220	5,827	......	6,000	229	5,747
Georgia	313	425	312	850	277	467
Illinois	204	28,574	215½	32,951	219½	34,585
Indiana	220	5,489	190	5,879	224	6,436
Indian Territory	238	2,571	221½	2,891	311	3,257
Iowa	213	8,130	224	8,124	236	8,170
Kansas	210	4,523	222	6,201	208½	6,559
Kentucky	219	5,259	225	6,355	217	6,724
Maryland	244	3,842	244	3,891	225	3,886
Michigan	229	180	205	223	195	230
Missouri	229	5,971	218	6,199	230	5,893
Montana	218	1,251	......	1,119	258	1,158
Nevada						
New Mexico	192	827	265	806	223	1,083
North Carolina	200	80	254	80	160	90
North Dakota					216	54
Ohio	201	20,576	206	22,182	212	22,576
Oregon	305	208	125	100	120	90
Pennsylvania bituminous	232	61,333	223	63,661	223	66,655
Tennessee	263	5,082	230	5,097	240	4,926
Texas	241	674	225	787	208	871
Utah	289	429	......	621	230	646
Virginia	296	1,295	246	820	192	836
Washington	270	2,206	211	2,447	247	2,564
West Virginia	227	12,236	237	14,227	228	14,867
Wyoming	246	3,272	......	3,411	225	3,133
Total	226	192,204	*a* 223	205,803	219	212,893
Pennsylvania anthracite	200	126,000	203	126,350	198	129,050
Grand total	216	318,204	215	332,153	212	311,943

a General average obtained from the average days made in the different States, exclusive of Colorado, Montana, Utah, and Wyoming.

Labor statistics of coal mining since 1890—Continued.

State or Territory.	1893.		1894.		1895.	
	Number of days active.	Average number employed.	Number of days active.	Average number employed.	Number of days active.	Average number employed.
Alabama	237	11,294	238	10,859	244	10,346
Arkansas	151	1,559	134	1,493	176	1,218
California	208	158	232	125	262	190
Colorado	188	7,202	155	6,507	182	6,125
Georgia	342	736	304	729	312	848
Illinois	229	35,390	183	38,477	182	38,630
Indiana	201	7,644	149	8,603	189	8,530
Indian Territory	171	3,446	157	3,101	164	3,212
Iowa	204	8,863	170	9,995	189	10,066
Kansas	147	7,310	164	7,339	159	7,482
Kentucky	202	6,581	145	8,083	146	7,865
Maryland	240	3,935	215	3,974	248	3,912
Michigan	154	162	224	223	186	320
Missouri	206	7,375	138	7,523	163	6,299
Montana	242	1,401	192	1,782	223	2,184
Nevada			60	2		
New Mexico	229	1,011	182	985	190	1,383
North Carolina	80	70	145	95	226	61
North Dakota	193	88	156	77	139	65
Ohio	188	23,931	136	27,105	176	24,644
Oregon	192	110	243	88	69	414
Pennsylvania bituminous	190	71,931	165	75,010	206	71,130
Tennessee	232	4,976	210	5,542	224	5,120
Texas	251	996	283	1,062	171	1,642
Utah	226	576	199	671	203	670
Virginia	253	961	234	1,635	225	2,158
Washington	241	2,757	207	2,662	224	2,840
West Virginia	219	16,524	186	17,824	195	19,159
Wyoming	189	3,378	190	3,032	184	3,449
Total	204	230,365	171	244,603	194	239,962
Pennsylvania anthracite	197	132,944	190	131,603	196	142,917
Grand total	201	363,309	178	376,206	195	382,879

AVERAGE PRICES.

The following table will be of interest as showing the fluctuations in the average prices ruling in each State since 1886. Prior to that year the statistics were not collected with sufficient accuracy to make a statement of the average prices of any practical value. These averages are obtained by dividing the total value by the total product, except for the years 1886, 1887, and 1888, when the item of colliery consumption was not considered:

Average prices for coal at the mines since 1886.

State or Territory.	1886.	1887.	1888.	1889.	1890.
Alabama	$3.09	$1.30	$1.15	$1.11	$1.03
Arkansas	1.60	1.68	1.50	1.42	1.29
California	3.00	3.00	4.00	2.36	2.56
Colorado	2.35	2.20	2.20	1.51	1.40
Georgia	1.50	1.50	1.50	1.50	1.04
Illinois	1.11	1.09	1.12	.97	.93
Indiana	1.15	1.34	1.40	1.02	.99
Indian Territory	1.60	1.87	1.88	1.76	1.82
Iowa	1.25	1.34	1.30	1.33	1.24
Kansas	1.20	1.40	1.50	1.48	1.30
Kentucky	1.15	1.15	1.20	.99	.92
Maryland	.95	.95	.95	.86	.86
Michigan	1.50	1.50	1.66	1.71	1.99
Missouri	1.30	1.34	2.21	1.36	1.24
Montana	3.50	3.50	3.50	2.42	2.42
Nevada	......	......	......	......	......
New Mexico	3.00	3.00	3.00	1.79	1.34
North Carolina	......	......	......	......	1.74
North Dakota	1.59	1.50	3.50	1.43	1.40
Ohio	.95	.88	.93	.93	.94
Oregon	2.50	2.20	3.00	......	2.89
Pennsylvania bituminous	.80	.90	.95	.77	.84
Tennessee	1.15	1.30	1.10	1.21	1.10
Texas	1.85	2.00	2.05	2.66	2.53
Utah	2.10	2.00	2.10	1.59	1.74
Virginia	1.00	.94	1.00	.93	.75
Washington	2.25	2.20	3.00	2.32	2.71
West Virginia	.94	.95	1.10	.82	.84
Wyoming	3.00	3.00	3.00	1.26	1.70
Total bituminous	a 1.06	a 1.12	a 1.00	1.00	.99
Pennsylvania anthracite	a 1.95	a 2.01	a 1.95	1.44	1.43
General average	a 1.30	a 1.45	a 1.42	1.13	1.12

a Exclusive of colliery consumption.

Average prices for coal at the mines since 1886—Continued.

State or Territory.	1891.	1892.	1893.	1894.	1895.
Alabama	$1.07	$1.05	$0.99	$0.93	$0.90
Arkansas	1.19	1.24	1.34	1.22	1.25
California	2.20	2.46	2.31	2.31	2.33
Colorado	1.37	1.62	1.24	1.24	1.20
Georgia	1.50	.99	.98	.85	.83
Illinois	.91	.91	.89	.89	.80
Indiana	1.03	1.08	1.07	.96	.91
Indian Territory	1.74	1.71	1.79	1.59	1.43
Iowa	1.27	1.32	1.30	1.26	1.20
Kansas	1.31	1.31½	1.27	1.23	1.20
Kentucky	.93	.92	.86	.88	.86
Maryland	.81	.89	.88	.77	.81
Michigan	1.66	1.56	1.79	1.47	1.60
Missouri	1.23	1.23	1.23	1.17	1.12
Montana	2.27	2.36	1.99	2.04	1.89
Nevada	....	....	....	3.15	....
New Mexico	1.68	1.62	1.47	1.57	1.49
North Carolina	1.93	1.44	1.50	1.76	1.66
North Dakota	1.40	.96	1.13	1.12	1.07
Ohio	.94	.94	.92	.83	.79
Oregon	3.00	4.29	3.57	3.87	3.36
Pennsylvania bituminous	.87	.84	.80	.74	.72
Tennessee	1.11	1.13	1.08	.97	.93
Texas	2.40	2.32	2.28	2.32	1.88
Utah	1.80	1.56	1.48	1.40	1.31
Virginia	.83	.86	.84	.76	.63
Washington	2.31	2.28	2.31	2.33	2.16
West Virginia	.80	.80	.77	.75	.68
Wyoming	1.53	1.27	1.35	1.31	1.33
Total bituminous	.99	.99	.96	.91	.86
Pennsylvania anthracite	1.46	1.57	1.59	1.52	1.41
General average	1.13	1.16	1.14	1.09	1.02

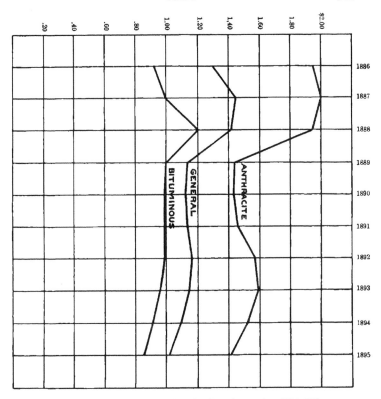

Fig. 1.—Variations in average prices of coal per short ton from 1886 to 1895.
(Prices for 1886, 1887, and 1888 do not include colliery consumption.)

IMPORTS AND EXPORTS.

The following tables have been compiled from official returns to the Bureau of Statistics of the Treasury Department, and show the imports and exports of coal from 1867 to 1895, inclusive. The values given in both cases are considerably higher than the average "spot" rates by which the values of the domestic production have been computed.

The tariff from 1824 to 1843 was 6 cents per bushel, or $1.68 per long ton; from 1843 to 1846, $1.75 per ton; 1846 to 1857, 30 per cent ad valorem; 1857 to 1861, 24 per cent ad valorem; 1861, bituminous and shale, $1 per ton; all other, 50 cents per ton; 1862 to 1864, bituminous and shale, $1.10 per ton; all other, 60 cents per ton; 1864 to 1872, bituminous and shale, $1.25 per ton; all other, 40 cents per ton. By the act of 1872 the tariff on bituminous coal and shale was made 75

cents per ton, and so continued until the act of August, 1894, changed
it to 40 cents per ton. On slack or culm the tariff was made 40 cents
per ton by the act of 1872; was changed to 30 cents per ton by the act
of March, 1883, and so continued until the act of August, 1894, changed
it to 15 cents per ton. Anthracite coal has been free of duty since
1870. During the period from June, 1854, to March, 1866, the reci-
procity treaty was in force, and coal from the British Possessions in
North America was admitted into the United States duty free.

The exports consist both of anthracite and bituminous coal, the
amount of bituminous being the greater in the last few years. They
are made principally by rail over the international bridges and by lake
and sea to the Canadian provinces. Exports are also made by sea to
the West Indies, to Central and South America, and elsewhere.

The imports are principally from Australia and British Columbia to
San Francisco, from Great Britain to the Atlantic and Pacific coasts,
and from Nova Scotia to Atlantic Coast points.

Coal imported and entered for consumption in the United States, 1867 to 1895.

Year ending—	Anthracite.		Bituminous and shale.	
	Quantity.	Value.	Quantity.	Value.
	Long tons.		*Long tons.*	
June 30, 1867			509, 802	$1, 412, 597
1868			394, 021	1, 250, 513
1869			437, 228	1, 222, 119
1870			415, 729	1, 103, 965
1871	973	$4, 177	430, 508	1, 121, 914
1872	390	1, 322	485, 063	1, 279, 686
1873	2. 221	10, 764	460, 028	1, 548, 208
1874	471	3, 224	492, 063	1, 937, 274
1875	138	963	436, 714	1, 791, 601
1876	1, 428	8, 560	400, 632	1, 592, 846
1877	630	2, 220	495, 816	1, 782, 941
1878	158	518	572, 846	1, 929, 660
1879	488	721	486, 501	1, 716, 209
1880	8	40	471, 818	1, 588, 312
1881	1, 207	2, 628	652, 963	1, 988, 199
1882	36	148	795, 722	2, 141, 373
1883	507	1, 172	645, 924	3, 013, 555
1884	1, 448	4, 404	748, 995	2, 494, 228
1885	4, 976	15, 848	768, 477	2, 548, 432
Dec. 31, 1886	2, 039	4, 920	811, 657	2, 501, 153
1887	14, 181	42, 983	819, 242	2, 609, 311
1888	24, 093	68, 710	1, 085, 647	3, 728. 060
1889	20, 652	117, 434	1, 001, 374	3, 425, 347
1890	15, 145	46, 695	819. 971	2, 822, 216
1891	37, 607	112, 722	1, 363, 313	4, 561, 105
1892	65, 058	197, 583	1, 143, 304	3, 744, 862
1893	53, 768	148, 112	*a* 1, 082, 993	3, 623, 892
1894	90, 068	234, 024	*b* 1, 242. 714	3, 785, 513
1895	141, 337	328, 705	*c* 1. 212. 023	3, 626. 623

a Including 14,632 tons of slack or culm, valued at $16,906.
b Including 30,453 tons of slack or culm, valued at $32,267.
c Including 18,174 tons of slack or culm, valued at $15,309.

Coal of domestic production exported from the United States, 1867 to 1895.

Year ending—	Anthracite.		Bituminous and shale.	
	Quantity.	Value.	Quantity.	Value.
	Long tons.		*Long tons.*	
June 30, 1867...........	192,912	$1,333,457	92,189	$512,742
1868.............	192,291	1,082,745	86,367	433,475
1869.............	283,783	1,553,115	....	....
1870.............	121,098	803,135	106,820	503,223
1871.............	134,571	805,169	133,380	564,067
1872.............	259,567	1,375,342	141,311	586,264
1873.............	312,180	1,827,822	242,453	1,086,253
1874.............	401,912	2,236,084	361,490	1,587,666
1875.............	316,157	1,791,626	203,189	828,943
1876.............	337,931	1,869,434	230,144	850,711
1877.............	418,791	1,891,351	321,665	1,024,711
1878.............	319,477	1,006,843	340,661	1,352,624
1879.............	386,916	1,427,886	276,000	891,512
1880.............	392,626	1,362,901	222,634	695,179
1881.............	462,208	2,091,928	191,038	739,532
1882.............	553,742	2,589,887	314,320	1,102,898
1883.............	557,813	2,648,033	463,051	1,593,214
1884.............	649,040	3,053,550	646,265	1,977,959
1885.............	588,461	2,586,421	683,481	1,989,541
Dec. 31, 1886.............	667,076	2,718,143	544,768	1,440,631
1887.............	825,486	3,469,166	706,364	2,001,966
1888.............	969,542	4,325,126	860,462	2,529,472
1889.............	857,632	3,636,347	935,151	2,783,592
1890.............	794,335	3,272,697	1,280,930	4,004,995
1891.............	861,251	3,577,610	1,615,869	5,104,850
1892.............	851,639	3,722,903	1,645,869	4,999,289
1893.............	1,333,287	6,241,007	2,324,591	6,009,801
1894.............	1,440,625	6,359,021	2,195,716	4,970,270
1895.............	1,470,710	5,937,130	2,211,983	4,816,847

WORLD'S PRODUCT OF COAL.

In the following table is given the coal product of the principal countries for the years nearest the one under review for which figures could be obtained. For the sake of convenience the amounts are expressed in the unit of measurement adopted in each country and reduced for comparison to short tons of 2,000 pounds. In each case the year is named for which the product is given.

The world's product of coal.

Country.	Usual unit in producing country.	Equivalent in short tons.
Great Britain (1895) ....long tons..	189, 661, 362	212, 320, 725
United States (1895)..............do....	172, 426, 366	193, 117, 530
Germany (1895)...............metric tons..	103, 876, 813	114, 524, 186
France (1894) ....do....	27, 459, 137	30, 273, 699
Austria-Hungary (1893) ....do....	30, 449, 304	33, 570, 358
Belgium (1895).......................do....	20, 414, 849	22, 507, 371
Russia (1893).......................do....	7, 535, 000	8, 307, 337
Canada (1895) ....short tons..	3, 512, 504	3, 512, 504
Japan (1893) ....do....	3, 400, 000	3, 400, 000
Spain (1895)..................metric tons..	1, 774, 560	1, 956, 452
New Zealand (1894)............short tons..	719, 546	719, 546
Sweden (1894)................metric tons..	214, 000	235, 935
Italy (1894) ....do....	271, 295	299, 103
Other countries	....	4, 126, 553
Total.......................	....	628, 805, 239
Percentage of the United States..............	....	31

The steady advance of the United States in industrial development
is well illustrated in the following tables showing the world's production of coal for twenty-eight years.   In 1868 and 1869, when the total output of the world was about 225,000,000 tons, the United States yielded
but 14 per cent.   In 1892, 1893, 1894, and 1895 the world's output has
exceeded half a billion tons each year, of which the United States has
contributed an average of 30 per cent, having more than doubled its
percentage.   Great Britain, whose mines furnished more than 50 per
cent of the world's product in 1868, now barely exceeds the percentage
of the United States.

World's production of coal, by countries, since 1868.

Year.	United States.		Great Britain.	
	Long tons.	Short tons.	Long tons.	Short tons.
1868.............	28,258,000	31,648,960	103,141,157	115,518,096
1869.............	28,268,000	31,660,160	107,427,557	120,318,864
1870.............	32,863,000	36,806,560	110,431,192	123,682,935
1871.............	41,384,000	46,350,080	117,352,028	131,434,271
1872.............	45,416,000	50,865,920	123,497,316	138,316,994
1873.............	51,004,000	57,124,480	128,680,131	144,121,747
1874.............	46,916,000	52,545,920	126,590,108	141,780,921
1875.............	46,686,000	52,288,320	133,306,485	149,303,263
1876.............	47,500,000	53,200,000	134,125,166	150,220,186
1877.............	53,948,000	60,421,760	134,179,968	150,281,564
1878.............	51,655,000	57,853,600	132,612,063	148,525,511
1879.............	59,333,000	66,452,960	133,720,393	149,766,840
1880.............	63,822,830	71,481,569	146,969,409	164,605,738
1881.............	76,865,357	85,881,030	154,184,300	172,686,416
1882.............	92,219,454	103,285,789	156,499,977	175,279,974
1883.............	102,867,969	115,212,125	163,737,327	183,385,806
1884.............	106,906,295	119,735,051	160,757,779	180,048,712
1885.............	99,069,216	110,957,522	159,351,418	178,473,588
1886.............	100,663,753	112,743,403	157,518,482	176,420,700
1887.............	116,049,604	129,975,557	162,119,812	181,574,189
1888.............	132,731,609	148,659,402	169,935,219	190,327,445
1889.............	126,097,780	141,229,514	176,916,724	198,146,731
1890.............	140,882,729	157,788,657	181,614,288	203,408,003
1891.............	150,505,954	168,566,668	185,479,126	207,736,621
1892.............	160,115,242	179,329,071	181,786,871	203,601,296
1893.............	162,814,977	182,352,774	164,325,795	184,044,890
1894.............	152,447,791	170,741,526	188,277,525	210,870,828
1895.............	172,426,366	193,117,530	189,661,362	212,320,725

World's production of coal, by countries, since 1868—Continued.

Year.	Germany.		France.	
	Metric tons.	Short tons.	Metric tons.	Short tons.
1868	32, 879, 123	36, 249, 233	13, 330, 826	14, 697, 236
1869	34, 343, 913	37, 864, 164	13, 509, 745	14, 894, 494
1870	34, 003, 004	37, 488, 312	13, 179, 788	14, 530, 716
1871	37, 856, 110	41, 736, 361	13, 240, 135	14, 597, 249
1872	42, 324, 467	46, 662, 725	16, 100, 773	17, 751, 102
1873	46, 145, 194	50, 875, 076	17, 479, 341	19, 270, 973
1874	46, 658, 145	51, 440, 605	16, 907, 913	18, 640, 974
1875	47, 804, 054	52, 703, 970	16, 956, 840	18, 694, 916
1876	49, 550, 461	54, 629, 383	17, 101, 448	18, 854, 346
1877	48, 229, 882	53, 173, 445	16, 804, 529	18, 526, 993
1878	50, 519, 899	55, 698, 188	16, 960, 916	18, 699, 410
1879	53, 470, 716	58, 951, 464	17, 110, 979	18, 864, 854
1880	59, 118, 035	65, 177, 634	19, 361, 564	21, 346, 124
1881	61, 540, 485	67, 848, 385	19, 765, 983	21, 791, 996
1882	65, 378, 211	72, 079, 478	20, 603, 704	22, 715, 584
1883	70, 442, 648	77, 663, 019	21, 333, 884	23, 520, 607
1884	72, 113, 820	79, 505, 487	20, 023, 514	22, 075, 924
1885	73, 675, 515	81, 227, 255	19, 510, 530	21, 510, 359
1886	73, 682, 584	81, 235, 049	19, 909, 894	21, 950, 658
1887	76, 232, 618	84, 046, 461	21, 287, 589	23, 469, 567
1888	81, 960, 083	90, 360, 992	22, 602, 894	24, 919, 691
1889	84, 788, 609	93, 479, 441	24, 303, 509	26, 794, 619
1890	89, 051, 527	98, 179, 309	26, 083, 118	28, 756, 638
1891	94, 252, 278	103, 913, 136	26, 024, 893	28, 692, 444
1892	92, 544, 030	102, 029, 793	26, 178, 701	28, 862, 018
1893	95, 426, 153	105, 207, 334	25, 650, 981	28, 280, 207
1894	98, 876, 105	109, 010, 906	27, 459, 137	30, 273, 699
1895	103, 876, 813	114, 524, 186	(a)	(a)

a Latest figures available have been used in making up the total for the year.

World's production of coal, by countries, since 1868—Continued.

Year.	Austria-Hungary.		Belgium.	
	Metric tons.	Short tons.	Metric tons.	Short tons.
1868.............	7, 021, 756	7, 741, 486	12. 298, 589	13, 559, 194
1869.............	7, 663. 043	8, 448, 505	12, 943, 994	14, 270. 753
1870.............	8, 355. 945	9, 212, 429	13. 697, 118	15. 101, 073
1871.............	8. 437, 401	9, 302, 235	13, 733, 176	15, 140. 827
1872.............	8, 825, 896	9, 730, 550	15, 658, 948	17, 263, 990
1873.............	10, 104. 769	11, 140, 508	15, 778, 401	17, 395, 687
1874.............	12, 631, 364	13, 926, 079	14, 669, 029	16. 172, 604
1875.............	13, 062, 738	14, 395, 137	15, 011, 331	16, 549, 992
1876.............	13, 000, 000	14, 327, 300	14, 329, 578	15, 798, 360
1877.............	13, 500, 000	14, 883, 750	13, 669, 077	15, 070, 157
1878.............	13, 990, 000	15, 324, 750	14, 899. 175	16, 426, 340
1879.............	14, 500, 000	15, 986, 250	15, 447, 292	17, 030, 640
1880.............	14, 800, 000	16. 317, 000	16, 886, 698	18, 617, 585
1881	15, 304, 813	16, 873, 556	16, 873, 951	18, 603, 531
1882.............	15, 555, 292	17, 149, 709	17, 590, 989	19, 394, 065
1883.............	17, 047, 961	18, 795, 377	18, 177, 754	20, 040, 974
1884.............	18, 000, 000	19, 845, 000	18, 051, 499	19, 901, 778
1885.............	20, 435, 463	22, 530, 098	17, 437, 603	19, 224, 957
1886.............	20, 779, 441	22, 909, 334	17, 285, 543	19, 057, 311
1887.............	21, 879, 172	24, 121, 787	18, 378, 624	20, 262, 433
1888.............	23, 859, 608	26, 305, 218	19, 218, 481	21, 188, 375
1889.............	25, 328, 417	27, 924, 580	19, 869, 980	21, 906, 653
1890.............	27, 504, 032	30, 323, 195	20, 365, 960	22, 453, 471
1891.............	28, 823, 240	31, 777, 622	19, 675, 644	21, 692, 398
1892.............	29, 037, 978	32, 014. 371	19, 583, 173	21, 590, 448
1893.............	30, 449, 304	33, 570, 358	19, 410, 519	21, 400, 097
1894.............	(a)	(a)	20, 458, 827	22, 555, 857
1895.............	(a)	(a)	20, 414, 849	22, 507, 371

a Latest figures available have been used in making up the total for the year.

World's production of coal, by countries, since 1868—Continued.

Year.	Russia.		Other countries.	Total.	Per cent of United States.
	Metric tons.	Short tons.	Short tons.	Short tons.	
1868...............	....	....	1, 152, 665	220, 566, 870	14. 35
1869...............	....	....	1, 107, 395	228, 564, 335	13. 85
1870...........	696, 673	768, 082	1, 086, 717	238, 676, 824	15. 42
1871...........	....	....	1, 128, 822	259, 689, 845	17. 85
1872...........	....	....	1, 293, 835	281, 885, 116	18. 04
1873...........	....	....	1, 514. 191	301, 442, 662	18. 95
1874...........	....	....	2, 697, 160	297, 204, 263	17. 68
1875...........	1, 709, 718	1, 884, 964	2, 638, 491	308, 459, 053	16. 95
1876...........	....	....	2, 601, 761	309, 631, 336	17. 18
1877...........	....	....	2, 823, 109	315, 180, 778	19. 17
1878...........	2, 483, 575	2, 738, 141	3, 176, 050	318, 441, 990	18. 17
1879...........	2. 874 790	3, 169, 456	3, 362, 605	333, 585, 069	19. 92
1880...........	3, 238, 470	3, 570, 413	3, 621, 342	364, 737, 405	19. 60
1881...........	3, 439, 787	3, 792, 365	5, 185, 974	392, 663, 253	21. 87
1882...........	3, 672, 782	4, 049, 242	6, 128, 631	420, 082, 472	24. 58
1883...........	3, 916, 105	4, 317, 506	6, 930, 279	449, 865, 693	25. 61
1884...........	3, 869, 689	4, 266, 332	7, 367, 309	452, 745, 593	26. 45
1885...........	4, 207, 905	4, 639, 215	7, 570, 507	446, 133, 501	24. 87
1886...........	4, 506, 027	4, 967, 895	9, 058, 136	448, 342, 486	25. 15
1887...........	4, 464, 174	4, 921, 752	9, 838, 438	478, 210, 184	27. 18
1888...........	5, 187, 312	5, 719, 011	10, 848, 759	518, 328, 893	28. 68
1889...........	6, 215, 577	6, 852, 674	11, 779, 474	528, 113, 686	26. 74
1890...........	6, 016, 525	6, 633, 219	12, 048, 616	559, 591, 108	28. 20
1891...........	6, 233, 020	6, 871, 905	13, 789, 657	583, 040, 451	28. 93
1892...........	6, 816, 323	7, 514, 996	13, 603, 435	588, 545, 428	30. 47
1893...........	7, 535, 000	8, 307, 337	13, 087, 484	576, 250, 481	31. 64
1894...........	(a)	(a)	14, 516, 903	599, 847, 414	28. 45
1895...........	(a)	(a)	14, 250, 093	628, 805, 239	30. 71

a Latest figures available have been used in making up the total for the year.

The following table shows in detail the production of the countries included under "other countries" in the preceding statement.

Product of minor coal-producing countries since 1868.

Year.	New South Wales.		Queensland.		New Zealand.	
	Long tons.	Short tons.	Long tons.	Short tons.	Long tons.	Short tons.
1868	954,231	1,068,739	19,611	21,964		
1869	919,774	1,030,147	11,120	12,454		
1870	868,564	972,791	22,639	25,356		
1871	898,784	1,006,638	17,000	19,040		
1872	1,012,426	1,133,917	27,727	31,054		
1873	1,192,862	1,336,005	33,613	37,647		
1874	1,304,567	1,461,115	43,443	48,656		
1875	1,329,729	1,489,296	32,107	35,960		
1876	1,319,918	1,478,308	50,627	56,702		
1877	1,444,271	1,617,584	60,918	68,228		
1878	1,575,497	1,764,556	52,580	58,890	162,218	181,684
1879	1,583,381	1,773,387	55,012	61,613	231,218	258,964
1880	1,466,180	1,642,122	58,052	65,018	299,923	335,913
1881	1,769,597	1,981,949	65,612	73,485	337,262	377,733
1882	2,109,282	2,362,396	74,436	83,368	378,272	423,665
1883	2,521,457	2,824,032	104,750	117,320	421,764	472,376
1884	2,749,109	3,079,002	120,727	135,214	480,831	538,531
1885	2,878,863	3,224,327	209,698	234,862	511,063	572,390
1886	2,830,175	3,169,796	228,656	256,094	534,353	598,475
1887	2,922,497	3,273,197	238,813	267,470	558,620	625,654
1888	3,203,444	3,587,857	311,412	348,781	613,895	687,562
1889	3,655,632	4,094,308	265,507	297,368	586,445	656,818
1890	3,060,876	3,428,181	338,344	378,945	637,397	713,885
1891	4,037,929	4,522,480	271,603	304,195	668,794	749,049
1892	3,780,968	4,234,684	265,086	296,896	673,315	754,113
1893	3,278,328	3,671,727	264,403	296,131	691,548	774,534
1894	3,672,076	4,112,725	270,705	303,190	719,546	805,892
1895						

Product of minor coal-producing countries since 1868—Continued.

Year.	Victoria.		Canada (Short tons).	India.	
	Long tons.	Short tons.		Long tons.	Short tons.
1868					
1869					
1870					
1871					
1872					
1873					
1874			1,058,446		
1875			984,905		
1876			933,803		
1877			1,002,395		
1878			1,034,081		
1879			1,123,863		
1880			1,424,635		
1881			1,487,182	997,543	1,117,248
1882			1,811,708	1,130,242	1,265,871
1883			1,806,259	1,315,976	1,473,893
1884			1,950,080	1,266,312	1,418,269
1885			1,879,470	1,294,221	1,449,528
1886			2,091,976	1,401,295	1,569,450
1887			2,418,494	1,560,393	1,747,640
1888			2,658,134	1,802,876	2,019,221
1889	14,421	16,152	2,719,478	2,045,359	2,290,802
1890	20,750	23,240	3,117,661	2,168,521	2,428,744
1891	22,834	25,574	3,623,076	2,328,577	2,608,006
1892	23,363	26,166	3,292,547	2,537,696	2,842,220
1893	91,726	102,733	3,201,742	2,529,855	2,833,438
1894	171,659	192,258	3,903,913		
1895			3,512,504		

Product of minor coal-producing countries since 1868—Continued.

Year.	Spain.		Italy.		Sweden.	
	Metric tons.	Short tons.	Metric tons.	Short tons.	Metric tons.	Short tons.
1868.....	....	....	56, 201	61, 962	....	....
1869.....	....	....	58, 770	64, 794	....	....
1870.....	....	....	80, 336	88, 570	....	....
1871.....	....	....	93, 555	103, 144	....	....
1872.....	....	....	116, 884	128, 864	....	....
1873.....	....	....	127, 473	140, 539	....	....
1874.....	....	....	116, 955	128, 943	....	....
1875.....	....	....	116, 399	128, 330	....	....
1876.....	....	....	120, 588	132, 948	....	....
1877.....	....	....	122, 360	134, 902	....	....
1878.....	....	....	124, 117	136, 839	....	....
1879.....	....	....	131, 318	144, 778	....	....
1880.....	....	....	139, 369	153, 654	....	....
1881.....	....	....	134, 582	148, 377	....	....
1882.....	....	....	164, 737	181, 623	....	....
1883.....	....	....	214, 421	236, 399	....	....
1884.....	....	....	223, 322	246, 213	....	....
1885.....	....	....	190, 413	209, 930	....	....
1886.....	1, 104, 079	1, 104, 079	243, 325	268, 266	....	....
1887.....	1, 038, 305	1, 144, 731	327, 665	361, 251	....	....
1888.....	1, 036, 565	1, 142, 813	366, 794	404, 390	....	....
1889.....	1, 153, 755	1, 272, 015	390, 320	432, 533	....	....
1890.....	1, 212, 089	1, 336, 328	376, 326	415, 500	187, 512	206, 132
1891.....	1, 287, 988	1, 420, 007	289, 286	318, 938	198, 033	218, 331
1892.....	1, 461, 196	1, 610, 969	295, 713	326, 024	199, 380	219, 816
1893.....	1, 484, 794	1, 636, 986	317, 249	349, 767	199, 933	220, 426
1894.....	1, 657, 010	1, 830, 853	271, 295	299, 103	213, 633	235, 532
1895.....	1, 774, 560	1, 956, 452	....	....	....	....

COAL TRADE REVIEW.

A review of the coal-mining industry in 1895 presents some interesting features, principal among which was a largely increased production in the face of badly demoralized prices. What developed this condition is difficult to determine. Lack of cooperation among the anthracite producers and carriers was responsible for the unsatisfactory results of the year's business in anthracite circles. Desultory efforts were made to restrict production during the early months of the year and to establish community interests on a profitable basis, but harmonious action could not be obtained before the middle of May, the percentage

17 GEOL, PT 3——21

of the distribution among the initial carriers being the bone of conten-
tion.   In May an agreement was concluded among the operators
according to which the mines were to be operated three days in the
week.   If this agreement was lived up to at all there is no doubt
that during the three days the mines were pushed to their utmost
capacity, for in the week ending May 18 the output was more than
80 per cent of the product of the corresponding week in 1894, when
the anthracite collieries were unable to supply the demand made upon
them because of the bituminous famine occasioned by the great strike.
In the week ending May 25 there was an actual increase over the
corresponding week in 1894 of anthracite shipments.   For the entire
month of May the shipments were but 95,000 tons less than for the
same month in 1894, and as the output was—with the mines running but
three days in the week—more than the market demanded, it is evident
that the capacity of the mines is from 50 to 75 per cent more than the
actual production.   In making this estimate allowance is made for the
fact that when the collieries are working full time the average miner
does not work more than five days in the week, and when the mines are
on half time the miners work all the time possible.   In four weeks of
June the output was 1,003,853 tons, or about 20 per cent less than the
tonnage for the same period in 1894, but there was no improvement in
prices, the market being still glutted.   At the end of June, or say for
the first six months of 1895, the anthracite production was a million
and a quarter tons more than during the first six months of 1894, when
the demand for anthracite was exceptionally brisk, to take the place of
bituminous fuel cut off by the strike.

On April 8 the anthracite sales agents met in New York and issued
a circular of "opening prices" for free-burning coal for 1895 as follows:
Broken, $3.35; egg, $3.35; stove, $3.50; chestnut, $3.35.   As will be
seen from the following table, these were, with the exception of chestnut in 1890, the lowest opening circular prices in eight years.

Opening circular prices for free-burning coal for a series of years.

Year.	Broken.	Egg.	Stove.	Chestnut.
1888	$3.75	$4.00	$4.25	$4.25
1889	3.75	3.90	4.15	4.00
1890	3.40	3.50	3.50	3.25
1891	3.50	3.60	3.75	3.50
1892	3.65	3.75	3.90	3.65
1893	3.90	3.90	4.15	4.15
1894	3.50	3.50	3.75	3.75
1895	3.35	3.35	3.50	3.35

Low as these prices were they were not maintained, nor could they
be, in a continual glut of anthracite fuel.   In the beginning of July

there was a larger stock of coal on hand at tide-water points than ever before at that time. During July and August sales of stove-size anthracite were reported at $2.75 per ton free on board cars at New York loading ports. Toward October 1 a firmer tone manifested itself, due partly to the usual increased demand at the approach of cooler weather and partly to an attempt to force an advance in prices by cooperation. Higher prices could not, however, be maintained in a continued redundant supply, and the year closed with prices weak and with a determination on the part of producers to operate on half time, so that with the beginning of 1896 the industry might be placed upon a firmer basis. From the consumer's standpoint the anthracite trade in 1895 was very gratifying. Hard coal was cheaper than at any time in the history of the industry. But to the miner, to the operator, and to the carriers the year was one of meager wages, unprofitable sales, and actual loss in freights.

In bituminous circles conditions similar to those in the anthracite trade existed, except that there was not at any time any concerted effort on the part of producers to restrict the output to the market demands. Some attempts were made in certain districts—notably the Pittsburg, northern West Virginia, and Ohio—to curtail production; but as consumers were able without much trouble to obtain fuel from other regions, and as this meant loss of legitimate trade to the conservative districts the attempts were without practical result and were short-lived. The year was marked by an uncontrolled and uncontrollable desire to secure a large tonnage regardless of demand and price. The low prices of bituminous coal, taken in connection with cheap iron ores, enabled manufacturers of pig iron to make iron at unprecedentedly low prices. Consumers of iron and steel realized that now was the time to buy, and a brief season of activity was inaugurated. When prices stiffened somewhat in response to the quickened demand buyers withheld their orders and the industry fell back to its previous demoralized condition. The iron boom of 1895, if such it may be called, began in May and ended in October. It was neither long enough nor strong enough to advantageously affect the coal business, whose history for 1895 is concisely shown in the tables of production and value.

In the early part of December a convention of operators and miners was held in Pittsburg, Pa., for the purpose of establishing a uniform scale of wages to be paid in the railroad mines of the region. A provisional agreement adopted at that meeting, as reported to the Coal Trade Journal, was as follows:

That the price of mining coal screened over a 1¼-inch screen shall be 64 cents per ton of 2,000 pounds from January 1 to March 1, 1896, and 70 cents from that time until December 1, 1896; that the day and deadwork scale agreed to at the joint convention of October, 1895, is hereby reaffirmed. It is further agreed that this contract is contingent on the following conditions: That all stores owned by the coal companies and the individual operators be abolished in accordance with a joint resolution of October 12, 1895, as follows: That all stores be abolished January 1, 1896, and that after that date no mine superintendent, mine clerk, or mine boss shall be directly or indirectly interested in or connected with such stores; that whatever company stores exist after that date, if deductions are made from miners' wages in the interest of any stores directly or indirectly, the employer shall be regarded as keeping company store, and shall pay 20 cents extra per ton for mining; that there shall be no limit on wagons at any mine; that the recognized screen of the Pittsburg district shall not exceed 60 superficial feet, with 1¼ inches between continuous flat bars. Screens shall be free from obstructions, and back-acting screens shall be considered as screens with obstructions. Operators shall recognize the rights of miners to have check weighmen of their own selection, whose wages shall be deducted by the company from the miners' wages. It is further provided that the check weighmen must not interfere with the business of the company nor be members of the mine committee.

That a committee of five operators and five miners shall be appointed, to which shall be referred all questions of difference arising under the contract, and that said committee shall, before January 15, 1896, canvass the situation, and if it finds that the above provisions have been practically complied with, and the New York and Cleveland Gas Coal Company is paying the district price of 64 cents per ton for mining, then the committee shall declare this contract in effect; but if the said company is not paying the district price of 64 cents per ton for mining, then the price to be paid shall be the price paid by the New York and Cleveland Gas Coal Company during the existence of this contract.

The pay days shall be on the 10th and 25th of each month. On the 10th the miners shall be paid the wages earned during the last fifteen days of the preceding month, and on the 25th the wages earned during the first fifteen days of the current month, provided, however, that nothing in this contract shall be construed to prevent operators who now pay every two weeks from continuing to do so.

The machine-mining contract is as follows:

Harrison, Ingersoll, or pick machine cutting to be one-fifth the price of pick mining, and loading to be one-half; Jeffrey chain and cutter bar machine cutting to be one-eighth of the price for pick mining, and loading one-half. That we recommend the price for driving entry or narrow work with machines to be for the Jeffrey chain bar machine 3 cents per ton over and above the regular price; for loading, 13 cents per ton, and for the Harrison or pick machine to be 5 cents per ton; where it is preferred to pay no yardage the price on the Harrison machine for cutting and loading is to be 30 per cent less than the regularly established district price for yardage of pick mining, and for the Jeffrey chain or bar to be 37 per cent less, to be divided between the cutter and the loader in the same relative proportion that he is paid for room work; where the entries are not of sufficient width to enable the machine miner to turn in his room, in this the operator shall pay pick prices for any entry work. The price to be paid for room turning, with all machines, to be $2, based on a 64-cent rate of pick mining, of which the cutter is to receive one-third and the loader two-thirds. That the relative price of differential between the thick and vein shall be the same relative differential as in 1892, which would make a difference of 14 cents per ton in the Youghiogheny Valley and 13 cents per ton in the Monongahela Valley when mining in the thin veins is 64 cents per ton, and to advance and decline with this percentage of difference. The standing committee is given power to decide any question that may arise as to the geographic line of thick or thin vein mines.

This agreement was contingent upon the condition that operators representing 95 per cent of the output of the district should sign. Articles of agreement were drawn up for signature. This agreement contained some amendments to the foregoing report, provided penalties for nonobservance, and at considerable length covered all points thought desirable. It provided for a "Uniformity commission" to be composed of nine members selected by the subscribers, with authority and power to enforce awards, judgments, etc., to investigate conditions prevailing at the mines of the subscribers so far as they affected the earnings of miners, inspect scales, screens, pay rolls, etc., and to act upon any complaints made by any of the subscribers. It was generally hoped and believed that the establishment of a uniform rate of wages would compel the maintenance of selling prices and forbid disastrous competition.

Up to the end of March the efforts to bring the agreement to a successful issue were made, and until the very last day of that month the parties at interest expected the agreement to be signed by the necessary 95 per cent, but at the last moment the whole matter fell through for lack of one or two signatures, and at the time of writing this report (June, 1896) there is little hope for its resuscitation.

A comprehensive understanding of the coal trade throughout the United States may be obtained from the following pages, which contain contributions from and reports of secretaries of boards of trade and other recognized authorities. They show the movements of coal from the mines to the trade centers, the tendency of prices, and other information of interest to the trade.

NEW YORK, N. Y.

Mr. F. E. Saward's annual report, The Coal Trade, contains the following review of the coal trade of that city:

The Empire City is the point where more coal is dealt in in the course of the year than anywhere else except the city of London, England. In its vicinity are the shipping ports of millions of tons of every grade and quality of anthracite and bituminous coals, so that 15,000,000 tons is an underestimate of the sales actually consummated at this point. The several shipping points on the New Jersey shore of the Hudson, the Kill von Kull, and Raritan Bay, known as South Amboy, Perth Amboy, Port Reading, Elizabethport, Port Johnston, Port Liberty, Jersey City, Hoboken, and Weehawken, are feeders to the trade of the metropolis for local use and for shipment to Eastern ports. The docks of the Pennsylvania Coal Company, at Newburg, N. Y., the Delaware and Hudson Canal, at Rondout, N. Y., the Erie, at Piermont, N. Y., and the Ontario and Western, at Cornwall, N. Y., also furnish tribute to the trade of the firms doing business here.

The quantity used locally is set down at 6,000,000 tons, to which may be added 2,750,000 tons for Jersey City and Brooklyn, really but part of the metropolis.

Bituminous coal comes in schooners and steam colliers from Norfolk, Newport News, and Baltimore, and in barges from South Amboy, Port Reading, and Port Liberty, N. J., and is used locally for all the purposes to which it is adapted. An approximate statement of the bituminous coal loaded into ocean steamers at this port shows that there are over 1,500,000 gross tons so taken; of this perhaps 150,000 tons is "Pocahontas" coal and the remainder is "Clearfield."

Prices ranged very low during the year, for the reason, perhaps only too well known, that the "tonnage" was more of an object in the view of some of the producers than the price. There was no attempt made to adhere to the agreements made from time to time in regard to what would constitute a sufficient amount to meet the requirements of the month next ensuing after the agreement was entered into. As a consequence the market value of anthracite dropped to figures below what it has sold for in several years.

List prices of anthracite at tide-water ports near New York have been nominally as follows within the past year:

List prices of anthracite in New York, 1895.

Date.	Broken.	Egg.	Stove.	Chestnut.
January 1	$3.10	$3.20	$3.35	$3.25
April 1	3.35	3.35	3.50	3.35
September 27..................	3.10	3.40	3.40	3.15
October 10	3.25	3.65	3.65	3.30
October 18	3.35	3.65	3.75	3.40
October 24	3.75	3.90	4.15	3.90

None of these list prices were realized at the dates named. Nominally the free-on-board prices at New York ports in July were $2.75 for grate, egg, or chestnut, with $2.85 for stove. At the same time it is well known that coal was delivered in company boats and barges that did not realize any such figure; in fact, it is stated that about $2.30 for broken, $2.40 for egg, $2.50 for stove, and $2.35 for chestnut was a rate realized for some coal sold during that month. In the latter part of August it seemed as if there was a change for the better; the demand was large for coal at so low a price, and there was a stiffening of asking prices to, say, $3 per ton free on board for stove, which was a reaction from the very low prices. Then the Delaware, Lackawanna and Western Railroad came out boldly with a quotation of $3.25, and the others followed. This served as a spur to the market, and the several advances were as per the schedule. During the rush for coal that usually takes place in September and October the market was cleverly worked, and some coal no doubt sold at $4 per ton free on board. By the middle of November the "boom" was largely off and prices receded, and broken closed at $3, egg $3.15, stove $3.50, with chestnut $3.35.

Following is said to be the average price obtained for anthracite stove coal free on board at the New York loading ports by one concern:

Monthly prices for anthracite coal at New York for four years.

Month.	1895.	1894.	1893.	1892.
January......................	$3.30	$4.15	$4.50	$3.75
February	3.25	3.95	4.55	3.65
March.......................	3.20	3.85	4.25	3.70
April........................	3.05	3.60	4.00	3.75
May..........................	3.00	3.55	4.00	3.90
June.........................	3.00	3.55	4.00	4.00
July	2.80	3.55	4.00	4.20
August.......................	2.75	3.55	4.10	4.20
September	2.80	3.40	4.20	4.35
October	3.15	3.40	4.20	4.45
November	3.50	3.40	4.30	4.60
December	3.45	3.30	4.25	4.55
Average................	3.10	3.60	4.19	4.09

This yearly average is merely that of the mean of the twelve monthly prices. If quantity at each price were the same it would still stand, but not otherwise. At any rate it is indicative of the great loss in the past two years.

The nominal opening prices were as below, free on board at the loading ports, in the beginning of the years named:

Opening prices for free-burning anthracite coal at New York for six years.

Year.	Broken.	Egg.	Stove.	Chestnut.
1890...............................	$3.40	$3.50	$3.50	$3.25
1891...............................	3.50	4.60	3.75	3.50
1892...............................	3.65	3.75	3.90	3.65
1893...............................	3.90	3.90	4.15	4.15
1894...............................	3.50	3.50	3.75	3.75
1895...............................	3.35	3.35	3.50	3.35

In the race for tonnage all the companies suffered financially, so that their earnings were smaller in the aggregate, with some of them showing an actual loss of 10 or 15 cents per ton.

In the spring of the year the soft coal producers sending to the seaboard put their prices at $2 free on board vessels at all loading points, with, say, $3 at New York alongside; while for tonnage shipped at the loading ports near New York a less rate was made, according to quality. It was a very disastrous year for this trade, and there was coal sold that did not net anything like the prices agreed upon; in fact, this whole scheme of prices was more honored in the breach than the observance. Sometimes one might get cargoes of coal at New York and the east at the rates agreed upon for the free-on-board and the New York prices, respectively. All the districts shipping here made large increases in their production. At the close prices were as follows: Norfolk and Newport News, $1.90 to $2.15; Baltimore, $2 to $2.20; Philadelphia, $1.75 to $2.20; New York Harbor shipping ports, $2.20 to $2.65; alongside New York Harbor, $2.40 to $2.75, according to quality.

A fair exhibit of the course of prices of the best Georges Creek coal is shown below:

Prices for Georges Creek (Cumberland) coal at New York.

Year.	Per ton.	Year.	Per ton.
1889.......................	$3.50	1893.......................	$3.25
1890.......................	3.50	1894.......................	3.00
1891.......................	3.50	1895.......................	2.75
1892.......................	3.40	.	

The soft coal for "bunker" use that is put into the "ocean greyhounds" and other vessels plying to all parts of the world from this port is a feature that is looked after by the producers of coal in Pennsylvania, Maryland, and the Virginias most earnestly. Competition for this trade brings the prices down to a figure that is much less than it should be to pay a fair recompense to the miner, the carrier, and the producer. The principal lines and their yearly tonnage are given below:

Annual tonnage of coal used by steamship companies out of New York.

Company.	Tons.	Company.	Tons.
Anchor Line	50,000	C. H. Mallory & Co	80,000
Atlas Line	30,000	North German Lloyd Co..	120,000
Cromwell Line	20,000	Phelps Bros. & Co	30,000
Clyde Steamship Co	30,000	Red Star Line	40,000
Cunard Steamship Co	100,000	National Line	25,000
French Line	70,000	Morgan Line	60,000
Funch, Eyde & Co	40,000	White Star Line	75,000
Hamburg Line	100,000	Spanish Line	20,000
American Line	75,000	Standard Oil Co	30,000
Guion Line	25,000	United States and Brazil	
New York and Cuba Mail		Mail Line	20,000
Steamship Co	40,000	Tramp steamers	200,000
Pacific Mail Steamship		Lines taking 20,000 tons.	170,000
Co	20,000		

Retail prices followed the downward course of the wholesale market, and there was a great deal of coal sold at $4 per ton at certain times, while in Brooklyn, where the competition seemed to be very keen between the representatives of two of the large producing and carrying companies, the price went to a lower figure; at a time in the summer stove coal was offered at $3 per ton in the yard by one concern. Evidently the consumer very largely benefited by the reduction in the wholesale and retail prices. The annual election of the Retail Coal Exchange of New York resulted in James Morrison being chosen as president; G. D. Curtis, first vice-president; C. T. Leonard, second vice-president; J. Rodenburg, jr., treasurer; and George Stewart, secretary. The meetings have been well attended and much good results therefrom, though no action on the all-important question of price can be taken in view of the anticombine laws of the State of New York.

BOSTON, MASS.

Mr. Elwyn G. Preston, secretary of the Boston Chamber of Commerce, presents the following review of the coal trade of that city:

The receipts of coal at Boston for the past thirteen years have been as follows:

Receipts of coal at Boston for thirteen years.

Year.	Domestic.			Foreign.	Total.
	By water.		All rail (largely bituminous).		
	Anthracite.	Bituminous.			
	Long tons.	*Long tons.*	*Long tons.*	*Long tons.*	*Long tons.*
1883					2,273,068
1884					2,225,740
1885					2,221,220
1886				44,464	2,500,000
1887				13,966	2,400,000
1888	2,057,279	1,004,195		10,081	3,071,555
1889	1,647,348	914,966		5,538	2,567,852
1890	1,740,564	964,857		14,072	2,719,493
1891	2,039,443	1,070,088		5,842	3,115,373
1892	2,163,984	919,815		1,416	3,085,215
1893	2,227,086	1,100,384	50,000	17,097	3,394,567
1894	2,237,599	958,701	71,303	41,779	3,309,382
1895	2,518,441	977,762	90,999	21,009	3,608,211

From the above table it will be observed that the receipts of coal at the port of Boston for 1895 were larger than during any previous year. As an evidence of the improvement in general business conditions and renewed activity on the railroads these figures are instructive. Of the total amount of coal received, 1,029,513 tons, or 28 per cent, were forwarded to interior New England points, making the consumption of the city of Boston 2,578,698 tons, as compared with 2,316,743 tons during 1894. The demand for coal has been fairly steady throughout the year, but prices have at times been badly demoralized.

An attempt made early in April to bring all retail dealers in Boston and suburbs into a combination to maintain prices was defeated owing to lack of cooperation on the part of several large dealers, and a rate war ensued that brought retail prices for a time down to cost figures. The effect of the cut in prices was to stimulate trade for a short time and crowd into a few weeks business that would ordinarily have been distributed over a large part of the year. This resulted in an unusually quiet period during the late spring and early summer.

The receipts of foreign coal, namely, coal from the provinces, were not as large as last year, notwithstanding the efforts that have been made to create a market here for provincial coal.

Carriers' rates have not covered so wide a range as during 1894, and on the whole a higher average has obtained. The range of published rates has been as follows:

Coal freights to Boston, Mass.

From—	Per ton.
Philadelphia	$0.60 to $1.00
Baltimore	.60 1.10
Norfolk and Newport News	.60 1.00
New York	.45 .75

The lowest rates were quoted in September and October, the highest being reached several times during the year.

The year opened with stove coal quoted at $5.25 per ton at retail. April witnessed a sharp decline in price to $4.20, with occasional sales at $4, or even lower. Prices rallied in May to $5, where they remained during the summer months, advancing to $5.50 in October and $5.75 in November, closing the year at the latter figure.

Georges Creek Cumberland coal was quoted at $3.50 to $3.55 in January, with prices becoming easier as the season progressed. A temporary advance was made in April to $3.65, but prices soon fell off to $3.35 to $3.40, with further reductions during the summer to $3.05 to $3.10. In November prices advanced to $3.25, with a further advance to $3.45 in December, at which latter figure the year closed.

The following table shows the receipts of coal by months during the year 1895:

Monthly receipts of coal at Boston during 1895.

Month.	Domestic.		All rail (anthracite and bituminous.)	Foreign.	Total.
	By water.				
	Anthracite.	Bituminous.			
January	121,520	60,873	8,755	1,292	192,440
February	80,381	47,933	9,745	999	139,058
March	188,351	88,896	10,601	131	287,979
April	244,614	80,663	5,380	526	331,183
May	313,242	100,023	6,165	531	419,961
June	193,819	77,031	6,815	....	277,665
July	266,113	116,947	7,973	534	391,567
August	217,656	93,351	7,430	3,727	322,164
September	193,802	82,392	5,056	....	281,250
October	260,017	78,141	4,824	5,762	348,744
November	225,913	70,275	7,819	2,975	306,982
December	213,013	81,237	10,436	4,532	309,218
Total	2,518,441	977,762	90,999	21,009	3,608,211

PHILADELPHIA, PA.

The following interesting contribution in regard to the coal trade of Philadelphia has been prepared by Mr. John S. Arndt, financial editor of the Inquirer:

The natural advantages of Philadelphia as a coal-shipping port have commanded recognition from the very inception of railroads in the State of Pennsylvania. It was this idea, indeed, that was largely instrumental in inducing the enlistment of capital in constructing the two great railroad systems in the eastern portion of the State, the Philadelphia and Reading and the Pennsylvania. It was clearly perceived that for certain competitive markets that transportation route was the best which united a short land carriage with a not too long water carriage, inasmuch as transportation on land must always be more costly than transportation on water. With eastern New England as the objective point this condition applied exactly in favor of Philadelphia as a shipping port. And this expectation has been amply justified by the result. From the beginning the anthracite trade of New England east of Cape Cod has been largely secured to Philadelphia through the Reading Railroad, and when soft coal came into general use as a steam fuel the bituminous trade of that section was secured through the Pennsylvania Railroad. The same advantage has enabled Philadelphia to enter into competition with Baltimore for the anthracite trade of the southern seaboard. In these markets the railroads centering in Philadelphia must always be prominent, whatever be their position in the trade of New York City and State. The favorable location of Philadelphia as regards the markets referred to may be seen by a glance at the following tables, showing the distance from the coal regions to all tide-water shipping ports and the distance from those ports by the most direct sea route to Boston:

Distance in miles from anthracite regions to shipping ports.

From—	To—			
	Philadelphia.	Port Liberty.	Amboy.	Hoboken.
Schuylkill	93	173		
Lehigh	114	147	146	
Wyoming	154	179	186	144

Distance in miles from bituminous regions to shipping ports.

From—	To—					
	Philadelphia.	Baltimore.	Amboy.	Port Liberty.	Lamberts Point.	Newport News.
Cumberland	308	200	368			
Clearfield	270		330			
Beech Creek	291			311		
West Virginia Central	345	238	405			
Pocahontas					390	
Chesapeake and Ohio						410

Distance from shipping ports to Boston.

From—	Knots.	From—	Knots.
Philadelphia	456	Hoboken	278
Baltimore	649	Lamberts Point	516
Amboy	270	Newport News	524
Port Liberty	276		

It thus appears that Philadelphia is 50 miles nearer the anthracite coal fields than any other shipping port. And this advantage is strengthened by the favorable gradients of the Reading Railroad, which is the short line to the anthracite regions. The railroad follows the course of the Schuylkill River for the entire distance, thus having a steady and easy descent with absolutely no adverse grades. Other ports, and indeed Philadelphia itself from every region but the Schuylkill, must be reached over a diversified country in which unfavorable grades are more or less numerous. Thus favored by nature, the traffic situation of the Reading Railroad is an ideal one. The freight is secured in train loads, the grade is with the traffic, and the haul is short. It is not only a theory but an established practice that the Reading locomotives haul as many loaded cars to tide water as they can haul back empty. The cars can make two round trips a week. Quick dispatch and economy of operation have therefore always marked the management of the property. It is true there is a disadvantage in the water carriage. Philadelphia is 175 miles farther away from Boston by water than New York City is, and vessel owners demand from 5 to 20 cents a ton more freight than they do from New York. But even with this higher cost the superior advantage of the short land haul has always enabled Philadelphia to maintain its hold on the New England market.

In regard to the bituminous trade the position of Philadelphia is hardly as good as that of Baltimore, which is 70 miles nearer the mines. But some compensation is secured in the fact that the water carriage is decidedly in favor of this city and especially from the fact that there is always an adequate supply of vessels here. Philadelphia secures its supply of ice from the rivers of Maine, and having a large population this business attracts a considerable number of vessels. They are all loaded with coal for the return voyage. Baltimore also secures part of its ice from Maine, but not requiring so large a quantity of the Maine ice does not receive the service of as many vessels. Water freights from this port are always lower than from Baltimore, and this in part, if not fully, makes up for the longer rail haul. This port has always been able to maintain its position in the Eastern bituminous trade against Baltimore, and therefore against all other shipping ports.

SHIPPING TERMINALS OF THE READING RAILROAD.

With a full appreciation of the strong geographical position of the city and with a prophetic insight into the future, the first managers of the Philadelphia and Reading Railroad made ample provision for the

growth of the anthracite coal trade. To the sagacity and persistence
of Mr. Moncure Robinson, the chief engineer of construction, is due
the conception of securing the extensive terminals at Port Richmond.
After fifty-five years of growth the property originally acquired is still
more than ample for the business of the road. The Port Richmond
yard begins about 3 miles north of the business center of the city and
extends north along the Delaware water front for a distance of 5,400
feet, or rather more than a mile. It has an average depth of 1,600 feet.
It includes, therefore, about 200 acres. A short distance outside the
limits of the property is an extensive shifting yard, where the loaded
cars are separated into drafts to be run out upon the piers, and where
the empty cars are made up into trains again to be returned to the
mines. Twelve tracks lead into the Port Richmond yard, in which are
58 miles of track, affording ample room for the movement of traffic.

Port Richmond is now in a transition state. Several years ago, when
there were many individual shippers over the road and when the business
was conducted in vessels of from 300 to 500 tons capacity, there were
twenty-three piers on the property, all in constant use. But now that
the Philadelphia and Reading Coal and Iron Company is the only shipper
a great number of piers is not required, and since the vessels employed
have a capacity of from 1,000 to 2,500 tons, larger piers are necessary.
Nearly all the old small piers have been torn down or are in process of
demolition, and there are now but thirteen piers. Of these, three are
used for merchandise, two for iron ore, and eight for coal. Three of
these eight coal piers are of the most modern construction and are
equal to any on the coast. They are capable of accommodating with
ease any vessel that has yet entered the capes of the Delaware. They
are about 550 feet long and are double piers, that is, vessels can lie on
each side. There are berths for two vessels on each side, so that each
pier can serve four vessels at once. Should occasion require, the piers
can be extended 200 feet, as the harbor improvements now being made
have enabled the port wardens to extend their pier line. On each pier
are four tracks. The two outside tracks are devoted to loaded cars,
which after being unloaded roll on by gravity to the extreme end of
the pier. Then they pass over self-operating switches and are shunted
back on the two inside tracks, over which they pass by the force of
gravity to the yard. The loaded car is weighed upon arriving at the
pier. The contents are unloaded by dropping the bottom of the hop-
per; the coal passes over a screen into chutes and is discharged directly
into vessels. These chutes are arranged at convenient intervals along
the pier so that the two, three, or four hatches of a vessel can be loaded
at once. In addition to these three large piers are five smaller ones
adopted for vessels of moderate capacity. They are also double piers,
but have only three tracks upon them, one track being sufficient for all
the unloaded cars, and they can accommodate but one vessel on each side
at a time. Four of the five small piers are used for anthracite shipments, the other being given up to the bituminous trade. The depth

of water all along the pier line is 26 feet, although occasional dredging has to be done to maintain this depth.

There are abundant and excellent facilities for the economical storage of coal. Near the bulkhead line is sufficient space for the storage of about 150,000 tons, which is deposited by dumping from the cars. Four traveling conveyors, operating on the principle of the crane, are used to pick up the coal and replace it in cars when it is desired to transfer it into vessels. These conveyors have a capacity of 1,000 tons per day each, and being mounted upon railroad trucks move readily with their own steam to any part of the yard. There is besides a stationary double-conveyor plant, which is capable of picking up and moving into pockets 2,000 tons a day, and from these pockets the coal passes into cars. Finally, should occasion require, the coal can be removed by wheelbarrows directly into vessels. All these appliances are for handling the coal dumped near the water's edge. There is in addition, in a remote part of the yard, a considerable space given over to the storage of coal in immense heaps, some of them containing as much as 40,000 tons. Six stationary conveyors of the most approved type are operated here, having an aggregate capacity of 180,000 tons. It is asserted that coal can be piled by means of these conveyors at an expense of not over 2 cents per ton, while the cost of picking up and replacing in cars is not more than 1 cent additional. These facilities, however, are not used to their fullest extent, as the company has two storage yards in the mining region with a combined capacity of over 1,000,000 tons, and only a moderate working stock is kept at Port Richmond.

Nearly all of the coal shipped from this yard is transported in the company's own fleet. At the present time this fleet consists of 3 ocean-going tugs, 7 steamers, one of 600 tons burden and the others of from 1,400 to 1,650 tons burden, and 31 barges of a capacity of from 1,000 to 1,450 tons each. Each steamer is expected to tow one loaded barge and each tugboat tows three barges. The company occasionally charters sailing vessels to accommodate customers in Southern ports and those in New England towns, who are better served in this way. The effort is made to concentrate all the coastwise business at Port Richmond, but some has to be done from New York Harbor. Light-draft vessels of small capacity are not always plentiful here, while they are generally in good supply at New York. At Port Reading, a few miles north of Amboy, on Staten Island Sound, the company has established another shipping depot, and here small vessels are loaded. It is also a convenient distributing point for the New York City and Long Island Sound trade; but it is distinctly a port of secondary importance, just as Amboy is in the bituminous trade of the Pennsylvania Railroad.

SHIPPING TERMINALS OF THE PENNSYLVANIA RAILROAD.

The Greenwich coal piers of the Pennsylvania Railroad are located on the Delaware River about 3 miles south of the business center of the city. The property has a water front of about three-quarters of a mile and has a depth from the water line of about 1,500 feet. Beyond the bulkhead line project five piers to a distance of from 500 to 650 feet. Four are double piers, and on each side there are berths for two vessels. Only one side of the fifth pier is available, the other side being shut off by a freight slip. The piers, therefore, have room to load eighteen vessels at once. The four double piers are used exclusively for the shipments of bituminous coal, while all the anthracite coal is shipped over the single pier, although bituminous coal is also shipped over it. The piers are of the latest design and are kept in the highest state of efficiency. They are built upon an easy gradient, the highest point being at the extreme end. Upon each pier are four tracks. The requirements of the company's business necessitate a different arrangement of tracks from that followed at Port Richmond. All of the coal shipped over the Port Richmond wharves is mined by the Philadelphia and Reading Coal and Iron Company, while fifty or sixty different shippers use the facilities at Greenwich. At the latter place, therefore, a good deal of shifting is necessary not only in the yard, but on the piers themselves. Therefore, instead of having one or two depressed tracks in the center of the pier, the tracks on the Greenwich piers are all on the same level. The inside tracks are used as sidings, upon which loaded cars are pushed upon the piers and from which they are switched as the coal is required for shipment upon the outside tracks.

Upon each side of each pier are seven chutes, over which the coal is run from the cars directly into the vessels below. Any vessel, no matter what the position of its hatches, can easily find a position where all can be loaded at once. The depth of water is 24 feet, but the bottom is soft, so that almost any vessel that floats can obtain a cargo. Most of the business is done in sailing vessels and barges. As the business is divided up among so many shippers, no one of them has found it desirable to establish a line of barges, and all the carrying business as yet is done by outside vessel owners. Some of the craft are very large. One or two barges carrying 4,500 tons find regular employment, and quite a number have a capacity of between 2,500 and 3,000 tons. The business at Greenwich is steadily growing. It has quadrupled in fifteen years, and now 3,000,000 tons of coal are annually shipped there, giving employment to 500 men besides the train crews and yardmen. There is, of course, no storage room, soft coal being so cheap as not to permit of more than one handling, and it therefore remains in the cars until ready for shipment.

SHIPPING TERMINALS OF THE BALTIMORE AND OHIO RAILROAD.

It is only a few years since the Baltimore and Ohio Railroad secured an entrance into Philadelphia, and its coal terminals as yet are not large. About a mile north of Greenwich the company has established its coal shipping depot. It owns a tract of land having a frontage of about 300 feet on the Delaware River, and of about the same depth, and upon this property it has constructed one pier. It is about 600 feet long, and along 500 feet the depth of water is sufficient for shipping purposes. The pier has just been completed and is well planned and constructed. It is a double pier and will accommodate one vessel and one barge on each side. It has three tracks. The loaded cars are pushed out upon the outside tracks, the contents dumped and loaded into vessels by means of chutes, and the cars are passed along to the end of the pier, returning thence to the yard on the one inside track. Although the rail haul from the Cumberland regions to Philadelphia is much farther than to Baltimore, yet for certain reasons it is sometimes desirable to send coal here for shipment. The business is steadily growing and the pier is in constant use. It is capable of shipping 500,000 tons a year without difficulty, but it has not been called upon for this amount of service yet.

THE COAL TRADE, 1895.

The distribution of coal in and through Philadelphia was much greater in the calendar year 1895 than in the calendar year 1894. This increase, which exceeded 15 per cent, was due to three general causes:

First. The winter of 1894-95 was more severe than usual, the spring was cold and late, and there was a greater consumption of coal in dwellings.

Second. The extremely low price of anthracite coal during the summer months prompted consumers to lay in larger stocks than usual.

Third. The revival in manufacturing caused an increased demand for fuel for steam-raising purposes. Yet in spite of this enlarged demand for coal all through the Eastern States prices were lower than for many years. It is credibly reported that anthracite stove coal sold here free on board vessels for shipment beyond the capes of the Delaware as low as $2.65 per ton, and it is admitted that bituminous coal sold free on board at $1.65. The open war in the anthracite trade and the complete demoralization that prevailed in the bituminous trade are the causes of these extraordinarily low prices, which really represented losses to the miner and the carrying company. The shipments from this port to New England, however, were larger in 1895 than in any recent year, if not in any year on record. In the anthracite trade the Philadelphia and Reading Company pushed the fight in the New England States and shipped coal in unusual quantities, while in the bituminous trade the Pennsylvania and Beech Creek roads were favored by the strike in the Norfolk and Western region. In 1894 the miners in the Clearfield region went out on a strike, and the bituminous shipments from this port were curtailed and did not exceed those in 1893. But in 1895 the roads serving the Clearfield district had a decided advantage, and not only recovered all their old trade but secured some that had been supplied by their Southern competitor. Despite this increased pressure upon the vessel tonnage, the supply of vessels was adequate to all demands. The water freight rates to Boston were quite as low as in 1894, many charters being made as low as 50 cents per ton, although 55 and 60 cents were more common quotations, and at times 75 cents was willingly paid.

The local consumption of anthracite coal in the year 1895 was 3,960,000 long tons as against 3,540,000 tons in 1894, an increase of 420,000 tons. A small amount of this increase was in the domestic sizes, but the growing demand for anthracite as a steam fuel accounted for most of the gain. It was the most unsatisfactory year for the producing interests since 1879. Prices sunk to a level that has rarely been reached before. The price circulars do not tell the story of the extreme demoralization that existed. Only three circulars were issued during the year, on January 1, October 1, and November 1, and they show little change from each other or from the preceding year. The circulars issued by the Philadelphia and Reading Coal and Iron Company in 1895 and in 1894 are as follows:

Local prices of anthracite coal for Philadelphia in 1894 and 1895.

Kind of coal.	1894.			1895.		
	Jan.	Apr.	June.	Jan.	Oct.	Nov.
Lump and steamboat	$2.50	$2.50	$2.50	$2.50	$2.50	$2.50
Broken	2.25	2.15	2.20	2.20	2.00	2.25
Egg	2.50	2.25	2.30	2.30	2.40	2.65
Stove..................	2.80	2.50	2.55	2.55	2.50	2.75
Chestnut	2.70	2.40	2.40	2.40	2.15	2.50
Pea	1.35	1.40	1.40	1.40	1.30	1.30
Buckwheat	.75	.85	.85	.85	.85	.85

These prices are subject to the usual agents' commission of 10 cents per ton.

The market was weak from January until September. With almost every month the concessions from the price circular grew larger. The producing companies made several attempts to hold prices up, but with every fresh dip in the tide-water market the attempt had to be abandoned. High prices would simply invite a flood of coal that should naturally go to tide water. In the latter part of August and the first part of September coal was being sold openly by the companies at $1.60 for broken, $1.70 for egg, $1.95 for stove, $1.80 for chestnut, $1.10 for pea, and 65 cents for buckwheat, or, say, 60 cents a ton below the circular. Occasional sales were reported at 10 and 20 cents a ton below these low prices, but they were not general and were usually attended by exceptional circumstances. In the latter part of September the market turned sharply; in October it became firm, and the price circular issued November 1, which has been lived up to ever since, marked the return of the trade to normal conditions. There was no change in anthracite freight rates during the year. The prices quoted above are for coal at the mines, the purchaser being required to pay the freight rate in addition. All shippers selling in the Philadelphia market adopt this rule except the coal companies controlled by the Pennsylvania Railroad, which sell at a delivered price. The freight rates were:

Freight rates from anthracite regions to Philadelphia.

Region.	Prepared sizes.	Pea.	Buck-wheat.
Schuylkill	$1.70	$1.40	$1.25
Lehigh	1.75	1.45	1.30
Wyoming	1.80	1.50	1.35

The important economic development of the year was the further demonstration of the growing value of the small sizes of anthracite. Particular attention has been given of late by the companies selling anthracite in Philadelphia to the preparation of pea and buckwheat coal. The slate and dirt are removed by "jigging" at the breakers and washeries, and these two sizes reach the market in just as good condition as the so-called prepared sizes. A stricter classification has been adopted, and what would have passed for small chestnut a few years ago is now called No. 1 pea. This size is now very largely used by families, and is steadily growing in favor as a domestic fuel. It makes a quick fire, and many housekeepers prefer it to stove or chestnut, when once they have learned to regulate its use. The low price of the coal, $1.50 per ton below stove and chestnut, is another argument in favor of its extended use, and this applies with especial force to this city, where the industrial population is large, and where almost every family lives under its own roof. Among manufacturers anthracite has made still further inroads upon bituminous. Practically every large industrial establishment near the built-up portions of the city now uses anthracite for steam purposes. Pea coal is sold delivered for $2.50 per ton, buckwheat for $2, and rice for $1.60. While possibly not equal to good bituminous coal, pound for pound, for steam raising, yet buckwheat and rice are cheaper, and the argument of cleanliness has carried the day in favor of these sizes. The sugar refineries, oil refineries, and other large establishments where much coal is consumed are all equipped with automatic stokers, by means of which the small sizes can be fed to furnaces with perhaps better advantage than the lumpy bituminous. The power houses of the street trolley railways all use pea or buckwheat, and the use of bituminous has been relegated largely to those establishments where either soft coal is necessary or where soot does not occasion complaint. Yet it is interesting to note that one woolen goods manufacturer, whose factory is in the suburbs, has changed his grate bars in the past year and abandoned anthracite for bituminous.

The local bituminous coal trade also showed a gain for the year. The consumption in Philadelphia in 1895 was about 1,060,000 tons, as against 845,000 tons in 1894, an increase of about 215,000 tons. There was no important extension of its use, however, except the case of the woolen manufacturer above referred to be considered important, and the increased demand came almost entirely from the larger requirements of old consumers. Of the quantity sold, 286,000 tons were taken by the city gas works, a considerable quantity was used for blacksmithing purposes, another considerable amount was used for heating in iron-working establishments, and the quantity left for steam-raising purposes is therefore comparatively small. It was used in many instances mixed in with anthracite. The price of bituminous coal ruled low throughout the year. It sold delivered on tracks at from $2.35 to $2.50 per ton, or from 15 to 20 cents below the prices of 1894, and from 25 to 35 cents below the prices of 1893. The year opened with the market weak, and it did not recover as the year advanced. Since the close of the year, however, prices have risen.

The export business showed a slight improvement. Nearly all the coal exported through Philadelphia goes to the West Indies. Steamers bringing iron ore to this port from Santiago de Cuba for the use of the Bethlehem Iron Company frequently take return cargoes of coal, and the same is true of the vessels bringing in raw sugar for the sugar houses here. But this trade has never been pushed, and it seems dependent upon the progress of our general trade relations with the West Indies and the Republics of South America. British coal seems to hold the markets of the Caribbean Sea, and until the United States secures a stronger commercial foothold there and the supply of vessels is larger the export business can hardly expand much.

Through the courtesy of the officers of the Philadelphia and Reading, Pennsylvania, and Baltimore and Ohio railroads, the data has been furnished from which the following statement has been compiled, showing with approximate correctness the distribution of the coal brought to Philadelphia in the years 1894 and 1895:

Distribution of coal at Philadelphia in 1894 and 1895.

	1894.		1895.	
	Anthracite.	Bituminous.	Anthracite.	Bituminous.
	Long tons.	*Long tons.*	*Long tons.*	*Long tons.*
Export.....................	20,635	362,468	23,068	411,009
Coastwise and harbor	1,420,000	2,400,000	1,750,000	2,710,000
Local	3,540,000	815,000	3,960,000	1,060,000
Total	4,980,635	3,607,468	5,733,068	4,181,009

BUFFALO, N. Y.

The following review of the coal trade of Buffalo is obtained from the annual report of Mr. William Thurstone, secretary of the Buffalo Merchants' Exchange:

The season at Buffalo in anthracite circles has been a remarkable one in many ways. The shipments of anthracite to the West were marked in the early part of the season by a slowness that made it appear that the docks in the West would be left with but little stock at the end of the season. The amount of coal in sight at the western ports during the spring made it appear to everybody that there would be little or no difficulty in placing all of the coal that could be sent forward. There was a spurt at the opening, but this was only temporary, and then the trade settled down to a dullness that was exceedingly unfavorable to the shippers. A large amount of coal was sent by rail to points that had before been handled from some of the Western ports. In the small places in Michigan and in the Western peninsula of Canada the dealers were getting coal by rail direct from Buffalo. The summer was well advanced before the Western men began to realize that there was likely to be a scarcity of coal during the winter, and then hurried visits were made here for the purpose of contracting for coal. However, the season closed with totals ahead of 1894.

The bituminous coal market passed through a season of tribulation. The labor troubles in the early part of the year caused the market to become unsettled, and although many of the consumers filled their storage room they found that the stock was not needed, and the extra production was almost a drug on the market. Other districts cared for the customers of the Pittsburg district while the men were on strike, and when the trade settled down to a normal condition it was found that the production was heavier than the demands of trade would warrant. Some of the mines closed down and others were run on short time, until in the Reynoldsville district the miners were almost at the point of starvation.

The following tables exhibit the receipts and shipments of anthracite, bituminous, and Blossburg (smithing) coal at Buffalo for a series of years:

Coal receipts at Buffalo for several years.

Year.	Anthracite.	Bituminous.	Blossburg.	Total.
	Tons.	Tons.	Tons.	Tons.
1842				1,800
1852				57,560
1862				239,873
1872				790,876
1882				3,021,791
1886	2,673,778	1,420,956	30,000	4,124,734
1887	3,497,203	1,776,217	25,000	5,298,420
1888	4,549,015	1,892,823	22,500	6,464,338
1889	4,338,570	2,198,327	22,500	6,559,397
1890	4,500,000	2,200,000	25,500	6,725,500
1891	4,800,000	2,450,000	25,500	7,275,000
1892	4,804,760	2,627,441	25,000	7,457,201
1893	4,770,546	2,896,614	25,000	7,692,160
1894	4,272,130	2,280,470	25,000	6,577,600
1895	4,764,038	2,727,308	25,000	7,516,346

Lake shipments of anthracite coal from Buffalo.

Year.	Tons.	Year.	Tons.
1883	1,467,778	1890	2,157,810
1884	1,431,081	1891	2,365,895
1885	1,428,086	1892	2,822,230
1886	1,531,210	1893	2,681,173
1887	1,894,060	1894	2,475,255
1888	2,514,906	1895	2,612,768
1889	2,151,670		

Lake shipments of bituminous and Blossburg coal from Buffalo.

Year.	Bituminous.	Blossburg.
	Tons.	Tons.
1887	8,706	10,000
1888	7,452	5,000
1889	11,673	5,000
1890	25,872	5,000
1891	34,066	5,000
1892	54,216	5,000
1893	15,000	7,500
1894	2,500	7,500
1895	2,000	2,500

Shipments of bituminous coal by canal.

Year.	Short tons.	Year.	Short tons.
1890	25,872	1893	19,336
1891	34,060	1894	8,840
1892	29,216	1895	4,259

Anthracite wholesale circular prices at Buffalo in 1895.

Date.	Free on board vessels at Buffalo.				On cars at Buffalo or Suspension Bridge.			
	Grate.	Egg.	Stove.	Chestnut.	Grate.	Egg.	Stove.	Chestnut.
January 1	$4.70	$4.95	$4.95	$4.95	$4.40	$4.65	$4.65	$4.65
May 3	4.05	4.20	4.20	4.20	3.75	3.90	3.90	3.90
September 15 (nom.)	3.85	3.80	3.80	3.80	3.35	3.50	3.50	3.50
October 1	4.30	4.55	4.55	4.55	4.00	4.25	4.25	4.25
October 24 to December 31	4.45	4.70	4.70	4.70	4.15	4.40	4.40	4.40

Anthracite retail prices at Buffalo in 1895.

Date.	Grate.	Egg.	Stove.	Nut.	Pea.	Bloss-burg.
January 1	$5.00	$5.25	$5.25	$5.25	$3.75	$4.00
May 3	4.40	4.50	4.50	4.50	3.75	4.00
August 15 (nom.)	3.75	4.00	4.00	4.00	3.50	4.00
October 1.................	4.50	4.75	4.75	4.75	4.00	4.00
October 24 to December 31	4.75	5.00	5.00	5.00	3.50	4.00

The range of prices during 1895 for bituminous, delivered to manufacturers, gas works, propeller lines, tugs, etc., was from $1.80 to $2.25 for gas, $1.40 to $1.50 for run of mine, $1.50 to $1.60 for lump and nut, and $1.60 to $1.70 for lump, per short ton, in car lots, on track; at retail, for choice for family use, was from $4 to $5.50 per short ton delivered.

The shipping docks and coal pockets at this port are:

Shipping docks and coal pockets at Buffalo.

Name.	Average shipping capacity daily.	Average capacity of pockets.
	Tons.	*Tons.*
Western New York and Pennsylvania R. R..............	2,500	3,000
Delaware and Hudson Canal Co...................	3,500	5,000
Delaware, Lackawanna and Western R. R..............	3,000	4,000
Lehigh docks Nos. 1 and 2....................	6,000	12,000
Erie docks (New York, Lake Erie and Western R. R.)...	2,500	3,000
Pennsylvania Coal Co............................	3,000	3,300
Reading docks............................	7,000	6,500
Total.........................	27,500	36.800

The distribution of exports of coal by lake from this port since 1886, as reported by the custom-house, was as follows:

Clearances of coal at Buffalo since 1886.

Destination.	1886.	1887.	1888.	1889.	1890.
	Tons.	*Tons.*	*Tons.*	*Tons.*	*Tons.*
Chicago	642,135	781,462	1,023,649	988,750	952,280
Milwaukee	376,615	376,876	549,831	497,895	451,550
Duluth	157,420	165,798	282,106	160,430	199,230
Superior.........	65,090	96,746	120,000	112,450	127,300
Toledo	55,290	84,563	83,850	52,725	96,230
Gladstone	....	....	39,575	36,520	30,215
Racine	25,263	16,565	29,695	33,410	29,130
Detroit	31,090	40,203	35,330	31,890	40,065
Green Bay.......	23,870	29,446	26,345	25,050	22,380
Other places.....	156,439	140,020	179,525	142,216	131,390
Total......	1,531,212	1,734,479	2,369,906	2,081,336	2,079,770

Clearances of coal at Buffalo since 1886—Continued.

Destination.	1891.	1892.	1893.	1894.	1895.
	Tons.	Tons.	Tons.	Tons.	Tons.
Chicago	957,805	1,179,635	1,180,245	1,119,187	1,019,461
Milwaukee	508,140	715,975	555,995	551,264	679,115
Duluth	257,625	318,580	278,515	212,664	209,825
Superior	162,075	200,680	197,063	198,284	290,740
Toledo	64,620	102,585	101,970	98,530	96,938
Gladstone	35,170	52,500	55,400	45,900	44,700
Racine	30,510	34,020	41,715	30,775	32,104
Detroit	24,560	22,500	15,075	9,491	6,362
Green Bay	29,015	35,300	57,800	20,335	36,175
Other places	295,375	190,555	239,895	168,825	205,318
Total	2,365,895	2,852,330	2,703,673	2,485,255	2,620,768

CLEVELAND, OHIO.

Mr. F. A. Scott, secretary of the transportation committee of the Cleveland Chamber of Commerce, furnishes the following history of the coal trade of that city:

The coal trade of Cleveland during the year 1895 has felt the effects of the general business depression, as many manufactories have not been running full time and have consequently required but a limited supply of fuel. Prices on bituminous coal have been low and on anthracite very erratic, and therefore the year's business, both to miners and dealers, has been unsatisfactory. Owing to these conditions the miners in the mining district tributary to Cleveland have not averaged more than half time during the year. The extraordinarily long winter season just passed has resulted in the depletion of the coal docks at the upper end of the lakes, and in the spring of 1896 they were almost bare of fuel on this account, and because there is a brighter prospect of heavy manufacturing during 1896 the dealers of this section look forward to an excellent trade during the current year.

Coal and coke receipts and shipments at Cleveland since 1887.

	1887.	1888.	1889.	1890.	1891.
Receipts:	Tons.	Tons.	Tons.	Tons.	Tons.
Bituminous	1,454,744	1,737,781	1,600,000	1,506,208	2,838,586
Anthracite	176,769	181,551	160,000	205,856	201,927
Coke	114,924	124,827	150,000	194,527	189,640
Total	1,746,437	2,044,159	1,910,000	1,960,591	3,230,153
Shipments:					
Anthracite by rail	20,296	29,735	25,000	29,056	34,910
Bituminous by rail	703,506	1,000,000	1,100,000	1,200,000	1,525,000
Bituminous by lake					
Total	723,802	1,029,735	1,125,000	1,229,056	1,559,910

Coal and coke receipts and shipments at Cleveland since 1887—Continued.

	1892.	1893.	1894.	1895.
Receipts:	Tons.	Tons.	Tons.	Tons.
Bituminous	3,651,080	3,603,984	2,715,540	2,842,333
Anthracite	259,150	262,266	207,604	201,022
Coke	351,527	235,248	298,061	432,216
Total	4,261,757	4,101,498	3,221,205	3,475,571
Shipments:				
Anthracite by rail ...	50,742	49,497	44,177	31,894
Bituminous by rail ...	} 1,728,831	24,128	30,000	64,908
Bituminous by lake..		1,257,326	1,106,000	1,125,624
Total	1,779,593	1,330,951	1,180,177	1,222,426

The Cuyahoga customs district includes the ports of Cleveland, Ashtabula, Fairport, and Lorain. The following table shows the clearances from this district for the past nine years:

Clearances of coal from the Cuyahoga (Ohio) district for nine years.

Year.	Tons.	Year.	Tons.
1887..............	1,433,035	1892..............	2,957,988
1888..............	1,855,260	1893..............	3,052,342
1889..............	2,020,996	1894..............	2,239,829
1890..............	2,328,663	1895..............	2,948,324
1891..............	2,635,461		

As previously explained, the figures for 1893, 1894, and 1895 include only the coal actually rehandled.

The following table shows the wholesale prices ruling at Cleveland during 1895:

Wholesale prices of coal at Cleveland, Ohio, in 1895.

Kind.	Average price per ton.	Kind.	Average price per ton.
Bituminous:		Bituminous—Continued.	
Massillon	$1.95	Coshocton............	$1.65
Palmyra	2.15	Hocking	1.65
Pittsburg	1.65	Anthracite:	
Salineville	1.50	Grate	1.10
Kentucky cannel	4.75	Egg.................	4.24
Goshen	1.55	Stove	4.24
Sherodsville..........	1.50	Chestnut............	4.24
Osnaburg	1.55		

TOLEDO, OHIO.[1]

The production and movement of coal in Ohio have not yet attained the activity of 1893. The reasons for a diminished movement in 1894 were found in a deficient recovery by the manufacturing industries of our country from the prostration of business in the previous year, and in the year that is under review extensive and long-continued strikes very seriously restricted the production at the Ohio mines. It was a serious loss to mining and the commerce of the railways engaged in transporting it. During the long and unproductive vacation, other coal mines entered the market, and not only supplied the demand at the time, but made engagements for future delivery, which have curtailed the Ohio movements. Of course all this is temporary, and in the coming year the business will return to its natural channels. The four great railways engaged in this commerce are a guaranty of this result. The harbor and bay channel is being greatly improved in depth, and every facility for inviting this coal traffic here will be used. A renewal of old-time receipts is hoped for in the coming year. The table below, gives a summary of receipts for ten years:

Coal receipts at Toledo since 1886.

	1886.	1887.	1888.	1889.
	Tons.	*Tons.*	*Tons.*	*Tons.*
Wabash R. R	12,598	9,637	10,375	8,586
Lake Shore and Michigan Southern Rwy.....................	165,382	206,099	201,064	35,693
Cincinnati, Hamilton and Dayton R. R.......................	8,198	11,741	37,831	51,746
Pennsylvania Co	201,427	330,020	339,750	234,675
Michigan Central R. R..........	9,594	13,864	16,504	19,935
Columbus, Hocking Valley and Toledo Rwy...................	1,039,200	955,620	1,358,025	923,745
Toledo, Ann Arbor and North Michigan Rwy...............	1,910	552	24,700	96
Toledo, St. Louis and Kansas City R. R......................	3,828	....	1,359	3,287
Toledo and Ohio Central Rwy...	404,684	590,000	637,000	706,950
Lake............................	87,120	117,921	140,963	90,282
Wheeling and Lake Erie Rwy...	391,086	451,813	755,155	763,055
Toledo, Columbus and Cincinnati Rwy.....................	15,832	5,446	2,014	2,210
Cincinnati, Jackson and Mackinaw R. R.....................	....	....	45	54
Total.....................	2,340,859	2,695,810	3,423,780	2,838,314

[1] Extract from the annual report of Mr. Denison B. Smith, secretary Toledo Produce Exchange.

Coal receipts at Toledo since 1886—Continued.

	1890.	1891.	1892.
	Tons.	Tons.	Tons.
Wabash R. R.	3,620	600	500
Lake Shore and Michigan Southern Rwy.	20,592	8,872	43,252
Cincinnati, Hamilton and Dayton R. R.	25,753	35,356	82,053
Pennsylvania Co.	214,765	172,325	92,894
Michigan Central R. R.	3,152	524	420
Columbus, Hocking Valley and Toledo Rwy.	931,716	604,039	394,895
Toledo, St. Louis and Kansas City R. R.	8,420	6,891	5,041
Toledo and Ohio Central Rwy.	820,049	300,429	450,000
Lake	133,813	83,800	112,199
Wheeling and Lake Erie Rwy.	853,940	1,007,042	1,080,000
Toledo, Columbus and Cincinnati Rwy.		35,064	30,000
Cincinnati, Jackson and Mackinaw R. R.	65		101
Total	3,021,886	2,754,943	2,291,355

	1893.	1894.	1895.
	Tons.	Tons.	Tons.
Wabash R. R.			1,000
Lake Shore and Michigan Southern Rwy.	31,110	22,126	38,000
Cincinnati, Hamilton and Dayton R. R.	100,000	72,000	30,000
Pennsylvania Co.	241,395	78,792	
Michigan Central R. R.			
Columbus, Hocking Valley and Toledo Rwy.	854,740	540,000	500,000
Toledo, St. Louis and Kansas City R. R.			
Toledo and Ohio Central Rwy.	984,000	767,670	721,914
Lake	134,750	116,000	124,000
Wheeling and Lake Erie Rwy.	1,100,000	914,220	520,060
Toledo, Columbus and Cincinnati Rwy.			
Cincinnati, Jackson and Mackinaw R. R.			
Total	3,445,995	2,510,808	1,934,914

CHICAGO, ILL.[1]

The following table shows the receipts of coal at and shipments from Chicago during 1894 and 1895, as collected by the Chicago bureau of coal statistics:

Receipts at Chicago.

Month.	Anthracite by lake.		Anthracite by rail.		Total anthracite.		1895.	
	1895.	1894.	1895.	1894.	1895.	1894.	Increase.	Decrease.
	Tons.	Tons.	Tons.	Tons.	Tons.	Tons.	Tons.	Tons.
January ...	....	....	43,624	51,326	43,624	51,326	....	7,702
February ..	....	....	35,083	34,893	35,083	34,893	190	....
March	....	....	36,324	26,998	36,324	26,998	9,326	....
April	16,236	18,449	39,176	15,206	55,412	33,655	21,757	....
May	83,245	117,572	11,340	53,829	94,585	171,401	....	76,816
June	129,400	134,797	15,292	53,512	144,692	188,309	....	43,617
July.......	93,458	180,350	41,810	15,639	135,268	195,989	....	60,721
August	99,335	131,408	56,993	56,152	156,328	187,560	....	31,232
September .	146,607	134,205	49,244	39,204	195,851	173,409	22,442	....
October ...	233,753	182,184	44,676	72,215	278,429	254,399	24,030	....
November .	243,423	224,395	40,821	58,492	284,244	282,887	1,357	....
December..	224,055	153,831	105,302	50,885	329,357	204,716	124,641	....
Total .	1,269,512	1,277,191	519,685	528,351	1,789,197	1,805,542	....	16,345

Month.	Pennsylvania.		1895.		Ohio.		1895.	
	1895.	1894.	Increase.	Decrease.	1895.	1894.	Increase.	Decrease.
	Tons.	Tons.	Tons.	Tons.	Tons.	Tons.	Tons.	Tons.
January ...	15,940	38,491	....	22,551	33,239	67,998	....	34,759
February..	15,212	24,833	....	9,621	24,724	56,476	....	31,752
March	19,843	26,116	....	6,273	29,879	43,448	....	13,569
April	13,177	28,436	....	15,259	21,591	53,249	....	31,658
May	7,075	14,391	....	7,316	6,331	22,503	....	16,172
June	8,281	21,219	....	12,938	15,953	25,772	....	9,819
July.......	9,541	13,346	....	3,805	15,075	11,840	3,235	....
August	15,467	47,795	....	32,328	17,138	60,987	....	43,849
September .	7,105	5,644	1,461	....	20,744	17,905	2,839	....
October ...	17,408	27,321	....	9,913	54,095	40,583	13,512	....
November .	18,109	20,102	....	1,993	58,342	37,321	21,021	....
December..	35,011	28,195	6,816	....	53,045	30,586	22,459	....
Total .	182,169	295,889	....	113,720	350,156	468,668	....	118,512

[1] By courtesy of the Black Diamond, Chicago, Ill.

Receipts at Chicago—Continued.

Month.	West Virginia and Kentucky.		1895.		Illinois.		1895.	
	1895.	1894.	Increase.	Decrease.	1895.	1894.	Increase.	Decrease.
	Tons.	Tons.	Tons.	Tons.	Tons.	Tons.	Tons.	Tons.
January ...	29,282	20,587	8,695	....	224,141	164,821	59,320	....
February ..	31,154	17,369	13,785	....	236,977	164,334	72,613	....
March	24,499	12,767	11,732	....	202,179	117,949	84,230	....
April	20,370	19,885	485	....	231,283	140,761	90,522	....
May	10,262	46,433	....	36,171	100,138	25,320	74,818	....
June	20,841	39,225	....	18,384	130,995	25,385	105,610	....
July	16,388	4,787	11,601	....	162,667	21,784	140,883	....
August	28,579	19,197	9,382	....	186,355	125,170	61,185	....
September .	29,787	24,524	5,263	....	186,326	147,164	39,162	....
October....	35,172	30,358	4,814	....	240,680	163,896	76,784	....
November .	42,085	34,173	7,912	....	247,040	216,497	30,543	....
December..	51,454	27,349	24,105	....	252,839	188,099	64,740	....
Total .	339,873	296,654	43,219	....	2,401,620	1,510,180	900,340	....

Month.	Indiana.		1895.		Coke.		1895.	
	1895.	1894.	Increase.	Decrease.	1895.	1894.	Increase.	Decrease.
	Tons.	Tons.	Tons.	Tons.	Tons.	Tons.	Tons.	Tons.
January ...	159,969	123,229	36,740	....	30,935	70,013	....	39,078
February ..	161,573	120,683	43,890	....	22,565	4,566	....	42,001
March	130,530	110,773	19,757	....	38,485	66,389	....	27,904
April	151,746	127,898	23,848	....	31,375	60,219	....	28,844
May	29,390	930	28,460	....	11,939	40,693	....	28,754
June	76,823	....	76,823	....	35,322	41,316	....	5,024
July	93,654	70,706	22,948	....	27,995	10,102	17,893	....
August	99,056	105,757	....	6,701	32,340	15,300	17,040	....
September .	105,293	78,278	27,015	....	20,034	14,061	5,973	....
October....	155,126	125,368	29,758	....	50,480	29,712	20,768	....
November .	179,719	149,259	30,460	....	27,780	17,161	10,619	....
December..	163,946	152,371	11,575	....	53,600	30,365	23,235	....
Total .	1,509,825	1,165,252	344,573	....	382,850	459,927	....	77,077

Shipments from Chicago.

Month.	Anthracite.		1895.		Bituminous and coke.		1895.	
	1895.	1894.	In-crease.	De-crease.	1895.	1894.	In-crease.	De-crease.
	Tons.	Tons.	Tons.	Tons.	Tons.	Tons.	Tons.	Tons.
January....	32,645	59,718	....	27,073	77,474	41,129	36,345	....
February...	33,499	42,981	....	9,482	94,711	34,576	60,135	....
March	19,600	28,494	....	8,894	82,374	23,817	58,557	....
April.......	12,692	15,511	....	2,819	65,960	34,123	31,837	....
May	10,872	69,453	....	58,581	40,646	14,209	26,437	....
June........	10,080	34,853	....	24,773	55,634	11,911	43,723	....
July	28,223	....	28,223	....	50,782	....	50,782	....
August.....	30,162	37,040	....	6,878	56,362	6,013	50,349	....
September..	41,114	15,780	25,334	....	66,804	101,247	....	34,443
October....	36,291	54,886	....	18,595	111,525	81,578	29,947	....
November..	32,910	53,355	....	20,445	94,694	85,262	9,432	....
December..	49,622	40,896	8,726	....	104,506	81,300	23,206	....
Total .	377,710	452,967	....	115,257	901,472	515,165	386,307	....

The following table gives a correct statement of the anthracite coal received at this market during the season of 1895, as obtained from custom-house reports and compared with the actual weights as shown on the books of the different consignees:

Lake receipts of anthracite coal at Chicago.

	Tons.
O. S. Richardson & Co ......:	237,630
E. L. Hedstrom & Co	234,420
Robert Law.......................................	186,339
Lehigh Valley Coal Co..............................	132,743
Coxe Bros. & Co...................................	124,000
Philadelphia and Reading Coal and Iron Co...............	107,915
Peabody Coal Co	84,247
Delaware and Hudson Canal Co......................	61,401
Youghiogheny and Lehigh Coal Co...................	52,500
William Drieske	29,500
Pennsylvania Coal Co	10,800
Drieske & Hinners	8,017
Total...................................	1,269,512

Summary of Chicago coal and coke trade for 1894 and 1895.

	1895.	1894.
	Tons.	*Tons.*
Stock of anthracite coal on hand January 1	604, 655	580, 430
Receipts of anthracite by lake	1, 269, 512	1, 277, 191
Receipts of anthracite by rail	519, 685	528, 351
Receipts of bituminous coal	4, 783, 643	3, 732, 694
Receipts of coke	382, 850	459, 927
Shipments of anthracite to country	337, 710	452, 967
Shipments of bituminous coal to country	901, 172	390, 077
Shipments of coke	279, 874	125, 088
Local consumption—anthracite	1, 581, 986	1, 328, 350
Local consumption—bituminous	3, 882, 171	3, 342, 617
Local consumption—coke	102, 976	334, 839
Stock of anthracite on hand December 31	474, 156	604, 655

MILWAUKEE, WIS.

Mr. William J. Langson, secretary of the Milwaukee Chamber of Commerce, contributes the following report on the coal trade of that city:

The receipts and shipments of coal at Milwaukee during the year 1895 were larger than in any former year, exceeding the record of 1894 109,377 tons in receipts and 217,702 tons in shipments. The respective quantities of hard and soft coal received in each of the years named were as follows:

Receipts of coal at Milwaukee, Wis., in 1894 and 1895.

Kinds.	1895.	1894.
	Tons.	*Tons.*
Hard coal	853, 680	771, 786
Soft coal	592, 743	565, 260
Total	1, 446, 423	1, 337, 046

The increased shipments left local dealers with lighter stocks than usual at the beginning of the winter and helped to sustain a sharp advance in prices. Had not the winter been unusually mild there must have been a hard-coal famine in this city before the advent of fresh supplies by lake. The increased movement of coal is interpreted as one of the indications of better times.

Receipts of coal at Milwaukee for eleven years.

	1885.	1886.	1887.	1888.	1889.	1890.
By lake from—	Tons.	Tons.	Tons.	Tons.	Tons.	Tons.
Buffalo	392,003	395,971	464,972	631,263	542,167	510,598
Erie	50,915	41,847	61,222	74,610	47,862	46,378
Oswego	10,043	....	1,153	1,348	....	2,408
Cleveland	126,741	91,997	78,259	98,631	89,071	135,413
Ashtabula	35,360	11,096	38,881	23,105	48,599	24,671
Black River	5,549					
Lorain	19,452	12,417	11,757	13,533	15,367	15,351
Sandusky	19,307	57,412	46,606	19,733	51,816	26,193
Toledo	31,875	69,079	14,115	38,452	71,516	59,305
Charlotte	19,491	31,744	2,781	14,292	22,526	6,120
Fairport			10,517	30,253	5,552	11,100
Ogdensburg				7,700	4,953	7,026
Huron, Ohio				8,244	7,726	9,720
Other ports		2,679	4,331		588	a49,375
Total by lake	710,736	714,242	724,594	961,164	907,743	903,658
By railroad	65,014	45,439	118,385	161,079	72,935	92,999
Total receipts	775,750	759,681	842,979	1,122,243	980,678	996,657

	1891.	1892.	1893.	1894.	1895.
By lake from—	Tons.	Tons.	Tons.	Tons.	Tons.
Buffalo	659,388	819,570	629,243	658,978	755,831
Erie	55,202	65,190	78,947	97,995	86,332
Oswego	17,022	26,177	46,065	41,891	33,364
Cleveland	143,776	132,051	189,539	105,800	105,469
Ashtabula	22,726	30,549	38,317	58,179	99,521
Black River					
Lorain	3,983		18,406	22,552	27,017
Sandusky	10,692	19,039	5,360	7,250	5,179
Toledo	53,644	12,229	61,548	90,357	74,603
Charlotte	10,013	55,909	763		1,153
Fairport	5,775	5,359	16,483	122,573	126,955
Ogdensburg	5,179	18,134	1,635	2,065	
Huron, Ohio	12,307	12,173	26,312	3,275	11,229
Other ports	a6,949	19,485	1,800	18,395	9,950
Total by lake	1,006,656	1,210,865	1,117,448	1,229,310	1,336,603
By railroad	149,377	163,549	132,284	107,736	109,920
Total receipts	1,156,033	1,374,414	1,249,732	1,337,046	1,446,423

a Including cargoes from all ports not reported at the custom house.

Shipments of coal from Milwaukee for the past thirteen years.

Shipped by—	1883.	1884.	1885.	1886.	1887.
	Tons.	*Tons.*	*Tons.*	*Tons.*	*Tons.*
Chicago, Milwaukee and St. Paul Rwy	146,295	140,630	179,883	177,286	166,120
Chicago and Northwestern Rwy.	41,746	37,314	56,591	70,420	79,258
Wisconsin Central R. R.	6,725	7,469	8,943	11,745	18,953
Milwaukee, Lake Shore and Western Rwy	30,575	11,757	12,804	13,072	13,886
Milwaukee and Northern R. R.	10,075	7,556	10,872	12,011	15,627
Lake	355	335	184	269	1,595
Total	235,771	205,061	269,277	284,803	295,439

Shipped by—	1888.	1889.	1890.	1891.
	Tons.	*Tons.*	*Tons.*	*Tons.*
Chicago, Milwaukee and St. Paul Rwy	283,269	258,281	378,090	406,455
Chicago and Northwestern Rwy	107,193	97,207	103,279	114,847
Wisconsin Central R. R.	12,624	11,727	15,929	14,449
Milwaukee, Lake Shore and Western Rwy	16,146	25,413	5,884	7,998
Milwaukee and Northern R. R.	34,480	20,556	19,386	26,723
Lake	125	224	50	416
Total	453,837	413,408	522,618	600,888

Shipped by—	1892.	1893.	1894.	1895.
	Tons.	*Tons.*	*Tons.*	*Tons.*
Chicago, Milwaukee and St. Paul Rwy	252,168	321,960	246,620	398,053
Chicago and Northwestern Rwy	163,063	199,457	167,753	221,357
Wisconsin Central R. R.	14,930	10,967	12.377	17,990
Milwaukee, Lake Shore and Western Rwy	11,041			
Milwaukee and Northern R. R.	27,185			
Lake	757	609	6,018	3,070
Total	469,144	532,993	432,768	640,470

Receipts of coal at Milwaukee by lake and rail annually from 1862 to 1895, inclusive.

Year.	Tons.	Year.	Tons.
1862	21,860	1879	350,840
1863	43,215	1880	368,568
1864	44,503	1881	550,027
1865	36,369	1882	593,842
1866	66,616	1883	612,584
1867	74,568	1884	704,166
1868	92,992	1885	775,750
1869	87,690	1886	759,681
1870	122,865	1887	842,979
1871	175,526	1888	1,122,243
1872	210,194	1889	980,678
1873	229,784	1890	996,657
1874	177,655	1891	1,156,033
1875	228,674	1892	1,374,414
1876	188,444	1893	1,249,732
1877	264,784	1894	1,337,046
1878	239,667	1895	1,446,423

DULUTH, MINN.

Mr. Frank E. Wyman, secretary of the Duluth Board of Trade, has furnished the following interesting review of the coal trade of that city:

The movement of coal at the head of the lakes for 1895 did not equal that of either of the two years immediately preceding. Mild winters create no increase in the general demand for coal, and this portion of the country has been favored with mild winters of late. The spring of 1895 found perhaps 400,000 tons of coal on the docks. With this stock on hand it was late when cargoes began to come in. There was nothing in the movement during the season of lake navigation that is worthy of special mention. Receipts were only fair up to the closing of the lakes for the cold season. The winter of 1895-96 was by no means severe. Had it been, there might have been a shortage in coal that would have been quite generally felt. As it was, the demand for certain grades could not be met. Of the total receipts about 65 per cent was soft. Thirty cents a ton was the average price paid during the season for laying coal on the docks here from ports on the lower lakes that are tributary to the mines in Ohio, Pennsylvania, and West Virginia, whence comes most of the coal received here.

The various companies engaged in the trade here are continually making improvements in their facilities for handling coal. These improvements consist of extensions of their docks and the introduction of modern appliances for the rapid and economical handling of the coal. The general improvements made in the plants of the coal companies here in 1895 involved the expenditure of much money, nearly all of which went to labor at this point. The result is ample preparation for handling a continually growing volume of business.

Receipts of coal at Duluth, Minn., in 1895, by companies.

Company.	Tons.
Northwestern Fuel Co	475,000
Ohio Coal Co	300,000
Lehigh Coal and Iron Co	100,000
Pioneer Fuel Co	200,000
Philadelphia and Reading Coal and Iron Co	135,000
Youghiogheny and Lehigh Coal Co	175,000
Lehigh Valley Coal Co	125,000
St. Paul and Western Coal Co	200,000
Pennsylvania and Ohio Coal Co	75,000
Duluth and Iron Range Rwy. Co. (Two Harbors)	50,000
Total	1,835,000

The table following shows the development of the coal trade at the head of the lakes since 1878, and will be found of interest.

Coal receipts at Duluth, Minn., and Superior, Wis.

Year.	Tons.	Year.	Tons.
1878	31,000	1888	1,535,000
1881	163,000	1889	1,205,000
1882	260,000	1890	1,780,995
1883	420,000	1891	1,776,000
1884	372,000	1892	1,965,000
1885	595,000	1893	2,200,000
1886	736,000	1894	2,350,000
1887	912,000	1895	1,835,000

CINCINNATI, OHIO.

The Survey is indebted to Mr. Charles B. Murray, superintendent of the Chamber of Commerce, for the statement of coal receipts at Cincinnati since 1891. Statistics for previous years were furnished by the former superintendent, Col. S. D. Maxwell. Prior to 1892 the statistics in the following table were collected for fiscal years ending August 31. The figures for 1892, 1893, 1894, and 1895 are for calendar years. The receipts in 1891 from September 1 to December 31 are stated separately.

Receipts of coal at Cincinnati since September 1, 1871.

Year.	Pittsburg (Youghiogheny).	Kanawha.	Ohio River.	Canal.
	Bushels.	*Bushels.*	*Bushels.*	*Bushels.*
1871–72..........	19, 254, 716	....	*b*10, 359, 906	1, 104, 003
1872–73..........	24, 962, 373	....	*b*11, 075, 072	1, 162, 052
1873–74..........	24, 014, 681	....	*b*10, 398, 153	710, 000
1874–75..........	24, 225, 002	4, 476, 619	4, 277, 327	565, 352
1875–76..........	27, 017, 592	6, 004, 675	4, 400, 792	409, 358
1876–77..........	28, 237, 572	3, 631, 823	5, 141, 150	322, 171
1877–78..........	26, 743, 055	6, 386, 623	3, 288, 008	380, 768
1878–79..........	20, 769, 027	6, 134, 039	4, 068, 452	333, 549
1879–80..........	31, 750, 968	8, 912, 801	4, 268, 214	202, 489
1880–81..........	23, 202, 084	10, 715, 459	3, 151, 934	67, 684
1881–82..........	37, 807, 961	13, 950, 802	3, 560, 881	77, 336
1882–83..........	33, 895, 064	13, 260, 347	3, 309, 534	180, 621
1883–84..........	32, 239, 473	15, 926, 743	2, 956, 688	293, 010
1884–85..........	32, 286, 133	14, 588, 573	3, 007, 078	314, 774
1885–86..........	34, 933, 542	17, 329, 349	939, 746	205, 717
1886–87..........	37, 701, 094	20, 167, 875	338, 435	129, 503
1887–88..........	41, 180, 713	20, 926, 596	1, 533, 358	26, 098
1888–89..........	36, 677, 974	23, 761, 853	544, 940	12, 129
1889–90..........	42, 601, 615	19, 221, 196	454, 385	....
1890–91..........	43, 254, 460	19, 115, 172	1, 479, 670	15, 111
1891, 4 months	13, 766, 390	6, 288, 442	234, 940	....
1892 *a*	42, 272, 348	19, 214, 704	768, 588	....
1893 *a*	28, 643, 562	24, 971, 261	405, 202	....
1894 *a*	40, 156, 667	16, 398, 039	158, 334	....
1895 *a*	26, 675, 823	15, 106, 095	14, 400	....

Year.	Anthracite.	Other kinds.	Total.
	Bushels.	*Bushels.*	*Bushels.*
1871–72..........................	72, 171	....	30, 790, 796
1872–73..........................	75, 000	....	37, 274, 497
1873–74..........................	112, 000	....	35, 234, 834
1874–75..........................	248, 750	1, 597, 260	35, 390, 310
1875–76..........................	282, 578	2, 068, 322	40, 183, 317
1876–77..........................	376, 125	1, 913, 793	39, 622, 634
1877–78..........................	439, 350	1, 654, 425	38, 892, 229
1878–79..........................	768, 750	2, 136, 850	34, 210, 667
1879–80..........................	712, 075	2, 351, 699	48, 198, 246
1880–81..........................	770, 525	2, 336, 752	40, 244, 438
1881–82..........................	779, 925	3, 090, 715	59, 267, 620
1882–83..........................	977, 250	2, 997, 216	54, 620, 032

a Calendar year.   *b* Including Kanawha coal.

Receipts of coal at Cincinnati since September 1, 1871—Continued.

Year.	Anthracite.	Other kinds.	Total.
	Bushels.	*Bushels.*	*Bushels.*
1883–84	1, 085, 350	3, 910, 795	56, 412, 059
1884–85	1, 257, 900	2, 683, 864	54, 138, 322
1885–86	1, 287, 925	2, 720, 250	57, 416, 529
1886–87	1, 314, 775	3, 693, 850	63, 345, 532
1887–88	1, 328, 225	5, 710, 649	70, 705, 639
1888–89	1, 020, 525	3, 075, 000	65, 092, 421
1889–90	1, 001, 175	4, 709, 775	67, 988, 146
1890–91	1, 118, 671	7, 362, 698	72, 345, 782
1891, 4 months	402, 528	4, 437, 139	25, 129, 439
1892 *a*	1, 268, 170	13, 335, 006	76, 858, 816
1893 *a*	759, 626	25, 832, 374	80, 612, 025
1894 *a*	661, 548	19, 083, 527	76, 458, 115
1895 *a*	1, 227, 000	27, 119, 823	70, 143, 141

a Calendar year.

Receipts of coal at Cincinnati during the past fifteen years have been as follows:

Coal receipts at Cincinnati, Ohio.

Year.	Tons.	Year.	Tons.
1881	1, 492, 817	1889	2, 348, 055
1882	2, 197, 407	1890	2, 452, 253
1883	2, 025, 859	1891	2, 608, 923
1884	2, 092, 551	1892	2, 718, 809
1885	2, 008, 850	1893	2, 905, 071
1886	2, 130, 354	1894	2, 755, 137
1887	2, 350, 026	1895	2, 530, 061
1888	2, 551, 415		

The following review of the coal trade of Cincinnati is from the annual report of Mr. Murray:

The low stage of the Ohio River during a large part of the year precluded the usual movement of coal by water transportation, especially from the Pittsburg district, from which region the year's receipts were the smallest since 1881. While the movement from the Kanawha was not greatly reduced in comparison with the preceding year, it was the smallest in quantity since 1885. These conditions gave important impetus to the railroad traffic in coal, which was far in excess of any previous year, but the aggregate from all sources fell short of the preceding year, and in fact the records suggest the smallest total receipts since the year 1890.

Returns to the Chamber of Commerce indicate for the year a total of 70,143,000 bushels of coal received and 18,795,000 bushels shipped, leaving a net supply of 51,348,000 bushels. In 1894 the receipts were 76,458,000 bushels; shipments, 17,029,000;

leaving a net supply of 59,429,000 bushels. In 1893 the receipts were 80,612,000 bushels, the largest on record; shipments, 18,867,000; net supply, 61,755,000 bushels. The year closed with very small supplies on hand, the reserves being close to exhaustion.

Of the year's receipts of coal the arrivals by railroads were 27,263,000 bushels and shipments by railroads 15,673,000 bushels. For a period of five years prior to 1892 the receipts of coal by railroads averaged about 7 per cent of the total supply; in 1892 they exceeded 18 per cent, and for three years ending with 1894 the average was more than 25 per cent, and for 1895 represented about 40 per cent.

The year's receipts from the Pittsburg district were 26,676,000 bushels, compared with 40,156,000 in 1894; from Kanawha, 15,106,000 bushels, compared with 16,398,000 in 1894; the Pittsburg supply representing 38 per cent of the total receipts, Kanawha 21½ per cent, and all other 40½ per cent.

The year's range of prices of Pittsburg coal, afloat at Cincinnati, was 5½ to 6½ cents per bushel, the average being 6 cents, or $1.67 per ton; quotations were nominal a large part of the year from absence of offerings. This class of coal delivered to consumers had a range of $2.25 to $3 per ton, averaging $2.51, compared with $2.53 in 1894 and $3.07 in 1893; for ten years ending with 1894 the average was $3.05. The regulating influence of railroad supplies is reflected in the comparison of averages for recent years and those of earlier years which embraced extreme prices a portion of the year from scarcity of offerings.

A partial investigation in regard to the proportion of the local consumption of coal represented by household uses and for manufacturing purposes indicates that it is pretty evenly divided between the two channels, some dealers disposing of 40 to 50 per cent for household purposes and others a larger proportion.

The influence of low water in recent years in the Ohio and Kanawha rivers in restricting the movement of coal has made it plain that it is important to have measures of relief inaugurated. It is believed that much can be accomplished in this direction by the construction of a series of locks and dams, such as are now in use at Davis Island, below Pittsburg. While the railroads may be equal to modifying the urgency of such matters in an enlarged movement of coal, the fact remains that the water transportation is decidedly the cheaper, and the lower the cost of fuel the more encouragement and impetus is given to industrial operations along this valley.

The yearly range and average prices of Pittsburg coal, afloat and delivered, per bushel, based on weekly records, compared for ten years, is shown in the following compilation:

Prices of Pittsburg coal at Cincinnati.

[Per bushel.]

Year.	Afloat.			Delivered.		
	Lowest.	Highest.	Average.	Lowest.	Highest.	Average.
	Cents.	*Cents.*	*Cents.*	*Cents.*	*Cents.*	*Cents.*
1885-86	5¼	8	6.58	9	11	10.05
1886-87	6½	15	7.55	9½	16	11.04
1887-88	7	18	10.01	10¾	22	13.96
1888-89	6	8½	6.71	9	11¾	9.95
1889-90	6	8	6.78	9	10¾	9.69
1890-91	6½	8½	7.28	10	10¾	10.24
1892	6½	8½	7.49	9	12½	10.36
1893	6½	8¾	7.58	9	19¾	11.01
1894	5¼	9	6.34	7¼	10¾	9.11
1895	5½	6½	6.00	8⅛	10¾	9.00

The bulk of coal from the Kanawha, Virginia, and West Virginia regions sells at the same, or about the same, prices as are obtained for the product from the Pittsburg district.

The receipts of coke for the year were 2,353,000 bushels, and the quantity locally manufactured was 4,394,000 bushels, making a total of 6,747,000 bushels, compared with 7,060,000 bushels the preceding year. For city manufacture the average price for the year was 8 cents per bushel; of gas house, 8 cents; of Connellsville, $6.50 per ton.

ST. LOUIS, MO.

The following summary of the coal trade of St. Louis and vicinity for the year 1895 has been furnished by Mr. James Cox, secretary of the Business Men's League, an organization designed to extend the area of the city's trade and commerce and to protect it against transportation and other discriminations:

The year was a somewhat uneventful one in the coal trade of this city as compared with the preceding year, when the strike in the southern Illinois coal fields interfered at times very much with deliveries and caused prices to fluctuate considerably. The manufactories of St. Louis were exceptionally active during the year 1895, which fact was reflected in the coal receipts, which were very large, exceeding all previous records. In 1894 the receipts were only about 75,000,000 bushels. Last year the receipts exceeded 85,000,000 bushels. Almost all the railroads making a specialty of hauling coal into St. Louis had a share of the increase, the most remarkable gain being that of the St. Louis and Eastern road, which hauled in more than 12,000,000 bushels, as compared with less than 7,000,000 bushels in 1894. The Chicago, Peoria and St. Louis road also doubled its receipts.

All factories are (May, 1896) running full time and several are working extra hours, so that indications favor a maintained demand. Prices were very low indeed during the year, low enough, in fact, to induce several removals to this point on account of the economy in power producing. Standard Illinois coal, which was quoted two years ago as high as $1.95 a ton, sold as low as $1.20 during Christmas week of 1895. High-grade Illinois soft coal averaged 30 cents a ton cheaper than in the preceding year. Anthracite was very much lower during the year, and although prices stiffened a little during the early winter a great many orders were filled at fully $2 per ton less than two years ago. Coke, on the other hand, has ruled higher. Connellsville coke, which sold in 1893 and 1894 in the neighborhood of $5, has gone up to $5.75 and Indiana coke has had a similar advance. Gas coke is cheaper, but prices for the highest grade of coke are still at top notch, with indications of going higher. Anthracite coal is also stiffening in price.

The soft-coal market is so unsettled that there is no indication of an increase in prices; indeed, on large contracts lower figures are being made than actual quotations would indicate.

Almost the only item of interest to the coal trade of this city during the past year has been a systematic effort on the part of the Laclede Gas Company, which has a practical monopoly in the supply of gas, to encourage the use of its product for cooking purposes. The price of fuel gas has been reduced to 80 cents per thousand, and arrangements are made whereby heating and cooking stoves are supplied to occupants of dwellings on very tempting conditions. The use of electricity for illuminating purposes even in private houses is worthy of note, but the increase of gas for fuel purposes is equally significant. In the long run this is expected to have a marked effect on the demand for the better quality of coal, but at present the increase in population, which was probably 30,000 during 1895, has more than compensated for the loss of custom to the coal trade owing to the substitution of gas for fuel purposes.

Appended are the receipts of coal and coke at St. Louis during the last six years:

Coal and coke receipts at St. Louis since 1890.

Year.	Soft coal.	Hard coal.	Coke.
	Bushels.	Tons.	Bushels.
1890	69,477,225	124,335	9,919,850
1891	72,078,225	139,050	6,924,250
1892	82,302,228	187,327	8,914,400
1893	87,769,375	173,653	7,807,000
1894	74,644,375	186,494	6,365,900
1895	88,589,935	207,784	7,130,300

The following are the prices per ton of the most used grades of coal in car lots free on board in St. Louis in 1895:

Prices of coal at St. Louis during 1895.

	Highest.	Closing.		Highest.	Closing.
Standard Illinois...	$1.30	$1.20	Connellsville coke..	$5.75	$5.75
High grade Illinois.	1.67½	1.67½	New River coke....	4.55	4.55
Anthracite:			Indiana coke.......	3.80	3.55
Large egg......	5.75	5.75	Kentucky coke.....	3.80	3.55
Small	5.95	5.95	Gas coke..........	4.20	3.25

MOBILE, ALA.

The following statement regarding the coal trade of Mobile has been obtained from the Daily Register of that city and from information furnished by Mr. A. C. Danner, president of the Mobile Coal Company:

The coal business of Mobile is yearly improving, especially in steam coal. The large increase in the number of steamers which have entered this port in 1894 and the establishment of the Liverpool line have tended to develop more activity in the sale of steam coal. The fruit steamers use 2,500 tons a month, or about 30,000 tons a year. The home consumption in Mobile is about 7,000 tons.

The range of prices in Mobile for retail lots has been as follows: Alabama, $4 to $6.50; anthracite, $6.50 to $7 per ton; export coal, cargo lots, $2 to $2.10 per ton of 2,000 pounds free on board vessels at dock; tug coal, $2.50 in bunkers; bunker coal for steamers, $2.25 placed in bunkers and trimmed. Coke, car-load lots on cars, $4.50 per ton; retail, delivered, $6.50 per ton.

The total receipts during the year 1894-95 were 156,996 tons, as compared with 104,340 tons during 1893-94. This applies to Alabama coal alone. The importation of foreign coal was small, and barely reached 2,200 tons.

The following table shows the annual receipts of coal at Mobile since 1883:

Receipts of coal at Mobile, Ala., for thirteen years.

Year.	Alabama coal. (a)	Anthracite and English.	Total.
	Tons.	Tons.	Tons.
1883	25,304	1,229	26,533
1884	17,808	891	18,699
1885	40,301	775	41,076
1886	30,310	2,022	32,332
1887	39,232	910	40,142
1888	38,785	648	39,433
1889	43,620	1,454	45,074
1890	39,320	1,327	40,647
1891	51,267	1,775	53,042
1892	70,298	1,500	71,798
1893	90,000	4,130	94,130
1894	104,340	3,600	107,940
1895	156,996	4,200	161,196

a This does not include the amount of coal used by the railroads on their locomotives and at their shops.

In reference to the future of Mobile as a coal port, Mr. Danner calls attention to the completion of some of the Government work on the Warrior River. During the winter of 1895-96 three locks and dams on the upper Warrior, above Tuscaloosa, were completed and thrown open for navigation, thus extending the navigable part of the river up to the coal measures.

Two small mines have been opened on the river and several barge loads of coal have been towed from there to Mobile without difficulty or delay. The quantity brought down is small, only about 600 or 800 tons, but it has demonstrated that it is practicable to bring coal from the Alabama mines to Mobile by water, and it is hoped that this means of transportation will be used in the near future, so as to reduce the price of coal at Mobile.

NORFOLK, VA.

The following statement of coal handled at Lamberts Point coal piers has been furnished this office by the Chamber of Commerce of Norfolk:

Pocahontas coal shipments from Lamberts Point piers in six years.

Year.	Foreign.	Bunkers.	Coastwise.	Local.	Total.
	Long tons.	*Long tons.*	*Long tons.*	*Long tons.*	*Long tons.*
1890	37,723	102,755	941,019	71,010	1,152,507
1891	27,997	135,112	1,215,028	90,606	1,468,743
1892	25,653	129,627	1,400,984	98,034	1,654,298
1893	34,969	125,688	1,512,931	100,453	1,774,041
1894	44,328	105,382	1,810,480	96,841	2,057,031
1895	34,174	75,714	1,430,144	100,442	1,640,474

SAN FRANCISCO, CAL.

Mr. J. W. Harrison reports the trade for the year as follows:

The quantity of coal consumed in 1895 was greater than in any year since 1891, which shows very forcibly that our manufacturing interests have prospered. This is mainly attributable to the very low prices for fuel which ruled, they being the lowest known to the trade, and the outlook is that low prices will prevail for several months to come. With reduced freight rates from Australia, and their best grades of steam coal quoted at $1.75 per ton, our large consumers are assured cheap fuel, which is the principal factor in establishing the prosperity of our leading industries. Swansea anthracite coal is becoming very popular as a steam producer, the best evidence of which is that we have imported 65,000 tons more than in 1894. This grade is favored by the Department, being admitted free of duty, while bituminous pays 40 cents per ton. Crude oil is now being utilized at several of our factories, on the grounds of economy, but with coal at present figures the saving is very slight; besides, the amount produced is not sufficient to alarm our coal importers. The gas companies are liberal consumers of this oil, which combined with anthracite is an economical gas producer; in fact, their purchases of bituminous coal are very light. The reduced values of all characters of Australian and English coal are materially interfering with our northern collieries, hence their output is being diminished.

The following table of prices will show the fluctuations of foreign coals for "spot" cargoes; the changes were:

Monthly prices for coal at San Francisco in 1895.

Kind.	Jan.	Apr.	May.	Aug.	Nov.	Dec.
Australian (gas).........	$5.75	$6.00	$5.75	$5.40	$5.30	$5.20
English steam..........	6.25	6.25	6.00	5.75	6.00	6.00
Scotch splint...........	7.00	7.00	6.50	7.00	6.75	6.50
West Hartley	6.25	6.50	6.25	6.25	6.00	6.00

The various sources from which we have derived our supplies are as follows:

Sources of coal consumed in California.

Source.	1890.	1891.	1892.
	Tons.	Tons.	Tons.
British Columbia	441,759	652,657	554,600
Australia	194,725	321,197	314,280
English and Welsh..................	35,662	168,586	210,660
Scotch............................	1,610	31,840	24,900
Eastern (Cumberland and anthracite)	32,550	42,210	35,720
Franklin, Green River, and Cedar River..............................	216,760	178,230	164,930
Carbon Hill and South Prairie.......	191,109	196,750	218,390
Mount Diablo and Coos Bay........	74,210	90,684	66,150
Japan, etc	13,170	20,679	4,220
Total	1,204,555	1,702,833	1,593,850

Source.	1893.	1894.	1895.
	Tons.	Tons.	Tons.
British Columbia..................	588,527	647,110	651,295
Australia	202,017	211,733	268,960
English and Welsh..................	151,269	157,562	201,180
Scotch	18,809	18,636	4,098
Eastern (Cumberland and anthracite)	18,960	16,640	26,863
Franklin, Green River, and Cedar River..............................	167,550	153,199	150,888
Carbon Hill and South Prairie.......	261,435	241,974	256,267
Mount Diablo and Coos Bay	63,460	65,263	84,954
Japan, etc	7,758	15,637	9,015
Total	1,479,785	1,527,754	1,653,520

To insure a correct statement of the entire amount of coal consumed, the arrivals by water at San Pedro, Port Los Angeles, San Diego, and Santa Barbara, aggregating 199,130 tons, have been included.

The total amount of coke imported is 24,688 tons—all foreign—mainly from England and Belgium. The owners of the Union mine at Comox, British Columbia, are fitting up ovens, etc., on a large scale, with a view to supplying this market with coke, as the coal is reputed to be well adapted for coke producing. It will be several months before they are fully equipped.

SEATTLE, WASH.

The Trade Register has each year recorded the mine outputs of the State and the total receipts from the mines shipping directly to Seattle. The State output for 1893 was 1,264,877 tons, of which Seattle handled 461,034 tons. The State output for 1894 was 1,106,470 tons, of which Seattle handled 437,939 tons. The Seattle Coal and Iron Company principally supplies the home demand, and this year has resumed cargo shipments to San Francisco, and also ships to British Columbia. The Black Diamond Company and the Oregon Improvement Company also ship to San Francisco and sell locally, while the new Renton coal mines have recently added to the Seattle receipts and will produce regularly next year. It is worthy of note here that the Cedar Mountain mine has resumed operations this month, after a long idleness. The outputs for 1895 of the three principal mines shipping to Seattle are as follows, by months:

Shipments of coal from Washington mines to Seattle in 1895, by months.

Month.	Seattle Coal and Iron Co.	Oregon Improvement Co.	Black Diamond Co.
	Tons.	Tons.	Tons.
January	9,817	13,537	9,750
February	6,023	14,445	7,714
March	6,038	10,775	12,700
April	5,967	15,725	3,913
May	8,052	13,968	8,860
June	8,678	12,705	6,091
July	2,843	8,199	7,778
August	8,000	9,323	5,500
September	5,320	11,419	10,411
October	7,980	18,193	6,312
November	9,482	11,418	12,543
December (a)	12,000	12,500	10,000
Total	90,200	152,207	101,572

a Estimated.

To these are to be added about 20,000 tons from the other mines, making the total for the year 363,979 tons, against 437,939 tons in 1894. The falling off was due to the fire disasters at the Oregon Improvement Company mines. Seattle handles and ships far more coal than any other town in the State, and King County produces nearly half of the output of the State.

PRODUCTION OF COAL, BY STATES.

ALABAMA.

Total product in 1895, 5,693,775 short tons; spot value, $5,126,822.

Owing to the brief but, while it lasted, very pronounced renewal of activity in the iron industry which took place during the spring and summer (from May to September) of 1895, the coal-mining industry of Alabama experienced a sympathetic impetus of noteworthy importance. The production of pig iron in the State increased from 556,314 long tons in 1894 to 835,851 long tons in 1895, a gain of 279,537 long tons, or just about 50 per cent. The product of coal increased 1,296,597 short tons, or 29 per cent, from 4,397,178 short tons in 1894 to 5,693,775 short tons in 1895.

Alabama ranks fifth as a coal-producing State and fourth in the manufacture of pig iron. Pennsylvania, Ohio, and Illinois precede Alabama in iron making, and in all three States the output of pig iron in 1895 was largely in excess of that of 1894—Pennsylvania by 37 per cent, Ohio by 64 per cent, and Illinois by 66 per cent. But in Pennsylvania only was there an increase in coal production at all commensurate with the increased iron product. The increase of Ohio's coal product was but 12 per cent; that of Illinois less than 4 per cent. Pennsylvania increased her bituminous coal product 25 per cent. The reason for this is readily explained. Very little of the coal mined in Ohio or Illinois produces a high grade of furnace coke, and nearly all the coke used in the furnaces of these States is made from coal drawn from Pennsylvania mines. The percentage of increase for the three States combined was, for pig iron, 47 per cent; and for coal, 18 per cent. Bringing the relative increases in the production of coal and pig iron in these States to a unit and comparing them, it is seen that in Alabama there is an increase of 6 short tons of coal for each additional long ton of pig iron. In the other three States taken together there is an increase of 4.5 short tons of coal for each increased ton of pig iron. The larger percentage yield of coal in coke, and the superior quality of Pennsylvania coke compared with that of Alabama, will partly account for this difference.

Alabama was not one of the exceptions to the general rule in 1895, the value of the coal product showing a comparative decline in value, the average price per ton decreasing from 93 cents in 1894 to 90 cents in

1895. The total increase in the value of the product in 1895 over that of 1894 was $1,041,287.

In the following tables is shown the details of production during 1894 and 1895:

Coal product of Alabama in 1894, by counties.

County.	Loaded at mines for shipment.	Sold to local trade and used by employes.	Used at mines for steam and heat.	Made into coke.	Total product.	Total value.	Average price per ton.	Average number of days active.	Average number of employees.
	Short tons.	*Short tons.*	*Short tons.*	*Short tons.*	*Short tons.*				
Bibb	379,488	4,250	15,190	2,133	401,061	$401,061	$1.00	204	1,089
Blount		6,000		2,000	8,000	8,000	1.00	75	45
Jackson		6,011			6,011	15,028	2.50	257	6
Jefferson	1,805,269	11,744	82,959	866,330	2,766,302	2,477,795	.90	272	6,567
St. Clair	34,167	950	5,200	3,200	43,517	42,135	.96	225	98
Shelby	72,904	350	3,365		76,619	110,600	1.44	114	405
Tuscaloosa	129,999	1,400	6,720	52,962	191,081	201,754	1.06	261	363
Walker	843,227	5,066	16,970	26,690	891,953	812,528	.91	180	2,252
Winston	4,494	140			4,634	4,634	1.00	140	34
Small mines		8,000			8,000	12,000			
Total	3,269,548	43,911	130,404	953,315	4,397,178	4,085,535	.93	238	10,859

Coal product of Alabama in 1895, by counties.

County.	Number of mines.	Loaded at mines for shipment.	Sold to local trade and used by employes.	Used at mines for steam and heat.	Made into coke.	Total product.	Total value.	Average price per ton.	Average number of days active.	Average number of employees.
		Short tons.	*Short tons.*	*Short tons.*	*Short tons.*	*Short tons.*				
Bibb	3	600,006	4,765	25,180	23,781	653,732	$653,732	1.00	198	1,259
Jefferson	22	1,879,665	249,540	75,926	1,521,194	3,726,325	3,249,287	.87	267	5,825
St. Clair	2	30,531	125	150		30,806	14,893	.48	126	96
Shelby	5	50,524	100	2,130		52,754	91,350	1.73	169	198
Tuscaloosa	6	130,851	574	2,965	73,727	208,117	202,512	.97	282	612
Walker	23	855,556	4,947	30,670	55,068	946,241	847,748	.90	210	2,231
Blount Etowah Winston	3	63,300	4,500			67,800	55,300	.82	252	125
Small mines			8,000			8,000	12,000	1.50		
Total	64	3,610,433	272,551	137,021	1,673,770	5,693,775	5,126,822	.90	244	10,346

The following table shows the annual output of coal in the State since 1870, with the exception of 1871 and 1872, for which no statistics were obtained:

Annual coal product of Alabama since 1870.

Year.	Short tons.	Value.	Average price per ton.	Average number of days worked.	Average number of employees.
1870	13,200				
1873	44,800				
1874	50,400				
1875	67,200				
1876	112,000				
1877	196,000				
1878	224,000				
1879	280,000				
1880	380,800				
1881	420,000				
1882	896,000				
1883	1,568,000				
1884	2,240,000				
1885	2,492,000				
1886	1,800,000	$2,574,000	$1.43		
1887	1,950,000	2,535,000	1.30		
1888	2,900,000	3,335,000	1.15		
1889	3,572,983	3,961,491	1.10	248	6,975
1890	4,090,469	4,202,469	1.03	217	10,642
1891	4,759,781	5,087,596	1.07	268	9,302
1892	5,529,312	5,788,898	1.05	271	10,075
1893	5,136,935	5,096,792	.99	237	11,294
1894	4,397,178	4,085,535	.93	238	10,859
1895	5,693,775	5,126,822	.90	244	10,346

It will be seen from the above table that the product in 1894 is the smallest since 1890, and the total value less than in any year since 1889. The average price obtained in 1895 was the lowest in the history of coal mining in the State.

In the following table is shown the coal product in Alabama, by counties, for a period of seven years, with the increase or decrease in each county during 1895 as compared with 1894:

Coal product of Alabama, by counties, since 1889.

County.	1889.	1890.	1891.	1892.	1893.
	Short tons.	Short tons.	Short tons.	Short tons.	Short tons.
Bibb	500,525	221,811	619,809	793,469	806,214
Blount					
Dekalb					40
Etowah					
Jackson					
Jefferson	2,437,446	2,665,060	2,905,343	3,399,274	3,093,277
St. Clair	40,557	33,653	66,096	24,950	72,000
Shelby	84,333	25,022	34,130	27,968	55,339
Tuscaloosa	16,141	65,517	142,184	168,039	167,516
Walker	488,226	767,346	980,219	1,103,612	927,349
Winston					3,200
Small mines	5,255	12,000	12,000	12,000	12,000
Total	3,572,983	4,090,409	4,759,781	5,529,312	5,136,935

County.	1894.	1895.	Increase in 1895.	Decrease in 1895.
	Short tons.	Short tons.	Short tons.	Short tons.
Bibb	401,061	653,732	252,671	
Blount	8,000	62,400	54,400	
Dekalb				
Etowah		900	900	
Jackson	6,011			6,011
Jefferson	2,766,302	3,726,325	960,023	
St. Clair	43,517	30,806		12,711
Shelby	76,619	52,754		23,865
Tuscaloosa	191,081	208,117	17,036	
Walker	891,953	946,241	54,288	
Winston	4,634	4,500		134
Small mines	8,000	8,000		
Total	4,397,178	5,693,775	a 1,296,597	

a Net increase.

Previous to 1889 the statistics of coal production in Alabama did not show the value by counties nor the average prices. It is, however, interesting to note the almost uniform decline in values in every county since that year, as is shown in the following table. The seemingly increased price in Shelby County in 1890, 1891, and 1892 was due to the fact that one of the largest mines was shut down during those years. Its resumption in 1893 brought down the average price to some extent, and the increased production in 1894 caused a further decline. This mine was idle again in 1895, and an increase in the average price per ton for the county is shown.

Average prices for Alabama coal at the mines since 1889, by counties.

County.	1889.	1890.	1891.	1892.	1893.	1894.	1895.
Bibb	$1.20	$1.10	$1.17	$1.08	$1.00	$1.00	$1.00
Blount							.80
Jefferson	1.07	1.00	1.04	1.03	.98	.90	.87
St. Clair	1.25	1.18	1.14	1.10	1.06	.96	.48
Shelby	1.79	2.50	2.60	2.61	1.82½	1.44	1.73
Tuscaloosa	1.23	1.05	1.03	1.07	1.05	1.06	.97
Walker	1.04	1.00	1.03	1.02	.98	.91	.90
General average	1.10	1.03	1.07	1.05	.99	.93	.90

In the above table only those counties are considered whose annual product exceeds 10,000 tons. Instead of discussing each county by itself, the foregoing tables have been given as showing in compact form the essential matters of interest in regard to the product and value for a series of years. Similarly the following table shows the statistics of the number of men employed and the average working time in counties producing more than 10,000 tons in each year.

Statistics of labor employed and working time at Alabama coal mines.

County.	1890.		1891.		1892.	
	Average working days.	Average number employed.	Average working days.	Average number employed.	Average working days.	Average number employed.
Bibb	250	1,340	243	1,175	290	1,500
Blount						
Jefferson	267	6,209	274	5,405	289	5,860
St. Clair	250	1,340	242	180	200	75
Shelby	200	150	265	200	225	150
Tuscaloosa	157	268	287	298	261	281
Walker	210	1,509	219	2,044	217	2,209
The State	217	10,642	268	9,302	271	10,075

*Statistics of labor employed and working time at Alabama coal mines—*Continued.

County.	1893.		1894.		1895.	
	Average working days.	Average number employed.	Average working days.	Average number employed.	Average working days.	Average number employed.
Bibb	216	1,280	204	1,089	198	1,259
Blount					275	95
Jefferson	258	7,033	272	6,567	267	5,825
St. Clair	198	135	225	98	126	96
Shelby	200	255	114	405	169	198
Tuscaloosa	247	412	261	363	282	612
Walker	187	2,158	180	2,252	210	2,231
The State	237	11,294	238	10,859	241	10,346

ARKANSAS.

Total product in 1895, 598,322 short tons; spot value, $751,156.

The coal product of Arkansas in 1895 was the largest in the history of the State, being 85,696 short tons, or about 17 per cent in excess of that of 1894, and 23,559 short tons, or about 4 per cent more than that of 1893, the year of largest previous production. The value of the product in 1895, while greater than that of 1894 by $119,168, was $22,191 less than that of 1893.

Outside of the fact of an increased output and a slight advance in value there were no developments of particular note during the year. The increased activity was due to improved industrial conditions incident to immigration and increased population.

In the tables below the statistics of coal production in Arkansas in 1894 and 1895 are shown, together with the distribution of the product for consumption:

Coal product of Arkansas in 1894, by counties.

County.	Number of mines.	Loaded at mines for shipment.	Sold to local trade and used by employees.	Used at mines for steam and heat.	Total product.	Total value.	Average price per ton.	Average number of days active.	Average number of employees.
		Short tons	*Short tons*	*Short tons*	*Short tons*				
Franklin									
Johnson	3	143,618	610	3,500	147,728	$172,357	$1.17	192	372
Pope	2	16,363	300	1,125	17,788	52,289	2.94	229	62
Sebastian	8	328,096	960	12,054	341,110	395,342	1.16	108	1,059
Small mines			6,000		6,000	12,000	2.00		
Total	13	488,077	7,870	16,679	512,626	631,988	1.22	134	1,493

17 GEOL, PT 3——24

Coal product of Arkansas in 1895, by counties.

County.	Number of mines.	Loaded at mines for shipment.	Sold to local trade and used by employees.	Used at mines for steam and heat.	Total product.	Total value.	Average price per ton.	Average number of days active.	Average number of employees.
		Short tons	Short tons	Short tons	Short tons				
Franklin ...... Pope........... }	3	123,012	1,000	1,000	125,012	$176,114	$1.41	251	240
Johnson	2	125,926	1,000	1,000	127,926	153,311	1.20	193	220
Sebastian	8	327,174	6,935	5,275	339,384	409,731	1.21	148	758
Small mines ...	......	......	6,000	......	6,000	12,000	2.00	......	......
Total	13	576,112	14,935	7,275	598,322	751,156	1.25	176	1,218

According to the Tenth Census of the United States (1880) the coal output of Arkansas was 14,778 short tons, worth at the mines $33,535. No statistics were obtained in 1881. Since 1882 the statistics of production, as far as have been ascertained, have been as follows:

Annual production of coal in Arkansas since 1882.

Year.	Short tons.	Value.	Average price per ton.	Average number of days worked.	Average number of employees.
1882................	5,000	......	......	......	......
1883................	50,000	......	......	......	......
1884................	75,000	......	......	......	......
1885................	100,000	......	......	......	......
1886................	125,000	$200,000	$1.60	......	......
1887................	129,600	194,400	1.50	......	......
1888................	276,871	415,306	1.50	......	978
1889................	279,584	395,836	1.42	......	677
1890................	399,888	514,595	1.29	214	938
1891................	542,379	647,560	1.19	214	1,317
1892................	535,558	666,230	1.24	199	1,128
1893................	574,763	773,347	1.34	151	1,559
1894................	512,626	631,988	1.22	134	1,493
1895................	598,322	751,156	1.25	176	1,218

In the following table is shown the annual product since 1887, by counties:

Coal product of Arkansas since 1887, by counties.

County.	1887.	1888.	1889.	1890.	1891.
	Short tons.	Short tons.	Short tons.	Short tons.	Short tons.
Franklin	....	....	....	....	....
Johnson	81,900	106,037	105,998	89,000	80,000
Pope	8,200	10,240	6,014	4,000	5,000
Sebastian	39,500	160,594	165,884	300,888	451,379
Small mines	....	....	a 1,688	6,000	6,000
Total	129,600	276,871	279,584	399,888	542,379

County.	1892.	1893.	1894.	1895.
	Short tons.	Short tons.	Short tons.	Short tons.
Franklin	....	9,879	147,728	252,938
Johnson	91,960	97,733		
Pope	17,500	12,250	17,788	
Sebastian	420,098	448,901	344,110	339,384
Small mines	6,000	6,000	6,000	6,000
Total	535,558	574,763	512,626	598,322

a Product of Franklin County according to Eleventh Census.

CALIFORNIA.

Total product in 1895, 75,453 short tons; spot value, $175,778.

California's coal product in 1895 shows an increase of 8,206 short tons, or about 12 per cent, over that of 1894. This was the first year since 1889 that an increase over the preceding year was obtained. In 1889, the year of largest production, the output was 121,820 short tons. Each succeeding year showed a steady decrease until 1894, when the product was 67,247 short tons, the smallest yield in any year of which there is any record, with one exception, 1887, when the output was reported at 50,000 tons.

The value of the product in 1895 was $175,778, against $155,620 in 1894, an increase of $20,158, or about 13 per cent.

The following tables exhibit the statistics of coal production in California during 1894 and 1895:

Coal product of California in 1894.

County.	Number of mines.	Loaded at mines for shipment.	Sold to local trade and used by employees.	Used at mines for steam and heat.	Total product.	Total value.	Average price per ton.	Average number of days active.	Average number of employees.
		Short tons	*Short tons*	*Short tons*	*Short tons*				
Contra Costa..	2	34,720	112	4,368	39,200	$99,310	$2.53	220	96
Amador.......									
Fresno........	4	18,016	8,031	2,000	28,017	56,310	2.01	270	29
San Diego.....									
Total....	6	52,736	8,143	6,368	67,247	155,620	2.31	232	125

Coal product of California in 1895, by counties.

County.	Number of mines.	Loaded at mines for shipment.	Sold to local trade and used by employees.	Used at mines for steam and heat.	Total product.	Total value.	Average price per ton.	Average number of days active.	Average number of employees.
		Short tons	*Short tons*	*Short tons*	*Short tons*				
Contra Costa...	2	41,220	1,191	2,842	45,253	$121,247	2.68	251	135
Amador									
Orange	3	19,220	10,980	....	30,200	54,531	1.81	288	55
Riverside......									
Total	5	60,440	12,171	2,842	75,453	175,778	2.33	262	190

The following table shows the total output of California since 1883, with the value when it has been reported, and the statistics of the number of employees and the average working time during the past six years:

Coal product of California since 1883.

Year.	Short tons.	Value.	Average price per ton.	Average number of days active.	Average number of employees.
1883..............	76,162	....	....	....	....
1884..............	77,485	....	....	....	....
1885..............	71,615	....	....	....	....
1886..............	100,000	$300,000	$3.00	....	....
1887..............	50,000	150,000	3.00	....	....
1888..............	95,000	380,000	4.00	....	....
1889..............	121,820	288,232	2.36	....	....
1890..............	110,711	283,019	2.56	301	364
1891..............	93,301	204,902	2.20	222	256
1892..............	85,178	209,711	2.46	204	187
1893..............	72,603	167,555	2.31	208	158
1894..............	67,247	155,620	2.31	232	125
1895..............	75,453	175,778	2.33	262	190

COLORADO.

Total product in 1895, 3,082,982 short tons; spot value, $3,675,185.

Of the coal-producing States west of the Mississippi River, Colorado stands in second place, being preceded by Iowa. She ranks tenth among the coal-mining States of the country. In 1894 the coal-mining interests of the State suffered severely from the effects of the great strike of that year, and the output decreased from 4,102,389 short tons to 2,831,409 short tons, a loss of 1,270,980 tons, or about 30 per cent. The industry recovered somewhat in 1895, gaining 251,573 tons on the output of 1894, but still falling more than a million tons short of the product of 1893.

The value of the product in 1895 was $158,845 more than in 1894, but less in proportion to the amount of coal produced, the average price per ton for the State declining from $1.24 in 1894 to $1.20 in 1895, due to the prevalent low values.

Among the important coal-producing counties of the State, Las Animas is by far the largest, yielding 40 per cent of the total product of the State, and more than the three next in importance combined. These are Huerfano, Boulder, and Fremont, in the order named, Huerfano having exchanged places with Boulder County in 1895.

The details of production during 1894 and 1895 will be found in the following tables:

Coal product of Colorado in 1894, by counties.

County.	Number of mines	Loaded at mines for shipment.	Sold to local trade and used by employees.	Used at mines for steam and heat.	Made into coke.	Total product.	Total value.	Average price per ton.	Average number of days active.	Average number of employees.
		Short tons.	*Short tons.*	*Short tons.*	*Short tons.*	*Short tons.*				
Arapahoe..	1	....	539	20	....	559	$839	$1.50	125	2
Boulder....	12	377,877	9,087	32,770	....	419,734	536,190	1.28	150	1,091
Delta	3	1,797	1,900	....	....	3,697	5,545	1.50	143	9
El Paso....	1	27,668	600	2,000	....	30,268	35,453	1.17	241	70
Fremont...	4	226,940	3,334	15,342	....	245,616	409,966	1.67	104	1,580
Garfield ...	2	73,335	32	2,296	....	75,663	85,767	1.13	142	122
Gunnison..	5	125,644	792	5,410	68,479	200,325	330,517	1.65	156	332
Huerfano..	6	373,199	1,766	33,080	....	408,045	441,130	1.08	186	753
Jefferson ..	2	30,000	1,108	3,000	....	34,108	68,216	2.00	162	25
La Plata...	6	41,672	8,519	302	3,078	53,571	87,346	1.63	46	349
Las Animas	10	807,772	14,658	14,984	316,449	1,153,863	1,167,174	1.01	199	1,699
Mesa	2	25,000	6,000	250	500	31,750	63,500	2.00	223	46
Montezuma	3	....	235	....	....	235	1,050	4.47	110	6
Montrose ..	1	....	100	....	....	100	125	1.25	80	1
Park......	1	28,094	....	849	....	28,943	91,170	3.15	231	108
Pitkin.....	1	2,793	67	2,111	92,753	97,724	110,117	1.13	266	535
Rio Blanco.	4	....	1,680	....	....	1,680	4,310	2.57	172	10
Routt......	12	560	2,150	....	....	2,710	3,853	1.42	75	24
Weld	3	38,697	4,121	....	....	42,818	74,072	1.73	145	145
Total ..	79	2,181,048	56,688	112,414	481,259	2,831,409	3,516,340	1.24	155	6,507

Coal product of Colorado in 1895, by counties.

County.	Number of mines	Loaded at mines for shipment.	Sold to local trade and used by employees.	Used at mines for steam and heat.	Made into coke.	Total product.	Total value.	Average price per ton.	Average number of days active.	Average number of employees.
		Short tons.	Short tons.	Short tons.	Short tons.	Short tons.				
Boulder....	13	356,360	7,755	13,280	....	377,395	$521,985	$1.38	160	868
Delta......	3	1,610	2,854	50	....	4,514	6,234	1.38	265	10
El Paso...	2	47,940	750	3,150	....	51,840	52,994	1.02	219	117
Fremont...	5	293,262	3,976	18,106	....	315,344	526,434	1.67	150	1,016
Garfield ...	3	152,345	204	12,379	109,343	274,271	293,926	1.07	246	398
Gunnison .	7	160,338	981	6,126	71,737	239,182	380,754	1.60	238	393
Huerfano..	6	354,744	2,056	29,896	....	386,696	402,905	1.04	167	816
La Plata...	7	92,528	8,431	310	4,830	106,099	155,107	1.42	80	502
Las Animas	9	922,861	11,354	15,583	303,351	1,253,149	1,212,527	.97	214	1,839
Mesa	2	40,000	1,000	150	....	41,150	77,225	1.88	290	47
Montezuma	3	....	190	....	....	190	790	4.16	54	5
Rio Blanco.	4	....	1,761	....	....	1,761	3,177	1.80	187	6
Routt......	16	....	2,752	15	....	2,767	4,396	1.59	63	27
Weld	5	23,590	4,344	....	....	27,934	35,306	1.26	220	74
Arapahoe.. } Montrose .. }	2	....	680	10	....	690	1,425	2.07	71	7
Total ..	87	2,445,578	49,088	99,055	489,261	3,082,982	3,675,185	1.20	182	6,125

In the table below is shown the total product of the State, by counties, since 1887, with the increases and decreases in 1895 as compared with 1894.

Coal product of Colorado since 1887, by counties.

[Short tons.]

County.	1887.	1888.	1889.	1890.	1891.	1892.
Arapahoe.....	16,000	1,700	823	700	1,273	654
Boulder	297,338	315,155	323,096	425,704	498,494	545,563
Dolores.......	1,000	200	....	800	3,475	....
El Paso.......	47,517	44,114	54,212	25,617	34,364	23,014
Fremont......	417,326	438,789	274,029	397,418	545,789	538,887
Garfield	30,000	115,000	239,292	183,884	191,994	277,794
Gunnison.....	243,122	258,374	252,442	229,212	261,350	225,260
Huerfano.....	131,810	159,610	333,717	427,832	494,466	541,733
Jefferson	12,000	9,000	10,790	10,984	17,910	21,219
Las Animas...	506,540	706,455	993,534	1,154,668	1,219,224	1,171,069
La Plata......	22,880	33,625	34,971	43,193	72,471	81,500
Mesa	....	300	1,100	1,000	5,000	5,050
Park	23,421	46,588	41,823	49,594	52,626	76,022
Pitkin........	4,000	28,113	....	74,362	91,642	....
Weld.........	39,281	28,054	28,628	46,417	22,554	2,205

Coal production of Colorado since 1887, by counties—Continued.

[Short tons.]

County.	1887.	1888.	1889.	1890.	1891	1872.
Routt			1,491	705	....	330
Larimer			100	1,500	....	
Douglas	3,500	400	260	700	....	200
San Miguel ...			1,800	1,500	....	
Delta.........			1,357	775	....	200
Montezuma...			816	238	....	30
Montrose						
Rio Blanco ...			2,900	200	....	100
Total...	1,795,735	2,185,477	2,597,181	3,077,003	3,512,632	3,510,830

County.	1893.	1894.	1895.	Increase in 1895.	Decrease in 1895.
Arapahoe	633	559	540	....	19
Boulder.......	663,220	419,734	377,395	....	42,339
Dolores					
El Paso	19,415	30,268	51,840	21,572	....
Fremont	536,787	245,616	315,344	69,728	....
Garfield.......	212,918	75,663	274,271	198,608	....
Gunnison	258,539	200,325	239,182	38,857	....
Huerfano	521,205	408,045	386,696	....	21,349
Jefferson......	1,895	34,108	....	....	34,108
Las Animas ...	1,587,338	1,153,863	1,253,149	99,286	....
La Plata......	104,992	53,571	106,099	52,528	....
Mesa..........	18,100	31,750	41,150	9,400	....
Park..........	39,095	28,943	....	....	28,943
Pitkin	99,211	97,724	....	....	97,724
Weld	35,355	42,818	27,934	....	14,884
Routt.........	816	2,710			
Larimer					
Douglas.......	200				
San Miguel....			9,382	960	....
Delta	2,580	3,697			
Montezuma ...	90	235			
Montrose......		100			
Rio Blanco....		1,680			
Total ...	4,102,389	2,831,409	3,082,982	a 251,573	....

a Net increase.

In connection with the above table it will be of interest to note the variations in the average prices in each county. The statistics of value by counties were not obtained prior to 1889, when the Eleventh Census was taken. Since that year, with the exception of 1891, the statistics have been collected in that way by the Geological Survey, and the average prices for six years are shown in the following table. Only those counties are considered whose product averages 10,000 tons or over:

Average prices for Colorado coal since 1889 in counties producing 10,000 tons or over.

County.	1889.	1890.	1892.	1893.	1894.	1895.
Boulder	$1.53	$1.32	$1.36	$1.28	$1.28	$1.38
El Paso	1.27	1.10	1.25	1.20	1.17	1.02
Fremont	2.12	1.54	1.92	1.60	1.67	1.67
Garfield	1.64	1.46	2.00	1.19	1.13	1.07
Gunnison	2.28	1.95	1.84	1.67	1.65	1.60
Huerfano	1.37	1.31	2.00	1.15	1.08	1.04
Jefferson	2.54	2.99	1.90	2.50	2.00	....
La Plata	1.91	2.76	1.76	1.45	1.63	1.42
Las Animas	1.16	1.16	1.22	1.01¼	1.01	.97
Park	2.49	3.00	2.40	2.50	3.15	....
Pitkin	....	1.45	....	1.12	1.13	....
Weld	1.51	1.38	2.00	1.49	1.73	1.26
The State	1.54	1.40	1.62	1.24	1.24	1.20

In the following table is shown the number of men employed during 1890, 1892, 1893, 1894, and 1895, in counties producing 10,000 tons or over, together with the average working time for the past four years:

Statistics of labor employed and working time at Colorado coal mines.

County.	1890.		1892.		1893.	
	Average number employed.	Average working days.	Average number employed.	Average working days.	Average number employed.	
Boulder	979	193	1,128	142	1,143	
El Paso	54	200	40	143	88	
Fremont	1,049	195	1,040	182	1,268	
Garfield	334	248	423	121	300	
Gunnison	389	259	368	168	576	
Huerfano	907	253	947	172	999	
Jefferson	79	233	50	250	7	
La Plata	97	288	124	235	152	
Las Animas	1,531	246	1,450	229	2,243	
Park	150	266	140	236	185	
Pitkin	96	....	....	211	115	
Weld	118	300	4	217	79	
The State	5,827	229	5,747	188	7,202	

Statistics of labor employed and working time at Colorado coal mines—Continued.

County.	1894.		1895.	
	Average working days.	Average number employed.	Average working days.	Average number employed.
Boulder	150	1,091	160	868
El Paso	241	70	219	117
Fremont	104	1,580	150	1,016
Garfield	142	122	246	398
Gunnison	156	332	238	393
Huerfano	186	753	167	816
Jefferson	162	25	....	....
La Plata	46	349	80	502
Las Animas	199	1,699	214	1,839
Park	231	108	....	....
Pitkin	266	135	....	....
Weld	145	145	220	74
The State	155	6,507	182	6,125

The State is divided, for sake of convenience, into four geographical divisions, known, respectively, as the northern, central, southern, and western. The first mentioned contains the counties of Arapahoe, Boulder, Jefferson, Larimer, Routt, and Weld. The central division embraces Douglas, El Paso, Fremont, and Park counties. The southern division contains the counties of Dolores, Huerfano, La Plata, and Las Animas, while Delta, Garfield, Gunnison, Mesa, Montezuma, Montrose, Pitkin, Rio Blanco, and San Miguel counties lie in the western district.

The following table shows the annual product of coal in Colorado since 1864, that for the years previous to 1877 being given by counties and subsequent to 1878 by districts:

Coal product of Colorado from 1864 to 1895.

Year.	Locality.	Product.
		Short tons.
1864	Jefferson and Boulder counties	500
1865	do	1,200
1866	do	6,100
1867	do	17,000
1868	do	10,500
1869	do	8,000
1870	do	13,500
1871	do	15,600

Coal product of Colorado from 1864 to 1885—Continued.

Year.	Locality.	Product.	
		Short tons.	
1872......	Jefferson and Boulder counties	14,200	
	Weld County............................	54,340	
			68,510
1873......	Jefferson and Boulder counties...........	14,000	
	Weld County............................	43,790	
	Las Animas and Fremont counties........	12,187	
			69,977
1874......	Jefferson and Boulder counties...........	15,000	
	Weld County............................	44,280	
	Las Animas and Fremont counties........	18,092	
			77,372
1875......	Jefferson and Boulder counties...........	23,700	
	Weld County............................	59,860	
	Las Animas and Fremont counties........	15,278	
			98,838
1876......	Jefferson and Boulder counties...........	28,750	
	Weld County............................	68,600	
	Las Animas and Fremont counties........	20,316	
			117,666
1877......	....	....	160,000
1878......	Northern division.......................	87,825	
	Central division........................	73,137	
	Southern division	39,668	
			200,630
1879......	Northern division.......................	182,630	
	Central division........................	70,647	
	Southern division	69,455	
			322,732
1880......	Northern division.......................	123,518	
	Central division........................	136,020	
	Southern division	126,403	
	Western division	1,064	
	Unreported mines	50,000	
			437,005
1881......	Northern division	156,126	
	Central division	174,882	
	Southern division	269,045	
	Western division	6,691	
	Unreported mines	100,000	
			706,744
1882......	Northern division	300,000	
	Central division	243,694	
	Southern division	474,285	
	Western division	43,500	
			1,061,479
1883......	Northern division	243,903	
	Central division	396,401	
	Southern division.......................	501,307	
	Western division	87,982	
			1,229,593

*Coal product of Colorado from 1864 to 1895—*Continued.

Year.	Locality.	Product.
		Short tons.
1884......	Northern division	253, 282
	Central division	296, 188
	Southern division	483, 865
	Western division	96, 689
		1, 130, 024
1885......	Northern division	242, 846
	Central division	416, 373
	Southern division	571, 684
	Western division	125, 159
		1, 356, 062
1886......	Northern division	260, 145
	Central division	408, 857
	Southern division	537, 785
	Western division	161, 551
		1, 368, 338
1887......	Northern division	364, 619
	Central division	491, 764
	Southern division	662, 230
	Western division	273, 122
		1, 791, 735
1888......	Northern division	353, 909
	Central division	529, 891
	Southern division	899, 690
	Western division	401, 987
		2, 185, 477
1889......	Northern division	364, 928
	Central division	370, 324
	Southern division	1, 362, 222
	Western division	499, 707
		2, 597, 181
1890......	Northern division	486, 010
	Central division	473, 329
	Southern division	1, 626, 493
	Western division	491, 171
		3, 077, 003
1891......	Northern division	540, 231
	Central division	632, 779
	Southern division	1, 789, 636
	Western division	549, 986
		3, 512, 632
1892......	Northern division	569, 971
	Central division	638, 123
	Southern division	1, 794, 302
	Western division	508, 434
		3, 510, 830
1893......	Northern division	701, 919
	Central division	694, 708
	Southern division	2, 213, 535
	Western division	492, 227
		4, 102, 389

Coal product of Colorado from 1864 to 1895—Continued.

Year.	Locality.	Product.	
		Short tons.	
1894......	Northern division	499,929	
	Central division	304,827	
	Southern division	1,615,479	
	Western division	411,174	
			2,831,409
1895......	Northern division	408,636	
	Central division	367,184	
	Southern division	1,745,944	
	Western division	561,218	
			3,082,982

GEORGIA.

Total product in 1895, 260,998 short tons; spot value, $215,863.

The entire product of Georgia continues to come from but two counties, Dade and Walker, which contain within their boundaries the northern extreme of the Warrior coal field of Alabama. The output in 1895 shows a decided decrease from that of 1894—93,113 short tons, or about 26 per cent. The production of the State has been nearly evenly divided between the two counties for the past three years, and the loss during 1895 was experienced in practically equal proportions by both. The following table exhibits the tendency of coal production in the State, with the distribution of the product, value, etc., since 1889:

Coal product of Georgia since 1889.

Year.	Loaded at mines for shipment.	Sold to local trade and used by employees.	Used at mines for steam and heat.	Made into coke.	Total product.	Total value.	Average price per ton.	Average number of days worked	Average number of employees
	Short tons.	*Short tons.*	*Short tons.*	*Short tons.*	*Short tons.*				
1889..........	46,131	158	15,000	164,645	225,934	$338,901	$1.50	....	......
1890..........	57,949	....	....	170,388	228,337	238,315	1.04	313	425
1891..........	15,000	1,000	5,000	150,000	171,000	256,500	1.50	312	850
1892..........	52,614	250	3,756	158,878	215,498	212,761	.99	277	467
1893..........	196,227	....	4,869	171,644	372,740	365,972	.98	342	736
1894..........	178,610	....	8,978	166,523	354,111	299,290	.85	304	729
1895..........	135,692	150	6,256	118,900	260,998	215,863	.83	312	a 848

a Includes 500 State convicts.

The following table shows the total annual product since 1884:

Coal product of Georgia since 1884.

Year.	Short tons.	Year.	Short tons.
1884	150,000	1890	228,337
1885	150,000	1891	171,000
1886	223,000	1892	215,498
1887	313,715	1893	372,740
1888	180,000	1894	354,111
1889	225,934	1895	260,998

ILLINOIS.

The fourteenth annual coal report of the statistics relating to the production of coal in the State of Illinois, and being for the year 1895, is herewith presented.

It is, necessarily, a continuation of the former reports on the same subject. The data upon which the calculations are based, the sources from which the information is obtained, as well as the method of arranging and tabulating the same, are identical with those of previous reports, thus presenting not only the most complete and accurate history of the subject possible for the past year, but allowing comparisons to be made through a long series of years, by which means averages and percentages may be obtained and conclusions reached which could be arrived at in no other way.

Those parts of the report which deal with the physical characteristics of the mines, such as the depths of shafts, thickness of seams, systems of working, ventilation, and equipments, are based upon observations made by the State inspectors of mines.

The information relating to the output of coal, its value, number of men employed, wages paid, etc., is furnished by the operators. Each mine reports the various facts which are used as a basis for the calculations to the State inspector of mines for the district in which the mine is located. The inspector, in turn, verifies the information, where possible, tabulates it upon blank schedules furnished for that purpose, assembles the individual mines by the counties in which they are located, and, finally, combines the whole into a recapitulation which embraces the entire district. From these schedules this report is compiled, and, as throughout the whole series of reports the data upon which the calculations are based, the sources of information, and the methods of computation have been uniform and practically identical, it may be assumed that the facts as given for any particular year, as well

---

[1] Abstracted from advance sheets of the report of Mr. George A. Schilling, secretary of the bureau of labor statistics of Illinois.

as the comparisons and deductions drawn from parallel tables extending through a long series of years, are accurate and trustworthy.

For detailed information in regard to the business of the past year reference must be had to the various tables which follow, and to the reports of the inspectors of mines for their respective districts, but an epitomized statement, which, for convenience, is compared with that of the year next preceding, will be found in the following summary:

Comparative statement of coal production in Illinois in 1894 and 1895.

Subject of inquiry.	1894.	1895.	Increase in 1895 over 1894.	Decrease in 1895 from 1894.
Number of counties in which coal is mined	56	54		2
Number of mines and openings of all kinds	836	847	11	
Number of shipping mines	319	319		
Number of mines in local trade	517	555	38	
Number of tons of coal mined, all grades	17,113,576	17,735,864	622,288	
Number of tons of lump coal (2,000 pounds)	13,865,284	14,045,962	180,678	
Number of tons of other grades of coal	3,248,292	3,689,902	441,610	
Number of tons of nut coal included in other grades	479,595	897,942	418,347	
Number of acres worked out (estimated)	2,818.01	2,950.69	138.68	
Numbers of employees of all kinds	38,477	38,630	153	
Number of miners	31,595	31,515		80
Number of other employees, including boys	6,882	7,115	233	
Number of boys over 14 years of age under ground	701	811	110	
Number of employees under ground	32,046	34,648	2,602	
Number of employees above ground	6,431	3,982		2,449
Average number of days active operation—shipping mines	183.1	182.2		.9
Aggregate home value of total product	$15,282,111	$14,239,157		$1,042,954
Aggregate home value of lump coal	$13,998,588	$13,090,836		$907,752
Aggregate value of other grades of coal	$1,283,531	$1,148,321		$135,210

Comparative statement of coal production in Illinois in 1894 and 1895—Continued.

Subject of inquiry.	1894.	1895.	Increase in 1895 over 1894.	Decrease in 1895 from 1894.
Average value of lump coal per ton at the mine	$1.0096	$0.932	....	$0.0776
Average value of other grades of coal at the mine	$0.3951	$0.349	....	$0.0461
Average price paid for hand mining—the year	$0.671	$0.573	....	$0.098
Average price paid for hand mining—summer	$0.6435	$0.516	....	$0.1275
Average price paid for hand mining—winter	$0.6847	$0.596		$0.887
Number of tons of lump coal mined by hand	7,368,850	7,868,006	499,156	....
Number of tons mined by hand—wages paid by the day	1,280,850	1,100,540	....	180,310
Number of tons mined by hand—paid by gross weight	2,727,331	2,934,998	207,667	....
Number of mining machines in use	296	322	26	....
Number of tons of coal, all grades, mined by machines	3,396,139	3,531,436	135,297	....
Number of tons of lump coal mined by machines	2,496,793	2,469,804	....	26,989
Number of tons of other grades mined by machines	758,781	824,235	65,454	....
Number of kegs of powder used	318,263	324,888	6,625	....
Number of men killed	72	75	3	....
Number of wives made widows	41	42	1	....
Number of children left fatherless	114	111	....	3
Number of men injured so as to lose time	521	605	84	....
Number of tons of coal mined to each life lost	237,689	236,478	....	1,211
Number of tons of coal mined to each man injured	32,817	29,312	....	3,535
Number of employees to each life lost	534	515		19
Number of employees to each man injured	74	64	....	10
Number of new mines opened and old ones reopened	156	115		46
Number of mines closed or abandoned	108	78	....	30

There are two less coal-producing counties this year than last. The two counties to drop out are Cumberland, in the fourth district, and Franklin, in the fifth, but the amount of coal produced in these counties was insignificant, and was never great enough to be a factor in any of the calculations. The same may be said of several other counties which lie adjacent to the large coal-producing counties, and in which mining is carried on in a small and intermittent way, so that the number of coal-producing counties in the State is liable to fluctuations from year to year without in any way affecting the general results.

The total production of coal for the year was 17,735,864 tons, an excess of 622,288 tons over that of 1894, and the largest in the history of the State with the single exception of 1893, when the total output was 19,949,564 tons. The increase of tonnage for 1895 was mainly in the second and fourth districts, which show an increase, respectively, of 291,675 and 439,461 tons. The first district also gained slightly, recording 50,467 more tons than last year; while in the third and fifth districts there was a loss of 125,658 and 33,657 tons, respectively.

While the tonnage of 1895 is larger than that of 1894, the prices have not been so satisfactory; the aggregate value, at the mine, of the total product for the past year being $14,239,157, as against $15,282,111 for the previous year. Upon whom this loss fell is shown by the fact that, while the operators received an average of 7.76 cents less per ton for the coal, the miners were paid an average of 9.81 cents less per ton for mining it.

The total number of men employed in and about the mines was 38,630, the largest in the history of the State, but the average number of days of active operation was the lowest recorded.

The total number of mining machines in use in 1895 was 322, an increase of 26 over 1894. Their use is confined, as in former years, entirely to the thick seams in the third, fourth, and fifth districts. The number of mines which use machines exclusively in the production of coal is 32, and these are confined to seven counties. These few mines use 283 machines, or 88 per cent of the entire number in use in the State.

The most deplorable feature of the year's record is the large number of accidents that have occurred. The mine inspectors have insisted on a more careful reporting of casualties, and their requirements have been generally observed and complied with, especially in localities where various forms of casualty insurance is carried by the miners. But this alone does not account for the increase in the number of accidents reported; nor has this increase, steady and constant through the series of years, merely kept pace with, it has outrun, the increase in tonnage.

During the ten years next preceding this report there has been an average of 270,473 tons of coal produced for each life lost. In 1895 75 men were killed, one for every 236,478 tons mined; 144 persons were left helpless and dependent, widowed and fatherless by these accidents—one for every 123,166 tons of coal produced.

NUMBER AND RANK OF MINES.

The following table shows the rank of the mines throughout the State, the shipping mines being mainly large concerns with costly plants, while the local mines are, for the most part, small, and with an output comparatively insignificant.

Keeping this fact in mind, it will be seen that the fluctuation in the number of local mines, from year to year, is of comparatively small importance, and, though the whole number of mines is greater by 11 than last year, the increase has been wholly in the number of local mines and the total output remains practically unchanged.

Taking the mines by districts, we find that there was a decrease in the number of shipping mines in the first and third districts, which was offset by an increase in the second, fourth, and fifth.

Number of shipping coal mines in Illinois, 1887 to 1895, by districts.

Year.	First.		Second.		Third.		Fourth.		Fifth.		Total.	
	Shipping.	Local.	Shipping.	Local.	Shipping.	Local.	Shipping.	Local.	Shipping.	Local.	Shipping.	Local.
1887	44	24	30	245	77	159	58	53	83	35	292	516
1888	37	33	32	235	81	156	57	51	106	45	313	520
1889	36	36	31	233	89	157	57	41	119	55	332	522
1890	37	42	32	222	93	180	55	82	110	83	327	609
1891	38	32	31	233	90	183	56	70	112	73	327	591
1892	37	33	30	210	85	171	57	52	101	63	310	529
1893	38	33	27	197	84	152	59	45	102	51	310	478
1894	39	33	32	209	84	167	66	64	98	44	319	517
1895	a33	49	34	212	79	183	67	67	106	44	a319	555
Averages	38	35	31	222	85	168	59	58	104	55	317	537
Increase		25	4		2	24	9	14	23	9	27	39
Decrease	11			33								

a Includes one mine abandoned late in the year.

The two following tables, in which the mines of the State are classified according to their tonnage, will be of interest, both as showing the location and grouping of the different classes of mines, and indicating the correctness of the conclusions deduced from the foregoing tables. It will be seen that, dividing the mines into two classes—those producing less and those producing more than 50,000 tons—the fourth district has much the larger number of the more extensive plants, though standing third in the total number of mines, and the second district, standing nearly at the top of the list as regards the number of mines, stands last in the number of mines with an output of over 50,000 tons. These tables also show that the variation in the number of large mines

17 GEOL, PT 3——25

is inconsiderable and has shown a steady and very uniform, if slow, growth through the series of years, reaching the climax in 1893, and falling in 1894 from the effects of the labor troubles and general business depression, but at present stationary.

Classification of Illinois coal mines according to output of lump coal.

District.	Number of mines producing—								
	Less than 1,000 tons.			From 1,000 to 10,000 tons.			From 10,000 to 50,000 tons.		
	1893.	1894.	1895.	1893.	1894.	1895.	1893.	1894.	1895.
First	12	11	16	23	24	30	15	17	16
Second	131	133	130	71	88	94	12	11	7
Third	96	103	113	74	89	100	52	44	35
Fourth	21	50	45	29	21	19	14	28	27
Fifth	25	18	21	40	32	39	53	69	66
The State	285	315	325	237	254	282	146	169	151
Increase		30	10		17	28		23	
Decrease	50				5			8	18
Per cent of increase		10.5	3.1		7.2	11.02		15.8	
Per cent of decrease	14.9			2.1			5.2		10.65

District.	Number of mines producing—								
	From 50,000 to 100,000 tons.			Over 100,000 tons.			Total number of mines.		
	1893.	1894.	1895.	1893.	1894.	1895.	1893.	1894.	1895.
First	10	11	11	11	9	7	71	72	80
Second	4	4	7	6	5	5	224	241	243
Third	11	12	10	3	3	4	236	251	262
Fourth	26	20	22	14	11	11	101	130	124
Fifth	29	19	17	6	4	3	153	142	146
The State	80	66	67	40	32	30	788	836	b855
Increase	11		1	1				a48	a19
Decrease		14			8	2	a51		
Per cent of increase	15.9		1.5	2.6				a6.09	a2.3
Per cent of decrease		17.5			20.		6.2	a6.8	

a Net increase and net decrease in the total mines of each year compared with the year previous.
b Nineteen mines which failed to report tonnage are omitted; real total is 874.

Classification of Illinois coal mines according to output of lump coal for thirteen years.

Year.	Less than 1,000 tons.	From 1,000 to 10,000 tons.	From 10,000 to 50,000 tons.	From 50,000 to 100,000 tons.	Over 100,000 tons.	Total number of mines.	Increase.	Decrease.
			Number of mines producing—					
1883...............	209	233	133	39	25	639	....	....
1884...............	262	273	148	38	20	741	102	....
1885...............	286	290	143	40	19	778	37	....
1886...............	316	280	135	44	14	789	11	....
1887...............	320	278	141	42	20	801	12	....
1888...............	327	271	151	47	25	822	21	....
1889...............	321	316	139	55	23	854	32	....
1890...............	398	301	155	54	28	936	82	....
1891...............	405	263	164	55	31	918	....	18
1892...............	335	242	154	69	39	839	....	79
1893...............	285	237	146	80	40	788	....	51
1894...............	315	254	169	66	32	836	48	....
1895...............	325	282	151	67	30	a 855	19	....
Increase 1895 over 1883............	116	49	18	28	5	216	364	148
Per cent of increase..........	55.02	21	15	71.7	20	33.08	....	....

a Nineteen mines which failed to report tonnage are omitted; real total is 874.

Using the same classification as in preceding tables, the following will show the proportion of total output produced by each class of mines. The tonnage here given is for the total amount of lump coal which is the standard, commercial grade of coal, and in tons of 2,000 pounds. It will be noticed that those mines which produce less than 10,000 tons, though constituting over 70 per cent of the whole number, yield only 7.36 per cent of the total product, and this proportion has been very uniform throughout a period of five years.

Classification of the lump-coal product of Illinois in 1895.

District.	Over 100,000 tons.		From 50,000 to 100,000 tons.		From 10,000 to 50,000 tons.		Less than 10,000 tons.		Total number of mines and tons.	
	No.	Tons.	No.	Tons.	No.	Tons.	No.	Tons.	No.	Tons.
			Lump coal, mines producing—							
First............	7	994,695	11	866,173	16	339,249	46	92,286	80	2,294,063
Second..........	5	707,319	7	529,908	7	122,542	224	313,227	243	1,673,056
Third............	4	691,778	10	730,035	35	733,980	213	387,724	262	2,543,517
Fourth	11	1,683,202	22	1,584,225	27	802,017	64	85,096	124	4,154,538
Fifth	3	393,603	17	1,196,038	66	1,636,962	60	154,185	146	3,380,788
The State..	30	4,470,737	67	1,906,444	151	3,634,750	607	1,032,518	a 855	14,045,962

Classification of the lump-coal product of Illinois—Continued.

MINES AND AVERAGES.

Year.	Lump coal, mines producing—								Total number of mines and tons.	
	Over 100,000 tons.		From 50,000 to 100,000 tons.		From 10,000 to 50,000 tons.		Less than 10,000 tons.			
	No.	Tons.	No.	Tons.	No.	Tons.	No.	Tons.	No.	Tons.
1895.............	30	149,025	67	73,230	151	24,071	607	1,701	a855	16,428
1894.............	32	132,768	66	68,748	169	24,599	569	1,621	836	16,585
1893.............	40	150,287	80	69,443	146	25,200	522	1,667	788	20,488
1892.............	39	142,077	69	67,787	154	23,272	577	1,610	839	17,558
1891.............	31	137,855	55	69,745	164	23,015	668	1,564	918	14,118

PERCENTAGES.

Year.	P.ct.	Per cent.	P.ct.	Per cent.	P.ct.	Per cent.	P.ct.	Per cent.	P.ct.	Per cent.
1895.............	3.5	31.83	7.8	34.93	17.7	25.89	71	7.36	100	100
1894.............	3.8	30.6	7.9	32.7	20.2	30	68.1	6.7	100	100
1893.............	5.1	37.3	10.2	31.5	18.5	22.8	66.2	5.4	100	100
1892.............	4.6	37.6	8.2	31.8	18.4	24.3	68.8	6.3	100	100
1891.............	3.4	33	6	29.6	17.9	29.1	72.8	8.3	100	100

a Nineteen mines which failed to report tonnage are omitted as follows: First district, 2; second district, 3; fourth district, 10; fifth district, 4.

Again dividing the mines into two classes, those producing more and those producing less than 50,000 tons, we find that the former class, comprising 11.35 per cent of the whole number, produces 66.76 per cent of the entire yield of coal—an average of 96,672 tons to each mine—while those mines in the latter class, constituting 88.65 per cent of the whole number, produce only 33.23 per cent of the whole, which very closely coincides with the percentages for the period of nine years as shown.

Annual lump-coal product of Illinois since 1887.

Year.	Mines producing over 50,000 tons of lump coal.				
	Number.	Short tons.	Average number of tons per mine.	Per cent of whole number of mines.	Per cent of total product.
1887.....................	62	5,949,894	95,966	7.74	57.90
1888.....................	72	7,188,507	99,840	8.76	60.61
1889.....................	78	7,235,577	92,764	9.13	62.39
1890.....................	81	8,011,777	98,911	8.65	63.39
1891.....................	86	8,109,485	94,296	9.37	62.57
1892.....................	108	10,218,279	94,614	12.87	69.37
1893.....................	120	11,563,728	96,364	15.23	71.77

*Annual lump-coal product of Illinois since 1887—*Continued.

Mines producing over 50,000 tons of lump coal.

Year.	Number.	Short tons.	Average number of tons per mine.	Per cent of whole number of mines.	Per cent of total product.
1894	98	8,785,908	89,652	11.72	63.37
1895	a 97	9,377,181	96,672	11.35	66.76
Average 9 years	82	8,555,037	95,453		
Percentage 9 years				10.49	64.73
Average 8 years	88	8,382,894	95,125		
Percentage 8 years				10.38	64.46
Average 7 years	87	8,325,321	96,009		
Percentage 7 years				10.19	64.63
Average 6 years	81	7,785,587	95,921		
Percentage 6 years				9.42	63.07

Mines producing less than 50,000 tons of lump coal.

Year.	Number.	Short tons.	Average number of tons per mine.	Per cent of whole number of mines.	Per cent of total product.
1887	739	4,328,996	5,858	92.26	42.10
1888	750	4,666,681	6,222	91.25	39.36
1889	776	4,362,386	5,622	90.87	37.61
1890	855	4,626,587	5,411	91.35	36.61
1891	832	4,850,739	5,883	90.63	37.43
1892	731	4,512,684	6,173	87.13	30.63
1893	668	4,549,171	6,810	84.77	28.23
1894	738	5,079,376	6,883	88.28	36.63
1895	a 758	4,667,268	6,157	88.65	33.23
Average 9 years	761	4,627,099	6,085		
Percentage 9 years				89.52	35.27
Average 8 years	786	4,622,078	6,073		
Percentage 8 years				89.62	35.54
Average 7 years	764	4,556,749	6,148		
Percentage 7 years				89.81	35.37
Average 6 years	781	4,558,012	5,840		
Percentage 6 years				90.58	36.93

a Nineteen mines which failed to report tonnage are omitted throughout.

The three following tables give detailed information concerning shipping and local mines and their relative importance as factors in the production of coal.

The first table deals with shipping mines, the whole number of which is 319, the same as 1894; this number, however, includes one mine which, though active through the greater part of the year, was abandoned toward its close. This class comprises 36.5 per cent of all the mines, as against 38.2 per cent in 1894, and furnishes 93.5 per cent of the total product as against 94.1 per cent the preceding year. The aggregate number of tons is 472.277 more than 1894; the average number of tons per mine is 668 greater, while the average number of running days is three less.

The second table is a parallel table dealing with local mines. The whole number in this class is 555, or 38 more than 1894. This class comprises 63.5 per cent of the whole number of mines as against 61.8 per cent in 1894, and furnishes 6.5 per cent of the total tonnage as against 5.9 the previous year. The total tonnage of this class of mines exceeds that of 1894 by 150,011 tons, the average per mine is practically the same (12 tons less), and the average number of running days is two less.

Statistics of production in Illinois, by shipping mines, in 1895.

District.		Shipping mines.						
	Number.	Total output, all grades.	Total lump coal.	Per cent of whole number of mines.	Per cent of total tonnage.	Per cent of total lump.	Average number of tons of lump coal per mine.	Average number of days worked.
		Tons.	*Tons.*					
First a........	33	2,564,276	2,137,186	40.3	93.7	93.2	64,763	145
Second	34	1,731,587	1,416,544	13.8	86.8	84.7	41,663	161
Third.........	79	2,675,458	2,278,335	30.2	90.6	89.6	28,840	157
Fourth	67	5,555,219	4,096,993	50	99	98.6	61,149	186
Fifth b	106	4,052,350	3,085,191	70.7	91.3	91.3	29,953	182
The State...	319	16,578,890	13,014,249	36.5	93.5	92.7	41,184	171

a Includes one mine abandoned during the year.   b Three mines made no report.

Statistics of production in Illinois, by local mines, in 1895.

District.		Local mines.						
	Number.	Total output, all grades.	Total lump coal.	Per cent of whole number of mines.	Per cent of total tonnage.	Per cent of total lump.	Average number of tons of lump coal per mine.	Average number of days worked.
		Tons.	*Tons.*					
First a	49	171,435	156,877	59.7	6.3	6.8	3,338	182
Second........	212	263,711	256,512	86.2	13.2	15.3	1,210	145
Third.........	183	276,802	265,182	69.8	9.4	10.4	1,449	165
Fourth	67	57,545	57,545	50	1	1.4	859	118
Fifth b	44	387,481	295,597	29.3	8.7	8.7	6,874	174
The State.	555	1,156,974	1,031,713	63.5	6.5	7.3	1,869	155

a One mine made no report.   b One new mine made no report.

The following is a condensation of the two preceding tables and a comparison of percentages and averages through a period of six years.

This illustrates the uniformity, both in number and product, of the more important mines throughout the State, as well as the constant character of the ratio between the two classes.

It will be noticed that the percentage of tons of lump coal in the shipping mines is slightly and uniformly below that of the total product, while in the local mines the reverse is true.

Percentage of coal product, by shipping and local mines, in Illinois for six years.

Year.	Shipping mines.					Local mines.				
	Number.	Per cent of whole number of mines.	Per cent of total product.	Per cent of lump coal.	Average number of lump tons per mine.	Number.	Per cent of whole number of mines.	Per cent of total product.	Per cent of lump coal.	Average number of lump tons per mine.
			Tons.					*Tons.*		
1890.....	327	34.9	93.6	......	34,176	609	65.1	6.4	......	1,328
1891.....	327	35.6	95.5	92	37,850	591	64.4	4.5	8	987
1892.....	309	36.8	95.1	94	45,356	530	63.2	4.9	6	1,295
1893.....	310	39.3	96.5	96	49,776	478	60.7	3.5	4	1,427
1894.....	319	38.2	94.1	93	40,416	517	61.8	5.9	7	1,881
1895...: .	a 319	36.5	93.5	92.7	41,184	555	63.5	6.5	7.3	1,869

a Includes one mine abandoned during the year.

OUTPUT FOR THE YEAR.

The total amount of lump coal produced in 1895 was 14,045,962 tons, a gain of 180,678 tons over 1894. This gain was wholly in the second and fourth districts, the others showing a loss. The following table is a comparative statement of the output of lump coal for the State and by districts for a period of six years. For this period the State, as a whole, shows an increase of 1,085,738 tons in the output, and this gain is shared by all the districts except the first, which alone shows a steady decline:

Total tonnage of lump coal, with gains and losses, for six years, by districts.

District.	Output of lump coal, by districts.				
	1890.	1891.	1892.	1893.	1894.
	Tons.	*Tons.*	*Tons.*	*Tons.*	*Tons.*
First........	2,303,326	3,701,652	2,965,067	2,913,144	2,367,298
Second.....	1,002,600	1,215,883	1,461,224	1,708,909	1,449,356
Third	2,375,970	2,336,500	2,711,574	2,860,299	2,569,268
Fourth.....	3,716,464	3,532,233	4,090,921	4,508,382	4,877,110
Fifth	3,240,004	3,173,956	3,502,177	4,122,165	3,602,252
Total ..	12,638,316	12,960,224	14,730,963	16,112,899	13,865,284
Net gain ...	a 1,040,401	321,860	1,770,739	1,381,936	....
Net loss	....	....	....	....	2,247,615

a Gain over 1889.

Total tonnage of lump coal, with gains and losses, for six years, by districts—Continued.

District.	1895.	1893-94.		1894-95.	
		Gain.	Loss.	Gain.	Loss.
	Tons.	*Tons.*	*Tons.*	*Tons.*	*Tons.*
First.......	2,294,063	....	545,846	....	73,235
Second.....	1,673,056	....	259,553	223,700	....
Third	2,543,517	....	291,031	....	25,751
Fourth.....	4,154,538	....	631,272	277,428	....
Fifth	3,380,788*	....	519,913	....	221,464
Total ..	14,045,962	....	2,247,615	501,128	320,450
Net gain ...	180,678	....	....	180,678	....
Net loss	....	....	2,247,615	....	....

To illustrate this subject more thoroughly, the following table gives the percentages of increase or decrease in output of lump coal for the State and by districts for a period of seven years. In order that the comparison may be more exhaustive and the variations be located more exactly, the average percentages for periods of seven, six, five, and four years are also given:

Percentages of increase and decrease in tonnage of lump coal for seven years (1889–1895), by districts.

Year.	First district.		Second district.		Third district.	
	Increase.	Decrease.	Increase.	Decrease.	Increase.	Decrease.
1889.........................	13.73	....	18.14	....		6.91
1890.........................	9.86	....	8.5		15.88	....
1891.....................	17.29	....	21.27	....	....	1.26
1892.........................	9.75	....	18.53	....	16.05	....
1893.........................	1.78	....	16.95	....	5.48	....
1894.........................	18.74	....	15.19	....	....	10.18
1895.........................	3.09	....	15.43	....	1	....
Seven years	20.28	....	27.83	....	16.03	....
Six years...........	17.74	....	31.71	....	17.2	....
Five years........	1.23	....	32.15	....	30.57	
Four years	3.03	....	12.99	....	23.7	....

Percentages of increase and decrease in tonnage of lump coal for seven years (1889-1895), by districts—Continued.

Year.	Fourth district.		Fifth district.		The State.	
	Increase.	Decrease.	Increase.	Decrease.	Increase.	Decrease.
1889	10.88	....	4.81	....	....	2.22
1890	17.43	....	17.2	....	8.97	....
1891	....	5.22	....	2.08	2.55	....
1892	15.82	....	10.34	....	13.51	....
1893	10.2	....	17.7	....	9.38	....
1894	....	14	....	12.61	....	13.95
1895	7.16	....	....	6.15	1.3	....
Seven years	45.89	....	28.18	....	18.48	....
Six years	35.82	....	36.58	....	16.96	....
Five years	57.94	....	56.28	....	35.93	....
Four years	43.31	....	32.78	....	24.26	....

The total output of coal for the State is 17,735,864 tons, leaving 3,689,902 tons other than lump coal. Much of this is of a merchantable quality, but it brings much less per ton in the market than lump. The following table will show the total product of the State by districts, together with the percentage of lump coal to the whole, and for a period of five years. It will be seen that the percentage for the State is the smallest for the entire period, and that the third district was the only one to gain in this respect, though the fourth is very nearly the same, the decimal being in favor of 1894. For the State the percentage of nut and other grades is 20.75, as against 18.98 in 1894.

Total product and percentage of lump coal for five years.

District.	1891.		1892.		1893.	
	Total product.	Percentage of lump grade.	Total product.	Percentage of lump grade.	Total product.	Percentage of lump grade.
	Tons.		Tons.		Tons.	
First	3,082,915	87.63	3,458,066	85.74	3,394,686	85.81
Second	1,440,266	82.73	1,733,608	84.29	2,000,664	85.42
Third	2,794,004	83.54	3,260,951	83.15	3,397,433	84.19
Fourth	4,428,109	79.64	5,117,600	79.94	5,784,866	77.93
Fifth	3,915,404	81.06	4,292,051	81.60	5,371,915	76.73
The State	15,660,698	82.76	17,862,276	82.47	19,949,564	80.77

Total product and percentage of lump coal for five years—Continued.

District.	1894.		1895.	
	Total product.	Percentage of lump grade.	Total product.	Percentage of lump grade.
	Tons.		*Tons.*	
First	2,685,244	88.16	2,735,711	83.86
Second	1,703,623	85.07	1,995,298	83.85
Third	3,077,918	83.47	2,952,260	86.15
Fourth	5,173,303	74.95	5,612,764	74.02
Fifth	4,473,488	80.52	4,439,831	76.15
The State	17,113,576	81.02	17,735,864	79.25

Continuing and extending the investigation, the following table shows the total tonnage, all grades, and also the whole number of mines operated and men employed each year for a period of fourteen years. It will be seen that the industry has made great advancement in this time.

The increase in the number of mines has been 170; in the output, 6,718,795 tons, and in the number of men employed, 18,340.

Although the number of men employed is greater, they have averaged less days' work in the year and for less remuneration.

In 1882 the miners received an average of over 80 cents per ton for mining coal, and produced an average of 543 tons to each man, while in 1895 they received an average of a little over 57 cents per ton and produced an average of only 445 tons per man, a decrease in earnings of over 58 per cent.

Total number of mines, men, and product, lump and other grades, since 1882.

Year.	Whole number of mines.	Whole number of men employed.	Total product in tons (2,000 pounds).	Total tons of lump coal.	Total tons of other grades.
1882	704	20,290	11,017,069	9,115,653	1,901,506
1883	639	23,939	12,123,456	10,030,991	2,092,465
1884	741	25,575	12,208,075	10,101,005	2,107,070
1885	778	25,946	11,834,459	9,791,874	2,402,585
1886	787	25,846	11,175,241	9,246,435	1,928,806
1887	801	26,804	12,423,066	10,278,890	2,144,176
1888	822	29,410	14,328,181	11,855,188	2,472,993
1889	854	30,076	14,017,298	11,597,963	2,419,335
1890	936	28,574	15,274,727	12,638,364	2,636,363
1891	918	32,951	15,660,698	12,960,224	2,700,474
1892	839	33,632	17,062,276	14,730,963	3,131,313
1893	788	35,390	19,949,564	16,112,899	3,836,655
1894	836	38,477	17,113,576	13,865,284	3,248,292
1895	871	38,630	17,735,864	14,045,962	3,689,902

The following table, being a list of the counties which have produced over 200,000 tons of coal in the past year, will indicate and locate the activity of this industry in the various portions of the State. It will be noted that Macoupin County has again passed St. Clair, and that while there are, as in 1894, six counties each producing more than 1,000,000 tons, Christian County has dropped out of this class, and her place has been taken by Vermilion. This list contains 21 counties, as against 20 last year, Marshall County having been added:

Counties which have produced more than 200,000 tons of coal, arranged in order of their rank, for the years 1894 and 1895.

	Year 1894.				Year 1895.		
District.	County.	Rank.	Total product, all grades.	District.	County.	Rank.	Total product, all grades.
			Tons.				Tons.
5	St. Clair........	1	1,623,684	4	Macoupin	1	1,948,992
4	Macoupin	2	1,575,045	5	St. Clair.......	2	1,479,106
4	Sangamon.....	3	1,142,299	4	Sangamon.....	3	1,318,092
1	Lasalle........	4	1,134,097	1	Grundy	4	1,261,838
1	Grundy	5	1,130,420	3	Vermilion	5	1,177,375
4	Christian......	6	1,005,500	1	Lasalle........	6	1,084,552
3	Vermilion	7	989,813	4	Madison.......	7	978,161
4	Madison.......	8	889,768	2	Bureau........	8	834,541
2	Bureau........	9	878,937	5	Jackson.......	9	739,661
5	Jackson.......	10	766,514	4	Christian......	10	735,361
3	Peoria	11	611,792	5	Perry	11	587,444
3	Fulton	12	557,703	5	Marion........	12	538,900
5	Perry	13	530,490	3	Fulton	13	468,792
5	Marion........	14	478,757	2	Mercer	14	462,011
5	Williamson....	15	437,157	5	Williamson....	15	461,475
2	Mercer	16	374,003	3	Peoria	16	437,457
1	Livingston	17	342,127	2	Marshall	17	346,281
3	Menard	18	295,852	5	Clinton	18	284,487
4	Macon	19	227,820	3	Menard	19	277,738
5	Clinton	20	200,920	1	Livingston	20	267,133
				4	Macon	21	231,000
	Total..........		15,192,698		Total..........		15,920,397

In order that the comparisons may be complete, the following table gives a list of all the counties which have produced over 200,000 tons in any one year for the past five years, their average production per year for five years, and their rank as determined thereby:

Rank of counties according to output of all grades of coal for five years.

District.	County.	Rank of counties for the year—					Rank for average tons for five years.	Average tons of counties for five years.
		1891.	1892.	1893.	1894.	1895.		
4	Macoupin	2	1	2	2	1	1	1,759,317
5	St. Clair	1	2	1	1	2	2	1,718,464
1	Lasalle	3	3	3	4	6	3	1,327,191
4	Sangamon	4	5	4	3	3	4	1,202,671
1	Grundy	5	4	5	5	4	5	1,135,234
3	Vermilion	6	6	7	7	5	6	1,003,402
2	Bureau	9	7	6	9	8	7	900,262
4	Madison	7	8	8	8	7	8	882,580
4	Christian	8	10	11	6	10	9	813,238
5	Jackson	10	9	9	10	9	10	796,758
5	Perry	11	14	10	13	11	11	608,661
3	Fulton	13	11	12	12	13	12	589,916
3	Peoria	12	12	13	11	16	13	573,291
5	Marion	15	15	15	14	12	14	439,271
1	Livingston	14	13	14	17	20	15	428,554
5	Williamson	20	17	16	15	15	16	369,199
2	Mercer	16	16	17	16	14	17	368,424
2	Marshall					17	18	346,281
3	Menard	21	18	18	18	19	19	269,101
5	Clinton			20	20	18	20	246,834
4	Macon	19	19	19	19	21	21	234,672
1	Will	17					22	233,603
3	McLean	18	20	21			23	219,109
	Total	21	20	21	20	21	23	15,815,750

In the following table will be found all the coal-producing counties of the State, named and assembled by districts, together with the output of each in the different grades of coal from 1887 to 1895:

Output of coal in Illinois, by counties, for nine years.

District.	Lump coal.		
	1887.	1888.	1889.
	Short tons.	*Short tons.*	*Short tons.*
First district	2,686,829	2,877,794	2,530,453
Counties:			
Grundy......................	792,954	862,866	698,033
Kankakee	97,000	82,000	67,380
Lasalle	1,125,235	1,090,435	1,039,703
Livingston	387,600	495,388	382,965
Will........................	284,040	347,105	342,372
Second district..................	1,069,027	1,293,187	1,087,848
Counties:			
Bureau	459,580	635,097	493,730
Hancock.....................	6,208	6,515	6,028
Henry	117,533	108,831	101,716
Knox	64,324	57,013	57,588
Marshall....................	73,928	87,013	59,784
McDonough	110,103	104,274	98,386
Mercer	127,708	167,931	175,690
Rock Island	85,282	57,872	47,363
Schuyler	22,686	34,403	16,243
Stark.......................	17,865	18,690	19,171
Warren.....................	13,810	15,518	12,149
Third district....................	1,781,395	2,192,121	2,050,349
Counties:			
Cass	2,325	7,300	4,414
Fulton......................	337,215	461,589	366,577
Logan	159,000	174,330	138,700
McLean	141,700	117,110	129,322
Menard.....................	155,621	181,075	181,621
Peoria......................	452,123	533,817	454,731
Tazewell	51,847	59,324	67,973
Vermilion	359,119	499,076	537,411
Woodford...................	122,415	158,500	169,600

Output of coal in Illinois, by counties, for nine years—Continued.

District.	Lump coal.		
	1887.	1888.	1889.
	Short tons.	*Short tons.*	*Short tons.*
Fourth district..............	2,568,291	2,854,540	3,164,835
Counties:			
Bond	36,076	38,200	59,724
Calhoun	....	1,036	1,078
Christian	149,973	147,030	249,774
Coles	34,612	27,210	....
Effingham	....	....	....
Greene...................	12,578	14,494	19,048
Jasper...................			
Jersey	2,684	3,949	4,040
Macon	118,183	280,805	233,309
Macoupin................	926,588	1,016,624	1,202,187
Madison	521,705	512,948	490,181
Montgomery	10,220	14,295	24,425
Morgan..................	6,669	12,545	13,019
Pike.....................			
Richland	....	....	
Sangamon	730,391	764,970	846,012
Scott	9,802	12,491	15,028
Shelby	8,810	7,943	7,010
Fifth district	2,173,348	2,637,546	2,764,478
Counties:			
Clinton...................	55,238	66,463	121,557
Franklin.................	....	....	....
Gallatin	31,437	45,374	30,044
Hardin	....	....	....
Hamilton	....	....	....
Johnson	28,000	28,210	3,000
Jackson	375,718	445,575	477,474
Jefferson			
Marion	98,915	156,975	180,777
Perry....................	319,552	306,235	381,347
Randolph................	74,263	167,321	98,202
Saline	19,518	32,550	35,496
St. Clair	1,018,149	1,184,579	1,198,100
Washington	40,220	43,600	36,220
Williamson	112,338	160,664	202,261
State totals..............	10,278,890	11,855,188	11,597,963

Output of coal in Illinois, by counties, for nine years—Continued.

District.	Lump coal.		1891—All grades.
	1890.	1891.	
	Short tons.	*Short tons.*	*Short tons.*
First district................	2,303,326	2,701,652	3,082,915
Counties:			
Grundy..................	654,017	861,507	921,907
Kankakee	62,460	84,808	90,908
Lasalle	926,214	1,174,961	1,378,168
Livingston..............	372,504	355,800	458,329
Will....................	288,131	224,576	233,603
Second district..............	1,002,600	1,215,883	1,440,266
Counties:			
Bureau	372,701	612,292	701,064
Hancock................	6,948	6,740	6,740
Henry	98,734	116,173	131,986
Knox	51,653	44,974	44,974
Marshall...............	56,574	53,319	65,219
McDonough.............	83,401	73,596	81,732
Mercer.................	238,290	222,237	314,360
Rock Island............	39,696	38,654	41,540
Schuyler...............	21,836	15,369	20,122
Stark..................	18,672	20,157	20,157
Warren................	14,095	12,372	12,372
Third district..............	2,375,970	2,336,500	2,794,004
Counties:			
Cass	4,650	5,680	6,466
Fulton	404,417	391,721	484,117
Logan..................	164,650	155,048	176,052
McLean	173,492	184,629	230,129
Menard	230,662	171,784	204,583
Peoria.................	482,725	498,601	564,119
Tazewell	81,141	85,692	107,252
Vermilion	704,509	728,156	880,466
Woodford	129,724	115,189	140,820
Fourth district..............	3,716,464	3,532,233	4,428,109
Counties:			
Bond...................	66,746	76,067	102,535
Calhoun................	1,468	2,773	2,773
Christian...............	439,451	513,315	718,326
Coles..................			

Output of coal in Illinois, by counties, for nine years—Continued.

District.	Lump coal.		1891—All grades.
	1890.	1891.	
Counties—Continued.	Short tons.	Short tons.	Short tons.
Effingham	796	a 487	a 487
Greene	11,714	16,442	16,442
Jasper	152	(b)	(b)
Jersey	7,500	4,252	4,252
Macon	179,050	126,569	207,286
Macoupin	1,369,919	1,119,380	1,461,344
Madison	646,228	600,294	719,308
Montgomery	58,617	94,975	107,190
Morgan	16,601	6,584	7,610
Pike	135	(b)	(b)
Richland	154	(b)	(b)
Sangamon	879,888	912,643	1,051,604
Scott	20,022	14,255	14,755
Shelby	18,023	14,197	14,197
Fifth district	3,240,004	3,173,956	3,915,404
Counties:			
Clinton	170,416	146,903	174,166
Franklin	700	200	200
Gallatin	52,383	31,119	34,462
Hardin	40	24	24
Hamilton	450	280	280
Johnson	12,110	424	424
Jackson	580,521	477,330	681,859
Jefferson	2,100	1,104	1,104
Marion	218,499	251,283	321,652
Perry	497,768	457,431	604,152
Randolph	134,699	162,717	172,321
Saline	45,845	38,729	54,269
St. Clair	1,332,978	1,389,429	1,595,839
Washington	25,160	56,500	68,200
Williamson	166,335	160,483	206,452
State totals	12,638,364	12,960,224	15,660,698

a Includes Jasper, Pike, and Richland counties.
b Included in Effingham County.

Output of coal in Illinois, by counties, for nine years—Continued.

District.	1892.		
	Lump coal.	Other grades.	All grades.
	Short tons.	*Short tons.*	*Short tons.*
First district......................	2,965,067	492,999	3,458,066
Counties:			
Grundy	1,108,419	66,665	1,108,419
Kankakee	81,793	10,365	92,158
Lasalle	1,261,467	282,844	1,544,311
Livingston	404,491	128,176	532,667
Will........................	108,897	4,949	113,846
Second district	1,461,224	272,384	1,733,608
Counties:			
Bureau	809,009	134,487	943,496
Hancock.....................	5,380	....	5,380
Henry	142,762	13,974	156,736
Knox	43,137	....	43,137
Marshall	64,276	14,300	78,576
McDonough	82,001	9,126	91,127
Mercer	233,244	95,298	328,542
Rock Island	34,017	2,092	36,109
Schuyler....................	13,685	3,107	16,792
Stark......................	22,349	....	22,349
Warren.....................	11,364	....	11,364
Third district..................	2,711,574	549,377	3,260,951
Counties:			
Cass	13,270	2,060	15,330
Fulton	535,288	131,185	666,473
Logan	163,002	24,354	187,356
McLean.....................	170,912	51,460	222,372
Menard	237,419	48,276	285,695
Peoria	541,659	91,280	632,939
Tazewell	94,190	25,966	120,156
Vermilion..................	827,893	144,696	972,589
Woodford	127,941	30,100	158,041
Fourth district.................	4,090,921	1,026,679	5,117,600
Counties:			
Bond.......................	92,308	29,504	121,812
Calhoun....................	4,637	....	4,637
Christian	525,746	241,608	767,354
Coles	....	....	....

Output of coal in Illinois, by counties, for nine years—Continued.

District.	1892.		
	Lump coal.	Other grades.	All grades.
Counties—Continued.	*Short tons.*	*Short tons.*	*Short tons.*
Effingham..................	a 302	....	302
Greene......................	19,870	....	19,870
Jasper	(b)	....	....
Jersey	3,378	....	3,378
Macon	198,375	28,645	227,020
Macoupin	1,434,021	389,115	1,823,136
Madison....................	703,980	169,790	873,770
Montgomery	119,850	28,020	147,870
Morgan	4,266	....	4,266
Pike	(b)	....	....
Richland...................	(b)	....	....
Sangamon..................	951,517	139,497	1,091,014
Scott.......................	17,006	500	17,506
Shelby	15,665	....	15,665
Fifth district..............	3,502,177	789,874	4,292,051
Counties:			
Clinton	156,376	35,497	191,873
Franklin....................	200	....	200
Gallatin....................	13,782	720	14.502
Hardin.....................			
Hamilton	220	....	220
Johnson....................	2,200	....	2,200
Jackson....................	674,161	195,353	869,514
Jefferson	100	....	100
Marion.....................	306,019	70,500	376,519
Perry	362,926	98,142	461,068
Randolph	160,532	8,447	168,979
Saline......................	41,992	19,610	61.602
St. Clair	1,519,472	240,350	1,759.822
Washington................	54,183	8,783	62.966
Williamson	210,014	112,472	322.486
State totals	14,730,963	3,131,313	17,862.276

a Includes Jasper, Pike, and Richland counties.
b Included in Effingham County.

Output of coal in Illinois, by counties, for nine years—Continued.

District.	1893.		
	Lump coal.	Other grades.	All grades.
	Short tons.	*Short tons.*	*Short tons.*
First district......................	2, 913, 144	481, 542	3, 394, 686
Counties:			
Grundy.......................	1, 106, 574	80, 345	1, 186, 919
Kankakee	83, 700	5, 000	88, 700
Lasalle	1, 242, 566	252, 260	1, 494, 826
Livingston	402, 370	140, 146	542, 516
Will........................	77, 934	3, 791	81, 725
Second district..................	1, 708, 909	291, 755	2, 000, 664
Counties:			
Bureau	976, 572	166, 698	1, 143, 270
Hancock.....................	5, 060	....	5, 060
Henry	148, 324	7, 937	156, 261
Knox	49, 808	....	49, 808
Marshall.....................	78, 700	13, 444	92, 144
McDonough	92, 096	10, 830	102, 926
Mercer	273, 390	89, 816	363, 206
Rock Island.................	34, 058	250	34, 308
Schuyler.....................	15, 955	2, 780	18, 735
Stark........................	23, 070	....	23, 070
Warren	11, 876	....	11, 876
Third district..................	2, 860, 299	537, 134	3, 397, 433
Counties:			
Cass	21, 370	1, 780	23, 150
Fulton	610, 854	161, 643	772, 497
Logan	157, 699	31, 620	189, 319
McLean	153, 027	51, 800	204, 827
Menard	230, 296	51, 339	281, 635
Peoria	537, 928	82, 221	620, 149
Tazewell	113, 597	15, 360	128, 957
Vermilion	873, 597	123, 171	996, 768
Woodford	161, 931	18, 200	180, 131
Fourth district	4, 508, 382	1, 276, 484	5, 784, 866
Counties:			
Bond........................	56, 120	22, 480	78, 600
Calhoun.....................	4, 584	....	4, 584
Christian....................	593, 602	246, 018	839, 650
Coles.......................	....	....	....

Output of coal in Illinois, by counties, for nine years—Continued.

District.	1893.		
	Lump coal.	Other grades.	All grades.
Counties—Continued.	*Short tons.*	*Short tons.*	*Short tons.*
Effingham....................	520	....	520
Greene.....................	10,995	....	10,995
Jasper	(a)	(a)	(a)
Jersey	5,904	....	5,904
Macon	237,442	42,791	280,233
Macoupin	1,509,594	478,475	1,988,069
Madison....................	758,288	193,606	951,894
Montgomery	123,920	51,792	175,712
Morgan	2,142	....	2,142
Pike	(a)	(a)	(a)
Richland..................	(a)	(a)	(a)
Sangamon..................	1,170,854	239,492	1,410,346
Scott......................	22,157	600	22,757
Shelby....................	12,260	1,200	13,460
Fifth district..............	4,122,165	1,249,750	5,371,915
Counties:			
Clinton	174,994	80,101	255,095
Franklin..................	120	....	120
Gallatin..................	14,972	2,485	17,457
Hardin....................			
Hamilton	244	....	244
Johnson...................			
Jackson	674,943	251,299	926,242
Jefferson	90	....	90
Marion....................	352,793	127,736	480,529
Perry	620,502	239,649	860,151
Randolph	161,565	9,490	171,055
Saline....................	24,929	11,507	36,436
St. Clair..................	1,778,787	355,083	2,133,870
Washington...............	63,500	8,700	72,200
Williamson...............	254,726	163,700	418,426
State totals..............	16,112,899	3,836,665	19,949,564

a Included in Effingham County.

Output of coal in Illinois, by counties, for nine years—Continued.

District.	1894.		
	Lump coal.	Other grades.	All grades.
	Short tons.	*Short tons.*	*Short tons.*
First district..................	2,367,298	317,946	2,685,244
Counties:			
Grundy....................	1,052,233	78,187	1,130,420
Kankakee	50,883	7,000	57,883
Lasalle	968,243	165,854	1,134,097
Livingston	276,654	65,473	342,127
Will......................	19,285	1,432	20,717
Second district..................	1,449,356	254,267	1,703,623
Counties:			
Bureau	743,764	135,173	878,937
Hancock..................	10,290	25	10,315
Henry	105,453	6,187	111,640
Knox	50,581	949	51,530
Marshall..................	117,612	17,084	134,696
McDonough	50,223	3,144	53,367
Mercer....................	286,445	87,558	374,003
Rock Island	40,041	1,600	41,641
Schuyler..................	11,774	2,054	13,828
Stark.....................	22,182	443	22,625
Warren	10,991	50	11,041
Third district..................	2,569,268	508,650	3,077,918
Counties:			
Cass	13,300	5,600	18,900
Fulton....................	444,896	112,807	557,703
Logan	154,025	32,275	186,300
McLean...................	125,053	42,241	167,294
Menard	235,873	59,979	295,852
Peoria	517,957	93,835	611,792
Tazewell	85,399	8,200	93,599
Vermilion	842,615	147,198	989,813
Woodford	150,150	6,515	156,665
Fourth district..................	3,877,110	1,296,193	5,173,303
Counties:			
Bond	54,091	25,500	79,591
Calhoun	3,478	....	3,478
Christian	671,278	334,222	1,005,500
Coles	....	....	....

Output of coal in Illinois, by counties, for nine years—Continued.

District.	1894.		
	Lump coal.	Other grades.	All grades.
Counties—Continued.	*Short tons.*	*Short tons.*	*Short tons.*
Effingham	5, 440	....	a5. 440
Greene......................	18, 400	200	18. 600
Jasper	....	....	....
Jersey	2, 238	....	2, 238
Macon	190, 388	37, 432	227. 820
Macoupin..................	1, 173, 392	401, 653	1. 575, 045
Madison	682, 520	207, 248	889, 768
Montgomery	122, 742	55, 298	178, 040
Morgan	....	....	....
Pike.......................	....	....	....
Richland	....	....	....
Sangamon	912, 700	229, 599	1, 142, 299
Scott	18, 525	500	19, 025
Shelby.....................	21, 909	4, 541	26, 450
Fifth district..................	3, 602, 252	871, 236	4, 473, 488
Counties:			
Clinton	150, 159	50, 761	200, 920
Franklin....................	....	....	....
Gallatin	153, 116	2, 235	155, 351
Hardin	....	....	....
Hamilton	620	....	b620
Johnson	....	....	....
Jackson	566, 540	199, 974	766, 514
Jefferson...................	....	....	....
Marion	354, 670	124, 087	478. 757
Perry	394, 702	135, 788	530. 490
Randolph	180, 971	12, 276	193, 247
Saline	24, 864	12, 049	36, 913
St. Clair	1, 427, 714	195, 970	1. 623, 684
Washington.................	48, 435	1, 400	49, 835
Williamson	300, 461	136, 696	437. 157
State totals	13, 865, 284	3, 248, 292	17. 113. 576

a Includes Cumberland, Jasper, Morgan, Pike, and Richland counties.
b Includes Franklin and Jefferson counties.

Output of coal in Illinois, by counties, for nine years—Continued.

District.	1895.		
	Lump coal.	Other grades.	All grades.
	Short tons.	*Short tons.*	*Short tons.*
First district	2, 294, 063	441, 648	2, 735, 711
Counties:			
Grundy......................	1, 126, 810	135, 028	1, 261, 838
Kankakee	54, 658	28, 855	83, 513
Lasalle	881, 773	202, 779	1, 084, 552
Livingston	197, 847	69, 286	267, 133
Will........................	32, 975	5, 700	38, 675
Second district................	1, 673, 056	322, 242	1, 995, 298
Counties:			
Bureau	716, 313	118, 228	834, 541
Hancock....................	10, 186	88	10, 274
Henry	127, 484	8, 483	135, 967
Knox........................	55, 502	2, 828	58, 330
Marshall....................	275, 070	71, 211	346, 281
McDonough	49, 709	3, 678	53, 387
Mercer......................	384, 681	113, 330	462, 011
Rock Island.................	42, 237	3, 348	45, 585
Schuyler....................	11, 552	1, 048	12, 600
Stark.......................	22, 131	....	22, 131
Warren.....................	14, 191	....	14, 191
Third district.................	2, 543, 517	408, 743	2, 952, 260
Counties:			
Cass........................	14, 120	5, 000	19, 120
Fulton......................	379, 438	89, 354	468, 792
Logan	163, 975	18, 000	181, 975
McLean.....................	137, 095	27, 045	164, 140
Menard.....................	235, 199	42, 539	277, 738
Peoria......................	381, 883	55, 574	437, 457
Tazewell	82, 086	12, 020	94, 106
Vermilion	1, 033, 305	144, 070	1, 177, 375
Woodford	116, 416	15, 141	131, 557
Fourth district............	4, 154, 538	1, 458, 226	5, 612, 764
Counties:			
Bond	66, 797	26, 718	93, 515
Calhoun	9, 200	....	9, 200
Christian	496, 235	239, 126	735, 361
Coles	....	....	....
Effingham	....	....	....

Output of coal in Illinois, by counties, for nine years—Continued.

District.	1895.		
	Lump coal.	Other grades.	All grades.
Counties—Continued.	*Short tons.*	*Short tons.*	*Short tons.*
Greene	11, 345	....	11, 345
Jasper			
Jersey			
Macon	190, 000	41, 000	231, 000
Macoupin	1, 406, 372	542, 620	1, 948, 992
Madison	721, 561	256, 600	978, 161
Montgomery	147, 452	50, 390	197, 842
Morgan			
Pike	*a* 7, 800	....	7, 800
Richland			
Sangamon	1, 033, 923	284. 169	1, 318, 092
Scott	17, 280	450	17, 730
Shelby	46, 573	17, 153	63, 726
Fifth district	3, 380, 788	1, 059, 043	4, 439, 831
Counties:			
Clinton	216, 655	67, 832	284, 487
Franklin			
Gallatin	11, 590	8, 740	20, 330
Hardin			
Hamilton	4, 645	....	4, 645
Johnson			
Jackson	538, 241	201, 420	739, 661
Jefferson	27, 080	800	27, 880
Marion	395, 869	143, 031	538, 900
Perry	393, 260	194, 184	587, 444
Randolph	161, 481	33, 000	194, 481
Saline	30, 628	14, 574	45, 202
St. Clair	1, 267, 862	211, 244	1, 479, 106
Washington	50, 220	6, 000	56, 220
Williamson	283, 257	178, 218	461, 475
State totals	14, 045, 962	3, 689, 902	17, 735, 864

a Includes Cumberland, Effingham, Jasper, and Jersey counties.

The consideration of this phase of the subject—product and tonnage—is completed by the following tables, which are, practically, summaries of the information contained in the preceding one:

Number of mines, employees, and tons raised, in each district and the State, for each of the thirteen years, on the basis of all grades of product.

Year.	First.			Second.		
	Mines.	Employees.	Coal.	Mines.	Employees.	Coal.
			Tons.			Tons.
1883...............	93	7,566	3,015,544	229	3,211	1,004,977
1884...............	84	8,013	3,030,407	264	3,616	890,273
1885...............	74	7,463	3,044,943	236	3,391	873,911
1886...............	69	7,613	2,812,100	262	3,599	851,728
1887...............	68	7,915	3,247,302	275	4,068	1,292,026
1888...............	70	8,623	3,478,106	267	4,911	1,562,946
1889...............	72	9,018	3,058,305	264	4,498	1,314,773
1890...............	79	8,258	2,783,700	254	4,099	1,211,742
1891...............	70	9,128	3,082,915	264	5,089	1,440,266
1892...............	70	9,572	3,458,066	240	4,865	1,733,608
1893...............	71	8,831	3,394,686	224	5,794	2,000,664
1894...............	72	10,280	2,685,244	241	6,714	1,703,623
1895...............	82	9,644	2,735,711	246	7,184	1,995,298

Year.	Third.			Fourth.		
	Mines.	Employees.	Coal.	Mines.	Employees.	Coal.
			Tons.			Tons.
1883...............	92	4,070	2,036,662	95	4,417	3,660,086
1884...............	171	5,018	2,336,080	104	3,781	3,389,136
1885...............	209	5,213	2,189,264	104	4,950	3,161,808
1886...............	223	4,870	1,835,193	109	5,197	3,323,424
1887...............	236	4,903	2,152,994	111	4,934	3,104,520
1888...............	237	5,250	2,649,397	108	5,086	3,449,997
1889...............	246	5,117	2,478,052	98	5,679	2,825,020
1890...............	273	5,171	2,871,597	137	5,685	4,491,718
1891...............	273	6,458	2,794,004	126	5,881	4,428,109
1892...............	256	6,453	3,260,951	109	6,542	5,117,600
1893...............	236	6,964	3,397,433	104	7,021	5,784,866
1894...............	251	7,112	3,077,918	130	7,750	5,173,303
1895...............	262	6,607	2,952,260	134	8,005	5,612,764

Number of mines, employees, and tons raised, in each district and the State, for each of the thirteen years, on the basis of all grades of product—Continued.

Year.	Fifth.			The State.		
	Mines.	Employees.	Coal.	Mines.	Employees.	Coal.
			Tons.			*Tons.*
1883............	130	4,695	2,406,227	639	23,939	12,123,456
1884............	118	4,147	2,572,262	741	25,575	12,208,075
1885............	126	4,429	2,564,653	778	25,946	11,834,459
1886............	126	4,567	2,352,794	787	25,846	11,175,241
1887............	118	4,984	2,626,708	801	26,804	12,423,066
1888............	151	5,537	3,187,738	822	29,410	14,328,181
1889............	174	5,764	3,341,148	854	30,076	14,017,298
1890............	193	5,361	3,915,869	936	28,574	15,274,727
1891............	185	6,395	3,915,404	918	32,951	15,660,698
1892............	164	6,200	4,292,051	839	33,632	17,862,276
1893............	153	6,780	5,371,915	788	35,390	19,949,564
1894............	142	6,621	4,473,488	836	38,477	17,113,576
1895............	150	7,190	4,339,831	874	38,630	17,735,864

NUMBER OF EMPLOYEES.

The two following tables give detailed information concerning the number of employees in and about the mines for a period of thirteen years:

Total number of employees in and about the mines by districts for thirteen years.

Year.	First.	Second.	Third.	Fourth.	Fifth.	The State.
1883..................	7,566	3,211	4,079	4,417	4,675	23,939
1884..................	8,013	3,616	5,018	4,781	4,147	25,575
1885..................	7,463	3,391	5,213	4,950	4,429	25,446
1886..................	7,613	3,599	4,870	5,197	4,567	25,846
1887..................	7,915	4,068	4,903	4,934	4,984	26,804
1888..................	8,623	4,914	5,250	5,086	5,537	29,410
1889..................	9,014	4,498	5,117	5,679	5,764	30,076
1890..................	8,258	4,099	5,171	5,685	5,361	28,574
1891..................	9,128	5,089	6,458	5,881	6,395	32,951
1892..................	9,572	4,865	6,453	6,542	6,200	33,632
1893..................	8,831	5,794	6,964	7,021	6,780	35,390
1894..................	10,280	6,714	7,112	7,750	6,621	38,477
1895..................	9,644	7,184	6,607	8,005	7,190	38,630
Net increase.....	2,078	3,973	2,537	3,588	2,515	14,691
Per cent increase.	27.46	123.73	62.33	81.23	53.80	61.37

DAYS OF ACTIVE OPERATION.

In arriving at the average number of days during which the mines are in active operation all the small and new mines are excluded from the calculations, and the estimates are based on information received from each mine and from all mines of sufficient importance to make them valuable as factors in arriving at the correct result. In 1894 these calculations were based on the running time of 295 mines, representing 91.9 per cent of the total tons and 81.2 per cent of total number of employees, while this year 278 mines are considered, representing 88.2 per cent of the total tons and 80.7 per cent of the number of employees, and it is found that the average running time is slightly less than in 1894. The following table shows the average running time by districts, and for five years, of shipping mines producing over 1.000 tons and working more than 100 days:

Shipping mines producing 1,000 tons or more, and working 100 days or more, with average number of days and average number of total tons produced by districts for five years.

District.	1895.			1894.			1893.		
	Mines.	Average number of days.	Average number of tons, all grades.	Mines.	Average number of days.	Average number of tons, all grades.	Mines.	Average number of days.	Average number of tons, all grades.
First.........	26	159.4	90,073	35	161.5	69,019	38	220	86,860
Second.......	28	176.1	58,393	26	171	51,794	26	228	65,214
Third ..:.....	66	173	33,846	81	182.9	33,735	80	215	39,316
Fourth.......	64	188.5	85,869	63	194.7	81,195	56	251	102,027
Fifth.........	94	192.6	42,028	90	186.9	45,762	101	233	52,366
The State.	278	182.2	56,320	295	183.1	53,318	301	229.6	63,818

District.	1892.			1891.		
	Mines.	Average number of days.	Average number of tons, all grades.	Mines.	Average number of days.	Average number of tons, all grades.
First	35	218.3	81,026	36	207.6	82,961
Second ..:............	29	214.8	43,731	28	214.6	43,710
Third	84	203.8	29,241	88	193	28,524
Fourth	55	239.9	72,771	53	238.8	80,275
Fifth.................	96	221.8	35,204	106	225	36,096
The State	299	219.5	46,630	311	215.6	47,595

The following table includes all mines, both shipping and local, which produce more than 1,000 tons and work more than 100 days; the average number of running days, while slightly larger than in the former table, is sufficiently near the same to demonstrate its accuracy:

All mines producing 1,000 tons or more, and working 100 days or more, with average number of days and average number of total tons produced, for five years, by districts.

District.	1895.			1894.			1893.		
	Mines.	Average number of days.	Average number of tons, all grades.	Mines.	Average number of days.	Average number of tons, all grades.	Mines.	Average number of days.	Average number of tons, all grades.
First.........	59	184.1	42,469	56	177.7	46,067	60	213	56,459
Second.......	109	189.5	16,836	107	187	14,371	93	225	20,794
Third........	142	184.8	17,279	145	187.8	20,264	136	213	24,508
Fourth.......	78	185.9	70,924	80	191	64,404	80	249	72,132
Fifth.........	118	195.9	36,459	119	195.6	36,751	128	223	41,843
The State.	506	188.5	32,863	507	188.9	32,703	497	225.5	39,801

District.	1892.			1891.		
	Mines.	Average number of days.	Average number of tons, all grades.	Mines.	Average number of days.	Average number of tons, all grades.
First	59	207.5	57,777	53	200.9	57,570
Second	91	268	17,132	93	215.4	14,901
Third	144	239.9	22,152	146	201	18,483
Fourth	81	240	62,592	85	233.5	51,236
Fifth	120	227.7	35,477	127	227.8	30,727
The State.............	495	217.7	35,523	504	215.8	30,506

For convenience of reference the information contained in the two foregoing tables is presented in the following table in a condensed form. The lowest average value per ton for the past year was obtained in the fifth district, which is true of the entire series of years, excepting only 1894, when the price was a fraction of a cent above that in the fourth district, which in turn has as uniformly ranked next to the lowest.

Average value of lump coal per ton of 2,000 pounds at the mines.

Year.	Total lump coal.	First district.	Second district.	Third district.	Fourth district.	Fifth district.	The State.	In- crease.	De- crease.
	Tons.							*Cents.*	*Cents.*
1882	9,115,653	$1.75	$1.87	$1.43	$1.33	$1.31	$1.51	....	....
1883	10,030,991	1.59	1.97	1.45	1.32	1.26	1.48	....	3
1884	10,101,005	1.49	1.75	1.31	1.09	.961	1.26	....	22
1885	9,791,874	1.41	1.71	1.25	.985	.894	1.17	....	9
1886	9,246,435	1.32	1.57	1.16	.969	.862	1.10	....	7
1887	10,278,890	1.316	1.497	1.095	.887	.823	1.085	....	1.5
1888	11,855,188	1.309	1.473	1.138	.947	.857	1.123	3.8	....
1889	11,597,963	1.355	1.432	1.104	.965	.867	1.078	....	4.5
1890	12,638,364	1.302	1.477	1.065	.873	.811	1.019	....	5.9
1891	12,960,224	1.298	1.426	1.032	.853	.757	1.008	....	1.1
1892	14,730,963	1.323	1.432	1.053	.836	.817	1.029	2.1	....
1893	16,112,899	1.333	1.455	1.074	.836	.803	1.025	....	.4
1894	13,865,284	1.316	1.416	1.043	.821	.826	1.009	....	1.6
1895	14,045,962	1.205	1.302	.946	.765	.761	.932	....	7.7
Net decrease .	a 4,930,309	.545	.568	.484	.565	.549	.578	....	57.80
Per cent of decrease....	a 54.9	31.14	30.37	33.85	42.41	41.91	38.28	....	....

a Increase.

INDIANA.

Total product in 1895, 3,995,892 short tons; spot value, $3,642,623.

In 1895 Indiana produced more coal than in any year in her history, gaining 571,971 short tons, or about 16 per cent over the output of 1894, and more than 200,000 tons over that of 1893, when the largest previous product was obtained. The general decline in values was felt in the coal-mining industry of the State sufficiently to show a fall of 5 cents per ton in the average price—from 96 cents in 1894 to 91 cents in 1895. The aggregate value of the product, while greater than that of 1894, was less than that of 1893 by $412,749.

Among the producing counties Clay ranks first, with a tonnage in 1895 of 1,223,186, or nearly 33 per cent of the total output of the State. Forty-three per cent of the product was contributed in nearly equal amounts by Parke, Sullivan, Greene, and Vigo counties in the order named, each producing more than 400,000 tons. Vermilion County, with an output of 306,000, was sixth in importance, and Pike County, with a product of 232,950 short tons, held seventh place.

From an effort made by the operators in the "block" coal districts of Indiana to reduce the rate paid for mining coal in accordance with the reduced price, a strike was precipitated about the 1st of May, but it was not of great length, a compromise being effected by which the operators were to continue the old rate of 60 cents per ton until July 1, when the controversy was renewed, and finally settled by the men accepting a rate of 51 cents for screened coal and $1.65 per day for time men.

The details of production in 1894 and 1895 are shown in the following tables:

Coal product of Indiana in 1894, by counties.

County.	Number of mines.	Loaded at mines for shipment.	Sold to local trade and used by employees.	Used at mines for steam and heat.	Made into coke.	Total product.	Total value.	Average price per ton.	Average number of days active.	Average number of employees.
		Short tons.	Short tons.	Short tons.	Short tons.	Short tons.				
Clay.........	25	865,950	7,020	8,919	8,825	890,714	$1,008,293	$1.13	131	3,114
Daviess......	5	100,233	550	50	....	100,833	104,021	1.03	116	350
Fountain and Owen..	2	25,789	492	225	....	26,506	29,535	1.11	146	105
Gibson	2	15,521	3,600	500	....	19,021	14,865	.78	143	36
Greene	5	292,606	858	7,010	....	300,474	287,498	.96	141	576
Knox	2	18,076	9,641	1,145	....	28,862	24,133	.84	153	64
Parke	15	327,011	21,992	7,262	....	356,265	370,419	1.07	135	1,065
Pike.........	5	158,749	1,183	4,935	8,689	173,556	134,007	.77	148	348
Perry........	2	22,668	7,492	536	....	30,696	34,657	1.12½	168	93
Spencer	5	6,711	3,187	285	....	10,183	10,513	1.03	170	40
Sullivan	12	496,495	18,589	17,193	4,800	537,077	440,410	.82	152	885
Vanderburg .	5	55,286	108,923	11,672	....	175,881	168,987	.96	215	330
Vermilion ...	4	289,791	2,060	4,371	....	296,222	243,354	.82	165	710
Vigo.........	10	309,593	10,666	1,280	....	321,539	301,555	.95	196	740
Warrick.....	8	101,185	16,745	2,162	....	120,092	86,787	.72	199	147
Small mines .	....	....	36,000	....	....	36,000	36,000	....	....	....
Total ..	107	3,085,664	248,398	67,545	22,314	3,423,921	3,295,034	.96	149	8,603

Coal product of Indiana in 1895, by counties.

County.	Number of mines.	Loaded at mines for shipment.	Sold to local trade and used by employees.	Used at mines for steam and heat.	Made into coke.	Total product.	Total value.	Average price per ton.	Average number of days active.	Average number of employees.
		Short tons.	Short tons.	Short tons.	Short tons.	Short tons.				
Clay	31	1,184,484	19,570	19,132	....	1,223,186	$1,307,256	$1.07	195	3,319
Daviess....	3	80,580	600	200	....	81,380	76,658	.94	129	258
Greene	8	396,620	3,600	8,860	....	409,080	281,583	.69	180	646
Knox	3	14,946	10,106	1,391	....	26,443	26,023	.98	140	69
Parke......	16	444,088	24,692	10,829	....	479,609	472,357	.98	166	1,225
Pike	4	218,566	1,638	4,848	7,898	232,950	179,722	.77	191	392
Spencer....	10	5,609	4,920	350	....	10,879	10,960	1.01	129	61
Sullivan ...	8	325,699	106,500	18,968	2,000	453,167	379,873	.84	185	607
Vanderburg	5	38,220	144,040	10,450	....	192,710	199,296	1.03	233	281
Vermilion..	3	299,600	400	6,000	....	306,000	249,300	.81	245	572
Vigo	12	376,006	9,524	16,805	....	402,335	312,725	.78	187	869
Warrick...	12	87,758	27,033	6,462	....	121,253	87,495	.72	186	146
Gibson and Perry....	3	16,700	3,800	400	....	20,900	23,375	1.12	151	85
Small mines	....	....	36,000	....	....	36,000	36,000	....	....	....
Total.	117	3,488,876	392,423	104,695	9,898	3,995,892	3,642,623	.91	189	8,530

Previous to 1889 the statistics of production by counties were not obtained. The following table shows the annual product by counties since that year, with a statement of the increase or decrease in each county in 1895 as compared with 1894:

Coal product of Indiana since 1889, by counties.

[Short tons.]

County.	1889.	1890.	1891.	1892.	1893.
Clay	695,649	1,161,730	980,921	1,146,897	1,209,703
Daviess	191,585	189,696	155,358	174,560	319,787
Dubois	15,848	13,994	7,700	....	10,142
Fountain	41,141	24,000	23,700	13,888	4,000
Gibson	1,267	....	....	....	....
Greene	185,849	197,338	164,965	228,574	259,930
Knox	9,040	....	....	14,314	13,357
Martin	710	....	....	....	....
Owen	3,958	....	12,600	8,200	5,785
Parke	357,434	345,460	307,382	394,335	491,847
Perry	40,050	40,201	35,400	37,796	36,252
Pike	154,524	115,836	122,066	78,760	243,553
Spencer	18,456	11,656	15,340	8,426	7,647
Sullivan	317,252	286,323	181,434	316,893	290,482
Vanderburg	183,942	192,284	205,731	190,346	186,053
Vermilion	187,651	173,000	228,488	301,063	264,224
Vigo	371,903	429,160	400,255	307,113	350,143
Warren	2,160	....	....	....	....
Warwick	66,638	89,059	96,134	84,009	58,946
Small mines	....	36,000	36,000	40,000	40,000
Total	2,845,057	3,305,737	2,973,474	3,345,174	3,791,851

County.	1894.	1895.	Increase in 1895.	Decrease in 1895.
Clay	890,714	1,223,186	332,472	....
Daviess	100,833	81,380	....	19,453
Dubois	....	....	....	....
Fountain	18,931	....	....	18,931
Gibson	19,021	1,940	....	17,081
Greene	300,474	409,080	108,606	....
Knox	28,862	26,443	....	2,419
Martin	....	....	....	....
Owen	7,575	....	....	7,575
Parke	356,265	479,609	123,344	....
Perry	30,696	18,960	....	11,736
Pike	173,556	232,950	59,394	....

*Coal product of Indiana since 1889, by counties—*Continued.

[Short tons.]

County.	1894.	1895.	Increase in 1895.	Decrease in 1895.
Spencer	10,183	10,879	696	
Sullivan	537,077	453,167		83,910
Vanderburg	175,881	192,710	16,829	
Vermilion	296,222	306,000	9,778	
Vigo	321,539	402,335	80,796	
Warren				
Warrick	120,092	121,253	1,161	
Small mines	36,000	36,000		
Total	3,423,921	3,995,892	a571,971	

a Net increase.

The following table is of interest as showing the total amount and value of coal produced in the State from 1886 to 1895, and the total number of employees and average number of working days in each year since 1889:

Statistics of coal production in Indiana since 1886.

Year.	Short tons.	Value.	Average price per ton.	Number of days active.	Average number of employees.
1886	3,000,000	$3,450,000	$1.15		
1887	3,217,711	4,324,604	1.03		
1888	3,140,979	4,397,370	1.40		
1889	2,845,057	2,887,852	1.02		6,448
1890	3,305,737	3,259,233	.99	220	5,489
1891	2,973,474	3,070,918	1.03	190	5,879
1892	3,345,174	3,620,582	1.08	225	6,436
1893	3,791,851	4,055,372	1.07	201	7,644
1894	3,423,921	3,295,034	.96	149	8,603
1895	3,995,892	3,642,623	.91	189	8,530

In the following table is shown the total annual product of coal in the State since 1873:

Product of coal in Indiana from 1873 to 1895.

Year.	Short tons.	Year.	Short tons.
1873	1,000,000	1885	2,375,000
1874	812,000	1886	3,000,000
1875	800,000	1887	3,217,711
1876	950,000	1888	3,140,979
1877	1,000,000	1889	2,845,057
1878	1,000,000	1890	3,305,737
1879	1,196,490	1891	2,973,474
1880	1,500,000	1892	3,345,174
1881	1,771,536	1893	3,791,851
1882	1,976,470	1894	3,423,921
1883	2,560,000	1895	3,995,892
1884	2,260,000		

In accordance with the plan adopted in discussing the production in other States, the following tables are given to show the tendency in prices and the statistics of labor employed and average working time by counties for such years as they have been obtained. They include only those counties whose annual product averages 10,000 tons or over.

Average prices for Indiana coal since 1889 in counties averaging 10,000 tons or over.

County.	1889.	1890.	1891.	1892.
Clay	$1.14	$1.01	$1.15	$1.25
Daviess	1.02	1.04	1.12	1.11
Fountain	1.29	1.00	.99	.89
Gibson				
Greene	.91	.94	.91	.84
Knox				.84
Parke	1.05	1.09	1.13	1.09
Perry	1.18	1.05	1.10	.86
Pike	.83	.98	.90	.87
Spencer	1.15	.96	.88	.80
Sullivan	.94	.94	1.01	89
Vanderburg	1.16	1.02	1.09	1.06
Vermilion	.89	1.17	.98	.96
Vigo	.88	.80	.80	1.14
Warrick			.77	.81
The State	1.02	.99	1.03	1.08

Average prices for Indiana coal since 1889 in counties averaging 10,000 tons or over—Continued.

County.	1893.	1894.	1895.
Clay............................	$1.29	$1.13	$1.07
Daviess.........................	.97	1.03	.94
Fountain	1.00	1.08	....
Gibson	....	.78	....
Greene	.83	.96	.69
Knox	1.10	.84	.98
Parke	1.16	1.07	.98
Perry...........................	1.13	1.12½	1.12
Pike............................	.76	.77	.77
Spencer	.84	1.03	1.01
Sullivan	.88	.82	.84
Vanderburg	1.08	.96	1.03
Vermilion	.96	.82	.81
Vigo	.95	.95	.78
Warrick	.89	.72	.72
The State......................	1.07	.96	.91

Statistics of labor employed in Indiana coal mines.

County.	1889. Average number employed.	1890. Average number employed.	Average number of days worked.	1891. Average number employed.	Average number of days worked.	1892. Average number employed.	Average number of days worked.
Clay	2,592	2,179	218	2,346	181	2,797	239
Daviess	455	280	231	359	217	403	224
Fountain...........	41	48	260	252	40	30	315
Gibson	7	....				....	
Greene.............	296	250	218	154	300	335	227
Knox	22	....				28	138
Parke...............	591	558	254	510	255	639	228
Perry	109	100	250	95	190	88	227
Pike	340	235	170	230	198½	160	163
Spencer	29	39	261	46	204	13	310
Sullivan	556	588	181	544	130½	522	242
Vanderburg.........	318	454	262	338	228½	282	262
Vermilion	276	307	244	380	147	545	164
Vigo	629	280	161	487	244	491	217
Warrick	85	131	222	161	199	171	141
The State	6,448	5,489	220	5,879	190	6,436	225

Statistics of labor employed in Indiana coal mines—Continued.

County.	1893.		1894.		1895.	
	Average number employed.	Average number of days worked.	Average number employed.	Average number of days worked.	Average number employed.	Average number of days worked.
Clay	2,976	196	3,114	131	3,319	195
Daviess	553	213	350	116	258	129
Fountain	18	150	75	160	....	....
Gibson	......	......	36	143	....	....
Greene	391	203	576	141	646	180
Knox	37	183	64	153	69	140
Parke	1,091	202	1,065	135	1,225	166
Perry	100	198	93	168	80	148
Pike	365	211	348	148	392	191
Spencer	29	170	40	170	61	129
Sullivan	460	221½	885	152	607	185
Vanderburg	357	250	330	215	281	233
Vermilion	507	158	710	165	572	245
Vigo	579	217	740	196	869	187
Warrick	136	129	147	199	146	186
The State	7,644	201	8,663	119	8,530	180

INDIAN TERRITORY.

Total product in 1895, 1,211,185 short tons; spot value, $1,737,254.

The coal product of the Indian Territory in 1895 was 241,579 short tons, or 25 per cent more than in 1894, but still lacked about 40,000 tons of reaching the amount obtained in 1893. The effect of the depression in prices was shown in the Territory by a decline in the average price per ton from $1.59 in 1894 to $1.43 in 1895, and while the product increased 25 per cent the value advanced but 12½ per cent, or $195,961.

Several new mines were opened during 1895, and there is good reason to believe that the output in 1896 will show a considerable increase. The coal is of excellent quality, and the fields are reached by several important railroad lines, so that conditions are favorable for increased business in the region.

The following table exhibits the details of production during the past five years.

Coal product of the Indian Territory for five years.

Distribution.	1891.	1892.	1893.
	Short tons.	*Short tons.*	*Short tons.*
Loaded at mines for shipment	1,026,932	1,156,603	1,197,468
Sold to local trade and used by employees	9,405	10,840	9,231
Used at mines for steam and heat	22,163	18,089	21,663
Made into coke	32,532	7,189	23,745
Total	1,091,032	1,192,721	1,252,110
Total value	$1,897,037	$2,013,479	$2,235,209
Average number of employees	2,891	3,257	3,446
Average number of days worked	222	211	171

Distribution.	1894.	1895.
	Short tons.	*Short tons.*
Loaded at mines for shipment	923,581	1,173,399
Sold to local trade and used by employees	4,632	3,070
Used at mines for steam and heat	30,878	21,935
Made into coke	10,515	12,781
Total	969,606	1,211,185
Total value	$1,541,293	$1,737,254
Average number of employees	3,101	3,212
Average number of days worked	157	164

The first production of coal reported from the Indian Territory was made in 1885, in which year the total output was 500,000 short tons. It increased with each succeeding year until 1893, when it reached 1,252,110 tons, a gain of 150 per cent in eight years. In 1894 the operatives in the Territory took part in the great strike which paralyzed the industry for several months, and the product fell off 22 per cent to 969,606 short tons. Production returned to about its normal proportions in 1895, but without a proportionate increase in value.

Since 1885 the annual production has been as follows:

Product of coal in the Indian Territory from 1885 to 1895, inclusive.

Year.	Short tons.	Value.	Average price per ton.	Number of days active.	Number of employees.
1885..............	500,000	....	....	....	....
1886..............	534,580	$855,328	$1.60	....	....
1887..............	685,911	1,286,692	1.88	....	....
1888..............	761,986	1,432,072	1.89	....	....
1889..............	752,832	1,323,807	1.76	....	1,862
1890..............	869,229	1,579,188	1.82	238	2,571
1891..............	1,091,032	1,897,037	1.71	222	2,891
1892..............	1,192,721	2,043,479	1.71	211	3,257
1893..............	1,252,110	2,235,209	1.79	171	3,446
1894..............	969,606	1,541,293	1.59	157	3,101
1895..............	1,211,185	1,737,254	1.43	164	3,212

IOWA.

Total product in 1895, 4,156,074 short tons; spot value, $4,982,102.

The coal mining industry of Iowa in 1895 was marked by an increase in production of 188,821 short tons over that of 1894, but a decrease in value of $15,837, the average price declining from $1.26 in 1894 to $1.20 in 1895, in sympathy with the prevalent depression in values. There was an increase of 3 in the number of mines worked—174 in 1894 and 177 in 1895. This does not include the local banks worked on a small scale for purely domestic trade.

Comparing the statistics of labor employed in and about the mines during the past two years, it will be seen that while there was only a small increase in the total number of employees (9,995 to 10,066), there was an increase of 10 per cent in the average number of days worked—from 170 days in 1894 to 189 days in 1895.

For a description of the coal fields from which Iowa obtains her home supply the reader is referred to a paper on this subject by Mr. Charles R. Keyes, then assistant State geologist, in Mineral Resources for 1892; also for an account of mining methods in the State, to the report for 1894.

The statistics of production by counties in 1894 and 1895, together with the disposition of the product, are shown in the following tables.

Coal product of Iowa in 1894, by counties.

County.	Number of mines.	Loaded at mines for shipment.	Sold to local trade and used by employees.	Used at mines for steam and heat.	Total product.	Total value.	Average price per ton.	Average number of days active.	Average number of employees.
		Short tons.	*Short tons.*	*Short tons.*	*Short tons.*				
Appanoose.....	44	638,804	18,912	9,555	667,271	$852,124	$1.30	153	2,254
Boone..........	14	215,641	24,771	1,110	241,522	386,393	1.60	169	842
Dallas, Davis, and Greene...	4	10,147	4,132	1,142	15,421	26,104	1.65	186	62
Jasper	6	115,104	4,257	2,443	121,804	213,156	1.75	204	177
Jefferson.......	2	300	815	12	1,127	1,542	1.37	101	7
Keokuk........	13	129,694	10,837	2,219	142,750	162,786	1.14	128	551
Mahaska.......	14	1,053,142	84,301	15,545	1,152,988	1,357,448	1.18	199	2,396
Marion.........	12	99,088	8,942	665	108,695	114,623	1.05	121	329
Monroe	8	482,156	9,656	13,352	505,164	559,017	1.09	172	1,212
Polk	19	247,902	132,706	15,039	395,647	577,058	1.50	184	944
Taylor	2	13,880	900	....	14,780	27,343	1.85	212	52
Van Buren	5	21,658	1,859	102	23,619	32,257	1.37	174	78
Wapello........	8	228,228	48,403	1,952	278,583	304,661	1.09	167	541
Warren	5	5,409	7,232	8	12,649	20,015	1.58	177	32
Wayne..........	2	39,981	1,787	456	42,224	63,432	1.50	121	140
Webster	16	89,617	12,173	1,219	103,009	168,980	1.64	155	378
Small mines....	...	....	140,000	....	140,000	140,000	....	....	....
Total.....	174	3,390,751	511,683	64,819	3,967,253	4,997,939	1.26	170	9,995

Coal product of Iowa in 1895, by counties.

County.	Number of mines.	Loaded at mines for shipment.	Sold to local trade and used by employees.	Used at mines for steam and heat.	Total product.	Total value.	Average price per ton.	Average number of days active.	Average number of employees.
		Short tons.	*Short tons.*	*Short tons.*	*Short tons.*				
Appanoose.....	45	553,253	22,709	12,476	588,438	$737,907	$1.25	141	2,323
Boone	12	247,828	18,274	2,320	268,422	447,760	1.67	191	977
Greene.........	4	3,000	4,197	....	7,197	13,010	1.81	125	46
Jasper	5	150,000	5,573	134	155,707	196,477	1.26	242	278
Jefferson.......	2	400	1,440	....	1,840	2,335	1.27	176	11
Keokuk	12	249,124	11,750	5,520	266,394	277,769	1.04	167	563
Mahaska.......	14	979,674	26,837	10,112	1,016,623	1,134,922	1.12	208	2,144
Marion.........	13	181,615	9,874	2,279	193,768	195,628	1.01	200	471
Monroe.........	7	541,080	7,743	11,159	559,982	570,879	1.02	216	1,037
Polk	17	347,197	125,258	12,905	485,360	680,684	1.40	242	959
Taylor	3	12,180	1,843	30	14,062	26,638	1.89	236	38
Van Buren	4	7,800	1,990	106	9,896	13,582	1.37	193	31
Wapello........	9	206,969	50,892	3,649	261,510	291,746	1.12	183	541
Warren	5	197	5,899	20	6,116	9,145	1.50	165	20
Wayne	2	39,750	6,000	565	46,315	61,835	1.31	126	155
Webster	20	104,493	16,693	2,696	123,882	163,673	1.32	173	444
Dallas, Guthrie, and Story	3	6,298	3,848	416	10,562	19,012	1.80	198	28
Small mines....	...	....	140,000	....	140,000	140,000	....	....	....
Total.....	177	3,630,867	460,820	64,387	4,156,074	4,982,102	1.20	189	10,066

The State is divided into three inspection districts, known, respectively, as the first or southern, the second or northeastern, and the third or northwestern. The following table shows the annual production according to districts since 1883:

Total production of coal in Iowa, by districts, from 1883 to 1895, inclusive.

District.	1883.	1884.	1885.	1886.	1887.
	Short tons.	*Short tons.*	*Short tons.*	*Short tons.*	*Short tons.*
First........	1,231,444	1,165,803	1,294,971	1,416,165	1,598,062
Second......	1,654,267	1,583,468	1,379,799	1,890,784	1,989,095
Third.......	1,571,829	1,621,295	1,337,805	1,008,830	886,671
Total .	4,457,540	4,370,566	4,012,575	4,315,779	4,473,828

District.	1888.	1889.	1890.	1891.	1892.
	Short tons.	*Short tons.*	*Short tons.*	*Short tons.*	*Short tons.*
First........	1,712,443	1,497,685	1,536,978	1,229,512	1,398,793
Second......	2,211,274	1,720,727	1,626,193	1,814,910	1,666,224
Third.......	1,028,723	876,946	718,568	641,073	713,474
Small mines.	....	....	140,000	140,000	140,000
Total .	4,952,440	4,095,358	4,021,739	3,825,495	3,918,491

District.	1893.	1894.	1895.	Increase in 1895.
	Short tons.	*Short tons.*	*Short tons.*	*Short tons.*
First............	1,505,205	1,654,112	1,681,927	27,815
Second..........	1,734,666	1,417,512	1,438,724	21,182
Third............	592,358	755,599	895,423	139,824
Small mines......	140,000	140,000	140,000	....
Total.......	3,972,229	3,967,253	4,016,074	188,821

The counties comprised in each district and the product of each county since 1883 are shown in the following table:

Product of coal in the first inspection district of Iowa from 1883 to 1895, inclusive.

County.	1883.	1884.	1885.	1886.	1887.
	Short tons.	Short tons.	Short tons.	Short tons.	Short tons.
Appanoose	144,364	178,064	275,404	168,000	179,593
Adams	4,358	4,459	4,364	10,731	22,233
Cass	....	....	....	....	....
Davis	590	1,358	37,694	1,120	2,016
Jefferson	43,553	9,153	1,250	1,213	11,645
Lucas	546,360	460,017	492,750	594,450	529,758
Marion	101.903	108,735	112,012	158,697	238,218
Monroe	104,647	110,238	113,699	131,824	205,525
Montgomery	....	....	....	....	....
Page...........	838	1,130	2,037	1,736	1,993
Taylor	105	142	691	9,615	13,642
Van Buren	1,880	1,991	1,336	9,003	29,491
Wapello	266,360	269,607	210,461	265,564	304,722
Warren	14,367	15,374	14,364	26,132	27,772
Wayne..........	2,119	5,541	28.909	38,080	31,454
Total	1,231,444	1,165,803	1,294,971	1,416,165	1,598,062

County.	1888.	1889.	1890.	1891.	1892.
	Short tons.	Short tons.	Short tons.	Short tons.	Short tons.
Appanoose	235,495	285,194	284,560	409,725	411,984
Adams	21,075	13,457	(a)	(a)	(a)
Cass	....	280	(a)	(a)	(a)
Davis..........	2,016	3,825	(a)	(a)	(a)
Jefferson	10,514	8,123	351,600	800	1,000
Lucas..........	408,765	339,229			
Marion	258,330	145,180	153,506	165,867	134,400
Monroe	261,964	258,401	324,031	393,227	507,106
Montgomery	....	1,040	(a)	(a)	(a)
Page...........	3,842	2,768	(a)	(a)	(a)
Taylor	8,962	9,736	(a)	10,500	15,204
Van Buren	29,075	39,258	47,464	36,166	28,946
Wapello	426,042	359,199	341,932	165,827	231.472
Warren	19,155	14,515	8,470	2,000	3,600
Wayne..........	27,208	17,480	25,415	45,000	62,078
Total	1,712,443	1,497,685	b1,536,978	b1,229,512	b1.398.793

a Included in product of small mines.
b Exclusive of product of small mines.

Product of coal in the first inspection district of Iowa from 1883 to 1895—Continued.

County.	1893.	1894.	1895.	Increase.	Decrease.
	Short tons.	*Short tons.*	*Short tons.*	*Short tons.*	*Short tons.*
Appanoose........	489,920	667,271	588,438	....	78,833
Adams...........	(a)	(a)	(a)	....	....
Cass.............	(a)	(a)	(a)	....	....
Davis............	(a)	(a)	(a)	....	....
Jefferson......... ⎫ Lucas............ ⎭	482	1,127	1,840	713	....
Marion	111,145	108,695	193,768	85,073	....
Monroe	570,905	505,164	559,982	54,818	....
Montgomery	(a)	(a)	(a)	....	....
Page.............	(a)	(a)	(a)	....	....
Taylor...........	10,990	14,780	14,062	....	718
Van Buren.......	22,867	23,619	9,896	....	13,723
Wapello	230,460	278,583	261,510	....	17,073
Warren	3,000	12,649	6,116	....	6,533
Wayne...........	65,436	42,224	46,315	4,091	....
Total	b 1,505,205	b 1,654,112	b 1,681,927	c 27,815	....

a Included in product of small mines.   *b* Exclusive of product of small mines.   *c* Net increase.

Product of coal in the second inspection district of Iowa from 1883 to 1895.

County.	1883.	1884.	1885.	1886.	1887.
	Short tons.	*Short tons.*	*Short tons.*	*Short tons.*	*Short tons.*
Mahaska.........	1,038,673	1,044,640	851,319	953,525	1,148,614
Keokuk..........	560,045	482,652	417,554	610,741	670,888
Jasper	51,389	51,896	101,276	320,358	159,083
Scott	4,160	4,280	6,650	3,360	9,670
Marshall........	....	....	....	448	224
Hardin	....	....	....	2,240	504
Muscatine	....	....	....	112	112
Total	1,654,267	1,583,468	1,379,799	1,890,784	1,989,096

County.	1888.	1889.	1890.	1891.	1892.
	Short tons.	*Short tons.*	*Short tons.*	*Short tons.*	*Short tons.*
Mahaska	936,299	1,056,477	1,103,831	1,231,405	1,141,131
Keokuk	607,002	455,162	349,318	316,303	361,233
Jasper...........	308,200	199,152	173,044	267,202	163,860
Scott	10,170	9,446	(b)	(b)	(b)
Hardin	1,120	490	(b)	(b)	(b)
Total	a 2,211,274	1,720,727	c 1,626,193	c 1,814,910	c 1,666,224

a Includes 348,483 tons nut coal not included in county distribution.
b Included in product of small mines.   *c* Exclusive of product of small mines.

Product of coal in the second inspection district of Iowa from 1883 to 1895—Continued.

County.	1893.	1894.	1895.	Increase.	Decrease.
	Short tons.	*Short tons.*	*Short tons.*	*Short tons.*	*Short tons.*
Mahaska........	1,419,930	1,152,988	1,016,623	....	136,365
Keokuk.........	152,097	142,750	266,394	123,644	....
Jasper.........	162,639	121,804	155,767	33,903	....
Scott	(a)	(a)	(a)	....	....
Hardin	(a)	(a)	(a)	....	....
Total......	b 1,734,666	b 1,417,542	b 1,438,724	c 21,182	....

a Included in product of small mines.
b Exclusive of product of small mines.
c Net increase.

Product of coal in the third inspection district of Iowa from 1883 to 1895.

County.	1883.	1884.	1885.	1886.	1887.
	Short tons.	*Short tons.*	*Short tons.*	*Short tons.*	*Short tons.*
Boone	523,019	529,842	513,174	330,366	187,116
Dallas	42,793	41,647	36,944	24,624	45,270
Greene.........	99,513	107,886	100,337	131,643	118,601
Guthrie.........	....	5,809	5,148	19,257	20,502
Hamilton	2,238	2,103	1,028	3,710	7,469
Polk.............	625,879	694,312	518,442	378,520	341,705
Webster	278,387	239,696	162,732	120,710	163,768
Story	....	....	....	....	2,240
Total	1,571,829	1,621,295	1,337,805	1,008,830	886,671

County.	1888.	1889.	1890.	1891.	1892.
	Short tons.	*Short tons.*	*Short tons.*	*Short tons.*	*Short tons.*
Boone	156,959	174,392	153,229	151,659	139,820
Dallas..........	54,457	67,055	33,466	48,710	26,550
Greene	122,127	51,438	45,192	53,215	43,360
Guthrie..........	20,922	12,275	(a)	(a)	(a)
Hamilton	7,257	....	....	....	....
Polk	336,749	434,047	367,852	309,467	388,590
Webster	178,881	137,739	118,829	78,022	115,154
Story.............	2,240	....	....	....	....
Total	b 1,028,723	876,946	c 718,568	c 641,073	c 713,474

a Included in product of small mines.
b Includes 149,131 tons nut coal not included in county distribution.
c Exclusive of product of small mines.

Product of coal in the third inspection district of Iowa from 1883 to 1895—Continued.

County.	1893.	1894.	1895.	Increase.	Decrease.
	Short tons.	*Short tons.*	*Short tons.*	*Short tons.*	*Short tons.*
Boone	172,070	241,522	268,422	26,900	....
Dallas...........	13,461	10,201	6,061	....	4,140
Greene	18,000	5,220	7,197	1,977	....
Guthrie..........	(a)	(a)	1,600	1,600	....
Hamilton	....	....	....	....	....
Polk	271,731	395,647	485,360	89,713	....
Webster	117,096	103,009	123,882	20,873	....
Story	....	....	2,901	2,901	....
Total	*b* 592,358	*b* 755,599	*b* 895,423	*c* 139,824	....

a Included in product of small mines.   b Exclusive of product of small mines.   c Net increase.

The product in some of the earlier years in the history of coal mining has already been referred to. Below is given in tabular form the output in all the years for which figures are obtainable, with the value and average price per ton when known, and the statistics of labor employed during the past seven years.

Product of coal in Iowa from 1860 to 1895, inclusive.

Year.	Short tons.	Value.	Average price per ton.	Number of days active.	Number of employees.
1860...............	48,263	$92,180	$1.91	....	....
1865...............	69,574	....	....	....	....
1866...............	99,320	....	....	....	....
1868...............	241,453	....	....	....	....
1870...............	283,467	....	....	....	....
1875...............	1,231,547	2,500,140	2.03	....	....
1880...............	1,461,166	2,507,453	1.72	....	....
1882...............	3,920,000	....	....	....	....
1883...............	4,457,540	....	....	....	....
1884...............	4,370,566	....	....	....	....
1885...............	4,012,575	....	....	....	....
1886...............	4,315,779	5,391,151	1.25	....	....
1887...............	4,473,828	5,991,735	1.34	....	....
1888...............	4,952,440	6,438,172	1.30	....	....
1889...............	4,095,358	5,426,509	1.33	....	9,247
1890...............	4,021,739	4,995,739	1.24	213	8,130
1891...............	3,812,495	4,807,999	1.27	224	8,124
1892...............	3,918,491	5,175,060	1.32	236	8,170
1893...............	3,972,229	5,110,160	1.30	204	8,863
1894...............	3,967,253	4,997,939	1.26	170	9,995
1895...............	4,156,074	4,982,102	1.20	189	10,066

It will be seen from the above table that the greatest range in the average price per ton during the past ten years has been 14 cents; the highest price being $1.34, in 1887, and the lowest $1.20, in 1895.

In the preceding tables the product for a series of years, by counties, has been given. In the following tables will be found the average price per ton for a period of seven years, and the statistics of labor and working time in counties producing 10,000 tons or over:

Average prices for Iowa coal since 1889, in counties producing 10,000 tons or over.

County.	1889.	1890.	1891.	1892.	1893.	1894.	1895.
Appanoose	$1.32	$1.38	$1.39	$1.51	$1.51	$1.30	$1.25
Boone	1.86	1.82	1.86	1.80	1.87	1.60	1.67
Dallas	1.66	1.70	1.60	1.71	1.82	1.60	....
Greene	1.74	1.63	1.40	1.76	2.00	2.00	....
Jasper	1.42	1.11	1.44	1.28	1.28	1.75	1.26
Keokuk	1.25	1.31	1.32	1.28	1.21	1.14	1.04
Lucas	1.23	1.25	....	....	....	....	....
Mahaska	1.16	1.06	1.06	1.15	1.11	1.18	1.12
Marion	1.28	1.26	1.16	1.17	1.21	1.05	1.01
Monroe	1.16	1.21	1.21	1.26	1.12	1.09	1.02
Polk	1.59	1.49	1.50	1.57	1.73	1.50	1.40
Taylor	2.07	....	2.15	2.00	2.02	1.85	1.89
Van Buren	1.39	1.29	1.29	1.32	1.36	1.37	1.37
Wapello	1.13	1.10	1.24	1.29	1.27	1.09	1.12
Wayne	1.47	1.25	1.52	1.49	1.47	1.50	1.31
Webster	1.63	1.54	1.71	1.61	1.67	1.64	1.32
The State	1.33	1.24	1.27	1.32	1.30	1.26	1.20

Statistics of labor employed and working time at Iowa coal mines.

County.	1890.		1891.		1892.	
	Average number employed.	Average working days.	Average number employed.	Average working days.	Average number employed.	Average working days.
Appanoose	1,080	165	1,419	207	1,213	184
Boone	465	191	484	196	534	189
Dallas	130	207	140	210	89	242
Greene	121	209	120	185	120	214
Jasper	335	246	416	256	426	274
Keokuk	1,018	184	795	204	610	285
Lucas	324	298	....	....	....	....
Mahaska	1,673	258	1,815	263	1,818	238
Marion	269	265	394	222	267	244

*Statistics of labor employed and working time at Iowa coal mines—*Continued.

County.	1890.		1891.		1892.	
	Average number employed.	Average working days.	Average number employed.	Average working days.	Average number employed.	Average working days.
Monroe	735	197	806	203	1,112	233
Polk	700	243	779	239	938	268
Taylor			35	241	54	223
Van Buren	108	280	85	207	92	226
Wapello	773	159	421	214	445	260
Wayne	60	180	130	205	140	232
Webster	307	182	273	182	302	247
The State	8,130	213	8,124	224	8,170	236

County.	1893.		1894.		1895.	
	Average number employed.	Average working days.	Average number employed.	Average working days.	Average number employed.	Average working days.
Appanoose	1,793	151	2,254	153	2,323	141
Boone	577	208	842	169	977	191
Dallas	55	159	43	172		
Greene	60	150	19	213		
Jasper	284	253	177	204	278	242
Keokuk	528	155	551	128	563	167
Lucas						
Mahaska	2,209	258	2,396	199	2,144	208
Marion	292	193	329	121	471	200
Monroe	1,103	214	1,212	172	1,037	216
Polk	697	211	944	184	959	242
Taylor	29	228	52	212	38	236
Van Buren	69	178	78	174	31	193
Wapello	603	174	541	167	541	183
Wayne	155	205	140	121	155	126
Webster	391	194	378	155	444	173
The State	8,863	204	9,995	170	10,066	189

KANSAS.

Total product in 1895, 2,926,870 short tons; spot value, $3,481,981.

During 1895 there were five States in which the coal production was less than in 1894. First and foremost of these was Kansas, whose output decreased 461,381 short tons, or 14 per cent from a total of 3,388,251 short tons the previous year. The value decreased from $4,178,998 to $3,481,981, a loss of $697,017 in exact proportion to the decrease in product, there being no change in the average price per ton. The aggregate decrease in tonnage of the five States whose product in 1894 exceeded that of 1895 was 797,258 short tons, of which Kansas was responsible for 461,381 tons, or 58 per cent.

In 1894, not considering local banks, 113 mines contributed to the coal product of Kansas. In 1895 the number was reduced to 106.

The following tables show the details of production in 1894 and 1895, by counties:

Coal product of Kansas in 1894, by counties.

County.	Number of mines.	Loaded at mines for shipment.	Sold to local trade and used by employees.	Used at mines for steam and heat.	Made into coke.	Total product.	Total value.	Average price per ton.	Average number of days active.	Average number of employees.
		Short tons.	Short tons.	Short tons.	Short tons.	Short tons.				
Cherokee	26	914,056	24,878	8,551	657	948,142	$1,075,480	$1.13	143	1,834
Crawford	25	1,520,953	14,547	18,753	......	1,554,253	1,669,789	1.07	167	2,723
Franklin	9	4,024	13,378	16	......	17,418	32,799	1.88	147	87
Leavenworth	4	301,421	77,272	17,166	108	395,967	591,661	1.49	197	1,406
Linn..........	6	22,408	3,185	274	......	25,867	31,088	1.20	91	132
Osage	39	300,036	21,390	763	......	322,189	609,324	1.89	159	1,129
Atchison, Coffey, and Labette....	4	3,500	915	....	......	4,415	8,857	2.01	266	28
Small mines..	......	......	120,000	....	......	120,000	120,000	1.00	......	......
Total ..	113	3,066,398	275,565	45,523	765	3,388,251	4,178,998	1.23	164	7,339

Coal product of Kansas in 1895, by counties.

County.	Number of mines.	Loaded at mines for shipment.	Sold to local trade and used by employees.	Used at mines for steam and heat.	Made into coke.	Total product.	Total value.	Average price per ton.	Average number of days active.	Average number of employees.
		Short tons.	Short tons.	Short tons.	Short tons.	Short tons.				
Cherokee	26	880,018	28,375	10,439	112	918,944	$1,122,785	$1.22	155	1,982
Crawford	28	1,316,237	20,252	18,125	......	1,354,614	1,378,996	1.02	161	3,098
Franklin	7	3,223	13,801	23	......	17,047	31,404	1.84	192	54
Leavenworth	3	158,760	70,343	29,683	275	259,060	385,475	1.49	182	1,019
Linn..........	4	9,389	4,616	46	......	14,051	15,492	1.10	115	71
Osage........	35	219,975	20,782	827	......	241,584	423,364	1.75	145	1,231
Atchison, Coffey, and Labette....	3	....	1,570	....	......	1,570	4,465	2.84	61	27
Small mines..	......	......	120,000	....	......	120,000	120,000	1.00	......	......
Total ..	106	2,587,602	279,739	59,142	387	2,926,870	3,481,981	1.20	159	7,482

The following table shows in condensed form the statistics of coal production in Kansas since 1880. It will be noted that the years 1893 and 1895 were the only exceptions to a continual annual increase in the product.

Coal product of Kansas since 1880.

Year.	Short tons.	Value.	Average price per ton.	Number of days active.	Number of men employed.
1880	550,000				
1881	750,000				
1882	750,000				
1883	900,000				
1884	1,100,000				
1885	1,212,057	$1,485,002	$1.23		
1886	1,400,000	1,680,000	1.20		
1887	1,596,879	2,235,631	1.40		
1888	1,850,000	2,775,000	1.50		
1889	2,221,043	3,296,888	1.48		5,956
1890	2,259,922	2,947,517	1.30	210	4,523
1891	2,716,705	3,557,305	1.31	222	6,201
1892	3,007,276	3,955,595	1.31¼	208	6,559
1893	2,652,546	3,375,740	1.27	147	7,310
1894	3,388,251	4,178,998	1.23	164	7,339
1895	2,926,870	3,481,981	1.20	159	7,482

In the following table is shown the total product of the State since 1885, by counties, with the increases and decreases during 1895 as compared with 1894:

Coal product of Kansas since 1885, by counties.

[Short tons.]

County.	1885.	1886.	1887.	1888.
Atchison				
Cherokee	371,930	375,000	385,262	450,000
Coffey				
Crawford	221,741	250,000	298,049	425,000
Franklin	14,518	15,000	18,080	25,000
Labette				
Leavenworth	120,561	160,000	195,480	210,000
Linn	5,556	8,900	12,400	17,500
Osage	370,552	380,000	393,608	415,000
Small mines	107,199	211,100	294,000	307,500
Total	1,212,057	1,400,000	1,596,879	1,850,000

Coal product of Kansas since 1885, by counties—Continued.

[Short tons.]

County.	1889.	1890.	1891.	1892.
Atchison	....	....	....	....
Cherokee	549, 873	724, 861	832, 289	825. 531
Coffey	18, 272	12, 200	1, 218	3, 664
Crawford	827, 159	900, 464	997, 759	1, 309, 246
Franklin	37, 771	9, 045	10, 277	11, 150
Labette	2, 541	4, 000	800	800
Leavenworth	245, 616	319, 866	380, 142	330, 166
Linn	25, 345	10, 474	38, 934	43. 913
Osage	446, 018	179, 012	355, 286	372, 806
Small mines	68, 448	100, 000	100, 000	110. 000
Total	2, 221, 043	2, 259, 922	2, 716, 705	3, 007, 276

County.	1893.	1894.	1895.	Decreases in 1895.
Atchison	....	3, 500	1, 200	2, 300
Cherokee	697, 521	948, 142	918, 944	29, 198
Coffey	1, 720	475	120	355
Crawford	1, 195, 868	1, 554, 253	1, 354, 614	199, 639
Franklin	11, 768	17, 418	17, 047	371
Labette	800	440	250	190
Leavenworth	309, 237	395, 967	259, 060	136, 907
Linn	46, 464	25, 867	14, 051	11, 816
Osage	279, 168	322, 189	241, 584	80, 605
Small mines	110, 000	120, 000	120, 000	....
Total	2, 652, 546	3, 388, 251	2, 926, 870	461, 381

In the preceding table the output by counties has been shown. The following tables indicate the tendency of prices for such years as they have been obtained, and the statistics of labor employed, together with the average working time:

Average prices for Kansas coal since 1889 in counties producing 10,000 tons or over.

County.	1889.	1890.	1891.	1892.	1893.	1894.	1895.
Cherokee	$1. 20	$1. 22	$1. 19	$1. 22	$1. 15	$1. 13	$1. 22
Crawford	1. 20	1. 24	1. 09	1. 08	1. 10	1. 07	1. 02
Franklin	2. 18	2. 00	1. 90	1. 85	1. 84	1. 88	1. 84
Leavenworth	1. 69	1. 60	1. 40	1. 60	1. 55	1. 49	1. 49
Linn	1. 32	1. 34	1. 23	1. 27	1. 22	1. 20	1 10
Osage	2. 03	1. 35	2. 04	2. 04	1. 85	1. 89	1. 45
The State .	1. 48	1. 30	1. 31	1. 31¼	1. 27	1. 23	1. 20

Statistics of labor employed and working time at Kansas coal mines.

County.	1890.		1891.		1892.	
	Average number employed.	Average working days.	Average number employed.	Average working days.	Average number employed.	Average working days.
Cherokee..............	1,413	186	1,609	180	1,777	183
Crawford	1,447	198	1,785	202	2,234	213
Franklin..............	47	224	48	207	57	180
Leavenworth...........	745	273	1,073	245	1,020	247
Linn	60	164	94	236	115	237
Osage.................	804	209	1,581	270	1,312	202
The State	4,523	210	6,201	222	6,559	208

County.	1893.		1894.		1895.	
	Average number employed.	Average working days.	Average number employed.	Average working days.	Average number employed.	Average working days.
Cherokee..............	1,978	106	1,834	143	1,982	155
Crawford	2,883	163	2,723	167	3,098	161
Franklin..............	57	162	87	147	54	192
Leavenworth...........	1,145	208	1,406	197	1,019	182
Linn	136	194	132	91	71	115
Osage'................	1,100	145	1,129	159	1,231	145
The State	7,310	147	7,339	164	7,482	159

KENTUCKY.[1]

Total product in 1895, 3,357,770 short tons; spot value, $2,890,247.

Kentucky increased her coal product in 1895 over 1894 by 246,578 short tons, or 8 per cent. The general decline in values was felt here as in nearly every other State, for while the tonnage increased 8 per cent the value increased only 5 per cent. A decline of 2 cents, from 88 to 86 cents, is shown in the average price for the State.

The number of small country banks in Kentucky is exceptionally large, more than 1,600 of them being reported by the Eleventh Census. Their aggregate output amounts to about 150,000 tons, and the product from this source has been estimated at about that figure each year since 1889, with the exception of 1894, when Mr. Norwood made a canvass of these mines for the Survey. His investigation showed an output from

---

[1] The statistics of coal production in Kentucky in 1894 and 1895 were collected by Mr. C. J. Norwood, chief inspector of mines, who, in connection with similar work for the State, acted as special agent for the Geological Survey. His valuable assistance is hereby gratefully acknowledged.

the local banks of 153,999 short tons, verifying the estimated product placed in these reports for the other years, as this factor is one not subject to changing trade conditions and is apt to be fairly regular.

Mr. Norwood, in addition to collecting the statistics for 1895, has contributed the following interesting discussion of the coal-mining industry in Kentucky during 1895:

In order that certain references made herein may be understood, it may be well to state that, for the convenience of the office of the State inspector of mines, in part, and in part because of differences in the general character of the coals and in the natural markets for certain groups of mines, the two coal fields have been divided into four districts, namely, the Western, the Northeastern, the Southeastern, and the Elkhorn. The Western district includes all the counties in the western coal field. The Southeastern district includes the counties of Bell, Knox, Laurel, Pulaski, Rockcastle, and Whitley, in which commercial mines are operated, and the counties of Clay, Clinton, Harlan, Jackson, Leslie, Madison, Perry, and Wayne. In the Northeastern district are included Boyd, Carter, Greenup, Johnson, Lawrence, and Lee counties, in which commercial mining is carried on, and the counties of Breathitt, Elliott, Estill, Magoffin, Martin, Menefee, Morgan, Powell, Rowan, and Wolfe. The Elkhorn district includes Floyd, Knott, Letcher, and Pike counties. In the latter district no commercial mining has yet been done, because of lack of transportation facilities, but it is regarded as the future seat of perhaps the most important operations—certainly with respect to coking coal—in the State.

The operations of 1895 were, upon the whole, no more satisfactory in Kentucky than elsewhere. The marked features were an increase in production of commercial coal and a decrease in selling value. The increase of production, however, was less of a real advance (except as regards cannel) than was the decline in price a positive retrogression. This is best shown by comparisons of production and selling value of the ordinary bituminous coal alone for 1895,[1] with the returns for the three preceding years, thus:

Bituminous product.

1895 shows a gain of 164,568 tons over 1892. In selling value per ton there was a decline of 5.87 cents.

1895 shows a loss of 120,689 tons from 1893. In selling value per ton there was a decline of 6.54 cents.

1895 shows a gain of 238,331 tons over 1894. In selling value per ton there was a decline of 3.50 cents.

The decline in selling value is chiefly due to increased competition encountered by the coals mined in the Western and Northeastern districts, but the Southeastern district has also suffered. To meet the

---

[1] A distinction is made between cannel and bituminous coal. Since the former constitutes only a small proportion of the total output, but brings a very much higher price per ton in the market, it is omitted from these comparisons. Prices indicated are for the coal sold.

falling value, efforts are making to reduce the cost of production, which, so far, have led to the extension of machine mining, the adoption of approved appliances for handling the output at the mines, and closer attention to mining economies rather than to reduction of mining rates, though there is also a tendency toward the latter. The increase of competition has also necessitated better methods of cleaning the coal for market, and along this line there has been a marked and general improvement.

The increase of output (bituminous and cannel) in 1895 occurred solely in the Eastern district. In the Western district there was a loss. Thus:

Increases and decreases in coal product of Kentucky in 1895, by districts.

	Tons.
Southeastern district, increment (a)	240,908.53
Northeastern district, increment (a)	32,354.76
Gross increment	273,263.29
Western district, decrement	22,687.88
Net increase	250,575.41

a In the table under "Coal fields of the United States," these two districts are included as one—the Eastern.

Analytical comparisons of the output returns for the last four years show that the loss in the Western district was essentially the extra tonnage mined there in 1894 on account of the long "sympathetic" strike, which involved nearly all other regions but did not materially affect this district. The gain in the Eastern field was principally a partial recovery from the loss of tonnage caused by the long strike of 1894. In Laurel County, the second in importance in the Southeastern district, however, a strike lasting five months occurred in 1895, and, when this is considered, it seems that the gain made in the Southeastern district indicates a positive advance for that mining region.

Low water in the Ohio River gave an impetus to trade for the Southeastern mines, the Laurel County mines participating in the benefits thereof from October 1. The output of Whitley County mines (including the larger part of the "Jellico region") was also stimulated by a betterment of conditions in the South. In addition to other causes, the improvement of the Southern iron trade resulted in the absorption of a large amount of coal for coking which hitherto entered into competition with the "Jellico" product for steam purposes. Moreover, the long drought prevented river coal from supplying the trade heretofore controlled by it, and certain railroad mines which were strong competitors of the Whitley mines in the markets of Georgia and the Carolinas were allowed to open up new markets for their product.

The production of the Northeastern district, while it shows a small gain over that for 1894, fell far short of the output for 1892 and 1893, respectively. Competition with West Virginia coal, the introduction of which was encouraged by the strike of 1894, and adverse freight rates seem to be seriously affecting mining operations in portions of this district.

In the Western district the output for 1895 was little less than that for 1893, and it exceeded that for 1892 by nearly 50,000 tons. The increase of tonnage in 1894 amounted to 11,379 tons, and the decrease in 1895 equaled 22,688 tons. It therefore seems, all things being considered, that the production of this district has held up fairly well. In reports concerning the trade, however, there are constant recurrences to increase of competition and consequent reduction of value per ton. It may be well to quote two of the statements received. First, one company reports a decrease in value, "owing to competition of mine owners who have no idea of the cost of coal." Second, another company says: "Decrease in production and value has been caused by poor business among manufacturers and partial suspension of a great many manufacturing establishments, thus curtailing the consumption and causing competition to be greater, and forcing prices down. The decrease, however, of output or value has not been very notable, except when compared with output and value during the general strike of miners. * * * No new markets have been opened to this field. We believe the field for western Kentucky coal is becoming more limited on account of the opening up of more railroads and mines in Alabama."

The following tables show the statistics of production in 1894 and 1895, with the distribution and value of the product:

Coal product of Kentucky in 1894, by counties.

County.	Loaded at mines for shipment.	Sold to local trade and used by employees.	Used at mines for steam and heat.	Made into coke.	Total product.	Total value.	Average price per ton.	Average number of days active.	Average number of employees.
	Short tons.	*Short tons.*	*Short tons.*	*Short tons.*	*Short tons.*				
Bell	61,384	1,100	538	....	63,022	$79,715	$1.27	208	192
Carter	77,581	6,705	980	....	85,266	116,199	1.37	110	516
Daviess	3,541	6,808	4	....	10,353	8,986	.87	142	33
Hancock	34,641	900	30	....	35,571	35,297	1.00	129	111
Henderson	53,505	25,660	909	....	80,074	70,601	.88	164	215
Hopkins	725,278	24,618	17,597	44,266	811,759	607,250	.75	182	1,535
Johnson	16,402	500	....	....	16,902	40,596	2.40	284	98
Laurel	249,446	10,357	1,374	....	261,177	209,981	.80	108	927
Lee	48,367	460	700	....	49,527	57,827	1.17	246	152
Muhlenberg	253,861	7,688	8,031	....	269,580	205,513	.76	195	642
Ohio	339,105	5,726	4,106	....	348,937	248,480	.70	147	673
Pulaski	49,421	747	1,497	....	51,665	51,813	1.00	90	339
Rockcastle	800	....	....	....	800	800	1.00	20	38
Union	103,072	24,196	3,817	3,500	134,585	117,497	.87	168	260
Webster	39,220	2,029	685	....	41,934	27,505	.66	98	89
Butler, Christian, and McLean	72,157	1,040	975	....	74,172	84,478	1.14	180	204
Boyd, Greenup, and Lawrence	195,049	2,364	2,316	....	199,729	178,386	.89	188	517
Knox and Whitley	412,017	6,338	3,785	....	422,140	414,391	.98	125	1,542
Small mines	....	153,999	....	....	153,999	194,617	1.27	....	....
Total	2,734,847	287,235	47,344	47,766	3,111,192	2,749,932	.88	145	8,083

Coal product of Kentucky in 1895, by counties.

County.	Number of mines.	Loaded at mines for shipment.	Sold to local trade and used by employees.	Used at mines for steam and heat.	Made into coke.	Total product.	Total value.	Average price per ton.	Average number of days active.	Average number of employees.
		Short tons.	*Short tons.*	*Short tons.*	*Short ton..*	*Short tons.*				
Bell........	5	76,132	1,982	936	324	79,374	$116,773	$1.47	137	275
Carter.....	8	94,976	5,618	1,435	....	102,029	116,391	1.14	162	328
Daviess....	2	4,211	8,576	111	....	12,898	6,877	.53	126	29
Hancock...	3	30,377	103	89	....	30,569	27,536	.90	106	82
Henderson.	6	53,075	23,134	2,904	....	79,113	70,797	.89	155	277
Hopkins...	11	709,573	22,152	16,497	40,214	788,436	541,489	.69	170	1,366
Johnson ...	3	10,561	....	118	....	10,679	25,928	2.43	242	50
Laurel.....	16	231,044	914	1,680	....	233,638	210,393	.90	100	1,000
Lee........	3	42,363	399	551	....	43,313	45,122	1.04	158	141
Muhlenberg.....	9	258,924	3,732	4,697	....	267,353	197,735	.74	114	583
Ohio.......	9	376,504	4,553	5,846	....	386,903	270,731	.70	160	724
Union	5	86,760	10,864	2,692	300	100,616	88,632	.88	169	224
Webster...	3	44,819	4,321	756	....	49,896	37,862	.76	166	81
Butler, Christian, and McLean.....	7	64,247	3,179	1,068	....	68,494	71,906	1.05	139	220
Greenup, Boyd, and Lawrence	6	222,502	1,155	4,102	....	227,759	180,233	.79	233	435
Knox and Whitley.	16	630,445	5,461	5,131	....	641,037	611,081	.95	158	1,606
Pulaski and Rockcastle....	8	76,097	7,885	1,681	....	85,663	83,261	.97	127	378
Small mines	......	....	150,000	....	....	150,000	187,500	1.25	......	......
Total..	120	3,012,610	254,028	50,294	40,838	3,357,770	2,890,247	.86	153	7,799

The following table exhibits the annual product of the State since 1873:

Annual coal product of Kentucky since 1873.

Year.	Short tons.	Year.	Short tons.
1873..................	300,000	1885..................	1,600,000
1874..................	360,000	1886..................	1,550,000
1875..................	500,000	1887..................	1,933,185
1876..................	650,000	1888..................	2,570,000
1877..................	850,000	1889..................	2,399,755
1878..................	900,000	1890..................	2,701,496
1879..................	1,000,000	1891..................	2,916,069
1880..................	1,000,000	1892..................	3,025,313
1881..................	1,100,000	1893..................	3,007,179
1882..................	1,300,000	1894..................	3,111,192
1883..................	1,650,000	1895..................	3,357,770
1884..................	1,550,000		

Since 1889 the product, by counties, has been as follows:

Coal product of Kentucky since 1889, by counties.

County.	1889.	1890.	1891.	1892.	1893.
	Short tons.	Short tons.	Short tons.	Short tons.	Short tons.
Bell	20, 095	....	15, 693	7, 971	43, 671
Boyd	163, 124	a 191, 600	179, 350	194, 470	162, 706
Butler	6, 489	b 44, 931	12, 871	18, 951	22, 719
Carter	172, 776	179, 379 .	145, 937	139, 351	105, 844
Christian	27, 281	....	34, 060	47, 895	34, 560
Daviess	30. 870	....	6, 711	8, 064	7, 546
Greenup	632	....	....	....	1, 964
Hancock	21, 588	....	16, 815	13, 393	5, 000
Henderson	65, 682	c 126, 640	124, 021	80, 661	103, 639
Hopkins	555, 119	604, 307	680, 386	730, 879	713, 809
Johnson	32, 347	21, 222	21, 522	24, 543	6, 205
Knox	48, 703	90, 000	100, 000	106, 031	161, 986
Laurel...............	280, 451	291, 178	308, 242	241, 129	193, 622
Lawrence.............	79, 787	....	80, 848	97, 000	95, 232
Lee..................	....	....	....	....	....
McLean..............	35, 177	....	25, 000	....	....
Muhlenberg..........	206, 855	240, 983	260, 315	277, 865	290, 270
Ohio.................	246, 253	267, 736	322, 411	310, 289	312, 658
Pulaski	84, 363	....	15, 810	10, 990	52, 897
Rockcastle...........	1, 432	....	....	9, 774	9, 010
Union	56, 556	67, 763	86, 678	127, 225	158, 194
Webster	32, 729	d 133, 216	33, 883	38, 207	37, 999
Whitley	184, 874	262, 541	265, 516	340, 615	337, 648
Small mines..........	46, 572	180, 000	180, 000	200, 000	150, 000
Total	2, 399, 755	2, 701, 496	2, 916, 069	3, 025, 313	3, 007, 179

County.	1894.	1895.	Increase 1895.	Decrease 1895.
	Short tons.	Short tons.	Short tons.	Short tons.
Bell..................	63, 022	79, 374	16, 352	....
Boyd	111, 659	170, 443	58, 784	....
Butler	19, 982	24, 501	4, 519	....
Carter	85, 266	102, 029	16, 763	....
Christian	38, 836	22, 159	....	16, 677
Daviess	10, 353	12, 898	2, 545	....
Greenup	1, 573	1, 403	....	170
Hancock	35, 571	30, 569	....	5, 002
Henderson	80, 074	79, 113	....	961
Hopkins	811, 759	788, 436	....	23, 323

a Includes Pulaski.
b Includes Christian, Crittenden, and Daviess.
c Includes Hancock and McLean.
d Includes Lawrence.

Coal product of Kentucky since 1889, by counties—Continued.

County.	1894.	1895.	Increase 1895.	Decrease 1895.
	Short tons.	*Short tons.*	*Short tons.*	*Short tons.*
Johnson...............	16,902	10,679	....	6,223
Knox..................	72,858	185,734	112,876	....
Laurel	261,177	233,638	....	27,539
Lawrence	86,497	55,913	....	30,584
Lee	49,527	43,313	....	6,214
McLean	15,354	21,834	6,480	....
Muhlenberg	269,580	267,353	....	2,227
Ohio	348,937	386,903	37,966	....
Pulaski	51,665	81,188	29,523	....
Rockcastle	800	4,475	3,675	....
Union.................	134,585	100,616	....	33,969
Webster	41,934	49,896	7,962	....
Whitley..............	349,282	455,303	106,021	....
Small mines	153,999	150,000	....	3,999
Total	3,111,192	3,357,770	*a* 246,578	....

a Net increase.

The following tables exhibit the average price per ton received for coal at the mines in counties producing 10,000 tons or over, the number of employees, and the average number of days worked:

Average prices for Kentucky coal since 1889 in counties producing 10,000 tons or over.

County.	1889.	1890.	1891.	1892.	1893.	1894.	1895.
Bell.............	$1.40	....	$1.25	$1.50	$0.87	$1.27	$1.47
Boyd.............	1.10	$0.84	.81	.74	.82	.80	.84
Butler	1.24	....	1.00	2.00	1.25	1.25	1.12
Carter	1.14	1.10	1.04	1.29	1.24	1.37	1.14
Christian	1.26	.86	1.16	.95	.97	1.25	1.18
Daviess	....	....	....	....	....	....	.53
Hancock	1.58	....	1.84	2.50	2.50	1.00	.90
Henderson	1.26	.89	.92	.86	.85	.88	.89
Hopkins	.78	.76	.73	.70	.66	.75	.69
Johnson..........	1.67	2.13	2.28	2.37	2.64	2.40	2.43
Knox	.84	.77	1.00	.79	.85	.80	.79
Laurel	.90	.95	1.00	.94	.89	.80	.90
Lawrence	1.34	1.25	1.00	1.15	1.38	.98	.60
Lee	....	....	....	....	....	1.17	1.04
Muhlenberg	.87	.80	.84	.89	.75	.76	.74
Ohio	.81	.78	.79	.83	.78	.70	.70
Pulaski	1.30	1.00	1.39	1.20	1.06	1.00	.97
Union............	1.13	1.08	1.26	1.01	.95	.87	.88
Webster	.80	.78	.88	.86	.74	.66	.76
Whitley..........	1.10	1.09	1.19	1.05	1.03	1.01	1.02
The State	.99	.92	.93	.92	.86	.88	.86

Statistics of labor employed and working time at Kentucky coal mines.

County.	1890.		1891.		1892.	
	Average number employed.	Average working days.	Average number employed.	Average working days.	Average number employed.	Average working days.
Bell			75	130	30	136
Boyd			300	287	300	285
Butler			45	200	65	192
Carter	459	237	437	227½	375	276
Christian			125	187	135	210
Daviess						
Hancock			100	80	100	275
Henderson			231	249	150	231
Hopkins	1,104	231	1,203	244	1,292	228
Johnson	110	267	153	280	157	291
Knox	200	240	215	200	225	185
Laurel	680	225	798	233	775	177
Lawrence			300	289	325	295
Lee						
Muhlenberg	495	213	586	215	555	219
Ohio	520	236	625	225	818	169
Pulaski			74	170	45	135
Union	131	189	289	161	313	191
Webster			67	226	64	194
Whitley	625	204	680	190	890	216
The State	5,259	219	6,355	225	6,724	217

*Statistics of labor employed and working time at Kentucky coal mines—*Continued.

County.	1893.		1894.		1895.	
	Average number employed.	Average working days.	Average number employed.	Average working days.	Average number employed.	Average working days.
Bell	194	177	192	208	275	137
Boyd	275	225	287	183	306	253
Butler	45	224	64	195	82	155
Carter	476	222	516	110	328	162
Christian	143	182	88	194	77	142
Daviess					29	126
Hancock	25	150	111	129	82	106
Henderson	194	185	215	164	277	155
Hopkins	1,264	232	1,535	182	1,366	170
Johnson	27	281	98	284	50	242
Knox	275	240	255	113	388	159
Laurel	654	223	927	108	1,000	100
Lawrence	380	244	226	194	99	213
Lee			152	246	141	158
Muhlenberg	597	173	642	105	583	114
Ohio	590	170	673	147	724	160
Pulaski	108	180	339	90	317	138
Union	332	181	260	168	224	169
Webster	52	215	89	98	81	166
Whitley	850	163	1,287	125	1,218	158
The State	6,581	202	8,083	145	7,799	153

MARYLAND.

Total product in 1895, 3,915,585 short tons; spot value, $3,160,592.

Compared with 1894 the coal output of Maryland shows an increase of 414,157 short tons, or 12 per cent in amount, and of $473,322, or a little over 17 per cent in value, Maryland being one of the few States in which there was any advance in the average price realized. But the advance was not sufficient to bring the price back to that realized prior to 1894. In 1893 the average price obtained was 88 cents per short ton, or 98 cents for a long ton of 2,240 pounds, which is the standard measure set by Maryland laws. In 1894, notwithstanding a smaller output and the temporary coal famine produced by the great strike of that year, the price declined to 86 cents per long ton, or 77 cents per short ton, recovering somewhat to 91 cents per long ton, or 81 cents per short ton in 1895.

Coal mining in Maryland is confined to two counties, Allegany and Garrett, the former being by far the most important. Of the product in 1895 Garrett County produced 111,501 short tons, not quite 3 per cent of the total.

The following table shows the statistics of production in Maryland since 1889. The figures are reduced to short tons for the sake of uniformity throughout the report.

Coal product of Maryland since 1889.

Year.	Loaded at mines for shipment.	Sold to local trade and used by employees.	Used at mines for steam and heat.	Total amount produced.	Total value.	Average price per ton.	Average number of days active.	Average number of employees.
	Short tons.	Short tons.	Short tons.	Short tons.				
1889	2,885,336	44,217	10,162	2,939,715	$2,517,474	$0.86	....	3,792
1890	3,296,393	52,621	8,799	3,357,813	2,890,572	.86	244	3,842
1891	3,771,584	36,959	11,696	3,820,239	3,082,515	.80	244	3,891
1892	3,385,384	30,955	3,623	3,419,962	3,063,580	.89	225	3,886
1893	3,676,137	26,833	13,071	3,716,041	3,267,317	.88	240	3,935
1894	3,435,600	51,750	14,078	3,501,428	2,687,270	.77	215	3,974
1895	3,840,091	59,950	14,644	3,915,585	3,160,592	.81	248	3,912

The following table shows the annual output of coal in Maryland since 1883:

Product of coal in Maryland from 1883 to 1895.

Year.	Short tons.	Value.	Average price per ton.	Average number of days active.	Average number of men employed.
1883	2,476,075				
1884	2,765,617				
1885	2,833,337				
1886	2,517,577	$2,391,698	$0.95		
1887	3,278,023	3,114,122	.95		
1888	3,479,470	3,293,070	.95		
1889	2,939,715	2,517,474	.86		3,702
1890	3,357,813	2,899,572	.86	244	2,842
1891	3,820,239	3,082,515	.80	244	3,891
1892	3,419,962	3,063,580	.89	225	3,886
1893	3,716,041	3,267,317	.88	240	3,935
1894	3,501,428	2,687,270	.77	215	3,974
1895	3,915,585	3,160,592	.81	248	3,912

The following tables, showing the shipments from the various mines in Maryland since 1883 and the total shipments from the Cumberland field (including the West Virginia mines in the field) since 1842, are obtained from the official reports of the Cumberland coal trade. The Maryland mining laws compel the use of the long ton as a basis of measurement, and the quantities in these tables are so expressed.

Shipments of coal from Maryland mines from 1883 to 1895.

[Long tons.]

Company.	1883.	1884.	1885.	1886.	1887.
Consolidation Coal Co.	456,238	689,212	710,064	675,652	936,799
New Central Coal Co..	210,850	210,140	203,814	149,561	181,906
Georges Creek Coal and Iron Co........	257,490	266,042	257,343	265,942	394,012
Maryland Union Coal Co.................	137,105	117,180	98,095	116,771	148,523
Borden Mining Co.....	151,665	162,057	179,537	137,747	192,636
Maryland Coal Co.....	235,854	295,736	365,319	288,742	316,518
American Coal Co.....	190,055	194,330	220,339	211,305	259,632
Potomac Coal Co......	139,723	169,463	196,280	156,757	209,793
Hampshire and Baltimore Coal Co.......	194,534	36,416	....	....	....
Atlantic and Georges Creek Coal Co. (Pekin mine)...........	69,000	75,467	64,938	7,321	....
Swanton Mining Co...	34,905	28,620	52,862	42,688	61,610
Blæn Avon Coal Co...	84,721	100,961	69,192	65,830	11,934
Piedmont Coal and Iron Co.............	4,619	1,250	32	1,678	....
Union Mining Co.....	5,024	5,310	5,641	6,824	7,500
National Coal Co......	38,998	42,680	48,307	62,637	117,775
Davis and Elkins mine.	....	74,437	58,002	58,382	82,667
James Ryan..........	....	....	....	....	3,608
George M. Hansel.....	....	....	....	....	1,989
Total..........	2,210,781	2,469,301	2,529,765	2,247,837	2,926,902

Company.	1888.	1889.	1890.	1891.	1892.
Consolidation Coal Co.	1,023,349	871,463	956,031	910,977	912,787
New Central Coal Co..	169,484	118,885	218,169	206,813	201,428
Georges Creek Coal and Iron Co........	437,992	311,258	351,310	356,927	297,632
Maryland Union Coal Co.................	106,620	....	....	....	....
Borden Mining Co.....	212,520	206,549	290,055	300,268	253,629
Maryland Coal Co.....	340,866	268,438	366,839	406,464	280,946
American Coal Co.....	287,058	297,537	386,731	449,631	384,681
Potomac Coal Co......	208,777	205,212	217,232	184,706	137,738
Atlantic and Georges Creek Coal Co. (Pekin mine)...........	6,375	3,884	752	....	....

Shipments of coal from Maryland mines from 1883 to 1895—Continued.

[Long tons.]

Company.	1888.	1889.	1890.	1891.	1892.
Swanton Mining Co...	58,383	40,748	41,401	33,029	5,162
Union Mining Co......	6,396	3,734	17,933	179,232	176,996
National Coal Co.....	76,592	72,571	60,206	....	....
Davis and Elkins mine.	98,443	18,089	....	....	....
George M. Hansel.....	3,559	113	....	....	....
Barton and Georges Creek Valley Co.....	69,857	123,429	175,838	201,124	201,365
Enterprise mine.......	399	288	11	....	....
Franklin Consolidated Coal Co. (a)	....	71,837	66,644	76,593	72,117
Big Vein Coal Co......	....	21,310	52,917	62,832	66,683
Piedmont-Cumberland Coal Co.............	....	2,493	29,003	42,439	14,564
Anthony Mining Co...	....	....	115	9,725	10,665
Total	3,106,670	2,637,838	3,231,187	3,420,760	3,016,393

Company.	1893.	1894.	1895.	Increase in 1895.	Decrease in 1895.
Consolidation Coal Co.	907,559	892,502	923,655	31,153	....
New Central Coal Co..	223,504	151,002	201,726	50,724	....
Georges Creek Coal and Iron Co.........	345,791	364,668	458,245	93,577	....
Borden Mining Co.....	367,725	265,548	244,878	....	20,670
Maryland Coal Co.....	356,820	351,542	449,234	97,692	....
American Coal Co.....	443,963	453,680	524,079	70,399	....
Potomac Coal Co......	121,258	108,977	123,708	14,731	....
Swanton Mining Co...	....	2,465	....	....	2,465
Union Mining Co......	205,210	173,548	184,916	11,368	....
Barton and Georges Creek Valley Co.....	193,545	165,886	190,826	24,940	....
Franklin Consolidated Coal Co. (a)	57,598	64,766	50,781	....	13,985
Big Vein Coal Co......	63,940	47,023	36,397	....	10,626
Piedmont-Cumberland Coal Co.............	17,869	6,483	9,537	3,054	....
Anthony Mining Co...	11,228	17,617	10,062	....	7,555
Atlantic and Georges Creek Coal Co......	....	....	4,714	4,714	....
Midland Mining Co...	....	....	240	240	....
Total	3,316,010	3,065,707	3,412,998	b 347,291	....

a Succeeded by Davis Coal and Coke Company in 1894.　　*b* Net increase.

Total shipments from the Cumberland coal field in

Year.	Frostburg region.						
	Cumberland and Pennsylvania R. R.				Cumberland Coal and Iron Company's railroad.		
	By Baltimore and Ohio R. R.	By Chesapeake and Ohio Canal.	By Pennsylvania R. R.	Total.	By Baltimore and Ohio R. R.	By Chesapeake and Ohio Canal.	Total.
	Long tons.	Long tons.	Long tons.	Long tons.	Long tons.	Long tons.	Long tons.
1842	757			757	951		951
1843	3,661			3,661	6,421		6,421
1844	5,150			5,156	9,734		9,734
1845	13,738			13,738	10,915		10,915
1846	11,240			11,240	18,555		18,555
1847	20,615			20,615	32,325		32,325
1848	36,571			36,571	43,000		43,000
1849	63,676			63,676	78,773		78,773
1850	73,783	3,167		76,950	119,023	875	119,898
1851	70,893	51,438		122,331	103,808	31,540	135,348
1852	128,534	46,357		174,891	139,925	19,362	159,287
1853	150,381	84,060		234,441	155,278	70,535	225,813
1854	148,953	63,731		212,684	173,580	92,114	265,694
1855	93,691	77,095		170,786	97,710	100,691	198,401
1856	86,994	80,387		167,381	121,945	105,149	227,094
1857	80,743	55,174		135,917	88,573	54,000	142,573
1858	48,018	166,712		214,730	66,009	87,539	153,548
1859	48,415	211,639		260,054	72,423	86,203	158,026
1860	70,669	232,278		302,947	80,500	63,600	144,100
1861	23,878	68,303		92,181	25,983	29,296	55,279
1862	71,745	75,206		146,951	41,096	23,478	64,574
1863	117,796	173,269		291,065	111,087	43,523	154,610
1864	287,126	194,120		481,246	67,676	64,522	132,198
1865	384,297	285,295		669,592	104,651	57,907	162,558
1866	592,938	291,019		883,957	52,251	52,159	104,410
1867	623,031	385,249		1,008,280	40,106	72,904	113,010
1868	659,115	424,406		1,083,521	100,345	57,919	158,264
1869	1,016,777	573,243		1,590,020	130,017	78,908	208,925
					2,092,660	1,192,224	3,284,884
					Eckhart Branch R. R.		
1870	909,511	520,196		1,429,707	114,404	83,941	198,345
1871	1,247,279	656,085		1,903,364	69,864	194,254	264,118
1872	1,283,956	612,537	22,021	1,918,514	26,586	203,666	230,252
1873	1,509,570	641,220	114,589	2,265,379	89,765	137,582	227,347
1874	1,295,804	631,882	67,671	1,995,357	113,670	135,182	248,852
1875	1,095,880	715,673	160,213	1,971,766	52,505	164,165	216,670
1876	939,262	443,435	131,866	1,514,563	15,285	189,005	204,290
1877	755,278	473,646	170,884	1,399,808	63,181	111,350	174,531
1878	823,801	486,038	145,864	1,455,703	99,455	123,166	222,621
1879	933,240	397,009	154,264	1,484,513	141,907	104,238	246,145
1880	1,055,491	471,800	213,446	1,740,737	197,525	131,325	328,850
1881	1,113,263	270,156	153,501	1,536,920	271,570	151,526	423,096
1882	576,701	115,344	91,574	783,619	199,183	76,140	275,323
1883	851,985	302,678	217,065	1,371,728	197,235	141,390	338,625
1884	1,193,780	150,471	199,138	1,543,389	289,884	124,718	414,602
1885	1,091,904	171,460	206,227	1,469,591	289,407	117,829	407,236
1886	1,131,949	115,531	141,520	1,389,000	243,321	113,791	357,112
1887	1,584,114	132,177	176,241	1,892,532	332,798	125,305	458,103
1888	1,660,406	155,216	193,046	2,008,668	374,888	95,191	470,079
1889	1,430,381	26,886	177,152	1,634,419	368,497	26,407	394,904
1890	1,511,418		291,704	1,803,122	522,334		522,334
1891	1,628,574	9,070	289,232	1,926,876	463,142	39,294	502,436
1892	1,426,994	93,705	214,011	1,734,710	349,207	170,116	519,323
1893	1,332,634	135,409	360,807	1,828,850	341,321	201,947	543,268
1894	1,068,739	95,523	372,205	1,536,467	436,216	208,914	645,130
1895	1,193,834	101,076	255,133	1,550,043	464,407	212,534	676,941
Total	35,578,939	11,466,371	4,519,374	51,564,684	6,127,557	3,382,976	9,510,533

a Includes 112,837 tons used on line of Cumberland and Pennsylvania Railroad and its branches pany in locomotives, rolling mills, etc.

Maryland and West Virginia from 1842 to 1895.

Frostburg region.				Piedmont region.		Total.			
Georges Creek and Cumberland R. R.				Georges Creek R. R.	Hampshire R. R. by Baltimore and Ohio R. R.	Baltimore and Ohio R. R. and local.	Chesapeake and Ohio Canal.	Pennsylvania R. R.	Aggregate.
By Chesapeake and Ohio Canal.	By Pennsylvania R. R.	Local and Baltimore and Ohio.	Total.						
Long tons.	Long tons.	Long tons.	Long tons.	Long tons.	Long tons.	Long tons.	Long tons.	Long tons.	Long tons.
						1,708			1,708
						10,082			10,082
						14,890			14,890
						24,653			24,653
						29,795			29,795
						52,940			52,940
						79,571			79,571
						142,449			142,449
						192,806	4,042		196,848
						174,701	82,978		257,679
						268,459	65,719		334,178
				73,725		376,219	157,760		533,979
				181,303		503,836	155,845		659,681
				227,245	65,570	478,486	183,786		662,272
				269,210	42,765	502,330	204,120		706,450
				252,368	51,628	465,912	116,574		582,486
				218,318	63,060	395,405	254,251		649,656
				257,740	47,934	426,512	297,842		724,354
				289,298	52,564	493,031	295,878		788,909
				85,554	36,660	172,075	97,599		269,674
				69,482	36,627	218,950	98,684		317,634
				266,430	36,240	531,553	216,792		748,345
				44,552		399,354	258,642		657,996
				71,345		560,293	343,202		903,495
				90,964		736,153	343,178		1,079,331
				72,532		735,669	458,153		1,193,822
				88,658		848,118	482,325		1,330,443
				83,724		1,230,518	652,151		1,882,669
				2,190,673					
				Empire and West Virginia mines.					
				28,035	60,988	1,112,938	604,137		1,717,075
				81,218	96,453	1,494,814	850,339		2,345,153
				85,441	121,304	1,517,347	816,103	22,021	2,355,471
				77,582	103,793	1,780,710	778,802	114,589	2,674,101
				57,492	109,194	1,576,160	767,064	67,671	2,410,895
				63,537	90,800	1,302,237	879,838	160,698	2,342,773
				108,723	7,505	1,070,775	632,440	131,866	1,835,081
						818,459	584,996	170,884	1,574,339
					908	924,254	609,204	145,864	1,679,322
					51	1,075,198	501,247	154,264	1,730,709
				66,573		1,319,589	603,125	213,446	2,136,160
83,136	125,097	4,947	213,180	88,722		1,478,502	504,818	278,598	2,201,918
78,208	93,861	31,436	203,595	277,929		1,085,249	269,782	185,435	1,540,466
215,767	202,223	77,829	495,819	338,001		1,444,766	680,119	419,288	2,544,173
69,765	156,959	283,336	510,060	466,928		2,233,928	314,954	356,097	2,934,979
70,455	214,518	291,685	585,658	403,489		2,076,485	368,744	420,745	2,865,974
53,480	98,371	348,196	500,047	346,308		2,069,774	282,802	239,891	2,592,467
4,863	153,230	418,057	576,150	449,011		2,724,347	262,345	389,104	3,375,796
112	286,787	341,024	627,923	564,397		2,609,216	286,700	715,151	3,671,067
	365,029	243,487	608,516	576,047		2,357,585	57,459	798,842	3,213,886
	677,593	228,138	905,731	774,904		2,723,341		1,282,748	4,006,091
	763,845	229,266	993,111	959,673		2,855,225	51,121	1,474,087	4,380,433
	568,003	236,314	804,317	971,214		2,557,177	266,901	1,205,486	4,029,564
	741,954	201,938	943,892	1,031,797		2,423,159	338,107	1,586,541	4,347,807
	773,074	111,036	884,110	900,399		2,084,265	304,437	1,577,404	3,966,106
125	1,031,015	110,258	1,141,398	1,157,803		a2,418,554	314,551	1,793,080	4,526,185
585,001	6,251,559	3,156,947	9,993,507	9,875,223	1,475,969	57,262,187	16,729,656	13,903,800	87,895,643

and at Cumberland and Piedmont; also 276,237 tons used by the Baltimore and Ohio Railroad Com-

MICHIGAN.

Total product in 1895, 112,322 short tons; spot value, $180,016.

Coal mining in Michigan received a marked impetus in 1895, the product obtained exceeding that of any year since 1882, and reached a total of over 100,000 tons for the first time in twelve years. In 1880, 1881, and 1882 coal mining in the State was comparatively active, exceeding 125,000 tons each year, and reaching the maximum in 1882, with a total of 135,339 tons. After that it became irregular, fluctuating between 40,000 and 80,000 tons annually, according to the mildness or severity of the climate, until 1895, when in the general increase in coal production the output of Michigan rose again to 112,322 tons. More than this, the value increased in still greater proportion, noting an advance in the average price from $1.47 in 1894 to $1.60 in 1895.

The following tables show the details of production in Michigan for the past four years and the total output since 1887:

Coal product of Michigan for four years.

Year.	Loaded at mines for shipment.	Sold to local trade and used by employees.	Used at mines for steam and heat.	Total product.	Total value.	Average price per ton.	Average number of days active.	Average number of employees.
	Short tons.	*Short tons.*	*Short tons.*	*Short tons.*				
1892......	27,200	45,180	5,610	77,990	$121,314	$1.56	230	195
1893......	27,787	16,367	1,825	45,979	82,462	1.79	154	162
1894......	60,817	7,055	2,150	70,022	103,049	1.47	224	223
1895......	80,403	27,019	4,900	112,322	180,016	1.60	186	320

Coal product of Michigan from 1877 to 1895.

Year.	Short tons.	Year.	Short tons.
Previous to 1877......	350,000	1886...............	60,434
1877...............	69,197	1887...............	71,461
1878...............	85,322	1888...............	81,407
1879...............	82,015	1889...............	67,431
1880...............	129,053	1890...............	74,977
1881...............	130,130	1891...............	80,307
1882...............	135,339	1892...............	77,990
1883...............	71,296	1893...............	45,979
1884...............	36,712	1894...............	70,022
1885...............	45,178	1895...............	112,322

MISSOURI.

Total product in 1895, 2,372,393 short tons; spot value, $2,651,612.

The output of coal in Missouri reached its highest figure in 1888, a year of exceptional activity, particularly in the Western States. In that year Missouri's product amounted to 3,909,967 short tons. It has not exceeded 3,000,000 tons since that time. The product in 1895, while larger than that of 1894, was much below the average for the previous ten years. The average for the decade preceding 1895 was nearly 2,800,000 per year, more than 400,000 tons larger than the output during the past year.

The actual increase in the product of 1895 over 1894 was 127,354 short tons, or 6 per cent. The increase in value was only $17,048, or less than 1 per cent, there being a decline of 5 cents in the average price for the year, from $1.17 in 1894 to $1.12 in 1895.

The following tables exhibit the details of production in the past two years:

Coal product of Missouri in 1894, by counties.

County.	Number of mines.	Loaded at mines for shipment.	Sold to local trade and used by employees.	Used at mines for steam and heat.	Total product.	Total value.	Average price per ton.	Average number of days active.	Average number of employees.
		Short tons.	Short tons.	Short tons.	Short tons.				
Adair and Audrain.	6	15,922	9,049	100	25,071	$41,517	$1.66	199	87
Bates	17	260,044	14,476	5,186	279,706	289,665	1.04	83	919
Barton	5	131,977	6,675	1,325	139,977	147.712	1.06	195	412
Boone	3	10,000	7,860	300	18,160	28,200	1.55	200	50
Caldwell	3	23,343	2,155	806	26,304	46,301	1.76	228	115
Callaway	14	2,000	15,734	953	18,687	29,884	1.60	156	81
Cooper	2	2,155	48	40	2,243	5,236	2.33	90	20
Henry	14	152,945	4,841	623	158,409	179,413	1.13	156	327
Johnson	2	6,235	263	....	6,498	9,313	1.43	240	25
Lafayette	30	179,691	18,410	5,322	203,423	348,153	1.68	119	1,305
Linn	5	66,495	10,167	610	77,272	122,984	1.59	233	264
Macon	10	469,529	3,832	16,218	489,579	467,751	.96	183	1,387
Morgan	3	....	745	....	745	1,500	2.01	95	6
Putnam	3	111,415	2,180	3,060	116,655	141,262	1.21	146	486
Randolph	11	192,832	4,893	3,672	201,397	220,418	1.09	144	566
Ray	6	95,316	3,277	2,093	100,686	145,443	1.44	78	690
Vernon	10	234,636	2,662	6,915	244,213	241,938	.99	90	666
Chariton, Moniteau, Jackson, Montgomery, and St. Clair	5	720	15,234	60	16,014	27,874	1.28	147	117
Small mines	....	....	120,000	....	120,000	140,000	....	....	....
Total	149	1,955,255	242,501	47,283	2,245,039	2,634,564	1.17	138	7,523

Coal product of Missouri in 1895, by counties.

County.	Number of mines.	Loaded at mines for shipment.	Sold to local trade and used by employees.	Used at mines for steam and heat.	Total product.	Total value.	Average price per ton.	Average number of days active.	Average number of employees.
		Short tons.	*Short tons.*	*Short tons.*	*Short tons.*				
Adair	2	22,950	88	....	23,038	$28,598	$1.24	153	62
Audrain	2	26,346	11,310	730	38,386	55,501	1.45	238	72
Barton	3	50,735	224	441	51,400	56,277	1.09	172	150
Bates	11	349,852	2,389	2,500	354,741	324,301	.91	168	683
Boone	3	8,000	7,120	60	15,180	19,408	1.28	202	57
Caldwell	2	11,975	3,959	1,046	16,980	23,600	1.39	243	115
Callaway	8	2,000	17,165	4	19,169	28,936	1.51	205	73
Henry	10	51,077	4,069	282	55,428	80,609	1.45	115	173
Lafayette	26	243,412	16,764	3,751	263,927	369,866	1.40	147	1,015
Linn	5	86,584	11,774	677	99,035	151,576	1.53	234	282
Livingston	2	....	623	....	623	1,102	1.77	137	9
Macon	9	494,178	3,254	8,838	506,270	469,123	.93	152	1,346
Morgan	2	920	750	50	1,720	2,455	1.43	91	12
Randolph	10	207,482	16,605	4,010	228,097	241,310	1.06	187	602
Ray	8	127,077	4,072	2,532	133,681	192,409	1.44	132	559
Vernon	9	293,830	1,748	7,505	303,083	258,914	.85	149	542
Cooper, Grundy, Jackson, Johnson, Moniteau, Montgomery, Putnam, Ralls, Saline and St. Claire	12	128,034	9,176	4,425	141,635	207,627	1.46	172	547
Small mines	.....	....	120,000	....	120,000	140,000	.....	.....	.....
Total	124	2,104,452	231,090	36,851	2,372,393	2,651,612	1.12	163	6,299

The annual production since 1873 has been as follows:

Coal product of Missouri since 1873.

Year.	Short tons.	Year.	Short tons.
1873	784,000	1885	3,080,000
1874	789,680	1886	1,800,000
1875	840,000	1887	3,209,916
1876	1,008,000	1888	3,909,967
1877	1,008,000	1889	2,557,823
1878	1,008,000	1890	2,735,221
1879	1,008,000	1891	2,674,606
1880	1,680,000	1892	2,773,949
1881	1,960,000	1893	2,897,442
1882	2,240,000	1894	2,245,039
1883	2,520,000	1895	2,372,393
1884	2,800,000		

The following table contains the statistics of production by counties since 1889, with the increases and decreases in 1895 as compared with 1894:

Coal product of Missouri since 1889, by counties.

[Short tons.]

County.	1889.	1890.	1891.	1892.	1893.
Adair	18,592	16,000	10,940	11,138	20,893
Audrain	26,194	20,261	8,772	23,012	37,986
Barton	61,167	28,500	85,002	50,561	42,360
Bates	755,989	751,702	628,580	572,730	409,819
Boone	31,405	17,000	16,340	15,636	11,650
Caldwell	13,594	21,599	51,065	30,806	18,102
Callaway	16,053	5,331	22,458	21,710	24,266
Clay					12,724
Cooper	996			1,720	1,632
Grundy	23,401	24,000	30,000	27,300	37,633
Henry	180,118	109,768	102,866	89,769	100,415
Jasper	720				604
Johnson	12,841	5,950	4,500	5,680	11,009
Lafayette	348,670	347,688	277,393	324,848	339,668
Linn	6,992	1,300	26,994	40,622	93,207
Macon	446,396	540,061	592,105	668,146	688,479
Moniteau					520
Montgomery	12,300	13,584	16,129	16,689	12,000
Morgan	2,000	650	220	48	
Putnam	83,774	108,514	122,666	137,058	139,582
Randolph	221,463	269,372	274,520	149,608	214,490
Ray	220,530	278,118	213,539	235,298	220,418
St. Clair	6,880	5,050	2,500	6,500	336
Vernon	39,420	13,385	48,017	155,070	309,649
Other counties and small mines	28,328	157,388	140,000	150,000	150,000
Total	2,557,823	2,735,221	2,674,606	2,773,949	2,897,442

Coal product of Missouri since 1889, by counties—Continued.

[Short tons.]

County.	1894.	1895.	Increase in 1895.	Decrease in 1895.
Adair	10, 150	23, 038	12, 888	
Audrain	14, 921	38, 386	23, 465	
Barton	139, 977	51, 400		88, 577
Bates	279, 706	354, 741	75, 035	
Boone	18, 160	15, 180		2, 980
Caldwell	26, 304	16, 980		9, 324
Callaway	18, 687	19, 169	482	
Chariton	100			100
Cooper	2, 243	225		2, 018
Grundy		29, 340	29, 340	
Henry	158, 409	55, 428		102, 981
Jackson	6, 000	21, 300	15, 300	
Johnson	6, 498	250		6, 248
Lafayette	203, 423	263, 927	60, 504	
Linn	77, 272	99, 035	21, 763	
Livingston		623	623	
Macon	489, 579	506, 270	16, 691	
Moniteau	364	425	61	
Montgomery	8, 871	10, 881	2, 010	
Morgan	745	1, 720	975	
Putnam	116, 655	69, 044		47, 611
Ralls		9, 800	9, 800	
Randolph	201, 397	228, 097	26, 700	
Ray	100, 686	133, 681	32, 995	
Saline		150	150	
St. Clair	679	220		459
Vernon	244, 213	303, 083	58, 870	
Other counties and small mines	120, 000	120, 000		
Total	2, 245, 039	2, 372, 393	a 127, 354	

a Net increase.

The following tables are worthy of attention, as showing the tendency of prices during a series of years and the statistics of labor employed at Missouri coal mines during the same period.

Average prices for Missouri coal since 1889, in counties producing 10,000 tons or over.

County.	1889.	1890.	1891.	1892.	1893.	1894.	1895.
Adair............	$1.66	$1.70	$1.75	$1.75	$1.49	$1.48	$1.24
Andrain.........	1.47	1.61	1.57	1.50	1.40	1.50	1.45
Barton..........	1.35	1.06	1.22	1.29	1.12	1.06	1.09
Bates...........	1.14	1.02	1.04	1.00	1.01	1.04	.91
Boone...........	1.54	1.50	1.50	1.53	1.62	1.55	1.28
Caldwell........	1.97	1.98	2.15	2.20	1.98	1.76	1.39
Callaway	1.79	1.50	1.42	1.56	1.54	1.60	1.51
Grundy	2.05	2.05	2.05	2.05	2.05	....	1.95
Henry...........	1.55	1.48	1.33	1.41	1.45	1.13	1.45
Lafayette	1.60	1.55	1.55	1.60	1.52	1.68	1.40
Linn	1.88	....	1.19	1.56	1.62	1.59	1.53
Macon	1.23	1.11	1.02	1.04	1.06	.96	.93
Montgomery.....	1.42	1.35	1.35	1.36	1.35	1.25	1.25
Putnam	1.34	1.31	1.31	1.37	1.36	1.21	1.22
Randolph	1.29	1.14	1.06	1.07	1.10	1.09	1.06
Ray.............	1.57	1.52	1.62	1.54	1.51	1.44	1.44
Vernon..........	1.18	1.20	1.04	1.02	1.01	.99	.85
The State...	1.36	1.24	1.23	1.23	1.23	1.17	1.12

Statistics of labor employed and working time at Missouri coal mines.

County.	1890.		1891.		1892.	
	Average number employed.	Average working days.	Average number employed.	Average working days.	Average number employed.	Average working days.
Adair	48	280	40	300	40	300
Audrain................	70	205	33	180	60	224
Barton.................	90	231	263	221	149	179
Bates	1,315	215	1,077	235	663	207
Boone.................	46	290	53	257	38	273
Caldwell..............	77	294	194	230	158	244
Callaway	11	218	90	230	97	243
Grundy	50	200	90	297	140	275
Henry.................	311	207	286	218	246	219
Lafayette	1,056	217	850	206	949	233
Linn	....	....	90	240	135	249
Macon	1,027	259	1,198	228	1,489	252
Montgomery	33	200	37	260	40	195
Putnam	355	234	430	196	393	242
Randolph	635	229	535	249	371	227
Ray...................	687	241	753	178	694	206
Vernon................	44	118	139	131	186	166
The State	5,971	229	6,199	218	5,893	230

Statistics of labor employed and working time at Missouri coal mines—Continued.

County.	1893. Average number employed.	1893. Average working days.	1894. Average number employed.	1894. Average working days.	1895. Average number employed.	1895. Average working days.
Adair	81	188	28	226	62	153
Audrain	101	184	59	186	72	238
Barton	207	116	412	195	150	172
Bates	771	162	919	83	683	168
Boone	32	203	50	200	57	202
Caldwell	74	223	115	228	115	243
Callaway	127	218	81	156	73	205
Grundy	130	300	....	....	105	222
Henry	279	225	327	156	173	115
Lafayette	1,148	226	1,305	119	1,015	147
Linn	290	233	264	233	282	234
Macon	1,833	232	1,387	183	1,346	152
Montgomery	48	200	35	156	25	150
Putnam	460	236	486	146	301	148
Randolph	523	191	566	144	602	187
Ray	636	196	690	78	559	132
Vernon	537	126	666	90	542	149
The State	7,375	206	7,523	138	6,299	163

MONTANA.

Total product in 1895, 1,504,193 short tons; spot value, $2,850,906.

The annual coal product of Montana has shown an uninterrupted increase each year since 1887, and the output in 1895 shows a phenomenal gain of over 62 per cent, or 576,798 short tons over that of 1894. The value increased from $1,887,390 to $2,850,906, a gain of $963,516, or a little more than 50 per cent.

There was a decrease in the number of mines worked from 26 in 1894 to 22 in 1895, showing a tendency, noticed in some other States, toward greater production at the larger mines and the closing of smaller operations. The number of employees increased from 1,782 to 2,184 and the average working time from 192 to 223 days.

Coal product of Montana in 1894, by counties.

County.	Number of mines.	Loaded at mines for shipment.	Sold to local trade and used by employees.	Used at mines for steam and heat.	Made into coke.	Total product.	Total value.	Average price per ton.	Average number of days active.	Total number of employees.
		Short tons.	Short tons.	Short tons.	Short tons.	Short tons.				
Cascade	6	623,295	4,210	11,455	....	638,960	$1,238,001	$1.94	184	1,165
Choteau	6	705	2,177	10	....	2,892	11,089	3.83	92	28
Dawson	2	....	545	....	....	545	1,635	3.00	89	6
Fergus, Granite, Lewis and Clarke, and Meagher	5	900	563	25	....	1,488	4,840	3.25	50	22
Gallatin........	3	66,648	975	1,634	....	69,257	168,431	2.43	265	153
Park	4	169,623	4,430	4,200	36,000	214,253	463,394	2.16	198	408
Total.......	26	861,171	12,900	17,324	36,000	927,395	1,887,390	2.04	192	1,782

Coal product of Montana in 1895, by counties.

County.	Number of mines.	Loaded at mines for shipment.	Sold to local trade and used by employees.	Used at mines for steam and heat.	Made into coke.	Total product.	Total value.	Average price per ton.	Average number of days active.	Average number of employees.
		Short tons.	Short tons.	Short tons.	Short tons.	Short tons.				
Carbon	2	176,843	4,300	3,000	....	184,143	$388,924	$2.11	194	309
Cascade	5	650,027	8,050	15,800	40,000	713,877	1,238,035	1.72	235	1,341
Choteau	5	....	3,725	....	....	3,725	8,050	2.16	92	30
Dawson	2	....	600	....	....	600	1,650	2.75	120	4
Gallatin	3	95,992	793	1,613	....	98,398	204,122	2.07	245	235
Park	3	482,000	1,450	50	19,700	503,200	1,009,075	2.01	197	260
Lewis and Clarke and Meagher..	2	....	250	....	....	250	1,050	4.02	70	5
Total .	22	1,404,862	19,168	20,463	59,700	1,504,193	2,850,906	1.89	223	2,184

The following table shows the total output of coal in Montana since 1883, and the value of the product in the past six years:

Coal product of Montana since 1883.

Year.	Short tons.	Value.	Year.	Short tons.	Value.
1883	19,795	....	1890	517,477	$1,252,492
1884	80,376	....	1891	541,861	1,228,630
1885	86,440	....	1892	564,648	1,330,847
1886	49,846	....	1893	892,309	1,772,116
1887	10,202	....	1894	927,395	1,887,390
1888	41,467	....	1895	1,504,193	2,850,906
1889	363,301	....			

The development of the Montana coal fields on a commercial scale dates from 1889. Previous to that year the largest output was in 1885, when the product was 86,440 short tons. During 1893 extensive improvements were made at the Sandcoulee mines, in Cascade County; mining machines were introduced and the output of the county was increased over 100 per cent—from 242,120 short tons in 1892 to 516,460 short tons in 1893. The increase in this county in 1894 was more than three times the total increase in the State, the gain in Cascade County being in part offset by a decrease of over 90,000 tons, or about 30 per cent, in Park County. Cascade County shows a gain of about 75,000 tons in 1895; Park County increased its output by 288,947 short tons, or over 130 per cent, and Carbon County appears for the first time as a coal producer, with an output of 184,143 short tons.

The following tables show the product and value, by counties, since 1889, and the average price per ton and the statistics of labor and working time in the important producing counties:

Product and value of Montana coal since 1889, by counties.

County.	1889.		1890.	
	Product.	Value.	Product.	Value.
	Short tons.		*Short tons.*	
Cascade...............................	166,480	$339,226	200,435	$406,748
Choteau................................	820	2,160	800	2,000
Custer................................	3,470	9,129	10,228	26,417
Dawson................................	733	1,900	450	1,350
Fergus	460	1,380	1,200	5,740
Gallatin................................	43,838	104,377	51,452	119,084
Lewis and Clarke.......................	50	200	115	283
Missoula..............................	150	450		
Park................................	147,300	421,950	252,737	690,870
Total	363,301	880,773	517,477	1,252,492

County.	1891.		1892.		1893.	
	Product.	Value.	Product.	Value.	Product.	Value.
	Short tons		*Short tons*		*Short tons*	
Cascade	198,107	$396,219	242,120	$484,320	516,460	$907,640
Choteau	478	1,723	1,574	6,338	5,295	20,953
Dawson..................	250	625	335	1,000	440	1,320
Fergus	250	1,400	400	2,100	200	1,200
Gallatin	56,981	135,893	61,198	152,496	63,163	148,021
Lewis and Clarke........					125	666
Meagher..................	50	200	30	120	100	500
Park....................	285,745	692,570	258,991	684,473	306,526	691,816
Total	541,861	1,228,630	564,648	1,330,847	892,309	1,772,116

Product and value of Montana coal since 1889, by counties—Continued.

County.	1894.		1895.		Increase, 1895.		Decrease, 1895.	
	Product.	Value.	Product.	Value.	Product.	Value.	Product.	Value.
	Short tons.		*Short tons.*		*Short tons.*		*Short tons.*	
Carbon	....	....	184,143	$388,924	184,143	$388,924	......	......
Cascade	638,960	$1,238,001	713,877	1,238,035	74,917	34	......	......
Choteau	2,892	11,089	3,725	8,050	833	....	......	$3,039
Dawson	545	1,635	600	1,650	55	15	.. ..	......
Fergus	325	1,625	....	....	....	....	325	1,625
Gallatin	69,257	168,431	98,398	204,122	29,141	35,691	......	......
Granite...........	600	600	....	....	....	... .	600	600
Lewis and Clarke.	60	300	50	250	....	....	10	50
Meagher..........	503	2,315	200	800	....	....	303	1,515
Park	214,253	463,394	503,200	1,009,075	288,947	545,681	......	......
Total	927,395	1,887,390	1,504,193	2,850,906	a576,798	963,516	......	......

a Net increase.

Average prices for Montana coal since 1889 in counties producing 10,000 tons or over.

County.	1889.	1890.	1891.	1892.	1893.	1894.	1895.
Carbon...........	....	....	....	....	....	....	$2.11
Cascade.........	$2.04	$2.03	$2.00	$2.00	$1.76	$1.94	1.72
Gallatin.........	2.38	2.31	2.38	2.50	2.34	2.43	2.07
Park	2.86	2.73	2.43	2.64	2.31	2.16	2.01
The State .	2.42	2.42	2.27	2.36	1.99	2.04	1.89

Statistics of labor employed and working time at Montana coal mines.

County.	1890.		1891.		1892.	
	Average number employed.	Average working days.	Average number employed.	Average working days.	Average number employed.	Average working days.
Cascade.................	379	....	401	....	426	275
Gallatin................	120	....	139	....	146	298
Park....................	705	....	562	....	565	241
The State	1,251	....	1,119	....	1,158	258

Statistics of labor employed and working time at Montana coal mines—Continued.

County.	1893.		1894.		1895.	
	Average number employed.	Average working days.	Average number employed.	Average working days.	Average number employed.	Average working days.
Carbon					309	194
Cascade	634	247	1,165	184	1,341	235
Gallatin	151	278	153	265	235	245
Park	568	240	408	198	260	197
The State	1,401	242	1,782	192	2,184	223

NEBRASKA.

The southwestern corner of Nebraska contains a portion of the Western coal field, but the veins of coal being on the edge of the field are pinched to thin seams, varying from 6 to 22 inches. Some coal has been taken out in past years for local consumption, but with the development of the fields of Iowa, Kansas, and Missouri, more favored both as to quality and conditions for economical mining, and with the operators of these mines seeking a market for their surplus product, such little work as had been done on Nebraska coal deposits has been practically abandoned.

NEVADA.

During 1894 a small amount of coal (150 short tons) was mined in Esmeralda County, Nev., by Mr. William Groezinger, of Columbus. It was sold to the Columbus Borax Works at $2.50 per ton.

Mr. Groezinger writes that a coal field of considerable extent has been discovered about 20 miles from Candelaria. He states there are twelve different veins, varying in thickness from 4 to 12 feet, of semibituminous coal, some of which will make coke. The outcrops are badly weathered and decomposed, but the quality improves at greater depth. At present all the silver mines in the vicinity are shut down and there is no demand for the fuel. With a return to prosperity for the silver-mining industry, attention will be given to any properties promising an adequate and cheap supply of fuel.

Coal is also reported in the vicinity of Carlin, in Elko County, and a company of Nevada citizens has been organized, under the name of the Humboldt Coal Company, to exploit the deposits. No output had been obtained up to the close of 1895.

NEW MEXICO.

Total product in 1895, 720,654 short tons; spot value, $1,072,520.

The first report of coal production in New Mexico was contained in the inaugural volume of Mineral Resources, covering the calendar year

1882. No output was reported by the Tenth United States Census, 1880, and while it is probable that some coal was taken out by ranchmen and miners for their own use prior to 1882, there had been no development on a commercial scale until that year. The product reported for 1882 was 157,092 short tons. With the exception of 1886 it increased annually until 1888, when it reached a total of 626,665 short tons. The product decreased in the next two years, falling to 375,777 short tons in 1890, but recovered its normal proportions in 1892 and 1893. In 1894 the output was about 10 per cent less than in 1893. It increased again in 1895 to 720,654 short tons, a gain of 123,458 short tons, or a little more than 20 per cent, and exceeding by more than 50,000 tons the product of any previous year.

The statistics of production in the Territory during 1894 and 1895 are shown in the following tables:

Coal product of New Mexico in 1894, by counties.

County.	Number of mines.	Loaded at mines for shipment.	Sold to local trade and used by employees.	Used at mines for steam and heat.	Made into coke.	Total product.	Total value.	Average price per ton.	Average number of days active.	Average number of employees.
		Short tons.	Short tons.	Short tons.	Short tons.	Short tons.				
Bernalillo......	3	267,314	809	2,230	....	270,413	$388,103	$1.44	192	460
Colfax.........	3	109,989	3,501	1,495	....	114,985	143,925	1.25	111	136
Lincoln........	6	220	2,405	30	....	2,655	9,680	3.65	104	16
Rio Arriba and Union	2	18,000	20	3,000	....	21,020	26,290	1.25	289	26
San Juan	2	....	200	....	....	200	250	1.25	24	4
Santa Fe.......	4	166,000	1,271	7,610	13,042	187,923	367,609	1.96	193	343
Total	20	561,523	8,266	14,365	13,042	597,196	935,857	1.57	182	985

Coal product of New Mexico in 1895, by counties.

County.	Number of mines.	Loaded at mines for shipment.	Sold to local trade and used by employees.	Used at mines for steam and heat.	Made into coke.	Total product.	Total value.	Average price per ton.	Average number of days active.	Average number of employees.
		Short tons.	Short tons.	Short tons.	Short tons.	Short tons.				
Bernalillo........	5	304,989	1,463	2,224	.....	308,676	$440,750	$1.43	185	549
Colfax..........	3	180,773	3,863	2,466	......	187,102	224,218	1.20	151	332
Lincoln..........	3	....	3,125	....	....	3,125	12,337	3.95	149	7
Rio Arriba.......	2	27,250	1,500	3,250	....	32,000	49,000	1.53	284	40
San Juan ...... } Santa Fe....... }	9	182,622	3,094	3,352	683	189,751	346,215	1.83	218	455
Total	22	695,634	13,045	11,292	683	720,654	1,072,520	1.49	190	1,383

As will be seen in the foregoing tables there was an increase in the number of mines from 20 to 22. Bernalillo County had 3 mines running in 1894, and 5 in 1895. Lincoln County lost 3 and San Juan and Santa Fe together gained that number. There were about 400 more men employed in 1895 than in 1894, and there was also a slight increase in the average working time.

The following table shows the annual output of the Territory since 1882, with the value of the product since 1885. It is probable, however, that the values given for years prior to 1889 are too high. They were estimated on a basis of $3 per ton, which was evidently excessive:

Coal product of New Mexico since 1882.

Year.	Short tons.	Value.	Year.	Short tons.	Value.
1882..........	157,092	....	1889..........	486,943	$872,628
1883..........	211,347	....	1890..........	375,777	504,390
1884..........	220,557	....	1891..........	462,328	779,018
1885..........	306,202	$918,606	1892..........	661,330	1,074,251
1886..........	271,285	813,855	1893..........	665,094	979,044
1887..........	508,034	1,524,102	1894..........	597,196	935,857
1888..........	626,665	1,879,995	1895..........	720,654	1,072,520

In the following table the product since 1882 is shown by counties, together with the increase and decrease in 1895 as compared with 1894:

Coal product of New Mexico since 1882, by counties.

[Short tons.]

County.	1882.	1883.	1884.	1885.	1886.
Bernalillo..........	33,373	42,000	62,802	97,755	106,530
Colfax..........	91,798	112,089	102,513	135,833	87,708
Rio Arriba..........	12,000	17,240	11,203	14,958	7,000
Santa Fe..........	3,600	3,000	3,000	1,000	1,000
Socorro..........	16,321	37,018	41,039	56,656	69,047
Total..........	157,092	211,347	220,557	306,202	271,285

County.	1887.	1888.	1889.	1890.	1891.
Bernalillo..........	275,952	300,000	233,059	181,647	76,515
Colfax..........	154,875	227,427	151,464	151,400	295,089
Lincoln..........	....	....	1,255	1,175	1,000
Rio Arriba..........	11,000	12,000	13,650	12,175	7,350
Santa Fe..........	7,500	25,200	34,870	22,770	16,500
Socorro..........	58,707	62,038	52,205	....	65,574
Other counties..........	....	....	440	6,610	300
Total..........	508,034	626,665	486,943	375,777	462,328

Coal product of New Mexico since 1882, by counties—Continued.

[Short tons.]

County.	1892.	1893.	1894.	1895.	Increase, 1895.
Bernalillo	248, 911	278, 691	270, 413	308, 676	38, 263
Colfax	297, 911	249, 783	114, 985	187, 102	72, 117
Lincoln	3, 145	1, 962	2, 655	3, 125	470
Rio Arriba	20, 600	15, 500	a21, 020	32, 000	10, 980
Santa Fe	36, 780	118, 892	187, 923	b189, 751	1, 828
Socorro	53, 783	....	....	....	....
Other counties	200	266	200	....	....
Total	661, 330	665, 094	597, 196	720, 654	123, 458

a Including Union County.   b Including San Juan County.

The average price per ton and the statistics of labor and average working time in the more important counties for a series of years are shown in the following table:

Average prices for New Mexico coal since 1889 in counties producing 10,000 tons or over.

County.	1889.	1890.	1891.	1892.	1893.	1894.	1895.
Bernalillo	$1.70	$1.14	$1.47	$1.45	$1.42	$1.44	$1.43
Colfax	1.33	1.31	1.35	1.33	1.31	1.25	1.20
Rio Arriba	1.82	1.72	1.95	1.50	1.30	1.25	1.53
Santa Fe	2.14	2.29	2.13	2.63	2.13	1.96	1.83
Socorro	3.29	....	3.22	3.43	....	....	....
Territory..	1.79	1.34	1.68	1.62	1.47	1.57	1.49

Statistics of labor employed and working time at New Mexico coal mines.

County.	1890.		1891.		1892.	
	Average number employed.	Average working days.	Average number employed.	Average working days.	Average number employed.	Average working days.
Bernalillo	375	....	187	....	449	179
Colfax	360	....	384	....	370	261
Rio Arriba	20	....	20	....	35	270
Santa Fe...............	55	....	36	....	30	267
Socorro	....	....	175	....	180	253
Territory	827	....	806	....	1, 083	223

Statistics of labor employed and working time at New Mexico coal mines—Continued.

County.	1893.		1894.		1895.	
	Average number employed.	Average working days.	Average number employed.	Average working days.	Average number employed.	Average working days.
Bernalillo	370	196	460	192	549	183
Colfax	272	248	136	111	332	154
Rio Arriba	25	250	25	300	40	284
Santa Fe..............	328	257	343	193	455	218
Socorro						
Territory	1,011	229	985	182	1,383	190

NORTH CAROLINA.

Total product in 1895, 24,900 short tons; spot value, $41,350.

Although the production of coal in North Carolina during 1895 exceeded that of 1894 by nearly 50 per cent, the principal efforts were directed toward further developments of the Deep River field rather than increased production, which was chiefly incidental to the development work. Greater capacity has been added to the old Egypt mine, in Chatham County, and the name changed to Sterling No. 1. Another opening was made and styled Sterling No. 2, but the tonnage from this mine in 1895 did not add materially to the total for the State.

A contributor to the Manufacturers' Record, of Baltimore, writing of the Deep River field, claims that 35,000,000 tons may be mined from it, or, say, 350,000 tons per year for a century. The claim of superior quality is made for the coal after tests made on the locomotives of the Seaboard Air Line, to which it is easily accessible. It is stated that an order for 100 tons per day has been placed with the Langdon-Henszey Coal Mining Company by the Seaboard Air Line.

In addition to the mines in Chatham County, operations were begun at Glendon, in Moore County, in 1894, and 1,500 tons were produced there in 1895.

The history of coal mining in the State dates from 1889. The Egypt mines were opened in December of that year, and yielded 192 tons. Since that time the product annually has been as follows:

Coal product of North Carolina since 1889.

Year.	Short tons.	Value.	Year.	Short tons.	Value.
1889	192	$451	1893	17,000	$25,500
1890	10,262	17,864	1894	16,900	29,675
1891	20,355	39,635	1895	24,900	41,350
1892	6,679	9,599			

Coal product of North Carolina for five years.

Year.	Number of mines.	Loaded at mines for shipment.	Sold to local trade and used by employees.	Used at mines for steam and heat.	Total product.	Total value.	Average price per ton.	Average number of days active.	Average number of employees.
		Short tons.	Short tons.	Short tons.	Short tons.				
1891................	1	18,780	600	975	20,355	$39,635	$1.93	254	80
1892................	1	6,079	....		6,679	9,599	1.44	160	90
1893................	1	15,000	....	2,000	17,000	25,500	1.50	80	70
1894................	1	13,500	1,000	2,400	16,900	29,675	1.76	145	95
1895................	3	23,400	600	900	24,900	41,350	1.66	226	61

NORTH DAKOTA.

Total product in 1895, 38,997 short tons; spot value, $41,646.

The coals, or rather lignites, of North Dakota are of inferior quality when compared to the bituminous or true coals brought into the State from other regions, principally Montana. The market for Dakota lignites is limited to a practically local demand, and the output has never attained very large proportions, the highest figure having been reached in 1893, when 49,630 short tons were mined. The smallest product in twelve years was in 1887, when the output was 21,470 short tons.

The details of production in 1894 and 1895 and the total annual product since 1884 are shown in the following tables:

Coal product of North Dakota in 1894, by counties.

County.	Number of mines.	Loaded at mines for shipment.	Sold to local trade and used by employees.	Used at mines for steam and heat.	Total product.	Total value.	Average price per ton.	Average number of days active.	Average number of employees.
		Short tons.	Short tons.	Short tons.	Short tons.				
Morton...............	2	8,851	100	....	8,951	$10,294	$1.15	110	30
Stark................	4	25,100	2,924	....	28,024	30,055	1.07	211	31
Ward and McLean.	2	3,360	1,456	224	5,040	6,700	1.34	135	16
Total.........	8	37,311	4,480	224	42,015	47,049	1.12	156	77

Coal product of North Dakota in 1895, by counties.

County.	Number of mines.	Loaded at mines for shipment.	Sold to local trade and used by employees.	Total product.	Total value.	Average price per ton.	Average number of days active.	Average number of employees.
		Short tons	Short tons	Short tons				
McLean and Morton.....	4	13,720	617	14,337	$16,896	$1.18	110	40
Stark	4	21,660	3,000	24,660	24,750	1.00	202	22
Total	8	35,380	3,617	38,997	41,646	1.07	143	62

Coal product of North Dakota since 1884.

Year.	Short tons.	Year.	Short tons.
1884	35,000	1890	30,000
1885	25,000	1891	30,000
1886	25,955	1892	40,725
1887	21,470	1893	49,630
1888	34,000	1894	42,015
1889	28,907	1895	38,997

OHIO.

Total product in 1895, 13,355,806 short tons; spot value, $10,618,477.

The coal product of Ohio in 1895 was larger than in either 1893 or 1894, but still fell more than 200,000 tons short of the output in 1892, when the product reached the maximum total of 13,562,927 short tons. Compared with 1894, there was an increase in 1895 of 1,445,950 short tons, or about 12 per cent. The value increased a little less than 8 per cent, or $776,754, showing a comparative decline. The average price per ton declined from 83 cents in 1894 to 79 cents in 1895. The returns to the Survey show a reverse of the anomalous condition presented in 1894 regarding the number of employees and the average working time. In that year, with a decreased product of more than 1,300,000 tons compared with 1893, the average number of employees increased from 23,931 to 27,105, while the average working time was reduced by the great strike from 188 days in 1893 to 136 days in 1894. In 1895, on the other hand, with an increase in product greater than the loss the preceding year, the number of employees decreased to 24,644, while the average number of working days increased to 176. Reducing these figures to a unit for comparison, it will be seen that in 1893 there was the equivalent of 4,499,028 men for one day; in 1894, 3,930,225 men; and in 1895, 4,329,062 men. The average tonnage per man per day was in 1893, 2.95; in 1894, 3; and in 1895, 3.3. These figures are remarkably close, and show the general accuracy of the reports to the Survey and the statistical compilations. The small but gradual increase in the average tonnage per day per man may be accounted for by a larger production by mining machines. The report of Mr. R. M. Hazeltine, chief mine inspector of the State, for 1894 showed an increased product from machines in a year of much depression and a decreased total output.

PRODUCTION BY COUNTIES.

There are four counties in the State whose annual product has exceeded 1,000,000 tons for the past five years, and their average annual product has exceeded 1,500,000 tons each during that time. These counties are Athens, Hocking, Jackson, and Perry. Their combined product in 1895 was 6,738,539 short tons, a little more than half the total output of the State. Three of these counties, Athens, Hocking, and Perry, comprise what is known as the Hocking Valley district. Their combined product in 1895 was 4,733,155 short tons, 35 per cent of the total for the State. Jackson County, including the towns and and districts of Coalton, Jackson, and Wellston, produced 2,005,384 short tons in 1895, about 33 per cent more than in 1894, and 15 per cent of the State's total in 1895. Ten counties in the State produced more than half a million tons each during 1895. These in order of precedence were: (1) Jackson, (2) Perry, (3) Hocking, (4) Athens, (5) Guernsey, (6) Jefferson, (7) Belmont, (8) Stark, (9) Tuscarawas, and (10) Columbiana.

The statistics of production in 1894 and 1895, by counties, are shown in the following tables:

Coal product of Ohio in 1894, by counties.

County.	Number of mines.	Loaded at mines for shipment.	Sold to local trade and used by employees.	Used at mines for steam and heat.	Made into coke.	Total product.	Total value.	Average price per ton.	Average number of days active.	Total number of employees.
		Short tons.	Short tons.	Short tons.	Short tons.	Short tons.				
Athens	33	1,439,949	28,377	25,517	15,057	1,508,900	$1,123,887	$0.74	124	3,445
Belmont	31	797,687	105,312	3,285	....	906,284	640,110	.71	157	1,947
Carroll	7	258,648	2,800	1,845	....	263,293	204,099	.78	133	466
Columbiana.	23	537,967	16,507	3,806	....	558,280	431,251	.77	161	1,417
Coshocton ...	10	156,295	9,948	184	....	166,427	151,136	.91	168	451
Guernsey....	14	874,342	9,653	7,864	....	891,859	559,879	.63	165	1,880
Hocking	18	1,476,356	23,607	8,548	12,357	1,520,868	1,172,084	.77	122	2,549
Jackson	35	1,441,243	40,546	30,161	....	1,511,950	1,469,802	.97	142	3,803
Jefferson	32	745,706	84,897	2,920	17,677	851,200	607,880	.71	153	2,093
Lawrence....	7	25,319	31,860	....	....	57,179	58,567	1.03	134	198
Mahoning ...	8	32,156	10,077	515	....	42,748	59,722	1.40	138	206
Medina	5	105,587	1,000	4,200	....	110,787	125,569	1.13	150	351
Meigs	11	59,509	109,834	1,250	....	170,593	179,771	1.05	146	584
Muskingum .	15	95,636	13,683	15	....	109,334	97,171	.89	112	458
Perry........	56	1,523,996	62,184	12,845	....	1,599,025	1,240,084	.78	139	3,507
Portage......	3	85,413	2,593	2,088	....	90,094	137,343	1.52	182	249
Stark........	25	424,193	13,575	15,182	....	452,950	530,121	1.19	81	2,250
Summit......	3	8,258	6,144	108	....	14,510	24,187	1.67	126	80
Trumbull....	2	1,303	975	....	....	2,278	4,261	1.87	76	14
Tuscarawas .	24	458,202	23,922	2,874	26	485,024	319,653	.66	120	646
Vinton.......	6	41,307	1,093	1,000	....	43,400	40,600	.94	115	155
Wayne	3	25,178	2,674	2,190	....	30,042	36,520	1.22	83	184
Gallia, Harrison, and Morgan....	3	22,152	679	....	....	22,831	18,426	.81	185	82
Small mines	....	....	500,000	....	....	500,000	600,000	....	....	....
Total..	374	10,636,402	1,101,940	126,397	45,117	11,909,856	9,841,723	.83	136	27,105

Coal product of Ohio in 1895, by counties.

County.	Number of mines.	Loaded at mines for shipment.	Sold to local trade and used by employees.	Used at mines for steam and heat.	Made into coke.	Total product.	Total value.	Average price per ton.	Number of days active.	Average number of employees.
		Short tons.	Short tons.	Short tons.	Short tons.	Short tons.				
Athens	27	1,307,250	9,211	27,824	28,941	1,433,226	$979,041	$0.68	155	2,556
Belmont	31	680,140	161,291	5,212		846,643	611,789	.72	197	1,302
Carroll	8	256,375	1,224	3,280		260,879	191,962	.74	148	482
Columbiana	21	574,525	38,537	4,592		617,654	481,890	.78	228	1,204
Coshocton	11	193,992	13,478	150		207,620	171,896	.83	175	395
Guernsey	17	866,673	15,280	4,628		886,581	513,837	.58	194	1,218
Harrison	2	2,100	1,372			3,472	2,981	.86	197	15
Hocking	19	1,566,747	2,800	7,800	10,638	1,587,985	1,053,203	.66	198	2,501
Jackson	47	1,883,556	90,738	30,290	800	2,005,384	1,798,665	.90	184	4,061
Jefferson	44	773,535	107,715	2,832	1,240	885.322	615,856	.70	136	1,989
Lawrence	8	55,230	32,052	1,220		88,502	81,098	.92	184	284
Mahoning	15	15,742	25,887	853		42,482	54,290	1.28	145	186
Medina	6	251,054	5,537	7,580		264,171	281,274	1.06	209	489
Meigs	13	82,638	99,091	2,347		184,076	172,409	.94	151	612
Muskingum	19	91,458	12,198	204		103,860	86,339	.83	194	279
Perry	53	1,661,748	29,059	21,137		1,711,944	1,323,181	.77	169	2,732
Portage	3	82,609	2,135	1,832		86,576	114,627	1.32	183	263
Stark	27	730,040	23,623	25,070	1,000	779,733	798,528	1.02	149	2,074
Summit	3	20,286	5,320			25,606	36,064	1.41	178	95
Trumbull	2	11,601	4,200			15,801	20,683	1.31	242	38
Tuscarawas	27	619,412	34,416	3,266		657,094	466,342	.71	180	1,354
Vinton	2	17,585	420			18,005	14,804	.83	226	38
Washington	2		3,489			3,489	3,057	.88	167	16
Wayne	5	104,890	3,751	2,160		110,801	121,151	1.09	174	392
Gallia and Morgan	3	24,500	4,400			28,900	23,420	.80	191	69
Small mines			500,000			500,000	600,000	1.20		
Total	415	11,933,686	1,227,224	152,277	42,619	13,355,806	10,618,477	.79	176	24,644

The following table shows the annual output of the State since 1884, by counties:

Coal product of Ohio since 1884, by counties.

[Short tons.]

County.	1884.	1885.	1886.	1887.	1888.
Athens	627,944	823,139	899,046	1,083,543	1,336,698
Belmont	643,129	744,446	573,779	721,767	1,108,106
Carroll	102,531	150,695	216,630	293,328	355,097
Columbiana	469,708	462,733	336,063	516,057	466,191
Coshocton	56,562	99,609	52,934	124,791	167,903
Gallia	20,372	16,383	17,424	15,365	16,722
Guernsey	375,427	297,267	433,800	553,613	383,728
Harrison			5,509	4,032	2,865
Hocking	372,694	656,441	741,571	853,063	1,086,538
Holmes	12,052	11,459	12,670	10,526	8,121
Jackson	831,720	791,608	856,740	1,134,705	1,088,761
Jefferson	316,777	271,329	275,666	293,875	243,178
Lawrence	176,412	145,916	166,933	143,559	137,806
Mahoning	241,599	275,944	313,040	272,349	231,035
Medina	77,160	152,721	252,411	225,487	198,452
Meigs	248,436	234,756	192,263	185,205	242,483
Morgan	7,636	5,536	4,370	4,100	
Muskingum	84,398	86,846	96,601	171,928	211,861
Noble			3,342	6,320	6,200
Perry	1,379,100	1,259,592	1,607,666	1,870,840	1,736,805
Portage	65,617	77,071	70,339	65,163	70,923
Sciota	3,650	2,440			
Stark	513,225	391,418	593,422	784,164	793,227
Summit	253,148	145,134	82,225	95,815	112,024
Trumbull	257,683	264,517	188,531	167,989	157,826
Tuscarawas	317,141	285,545	267,666	506,466	546,117
Vinton	69,740	77,127	60,013	89,727	108,695
Washington	5,600	5,000	5,500	1,880	2,432
Wayne	120,571	81,507	109,057	105,150	91,157
Total	7,640,062	7,816,179	8,435,211	10,300,807	10,910,951

Coal product of Ohio since 1884, by counties—Continued.

[Short tons.]

County.	1889.	1890.	1891.	1892.	1893.
Athens	1,224,186	1,205,455	1,482,294	1,400,865	1,597,685
Belmont	641,862	774,110	819,236	1,037,700	974,043
Carroll	351,782	328,967	313,543	367,055	261,327
Columbiana	596,824	567,595	621,726	520,755	467,314
Coshocton	166,599	177,700	189,469	228,727	244,605
Gallia	23,208	16,512	17,493	19,000	11,393
Guernsey	362,168	413,739	390,418	455,997	412,395
Harrison	33,721	8,600	3,960	3,220	2,640
Hocking	845,049	1,319,427	1,515,719	1,786,803	1,637,052
Jackson	926,874	970,878	1,475,939	1,833,910	1,826,572
Jefferson	271,830	491,172	697,193	932,477	1,077,779
Lawrence	102,656	77,004	76,235	71,376	36,512
Mahoning	240,563	256,319	200,734	205,105	173,704
Medina	136,061	139,742	160,184	101,440	153,100
Meigs	220,277	255,365	282,094	266,044	228,534
Morgan	8,060	....	....	12,000	10,000
Muskingum	214,005	229,719	160,154	177,488	205,966
Noble	38,400	6,850	3,800	300	....
Perry	1,565,786	1,921,417	1,785,626	1,452,979	1,438,123
Portage	78,117	70,666	69,058	76,398	89,431
Stark	851,994	836,449	917,995	856,607	926,200
Summit	50,726	112,997	140,079	147,847	28,989
Trumbull	108,120	47,714	83,950	30,187	15,681
Tuscarawas	683,505	589,875	736,297	777,215	698,527
Vinton	102,040	80,716	98,166	83,113	72,976
Washington	18,045	5,990	5,950	44,720	646
Wayne	84,178	38,528	21,371	73,599	62,452
Small mines	....	550,000	600,000	600,000	600,000
Total	9,976,787	11,494,506	12,868,683	13,562,927	13,253,646

Coal product of Ohio since 1884, by counties—Continued.

[Short tons.]

County.	1894.	1895.	Increase in 1895.	Decrease in 1895.
Athens.............	1,508,900	1,433,226	....	75,674
Belmont	906,284	846,643	....	59,641
Carroll............	263,293	260,879	....	2,414
Columbiana	558,280	617,654	59,374	....
Coshocton........	166,427	207,620	41,193	....
Gallia.............	12,894	12,900	6	....
Guernsey	891,859	886,581	....	5,278
Harrison	1,701	3,472	1,771	....
Hocking	1,520,868	1,587,985	67,117	....
Jackson...........	1,511,950	2,005,384	493,434	....
Jefferson	851,200	885,322	34,122	....
Lawrence	57,179	88,502	31,323	....
Mahoning	42,748	42,482	....	266
Medina	110,787	264,171	153,384	....
Meigs	170,593	184,076	13,483	....
Morgan	8,236	16,000	7,764	....
Muskingum	109,334	103,860	....	5,474
Perry	1,599,025	1,711,944	112,919	....
Portage	90,094	86,576	....	3,518
Stark	452,950	779,733	326,783	....
Summit	14,510	25,606	11,096	....
Trumbull	2,278	15,801	13,523	....
Tuscarawas	485,024	657,094	172,070	....
Vinton	43,400	18,005	....	25,395
Washington......	....	3,489	3,489	....
Wayne...........	30,042	110,801	80,759	....
Small mines......	500,000	500,000	....	....
Total	11,909,856	13,355,806	*a* 1,445,950	....

a Net increase.

Records of the total production of coal in Ohio extend only as far back as 1872, since which time the annual output has been as follows:

Annual coal product of Ohio since 1872.

Year.	Short tons.	Year.	Short tons.
1872.................	5, 315, 294	1884.................	7, 640, 062
1873.................	4, 550, 028	1885.................	7, 816, 179
1874.................	3, 267, 585	1886.................	8, 435, 211
1875.................	4, 864, 259	1887.................	10, 300, 708
1876.................	3, 500, 000	1888.................	10, 910, 951
1877.................	5, 250, 000	1889.................	9, 976, 787
1878.................	5, 500, 000	1890.................	11, 494, 506
1879.................	6, 000, 000	1891.................	12, 868, 683
1880.................	7, 000, 000	1892.................	13, 562, 927
1881.................	8, 225, 600	1893.................	13, 253, 646
1882.................	9, 450, 000	1894.................	11, 909, 856
1883.................	8, 229, 429	1895.................	13, 355, 806

Taken in connection with the preceding tables of production, the following tables, exhibiting the average prices and the statistics of labor for a series of years will be found of interest:

Average prices for Ohio coal since 1889 in counties producing 10,000 tons or over.

County.	1889.	1890.	1891.	1892.	1893.	1894.	1895.
Athens..........	$0. 81	$0. 83	$0. 85	$0. 85	$0. 83	$0. 74	$0. 68
Belmont........	.87	.78	.84	.84	.81	.71	.72
Carroll..........	.74	.85	.81	.83	.87	.78	.74
Columbiana.....	.79	.91	.96	.90	.88	.77	.78
Coshocton.......	.98	.90	1.00	1.01	1.00	.91	.83
Gallia..........	1.04	.90	.92	.92	.91	.85	.80
Guernsey........	.87	.68	.79	.72	.71	.63	.58
Hocking	.80	.81	.81	.85	.82	.77	.66
Jackson.........	1.03	1.00	1.06	.99	1.06	.97	.90
Jefferson	1.00	.83	.85	.92	.79	.71	.70
Lawrence	1.04	1.08	1.04	1.06	.94	1.03	.92
Mahoning	1.12	1.20	1.25	1.41	1.44	1.40	1.28
Medina..........	1.16	1.20	1.16	1.23	1.25	1.13	1.06
Meigs...........	1.02	1.24	.96	1.13	1.10	1.05	.94
Morgan							.80
Muskingum	.99	.86	.82	.91	.83	.89	.83
Perry	.84	.85	.84	.85	.85	.78	.77
Portage	1.27	1.59	1.52	1.52	1.55	1.52	1.32
Stark	1.26	1.30	1.25	1.22	1.24	1.19	1.02

Average prices for Ohio coal since 1889 in counties producing 10,000 tons or over—Cout'd.

County.	1889.	1890.	1891.	1892.	1893.	1894.	1895.
Summit	$1.83	$1.50	$1.38	$1.43	$1.73	$1.67	$1.41
Trumbull	1.64	1.20	1.41	1.54	1.54	1.87	1.31
Tuscarawas	.80	.85	.79	.85	.84	.66	.71
Vinton	1.03	1.07	1.05	1.02	.97	.94	.83
Wayne	1.23	1.07	1.15	1.39	1.27	1.22	1.09
The State ...	.94	.94	.94	.94	.92	.83	.79

Statistics of labor employed and working time at Ohio coal mines.

County.	1890.		1891.		1892.	
	Average number employed.	Average working days.	Average number employed.	Average working days.	Average number employed.	Average working days.
Athens	2,122	198	2,702	193	2,536	193
Belmont	1,401	201	1,276	238½	1,713	224
Carroll.................	642	188	589	200	595	214
Columbiana	987	219	1,031	251	932	223
Coshocton..............	327	237	284	265	386	229
Gallia	33	205	35	218	38	220
Guernsey...............	788	225	810	188	800	229
Hocking	1,625	240	1,674	241	2,099	216
Jackson	2,654	180	3,097	189	3,347	214
Jefferson	944	203	1,237	235	1,544	208
Lawrence	242	198	232	223	247	263
Mahoning	537	220	525	233½	484	206
Medina	310	219	314	221	175	255
Meigs	616	202	623	190	636	190
Muskingum	366	250	338	213	356	192
Perry	2,977	188	3,284	170	2,380	187
Portage	155	236	149	225	204	207
Stark	1,930	182	1,952	190	1,776	199
Summit	389	173	376	194	406	221
Trumbull	102	243	176	226	86	205
Tuscarawas	1,082	196	1,161	232	1,300	224
Vinton	186	241	197	206	197	198
Wayne.................	87	178	65	200	196	166
The State	20,576	201	22,182	206	22,576	212

Statistics of labor employed and working time at Ohio coal mines—Continued.

County.	1893.		1894.		1895.	
	Average number employed.	Average working days.	Average number employed.	Average working days.	Average number employed.	Average working days.
Athens	3,203	162	3,445	124	2,556	155
Belmont	1,684	199	1,947	157	1,302	197
Carroll	652	166	466	133	482	148
Columbiana	964	210	1,417	161	1,204	228
Coshocton	398	233	451	168	395	175
Gallia	36	176	40	160	9	200
Guernsey	993	176	1,880	165	1,218	194
Hocking	2,072	193	2,549	122	2,501	198
Jackson	3,188	201	3,803	142	4,061	184
Jefferson	2,033	194	2,093	153	1,989	136
Lawrence	142	143	198	134	284	184
Mahoning	419	196	206	138	186	145
Medina	349	228	351	150	489	209
Meigs	601	142	584	146	612	151
Morgan					60	190
Muskingum	388	214	458	112	279	194
Perry	2,585	178	3,597	139	2,732	169
Portage	252	217	249	182	263	183
Stark	2,105	161	2,250	81	2,074	149
Summit	90	256	80	126	95	178
Trumbull	53	128	14	76	38	212
Tuscarawas	1,329	234	646	120	1,354	180
Vinton	179	200	155	115	38	226
Wayne	168	167	184	83	392	174
The State	23,931	188	27,105	136	24,644	176

OREGON.

Total product in 1895, 73,685 short tons; spot value, $247,901.

With the exception of 1888 the coal output of Oregon in 1895 was the largest in the history of the State. The increased output in 1895 was due in part to greater activity at the Newport mine of the Oregon Coal and Navigation Company, and partly to the opening of two new mines on the Coquille river. It is anticipated that these, with one more mine opened in 1895, but not a producer up to the close of the year, will materially increase the product in 1896.

The following tables show the statistics of production for the past four years and the total output since 1885:

Coal product in Oregon in 1892, 1893, 1894, and 1895.

Distribution.	1892.	1893.	1894.	1895.
	Short tons.	*Short tons.*	*Short tons.*	*Short tons.*
Loaded at the mines for shipment	31,760	37,835	45,068	68,108
Sold to local trade and used by employees	2,353	3,594	2,171	5,294
Used at mines for steam and heat........................	548	254	282	283
Total product	34,661	41,683	47,521	73,685
Total value.....................	$148,546	$164,500	$183,914	$247,901
Total number of employees	90	110	88	414
Average number of days worked.	120	192	243	a 69

a The apparently large number of men employed and small average working time are due to the large force of men employed in developing the Beaver Hill mine, which was producing coal for shipment during only twenty days in 1895. The average time made at the Newport mines was over two hundred days per man.

Coal product of Oregon from 1885 to 1895.

Year.	Short tons.	Year.	Short tons.
1885....................	50,000	1891....................	51,826
1886....................	45,000	1892....................	31,661
1887....................	31,696	1893....................	41,683
1888....................	75,000	1894....................	47,521
1889....................	64,359	1895....................	73,685
1890....................	61,514		

Mr. J. S. Diller, of the United States Geological Survey, has made a reconnoissance of the geology of Oregon, and his full report will be found in Part I of this annual report. The following data relating to the coal fields of the State have been abstracted from Mr. Diller's report:

THE COAL FIELDS OF WESTERN OREGON.

Oregon has long been known as one of the coal-producing States of the Pacific Coast, but until this season no systematic attempt has been made to take a comprehensive view of the whole field to determine the geological position and areal distribution of the coal-bearing rocks. This could be done at the present time only in a preliminary way, inasmuch as the topographic maps of the country upon which to outline the productive districts have not yet been made. When the topographic surveys already well advanced about Roseburg and Coos Bay shall have been extended over the whole of Oregon west of the Cascade Range, and the maps published, it will be possible to show definitely the lateral extent of the coal regions.

The coal fields of Oregon, so far as yet known, all lie west of the Cascade Range and north of Rogue River. Most of them are among the mountains generally known in Oregon as the Coast Range, but others occur at the western foot of the Cascade Range. Four fields will be noticed here. (1) The Upper Nehalem coal field, in Columbia County; (2) the Lower Nehalem coal field, in Clatsop County; (3) the Yaquina coal field, in Lincoln County, and (4) the Coos Bay coal field, in Coos County. Traces of coal have been found in many other parts of the State. Some of them will be noted, although little can be said concerning their extent. It is not at all improbable, however, that other fields of considerable size will yet be discovered when the detailed explorations of the Geological Survey are made. Such explorations are necessarily slow. The luxuriance of the undergrowth, especially near the streams, with the abundance of fallen timber, renders the forest in many places upon the upland slopes of the Coast Range a veritable jungle. Exposures are few and meager and greatly enhance the difficulties which beset the geological observer.

The Upper Nehalem coal field.—The Upper Nehalem coal field is in Columbia County, within the drainage of the upper portion of the Nehalem River. It extends northeast and southwest a total length of about 13 miles, and has a width of 1 to 2 miles or more.

The Upper Nehalem coal field, while it has a length of over 10 miles, as far as yet known, is not over 2 miles in width, so that the whole area of the field is less than 20 square miles. Nevertheless, with two beds of coal, one 6 feet and the other 9 feet in thickness, it ought to yield a quantity of coal of commercial importance, if upon practical tests it is proved to be good enough to create a demand for it and if facilities for cheap transportation are obtained. Thus far no conveniences for transportation—not even a poor road—extends to the best outcrops.

About a ton of coal from the East Fork of Pebble Creek was taken out and sent to Portland, where it is said to have burned well in stoves, but so far as the writer knows its steam-producing power has never been measured.

Lower Nehalem coal field.—The Lower Nehalem coal field is situated north of the Nehalem River, near the county line between Clatsop and Tillamook, * * * embracing sections 16, 10, 2, and 36, which are all in a line extending northeast and southwest, and the coal exposed in them may all belong to the same bed. The coal field, as far as known, has a length of about 5 miles. The quality of the coal is good, but its thickness, as far as yet known, nowhere exceeds 22 inches. It occurs in strata so soft as to render timbering generally necessary, and is inclined at a considerable angle. In view of these facts, notwithstanding its good quality and nearness to tide water, above which it rises a few hundred feet, it can not be considered as promising commercial importance.

The Yaquina coal field.—This field is in Lincoln County, north of the Yaquina River and 6 miles from the coast. It borders Depot Slough upon the west, and has a length from north to south of about 5 miles, and a breadth of not over a mile. It contains, apparently, several beds of coal which belong to nearly the same horizon. Although it is not very far from marine transportation, it does not promise to be of considerable commercial importance.

The Coos Bay coal field.—The Coos Bay coal field is the most important in the State, and when thoroughly mapped will be a subject for later report. Thus far only a general reconnoissance has been made for this preliminary report and comparison with the other fields.

It is situated in Coos County, upon the borders of Coos Bay, with a length northeast and southwest of at least 20 miles and a breadth of 5 miles, so that its area is not less than 100 square miles. It is probable that future investigations may show this coal in a number of gulches. At one place the coal is exposed in a tunnel nearly 200 feet in length. It is greatly fissured, and the cracks contain a yellowish coating that makes the coal look muddy.

At the southwestern end of the field, near Riverton, a 3½-foot bed of coal has been opened by Mr. T. H. Timon. All the writer's information concerning this coal was derived from Mr. Timon and from Mr. E. C. Barnard, of the United States Geological Survey, who examined the mine. A tunnel is driven in the coal for several hundred feet. Mr. Timon reported the output for 1895 at 4,460 tons, and says the bed dips to the northeast at an angle of about 18 degrees. It is said to be good steam coal. The bed is only about 100 feet above the tide water one-fourth of a mile away. The coal is overlain by sandstone, has a small parting of the same material, and rests upon shale. The compact character of the coal enables it to be mined in large fragments. Its analysis, from a sample furnished by Mr. Timon, is No. 17 in the subsequent table. The good quality of the coal and its economic mining and shipment combine to render this a promising portion of the field. The bar at the mouth of the Coquille is, however, a shallow one, and is a serious impediment to commerce. Mr. Timon says that there are a number of persons prospecting for coal in that region, and several other veins will be worked when the bar at the mouth of the Coquille is improved enough to give them better freight rates.

Six miles north of Riverton and about 3½ miles northeast of the occurrence last described, is the Beaver Hill mine, opened within a year, and now actively operated by Mr. R. A. Graham, with Mr. J. L. Parker as superintendent, and a large force of men. A branch of railroad 1½ miles in length has been built to it from the main line of the Coos Bay, Roseburg and Eastern Railroad, near Coalton.

The bed is somewhat variable in thickness, and contains two thin partings of sandstone. The associated sandstones between which the coal appears are sometimes fossiliferous and comparatively soft, although firm enough to stand without timbering in many places.

The coal is brilliant black, with homogeneous structure, and has the composition given under No. 24 of the table. The large force of men is employed chiefly in developing, but the mine has not yet entered fully upon its career as a producer. During 1895 11,200 tons were shipped.

The strike of the bed varies considerably, but generally it is in a northeasterly and southwesterly direction, with a variable dip to the southeast, at an angle of about 40 degrees. The strata here are much disturbed, and the high angle at which they incline greatly increases the cost of mining the coal. Upon the surface the Beaver Hill bed has been traced along the strike for 8 or 10 miles.

The only coal mine of Oregon which has been continuously operated for a considerable time is the Newport. It has been worked for over forty years, and owes its success not so much to the quality of the coal as to the economical mining and management. It is now operated by Goodall, Perkins & Co., of San Francisco, with Mr. William Campbell as superintendent. The writer personally examined only one tunnel of the mine. All his information with reference to other portions of the mine and the Newport basin were kindly furnished by Mr. Campbell. The location is in sec. 9, T. 26 S., R. 13 W., where a ravine has cut into the middle of the shallow basin containing the coal at an elevation of about 100 feet above sea level. The bed of coal is about 5 feet 8 inches in thickness, and has two small sandstone partings of 6 inches each, leaving 4 feet 8 inches of solid coal. The total thickness varies greatly from place to place, especially about the islands which the coal encircles within the basin. The coal appears now to be contained in a shallow boat-shaped fold, which, according to Mr. Campbell, is about 4 miles long and 1¼ miles broad. The coal is said to crop out upon the surface around the edge of this synclinal basin (the Newport basin), and toward its center the coal is covered by 100 feet of sandstone. The opening of the mine is in a gulch near the center of the basin. The coal appears to dip gently toward this point from all directions. A stationary engine upon the outcropping edge of the bed pulls the empty cars into the mine, and the loaded cars run from all parts of the mine to the opening by gravity. The slopes of the ravine in which the mine opens afford a convenient position for gravity to aid in sifting, sorting, weighing, and loading the coal on the cars, which carry it by the comparatively gentle grade down Coal Slough to large bunkers on Coos Bay, near Marshfield, where it is easily transferred to vessels. The position of the coal bed and its situation with reference to the sea are very important factors in the cheap production of coal from the Newport mine.

The coal of this mine is brilliant black, breaking into small cubical blocks. It is in some places homogeneous, and at others irregularly streaked parallel to the bedding plane. The character of the vegetation from which the coal originated is shown by the occurrence of logs, which are sometimes completely changed to coal, and yet the woody structure is fully preserved. An analysis of a piece of coal in which the woody structure is distinct is No. 25 of the table. A comparison of this analysis with the one numbered 26, which was made of coal selected by Mr. Campbell as a representative sample of the Newport mine, will show how completely the wood has changed to coal. A comparison of these analyses with those numbered 27 and 28 shows an improvement in the quality of the coal. What is now mined contains considerably less moisture and sulphur than that analyzed by Mr. Price.

The bottom upon which the coal rests is chiefly sandstone and occasionally quite irregular, rising into the coal, sometimes cutting it off completely. The coal encircles several small areas. They were small islands in the swamp in which the vegetation accumulated to form the coal. One of these islands is shown at the mouth of the mine near the center of the basin, where the coal runs out completely, and the limiting sandstones come together with only dark tracings to mark the boundaries.

The outcropping coal about the edge of the Newport basin shows that the swamp in which the coal originated was of greater extent than the basin. The swamp may have extended more or less continuously throughout the whole coal field from the Coquille to North Slough. The rocks at that time were lying horizontally. The Newport basin originated at the time the rocks were folded. The upward folds, or anticlinals, were largely washed away, but the downward folds, the synclines or basins containing the coal, have been preserved. That the Newport coal is in a shallow synclinal there seems to be no doubt from the testimony of the mine itself, for the coal is reported to have been sufficiently prospected or removed to expose the form of the fold. The structure of the remainder of the coal field has not yet been wrought out. The dip of 18 degrees on the Coquille and 45 degrees at the Beaver Hill mine shows greater disturbance than at the Newport mine.

During the summer of 1895 there were only three mines, the Newport, the Beaver Hill, and the Timon, in active operation. Others have been operated in the past and some continued several years. (See Mr. Diller's complete report for details.)

Analyses of Oregon coals.

No.	Mois-ture.	Volatile matter.	Fixed carbon.	Ash.	Sul-phur.	Physical properties of coke.	Analyst.
	Per ct.	Per ct.	Per ct.	Per ct.	Per ct.		
1	2.56	46.29	48.49	2.74		....	
2	11.16	42.82	41.64	a4.38	4.32	Sooty; incoherent.	Peter Fireman.
3	10.83	41.05	43.17	a4.95	2.47	Partly brilliant and coherent.	Do.
4	10.03	43.40	29.98	b16.59	3.69	Sooty; noncoher-ent.	Do.
5	12.23	42.47	34.29	a11.01	3.19	.....do	Do.
6	10.07	44.52	32.18	a13.23	3.97	.....do	Do.
7	9.75	32.25	50.50	7.50		......|............	
8	9.53	42.73	42.29	5.45		......|............	J. H. Fisk.
9	9.00	37.83	45.17	8.00		......|............	W. H. Hampton.
10	19.75	33.20	42.59	4.73		......|............	Do.
11	8.08	41.26	46.81	a3.85	1.30	Partly brilliant and coherent.	Do.
12	8.86	40.06	46.79	a4.29	1.31	.....do	Do.
13	8.91	41.54	47.23	a2.34	.38	Sooty; slightly co-herent.	Do.
14	8.11	41.15	33.59	a17.15	.95	Sooty; noncoher-ent.	Do.
15	8.53	39.95	45.79	a5.73	2.00	Partly brilliant and coherent.	Do.
16	15.50	31.40	39.80	13.30		....	Sharpless & Winchell.
17	9.12	43.86	42.73	c4.29	.46	Coke; slightly co-herent.	Peter Fireman.
18	9.77	43.20	34.22	12.81	2.32	....	Sharpless & Winchell.
19	10.81	46.52	34.26	8.41			Do.
20	12.26	43.16	33.93	10.65			Do.
21	4.97	42.13	44.91	7.99	1.22		Do.
22	5.33	48.31	38.78	9.58			Do.
23	4.05	46.51	38.15	11.29			Do.
24	10.42	42.21	43.18	c4.19	.69	Sooty; very slight-ly coherent.	Peter Fireman.
25	9.78	42.57	44.19	a3.46	.91	Sooty; partly co-herent.	J. H. Fisk, W. H. Hampton.
26	11.94	41.48	37.85	a8.73	1.32	Sooty; noncoher-ent.	Do.
27	15.45	41.55	34.95	8.05	2.55	Will not coke......	Thomas Price.
28	17.27	44.15	32.40	6.18	1.37	.....do	Do.
29	11.00	41.00	44.50	3.00	.45	....	J. H. Fisk, W. H. Hampton.
30	20.09	32.59	41.98	5.34		.....|............	Do.
31	1.53	42.82	44.94	10.71	a4.49	Does not coke......	F. A. Good.
32	1.96	43.68	51.11	b3.25	1.66	Partly brilliant and coherent.	Peter Fireman.
33	4.66	38.54	39.00	d17.80	.44	.....do	Do.
34	1.08	24.40	34.71	39.81	.91	Coke, worthless...	F. A. Good.

a Red.　　　b Brown.　　　c Light brown.　　　d Light yellow.

Localities of coals given in table of analyses.

1. Astoria (Mineral Resources of the United States. 1882, p. 94)

Upper Nehalem coal field, Columbia County:

2. Pebble Creek. Sec. 34, T. 4 N., R. 4 W.
3. Pebble Creek. Sec. 34, T. 4 N., R. 4 W.
4. East Fork of Pebble Creek. Face at interior end of tunnel of Great Northern Coal Company.
5. East Fork of Pebble Creek. SW. ¼ of sec. 23, T. 4 N., R. 4 W., at bottom of canyon.
6. East Fork of Pebble Creek. NW. ¼ sec. 23, T. 4 N., R. 4 W., at bottom of side ravine.
7. East Fork of Pebble Creek. Face of tunnel, Great Northern Company's coal mine. Published by the company.
8. East Fork of Pebble Creek. Face of tunnel, Great Northern Company's mine. Published by the company.
9. Nehalem No. 1. Location not given. Published by Great Northern Coal Company.
10. Nehalem No. 2. Location not given. Published by Great Northern Coal Company.

Lower Nehalem coal field, Clatsop County:

11. Hodge Creek. Sec. 16, T. 3 N., R. 10 W.
12. Hodge Creek. Sec. 16, T. 3 N., R. 10 W.
13. Coal Creek. SW. ¼ of sec. 36, T. 4 N., R. 10 W.

Yaquina coal field, Lincoln County:

14. Shaw Place, 1½ miles west of Toledo. Sec. 13, T. 11 S., R. 11 W.
15. Four miles northwest of Toledo. Sec. 30, T. 10 S., R. 10 W.
16. Yaquina Bay. Noted by Sharpless & Winchell.

Coos Bay coal field, Coos County:

17. Riverton Coal (Timon's mine), Coos County.
18. Knight's mine, near Riverton—top.
19. Knight's mine, near Riverton—middle.
20. Knight's mine, near Riverton—bottom.
21. Coquille. Sec. 23, T. 27, R. 14—average.
22. Coquille. Sec. 23, T. 27, R. 14—above parting.
23. Coquille. Sec. 23, T. 27, R. 14—below parting.
24. Beaver Hill mine. Sec. 17, T. 27 S., R. 13 W.
25. Newport mine. Sec. 9, T. 26 S., R. 12 W. (Shows distinct woody structure; thrown out by picker.)
26. Newport mine. Sec. 9, T. 26 S., R. 12 W. (Selected by superintendent.)
27. Newport mine, Upper Bench. Sec. 9, T. 26 S., R. 12 W. (U. S. G. S., Min. Resources of U. S., 1887, p. 289.)
28. Newport mine, Lower Bench. Sec. 9, T. 26 S., R. 12 W. (U. S. G. S., Min. Resources of U. S., 1887, p. 289.)
29. Durham. Published by Great Northern Coal Company, of Portland.
30. Coos Bay. Exact location not given. Published by Great Northern Coal Company, of Portland.
31. Camas Mountain, Douglas County, Oreg. (Tenth Census U. S., Vol. XV, p. 788.)
32. Callahans, 11 miles west of Roseburg, Douglas County, Oreg.
33. Near mouth of Cavatts Creek, Douglas County, Oreg.
34. Blue Mountains, Oregon. (Tenth Census U. S., Vol. XV, p. 788.)

HINDRANCES TO THE DEVELOPMENT OF THE COAL FIELDS OF OREGON.

The coal fields of the Coast Range are covered by a growth of vegetation so dense as to greatly interfere with the coal prospector. The luxuriant undergrowth of vines and shrubs, amid large numbers of fallen trees in the forests, especially in the ravines, where abundant moisture lingers throughout the summer, completely covers the slopes. The soft sandstone and shales readily crumble to soil, and thus contribute to the more complete covering of the underlying strata. The coal-bearing strata are all soft, like the coal itself, and crop out upon the surface only along the lines of most rapid erosion—that is, along streams. In the gulches and ravines of small streams, where the force of the water in floods is not sufficient to sweep away the mass of logs and other rubbish, the outcrops are very few and prospecting especially tedious. But along the larger streams, as, for example, the Nehalem, which during freshets sweeps its bed, the rocks are well exposed.

The longer axes of the coal fields are more or less nearly parallel with the trend of the Coast Range, upon whose flanks they occur, and it would be expected that the streams descending from the range across the fields would give fine exposures, but the streams are generally so small that they afford meager outcrops.

While the dense floral envelope, by obscuring outcrops, hinders the prospecting of the coal fields, the presence of abundant timber is an advantage in supplying the demands of the work after the mines are once opened.

The greatest hindrance to the development of the Oregon coal fields is in the way of transportation. All the navigable rivers and bays of the Oregon coast are obstructed by bars, which greatly interfere with navigation.

Formerly the depth of low water on the bar in front of Coos Bay varied in different seasons with the shifting bar from 9 to 13 or 14 feet. Since the jetties have been built the channel has been improved. In the four years 1881–1885 the number of vessels crossing the bar was 1,118, of which 98 drew more than 13 feet of water.

The entrance to Coos Bay is regarded as one of the best along the Oregon coast, so that the obstacles interposed to navigation by bars at other places where not improved are still great.

The development of the Upper Nehalem coal field is, however, not hindered by marine obstruction, but by lack of proper facilities for transportation on land. Although the coal field is less than 30 miles from Portland, there is a divide between them which, taken in connection with the stream canyons and dense forests, presents considerable difficulty in the way of railroad construction. Until the railroad facilities are provided the Upper Nehalem coal field must remain undeveloped.

PENNSYLVANIA.

Total product in 1895, 96,621,933 long tons, or 108,216,565 short tons; spot value, $117,969,629. Anthracite: Total product, 51,785,122 long tons, or 57,999,337 short tons; spot value, $82,019,272. Bituminous: Total product, 44,836,811 long tons, or 50,217,228 short tons; spot value, $35,980,357.

In 1894 the total output from the anthracite and bituminous coal mines of Pennsylvania was 81,994,271 long tons, or 91,833,584 short tons, valued at $107,967,883, showing an increase in the output for 1895 of 14,627,662 long tons, equivalent to 16,382,981 short tons, or 15 per cent. The increase in value was $10,031,746, or 9 per cent. The great depression in values prevalent in 1895 is nowhere better illustrated than in the statistics of Pennsylvania coal production. As has been shown, the increase in production was 15 per cent over 1894, while the increase in value was only 9 per cent. When compared with the output of 1893, the difference is still more marked, for while the amount of coal produced in 1895 was over 9,000,000 long tons (or 10,000,000 short tons) in excess of the product of 1893, the value was about $3,000,000 less.

The production of anthracite coal in 1895 increased 5,426,978 long tons, or 6,078,215 short tons, over that of 1894, with a proportionally smaller increase in value of $3,531,209. The bituminous product increased 9,200,683 long tons, or 10,304,765 short tons, with an increase in value of $6,500,537.

Pennsylvania, as is well known, is by far the most important of the coal-producing States. It is so prominently ahead of every other producing State, having in the combined product of anthracite and bituminous coal more than six times the output of Illinois in 1895, which ranks second, that comparisons are only of interest when drawn with reference to the ratio of Pennsylvania's output to that of the total in the United States or of the combined product of the other States. It is not possible to carry such comparisons back to an earlier date than 1880, owing to incomplete statistics in a number of the States. During 1880 the total output of coal in the United States was 63,822,830 long tons, or 71,481,569 short tons, of which Pennsylvania produced 42,437,242 long tons, or 47,529,711 short tons, or practically two-thirds of the total.

The product of Pennsylvania coal has always exceeded 50 per cent of the total product of the United States, the lowest percentage being 52, in 1884 and 1888. The average percentage for the sixteen years from 1880 to 1895, inclusive, was 56. In the following table is shown the total product of Pennsylvania and the United States since 1880, with the percentage of the total produced by Pennsylvania in each year.

17 GEOL, PT 3——31

Product of Pennsylvania coal compared with total United States since 1880.

Year.	Total United States.	Pennsylvania.	Per cent of Pennsylvania to total.
	Short tons.	*Short tons.*	
1880	71,481,569	46,529,711	65
1881	85,881,030	54,320,018	63
1882	103,285,789	57,254,507	55
1883	115,212,125	62,488,190	54
1884	119,735,051	62,404,488	52
1885	110,957,522	62,137,271	56
1886	112,743,403	62,857,210	56
1887	129,975,557	70,372,857	54
1888	148,659,402	77,719,624	52
1889	141,229,514	81,719,059	58
1890	157,788,657	88,770,814	56
1891	168,566,668	93,453,921	55
1892	179,329,071	99,167,080	55
1893	182,352,774	98,038,267	54
1894	170,741,526	91,833,584	54
1895	193,117,530	108,216,565	56
Total for sixteen years	2,191,057,188	1,217,283,166	56

PENNSYLVANIA ANTHRACITE.

By JOHN H. JONES.

The production of anthracite coal in 1895 was larger by over three million tons than that of any previous year in the history of the trade. This, in the face of only mediocre trade conditions generally, resulted in complete demoralization of the anthracite trade and considerable losses to many of the mining and initial carrying companies.

The larger portion of this increase was produced in the last six months of the year, and during this period the overproduction was reflected to a greater extent in prices than in the first part of the year, although even during that period the prices received for anthracite coal were not remunerative, and in some cases did not even pay the expense of mining. The annual reports of the Philadelphia and Reading Coal and Iron Company and the Lehigh Valley Coal Company, which made their appearance during the early part of 1896, while this report was in preparation, furnished striking examples of the effects of the conditions referred to above.

The first of these companies gives a loss of 8.1 cents on each ton of coal mined during 1895, while in 1894 there was a profit of 3.3 cents per ton, showing the actual results to have been 11.4 cents less per ton in 1895 than in 1894.

The Lehigh Valley Coal Company's report shows a loss of 13.48 cents per ton on coal mined by themselves and purchased from individual operators.

Although in previous reports on anthracite production a description has always been given of the territory from which it is mined, it is thought advisable to include this description in the present report so that it may be complete in itself without reference to those of previous years.

The anthracite fields cover an area of something over 480 square miles, and are situated in the eastern middle part of the State, and extend about equal distances north and south of a line drawn through the middle of the State from east to west, in the counties of Carbon, Columbia, Dauphin, Lackawanna, Luzerne, Northumberland, Schuylkill, and Susquehanna, and known under three general divisions, viz, Wyoming, Lehigh, and Schuylkill regions. Geologically they are divided into well-defined fields or basins, which are again subdivided, for convenience of identification, into districts.

The Bernice basin, in Sullivan County, formerly classed as the western northern field, is now not considered strictly anthracite. In the tabular arrangement indicating the divisions of the fields, given below, the western northern is therefore omitted.

Geological field or basin.	Local district.	Trade region.
Northern	Carbondale Scranton Pittston Wilkesbarre Plymouth Kingston	Wyoming.
Eastern middle	Green Mountain Black Creek Hazleton Beaver Meadow Panther Creek	Lehigh.
Southern	East Schuylkill West Schuylkill Lorberry Lykens Valley	Schuylkill.
Western middle	East Mahanoy West Mahanoy Shamokin	

The above territory is reached by eleven so-called initial railroads, as follows:

Philadelphia and Reading Railroad Company.
Lehigh Valley Railroad Company.
Central Railroad Company of New Jersey.
Delaware, Lackawanna and Western Railroad Company.
Delaware and Hudson Canal Company's Railroad.
Pennsylvania Railroad Company.

Erie and Wyoming Valley Railroad Company.
New York, Lake Erie and Western Railroad Company.
New York, Ontario and Western Railroad Company.
Delaware, Susquehanna and Schuylkill Railroad Company.
New York, Susquehanna and Western Railroad Company.

The railroads named above are termed initial roads, and over them is shipped all coal from the several regions.

In another part of this report is given a table showing the shipments from the three trade regions, Wyoming, Lehigh, and Schuylkill, from the commencement of the industry down to and including 1895.

The total product of anthracite in 1895 was 51,785,122 long tons. Of this amount 46,511,477 tons were shipped over the initial lines named above to various markets. In addition to that shipped, 1,174,146 tons were sold to local trade at or a short distance from the mines, and 4,099,499 tons were used for steam and heat at collieries. The last item consists largely of culm and dirt and small sizes. Formerly in many cases no accurate record was kept of this coal, and it was necessary to estimate it. At the present time, since the small sizes have become marketable, more care is taken in keeping records of it, and there is, therefore, less approximation in the making up of this item. As, however, this coal does not come into market, and as it is, generally speaking, of a lower grade than that which is sold to consumers, it is not taken into account in giving the value of the coal at the mines.

The table following shows the total product, with its average value at the mines, number of persons employed, etc., in 1895 as compared with 1894:

Total product of Pennsylvania anthracite in 1894 and 1895.

Year.	Total product.	Value at mines.	Average per ton.	Average number of persons employed.	Average number of days worked.
	Long tons.				
1894	46,358,144	$78,488,063	$1.85	131,603	190
1895	51,785,122	82,019,272	1.72	142,917	196

The following tables give the details of total product as to shipments, local trade, and colliery consumption for the years 1894 and 1895, by counties:

Distribution of the anthracite product in 1894.

County.	Total product of coal of all grades.	Loaded at mines for shipment.	Sold to local trade or used by employees.	Used at mines for steam and heat.
	Long tons.	Long tons.	Long tons.	Long tons.
Susquehanna	418,375	368,375	20,000	30,000
Lackawanna	11,466,301	10,500,947	302,523	662,831
Luzerne	17,508,032	15,558,959	440,973	1,508,100
Carbon	1,581,268	1,391,883	23,872	165,513
Schuylkill	10,234,624	8,994,308	125,857	1,114,459
Columbia	593,569	504,973	12,624	75,972
Northumberland	3,944,713	3,526,530	88,163	330,020
Dauphin	608,262	542,225	20,768	45,269
Total	46,358,144	41,391,200	1,034,780	3,932,164

Distribution of the anthracite product in 1895.

County.	Total product of coal of all grades.	Loaded at mines for shipment.	Sold to local trade or used by employees.	Used at mines for steam and heat.
	Long tons.	Long tons.	Long tons.	Long tons.
Susquehanna	1,470,595	1,294,124	20,400	156,071
Lackawanna	546,990	471,774	11,125	64,091
Luzerne	712,856	569,187	68,548	75,121
Carbon	12,664,913	11,514,406	392,041	758,466
Schuylkill	19,239,498	17,272,082	450,963	1,516,453
Columbia	4,773,124	4,335,328	90,419	347,377
Northumberland	11,941,242	10,656,366	130,650	1,154,226
Dauphin	435,904	398,210	10,000	27,694
Total	51,785,122	46,511,477	1,174,146	4,099,499

Comparison can be made from the above tables of the relative increase in the production of each county in the anthracite region, as well as shipments, and other details of local and colliery consumption.

On the next page is given a table showing shipments from the commencement of the industry down to the present time, reference to which was made earlier in the report.

Annual shipments from the Schuylkill, Lehigh, and Wyoming regions from 1820 to 1895.

Years.	Schuylkill region.		Lehigh region.		Wyoming region.		Total.
	Long tons.	Per ct.	Long tons.	Per ct.	Long tons.	Per ct.	Long tons.
1820....	....	......	365	....	....	......	365
1821....	....	......	1,073	....	....	......	1,073
1822....	1,180	39.79	2,240	60.21	....	......	3,720
1823....	1,128	16.23	5,823	83.77	....	......	6,951
1824....	1,567	14.10	9,541	85.90	....	......	11,108
1825....	6,500	18.60	28,393	81.40	....	......	34,893
1826 ...	16,767	34.90	31,280	65.10	....	......	48,047
1827....	31,360	49.44	32,074	50.56	....	......	63,434
1828....	47,284	61.00	30,232	39.00	....	......	77,516
1829....	79,973	71.35	25,110	22.40	7,000	6.25	112,083
1830....	89,984	51.50	41,750	23.90	43,000	24.60	174,734
1831....	81,854	46.29	40,966	23.17	54,600	30.54	176,820
1832....	209,271	57.61	70,000	19.27	84,000	23.12	363,271
1833....	252,971	51.87	123,001	25.22	111,777	22.91	487,749
1834....	226,692	60.19	106,244	28.21	43,700	11.60	376,636
1835....	339,508	60.54	131,250	23.41	90,000	16.05	560,758
1836....	432,045	63.16	148,211	21.66	103,861	15.18	684,117
1837....	530,152	60.98	223,902	25.75	115,387	13.27	869,441
1838....	446,875	60.49	213,615	28.92	78,207	10.59	738,697
1839....	475,077	58.05	221,025	27.01	122,300	14.91	818,402
1840....	490,596	56.75	225,313	26.07	148,470	17.18	864,379
1841....	624,466	65.07	143,037	14.90	192,270	20.03	959,773
1842....	583,273	52.62	272,540	24.59	252,599	22.79	1,108,412
1843....	710,200	56.21	267,793	21.19	285,605	22.60	1,263,598
1844....	887,937	54.45	377,002	23.12	365,911	22.43	1,630,850
1845....	1,134,724	56.22	429,453	21.33	451,836	22.45	2,013,013
1846....	1,308,500	55.82	517,116	22.07	518,389	22.11	2,344,005
1847....	1,665,735	57.79	633,507	21.98	583,067	20.23	2,882,309
1848....	1,733,721	56.12	670,321	21.70	685,196	22.18	3,089,238
1849....	1,728,500	53.30	781,556	24.10	732,910	22.60	3,242,966
1850....	1,840,620	54.80	690,456	20.56	827,823	24.64	3,358,899
1851....	2,328,525	52.34	964,224	21.68	1,156,167	25.98	4,448,916
1852....	2,636,835	52.81	1,072,136	21.47	1,284,500	25.72	4,993,471
1853....	2,665,110	51.30	1,054,309	20.29	1,475,732	28.41	5,195,151
1854....	3,191,670	53.14	1,207,186	20.13	1,603,478	26.73	6,002,334
1855....	3,552,943	53.77	1,284,113	19.43	1,771,511	26.80	6,608,567
1856....	3,603,029	52.91	1,351,970	19.52	1,972,581	28.47	6,927,580
1857....	3,373,797	50.77	1,318,511	19.84	1,952,603	29.39	6,644,911
1858....	3,273,245	47.86	1,380,030	20.18	2,186,094	31.96	6,839,369
1859....	3,448,708	44.16	1,628,311	20.86	2,731,236	34.98	7,808,255
1860....	3,749,632	44.04	1,821,674	21.40	2,941,817	34.56	8,513,123
1861....	3,160,747	39.74	1,738,377	21.85	3,055,140	38.41	7,954,264

Annual shipments from the Schuylkill, Lehigh, and Wyoming regions from 1820 to 1895—
Continued.

Years.	Schuylkill region.		Lehigh region.		Wyoming region.		Total.
	Long tons.	Per ct.	Long tons.	Per ct.	Long tons.	Per ct.	Long tons.
1862....	3,372,583	42.86	1,351,054	17.17	3,145,770	39.97	7,869,407
1863....	3,911,683	40.90	1,894,713	19.80	3,759,610	39.30	9,566,006
1864....	4,161,970	40.89	2,054,669	20.19	3,960,836	38.92	10,177,475
1865....	4,356,959	45.14	2,040,913	21.14	3,254,519	33.72	9,652,391
1866....	5,787,902	45.56	2,179,364	17.15	4,736,616	37.29	12,703,882
1867....	5,161,671	39.74	2,502,054	19.27	5,325,000	40.99	12,988,725
1868....	5,330,737	38.52	2,502,582	18.13	5,968,146	43.25	13,801,465
1869....	5,775,138	41.66	1,949,673	14.06	6,111,369	44.28	13,836,180
1870....	4,968,157	30.70	3,239,374	20.02	7,974,660	49.28	16,182,191
1871....	6,552,772	41.74	2,235,707	14.24	6,911,242	44.02	15,699,721
1872....	6,694,890	34.03	3,873,339	19.70	9,101,549	46.27	19,669,778
1873....	7,212,601	33.97	3,705,596	17.46	10,309,755	48.57	21,227,952
1874....	6,866,877	34.09	3,773,836	18.73	9,504,408	47.18	20,145,121
1875....	6,281,712	31.87	2,834,605	14.38	10,596,155	53.75	19,712,472
1876....	6,221,934	33.63	3,854,919	20.84	8,424,158	45.53	18,501,011
1877....	8,195,042	39.35	4,332,760	20.80	8,300,377	39.85	20,828,179
1878....	6,282,226	35.68	3,237,449	18.40	8,085,587	45.92	17,605,262
1879....	8,960,829	34.28	4,595,567	17.58	12,586,293	48.14	26,142,689
1880....	7,554,742	32.23	4,463,221	19.05	11,419,279	48.72	23,437,242
1881....	9,253,958	32.46	5,294,676	18.58	13,951,383	48.96	28,500,017
1882....	9,459,288	32.48	5,689,437	19.54	13,971,371	47.98	29,120,096
1883....	10,074,726	31.69	6,113,809	19.23	15,604,492	49.08	31,793,027
1884....	9,478,314	30.85	5,562,226	18.11	a15,677,753	51.04	30,718,293
1885....	9,488,426	30.01	5,898,634	18.65	a16,236,470	51.34	31,623,530
1886....	9,381,407	29.19	5,723,129	17.89	a17,031,826	52.82	32,136,362
1887....	10,609,028	30.63	4,347,061	12.55	a19,684,929	56.82	34,641,018
1888....	10,654,116	27.93	5,639,236	14.78	a21,852,366	57.29	38,145,718
1889....	10,486,185	29.28	6,294,073	17.57	a19,036,835	53.15	35,817,093
1890....	10,867,822	29.68	6,329,658	17.28	a19,417,979	53.04	36,615,459
1891....	12,711,258	31.50	6,381,838	15.78	a21,325,240	52.72	40,448,336
1892....	12,626,784	30.14	6,451,076	15.40	a22,815,480	54.46	41,893,340
1893....	12,357,444	28.68	6,892,352	15.99	23,839,741	55.33	43,089,537
1894....	12,035,005	29.08	6,705,434	16.20	22,650,761	54.72	41,391,260
1895....	14,269,932	30.68	7,298,124	15.69	24,943,421	53.63	46,511,477
Total 76 years..	328,394,119	34.47	168,557,218	17.70	455,573,543	47.83	952,524,880

a Includes Loyalsock field.

In the following pages is given a directory of the anthracite mines in Pennsylvania, with names of operators, post-office addresses, etc.

Directory of anthracite coal mines in Pennsylvania.

NORTHERN COAL FIELD.

Map No.	Name of mine	Local district	Inspector's district	Location				Operator	
				Township, etc.	County.	Railroad.	Nearest shipping station.	Name.	Post-office address.
15	Erie	Carbondale	1	Carbondale Twp.	Lackawanna	D. and H. C. Co. R. R.	Glenwood	Hillside Coal and Iron Co.	Scranton.
16	Glenwood	do	1	do	do	do	do	do	Do.
17	Keystone	do	1	do	do	do	Archbald	do	Do.
21	Raymond	do	1	Blakely Twp.	do	do	do	Raymond Coal Co.	Do.
23	Pierce	do	1	do	do	D., L. and W. R. R.	Winton	Pierce Coal Co., Limited.	Winton.
18	Edgerton	do	1	do	do	Erie R. R.	Jermyn	Edgerton Coal Co., Limited.	Jermyn.
25	Sterrick Creek	do	1	do	do	N. Y., S. and W. R. R.	Winton	Sterrick Creek Coal Co.	Peckville.
26	Jermyn No. 3	do	1	do	do	do	Dickson	John Jermyn	Scranton.
35	Jermyn No. 4	do	1	do	do	do	do	do	Do.
28	Marshwood	do	1	do	do	Erie R. R.	Peckville	Moosic Mountain Coal Co.	Marshwood.
43	Murray	do	1	Dunmore Twp.	do	D., L. and W. R. R.	Scranton	Murray, Carney & Co.	Dunmore.
5	Northwest	do	1	Fell Twp.	do	Erie R. R.	Carbondale	Northwest Coal Co	Scranton.
27	White	do	1	Blakely Twp.	do	N. Y., S. and W. R. R.	Winton	Winton Coal Co., Limited.	Do.
24	Mount Jessup	do	1	do	do	D., L. and W. R. R. and N. Y., O. and W.R.R.	do	Mount Jessup Coal Co., Limited.	Peckville.
53	Olyphant	do	1	do	do	D. and H. C. Co. R. R.	Olyphant	D. & H. Canal Co.	Providence.
34	Eddy Creek	do	1	do	do	do	do	do	Do.
29	Grassy Island	do	1	do	do	do	Archbald	do	Do.
20	White Oak	do	1	do	do	do	Jermyn	do	Do.
19	Jermyn Shaft	do	1	Carbondale Twp.	do	do	Jermyn	do	Do.
11	Coal Brook	do	1	do	do	do	Carbondale	do	Do.
12	No. 1 Shaft	do	1	do	do	do	do	do	Do.
13	No. 3 Shaft	do	1	do	do	do	do	do	Do.

Directory of anthracite coal mines in Pennsylvania—Continued.

NORTHERN COAL FIELD—Continued.

Map No.	Name of mine	Local district	Inspectors' district	Township, etc.	County	Railroad	Nearest shipping station	Operator — Name	Post-office address
10	Racket Brook	Carbondale	1	Carbondale Twp	Lackawanna	D. and H. C. Co. R. R.	Carbondale	D. & H. Canal Co.	Providence.
14	Powderly	do	1	do	do	do	do	do	Do.
3	Clinton	do	1	Fell Twp	do	Erie R. R	Forest City	do	Do.
26	Dolph	do	1	Blakely Twp	do	L. V. R. R.	Jessup	Dolph Coal Co., Limited	Scranton.
32	Lackawanna	do	1	do	do	N. Y., O. and W. R. R.	Olyphant	Lackawanna Coal Co., Lim.	Do.
31	Ontario	do	1	do	do	do	Peckville	N. Y. and Scranton Coal Co.	Peckville.
2	Forest City	do	1	Forest City	Susquehanna	Erie R. R	Forest City	Hillside Coal and Iron Co.	Scranton.
1	Clifford	do	1	do	do	do	do	do	Do.
	West Ridge	do	1	do	Lackawanna	N. Y., O. and W. R. R.	West Ridge	West Ridge Coal Co.	Do.
	Riverside	do	1	Archbald	do	do	Winton	Riverside Coal Co.	Do.
68	Archbald	Scranton	2	Lackawanna Twp	do	D., L. and W. R. R.	Scranton	D., L. and W. R. R. Co.	Do.
63	Bellevue	do	2	do	do	do	Bellevue	do	Do.
	Amchincloss	do	2	do	do	do	do	do	Do.
	Bliss	do	2	do	do	do	do	do	Do.
60	Brisbin	do	2	3d ward, Scranton	do	do	Scranton	do	Do.
58	Cayuga	do	2	do	do	do	do	do	Do.
66	Central	do	2	15th ward, Scranton	do	do	do	do	Do.
64	Continental	do	2	Lackawanna Twp	do	do	do	do	Do.
64	Dodge	do	2	do	do	do	Bellevue	do	Do.
67	Hampton	do	2	do	do	do	Scranton	do	Do.
71	Holden	do	2	do	do	do	Taylorville	do	Do.
65	Hyde Park	do	2	5th ward, Scranton	do	do	Scranton	do	Do.
62	Oxford	do	2	do	do	do	do	do	Do.

Directory of anthracite coal mines in Pennsylvania—Continued.

NORTHERN COAL FIELD—Continued.

Map No.	Name of mine	Location					Nearest shipping station	Operator	
		Local district	Inspector's district	Township, etc.	County.	Railroad.		Name.	Post-office address.
73	Pyne	Scranton	2	Lackawanna Twp	Lackawanna	D., L. and W. R. R.	Taylorville	D., L. & W. R. R. Co	Scranton.
78	Sloan	do	2	do	do	do	Scranton	do	Do.
44	Storrs	do	2	Blakely Twp	do	do	Priceville	do	Do.
72	Taylor	do	2	Lackawanna Twp	do	do	Taylorville	do	Do.
61	Diamond No. 1	do	2	21st ward, Scranton	do	do	Scranton	do	Do.
	Diamond No. 2	do	2	do	do	do	do	do	Do.
	Tripp Shaft	do	2	do	do	do	do	do	Do.
38	Dunmore No. 1	do	1	Dunmore Twp	do	E. and W. V. R. R.	Dunmore	Pennsylvania Coal Co	Dunmore.
41	Dunmore No. 5	do	1	do	do	do	do	do	Do.
	Bunker Hill	do	2	do	do	do	do	do	Do.
30	Blue Ridge	do	1	Old Forge Twp	do	N. Y., O. and W. R. R.	Peckville	Blue Ridge Coal Co	Peckville.
	Austin	do	2	do	do	L. V. R. R.	Lackawanna	Austin Coal Co	Scranton.
40	Gypsy Grove No. 3	do	2	Dunmore Twp	do	E. and W. V. R. R.	Dunmore	Pennsylvania Coal Co	Dunmore.
	Gypsy Grove No. 4	do	1	do	do	do	do	do	Do.
52	Pine Brook	do	2	7th ward, Scranton	do	D., L. and W. R. R.	Scranton	Lackawanna Land C. Co.	Scranton.
53	Capouse	do	2	21st ward, Scranton	do	do	do	do	Do.
76	Greenwood No. 1	do	2	Lackawanna Twp	do	N. Y., S. and W. R. R.	Peckville	Greenwood Coal Co., Lim.	Do.
77	Greenwood No. 2	do	2	do	do	do	Minooka	do	Do.
80	Jermyn Nos. 1 and 2	do	1	Old Forge Twp	do	I. V. R. R.	Taylorville	Jermyn & Co	Do.
37	Pancoast	do	1	Blakely Twp	do	D. L. and W. R R	Dickson City	Pancoast Coal Co	Do.
56	Providence	do	2	2d ward, Scranton	do	do	Green Ridge	Providence Coal Co., Lim.	Do.
79	Sibley	do	2	Old Forge Twp	do	L. V. R. R.	Lackawanna	Elliot, McClure & Co	Do.
42	Spencer	do	2	Dunmore Twp	do	do	Dunmore	A. D. and F. M. Spencer	Dunmore.

Directory of anthracite coal mines in Pennsylvania—Continued.

NORTHERN COAL FIELD—Continued.

Map No.	Name of mine.	Local district.	Inspectors district.	Township, etc.	County.	Railroad.	Nearest shipping station.	Name.	Post-office address.
				Location.				**Operator.**	
74	Meadow Brook	Scranton	2	20th ward, Scranton	Lackawanna	D., L. and W. R. R	Taylorville	William Connell & Co	Scranton.
75	National	do	2	Lackawanna Twp	do	do	do	do	Do.
49	Stafford	do	2	13th ward, Scranton	do	D. and H. C. Co. R. R.	Green Ridge	D. and H. Canal Co	Providence.
46	Manville	do	2	1st ward, Scranton	do	do	Providence	do	Do.
45	Leggitts Creek	do	1	do	do	do	do	do	Do.
48	Marvine	do	2	2d ward, Scranton	do	do	do	do	Do.
48	Von Storch	do	2	do	do	do	do	do	Do.
47	Dickson	do	2	do	do	Erie R. R	do	O. S. Johnson	Scranton.
50	Green Ridge	do	2	Dunmore Twp	do	do	Green Ridge	do	Do.
	Richmond, Nos. 3, 4	do	1	Scranton Twp	do	N. Y., O. and W. R. R	Providence	Elk Hill Coal and Iron Co	Do.
57	Mount Pleasant	do	2	14th ward, Scranton	do	D., L. and W. R. R	Scranton	Wm. T. Smith	Do.
81	William A	Pittston	2	Old Forge Twp	do	L. V. R. R	Lackawanna	Connell Coal Co	Do.
	Lawrence	do	2	do	do	do	do	do	Do.
88	Katy-Did	do	3	do	do	E. and W. V. R. R	Moosic	Robertson & Co	Moosic.
87	Central No. 13	do	3	do	do	do	Pleasant Valley	Pennsylvania Coal Co	Dunmore.
	Law Shaft	do	3	Pittston Twp	do	do	do	do	Do.
86	Old Forge	do	2	Old Forge Twp	do	do	Lackawanna	do	Do.
109	Ewen Breaker	do	3	Jenkins Twp	Luzerne	do	Pittston	do	Do.
110	Shaft No. 4	do	3	do	do	do	do	do	Do.
110	Breaker No. 6	do	3	do	do	do	Port Blanchard	do	Do.
	Breaker No. 8	do	3	Hughestownboro	do	do	Pittston	do	Do.
99	Breaker No. 10	do	3	do	do	do	do	do	Do.

a Operated jointly with Delaware, Lackawanna and Western Railroad Company.

Directory of anthracite coal mines in Pennsylvania—Continued.

NORTHERN COAL FIELD—Continued.

Map No.	Name of mine	Local district	Inspectors district	Location				Operator	
				Township, etc.	County.	Railroad.	Nearest shipping station.	Name.	Post-office address.
111	Breaker No. 14	Pittston	3	Jenkins Twp	Luzerne	E. and W. V. R. R.	Port Blanchard	Pennsylvania Coal Co	Dunmore.
100	Barnum	do	3	Marey Twp	do	do	Pittston Junction	do	Do.
112	Laflin	do	3	Jenkins Twp	do	C. R. R. of New Jersey and L. V. R. R.	Laflin	Amora Coal Co	Wilkesbarre.
91	Avoca	do	3	Pittston Twp	do	L. V. R. R.	Avoca	Avoca Coal Co., Limited	Avoca.
90	Langcliffe	do	3	Pittston	do	do	do	Langcliffe Coal Co	Do.
101	Twin	do	3	do	do	do	Pittston	Newton Coal Mining Co	Pittston.
	Ravine	do	3	do	do	do	do	do	Do.
102	Seneca	do	3	do	do	do	do	do	Do.
98	Mosier	do	3	Marey Twp	do	do	do	do	Do.
168	Hunt	do	3	Kingston Twp	do	D., L. and W. R. R.	Wyoming	Race & Shaffer	Scranton.
83	Hallstead	do	3	Marey Twp	do	do	Duryea	D., L. and W. R. R. Co	Do.
55	Butler	do	3	Pittston Twp	do	L. V. R. R.	Pittston	Butler Mine Co., Limited	Pittston.
106	Schooley	do	3	Exeter Twp	do	do	West Pittston	do	Do.
84	Columbia	do	3	Marey Twp	do	D., L. and W. R. R and L. V. R. R.	Duryea	Columbia Coal Co	Do.
85	Phœnix	do	3	do	do	do	do	do	Do.
82	Babylon	do	3	do	do	L. V. R. R.	Coxton	Babylon Coal Co	Scranton.
89	Consolidated	do	3	Pittston Twp	do	E. and W. V. R. R.	Moosic	Hillside Coal and Iron Co	Do.
103	Clear Spring	do	3	West Pittston	do	D. L. and W	West Pittston	Clear Spring Coal Co	Pittston.
	Louse	do	3	do	do	L. V. R. R.	do	Raub Coal Co	Do.
94	Elmwood	do	3	Pittston Twp	do	L. V. R. R.	Avoca	Florence Coal Co., Limited	Dupont.
96	Abbott No. 2	do	3	do	do	C. R. R. of New Jersey	Pittston	Abbott Coal Co	Pittston.

Directory of anthracite coal mines in Pennsylvania—Continued.

NORTHERN COAL FIELD—Continued.

Map No.	Name of mine	Local district	Inspector's district	Township, etc.	County	Railroad	Nearest shipping station	Name	Post-office address
133	Ridgewood	Pittston	3	Plains Twp	Luzerne	N. Y., S. and W. R. R.	Mill Creek	Keystone Coal Co	Wilkesbarre.
104	Stevens	do	3	Exeter Twp	do	L. V. R. R.	Exeter	Stevens Coal Co	Scranton.
10?	Mount Lookout	do	3	do	do	D., L. and W. R. R. and L. V. R. R.	do	Mount Lookout Coal Co	Do.
105	Morning Star	do	3	do	do	L. V. R. R.	Wyoming	J. A. Hutchins	Wyoming.
	Exeter	do	3	Pittston Twp	do	do	West Pittston	Lehigh Valley Coal Co	Wilkesbarre.
9?	Heidelberg No. 1	do	do	do	do	do	do	do	Do.
9?	Heidelberg No. 2	do	do	do	do	do	do	do	Do.
	Spring Brook	do	3	Old Forge Twp	do	D. and H. C. Co. R. R.	Moosic	Whitney & Kemmerer	Philadelphia.
133	Diamond No. 1	Wilkesbarre	4	Wilkesbarre	do	C. R. R. of New Jersey	Ashley	L. and W. Coal Co	Wilkesbarre.
132	Hollenback No. 2	do	4	do	do	do	Wilkesbarre	do	Do.
134	Empire No. 4	do	4	do	do	do	Ashley	do	Do.
137	S. Wilkesbarre No. 5	do	4	do	do	do	S. Wilkesbarre	do	Do.
135	Stanton No. 7	do	4	do	do	do	Ashley	do	Do.
138	New Jersey No. 8	do	4	Hanover Twp	do	do	do	do	Do.
139	Sugar Notch No. 9	do	4	do	do	do	Sugar Notch	do	Do.
	Maxwell No. 20	do	4	Newport Twp	do	do	Wanamie	do	Do.
143	Wanamie No. 18	do	4	do	do	do	Alden	Alden Coal Co	Alden.
142	Alden	do	4	do	do	do	Leo	Newport Coal Co	Wilkesbarre.
146	Mellville	do	4	do	do	do	Ashley	Red Ash Coal Co	Do.
130	Red Ash No. 1	do	4	Wilkesbarre Twp	do	do	do	do	Do.
131	Red Ash No. 2	do	4	do	do	do			Do.
144	Colliery No. 1	do	4	Hanover Twp	do	P. R. R.	Nanticoke	Susquehanna Coal Co	Do.

Directory of anthracite coal mines in Pennsylvania—Continued.

NORTHERN COAL FIELD—Continued.

Map No.	Name of mine.	Location.						Operator.	
		Local district.	Inspector's district.	Township, etc.	County.	Railroad.	Nearest shipping station.	Name.	Post-office address.
145	Colliery No. 2	Wilkesbarre	4	Hanover Twp	Luzerne	P. R. R	Nanticoke	Susquehanna Coal Co	Wilkesbarre.
146	Colliery No. 5	do	4	do	do	do		do	Do.
147	Colliery No. 6	do	4	Newport Twp	do	do	Glen Lyon	do	Do.
117	Bennett	do	3	Plains Twp	do	C. R. R. of New Jersey	Mill Creek	Thomas Waddell & Co	Pittston.
141	Warrior Run	do	4	Hanover Twp	do	L. V. R. R	Warrior Run	A. J. Davis & Co	Wilkesbarre.
149	West End No. 1	do	3	Conyngham Twp	do	P. R. R. and C. R. R. of New Jersey	Mocanaqua	West End Coal Co	Shickshinny.
140	Mallet	do	4	Hanover Twp	do	C. R. R. of New Jersey	Sugar Notch	Hanover Coal Co	Wilkesbarre.
118	Abbott	do	3	Plains Twp	do	L. V. R. R	Miners Mills	Lehigh Valley Coal Co	Do.
129	Hillman Vein	do	4	Wilkesbarre Twp.	do	do	Wilkesbarre	Hillman Vein Coal Co	Do.
136	Franklin	do	3	do	do	do	Ashley	Lehigh Valley Coal Co	Do.
119	Enterprise	do	4	Plains Twp.	do	do	Port Bowkley	do	Do.
130	Henry	do	3	do	do	do	do	do	Do.
122	Prospect	do	3	do	do	do	do	do	Do.
121	Dorrance	do	3	Wilkesbarre Twp	do	do	do	do	Do.
	Wyoming	do	3	Plains Twp.	do	do	do	do	Do.
115	Mill Creek	do	3	do	do	D. and H. C. Co. R. R.	Mill Creek	D. and H. Canal Co	Providence.
116	Algonquin	do	3	do	do	do	Miners Mills	Algonquin Coal Co	Wilkesbarre.
125	Laurel Run	do	3	Wilkesbarre Twp.	do	do	Parsons	N. Y., S. & W. R. R. Co	Do.
126	Baltimore Slope	do	4	do	do	do	do	D. and H. Canal Co	Providence.
	Bal. Red Ash No. 2	do	4	do	do	do	do	do	Do.
127	Baltimore Tunnel	do	4	do	do	do	Wilkesbarre	do	Do.
128	Conyngham	do	4	do	do	do	do	do	Do.

Directory of anthracite coal mines in Pennsylvania—Continued.

NORTHERN COAL FIELD—Continued.

Map No.	Name of mine	Local district.	Inspectors district.	Location.				Operator.	
				Township, etc.	County.	Railroad.	Nearest shipping station.	Name.	Post-office address.
114	Delaware	Wilkesbarre	3	Plains Twp	Luzerne	D. and H. Co. R. R.	Mill Creek	D. & H. Canal Co	Providence.
168	Lance No. 11	Plymouth	4	Plymouth	do	D., L. and W. R. R.	Plymouth	L. and W. Coal Co	Do.
169	Nottingham No. 15	do	4	do	do	do	do	do	Do.
170	Reynolds No. 16	do	4	do	do	do	do	do	Do.
172	Avondale	do	4	Plymouth Twp	do	do	Avondale	D., L. and W. R. R. Co	Scranton.
160	Woodward	do	4	do	do	do	Kingston	do	Do.
166	Dodson	do	4	do	do	do	Plymouth	John C. Haddock	Wilkesbarre.
155	East Boston	do	3	Kingston	do	D., L. and W. R. R., P. R. R., and L. V. R. R.	Kingston	W. G. Payne & Co	Kingston.
171	Parrish	do	4	Plymouth	do	C. R. R. of New Jersey	Plymouth	Parrish Coal Co	Plymouth.
	Buttonwood	do	4	do	do	do	do	do	Do.
173	Colliery No. 3	d.	4	West Nanticoke	do	D., L. and W. R. R.	West Nanticoke	Susquehanna Coal Co	Wilkesbarre.
	Salem	do	4	Shickshinny	do	do	Shickshinny	E. S. Stackhouse	Shickshinny.
161	Boston	do	4	Plymouth Twp	do	D. and H. C. Co. R. R	Plymouth	D. and H. Canal Co	Providence.
162	Plymouth No. 2	do	4	do	do	do	do	do	Do.
163	Plymouth No. 3	do	4	do	do	do	do	do	Do.
164	Plymouth No. 4	do	4	do	do	do	do	do	Do.
165	Plymouth No. 5	do	4	do	do	do	do	do	Do.
159	Pettebone	Kingston	3	Kingston	do	D., L. and W. R. R	do	D., L. and W. R. R. Co	Do.
156	Kingston No. 1	do	3	Kingston Twp	do	do	do	Kingston Coal Co	Kingston.
158	Kingston No. 2	do	3	Plymouth	do	do	do	do	Do.
	Kingston No. 3	do	3	do	do	do	do	do	Do.
157	Kingston No. 4	do	3	Kingston Twp	do	do	do	do	Do.

Directory of anthracite coal mines in Pennsylvania—Continued.

NORTHERN COAL FIELD—Continued.

Map No.	Name of mine	Local district	Inspector's district	Location Township, etc.	County	Railroad	Nearest shipping station	Operator Name	Post-office address
167	Gaylord	Kingston	4	Plymouth Twp	Luzerne	D., L. and W. R. R.	Plymouth	Kingston Coal Co	Kingston.
152	Harry E	do	3	Kingston Twp	do	do	Bennett	Simpson & Watkins	Wilkesbarre.
151	Forty Fort	do	3	do	do	D., L. and W. R. R. and L. V. R. R.	Maltby	do	Do.
154	Black Diamond	do	3	do	do	do	Kingston	John C. Haddock	Do.
153	Mill Hollow	do	3	do	do	do	Bennett	Thomas Waddell	Pittston.
150	Maltby	do	3	do	do	do	Maltby	Lehigh Valley Coal Co	Wilkesbarre.

EASTERN MIDDLE COAL FIELD.

Map No.	Name of mine	Local district	Inspector's district	Location Township, etc.	County	Railroad	Nearest shipping station	Operator Name	Post-office address
175	Upper Lehigh No. 2	Green Mountain	5	Butler Twp	Luzerne	C. R. R. of New Jersey	Upper Lehigh	Upper Lehigh Coal Co	Upper Lehigh.
176	Upper Lehigh No. 4	do	5	do	do	do	do	do	Do.
191	Milnesville	Black Creek	5	Hazle Twp	do	L. V. R. R.	Hazleton	A. S. Van Wickle & Co	Milnesville.
188	Lattimer No. 1	do	5	do	do	do	do	Calvin Pardee & Co	Hazleton.
189	Lattimer No. 2	do	5	do	do	do	do		
190	Lattimer No. 3	do	5	do	do	do	do		
192	Hollywood	do	5	do	do	do	do		Do.
177	Sandy Run	do	5	Foster Twp	do	C. R. R. of New Jersey	Sandy Run	M. S. Kemmerer & Co	Sandy Run.
178	Highland No. 1	do	5	do	do	L. V. R. R.	Highland	G. B. Markle & Co	Jeddo.
179	Highland, Nos. 2, 5	do	5	do	do	do	do	do	Do.
184	Jeddo No. 3	do	5	Hazle Twp	do	do	Jeddo	do	Do.
185	Jeddo No. 4	do	5	do	do	do	do	do	Do.

Directory of anthracite coal mines in Pennsylvania—Continued.

EASTERN MIDDLE COAL FIELD—Continued.

Map No.	Name of mine	Local district	Inspectors' district	Location				Operator	
				Township, etc.	County.	Railroad.	Nearest shipping station.	Name.	Post-office address.
195	Derringer	Black Creek	5	Black Creek Twp.	Luzerne	D., S. and S. R. R.	Derringer	Coxe Bros. & Co	Drifton.
180	Drifton No. 1	do	5	Foster Twp.	do	do	Drifton	do	Do.
181	Drifton No. 2	do	5	do	do	do	do	do	Do.
181	Drifton No. 3	do	5	Hazle Twp.	do	do	do	do	Do.
183	Eckley No. 5	do	5	Foster Twp.	do	do	Eckley	do	Do.
182	Eckley No. 10	do	5	do	do	do	do	do	Do.
196	Gowen	do	5	Black Creek Twp.	do	do	Gowen	do	Do.
194	Tomhicken	do	5	Sugar Loaf Twp.	do	do	Tomhicken	do	Do.
	Oneida, Nos. 1, 2, and 3	do	6	North Union	Schuylkill	do	Oneida	do	Do.
197	Hazlebrook	Hazleton	5	Foster Twp.	Luzerne	L. V. R. R.	Hazlebrook	J. S. Wentz & Co	Mauch Chunk.
209	Humboldt	do	5	Hazle Twp.	do	do	Hazleton	Lindeman, Skeer & Co	S. Bethlehem.
201	East Sugar Loaf No. 1	do	5	do	do	do	Stockton	do	Do.
200	East Sugar Loaf, Nos. 2 and 4.	do	5	do	do	do	do	do	Do.
199	East Sugar Loaf, Nos. 5 and 6.	do	5	do	do	do	do	do	Do.
208	Harwood	do	5	do	do	D., S. and S. R. R.	Hazleton	Calvin Pardee & Co	Harwood Mines.
198	Stockton	do	5	do	do	do	Stockton	Coxe Bros. & Co	Drifton.
207	Cranberry	do	5	do	do	L. V. R. R.	Hazleton	A. Pardee & Co	Hazleton.
205	Hazleton, Nos. 1, 2.	do	7	Hazleton	do	do	do	Lehigh Valley Coal Co	Do.
204	Hazleton, Nos. 3, 5.	do	7	do	do	do	do	do	Do.

Directory of anthracite coal mines in Pennsylvania—Continued.

EASTERN MIDDLE COAL FIELD—Continued.

Map No.	Name of mine	Local district	Inspectors district	Location				Operator	
				Township, etc.	County	Railroad	Nearest shipping station.	Name.	Post-office address.
206	Hazleton No. 6	Hazleton	5	Hazleton	Luzerne	L. V. R. R.	Hazleton	Lehigh Valley Coal Co	Hazleton.
217	Beaver Brook	Beaver Meadow.	5	...do	...do	L. V. R. R. and C. R. R. of New Jersey.	Audenried	C. M. Dodson & Co	Audenried.
211	Beaver Meadow	...do	5	Banks Twp	Carbon	D., S. and S. R. R. and L. V. R. R.	Beaver Meadow	Coxe Bros. & Co	Drifton.
218	Honeybrook No. 2	...do	5	...do	...do	C. R. R. of New Jersey.	Treskow	L. and W. Coal Co	Wilkesbarre.
219	Honeybrook No. 4	...do	6	Klein Twp	Schuylkill	...do	Audenried	...do	Do.
220	Honeybrook No. 5	...do	6	...do	...do	...do	...do	...do	Do.
221	Silver Brook No. 1	...do	6	...do	...do	L. V. R. R	Silver Brook	Silver Brook Coal Co	Mauch Chunk.
	Silver Brook No. 2	...do	6	...do	...do	...do	...do	...do	Do.
212	Coleraine	...do	5	Banks Twp.	Carbon	...do	Beaver Meadow	A. S. Van Wickle & Co	Milnesville.
210	Evans	...do	5	...do	...do	...do	...do	Evans Mining Co	Beaver Meadow.
216	Spring Brook	...do	5	Jeanesville	...do	...do	Audenried	Lehigh Valley Coal Co	Wilkesbarre.
213	Spring Mount No. 1	...do	5	...do	...do	...do	Jeanesville	...do	Do.
214	Spring Mount No. 4	...do	5	...do	Luzerne	...do		...do	Do.

WESTERN MIDDLE COAL FIELD.

Map No.	Name of mine	Local district	Inspectors district	Township, etc.	County	Railroad	Nearest shipping station.	Name.	Post-office address.
235	Elhangowan	East Mahanoy	6	Mahanoy Twp	Schuylkill	P. a. R. R. R.	St. Nicholas	P. and R. Coal and Iron Co	Pottsville.
230	Elmwood	...do	6	...do	...do	...do	Mahanoy City	...do	Do.
236	Knickerbocker	...do	6	...do	...do	...do	Yatesville	...do	Do.
229	Mahanoy City	...do	6	Mahanoy City	...do	...do	Mahanoy City	...do	Do.

Directory of anthracite coal mines in Pennsylvania—Continued.

WESTERN MIDDLE COAL FIELD—Continued.

Map No.	Name of mine.	Location.						Operator.	
		Local district.	Inspectors' district.	Township, etc.	County.	Railroad.	Nearest shipping station.	Name.	Post-office address.
228	North Mahanoy	East Mahanoy	6	Mahanoy Twp	Schuylkill	P. and R. R. R.	Mahanoy City	P. and R. Coal and Iron Co	Pottsville.
227	Schuylkill	do	6	do	do	do	St. Nicholas	do	Do.
233	Suffolk	do	6	do	do	do	do	do	Do.
232	St. Nicholas	do	6	do	do	do	do	do	Do.
231	Tunnel Ridge	do	6	do	do	do	Mahanoy City	do	Do.
330	Middle Lehigh	do	7	do	do	L. V. R. R.	New Boston	Mill Creek Coal Co	New Boston.
223	Buck Mountain	do	6	do	do	do	Buck Mountain	do	Do.
331	Morea	do	8	do	do	P. R. R. and L. V. R. R.	Morea	Dodson Coal Co	Morea Colliery.
225	Park No. 2	do	6	do	do	L. V. R. R.	Park Place	Lentz, Lilly & Co	Park Place.
226	Springdale	do	6	do	do	do	do	do	Do.
224	Primrose	do	6	do	do	do	Mahanoy City	Lehigh Valley Coal Co	Wilkesbarre.
234	Maple Hill	do	6	do	do	P. and R. R. R.	St. Nicholas	P. and R. Coal and Iron Co	Pottsville.
284	Alaska	West Mahanoy	7	Mount Carmel Twp	Northum'l'd	do	Alaska	do	Do.
283	Locust Gap	do	7	do	do	do	Locust Gap	do	Do.
282	Locust Spring	do	7	do	do	do	do	do	Do.
279	Merriam	do	7	do	do	do	Locust Summit	do	Do.
280	Monitor	do	7	do	do	do	Locust Gap	do	Do.
281	Reliance	do	7	do	do	do	Mount Carmel	do	Do.
276	Mount Carmel	do	7	do	do	P. and R. R. R., N. C. R. R. and L. V. R. R.	do	Thomas M. Righter & Co	Do.
274	Columbus, Nos. 1, 2	do	7	N. Conyngham Twp	Columbia	L. V. R. R.	do	Shaefer, Beckel & Co	Do.
271	Centralia	do	7	do	do	do	Centralia	Lehigh Valley Coal Co	Wilkesbarre.

Directory of anthracite coal mines in Pennsylvania—Continued.

WESTERN MIDDLE COAL FIELD—Continued.

Map No.	Name of mine	Local district	Inspector's district	Township, etc.	County	Railroad	Nearest shipping station	Name. (Operator)	Post-office address.
272	Logan	West Mahanoy	7	N. Conyngham Twp.	Columbia	L. V. R. R.	Centralia	Lehigh Valley Coal Co.	Wilkesbarre.
273	Morris Ridge	do	7	do	do	do	Mount Carmel	Morris Ridge Coal Co.	Shamokin.
268	North Ashland	do	7	do	do	P. and R. R. R.	Continental	P. and R. Coal and Iron Co.	Pottsville.
278	Potts	do	7	do	do	do	Locust Dale	do	Do.
270	Continental a	do	7	do	do	L. V. R. R.	Centralia	Lehigh Valley Coal Co.	Wilkesbarre.
271	Locust Run	do	7	do	Schuylkill	P. and R. R. R.	Ashland	P. and R. Coal and Iron Co.	Pottsville.
267	Bast	do	7	Butler Twp.	do	do	do	do	Do.
247	Bear Ridge	do	6	West Mahanoy Twp.	do	do	Mahanoy Plane	do	Do.
238	Boston Run	do	6	Mahanoy Twp.	do	do	St. Nicholas	do	Do.
237	Bear Run	do	6	do	do	do	Gilberton	do	Do.
241	Gilberton	do	6	West Mahanoy Twp.	do	do	Gilberton	do	Do.
290	Girard Mammoth	do	6	do	do	do	Raven Run	do	Do.
263	Girard	do	6	Butler Twp.	do	do	Girardville	do	Do.
262	Hammond	do	6	do	do	do	Conner	do	Do.
248	Indian Ridge	do	6	West Mahanoy Twp.	do	do	Shenandoah	do	Do.
252	Kohinoor	do	6	do	do	do	Shenandoah	do	Do.
277	Keystone	do	7	Butler Twp.	do	do	Locust Dale	do	Do.
249	Shenandoah City	do	6	West Mahanoy Twp.	do	do	Shenandoah	do	Do.
266	Tunnel	do	7	Butler Twp.	do	do	Ashland	do	Do.
250	Turkey Run	do	6	West Mahanoy Twp.	do	do	Shenandoah	do	Do.
251	West Shenandoah	do	6	do	do	do	do	do	Do.
264	Preston No. 2	do	7	Butler Twp.	do	do	Girardville	do	Do.

a The mine extends into Northumberland County.

Directory of anthracite coal mines in Pennsylvania—Continued.

WESTERN MIDDLE COAL FIELD—Continued.

Map No.	Name of mine	Local district	Inspectory district	Township, etc.	County	Railroad	Nearest shipping station	Operator Name	Post office address.
295	Preston No. 3	West Mahanoy	7	Butler Twp	Schuylkill	P. and R. R. R.	Girardville	P. and R. Coal and Iron Co	Pottsville.
260	Big Mine Run	do	7	do	do	do	Ashland	Lehigh Valley Coal Co	Ashland.
253	Cambridge	do	6	West Mahanoy Twp	do	do	Shenandoah	Cambridge Coal Co	Shenandoah.
242	Draper	do	6	do	do	do	Gilberton	P. and R. Coal and Iron Co	Pottsville.
239	Furnace	do	6	do	do	do	Gilberton	Furnace Coal Co	Gilberton.
254	Kehley Run	do	6	do	do	do	Shenandoah	Thomas Coal Co	Philadelphia.
245	Lawrence	do	6	do	do	do	Shenandoah	Lawrence Coal Co	Pottsville.
255	William Penn	do	6	do	do	P. R. R.	Mahanoy Plane	William Penn Coal Co	Shaft.
258	Packer No. 2	do	6	do	do	L. V. R. R.	Shaft	Lehigh Valley Coal Co	Wilkesbarre.
256	Packer No. 3	do	6	do	do	do	Lost Creek	do	Do.
257	Packer No. 4	do	6	do	do	do	Shenandoah	do	Do.
259	Packer No. 5	do	6	Butler Twp	do	do	Girardville	do	Do.
265	Bear Valley	Shamokin	7	Coal Twp	Northum'l'd	P. and R. R. R.	Shamokin	P. and R. Coal and Iron Co	Pottsville.
263	Buck Ridge	do	7	do	do	do	Greenback	do	Do.
261	Burnside	do	7	do	do	do	Shamokin	do	Do.
299	Henry Clay	do	7	do	do	do	do	do	Do.
306	North Franklin	do	7	Zerbe Twp	do	do	Treverton	Mineral R. R. & Mining Co	Wilkesbarre.
297	Cameron	do	7	Coal Twp	do	N. C. Rwy.	Shamokin	do	Do.
296	Luke Fidler	do	7	do	do	do	Lancaster Switch	Union Coal Co	Shamokin.
290	Hickory Ridge	do	7	do	do	do	do	do	Do.
291	Hickory Swamp	do	7	Mount Carmel Twp	do	do	Mount Carmel	do	Do.
286	Richards	do	7	do	do	do	do	do	Do.

Directory of anthracite coal mines in Pennsylvania—Continued.

WESTERN MIDDLE COAL FIELD—Continued.

Map No.	Name of mine.	Local district.	Inspectors district.	Township, etc.	County.	Railroad.	Nearest shipping station.	Operator. Name.	Operator. Post-office address.
287	Enterprise	Shamokin	7	Coal Twp	Northumb'l'd	P. and R. R. R.	Excelsior	Enterprise Coal Co	Scranton.
288	Excelsior	do	7	do	do	do	do	Excelsior Coal Co	Excelsior.
289	Corbin	do	7	do	do	do	do	do	Do.
292	Colbert	do	7	do	do	N. C. Rwy	Lancaster Switch	Shipman-Deg Coal Co	Shamokin.
302	Neilson	do	7	do	do	P.&R.R.R.and P.R.R	Shamokin	J. Langdon & Co	Elmira, N. Y.
	Natalie	do	7	do	do	do	do	Natalie Anthracite Coal Co	Mount Carmel.
275	Midvalley	do	7	Mount Carmel Twp	do	L. V. R. R.	Mount Carmel	Midvalley Coal Co	Wilburton.

SOUTHERN COAL FIELD.

Map No.	Name of mine.	Local district.	Inspectors district.	Township, etc.	County.	Railroad.	Nearest shipping station.	Operator. Name.	Operator. Post-office address.
307	Colliery No. 1	Panther Creek	5	Packer Twp	Carbon	C. R. R. of New Jersey	Nesquehoning	Lehigh C. and N. Co	Lansford.
308	Colliery No. 4	do	5	do	do	do	Lansford	do	Do.
309	Colliery No. 5	do	5	do	do	do	do	do	Do.
	Colliery No. 6	do	5	do	do	do	do	do	Do.
311	Colliery No. 8	do	8	Rahn Twp	Schuylkill	do	Coaldale	do	Do.
310	Colliery No. 9	do	5	Packer Twp	Carbon	do	do	do	Do.
313	Colliery No. 10	do	8	Rahn Twp	Schuylkill	do	Tamaqua	do	Do.
314	Colliery No. 11	do	8	do	do	do	do	do	Do.
312	Colliery No. 12	do	8	do	do	do	Coaldale	do	Do.
315	Colliery No. 13	do	8	do	do	do	Tanaqua	do	Do.
337	Beechwood	E. Schuylkill	8	Newcastle Twp	do	P. and R. R. R.	Pottsville	P. and R. Coal and Iron Co	sville.
327	Eagle	do	8	East Norwegian Twp	do	do	St. Clair	do	Do.

Directory of anthracite coal mines in Pennsylvania—Continued.

SOUTHERN COAL FIELD—Continued.

Map No.	Name of mine	Location						Operator	
		Local district.	Inspectors district.	Township, etc.	County.	Railroad.	Nearest shipping station.	Name.	Post-office address.
321	Eagle Hill	E. Schuylkill	8	Blythe Twp	Schuylkill	P. and R. R. R.	Cumbola	P. and R. Coal and Iron Co.	Pottsville.
316	East Lehigh	do	8	Tamaqua	do	do	Tamaqua	Mitchell & Shepp	Tamaqua.
356	Flowery Field	do	8	Newcastle Twp	do	do	St. Clair	Geo. U. Sturdevant	St. Clair.
321	Kaska William	do	8	Blythe Twp	do	do	Middleport	T. M. Dodson Coal Co.	S. Bethlehem.
	Palmer Vein	do	8	do	do	do	do	P. F. Kelly	Lansford.
325	Pine Forest	do	8	East Norwegian Twp	do	do	Mill Creek	P. and R. Coal and Iron Co	Pottsville.
322	Silver Creek	do	8	Blythe Twp	do	do	Patterson	do	Do.
326	Mount Hope	do	8	East Norwegian Twp	do	do	St. Clair	G. B. Linderman & Co.	S. Bethlehem.
318	York Farm	do	8	do	do	do	do	Lehigh Valley Coal Co	Wilkesbarre.
344	Glendower	W. Schuylkill	8	Foster Twp	do	do	Glen Carbon	P. and R. Coal and Iron Co	Pottsville.
350	Otto	do	8	Reilly Twp	do	do	Branch Dale	do	Do.
342	Thomaston	do	8	Cass Twp	do	do	Heckscherville	do	Do.
349	Phenix Park	do	8	do	do	do	Llewellyn	do	Do.
313	Richardson	do	9	Foster Twp	do	do	Glen Carbon	do	Do.
339	Ellsworth	do	8	Newcastle Twp	do	do	Broad Mountain	do	Broad Mountain.
	Albright	do	8	Cass Twp	do	do	Llewellyn	Albright Coal Co	Pottsville.
	Stoddart	do	8	do	do	do	Gilberton	Stoddart Coal Co	Gilberton.
345	Oak Hill	do	8	do	do	do	Minersville	Leisuring & Co.	Minersville.
352	Blackwood	do	8	do	do	L. V. R. R.	Blackwood	Lehigh Valley Coal Co.	Wilkesbarre.
354	East Franklin	do	8	Tremont Twp	do	P. and R. R. R.	Tremont	P. and R. Coal and Iron Co.	Pottsville.
353	Middle Creek	Lykens Valley	8	Frailey Twp	do	do	Swatara Switch	do	Do.
359	West Brookside	do	8	Porter Twp	do	do	Brookside	do	Do.

Directory of anthracite coal mines in Pennsylvania—Continued.

SOUTHERN COAL FIELD—Continued.

Map No.	Name of mine.	Local district.	Inspectors district.	Location. Township, etc.	County.	Railroad.	Nearest shipping station.	Operator. Name.	Post-office address.
355	Lincoln	Lykens Valley	8	Tremont Twp	Schuylkill	P. and R. R.	Lorberry Junc.	P. and R. Coal and Iron Co.	Pottsville.
356	North Brookside	do	8	Porter Twp	do	do	Good Spring	do	Do.
360	Good Spring	do	7	do	do	do	do	do	Do.
	Williamstown	do	7	Wiconisco Twp	Dauphin	N. C. Rwy	Williamstown	Summit Branch Railroad Co	Wilkesbarre.
361	Short Mountain	do	7	do	do	do	Lykens	Lykens Valley Coal Co	Do.

General offices of corporations named in foregoing directory.

Pennsylvania Coal Company, No. 1 Broadway, New York.

Lehigh and Wilkesbarre Coal Company, No. 143 Liberty street, New York.

Delaware, Lackawanna and Western Railroad Company, No. 26 Exchange place, New York.

Delaware and Hudson Canal Company, No. 21 Cortlandt street, New York.

Coxe Bros. & Co., No. 143 Liberty street, New York.

Philadelphia and Reading Coal and Iron Company, Reading Terminal, Philadelphia.

Lehigh Valley Coal Company, No. 228 South Third street, Philadelphia.

Lehigh Coal and Navigation Company, No. 226 South Third street, Philadelphia.

Hillside Coal and Iron Company, No. 21 Cortlandt street, New York.

New York, Susquehanna and Western Railroad Company, No. 26 Cortlandt street, New York.

Susquehanna Coal Company, Broad Street Station, Philadelphia.

Lykens Valley Coal Company, Broad Street Station, Philadelphia.

Mineral Railroad and Mining Company, Broad Street Station, Philadelphia.

Summit Branch Railroad Company, Broad Street Station, Philadelphia.

Union Coal Company, Erie, Pa.

New York, Ontario and Western Railroad Company, 56 Beaver street, New York.

Delaware, Susquehanna and Schuylkill Railroad Company, 143 Liberty street, New York.

In closing our report for the year 1894 reference was made to the efforts of prominent representatives of the trade looking toward a betterment of the conditions then prevailing, and which were growing so serious as to cause the gravest apprehensions, and it was then confidently expected that some satisfactory adjustment would be reached early in the year 1895. These efforts were, however, continued at intervals during the entire year of 1895 without definite results, the production meantime going forward at a rate not warranted by the demand, until the end of the year found the market overstocked to such an extent that the effects must be felt for several months to come, and will necessarily materially retard the good results which are so earnestly hoped to follow the contemplated improvement of the trade conditions in the near future. It is not thought necessary to rehearse in this report the accounts given in the public prints of "conferences," "propositions," etc., bearing upon this subject which were alleged to have taken place during the year further than to say that these accounts being entirely unofficial, and unfortunately so colored by prejudice either for or against the respective parties in interest, as to be useless in arriving at any fair comprehension of the situation.

Looked at from any standpoint, however, it is to be hoped that this great industry can be so conducted in the future as to prevent a recurrence of the conditions which have caused such enormous losses in the past both to the labor and the capital engaged in it, for assuredly no permanent good can come to the general community when such an important part of its industry is in an unhealthy and weakened state.

During the year under consideration no special events of a disturbing character, such as strikes, storms, or other interruptions, have taken place. It must be stated, however, that the general depression in business, and particularly in the iron trade in all its branches, contributed materially to the discouraging conditions surrounding the anthracite coal trade.

Mention was made in our previous report of the death, on May 13, 1895, of Hon. Eckley B. Coxe. It is also our duty to record the death of Mr. Edwin H. Mead, president and treasurer of the Pennsylvania Coal Company, which occurred February 3, 1895, at his home in South Orange, N. J. Mr. Mead was 73 years of age at the time of his death, and had been connected with the coal trade since 1840. He became identified with the Pennsylvania Coal Company in 1852 and was elected its president in 1888, succeeding Mr. George A. Hoyt.

PENNSYLVANIA BITUMINOUS COAL.

Total product in 1895, 50,217,228 short tons; spot value, $35,980,357.

The records of bituminous production in Pennsylvania for the earlier years of the industry are very incomplete. In fact, from 1840 to 1872 the only record extant is that of the shipments over some of the railroads, from a few of the districts, and these bear very little relation to the total product (see Mineral Resources, 1883–84, p. 84). For instance, the statement for 1873 shows the total shipments to have been about 4,600,000 long tons, whereas the total production for that year, the first for which any statistics were obtained, was 11,695,383 long tons. From 1873 to 1882 the product has been estimated in round numbers, the output in the latter year being about double that of 1873, approximately 22,000,000 long tons or 24,640,000 short tons. During the next decade the output increased each year, nearly doubling in 1892 the yield in 1882. In 1893 the output fell off 2,623,852 short tons, or between 5 and 6 per cent as compared with 1892. The first half of 1893 was favorable in the bituminous regions of Pennsylvania and operations were active; but later, when the unfavorable conditions of trade manifested themselves, production fell off and prices declined so severely that all of the benefits of the earlier months were overcome and the average price for the year was 4 cents lower than in 1892. The unfavorable conditions were still more pronounced in 1894, and this, added to the disastrous effects of the long strike in the spring and summer of the year, caused a diminution of over 4,000,000 tons, or about 10 per cent in the tonnage, while the value declined about 16 per cent. The average price per ton fell off from 80 cents in 1893 to 74 cents in 1894. Stimulated by the reaction in the iron industry during 1895, the production of bituminous coal in Pennsylvania received a remarkable impetus and the largest output in the history of the State was obtained. The activity in the iron business, however, was due principally to the exceedingly low prices at which it was being offered and not to any healthy recovery from the depressed condition of the previous two or three years. During the temporary improvement, or boom, in the iron industry of 1895 the prices of that commodity advanced somewhat, but this improvement in prices was not long lived, nor did its influence extend materially to its sister industry—coal mining—for, while the product increased something more than 25 per cent over the product in 1895, the value increased but 21 per cent and the average price declined from 74 cents in 1894 to 72 cents in 1895.

Outside of the phenomenally large increase in the production of bituminous coal in Pennsylvania during 1895, the principal feature of the year's business was the purchase by the H. C. Frick Coke Company of large interests which were formerly competitive. Principal among these were the mines and coking ovens of the McClure Coke Company; also those of the Fairchance Furnace Company and the Youngstown Coal and Coke Company. The purchase of these interests gives to the Frick Company practical control of the Connellsville region, so far as the fixing of the price and regulating the product are concerned. The production of the Connellsville region in 1895 was largely responsible for the greatly increased output in the State. The total increase in 1895 over 1894 was 10,304,765 short tons, of which Fayette and Westmoreland counties, comprising the Connellsville district, contributed 5,062,570 short tons, or nearly one-half. The combined product of these two counties in 1894 was 14,208,953 short tons, and in 1895, 19,271,523 short tons.

Notwithstanding the fact that the capacity of the already developed mines of the United States far exceeds the demand of a profitable market, and in spite of the fact that few of the mines are run to within 80 per cent of their capacity, no opportunity is lost to open any new territory that seems promising. The construction of the Pittsburg, Monongahela and Wheeling Railroad is a case in point. This road, when completed, will, it is said, open up new coal-mining territory in the vicinity of Pittsburg, and it is estimated that a million tons will be mined and shipped the first year after it is opened. This means the bringing in of that much or more mineral fuel to a market already crowded and from which it is difficult to obtain remunerative prices.

PRODUCTION BY COUNTIES.

There are four counties in Pennsylvania whose product in 1895 exceeded 5,000,000 tons. They were, in order of precedence, Fayette, Westmoreland, Allegheny, and Clearfield, and the first two came within less than 5 per cent of reaching a total of 10,000,000 each. The total product of the four counties was 31,103,024 short tons, more than 60 per cent of the total output of the State. Two other counties, Cambria and Jefferson, produce more than 4,000,000 tons each, and one, Washington, produced more than 3,500,000 tons. The total product from these seven counties amounted to 43,217,870 short tons, more than 86 per cent of the total output of the State, leaving but 14 per cent to be divided among the 18 other coal-producing counties, none of which produced more than 1,000,000 tons during the year.

The same anomalous position is presented by the labor statistics of coal production in Pennsylvania as have been observed in Ohio; that is, with a largely decreased production in 1894, the number of employees was increased from 71,931 in 1893 to 75,010 in 1894. With an increased production of more than 25 per cent in 1895, the number of employees decreased to 71,130. This was offset by a decrease in the average number of days worked in 1894 and increased working time for 1895. The average tonnage per man per day was about the same in 1893 and 1894 (3.22½) which was increased in 1895 to 3.42.

The following tables exhibit the statistics of bituminous coal production in Pennsylvania during 1894 and 1895 by counties:

Bituminous coal product of Pennsylvania in 1894, by counties.

County.	Number of mines.	Loaded at mines for shipment.	Sold to local trade and used by employees.	Used at mines for steam and heat.	Made into coke.	Total product.	Total value.	Average price per ton.	Average number of days active.	Average number of employees.
		Short tons.	*Short tons.*	*Short tons.*	*Short tons.*	*Short tons.*				
Allegheny ...	88	6,039,958	230,956	40,645	43,000	6,354,559	$4,684,407	$0.74	154	14,107
Armstrong ..	13	576,918	987	2,125	....	580,030	416,339	.72	168	1,153
Beaver	7	98,879	4,272	454	160	103,765	94,197	.91	146	312
Bedford	16	251,622	4,631	3,632	53,210	313,095	216,932	.69	144	855
Blair	7	238,482	3,195	5,080	9,400	256,157	191,567	.75	142	730
Butler	10	134,367	1,450	300	1,476	137,593	105,211	.76	111	457
Cambria	70	2,449,703	433,466	24,002	71,756	2,978,927	2,160,735	.73	165	6,220
Center.......	17	271,110	15,283	501	20,912	307,806	208,220	.68	111	855
Clarion	20	392,586	6,627	1,791	....	401,004	279,675	.70	201	926
Clearfield....	95	4,033,749	33,347	13,154	68,214	4,148,464	2,983,214	.72	134	9,654
Elk	5	307,518	4,290	2,165	85,050	399,023	341,873	.86	147	1,107
Fayette......	58	1,568,452	97,002	84,624	4,690,911	6,440,989	4,472,578	.69	198	8,847
Huntingdon	7	184,422	10,390	5,220	....	200,032	147,909	.74	133	478
Indiana......	11	392,053	980	265	5,250	398,548	291,885	.70	164	724
Jefferson	23	2,896,204	17,929	16,000	318,021	3,248,154	2,299,565	.71	164	5,184
Lawrence....	5	131,249	1,033	140	....	132,422	122,475	.92	165	490
Mercer	11	309,499	11,435	10,660	....	331,594	271,104	.82	121	1,014
Somerset	22	397,834	11,084	2,624	6,653	418,195	264,430	.63	150	731
Tioga........	6	481,333	12,997	9,560	670	704,560	956,483	1.36	149	2,213
Washington .	48	3,655,187	26,487	26,913	42,841	3,461,428	2,146,532	.62	159	6,880
Westmoreland	69	4,775,416	60,272	92,029	2,840,247	7,767,964	5,982,484	.77	202	11,517
Bradford										
Clinton										
Forest....... }	5	226,262	1,482	410	....	228,154	242,005	1.06	180	497
Lycoming ...										
McKean										
Small mines	....	....	600,000	....		600,000	600,000	....	....	....
Total ..	613	29,722,803	1,589,595	342,294	8,257,771	39,912,463	29,479,820	.74	165	75,010

Bituminous coal product of Pennsylvania in 1895, by counties.

County.	Number of mines.	Loaded at mines for shipment.	Sold to local trade and used by employees.	Used at mines for steam and heat.	Made into coke.	Total product.	Total value.	Average price per ton.	Average number of days active.	Average number of employees.
		Short tons.	*Short tons.*	*Short tons.*	*Short tons.*	*Short tons.*				
Allegheny ..	83	6,436,646	133,878	45,450	....	6,615,974	$4,885,184	$0.74	176	13,094
Armstrong .	13	630,709	5,148	6,952	....	642,809	450,669	.70	233	1,128
Beaver	7	175,523	8,061	512	....	184,096	142,494	.77	227	325
Bedford	10	296,346	69,305	2,337	50,000	417,988	264,417	.63	200	653
Blair	5	317,002	8,050	5,505	43,600	374,157	264,147	.71	248	650
Butler	12	217,720	13,484	1,900	....	233,104	160,696	.69	166	511
Cambria	70	3,510,150	538,564	26,832	213,711	4,289,257	2,854,352	.67	222	6,270
Center......	14	256,522	16,901	224	....	273,647	173,625	.63	101	579
Clarion	13	379,434	9,527	889	....	389,850	254,014	.65	230	665
Clearfield...	95	5,001,788	25,488	33,212	155,039	5,215,527	3,474,065	.67	190	8,604
Elk.........	4	635,841	3,201	3,101	....	642,143	733,473	1.14	247	1,024
Fayette.....	50	1,580,644	91,275	158,343	7,827,107	9,665,369	6,439,717	.67	256	7,745
Huntingdon	10	309,609	11,634	6,527	....	327,770	249,528	.76	230	606
Indiana.....	12	495,704	6,345	346	10,680	513,075	329,336	.64	181	672
Jefferson ...	22	3,753,076	14,802	22,279	458,172	4,248,329	2,770,568	.65	201	5,637
Lawrence...	7	267,748	1,518	513	....	269,779	211,241	.78	233	568
Lycoming ..	2	81,000	2,200	650	....	84,050	100,900	1.20	277	165
Mercer	12	513,280	9,382	12,380	....	535,042	396,027	.74	190	1,173
Somerset ...	24	504,611	10,105	2,145	7,894	524,755	310,542	.59	248	682
Tioga.......	9	776,601	16,843	6,671	976	801,091	927,479	1.16	173	2,128
Washington	44	3,537,496	14,798	20,877	4,089	3,577,260	2,373,490	.66	175	6,432
Westmoreland	67	5,293,154	122,441	110,236	4,080,323	9,606,154	7,440,685	.77	203	11,455
Bradford....										
Clinton ..... }	3	184,849	853	300	....	186,002	173,708	.77	206	359
McKean										
Small mines.	....	....	600,000	....	....	600,000	600,000	....	....	....
Total .	588	35,164,453	1,732,803	468,381	12,851,591	50,217,228	35,980,357	.72	206	71,130

The following table shows the total product since 1873:

Product of bituminous coal in Pennsylvania since 1873.

Year.	Short tons.	Year.	Short tons.
1873...................	13,098,829	1885...................	26,000,000
1874...................	12,320,000	1886...................	27,094,504
1875...................	11,760,000	1887...................	31,516,856
1876...................	12,880,000	1888...................	33,796,727
1877...................	14,000,000	1889...................	36,174,089
1878...................	15,120,000	1890...................	42,302,173
1879...................	16,240,000	1891...................	42,788,490
1880...................	21,280,000	1892...................	46,694,576
1881...................	22,400,000	1893...................	44,070,724
1882...................	24,610,000	1894...................	39,912,463
1883...................	26,880,000	1895...................	50,217,228
1884...................	28,000,000		

The production by counties was not reliably ascertained prior to 1886. The results obtained by the bureau of industrial statistics of the State for 1882, 1884, and 1885 were published in the earlier volumes of Mineral Resources, but owing to the failure of a number of mines to report their production, the statistics were very incomplete, the total for 1885, for instance, being more than 5,000,000 tons short of the actual product. Since 1886 the product by counties has been as follows:

Bituminous coal product of Pennsylvania since 1886, by counties.

[Short tons.]

County.	1886.	1887.	1888.	1889.
Allegheny	4, 202, 086	4, 680, 924	5, 575, 505	4, 717, 431
Armstrong	210, 856	235, 221	226, 093	289, 218
Beaver	208, 820	197, 863	63, 900	93, 461
Bedford	173, 372	311, 452	248, 159	257, 455
Blair	305, 695	287, 367	314, 013	215, 410
Bradford	206, 998	167, 416	163, 851	129, 141
Butler	162, 306	161, 764	194, 715	288, 591
Cambria	1, 222, 028	1, 421, 980	1, 540, 460	1, 751, 664
Cameron	3, 200	3, 000	700	2, 300
Center	313, 383	508, 255	382, 770	395, 127
Clarion	429, 544	593, 758	535, 192	596, 589
Clearfield	3, 753, 986	5, 180, 311	5, 398, 981	5, 224, 506
Clinton			32, 000	106, 000
Elk	526, 036	609, 757	555, 960	614, 113
Fayette	4, 494, 613	4, 540, 322	5, 208, 993	5, 897, 254
Greene	5, 600	3, 002	5, 323	53, 714
Huntingdon	313, 581	265, 479	281, 823	280, 133
Indiana	103, 615	207, 597	157, 285	153, 698
Jefferson	1, 023, 186	1, 693, 492	2, 275, 349	2, 896, 487
Lawrence	101, 154	125, 361	106, 921	143, 410
McKean	617	9, 214	10, 443	11, 500
Mercer	537, 712	539, 721	487, 122	575, 751
Somerset	349, 926	416, 240	370, 228	442, 027
Tioga	1, 384, 800	1, 328, 963	1, 106, 146	1, 036, 175
Venango	2, 500	2, 296	2, 000	6, 911
Washington	1, 612, 407	1, 751, 615	1, 793, 022	2, 364, 901
Westmoreland	5, 446, 480	6, 074, 486	6, 519, 773	7, 631, 124
Small mines		200, 000	240, 000	(a)
Total	27, 094, 501	31, 516, 856	33, 796, 727	36, 174, 089
Net increase		4, 422, 355	2, 279, 871	2, 377, 362

a Included in county distribution.

Bituminous coal product of Pennsylvania since 1886, by counties—Continued.

[Short tons.]

County.	1890.	1891.	1892.	1893.
Allegheny	4, 894, 372	5, 640, 669	6, 399, 199	6, 663, 095
Armstrong	380, 554	484, 000	583, 519	561, 039
Beaver	139, 117	129, 961	140, 835	150, 095
Bedford	445, 192	389, 257	552, 461	501, 507
Blair	298, 196	237, 626	259, 224	177, 902
Bradford	126, 687	68, 697	57, 708	42, 739
Butler	167, 578	211, 647	145, 729	156, 016
Cambria	2, 790, 954	2, 932, 973	3, 086, 554	3, 282, 467
Center	452, 114	526, 753	496, 521	458, 056
Clarion	512, 387	479, 887	569, 333	551, 158
Clearfield	6, 651, 587	7, 143, 382	6, 876, 785	6, 148, 758
Clinton	159, 000	130, 802	98, 242	94, 582
Elk	1, 121, 534	973, 600	731, 575	634, 165
Fayette	6, 413, 081	5, 782, 573	7, 260, 044	6, 261, 146
Huntingdon	322, 630	269, 021	333, 855	303, 547
Indiana	357, 580	456, 077	514, 463	380, 666
Jefferson	2, 850, 799	3, 160, 614	3, 706, 329	3, 885, 196
Lawrence	140, 528	164, 669	216, 561	196, 736
Lycoming			20, 515	53, 192
McKean	(a)	15, 345	21, 282	19, 169
Mercer	524, 319	526, 220	420, 145	499, 651
Somerset	522, 796	480, 194	509, 610	532, 688
Tioga	903, 997	1, 010, 872	999, 784	962, 248
Washington	2, 836, 667	2, 606, 158	2, 903, 235	3, 315, 146
Westmoreland	8, 290, 504	7, 967, 493	8, 791, 068	7, 439, 760
Small mines	1, 000, 000	1, 000, 000	1, 000, 000	800, 000
Total	42, 302, 173	42, 788, 490	46, 694, 576	44, 070, 724
Net increase	6, 128, 084	486, 317	3, 906, 086	b 2, 623, 852

a Included in product of small mines.
b Net decrease.

Bituminous coal product of Pennsylvania since 1886, by counties—Continued.

[Short tons.]

County.	1894.	1895.	Increase in 1895.	Decrease in 1895.
Allegheny	6, 354, 559	6, 615, 974	261, 415	....
Armstrong	580, 030	642, 809	62, 779	....
Beaver	103, 765	184, 096	80, 331	....
Bedford	313, 095	417, 988	104, 893	....
Blair	256, 157	374, 157	118, 000	....
Bradford	28, 027	52, 711	24, 684	....
Butler	137, 593	233, 104	95, 511	....
Cambria	2, 978, 927	4, 289, 257	1, 310, 330	....
Center	307, 806	273, 647	....	34, 159
Clarion	401, 004	389, 850	....	11, 154
Clearfield	4, 148, 464	5, 215, 527	1, 067, 063	....
Clinton	100, 000	95, 291	....	4, 709
Elk	399, 023	642, 143	243, 120	....
Fayette	6, 440, 989	9, 665, 369	3, 224, 380	....
Forest	123	....	....	123
Huntingdon	200, 032	327, 770	127, 738	....
Indiana	398, 548	513, 075	114, 527	....
Jefferson	3, 248, 154	4, 248, 329	1, 000, 175	....
Lawrence	132, 422	269, 779	137, 357	....
Lycoming	80, 160	84, 050	3, 890	....
McKean	19, 844	38, 000	18, 156	....
Mercer	331, 594	535, 042	203, 448	....
Somerset	418, 195	524, 755	106, 560	....
Tioga	704, 560	801, 091	96, 531	....
Washington	3, 461, 428	3, 577, 260	115, 832	....
Westmoreland	7, 767, 964	9, 606, 154	1, 838, 190	....
Small mines	600, 000	600, 000	....	....
Total	39, 912, 463	50, 217, 228	10, 350, 910	50, 145
Net increase	a4, 158, 261	10, 304, 765	10, 304, 765	....

a Net decrease.

In the following tables will be found a statement of the average prices which obtained in the different counties since 1889, and the statistics of labor and working time since 1890:

Average prices for Pennsylvania coal since 1889 in counties producing 10,000 tons or over.

County.	1889.	1890.	1891.	1892.	1893.	1894.	1895.
Allegheny	$0.85	$0.93	$1.03	$0.91	$0.82	$0.88	$0.74
Armstrong	.73	.72	.76	.76	.76	.72	.70
Beaver	1.18	1.05	1.00	1.01	.98	.91	.77
Bedford	.80	.80	.86	.82	.74	.69	.63
Blair	.98	.81	.87	.85	.77	.75	.71
Bradford	1.33	1.28	1.34	1.42	1.30	1.53	1.25
Butler	.97	.87	.89	.93	.81	.76	.69
Cambria	.77	.83	.80	.82	.79	.73	.67
Center	.79	.79	.75	.79	.75	.68	.63
Clarion	.72	.75	.75	.75	.72	.70	.65
Clearfield	.84	.85	.84	.81	.80	.72	.67
Clinton	....	.78	1.15	1.01	.76	.81½	.75
Elk	.81	.84	.83	.83	.79	.86	1.14
Fayette	.63	.77	.82	.77	.73	.69	.67
Huntingdon	.75	.77	.78	.75	.75	.74	.76
Indiana	.71	.82	.76	.77	.77	.70	.64
Jefferson	.73	.85	.88	.81	.74	.71	.65
Lawrence	1.05	1.02	1.02	1.02	1.03	.92	.78
Lycoming	....	....	....	1.12	1.22	1.23	1.20
McKean	....	....	1.05	1.10	1.10	.95	.95
Mercer	.89	.85	.90	.88	.89	.82	.74
Somerset	.70	.65	.71	.66	.63	.63	.59
Tioga	1.22	1.10	1.14	1.44	1.21	1.36	1.16
Washington	.66	.93	.87	.87	.78	.62	.66
Westmoreland	.74	.80	.87	.81	.82	.77	.77
The State	.77	.84	.87	.81	.80	.74	.72

17 GEOL, PT 3——33

Statistics of labor employed and working time at Pennsylvania coal mines.

County.	1890.		1891.		1892.	
	Average number employed.	Average working days.	Average number employed.	Average working days.	Average number employed.	Average working days.
Allegheny	9,036	198	11,194	199	11,223	225
Armstrong	661	251	805	230	964	246
Beaver	205	251	228	201½	323	210
Bedford	662	288	605	230	975	265
Blair	595	284	503	249	848	203
Bradford	292	196	169	228	122	206
Butler	314	237	342	240	358	169
Cambria	4,140	361	4,284	258	4,913	228
Center	623	230	823	200	767	181
Clarion	938	237	895	221	985	235
Clearfield	9,324	336	10,067	227	10,225	212
Clinton	200	265	181	291	175	175
Elk	1,181	255	1,622	229	1,265	230
Fayette	6,503	247	7,545	216½	7,952	239
Huntingdon	611	237	595	246	560	244
Indiana	668	245	561	227	656	191
Jefferson	3,971	245	4,172	237	4,567	232
Lawrence	307	232	327	236	368	250
Lycoming					60	252
McKean			42	230	28	304
Mercer	1,023	231	972	241	876	181
Somerset	646	225	531	266	577	238
Tioga	2,019	192	1,980	241	2,249	223
Washington	4,644	227	4,135	222	4,895	202
Westmoreland	12,080	228	11,083	221	10,724	234
The State	61,333	232	63,661	223	66,655	223

Statistics of labor employed and working time at Pennsylvania coal mines—Continued.

County.	1893.		1894.		1895.	
	Average number employed.	Average working days.	Average number employed.	Average working days.	Average number employed.	Average working days.
Allegheny	14,328	161	14,107	154	13,094	176
Armstrong	1,080	214	1,153	168	1,128	233
Beaver	318	215	312	148	325	227
Bedford	806	185	855	144	658	200
Blair	632	166	730	142	650	248
Bradford	83	167	90	134	109	299
Butler	276	208	497	111	511	166
Cambria	6,073	199	6,230	165	6,270	222
Center	743	193	855	111	579	161
Clarion	1,224	231	926	201	665	230
Clearfield	10,455	186	9,654	134	8,604	190
Clinton	175	163	190	153	175	140
Elk	1,244	195	1,107	147	1,024	247
Fayette	6,780	195	8,847	198	7,745	256
Huntingdon	487	182	478	133	606	230
Indiana	605	186	724	164	672	181
Jefferson	5,537	210	5,184	164	5,637	201
Lawrence	430	218	490	165	568	233
Lycoming	117	279	166	231	165	277
McKean	19	285	50	200	75	225
Mercer	981	187	1,014	121	1,173	190
Somerset	695	214	731	150	682	248
Tioga	2,425	214	2,213	149	2,128	173
Washington	6,058	184	6,889	159	6,432	175
Westmoreland	10,270	205	11,517	202	11,455	203
The State	71,931	190	75,010	165	71,130	206

SOUTH DAKOTA.

South Dakota appears for the first time in 1895 as a coal producer. The output was small, amounting to only 200 short tons. The coal is lignite and was mined in Fall River County, near the town of Edgemont. It was sold for $2 per ton for the local trade in the vicinity.

TENNESSEE.

Total product in 1895, 2,535,644 short tons; spot value, $2,349,032.

The conditions which prevailed in most of the other coal-producing States obtained also in Tennessee. These were an increased output in the face of a declining market and a consequent comparative loss in the value. The product was the largest in the history of the State, being 354,765 short tons in excess of that of 1894 and 121,966 short tons more than that of 1891, when the largest previous tonnage was obtained. The increase in value over 1894 was $229,551, considerably less in proportion than the increase in the product, the average price showing a decline of 4 cents per ton—from 97 cents in 1894 to 93 cents in 1895. There has been a steady decline in the value per ton since 1892, the total decrease amounting to 20 cents per ton. Since 1889 there has been a decline of 23 per cent in the average price. Such a condition would not seem to encourage increased production, but operators, to all appearance, have been inspired by an ambition to secure a large tonnage rather than, and at the expense of, remunerative prices.

The question of convict labor in the coal mines of Tennessee continues to be a disturbing element. There can be no doubt that the present arrangements, which provide for the employment of the convicts in mines owned by the State and under control of State officials, have more advantages and less disadvantages than the old convict lease system. The convicts themselves are better cared for, particularly from a sanitary standpoint, and the free miners are not brought into direct competition with their labor, nor into what they consider a degrading contact. This was one of the principal causes of labor disputes in the State, and led directly to the disastrous riots which took place at Briceville and Coal Creek in 1892 and 1893. On the other hand, while the trouble has been removed from the labor side, it has been taken up by the capital side, for operators claim that the product from the convict mines is put upon the market at prices with which they are unable to profitably compete. The operators, on the whole, claim not to be opposed to the State employing its convicts in its own mines, but insist upon an adherence to prices which it is necessary to obtain when hired labor is employed. It would seem that this is factious criticism. The output from the State mines in 1895 was less than 1 per cent of the State's total, and while this may have been offered on the market at less than what might be considered fair prices, the percentage of the total was so small that no cause for uneasiness should have been given.

During 1895 experiments with Anderson County (Coal Creek) coal for coke making were made at the ovens of the St. Bernard Coal and Coke Company, Earlington, Ky., with satisfactory results. The coal was ground and washed before coking, yielding a close, compact, silvery coke which showed upon analysis 85.97 per cent fixed carbon, 11.38 per cent ash, and 0.78 per cent sulphur. The operators in the Coal Creek region will build a battery of twenty-five beehive ovens, to be followed by a plant of by-product ovens. At present the product of coke in Anderson County is small, there being but 1,600 tons of coal made into coke in that county in 1895, and but 1,500 tons in 1894.

The following tables exhibit the details of production in Tennessee during 1894 and 1895 by counties:

Coal product of Tennessee in 1894, by counties.

County.	Number of mines.	Loaded at mines for shipment.	Sold to local trade and used by employees.	Used at mines for steam and heat.	Made into coke.	Total product.	Total value.	Average price per ton.	Average number of days active.	Average number of employees.
		Short tons.	Short tons.	Short tons.	Short tons.	Short tons.				
Anderson....	7	535,108	3,014	4,600	1,500	544,222	$527,671	$0.97	256	1,217
Campbell....	8	169,448	4,105	1,340	8,395	183,288	192,757	1.05	140	698
Claiborne....	4	142,145	550	....	24,458	167,153	157,377	.94	169	277
Grundy, Putnam, Franklin, White...	4	327,716	2,931	8,800	144,355	483,802	415,629	.86	224	1,229
Hamilton....	3	100,398	1,193	1,009	53,701	156,301	141,008	.90	218	441
Marion......	3	110,945	11,143	434	62,075	184,597	209,627	1.14	183	522
Morgan......	6	63,451	800	350	....	64,601	63,233	.98	145	373
Rhea........	3	4,386	7,751	3,360	108,618	124,115	125,823	1.01	253	209
Roane.......	2	3,456	11,238	2,800	101,393	118,887	118,887	1.00	307	210
Scott........	3	114,353	12,760	6,300	16,000	149,413	162,969	1.09	194	366
Small mines..	......	....	4,500			4,500	4,500			
Total..	43	1,571,406	59,985	28,993	520,495	2,180,879	2,119,481	.97	210	5,542

Coal product of Tennessee in 1895, by counties.

County.	Number of mines.	Loaded at mines for shipment.	Sold to local trade and used by employees.	Used at mines for steam and heat.	Made into coke.	Total product.	Total value.	Average price per ton.	Average number of days active.	Average number of employees.
		Short tons.	Short tons.	Short tons.	Short tons.	Short tons.				
Anderson....	9	422,551	4,508	2,709	1,600	431,368	$391,674	$0.91	248	1,118
Campbell....	9	309,168	12,129	1,518	17,580	340,395	350,907	1.03	174	1,128
Claiborne....	4	140,952	50	1,200	37,461	179,663	147,871	.82	179	284
Hamilton....	3	115,856	1,824	1,704	54,922	174,306	146,055	.84	220	335
Marion......	4	253,635	1,691	1,224	112,413	368,963	376,837	1.02	249	581
Morgan......	6	60,842	673	....	....	61,515	52,869	.86	134	209
Rhea........	2	3,936	9,405	3,360	93,116	109,817	76,838	.70	240	165
Scott........	3	114,817	7,287	3,155	15,597	140,856	153,967	1.09	193	331
Grundy, Putnam, Roane, and White..	4	386,299	9,856	10,607	317,499	724,261	647,514	.89	283	969
Small mines..	......	....	4,500	....	....	4,500	4,500			
Total..	44	1,808,056	51,923	25,477	650,188	2,535,644	2,349,032	.93	224	5,120

A glance at the foregoing tables will show that the decline in price was general throughout the State. Scott County was the only one in which no loss was shown.

Considering the increases and decreases in the product by counties it will be seen that Campbell and Marion counties are chiefly responsible for the increased product of the State. Their aggregate increase was over 340,000 short tons, which was, however, partly offset by a decrease of 112,854 tons in Anderson County. Grundy County increased its output by over 80,000 tons, and White County by about 26,000 tons. The changes in the other counties were immaterial.

In the following table is shown the total production, by counties, since 1889, with the increase and decrease in each county during 1895, as compared with the preceding year:

Coal product of Tennessee since 1889, by counties.

[Short tons.]

County.	1889.	1890.	1891.	1892.	1893.
Anderson...........	457,069	582,403	587,558	409,970	311,777
Campbell	123,103	126,367	159,937	289,605	262,503
Claiborne	(a)	(a)	73,738	137,219	181,530
Franklin...........	(b)	1,500	1,400	1,400	1,200
Grundy	400,107	349,467	398,936	358,023	294,013
Hamilton	241,067	277,896	243,298	105,283	155,523
Marion.............	203,923	213,202	271,809	241,974	211,594
Morgan	68,229	143,518	125,287	34,970	78,190
Putnam.............					
Rhea...............	149,194	211,465	213,649	133,424	96,531
Roane..............	c174,551	70,452	112,308	102,588	39,554
Scott..............	108,027	136,365	142,943	183,230	157,980
White..............	(b)	52,650	78,315	90,378	107,863
Other counties and small mines	419	4,300	4,500	4,000	4,000
Total	1,925,689	2,169,585	2,413,678	2,092,064	1,902,258
Net increase.......	....	243,896	244,093	d321,614	d189,806

a Developing.
b Included in Roane County.
c Includes Franklin and White counties.
d Net decrease.

Coal product of Tennessee since 1889, by counties—Continued.

[Short tons.]

County.	1894.	1895.	Increase in 1895.	Decrease in 1895.
Anderson............	544,222	431,368	....	112,854
Campbell	183,288	340,395	157,107	....
Claiborne	167,153	179,663	12,510	....
Franklin...........	3,000	....	....	3,000
Grundy	365,989	446,386	80,397	....
Hamilton	156,301	174,306	18,005	....
Marion.............	184,597	368,963	184,366	....
Morgan	64,601	61,515	....	3,086
Putnam	659	8,075	7,416	....
Rhea....	124,115	109,817	....	14,298
Roane..............	118,887	129,744	10,857	....
Scott..............	149,413	140,856	....	8,557
White.............	114,154	140,056	25,902	....
Other counties and small mines	4,500	4,500	....	....
Total	2,180,879	2,535,644	a 354,765	....
Net increase........	278,621	....	....	....

a Net increase.

In connection with the foregoing table the following statements of the average prices ruling in the important producing counties since 1889 and the statistics of labor and working time for the past six years should be considered:

Average prices for Tennessee coal since 1889 in counties producing 10,000 tons or over.

County.	1889.	1890.	1891.	1892.	1893.	1894.	1895.
Anderson........	$1.16	$1.17	$1.15	$1.11	$1.02	$0.97	$0.91
Campbell	1.15	1.22	1.27	1.19	1.25	1.05	1.03
Claiborne	....	....	1.19	1.04	.90	.94	.82
Grundy	.99	.94	.89	1.11	1.04	.90	.90
Hamilton	1.30	1.15	1.12	1.11	1.02	.90	.84
Marion..........	1.13	1.06	1.11	1.08	.98	1.14	1.02
Morgan	1.34	1.10	1.09	1.36	1.07	.98	.86
Rhea............	1.10	1.00	1.00	1.00	.89	1.01	.70
Roane...........	....	....	1.15	1.05	1.46	1.00	.80
Scott...........	1.34	1.29	1.25	1.24	1.40	1.09	1.09
White...........	....	....	1.31	1.25	1.03	1.03	.95
The State..	1.21	1.10	1.10½	1.13	1.08	.97	.93

Statistics of labor employed and working time at Tennessee coal mines.

County.	1890.		1891.		1892.	
	Average number employed.	Average working days.	Average number employed.	Average working days.	Average number employed.	Average working days.
Anderson	1,325	291	1,350	242	1,072	218
Campbell	251	212	451	145	732	213
Claiborne			165	172	276	207
Grundy	880	310	515	311	800	309
Hamilton	500	285	475	213	365	192
Marion	523	226	615	220	375	286
Morgan	363	258	363	250	156	148
Rhea	450	200	350	250	175	307
Roane			210	277	207	282
Scott	475	241	347	182	448	243
White			246	228	300	232
The State	5,082	263	5,097	230	4,926	240

County.	1893.		1894.		1895.	
	Average number employed.	Average working days.	Average number employed.	Average working days.	Average number employed.	Average working days.
Anderson	665	247	1,217	256	1,118	248
Campbell	936	175	698	140	1,128	174
Claiborne	280	142	277	169	284	179
Grundy	548	247	904	238	424	312
Hamilton	670	260	441	218	335	220
Marion	480	262	522	183	581	249
Morgan	272	224	373	145	209	134
Rhea	245	295	209	253	165	240
Roane	160	203	210	307	200	225
Scott	414	222	366	194	331	193
White	300	307	300	196	325	283
The State	4,976	232	5,542	210	5,120	224

The annual output of the State since 1873 has been as follows:

Coal product of Tennessee from 1873 to 1895.

Year.	Short tons.	Year.	Short tons.
1873	350,000	1885	1,440,957
1874	350,000	1886	1,714,290
1875	360,000	1887	1,900,000
1876	550,000	1888	1,967,297
1877	450,000	1889	1,925,689
1878	375,000	1890	2,169,585
1879	450,000	1891	2,413,678
1880	641,042	1892	2,092,061
1881	750,000	1893	1,902,258
1882	850,000	1894	2,180,879
1883	1,000,000	1895	2,535,644
1884	1,200,000		

TEXAS.

Total product in 1895, 484,959 short tons; total value, $913,138.

The principal features of the coal mining industry in Texas during 1895 were an increase in output of about 15 per cent over that of 1894, a decrease in value of 7 per cent compared with the previous year, and the marked developments of the lignite beds in the vicinity of Rockdale, Milam County. Milam County is credited with an output very little short of 100,000 tons, and this had much to do with the falling off in the total value. Competition among the lignite producers about Rockdale was very sharp during much of the year and prices were greatly demoralized, a regrettable state of affairs in a new mining community. The prices of bituminous coal mined in the State were fairly well maintained, though this product also felt, in some degree, the effects of the general depression.

Considerable attention was given in 1895 to the extensive lignite beds in the vicinity of Calvert, Robertson County, and work of a development nature was carried on by the Calvert Coal and Clay Company, with promises of this also becoming an important producing region. A market is found for the product among the cotton gins and other comparatively local industries using steam power, where lignite at low cost can be profitably used to the exclusion of bituminous coal. The physical properties of the lignites will not permit transportation to a great distance, nor will they stand much increased cost in the way of freight. Lignite coal is also mined in Medina County, the product from which added to that of Robertson and Milam counties made the total output of lignite in 1895 124,343 short tons.

The bituminous mines of Erath, Parker, Maverick, and Webb counties contributed their usual quota to the product of 1895. Mines have also been opened in Coleman, Montague, and Palo Pinto counties, and from the last mentioned an output of 12,500 tons was obtained in the four months the mines were operated.

The San Carlos mines in Presidio County did not get out any coal, commercially, before the close of the year, the first run over the tipple being made on January 3, 1896.

The following table shows the statistics of coal production in the State since 1889:

Coal product of Texas since 1889.

Distribution.	1889.	1890.	1891.	1892.
	Short tons.	Short tons.	Short tons.	Short tons.
Loaded at mines for shipment...	120,602	180,800	169,300	241,005
Sold to local trade and used by employees	6,552	1,840	900	4,460
Used at mines for steam and heat.	1,062	1,800	1,900	225
Total..................	128,216	184,440	172,100	245,690
Total value..................	$340,617	$465,900	$412,300	$569,333

Distribution.	1893.	1894.	1895.
	Short tons.	Short tons.	Short tons.
Loaded at mines for shipment......	300,064	417,281	475,157
Sold to local trade and used by employees	462	2,412	7,705
Used at mines for steam and heat....	1,680	1,155	2,097
Total..................	302,206	420,848	484,959
Total value	$688,407	$976,458	$913,138

The statistics of the production in 1895 in somewhat greater detail is shown in the following table:

Coal product of Texas in 1895, by counties.

County.	Number of mines.	Loaded at mines for shipment.	Sold to local trade and used by employees.	Used at mines for steam and heat.	Total product.	Total value.	Average price per ton.	Average number of days active.	Average number of employees.
		Short tons.	Short tons.	Short tons.	Short tons.				
Milam	6	97,492	2,185	....	99,677	$87,366	$0.88	213	146
Coleman, Earth, Medina, Montague, Parker, Palo Pinto, Robertson, and Webb........	8	377,665	5,520	2,097	385,282	825,772	2.14	167	1,496
Total	14	475,157	7,705	2,097	484,959	913,138	1.88	171	1,642

UTAH.

Total product in 1895, 471,836 short tons; spot value, $617,349.

The coal-mining industry of Utah is on the increase, notwithstanding the fact that the coal fields of Wyoming are about as near to the principal markets of Utah as the coal-producing districts of the Territory (now State) itself. In 1893, 1894, and 1895 the product was larger than in any previous year, that of 1894 being 4 per cent more than 1893, and 1895 exceeding that of 1894 by nearly 10 per cent. As in other States, values have declined. The average price for coal sold in 1893 was $1.48; in 1894, $1.40, and in 1895, $1.31. The details of production in 1894 and 1895 are shown in the following tables:

Coal product of Utah in 1894, by counties.

County.	Number of mines.	Loaded at mines for shipment.	Sold to local trade and used by employees.	Used at mines for steam and heat.	Made into coke.	Total product.	Total value.	Average price per ton.	Average number of days active.	Average number of employees.
		Short tons.	Short tons.	Short tons.	Short tons.	Short tons.				
Carbon	3	312,706	1,758	1,900	48,810	365,174	$512,389	$1.40	222	506
Emery and Morgan....	3	....	1,364	11	....	1,375	1,936	1.41	52	10
Sanpete......	2	1,800	1,107	40	....	2,947	6,843	2.32	70	30
Summit......	5	50,169	6,944	4,941	....	62,054	82,311	1.33	147	125
Total..	13	364,675	11,173	6,892	48,810	431,550	603,479	1.40	199	671

Coal product of Utah in 1895, by counties.

County.	Number of mines.	Loaded at mines for shipment.	Sold to local trade and used by employees.	Used at mines for steam and heat.	Made into coke.	Total product.	Total value.	Average price per ton.	Average number of days active.	Average number of employees.
		Short tons.	Short tons.	Short tons.	Short tons.	Short tons.				
Carbon	5	329,486	4,212	3,000	63,027	399,725	$503,529	$1.26	214	522
Iron	2	....	350	10	....	360	900	2.50	81	5
Sanpete.....	2	5,100	13,125	652	....	18,877	39,334	2.09	138	46
Summit.....	5	41,873	7,410	3,591	....	52,874	73,586	1.39	180	97
Total..	14	376,459	25,097	7,253	63,027	471,836	617,349	1.31	203	670

As shown in the above tables, Emery and Morgan counties, which contributed 1,375 tons to the product in 1894, yielded no coal in 1895. Mining was found to be unprofitable on account of lack of railroad facilities and the necessity of hauling by wagons a long distance to market. Iron County appears for the first time as a producer, with an output of 360 tons, which was sold to the local trade of Cedar City.

There are no records of the amount of coal produced in Utah prior to 1885. Since that time the annual output has been as follows:

Coal product of Utah since 1885.

Year.	Short tons.	Year.	Short tons.
1885	213,120	1891	371,045
1886	200,000	1892	361,013
1887	180,021	1893	413,205
1888	258,961	1894	431,550
1889	236,651	1895	471,836
1890	318,159		

VIRGINIA.

Total product in 1895, 1,368,324 short tons; spot value, $869,873.

Conditions similar to those of other States affected the coal-mining industry of Virginia, and there is presented an increase in production of 139,241 short tons, or 11 per cent over that of 1894, and an actual decrease in value of $63,703, or nearly 7 per cent. The average price per ton declined from 76 cents in 1894 to 63 cents in 1895. In 1893, two years previous, the average price was 84 cents per ton, showing a decline of 21 cents, or exactly 25 per cent in two years.

The first coal mined systematically in the United States was from the Richmond basin, in Virginia. As early as 1822 the amount of coal mined here was 48,214 long tons. In 1833, 142,587 long tons were produced. From 1833 to 1869 there is a blank in the records. In the latter year the product was 61,803 long tons, or 69.219 short tons. The Tenth United States Census reported an output of 43,079 short tons for the fiscal year ending June 30, 1880. All of the above figures represent the output of the State obtained from the Richmond basin. The output during 1880, 1881, and 1882 was estimated at 100,000 long tons, or 112,000 short tons, in each year, but this is an "estimate" merely. The development in the Pocahontas Flat Top coal field began in the fall of 1881, but owing to the wet season of 1882 and the lack of transportation facilities until the New River division of the Norfolk and Western Railroad was completed, in 1883, the first carload of coal was not shipped until the latter year. From 1883 the production of this field has grown to enormous proportions, the output in 1894 (including McDowell and Mercer counties, W. Va., and Tazewell and Wise counties, Va.) reaching 5,389,756 short tons. In 1895 the output from the Flat Top field was only 4,381,591 short tons, more than 1,000,000 tons less than in 1894. Four-fifths of the product in 1894 was from the districts north of the Bluestone River, in West Virginia, but the output from Virginia alone was 1,158,437 short tons. In 1895 West

Virginia's portion was less than three-fourths of the decreased total, while Virginia's quota increased to 1,298,862 short tons.

The increase in Virginia's product in 1895 was practically all from Tazewell County. The output from Wise County was not quite 6,000 tons more than in 1894, and there was a slight decrease in the aggregate output of the other coal-producing counties.

The following tables exhibit the details of production during the past two years:

Coal product of Virginia in 1894, by counties.

County.	Number of mines.	Loaded at mines for shipment.	Sold to local trade and used by employees.	Used at mines for steam and heat.	Made into coke.	Total product.	Total value.	Average price per ton.	Average number of days active.	Average number of employees.
		Short tons.	*Short tons.*	*Short tons.*	*Short tons.*	*Short tons.*				
Tazewell	2	635,708	1,120	3,360	187,518	827,706	$580,328	$0.70	302	825
Wise	13	326,086	4,029	616	....	330,731	230,637	.70	155	514
Chesterfield..										
Henrico	13	53,919	16,013	714	....	70,646	122,611	1.73	180	296
Montgomery.										
Pulaski......										
Total ..	28	1,015,713	21,162	4,696	187,518	1,229,083	933,576	.76	234	1,635

Coal product of Virginia in 1895, by counties.

County.	Number of mines.	Loaded at mines for shipment.	Sold to local trade and used by employees.	Used at mines for steam and heat.	Made into coke.	Total product.	Total value.	Average price per ton.	Average number of days active.	Average number of employees.
		Short tons.	*Short tons.*	*Short tons.*	*Short tons.*	*Short tons.*				
Montgomery.	5	269	1,032	....	....	1,301	$2,394	$1.84	87	14
Pulaski......	2	4,304	6,075	....	....	10,379	14,378	1.38	146	32
Tazewell	2	660,645	3,469	4,480	293,675	962,269	588,730	.61	305	1,077
Wise	11	320,243	4,382	924	11,044	336,593	192,713	.57	190	582
Chesterfield .										
Henrico......	2	38,739	215	16,934	1,894	57,782	71,658	1.24	90	453
Total ..	22	1,024,200	15,173	22,338	306,613	1,368,324	869,873	.63	225	2,158

The total production of coal in Virginia since 1880 has been as follows:

Coal product of Virginia since 1880.

Year.	Short tons.	Year.	Short tons.
1880	112,000	1888	1,073,000
1881	112,000	1889	865,786
1882	112,000	1890	784,011
1883	252,000	1891	736,399
1884	336,000	1892	675,205
1885	567,000	1893	820,339
1886	684,951	1894	1,229,083
1887	825,263	1895	1,368,324

WASHINGTON.

Total product in 1895, 1,191,410 short tons; spot value, $2,577,958.

The discovery of coal in what is now the most important producing region of the Pacific States was made in 1852. The first mine was opened on Bellingham Bay in 1854. The coal from this mine was sent to San Francisco, and was the only coal shipped out of the Territory (now State) of Washington until 1870, when exportation commenced at Seattle from the Seattle, Renton, and Talbot mines in the vicinity. In 1874 the product from the Seattle mines was 50,000 tons; from July 1, 1878, to July 1, 1879, the product was 155,900 tons. In the year ended December 31, 1879, the product was 137,207 short tons. The Renton mine, opened in 1874, produced, in 1875 and 1876, 50,000 short tons. The Talbot mine, opened in 1875, produced, in 1879, 18,000 short tons of coal. Records of the operations of Washington coal mines are incomplete, and entirely wanting from 1879 to 1884. The mining during this time was confined to King and Pierce counties. During the fiscal year ended June 30, 1885, the total product of the Territory is given at 380,250 short tons, of which King County is credited with 204,480 short tons and Pierce County with 175,770 short tons.

Coal mining in Washington received a sudden impetus in 1887 and 1888, practically reaching the limit of profitable production in the latter year, for in only two years since has the product of 1888 been exceeded. The product in 1887 was more than 75 per cent larger than in 1886, and that of 1888 more than 55 per cent larger than in 1887. The product in both 1890 and 1893 exceeded that of 1888 by about 50,000 tons, but these were the only years when it did so. The output has not fallen below 1,000,000 tons since it passed that figure in 1888. An increase of about 85,000 tons is shown in the product of 1895 over 1894, but it did not reach the tonnage of four previous years, 1888, 1890, 1892, and 1893.

The value of the product in 1895 was almost exactly the same as that of 1894, but slightly less, showing a decline in the average price from $2.33 to $2.16, the lowest price ever reached in the State.

The following tables show the details of production by counties in the past two years:

Coal product of Washington in 1894, by counties.

County.	Number of mines.	Loaded at mines for shipment.	Sold to local trade and used by employees.	Used at mines for steam and heat.	Made into coke.	Total product.	Total value.	Average price per ton.	Average number of days active.	Average number of employees.
		Short tons.	Short tons.	Short tons.	Short tons.	Short tons.				
King	7	379,433	6,708	36,535	....	422,676	$1,107,887	$2.62	244	919
Kittitas	2	221,292	2,559	8,729	....	232,580	490,860	2.11	125	809
Okanogan ..										
Pierce .... }	6	389,109	783	9,831	7,158	406,881	876,581	2.15	235	823
Skagit......										
Thurston ... }	4	40,398	772	1,758	1,405	44,333	103,113	2.33	292	111
Whatcom...										
Total ...	19	1,030,232	10,822	56,853	8,563	1,106,470	2,578,441	2.33	207	2,662

Coal product of Washington in 1895, by counties.

County.	Number of mines.	Loaded at mines for shipment.	Sold to local trade and used by employees.	Used at mines for steam and heat.	Made into coke.	Total product.	Total value.	Average price per ton.	Average number of days active.	Average number of employees.
		Short tons.	Short tons.	Short tons.	Short tons.	Short tons.				
King	10	400,326	12,940	22,705	....	435,971	$1,078,897	$2.47	218	1,045
Kittitas	2	270,673	2,545	8,316	....	281,534	485,520	1.72	182	877
Pierce	4	412,243	654	11,396	12,736	437,029	928,802	2.13	268	773
Skagit......	2	9,610	50	429	10,237	20,326	47,446	2.33	301	73
Thurston ... }	4	16,016	131	403	....	16,550	37,293	2.25	280	72
Whatcom...										
Total ...	22	1,108,868	16,320	43,249	22,973	1,191,410	2,577,958	2.16	224	2,840

The annual product since 1885 has been as follows :

Product of coal in Washington since 1885.

Year.	Total product.	Total value.	Average price per ton.	Average number of employees.	Average number of days worked.
	Short tons.				
1885.............	380, 250	....	....	....	
1886.............	423, 525	$952, 931	$2. 25	....	
1887.............	772, 601	1, 699, 746	2. 19	1, 571	....
1888.............	1, 215, 750	3, 647, 250	3. 00	....	
1889.............	1, 030, 578	2, 393, 238	2. 32	2, 657	
1890.............	1, 263, 689	3, 426, 590	2. 71	2, 006	270
1891.............	1, 056, 249	2, 437, 270	2. 31	2, 447	211
1892.............	1, 213, 427	2, 763, 547	2. 28	2, 564	247
1893.............	1, 264, 877	2, 920, 876	2. 31	2, 757	241
1894.............	1, 106, 470	2, 578, 441	2. 31	2, 662	207
1895.............	1, 191, 410	2, 577, 958	2. 16	2, 840	224

The total output of the State since 1887, by counties, with the increases and decreases in 1895, as compared with 1894, is shown in the following table:

Product of coal in Washington since 1887, by counties.

[Short tons.]

County.	1887.	1888.	1889.	1890.	1891.	1892.
King.........	339, 961	546, 535	415, 779	517, 492	429, 778	508. 467
Kittitas......	104, 782	220, 000	294, 701	445, 311	348, 018	285, 088
Okanogan....	....	....	....	....	....	....
Pierce	229, 785	276, 956	273, 618	285, 886	271, 053	364, 294
Skagit					1, 400	4, 703
Thurston.....	15, 295	42, 000	46, 480	15, 000	....	22, 119
Whatcom					6, 000	28, 756
Not specified .	82, 778	130, 259	....	....	....	....
Total ..	772, 601	1, 215, 750	1, 030, 578	1, 263, 689	1, 056, 249	1,213,427

County.	1893.	1894.	1895.	Increase in 1895.	Decrease in 1895.
King........	577, 731	422, 676	435, 971	13, 295	....
Kittitas.....	253, 467	232. 580	281, 534	48, 954	....
Okanogan...	....	50	....		50
Pierce	408, 074	406, 831	437, 029	30. 198	....
Skagit	2, 905	7. 537	20, 326	12, 789	....
Thurston....	....	26, 880	16. 550	....	20, 246
Whatcom ...	22, 700	9, 916		....	
Total .	1, 264, 877	1. 106, 470	1, 191. 410	a 84, 940	....

a Net increase.

In the following tables are shown the average prices ruling in each county since 1889, and the statistics of labor employed and average working time since 1890:

Average prices for Washington coal since 1889 in counties producing 10,000 tons or over.

County.	1889.	1890.	1891.	1892.	1893.	1894.	1895.
King	$2.55	$2.61	$2.35	$2.42	$2.22	$2.62	$2.47
Kittitas	2.64	2.76	2.22	2.11	2.71	2.11	1.72
Pierce	2.11¼	2.85½	2.33¼	2.26	2.25	2.15	2.13
Skagit	....	....	....	....	....	....	2.33
Thurston	1.79	2.00	....	2.01	....	2.28	} 2.25
Whatcom	....	....	3.00	2.68	2.40	2.23	
The State	2.32	2.71	2.31	2.28	2.31	2.33	2.16

Statistics of labor employed and working time at Washington coal mines.

County.	1890.		1891.		1892.	
	Average number employed.	Average working days.	Average number employed.	Average working days.	Average number employed.	Average working days.
King	1,098	292	1,285	226	1,296	265
Kittitas	489	259	501	148	500	178
Pierce	589	257	601	236	626	269
Thurston	30	240	....	....	42	223
Whatcom	....	....	30	150	70	305
The State	2,206	270	2,447	211	2,564	247

County.	1893.		1894.		1895.	
	Average number employed.	Average working days.	Average number employed.	Average working days.	Average number employed.	Average working days.
King	1,256	272	919	244	1,045	218
Kittitas	672	162	809	125	877	182
Pierce	756	260	818	237	773	268
Skagit	....	....	....	....	73	301
Thurston	....	....	38	245	} 72	} 280
Whatcom	56	291	43	328		
The State	2,757	241	2,662	207	2,840	221

WEST VIRGINIA.

Total product in 1895, 11,387,961 short tons; spot value, $7,710,575. West Virginia was one of the five States whose product decreased in 1895, the output being 239,796 short tons less than in 1894. Reference

17 GEOL, PT 3——34

was made in the report for 1894 to a strike then in progress in the Pocahontas region at the time of writing (May, 1895). This strike lasted from two to four months, the average time lost being about three months for all the mines in McDowell and Mercer counties, and is responsible for the loss of tonnage for the State. The total decrease in these two counties was 1,148,590 short tons—763,004 tons in McDowell County and 385,586 in Mercer County. The total tonnage for these two counties in 1894 was 4,231,319. The strike, lasting three months, caused a loss of one-fourth the working time for the year. This should have made a decrease of 1,057,830 short tons in the two counties. The actual decrease was 1,148,590 short tons. Part of this decrease was made up by an increase of nearly 700,000 tons in Fayette County, which reaped the benefits of the disturbance among her competitive neighbors.

The depression in values was markedly shown in West Virginia's coal product. The total output decreased 239,796 short tons, whereas the loss in value was only slightly less than $1,000,000. The average price per ton declined from 75 cents in 1894 to 68 cents in 1895.

The details of production in 1894 and 1895 are shown in the following table:

Coal product in West Virginia in 1894, by counties.

County	Number of mines.	Loaded at mines for shipment.	Sold to local trade and used by employees.	Used at mines for steam and heat.	Made into coke.	Total product.	Total value.	Average price per ton.	Average number of days active.	Average number of employees.
		Short tons.	Short tons.	Short tons.	Short tons.	Short tons.				
Barbour	2	7,616	2,104			9,720	$8,679	$0.89	223	20
Brooke	4	39,623	5,222	150		44,995	34,461	.77	205	100
Fayette	45	2,157,737	33,726	18,522	356,627	2,566,612	1,852,472	.72	164	4,594
Grant	2	6,104	459			6,563	4,510	.69	110	23
Harrison	10	235,173	2,782		17,679	255,634	182,653	.71	168	519
Kanawha	23	1,059,719	17,356	5,360	1,924	1,084,359	942,782	.87	155	2,706
Marion	11	1,154,744	6,743	13,482	224,929	1,399,808	1,198,514	.86	274	1,479
Marshall	4	145,513	10,407	400		156,320	113,337	.72½	177	220
Mason	9	65,577	72,470	2,755		140,802	122,036	.86	177	391
McDowell	29	2,088,249	26,313	8,842	1,034,965	3,158,369	2,104,466	.67	207	3,891
Mercer	7	786,363	5,620	8,450	272,517	1,072,950	761,190	.71	211	1,274
Mineral	6	559,829	3,163	278		563,270	432,234	.77	189	564
Monongalia	3	59,883	985	645	18,045	79,558	69,039	.87	181	164
Ohio	12	18,000	84,610	300		102,910	86,555	.84	166	249
Preston	4	35,884	829	246	3,895	40,854	27,960	.68	152	105
Putnam	4	201,625	16,363	2,150		220,138	247,082	1.12	158	530
Randolph	3	15,643	560			16,203	14,602	.90	93	120
Taylor	2	84,755	9,296	108	8,523	102,682	63,498	.62	204	158
Tucker	4	277,307	4,194	2,438	80,011	363,950	225,961	.62	179	390
Logan, Raleigh, and Wayne	3	116,970				116,970	89,759	.77	118	327
Small mines		125,000				125,000	125,000			
Total	187	9,116,314	428,202	64,126	2,019,115	11,627,757	8,706,808	.75	186	17,824

Coal product of West Virginia in 1895 by counties.

County.	Number of mines.	Loaded at mines for shipment.	Sold to local trade and used by employees.	Used at mines for steam and heat.	Made into coke.	Total product.	Total value.	Average price per ton.	Average number of days active.	Average number of employees.
		Short tons.	Short tons.	Short tons.	Short tons.	Short tons.				
Barbour.....	2	12,746	560	....	....	13,306	$10,686	$0.80	222	20
Brooke	3	64,039	10,652	150	....	74,841	54,167	.72	212	126
Fayette......	50	2,628,666	73,300	16,401	546,458	3,264,825	2,355,492	.72	201	5,537
Harrison	10	263,164	2,269	318	26,942	292,693	196,149	.67	212	513
Kanawha....	26	1,070,300	32,582	5,468	26,448	1,134,798	894,310	.79	161	2,738
Marion	11	916,407	10,717	13,531	316,908	1,257,563	805,801	.64	238	1,812
Marshall	4	177,992	15,695	390	....	194,077	130,661	.67	232	336
Mason.......	6	78,903	40,086	1,777	....	120,766	102,988	.85	167	367
McDowell ...	29	1,657,802	13,797	6,569	717,197	2,395,365	1,393,428	.55	199	3,955
Mercer	8	547,118	3,860	1,992	134,394	687,364	387,578	.56	169	1,148
Mineral......	6	667,536	7,777	297	....	675,610	424,643	.63	279	656
Monongalia..	2	42,949	668	668	23,225	67,510	51,941	.77	200	135
Ohio........	9	67,921	101,448	465	....	169,834	128,380	.76	227	221
Preston......	4	60,716	954	583	44,800	107,053	70,000	.65	225	208
Putnam	4	120,332	150	....	....	120,482	114,394	.95	112	438
Taylor.......	3	81,303	794	49	11,106	93,252	51,512	.55	159	180
Tucker	5	258,387	3,058	1,937	186,609	449,991	305,962	.68	188	488
Wayne	3	3,833	....	....	....	3,833	7,755	2.02	82	26
Grant,Logan, Mingo, Raleigh, and Randolph..	5	138,142	1,656	....	....	139,798	99,728	.71	173	255
Small mines .	....	....	125,000	....	....	125,000	125,000	....	....	....
Total ...	190	8,858,256	445,023	50,593	2,034,087	11,387,961	7,710,575	.68	195	19,159

In the following table will be found the total product of the State, by counties, since 1886, with the increases and decreases in 1895 as compared with 1894.

Coal product of West Virginia from 1886 to 1895, by counties.

[Short tons.]

County.	1886.	1887.	1888.	1889.
Brooke..............	22,880	40,366	11,568	31,119
Fayette.............	1,413,778	1,252,457	1,977,030	1,450,780
Harrison	234,597	154,220	109,515	174,115
Kanawha	876,785	1,126,839	863,600	1,218,236
McDowell..........	....	....	....	586,529
Marion.............	172,379	365,844	363,974	282,467
Marshall	251,333	92,368	47,702	47,706
Mason	150,878	140,968	72,410	185,030
Mercer	328,733	575,885	969,395	921,741

Coal product of West Virginia from 1886 to 1893, by counties—Continued.

[Short tons.]

County.	1886.	1887.	1888.	1889.
Mineral	361,312	478,636	456,361	493,464
Monongalia				74,031
Ohio	(a)	131,936	140,019	143,170
Preston	170,721	276,224	231,540	129,932
Putnam	(b)	53,200	145,440	218,752
Taylor	(c)	168,000	55,729	83,012
Tucker..............	22,400	24,707	62,517	173,492
Other counties and small mines				18,304
Total............	4,005,796	4,881,620	5,498,800	6,231,880

County.	1890.	1891.	1892.	1893.
Brooke..............	36,794	33,950	26,521	32,900
Fayette	1,591,298	2,307,421	2,455,400	2,652,860
Harrison	144,403	150,522	221,726	193,632
Kanawha	1,421,116	1,324,788	1,317,621	1,446,252
McDowell..............	956,222	1,267,136	1,696,975	2,166,478
Marion:..............	455,728	1,000,047	919,704	1,062,334
Marshall	123,669	193,703	118,974	158,997
Mason..............	145,314	159,990	159,644	153,633
Mercer	1,005,870	1,172,910	1,191,952	995,428
Mineral	573,684	693,574	582,402	653,025
Monongalia	31,360	31,000	48,900	38,600
Ohio	103,586	90,600	120,323	80,610
Preston	178,439	140,399	98,006	82,672
Putnam	205,178	94,230	89,886	209,881
Raleigh			95,824	92,330
Taylor	76,618	101,661	115,145	78,640
Tucker..............	245,378	358,734	359,752	476,372
Other counties and small mines	100,000	100,000	120,000	133,934
Total	7,394,654	9,220,665	9,738,755	10,708,578

a Included in product of Marshall County.
b Included in product of Mason County.
c Included in product of Harrison County.

Coal product of West Virginia from 1886 to 1895, by counties—Continued.

[Short tons.]

County.	1894.	1895.	Increase in 1895.	Decrease in 1895.
Barbour	9,720	13,306	3,586	
Brooke	44,995	74,841	29,846	
Fayette	2,566,612	3,264,825	698,213	
Grant	6,563	392		6,171
Harrison	255,634	292,693	37,059	
Kanawha	1,084,359	1,134,798	50,439	
Logan	11,611	24,648	13,037	
McDowell	3,158,369	2,395,365		763,004
Marion	1,399,898	1,257,563		142,335
Marshall	156,320	194,077	37,757	
Mason	140,802	120,766		20,036
Mercer	1,072,950	687,364		385,586
Mineral	563,270	675,610	112,310	
Mingo		26,370	26,370	
Monongalia	79,558	67,510		12,048
Ohio	102,910	169,834	66,924	
Preston	40,854	107,053	66,199	
Putnam	220,138	120,482		99,656
Raleigh	84,359	88,188	3,829	
Randolph	16,203	200		16,003
Taylor	102,682	93,252		9,430
Tucker	363,950	449,991	86,041	
Wayne	21,000	3,833		17,167
Other counties and small mines	125,000	125,000		
Total	11,627,757	11,387,961		a 239,796

a Net decrease.

The annual output since 1873 has been as follows:

Coal product of West Virginia since 1873.

Year.	Short tons.	Year.	Short tons.
1873	672,000	1885	3,369,062
1874	1,120,000	1886	4,005,796
1875	1,120,000	1887	4,881,620
1876	896,000	1888	5,498,800
1877	1,120,000	1889	6,231,880
1878	1,120,000	1890	7,394,654
1879	1,400,000	1891	9,220,665
1880	1,568,000	1892	9,738,755
1881	1,680,000	1893	10,708,578
1882	2,240,000	1894	11,627,757
1883	2,335,833	1895	11,387,961
1884	3,360,000		

The decrease in 1895 marks the first break in a series of fifteen years. In each year since 1881 until the close of 1894 the product of West Virginia has shown an uninterrupted gain, the total increase in fourteen years amounting to 10,059,757 short tons, an average of 718,554 short tons. The decrease in 1895 brings the total increase since 1881 down to 9,819,961 short tons, and the average for fifteen years down to 654,664 short tons, as shown in the following table:

Annual increase in the coal product of West Virginia since 1880.

Year.	Short tons.	Year.	Short tons.
1881 over 1880	112, 000	1892 over 1891	518, 090
1882 over 1881	560, 000	1893 over 1892	969, 823
1883 over 1882	95, 833	1894 over 1893	919, 179
1884 over 1883	1, 024, 167	Total increase in	
1885 over 1884	9, 062	fourteen years.	10, 059, 757
1886 over 1885	636, 734	Decrease in 1895......	239, 796
1887 over 1886	875, 824		
1888 over 1887	617, 180	Total increase in	
1889 over 1888	733, 080	fifteen years...	9, 819, 961
1890 over 1889	1, 162, 774	Average annual in-	
1891 over 1890	1, 826, 011	crease..............	654, 664

Uniformly with the discussion of the product of other States the following tables are given, showing the average price per ton and the statistics of labor employed and working time for a series of years:

Average prices for West Virginia coal since 1889 in counties producing 10,000 tons or over.

County.	1889.	1890.	1891.	1892.	1893.	1894.	1895.
Barbour..........	....	....	....	....	....	....	$0.80
Brooke..........	$0.73	$0.77½	$0.82½	$0.94	$0.88	$0.77	.72
Fayette	.90	.90	.85	.84	.80	.72	.72
Harrison	.66	.70	.72	.77	.67	.71	.67
Kanawha	.96	.96	.97	.92	.86	.87	.79
Logan	....	....	....	....	....	.64½	.60
Marion..........	.71	.69	.70	.74	.70	.86	.64
Marshall	.75	.81½	.80	.79	.78	.72½	.67
Mason	.91	.93	.90	.96	.93	.86	.85
McDowell	.67½	.71	.67½	.73	.70	.67	.55
Mercer	.64½	.75	.74	.76	.69	.71	.56
Mineral	.80	.87½	.84	.77	.82	.77	.63
Monongalia	.72	.64	.65	.72	.72	.87	.77
Ohio	.88½	.97	.78	.99	.82	.84	.76
Preston	.66	.72	.64	.67	.69	.68	.65
Putnam	1.12	.97	1.19	1.11	1.01	1.12	.95
Raleigh	....	....	....	.89	1.00	.78½	.78½
Randolph	....	....	....	....	1.00	.90	....
Taylor	.63½	.76	.60½	.61	.58	.62	.55
Tucker..........	.69½	.76	.64½	.70	.71	.62	.68
Wayne	....	....	....	....	....	.76	....
The State ...	.82	.84	.80	.80	.77	.75	.68

Statistics of labor employed and working time at West Virginia coal mines.

County.	1890.		1891.		1892.	
	Average number employed.	Average working days.	Average number employed.	Average working days.	Average number employed.	Average working days.
Barbour..............	....	......	....	......	....	......
Brooke..............	50	202	59	274	51	226
Fayette	2,824	225	3,823	245	4,102	252
Harrison	305	194	285	214	473	148
Kanawha	2,756	230	2,802	217	2,677	217
Marion..............	865	218	1,408	279	1,114	275
Marshall	175	265	190	257	210	199
Mason	480	229	311	236	338	215
McDowell	1,315	183	1,536	227	2,061	195
Mercer	1,465	217	1,510	244	1,621	211
Mineral	620	279	624	259½	500	244
Monongalia	55	260	50	260	72	308
Ohio	153	268	131	276	222	243
Preston	337	282	304	221	170	209
Putnam	375	194	526	143	483	180
Raleigh	....	......	....	......	120	167
Taylor	108	256	118	287	128	282
Tucker.............	353	309	550	306	525	306
The State	12,236	227	14,227	237	14,867	228

County.	1893.		1894.		1895.	
	Average number employed.	Average working days.	Average number employed.	Average working days.	Average number employed.	Average working days.
Barbour..............	....	......	....	......	20	222
Brooke..............	79	260	100	205	126	212
Fayette	4,487	224	4,594	164	5,537	201
Harrison	298	211	439	178	513	212
Kanawha	2,306	276	2,706	155	2,738	161
Logan..............	....	......	150	70	65	160
Marion..............	1,536	203	1,479	274	1,812	238
Marshall	245	194	220	177	336	232
Mason	376	194	391	177	367	167
McDowell	3,375	185	3,891	207	3,955	199
Mercer	1,281	209	1,274	211	1,148	169
Mineral	666	229	561	189	656	229

Statistics of labor employed and working time at West Virginia coal mines—Continued.

County.	1893.		1894.		1895.	
	Average number employed.	Average working days.	Average number employed.	Average working days.	Average number employed.	Average working days.
Monongalia	60	225	164	181	135	200
Ohio	135	221	249	166	221	227
Preston	200	110	105	152	208	225
Putnam	520	204	530	158	438	112
Raleigh	145	165	142	146	133	166
Randolph	8	100	120	93		
Taylor	105	260	158	204	180	159
Tucker	675	267	390	179	488	188
Wayne			35	210		
The State	16,524	219	17,824	186	19,159	195

WYOMING.

Total product in 1895, 2,246,911 short tons; spot value, $2,977,901.

Wyoming is one of five coal-producing States whose output in 1895 was less than that of 1894, and one of four in which there was an advance in the average value per ton. The other four States in which the product decreased were Georgia, Kansas, North Dakota, and West Virginia. The other three in which prices advanced were California, Maryland, and Michigan. This statement does not include the unimportant States of Nevada and South Dakota, the former of which produced 150 tons in 1894 and none in 1895, while the latter produced 200 tons in 1895, the first time in its history.

Compared with 1894, the coal product of Wyoming in 1895 shows a loss of 170,552 short tons. There has been a steady decrease in Wyoming's tonnage since 1892, and the output in 1895 was the smallest since 1890. The value of the product in 1895 was $192,491 less than that of the preceding year, the advance in price being only 2 cents a ton, from $1.31 in 1894 to $1.33 in 1895.

The decreases in 1895 were substantially all in Carbon and Sweetwater, the two principal coal-producing counties. The former lost a little more than 85,000 tons, and the latter about 230,000. These losses were partly made up by an increase of 114,172 tons in Uinta County and about 35,000 tons in the aggregate tonnage of the unimportant counties. An increase in Weston County and a decrease in Converse County were about equal.

The details of production in 1894 and 1895 are shown in the following tables:

Coal product of Wyoming in 1894, by counties.

County.	Number of mines.	Loaded at mines for shipment.	Sold to local trade and used by employees.	Used at mines for steam and heat.	Made into coke.	Total product.	Total value.	Average price per ton.	Average number of days active.	Average number of employees.
		Short tons.	Short tons.	Short tons.	Short tons.	Short tons.				
Carbon	6	419,896	4,554	11,900	....	436,350	$549,937	$1.26	179	539
Converse	2	69,000	1,700	3,300	....	74,000	110,500	1.50	229	140
Fremont......	3	....	1,925	10	....	1,935	4,270	2.22	137	7
Johnson.....	3	1,500	5,180	50	....	6,730	17,047	2.53	160	12
Sheridan.....	6	43,995	821	....	....	44,816	68,413	1.53	260	90
Sweetwater..	9	1,347,448	4,335	38,112	....	1,389,895	1,708,611	1.23	182	1,622
Uinta........	2	115,083	1,432	....	....	116,515	187,781	1.61	108	245
Crook and Weston....	3	313,012	1,535	18,990	13,685	347,222	523,833	1.50	261	377
Total ..	34	2,309,934	21,482	72,362	13,685	2,417,463	3,170,392	1.31	190	3,032

Coal product of Wyoming in 1895, by counties.

County.	Number of mines.	Loaded at mines for shipment.	Sold to local trade and used by employees.	Used at mines for steam and heat.	Made into coke.	Total product.	Total value.	Average price per ton.	Average number of days active.	Average number of employees.
		Short tons.	Short tons.	Short tons.	Short tons.	Short tons.				
Carbon	4	331,940	2,466	16,098	....	350,504	$438,501	$1.25	164	534
Converse	2	50,000	13,060	2,030	....	65,090	108,675	1.67	245	149
Crook........	2	8,000	1,650	....	....	9,650	14,700	1.52	275	14
Johnson	3	....	4,658	100	....	4,758	11,338	2.38	137	21
Sheridan.....	3	72,524	2,965	....	....	75,489	81,785	1.08	257	125
Sweetwater..	5	1,119,945	3,057	35,123	....	1,158,125	1,471,139	1.27	158	1,769
Uinta........	3	209,749	3,069	4,825	13,041	230,684	320,846	1.39	187	384
Fremont and Weston....	3	314,779	4,703	22,889	10,240	352,611	530,917	1.51	264	453
Total ...	25	2,106,937	35,628	81,065	23,281	2,246,911	2,977,901	1.33	184	3,449

In the following table is shown the total output in the State, by counties, since 1868, and the value of the total product since 1885:

Total product of coal in Wyoming, by counties.

[Short tons.]

Year.	Carbon County.	Sweetwater County.	Uinta County.	Weston County.
1868	6,560	365		
1869	30,482	16,933	1,967	
1870	54,915	20,945	29,435	
1871	31,748	40,566	75,014	
1872	59,237	34,677	127,831	
1873	61,164	44,700	153,836	
1874	55,880	58,476	104,705	
1875	61,750	104,664	134,394	
1876	69,060	134,952	130,538	
1877	74,343	146,494	122,016	
1878	62,418	154,282	116,500	
1879	75,424	193,252	132,315	
1880	100,433	244,460	182,918	
1881	156,820	270,425	200,936	
1882	200,123	287,510	211,276	
1883	248,380	304,495	190,163	
1884	319,883	318,197	219,351	
1885	226,863	328,601	234,657	
1886	214,233	359,234	255,888	
1887	288,358	465,444	361,423	
1888	338,947	732,327	369,333	
1889	199,276	857,213	309,218	
1890	305,969	978,827	350,278	200,024
1891	432,180	1,202,017	332,327	326,155
1892	499,787	1,265,441	330,104	344,300
1893	395,059	1,337,206	292,374	310,906
1894	436,350	1,389,895	116,512	341,822
1895	350,504	1,158,125	230,684	348,611

Total product of coal in Wyoming, by counties—Continued.

[Short tons.]

Year.	Converse County.	Other counties.	Total.	Value.
1868			6,925	
1869			49,382	
1870			105,295	
1871			147,328	
1872			221,745	
1873			259,700	
1874			219,061	
1875			300,808	
1876			334,550	
1877			342,853	
1878			333,200	
1879			400,991	
1880			527,811	
1881			628,181	
1882		8,855	707,764	
1883		36,651	779,689	
1884		45,189	902,620	
1885		17,207	807,328	$2,421,984
1886			829,355	2,488,065
1887		55,093	1,170,318	3,510,954
1888	29,933	11,000	1,481,540	4,444,620
1889	17,393	5,847	1,388,276	1,748,617
1890	25,748	9,520	1,870,366	3,183,669
1891	27,897	7,265	2,327,841	3,555,275
1892	45,907	18,300	2,503,839	3,168,776
1893	56,320	47,446	2,439,311	3,290,904
1894	74,000	58,884	2,417,463	3,170,392
1895	65,090	93,897	2,246,911	2,977,901

The following tables show the average prices per ton which have obtained in the more important counties since 1889, and the statistics of labor engaged in the production for six years:

Average price for Wyoming coal since 1889 in counties producing 10,000 tons or over.

County.	1889.	1890.	1891.	1892.	1893.	1894.	1895.
Carbon..........	$0.98	$1.75	$1.50	$1.11	$1.53	$1.26	$1.25
Converse........	1.78	1.74	1.77	1.63	1.58	1.50	1.67
Sheridan	1.50	1.50	1.00	....	1.67	1.53	1.08
Sweetwater	1.20	1.70	1.48	1.16	1.14	1.23	1.27
Uinta	1.56	1.78	1.71	1.56	1.74	1.61	1.39
Weston	....	1.45	1.50	1.50	1.50	1.50	1.51
The State..	1.26	1.70	1.53	1.27	1.35	1.31	1.33

Statistics of labor employed and working time at Wyoming coal mines.

County.	1890.		1891.		1892.	
	Average number employed.	Average working days.	Average number employed.	Average working days.	Average number employed.	Average working days.
Carbon..................	714	....	609	....	505	241
Converse.................	30	....	85	....	105	210
Sweetwater	1,672	....	1,754	....	1,643	198
Uinta	422	....	548	....	462	243
Weston	416	....	402	....	400	297
The State	3,272	....	3,411	....	3,133	225

County.	1893.		1894.		1895.	
	Average number employed.	Average working days.	Average number employed.	Average working days.	Average number employed.	Average working days.
Carbon..................	622	164	539	179	534	164
Converse.................	110	201	140	229	149	245
Sheridan	48	241	90	269	125	257
Sweetwater	1,729	179	1,622	182	1,769	158
Uinta	439	201	245	108	384	187
Weston	400	250	377	261	445	264
The State	3,378	189	3,032	190	3,449	184

EXPENSE OF COAL MINING.

In collecting the statistics of coal production in 1895 an effort was made to ascertain approximately the relative cost of mining bituminous coal, the total expenses, and the total value. The effort was only partially successful, but enough information has been obtained to form a basis for a fairly accurate estimate. In compiling these returns only such mines were considered whose product exceeded 10,000 tons, and all replies which showed any inconsistencies were excluded from the tabulation. The following table shows the results obtained from statements received from 425 mines producing over 10,000 tons each, and having a total output of 34,535,000 tons, or about 25 per cent of the entire bituminous coal product. The total selling value of the product shown in this table was $32,661,750, an average of 95 cents per ton, against an average price of 86 cents for the total bituminous coal product. The average wages received by the miners varied from 30 cents per ton in West Virginia to 78 cents in New Mexico, the general average being 48 cents, or practically exactly half of the selling price. The rate of wages paid the miners is shown to have represented 64 per cent of the total expense of mining the product and placing it on cars for shipment. This makes the total expense average 75 cents per ton, not considering the interest on invested capital. The total expenses computed as above for the 425 mines amounted to $25,970,110. Taking the Mineral Industries volume of the Eleventh United States Census as a basis for an estimate, the capital invested in these mines was approximately $80,000,000 on which an interest charge of 6 per cent would be $4,800,000, making the total expenses chargeable against the tonnage $30,770,110, and the actual net profit to operators less than $2,000,000. If we apply the same averages to the total bituminous product in 1895, it will be seen that out of $115,779,771 received for the coal there was paid out for mining coal $66,688,160, and the total expenses about $104,000,000. Interest charges, based on a capitalization of $320,000,000, would bring the total charges up to $123,200,000, more by $7,500,000 than the amount received. Leaving out the item of interest charges, there remains, after paying the other expenses, a balance of about $11,780,000 as the income of an invested capital of $320,000,000, a little more than 3½ per cent. It is not contended that these estimates are absolutely correct, but they are sufficiently approximate, and when taken in connection with the statistics of production and the review of the industrial conditions in the earlier pages of the report, show that the bituminous coal mining industry throughout the United States is not one of lucrative returns at the present time. Overproduction and sharp rivalry among competing districts are the causes leading to this result.

The distribution, by States, of the 425 mines furnishing the statistics from which the foregoing estimates have been made is a follows:

Statistics of 425 bituminous coal mines, showing tonnage, value, cost of mining, etc., in 1895.

State.	Number of mines.	Production.	Mining cost. Wages paid miners, per ton.	Per cent of total expenses, per ton.	Total expenses, per ton.	Selling price, per ton.	Total wages paid miners.	Total expenses.	Total selling price.
		Short tons.							
Alabama	19	2,710,000	$0.40	61	$0.66	$0.89	$1,086,680	$1,799,010	$2,406,670
Colorado.............	15	809,000	.60	56	1.07	1.23	484,550	866,850	991,540
Indiana.............	36	1,715,000	.64	73	.88	1.01	1,099,390	1,510,960	1,737,100
Indian Territory	4	563,000	.58	46	1.27	1.42	327,650	712,540	802,040
Iowa	39	1,786,000	.71	66	1.07	1.24	1,272,440	1,904,210	2,216,660
Kansas	25	1,536,000	.71	68	1.04	1.26	1,096,990	1,601,800	1,939,310
Maryland...........	5	820,000	.36	66⅝	.54	.73	292,800	448,780	601,900
Missouri.............	17	650,000	.77	68	1.13	1.31	503,520	733,850	854,690
Montana.............	3	1,180,000	.86	68	1.26	1.95	1,019,400	1,487,000	2,302,500
New Mexico	3	409,000	.78	68	1.14	1.49	319,610	465,760	608,610
Ohio	31	1,810,000	.53	66	.80	.95	963,910	1,446,900	1,713,850
Pennsylvania........	149	14,053,000	.38	67	.57	.73	5,378,810	8,041,860	10,188,940
Tennessee	15	782,000	.46	60	.77	.96	359,690	601,930	746,990
Texas	5	98,000	.67	64	1.04	1.42	65,600	102,100	139,100
Virginia.............	3	71,000	.50	74	.67	1.18	35,640	47,470	83,530
Washington	4	794,000	.90	47	1.90	2.30	714,450	1,511,100	1,828,520
West Virginia.......	44	4,211,000	.30	59	.51	.65	1,275,270	2,160,450	2,754,660
Wyoming.............	8	538,000	.70	71	.98	1.39	375,640	527,540	745,140
United States..	425	34,535,000	.48	64	.75	.95	16,672,040	25,970,110	32,661,750